THOMSON

COURSE TECHNOLOGY

Professional ■ Trade ■ Reference

$f^1(x_n)(x_n$

$x_{n+1} = x_n -$

$\dfrac{f(x_n)}{f^1(x_n}$

n

l_1

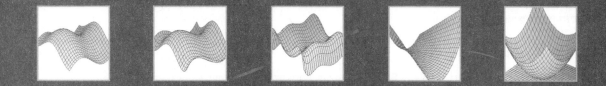

MATHEMATICS
FOR GAME DEVELOPERS

$$x_{n+1} = x_n - \frac{}{2(f^1(x_n))^2 - f(x_n)f^{11}(x_n)}$$

CHRISTOPHER TREMBLAY

SERIES EDITOR

ANDRÉ LaMOTHE, CEO, XTREME GAMES LLC

ISBN: 1-59200-038-X
Library of Congress Catalog Card Number: 2003105366
Printed in the United States of America
04 05 06 07 08 BH 10 9 8 7 6 5 4 3 2 1

THOMSON
™

COURSE TECHNOLOGY

Professional ■ Trade ■ Reference

Thomson Course Technology PTR, a division of
Thomson Course Technology
25 Thomson Place
Boston, MA 02210
http://www.courseptr.com

SVP, Thomson Course Technology PTR: Andy Shafran

Publisher:
Stacy L. Hiquet

Senior Marketing Manager:
Sarah O'Donnell

Marketing Manager:
Heather Hurley

Manager of Editorial Services:
Heather Talbot

Acquisitions Editor:
Mitzi Koontz

Senior Editor:
Mark Garvey

Associate Marketing Managers:
Kristin Eisenzopf and Sarah Dubois

Project Editor:
Kate Shoup Welsh

Technical Reviewers:
Kelly Dempski and Dave Astle

Thomson Course Technology PTR Market Coordinator:
Amanda Weaver

Copy Editors:
Kate Shoup Welsh and Sean Medlock

Interior Layout Tech:
Susan Honeywell

Cover Designer:
Mike Tanamachi

CD-ROM Producer:
Brandon Penticuff

Indexer:
Sharon Shock

Proofreader:
Sean Medlock

To the only things that truly matter:
family and friends

ACKNOWLEDGMENTS

So many people were involved in bringing this book to life, thanking each person individually would be a book in itself. Instead of subjecting you to that, I'll break the deserving into groups. From the early-on mathematicians to the old-school demo programmer gurus who taught me the secrets of the PC, I thank you all for the invaluable technical knowledge. Special thanks to the University of Ottawa professors who could actually teach, a rarity in an educator (especially in the engineering field). Thanks to my personal stress relievers (that is, the *Quake3* knobs on XO server), which were like caffeine when the hours were late. Special thanks to everyone who shepherded this book through production; I think the end result speaks for itself. Finally, I would like to thank every single reader out there, without whom none of this would be possible. After you've mastered the material here, I call on you to create some kick-ass demo to make us all proud!

ABOUT THE AUTHOR

CHRISTOPHER TREMBLAY lives in the California Bay Area, where he works for Motorola building a 3D graphics engine for cell phones to power next-generation games. He holds a degree in Software Engineering from the University of Ottawa, Canada, and is currently completing final courses for a mathematics degree. His work in the game industry includes game AI, core-networking, software rendering algorithms, 3D geometry algorithms, and optimization. Although most of his work is PC-based, a fair amount of it was done on embedded devices ranging from bottom-line TI-calculators to Z80 and 68K Palm processors to speedy PocketPC strong-arm processors, with games such as LemmingZ.

About the Series Editor

ANDRÉ LAMOTHE, CEO, Xtreme Games LLC, has been involved in the computing industry for more than 25 years. He wrote his first game for the TRS-80 and has been hooked ever since! His experience includes 2D/3D graphics, AI research at NASA, compiler design, robotics, virtual reality, and telecommunications. His books are top sellers in the game programming genre, and his experience is echoed in the Thomson Course Technology PTR *Game Development* series.

CONTENTS

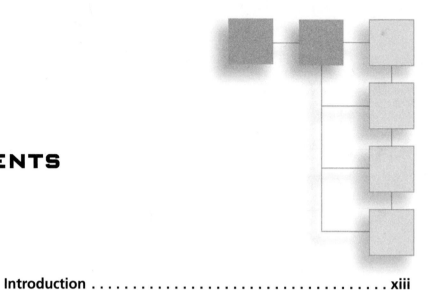

PART III: PLAYING WITH NUMBERS   293

PART IV: RENDERING AND LIGHTING   389

x   Contents

LETTER FROM THE SERIES EDITOR

Sometimes it seemed like this day—the day that *Mathematics for Game Developers* would be sent to press—would never come. Of the *Game Development* series, this title has been one the most challenging books to develop. Not only was it difficult to decide just what the book should include, but finding the perfect author—one who was knowledgeable in both mathematics and game development and at the same time a fantastic writer—was virtually a statistical impossibility! After a lot of searching, however, I did find the perfect author: Christopher Tremblay. This book exceeds my expectations and I hope it exceeds yours.

Within *Mathematics for Game Developers*, not only will you find the entire landscape of relevant, practical mathematics laid out in such a way that you can understand, you will also see how it is connected to game programming. The book begins by covering vectors, matrices, and complex number theory, and then shows how those fields of study can be applied to real 3D problems. When this framework is in place, the book then covers physics modeling and collision detection, followed by approximations, statistics, and probability—which are especially important when you consider that 99 percent of all computer graphics are based on simplified models or approximations. The core of the book, on 3D graphics, includes coverage of such topics as 3D graphics algorithms, visibility, rendering, and lighting techniques and their mathematical descriptions. Finally, the last chapters discuss mathematical optimizations as well as SIMD technology. (If you don't know what that means, then you'd better read this book!)

In conclusion, there are a lot of game development math books out there, but none that are as accessible as this one, that give you as much practical information for real game development.

Sincerely,

André LaMothe
Series Editor Course PTR *Game Development* Series

INTRODUCTION

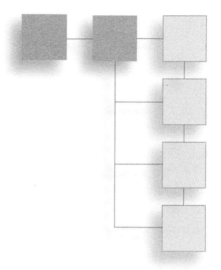

Math is a fundamental part of any game developer's programming arsenal. Without a strong understanding of math, you can easily waste days solving a problem in a game that, in reality, is as simple as 1-2-3. If you're considering programming a game that is even slightly complicated, you must realize that it is crucial to first master some basic concepts such as matrices and vectors.

This book is designed specifically for the game developer, *not* the mathematician. Most game programmers interested in learning about the math behind their work have two options:

- They can read a "true" math book—that is, a book that is geared for mathematicians. The problem with reading this type of book is that they not only tend to delve so deeply into each equation, losing you in the process, but they also provide you with no means to understand the material.
- They can read a "plug-and-play" book, which tend to present a glut of equations without showing how everything fits together.

This book falls somewhere in the middle. It clarifies how mathematical ideas fit together and apply to game programming, and includes only those proofs that help elucidate useful math concepts. Unlike most math books—including many math books for game programmers—this book is concerned less with *why* it works (for example, *proving* that one plus one equals two) as with *how* it works and what that implies.

One way this book simplifies key mathematical concepts is by providing examples. Another is by leveraging software to help solve algebraic equations. Instead of showing 200 ways to integrate a function or providing pages and pages of integral tables, this book recognizes that you simply need to understand the idea behind the operation and why the operation works.

note

Unless otherwise stated, the logic and deduction found throughout the book will stand for real numbers. Sometimes it will stand for complex numbers or even the more general cases, but overall, I won't bother covering the more general cases.

Beyond teaching you the mathematical concepts you need as a game programmer, this book aims to teach you to think for yourself, outside the box. In many cases, the best-known method for solving a problem won't be the simplest, fastest, or most efficient. Don't be afraid to try an unconventional approach; it just might make a dramatic difference in your game!

What You'll Find in This Book

In this book, you will find some unique solutions for dealing with real problems you'll likely face when programming many types of 3D games. Not only does this book show you how to solve these problem, it also explains why the solution works, which enables you to apply that solution to other problems that may crop up. Put another way, this book doesn't just show you how to solve problems; it teaches you how to *think* in order to solve problems.

The main topics that this book tackles are

- Fundamentals of mathematics
- Physics simulation
- Playing with numbers
- Rendering and lighting
- Optimization

How This Book Is Organized

The chapters in this book have been divided into five parts. The first part, "The Basics: A Professional Programmer's Mathematical Foundation," teaches you the basic math background that you will need to fully understand the material that comes later in the book. In this section, you'll examine the basic mathematical entities, their relationships, as well as their corresponding uses in games. In Part II, "Physics Simulations," you will explore the grand problem of motion and discover how you can make your world come alive using physics, collision detection, and a witty mind. The third part, "Playing with Numbers," looks at mathematics from a number-crunching point of view. It tackles various problems such as those seen in statistics for AI purposes, approximation for speedier functions, and interpolation for an ultra-smooth transition. Part IV, "Rendering and Lighting," looks at the rendering pipeline and how things can be modeled in an efficient manner. It discusses methods for rendering a game world that not only looks true-to-life but also displays quickly and efficiently. The last part, "Optimizations," takes a slightly less mathematical approach, discussing various techniques that can be used to optimize your code. It covers the use of fixed points for embedded devices, some dandy fast functions for basic math operations, and some crazy-fast approximations for well-known functions.

Coupled with the book comes a CD that includes a link to the open source GPL'ed library "SDL," which is used throughout the source code that accompanies various chapters of the book. Take your time to look at the source code, modify it, learn from it, and even innovate with it.

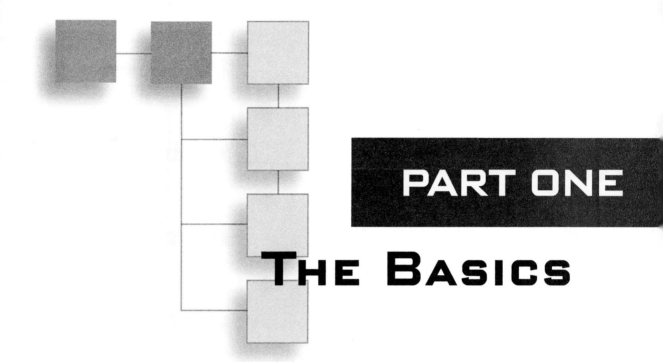

PART ONE

THE BASICS

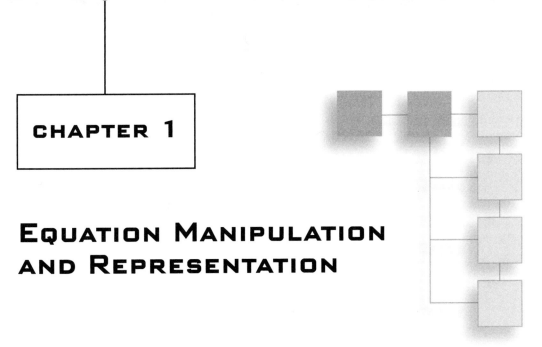

CHAPTER 1

EQUATION MANIPULATION AND REPRESENTATION

Contrary to popular belief, mathematics is not a universal language. Rather, mathematics is based on a strict set of definitions and rules that have been instated and to which meaning has been given. Indeed, arguably, logic is simply the process of someone else making you believe that what you know truly makes sense. In reality, a statement such as "1 + 1 = 2" is as "logical" as the statement that a chair is "a chair as we know it."

Likewise, mathematics for game programming, which is primarily an algebraic field, is also based on a set of definitions and rules. I assume that you already have reasonable knowledge of these algebraic rules; this chapter is meant to both refresh your algebraic knowledge and, perhaps, extend it a bit. That said, I hope that in addition to teaching you how to apply this set of definitions and rules to game programming, this book will open your mind to new ways of thinking about and representing problems. This chapter assumes that you know trigonometry and that you have taken a look at Appendix A, "Notation and Conventions," which enumerates a few interesting identities and refreshes your memory with regards to the relationships between trigonometric functions and a unit circle.

This chapter covers the following:

- Choosing a coordinate system
- Equation representation
- Using polynomial roots to solve equations
- Substitution

Choosing a Coordinate System

One important thing to consider when writing a game is the coordinate system you choose to use. As you'll discover, every coordinate system has its own purpose; that is, each one is geared toward performing certain tasks (this will become evident as I enumerate a few of them). So, although an infinite number of coordinate systems exists, a few stand out for writing games:

- Cartesian coordinates
- Polar coordinates
- Bipolar coordinates
- Cylindrical coordinates
- Spherical coordinates
- Linear coordinates

But wait, what exactly is a coordinate? You can define a coordinate as being a set of n variables that allows you to fix a geometric object. You should already be familiar with coordinates and also a few of these systems, but chances are that some of them will be new to you. Admittedly, not all of them are terribly useful for game programming, but I added them to expose you to a new spatial system, a new way of thinking.

note

All coordinates will be presented in a vector form <a, b, c, . . . > with length smaller or equal to n corresponding to the space's dimension.

Cartesian Coordinates

Without a doubt, the Cartesian coordinate system is the most widely known coordinate system. As shown in Figure 1.1, the Cartesian coordinate system is a rectilinear coordinate system—that is, a system that is rectangular in nature and thereby possesses what I will call rectangular coordinates. Each component in the Cartesian coordinate system is orthogonal. Geometrically speaking, this implies that each axis of the space is perpendicular (90°) to the other axis. Because of its rectangular nature, this system can naturally do translations by mere addition.

This coordinate system will be your reference point for all the other coordinate systems discussed here, and all conversions will be done from those other coordinate systems to this one. Note that as a convention, I will always place the x component on the horizontal axis, the y component on the vertical axis, and the z component on the perpendicular axis (that is, the axis coming out of the paper toward you). The interval of the components is $[-\infty, \infty]$. For the sake of example, I've plotted <1, 2, 3> on a 3D Cartesian system (feel free to do the same); the results are shown in Figure 1.2.

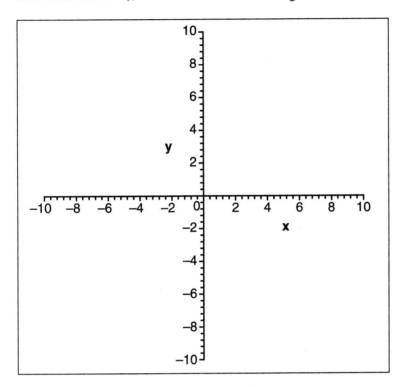

Figure 1.1
A 2D Cartesian coordinate system

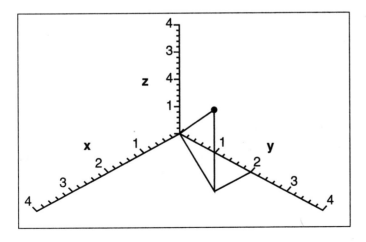

Figure 1.2
<1, 2, 3> plotted on a Cartesian system

Interestingly enough, this by no means implies that the Cartesian coordinate system you use should be such that x is horizontal, y is vertical, and so on. You could easily build a Cartesian coordinate system where, for example, the z and y axes are inverted. Just make sure to take this into account when plotting the coordinate. Similarly, you can define which side of the axis is negative and which one is positive, also called *handedness*, as illustrated in Figure 1.3. Typically, this only involves a change of sign in the depth axis, and this line is usually only drawn from the origin to the positive side of the axis, thus generating what looks like a house corner from the perspective of the inside or outside. For example, in 2D, using a 2D rendering library, the screen is arranged such that the y axis diminishes when moving up, but the x axis stays the same. This implies that the origin is at the top-left corner of the screen, instead of being at the bottom-left like a Cartesian coordinate system would yield. Math books sometimes like to place the 3D y axis as the depth component and the z axis as the height, but here I will stick to what the 3D libraries use.

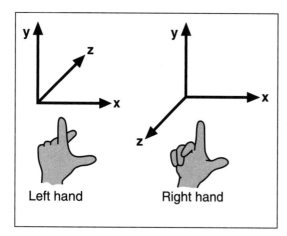

Figure 1.3
Right- and left-hand Cartesian coordinate system

tip

In Maple, you can use the plot([<functions(x)>], x=a..b, <options>) or plot3d([<functions>(x, y)], x=a..b, y=c..d) to plot graphs using Cartesian coordinates.

Polar Coordinates

Thanks to trigonometric primitives, the polar coordinate system is probably the second best-known coordinate system. As shown in Figure 1.4, the polar coordinate system is a radial coordinate system—that is, a system that is characterized by its distance relative to the center of the coordinate system. The polar coordinate system is a 2D coordinate system, and has the property of being cyclic in one component. It possesses two components: <r, φ>. r is the radial component, and it specifies the distance from the origin; φ is the angular coordinate, and represents the angle from an arbitrarily defined starting point.

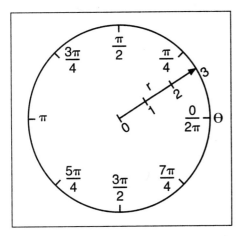

Figure 1.4
A polar coordinate system

Because of its circular nature, the polar coordinate system is very well adapted to rotations, which are performed naturally with an addition to the angular component. The range for this coordinate system is <[0, 2π), [0, ∞]>.

You can easily convert from polar coordinates to Cartesian coordinates with the following relationship:

$$x = r\cos(\theta)$$
$$y = r\sin(\theta)$$

Conversely, you can convert from Cartesian coordinates to polar coordinates with the following relationship:

$$r = \sqrt{x^2 + y^2}$$
$$\theta = \arctan\left(\frac{y}{x}\right)$$

Let's plot <1, 2> on a polar coordinate system; Figure 1.5 shows the results.

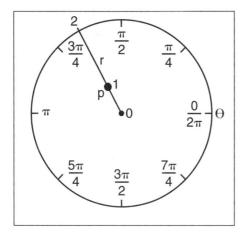

Figure 1.5
<1, 2> plotted on a polar system

tip

In Maple, you can append the coords=polar option to the plot function in order to plot graphs using polar coordinates.

Bipolar Coordinates

In a polar coordinate system, all coordinates are described with an angle and a length. A bipolar system, on the other hand, is described with two lengths or two angles. Although the bipolar coordinate system is not a very popular coordinate system for gaming purposes, it does have its uses and makes for a great way to look at things differently. Just as its name suggests, a bipolar coordinate system is minimally equipped with two centers, the distance between which can be a. For mathematical simplicity, let $a = 2c$.

Consider only the bipolar coordinate system, which is described with two lengths, r_1 and r_2, as illustrated in Figure 1.6. It may be a little confusing to see how you can pinpoint a coordinate with two lengths, but it is actually quite simple. The coordinate described by $< r_1, r_2 >$ is the point at which the two circles of radius r_1 and r_2, separated by a, intersect. As illustrated in Figure 1.6, for any two circles, there should be two intersections (assuming there is an intersection at all). As with the polar coordinate system, the range of the lengths is $[0, \infty]$.

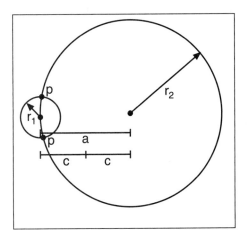

Figure 1.6
A bipolar coordinate system

You can convert from bipolar coordinates to Cartesian coordinates with the following relationship:

$$r = \sqrt{\frac{r_1^2 + r_2^2 - 2c^2}{2}}$$

$$\theta = \arctan\left(\frac{\sqrt{r_2^4 - 2(4c^2 + r_1^2)r_2^2 - (4c^2 - r_1^2)^2}}{r_1^2 - r_2^2}\right)$$

Conversely, you can convert from bipolar coordinates to Cartesian coordinates with the following relationship:

$$x = \frac{r_1^2 - r_2^2}{4c}$$

$$y = \pm\frac{\sqrt{16c^2 r_1^2 - (r_1^2 - r_2^2 + 4c^2)^2}}{4c}$$

One good use of this system is illustrated by the equation of an ellipse. An ellipse can easily be expressed in bipolar coordinates with its well-known relationship between its foci, $r_1 + r_2 = 2a$, as illustrated in Figure 1.7.

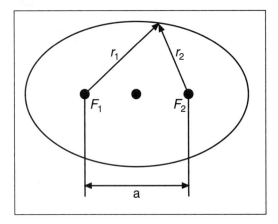

Figure 1.7
An ellipse using bipolar coordinates

Now that you have the basic idea, think a bit more about the new material and see what else you can come up with. The bipolar coordinate system shown here is cumbersome because it does not uniquely determine a single point in space. Try applying the same idea of intersection using angles instead. You will notice that they can uniquely determine a coordinate. You can also start to think about how this general idea can be applied to 3D to generate funky objects such as ellipsoids or smooth spherical-like objects. At this point, the stage is yours.

tip

In Maple, you can append the coords=bipolar option to the plot function in order to plot graphs using bipolar coordinates.

Cylindrical Coordinates

One rather interesting coordinate system for 3D coordinates is the cylindrical coordinate system, shown in Figure 1.8. This system mixes the polar coordinates with the Cartesian coordinates to get the best of both worlds when a mixture of both is required. As the name suggests, cylindrical coordinates are contained in the form of a cylinder, which is defined by three parameters: $<r, \phi, z>$. The first two parameters are associated with the polar space and have the same interpretation. The z component is associated with the Cartesian z coordinate, and also has the same purpose. This set of coordinates can be very useful when a rotation around one single axis is required, as well as when translations along the axis are required.

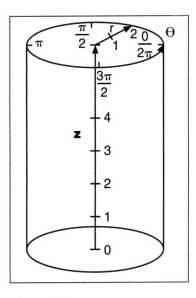

Figure 1.8
A cylindrical coordinate system

The ranges for the parameters are also the same as their two respective coordinate systems: $<[0, 2\pi), [0, \infty], [-\infty, \infty]>$. Converting from cylindrical to Cartesian is easily done with the same relationships established earlier:

$$x = r\cos(\theta)$$
$$y = r\sin(\theta)$$
$$z = z$$

From Cartesian to cylindrical, the conversion is as follows:

$$r = \sqrt{x^2 + y^2}$$
$$\theta = \arctan\left(\frac{y}{x}\right)$$
$$z = z$$

If you wanted to plot <1, 2, 3> on such a system, the results would be as shown in Figure 1.9.

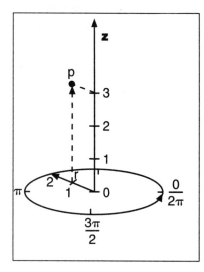

tip

In Maple, you can append the coords=cylindrical option to the plot3d function in order to plot graphs using cylindrical coordinates.

Figure 1.9
A coordinate plotted using cylindrical coordinates

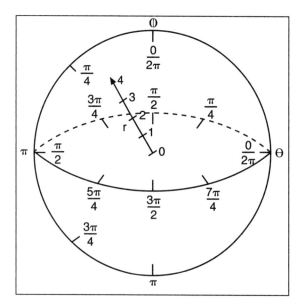

Figure 1.10
A spherical coordinate system

Spherical Coordinates

The next obvious progression from Cartesian to cylindrical is the spherical coordinate system illustrated in Figure 1.10. Whereas the cylindrical coordinates introduced an extra rectangular dimension to the polar coordinates to take care of the depth (or height, depending on your angle), the spherical coordinates introduce an extra component to the polar coordinates to uniquely access all coordinates in 3D. That being said, the spherical coordinates have three parameters: $<r, \phi, \theta>$.

This system can naturally do rotations around any two axes in 3D space with a mere addition. The range of the parameters is $<[0, \infty], [0, 2\pi], [0, \pi]>$. Notice that the second angle is not bound to 2π, which makes sense because if you were to allow it to comprise values greater than π, you would be in a situation where the coordinate would not be uniquely defined by the three parameters, and hence the redundancy would not be necessary.

By carefully looking at the geometry of the problem, and with some help from trigonometry, you can deduce that the conversion from spherical coordinates to Cartesian coordinates can be obtained with the following:

$$x = r\cos(\phi)\sin(\theta)$$
$$y = r\sin(\phi)\cos(\theta)$$
$$z = r\cos(\theta)$$

Conversely, you can convert from Cartesian to spherical coordinates with the following equation:

$$r = \sqrt{x^2 + y^2 + z^2}$$
$$\phi = \arctan\left(\frac{y}{x}\right)$$
$$\theta = \arctan\left(\frac{z}{r}\right)$$

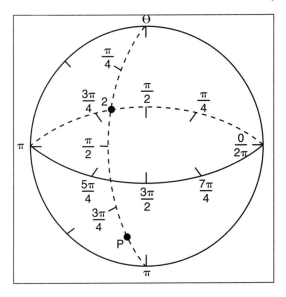

Once more, if you stand by your sample coordinate $<1, 2, 3>$, you obtain the plot in 3D space, as shown in Figure 1.11.

Figure 1.11
A coordinate plotted using spherical coordinates

tip
_____

In Maple, you can append the coords=spherical option to the plot3d function in order to plot graphs using spherical coordinates.
_____

Equation Representation

An equation is a formal statement of equality between two mathematical expressions. For example, a statement like $x = a + 1$ is an equation because it is composed of an equality between the expression x and $a + 1$. Equations can be represented in a few ways. This book focuses on three types of equations, each with its own pros and cons. As you will see, some representations are very well adapted to certain uses and, as with the various coordinate systems, each equation representation has its own way of "naturally" dealing with certain types of problems. In this section, you'll learn about the three types of equations on which this book focuses, and you'll see how to convert from one system to another (whenever possible). Understanding how to solve equations is a key and basic concept that will serve you throughout this book.

Do You Function Correctly?

By far the most widely known way to represent an equation is via a function. A _function_ can be sloppily defined as a relationship for which every set of input maps to one single value. Generally speaking, you have a function if one side of the equation has only one variable. When this is the case, the input parameters of the function are the variables on the opposite side of the equation.

A function is typically written as f(x, y, z), where x, y, z are the parameters of the function. For example, $f(x) = 2x + 1$ is an example of a function; more precisely, it is the equation of a line. Geometrically speaking, with a 2D function's graph plotted in a Cartesian coordinate in which x represents the horizontal axis, any given vertical line of infinite length should intersect with the graph no more than one time. This is also true for the general case. If you think in 3D, a very similar deduction can be put forward using a plane and a 3D graph. Once more, this is true because we claimed that a should have no more than one value per input set.

Here are a few examples of functions, followed by their graphs (see Figures 1.12 and 1.13).

$$y = \sqrt{x}$$
$$z = f(x, y)$$
$$= 3x - 4y$$

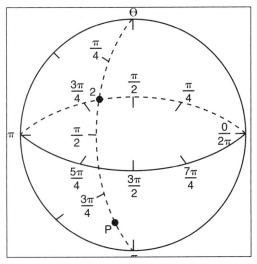

Figure 1.12
Graph of a square root

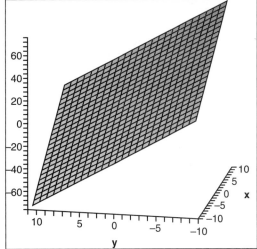

Figure 1.13
Graph of a 3D plane

---

tip

In Maple, you can assign values to variables via the assignment operator :=. Similarly, you can also define functions with this method. You may also unassign an operator with the command unassign('operator').

Parametric Notation

This equation description format is much less restrictive than a function because it does not force any variable to have only one value per input set. It enables you to freely describe the equation by giving one function for every coordinate in the coordinate system. Although these equations permit more liberal movement in space, some are somewhat cumbersome to deal with because they have more than one value per input set. Because these equations do not yield a unique value per input set, they obviously cannot be converted from a parametric form to a functional form. The following examples are equations in parametric form:

$$P_1 = \begin{cases} x = \cos(t) \\ y = \sin(t) \end{cases}$$

$$P_2 = \begin{cases} x = 3t \\ y = 4t \end{cases}$$

Converting a function to parametric notation is actually quite easy: Simply leave all the input parameters as is, and make the result of the function the last parameter. It does not come easier than this. Take the following as an example:

$$z = \sqrt{x^2 + y^2} \quad \rightarrow \quad \begin{cases} x = x \\ y = y \\ z = \sqrt{x^2 + y^2} \end{cases}$$

$$z = e^x + 3y \quad \rightarrow \quad \begin{cases} x = x \\ y = y \\ z = e^x + 3y \end{cases}$$

The challenge is when you want to convert from parametric to functional. The trick here is to isolate the parameters and substitute them into the other equations. In some cases, you can get a single equation by substituting every parameter, but you may sometimes end up in situations where you can no longer substitute. This is not always a problem; it simply implies that one of the variables is not really important in relation to the variable you have isolated for. Clearly, you may lose some information by doing this, but it will convert the equation to a function as required. For example, take the following equation of a plane in 3D:

$$f = \begin{cases} x = 3s \\ y = -3t \\ z = 2t \end{cases}$$

$$t = -\frac{y}{3}$$

$$z = 2t$$

$$= -\frac{2y}{3}$$

For this set of equations, you cannot isolate everything to one single variable—which means that either you cannot convert this equation to a function, or this equation will lose some information that cannot be expressed by functions in the conversion process (as is the case here). If you take a look at the graph of this equation (see Figure 1.14), you will notice that the x value is of no importance because regardless of the value in x, the height z is the same throughout. Consequently, the final functional equation becomes the last equation expressed above. Thus, given an arbitrary parameter y, you can compute z and arbitrarily choose x to yield any point satisfying the equality.

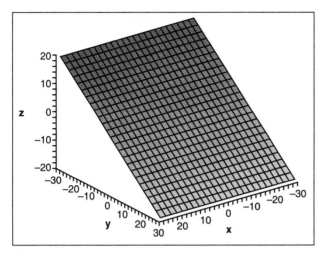

Figure 1.14
Graph of a plane

There is no easy conversion trick for very complicated equations. The best thing you can do is look at your function geometrically (if possible) to see whether it has only one value per axis. To make this possible, you might want to consider changing your coordinate system with the substitutions mentioned earlier in this section. The circle is obviously not a function because it has two values for any vertical or horizontal line, but if you change to polar coordinates, you can convert everything into a function, as shown here:

$$f = \begin{cases} x = r\cos(\theta) \\ y = r\sin(\theta) \end{cases}$$

$$r = \frac{y}{\sin(\theta)}$$

$$x = r\cos(\theta)$$

$$= \frac{y\cos(\theta)}{\sin(\theta)}$$

$$= \frac{y}{\tan(\theta)}$$

tip

Maple also accepts parametric input for equations using plots by issuing brackets around the function and defining each input set plus the range of the input parameters. To do so, issue the command Plot([$fx(s)$, $fy(s)$, $s=a..b$]); for 3D plots, the command is plot3d([$fx(s, t)$, $fy(s, t)$, $fz(s, t)$], $s=a..b$, $t=c..d$).

Chaotic Equations

The last types of equations are neither parametric nor functional—although they may look functional at first. The problem is, it is impossible to isolate one of their variables. For example, try to isolate any of the variables in $(8 + 2x + x^2 = y^2 - y)$ to yield a function; you will quickly discover that it is not possible. In general, these equations are not easy to convert into another representation—indeed, doing so is sometimes impossible algebraically.

This book doesn't focus much on these types of equations, but you will look at a few things about them in the chapters to come. Converting them from their original form to parametric or functional form requires various tactics and techniques. At the very least, you'll explore one method that, in fact, can solve the problem in the preceding paragraph and a family of similar problems.

Using Polynomial Roots to Solve Equations

Polynomials are equations of the form $y = a_n x^n + \dots a_i x^i + a_0 x^0$. This section focuses on finding the roots of a polynomial—in other words, solving algebraically for x in the equation $0 = a_n x^n + \dots a_i x^i + a_0$. As you will soon see, there is more to this than simply finding a finite set of solutions for x.

Quadratic Equations

Quadratic equations are second-order polynomial equations—in other words, equations of the form $ax^2 + bx + c = 0$, where $\{a, b, c\}$ are constants and x is a variable with a power of at most two (hence the word *second*). What's interesting with these equations is that you can easily determine the values for x. Specifically, x has two values, but they are not guaranteed to be real. The trick to isolating x comes from a process called "completing the square." (This process can also be useful when dealing with other problems.) The idea is to express the equation as a square of x plus some value. The benefit of doing so is that you can then determine the square root on each side to end up with one single value of x.

You are probably familiar with the following general root-finding quadratic equation:

$$x = \frac{-b \pm \sqrt{b^2 - 4ac}}{2a}$$

This equation is well known, and can be obtained by completing the square of the quadratic equation and isolating for x. A very similar result can also be obtained if you simply manipulate the equation a little differently. The advantage of having two different equations is that generally, the floating-point precision is more stable (more on this later in the book), as shown in the following proof:

$$a \cdot x^2 + b \cdot x + c = 0$$

$$a + \frac{b}{x} + \frac{c}{x^2} = 0$$

$$a + c\left(\frac{1}{x^2} + \frac{b}{cx}\right) = 0$$

$$c\left(\frac{1}{x^2} + \frac{b}{cx} + \frac{b^2}{4c^2} - \frac{b^2}{4c^2}\right) = -a$$

$$c\left(\frac{1}{x^2} + \frac{b}{cx} + \frac{b^2}{4c^2}\right) = \frac{b^2}{4c} - a$$

$$\left(\frac{1}{x} + \frac{b}{2c}\right)^2 = \frac{b^2}{4c^2} - \frac{4ca}{c^2}$$

$$\frac{1}{x} + \frac{b}{2c} = \pm\frac{\sqrt{b^2 - 4ac}}{2c}$$

$$\frac{1}{x} = \frac{-b \pm \sqrt{b^2 - 4ac}}{2c}$$

$$x = \frac{2c}{-b \pm \sqrt{b^2 - 4ac}}$$

The square is completed on the fourth line, where two canceling terms are added and one is pulled out of the parentheses so that the resulting equation can easily be converted to the square of some value, thereby reducing the power of x. This equation is really interesting because it is very similar to the previous one. Its bottom portion is exactly the same as the first one's top portion. This gives the interesting identity, which can yield more stable floating-point values for two different roots:

$$q = \frac{1}{2}\left(-b \pm \sqrt{b^2 - 4ac}\right)$$

$$x = \frac{q}{a} = \frac{c}{q}$$

Now that you have two solutions for a quadratic equation, you can actually do something with the equation $8 + 2x + x^2 = y^2 - y$, illustrated in Figure 1.15. As long as one of the variables is part of the quadratic equation, you can find the solution to the problem. In this case, both variables are part of a quadratic equation, which means that both variables can be isolated.

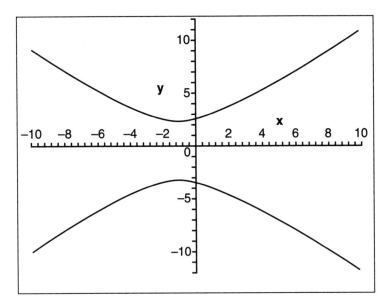

Figure 1.15
Graph of $8 + 2x + x^2 = y^2 - y$

Isolating for y yields a slightly nicer result, so let's proceed:

$$8 + 2x + x^2 = y^2 + y$$

$$0 = y^2 + y - (x^2 + 2x + 8) = ay^2 + by + c$$

$$y = \frac{-b \pm \sqrt{b^2 - 4ac}}{2a}$$

$$= \frac{-1 \pm \sqrt{1 + 4(x^2 + 2x + 8)}}{2}$$

$$= -\frac{1}{2} \pm \frac{\sqrt{33 + 4x^2 + 8x}}{2}$$

This is obviously not a function because it always has two values for any value of y. This equation is, however, a piecewise function, which means that by breaking this equation into pieces (in this case, two), you can construct well-defined functions. Obviously, by handling the plus/minus cases separately, you can do this. Later on, you will see how you can convert this equation into a pure function in certain conditions. Because the square root is defined only in real space for positive values, the discriminant, which is an expression distinguishing between two entities (here, $b^2 - 4ac$), must be greater than or equal to

0 for the solutions to be real. If the discriminant is 0, then two real solutions, which are exactly the same, exist. This is obvious because the square root of 0 is 0, and that 0 is not affected by a negative or positive sign.

Cubic Equation

If you managed to find a solution for a quadratic equation, one cannot help but think that a similar process can be performed to find a solution for a cubic equation. Sure enough, it is possible. The proof of this derivation is rather tedious, so I will skip it. Most of it is done by a set of variable substitutions, which you will see clearer examples of shortly, and by completing the cube.

A cubic equation is a polynomial of the form $x^3 + ax^2 + bx + c = 0$ where $\{a, b, c\}$ are constants and x is a variable. To calculate the solution of such an equation, you must compute things in a few steps, which mainly come from the substitutions the proof/derivation requires. You must first compute two values:

$$Q = \frac{a^2 - 3b}{9}$$

$$R = \frac{2a^3 - 9ab + 27c}{57}$$

Once you have these two values, you need to verify that $R^2 < Q^3$. If so, then the following holds:

$$\theta = \arccos\left(\frac{R}{\sqrt{Q^3}}\right)$$

$$x_1 = -2\sqrt{Q}\cos\left(\frac{\theta}{3}\right) - \frac{a}{3}$$

$$x_2 = -2\sqrt{Q}\cos\left(\frac{\theta + 2\pi}{3}\right) - \frac{a}{3}$$

$$x_3 = -2\sqrt{Q}\cos\left(\frac{\theta - 2\pi}{3}\right) - \frac{a}{3}$$

If $R^2 < Q^3$ fails, then you must precompute the following values:

$$A = -\operatorname{sgn}(R)^3\sqrt{|R| + \sqrt{R^2 - Q^3}}$$

$$B = \begin{cases} \dfrac{Q}{A} & A \neq 0 \\ 0 & A = 0 \end{cases}$$

The solution is then given by the following:

$$x_1 = (A+B) - \frac{a}{3}$$

$$x_2 = -\frac{(A+B)}{2} - \frac{a}{3} + i\frac{\sqrt{3}(A-B)}{2}$$

$$x_3 = -\frac{(A+B)}{2} - \frac{a}{3} - i\frac{\sqrt{3}(A-B)}{2}$$

Notice how only one real root exists in this scenario. In order to illustrate how this works, take the equation $x^3 + 5x^2 - 22x + 16$.

$$Q = \frac{5^2 - 3(-22)}{9} = \frac{91}{9}$$

$$R = \frac{2 \cdot 5^2 - 9 \cdot 5(-22) + 27 \cdot 16}{54}$$

$$= \frac{1472}{54}$$

$$= \frac{836}{27}$$

You may want to verify that $R^2 < Q^3$ (which is true in this case) so you can easily proceed to the next step:

$$\theta = \arccos\left(\frac{\frac{836}{27}}{\sqrt{\left(\frac{91}{9}\right)^3}}\right) = 0.2727278932$$

$$x_1 = -2\sqrt{\frac{91}{9}} \cos\left(\frac{0.2727278932}{3}\right) - \frac{5}{3} = -8$$

$$x_2 = -2\sqrt{\frac{91}{9}} \cos\left(\frac{0.2727278932 + 2\pi}{3}\right) - \frac{5}{3} = -2$$

$$x_2 = -2\sqrt{\frac{91}{9}} \cos\left(\frac{0.2727278932 - 2\pi}{3}\right) - \frac{5}{3} = 1$$

$x = \{-8, 1, 2\}$, which makes perfect sense if you verify by reversing the process and multi-plying $(x + 8)(x - 1)(x - 2)$. If you look at the curve this generates, you can see why I went with this algorithm. If the curve was such that it was only intersecting at one location, this is where you would have to resort to the second path.

Quartic Equation

As with quadratic and cubic equations, you can find a solution to a quartic equation by applying a set of substitutions and clever algebraic tricks to reduce the terms. The derivation can also make use of the Viéta formula, discussed in Chapter 11, "Educated Guessing with Statistics and Probability," or substitution combined with two passes to complete the square.

A quartic equation is the next logical step after the cubic polynomial equation. That being said, a quartic equation is of the form $x^4 + ax^3 + bx^2 + cx + d = 0$, where $\{a, b, c, d\}$ are constants and x is a variable. Due to the increasing complexity of the derivations, I have broken the solutions into finite steps. Let's start with a few precalculations:

$$P = b - \frac{3a^2}{8}$$

$$Q = \frac{a^3}{8} - \frac{ab}{2} + c$$

$$R = d - \frac{3a^4}{256} + \frac{a^2 b}{16} - \frac{ac}{4}$$

The next step is to solve a cubic equation by finding two of its non-zero real roots:

$$0 = y^3 + \frac{P \cdot y^2}{2} + \frac{(P^2 - 4R)y}{16} - \frac{Q^2}{64}$$

When you have this, let s and t be the square root of any two non-zero roots of the preceding equation (a real root is obviously easier to compute) to define the next two variables:

$$U = -\frac{Q}{8st}$$

$$V = \frac{a}{4}$$

Then, the four roots of the quartic equation are defined by the following:

$$x_1 = S + T + U - V$$
$$x_x = S - T - U - V$$
$$x_3 = -S - T + U - V$$
$$x_4 = -S + T - U - V$$

As an example, take $x^4 - 6x^3 - 9x^2 + 94x - 120 = 0$.

$$P = -9 - \frac{3(-6)}{8} = -\frac{45}{2}$$

$$Q = \frac{(-6)^3}{8} - \frac{(-6)(-9)}{2} + 94 = 40$$

$$R = d - \frac{3(-6)^4}{256} + \frac{(-6)^2(-9)}{16} - \frac{(-6)94}{4} = -\frac{231}{16}$$

$$0 = y^3 + \frac{\left(-\frac{45}{2}\right)y^2}{2} + \frac{\left(-\frac{45^2}{2} - 4\left(-\frac{231}{16}\right)\right)y}{16} - \frac{40^2}{64}$$

$$y = \left\{1, 4, \frac{25}{4}\right\}$$

$$S = 1$$
$$T = 4$$
$$U = -\frac{40}{8 \cdot 1 \cdot 4} = -\frac{5}{2}$$
$$V = -\frac{6}{4} = -\frac{3}{2}$$

$$x_1 = 1 + 4 - \frac{5}{2} + \frac{3}{2} = 2$$

$$x_2 = 1 - 4 + \frac{5}{2} + \frac{3}{2} = 3$$

$$x_3 = -1 - 4 - \frac{5}{2} + \frac{3}{2} = -4$$

$$x_4 = -1 + 4 + \frac{5}{2} + \frac{3}{2} = 5$$

Partial solutions for quintic equations also exist, but there is no known general solution for quintic equations. Generally, the trick to determining whether it's possible to find a solution for a given partially polynomial equation is always pretty much the same: Try to factor the equation in a binomial equation $(ax + b)^n$ that is a perfect power. When you have this, you can take the nth square root and x will be isolated. In order to get the equation on one side into this format, you will need to do a few substitutions, which is exactly what I'll talk about next.

tip

Maple can solve equations algebraically when a solution exists with the function solve(<function>, <variable>).

Substitution

Substitution is a very powerful tool that can be used to solve certain types of equations. You used substitution to some degree when learning about the various coordinate systems, but I think it's appropriate to take a more complete look at the methods and tricks you can use to simplify your equations—or even obtain a well-defined formula for equations that did not initially have one.

Substitution can be seen as a way to express the same idea as the original equation, but by distorting the path, which goes from A to B. In the coordinate systems, the input set is distorted to yield the new coordinate system. Your distortion does not always have to affect the final result, however. If you apply the inverse substitution you applied at the end of your algebraic process, you should not have changed anything when going from A to B. As an example, take the equation $2x^2 + 3x - 5$ and try to remove all the first-order terms in x with a substitution of $x = y + a$, where a is a real number:

$$f(x) = 2x^2 + 3x - 5$$
$$= 2(y+a)^2 + 3(y+a) - 5$$
$$= 2y^2 + 4ya + a^2 + 3y + 3a - 5$$
$$= 2y^2 + y(4a+3) + a^2 + 3a - 5$$

Now you want the first-order term to be 0, which implies the following:

$$4a + 3 = 0$$

$$a = -\frac{3}{4}$$

$$f(y) = 2y^2 + \frac{9}{16} + 3\left(-\frac{3}{4}\right) - 5$$

$$= 2y^2 - \frac{49}{8}$$

Geometrically speaking, the substitution applied is a horizontal translation of three quarters to the right. We did not actually change the function at all at this point because the equation is in terms of y and not in terms of x. If you want the equation to be a function of x, then you have to apply the reverse process: $y = x - a$. So for example, if you wanted to know the value of $f(x)$ for $x = 4$, you would have to compute $f(4 + \_)$ for $f(y)$, which gives 39, the same answer as $f(x)$ for $x = 4$. This method is particularly interesting for computational complexity because it successfully reduces a multiplication to a simple subtraction.

Substitution also enables you to convert an ugly equation into a function or parametric form with a rather interesting trick. Using this chapter's earlier example of a quadratic equation, suppose that you are interested only in the range of $x = [-10, 10]$ for that equation. By applying a substitution, you can make it such that the equation takes only positive values as input. Then, you can take advantage of this equation's symmetry in order to take care of both cases in the same equation. If you can achieve this, you will successfully convert the equation into a function. Observe the following logic:

$$y = -\frac{1}{2} \pm \frac{\sqrt{33 + 4x^2 + 8x}}{2}$$

Let's perform the substitution $x = s - 10$. This also changes the domain for x to $[-10 + 10, 10 + 10] = [0, 20]$:

$$y = -\frac{1}{2} \pm \frac{\sqrt{33 + 4(s-10)^2 + 8(s-10)}}{2}$$

$$t = -\frac{1}{2} \pm \frac{\sqrt{353 + 4s^2 - 72s}}{2}$$

In this equation, s is always expected to be greater than 0, so you can substitute s for the absolute value of s without changing anything. Also note that s^2 is always positive regardless of the sign of s. The trick to solve this one stems from the fact that you can store information using the sign of s by allowing it to span from $[-20, 20]$ and by adding extra logic in the equation to change the sign whenever s is negative. Observe the following change in the equation and its resulting graph (see Figure 1.16):

$$t = -\frac{1}{2} + \mathrm{sgn}(s)\frac{\sqrt{353 + 4s^2 - 72|s|}}{2}$$

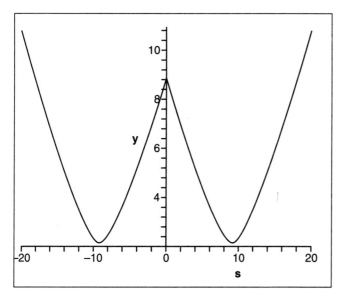

Figure 1.16
Graph of the new parametric equation

This does not solve the problem entirely; it simply generates another similar mirrored curve in the negative x quadrant. This is to be expected, though, because you know that a function can have only one value for any input, while the parametric notation does not have this limitation. The final trick to solve this as a parametric equation is simply to notice that s should always be positive, regardless of what happens. This last fact gives the following equation and graph (see Figure 1.17), which is exactly like the chapter's first equation, but translated by 10—which means that a substitution of $s = x + 10$ can convert your values for x into well-defined values for s.

$$f(s) = \left\langle |s|, -\frac{1}{2} + \operatorname{sgn}(s) \frac{\sqrt{353 + 4s^2 - 72|s|}}{2} \right\rangle$$

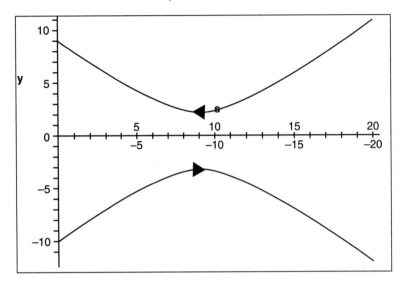

Figure 1.17
Final graph of the new parametric equation

If you distinguish the difference between +0 and −0 like the floating-point IEEE format does, this is a fully valid equation. If you cannot distinguish between these two, then you have a problem because 0 has no sign defined and, as a result, the equation is not defined.

tip

Maple can also perform substitutions via the evaluation function eval(<equation>, <var> = <function or value>). Sometimes, the equations Maple yields are not simplified, so simplify(<equation>) may come in handy. Another very useful tool is the expand(<equation>) function, which can break up the function powers and effectively undo some level of simplification.

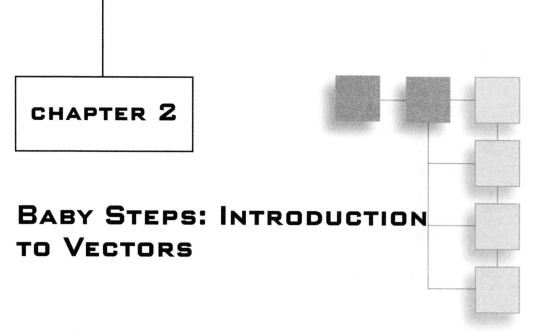

CHAPTER 2

BABY STEPS: INTRODUCTION TO VECTORS

You probably already know a good deal about vectors. In fact, you may be considering skipping this chapter altogether. My advice: Don't. This chapter will serve as a good review and reference for more advanced topics you will tackle later on. Along the way, you may also find some new and interesting ways of seeing things, which may open your eyes to some relationships between certain elements. I have also placed a few Easter eggs in this chapter if you think you know all there is to know about vectors.

note

Vectors are a very abstract concept and can be applied to many things. This book is interested in vectors primarily with regard to how they relate to real numbers; for this reason, some definitions and relations you'll find here work for real numbers only.

This chapter covers the following:

- Defining vectors
- Advanced vector operations and properties
- Vector spaces

O Vector, What Art Thou?

A vector is to math what an array is to programming. Both enable you to treat several pieces of information as a single element. With this pseudo-definition, you might think that a coordinate is a vector, but not quite directly. A vector has a direction and a magnitude, and does not have a fixed position in space. You could claim that a coordinate is a vector from the origin (more on this later). Because of this, and for practical reasons, this book will use the vectorial notation for coordinates (which is identified by a bold character). For example, suppose you wanted to assign a direction to a point in space. In that case, you would require two things: one coordinate and one vector.

note

Although vectors are not like coordinates per se, they are fairly similar to polar coordinates because both are described with a magnitude (length) and a direction (angle).

Another way to see a vector is to look at it as an offset coordinate, as was initially mentioned, with the stretched definition of a coordinate as being a vector from the origin. A vector is defined by n coordinates, where each component is typically assigned one axis in the coordinate system. You can also call these n-vectors. Most applications that use vectors use 2-vectors and 3-vectors.

Vectors are commonly expressed in a Cartesian coordinate system $<x, y, z, \ldots>$, but you can use the same principles in another coordinate system, such as in Polar coordinates, for example $<\theta, r>$. In fact, you can define a vector in any coordinate system. To do this, you use the concept of head and tail. A vector starts from its tail and ends at its head, as illustrated in Figure 2.1. In Cartesian coordinates, a vector is typically expressed as two coordinates in space—for example, **a** and **b**. The vector **ab** (that is, the vector between a and b in that very order), starts at **a** (the tail) and ends at **b** (the head). Thus, a coordinate **p** in a coordinate system can actually be viewed as the vector **0p**, where **0** is the origin.

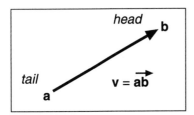

Figure 2.1
Vector properties

To compute the value of the vector, you would use the following:

$$\mathbf{ab} = \mathbf{b} - \mathbf{a}$$

Likewise, if you have a coordinate **a** and a vector **v**, you can find your second coordinate **b** by simply inverting the process:

$$\mathbf{b} = \mathbf{a} + \mathbf{v}$$

note

> The vector **ab** in the preceding equation is not to be confused with a times b. Throughout this book, I shall explicitly express the multiplication with a dot when confusion could arise.

It may sound confusing at first, but vectors use their own coordinate system, called a *vector space*, which is relative rather than absolute. For example, if you expand the first equation into components for the polar coordinate system, you get the following:

$$\mathbf{v} = \langle r, \theta \rangle = \langle a_r, a_\theta \rangle - \langle b_r, b_\theta \rangle$$

Geometrically, a vector can be seen as an arrow. The arrow indicates the direction, and therefore enables you to differentiate the tail and the head as shown in Figure 2.1. Because vectors do not actually possess an origin, the tail can be placed anywhere in coordinate space. The only restriction is that the head must lie at a given distance from the tail. For example, a vector <1, 2, 3>, which is written similarly to a coordinate, means that the tail is separated from the head by the signed numbers $<x = 1, y = 2, z = 3>$.

tip

> In Maple, you can define a vector by using triangular brackets, where the components are delimited by spaces. For example, a vector **s** = <1, 2, 3> would be defined as **s** = <1 2 3>.

Basic Operations and Properties

A vector by itself isn't all that useful. For any element to be useful, you need to define a set of operations you can apply to it. Quite clearly, the operations you define must have some type of usefulness, or else you are just doing math for the sheer pleasure of doing math and not for creating games.

Direction Inversion

A vector has a direction; that's a given. But how do you invert the direction of the vector? If you think about the problem geometrically, it is very simple. The head becomes the tail and the tail becomes the head. For example, suppose vector ab is defined and you want to determine the inverse of that vector. To do so, you simply swap a and b, and you get ba. It's as simple as that.

If you think of vectors in terms of Cartesian coordinates, inverting the vector is a simple matter of swapping the two coordinates—which, as it turns out, is the exact same thing as multiplying everything by −1. So in short, inverting the direction of a vector is pretty simple. You can simply multiply each of its coordinates by −1, and voilà.

Hi! My Name Is Norm

As mentioned previously, a vector is defined as having a magnitude and a direction. You already looked at various aspects of a vector's direction, but you haven't yet explored the issue of magnitude, also called norm.

The norm of a vector, which can be represented with either single bars or double bars, is defined as follows:

$$\sqrt[2]{|1|^2 + |-2|^2 + |3|^2} = \sqrt{1^2 + 2^2 + 3^2}$$

It may come as a surprise that although this equation is generally accepted as the definition of the norm of a vector, it is, in fact, only partially accurate. In truth, a norm in the general sense is defined as a function that attributes a length, size, or extent to the object being studied. It is not bound to one specific formula. The commonly used vector-norm, as stated in the preceding equation, fits just one group of norms called the *p*-norms. More specifically, it is defined as the 2-norm. The *p*-norm defined for *p* greater or equal to 1 is as follows:

$$\sqrt[2]{|1|^2 + |-2|^2 + |3|^2} = \sqrt{1^2 + 2^2 + 3^2}$$

Each of these norms is actually equivalent. That means if you choose any two vectors—say, s, and t—and if s's norm is smaller than t's, then the same will be true for any *p*-norm regardless of the value you choose for *p*. Similarly, you can state the opposite if t is smaller than s. Table 2.1 shows the norms computed with various values for *p* in the *p*-norm.

Table 2.1 p-Norm Values for $\mathbf{s} = <1, -2, 3>$

p	Expression	p-Norm Value
1	$\sqrt[1]{\lvert 1\rvert + \lvert -2\rvert + \lvert 3\rvert} = \lvert 1\rvert + \lvert -2\rvert + \lvert 3\rvert$	6
2	$\sqrt[2]{\lvert 1\rvert^2 + \lvert -2\rvert^2 + \lvert 3\rvert^2} = \sqrt{1^2 + 2^2 + 3^2}$	3.7416...
5	$\sqrt[5]{\lvert 1\rvert^5 + \lvert -2\rvert^5 + \lvert 3\rvert^5}$	3.0052...
∞	$\sqrt[\infty]{\lvert 1\rvert^\infty + \lvert -2\rvert^\infty + \lvert 3\rvert^\infty} = \max\left\{\lvert 1\rvert, \lvert -2\rvert, \lvert 3\rvert\right\}$	3

One thing that might have attracted your attention in Table 2.1 is the infinity (∞) norm. The ∞ norm is defined as the maximum absolute value of one component. If you look at the norms for increasing values of p, you can see that the value converges toward 3. This book has not yet covered convergence, so I won't go into it here, but keep your eyes open for Chapter 7, "Accelerated Vector Calculus for the Uninitiated."

To see the graphical representation of what various values of the p-norm do to an input value in 2D, take a look at Figure 2.2, which illustrates various values of p.

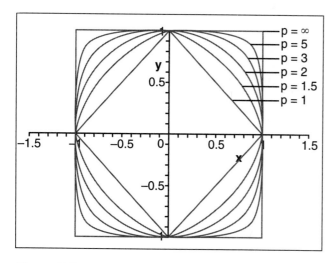

tip

In Maple, you can compute p-norms by issuing the norm command with the vector as well as p, like so: norm($\mathbf{s}$, p).

A lot has been said here about the p-norm, but by all means, it is not the only norm you can use. For a norm to be at all useful, you need it to follow a fixed set of rules, which are defined as follows:

Figure 2.2
p-norm applied for 2D vectors

a) $\|\mathbf{v}\| \geq 0$

b) $\|\mathbf{v}\| = 0 \leftrightarrow \mathbf{v} = 0$

c) $\|k\mathbf{v}\| = |k|\|\mathbf{v}\|$

d) $\|\mathbf{u} + \mathbf{v}\| \leq \|\mathbf{u}\| + \|\mathbf{v}\|$

Given these rules, you can come up with your own norm if you do not like the generally accepted 2-norm. The logic still stands. That said, nicer results can be obtained with the 2-norm simply because of its circular nature. For this reason, the rest of the book assumes the use of a 2-norm.

Before you move on, there is one more norm-related concept that you need to grasp: You can say that an element is normal if it is of norm 1. If the element is not normal, then you can normalize the vector by dividing by its norm. For example, if you wanted to normalize <1, −2, 3>, you would apply the following logic for the 2-norm:

$$\frac{\langle 1,-2,3 \rangle}{\|\langle 1,-2,3 \rangle\|_2} = \frac{\langle 1,-2,3 \rangle}{3.7416} = \langle 0.2672, -0.5345, 0.8017 \rangle$$

Thus, as soon as you need something related to the distance, the choice of norm truly is yours. Nothing really says that the 3-norm is better than all the other ones. The 2-norm is nice due to its circular nature, but the 1-norm and infinity norm can be equally useful— for example, in collision detection.

Vector Addition

One of the most fundamental operations is addition. Fortunately, vectors are a breeze to add. To understand how addition works with vectors, again think back to how the vector would be processed in a Cartesian world. If you added two vectors $\mathbf{s} = \mathbf{ab}$ and $\mathbf{t} = \mathbf{bc}$, you would have three coordinates: a, b, and c. Recall that a vector can be defined using two coordinates. If you were to add $\mathbf{s}$ and $\mathbf{t}$ in that order, the first vector's tail would thus be at a and its head would be at b; the second vector's tail would be at b and its head would be at c. The addition therefore takes the form of $\mathbf{s} + \mathbf{t} = \mathbf{ab} + \mathbf{bc} = \mathbf{ac}$ (the vector, or if you prefer, the offset between $\mathbf{a}$ and $\mathbf{c}$), as shown in Figure 2.3. This is the geometrical way of adding vectors. When you add two vectors, you must always append the tail of the second vector to the head of the first vector, because vectors do not work in an absolute world but in a world described by offsets.

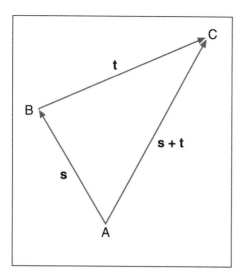

Figure 2.3
Vector addition

If you compute everything step by step, you get the following:

$$s = \langle b_1 - a_1, b_2 - a_2, \ldots, b_n - a_n \rangle$$
$$t = \langle c_1 - b_1, c_2 - b_2, \ldots, c_n - b_n \rangle$$
$$s + t = \langle b_1 - a_1 + c_1 - b_1, b_2 - a_2 + c_2 - b_2, \ldots, b_n - a_n + c_n - b_n \rangle$$
$$= \langle c_1 - a_1, c_2 - a_2, \ldots, c_n - a_n \rangle$$

Addition on vectors is defined such that you simply need to add every like component together. Thus, given vectors s and t, you can define their addition by the following equation:

$$s + t = \langle s_1 + t_1, s_2 + t_2, \ldots, s_n + t_n \rangle$$

Similarly, you can define their subtraction by simply inverting the second vector, hence multiplying all its components by -1. If you do this, you will quickly notice that given the addition rule, you can define the subtraction rule as follows:

$$s - t = s + (-t)$$

When you want to add vectors using their coordinates, you can simplify the expression as shown above. You can replace these two vectors by the more direct vector generated by the tail of the first one and the head of the second, as shown previously in Figure 2.2. If you think of vectors as offsets, you can clearly see that adding two offsets is really the same as expressing this as one offset (which is really the sum of the two initial offsets). For example, if Mike walks for two miles and then turns around and walks for one mile, he is one mile from his initial position. As a more complex example, consider if you were to take the summation of a set of vectors. You may be able to simplify them as follows:

$$s = (\mathbf{ab} + \mathbf{be}) + \mathbf{ed} + \mathbf{fg} - \mathbf{fa}$$
$$= \mathbf{ae} + \mathbf{ed} + \mathbf{fg} + \mathbf{af}$$
$$= (\mathbf{ae} + \mathbf{ed}) + (\mathbf{af} + \mathbf{fg})$$
$$= \mathbf{af} + \mathbf{ag}$$

Algebraically, vectors can be manipulated using many of the laws you take for granted with real numbers. Most notably, the following can be used:

a) $\mathbf{s} + \mathbf{t} = \mathbf{t} + \mathbf{s}$

b) $(\mathbf{s} + \mathbf{t}) + \mathbf{r} = \mathbf{s} + (\mathbf{t} + \mathbf{r})$

c) $(ab)\mathbf{s} = a(b\mathbf{s})$

d) $a(\mathbf{s} + \mathbf{t}) = a\mathbf{s} + a\mathbf{t}$

e) $(a + b)\mathbf{s} = a\mathbf{s} + b\mathbf{s}$

tip

In Maple, vector addition can be performed in the exact same way you would add any other element type (for example, **s** + **t**).

Advanced Operations and Properties

When I talk about advanced operations, "advanced" is a relative term. Advanced operations are just operations that are more complex than basic elementary math. Mathematicians have defined most of these operations by forcing them to abide by a given set of rules and by then proving various results given the rule set. This is very similar to what you saw with the norm, where the norm is generally defined with a set of rules and where you can define, if you wish, more specific cases of the general set.

The operations you will look at in this section fall under a second category. These operations are specific cases of a more general group. I discuss them here because, like the 2-norm, these operations have very interesting and meaningful properties that yield nice results.

Dot Product

Wrongfully, the dot product is sometimes called the inner product. Although this is partially correct, in that the dot product belongs to that family, it is not precise to say so. The dot product yields its name from its notation. Given two n-dimensional vectors $\mathbf{s}$ and $\mathbf{t}$, the dot product is defined as follows:

$$\mathbf{s} \bullet \mathbf{t} = \sum_{i=1}^{n} s_i t_i$$

Note that this is not the same as the dot you use while programming. In programming, the dot is a period; in this case, however, the dot is centered with the characters. Multiplication on variables is implicit, meaning that when the variables are connected as in the preceding equation, a multiplication is implied. You may sometimes, however, have to resort to using variables with more than one character, which yields confusion about the variables' names. It is therefore convenient to separate them with a dot, which is why you sometimes see equations written such that a dot separates two real variables that need to be multiplied. This is also sometimes applied to functions or multiplication between other types of elements. The dot product is actually the implied symbol in these cases because if you look at the function for $n = 1$, you will notice that the operation defines a simple multiplication.

By itself, the dot product is not interesting. What makes it interesting is an equation that the dot product satisfies. Notably, for two vectors $\mathbf{s}$ and $\mathbf{t}$, and theta, the angle between the two vectors, you get the following:

$$\mathbf{s} \bullet \mathbf{t} = \|\mathbf{s}\| \|\mathbf{t}\| \cos(\theta)$$

You can easily prove this by using the cosine law on a triangle with sides $\mathbf{s}$, $\mathbf{t}$, and $(\mathbf{s} - \mathbf{t})$. If, for example, you choose $\mathbf{s} = <1, -2, 3>$ and $\mathbf{t} = <0 -1, 2>$, you get the following results:

$$\mathbf{s} \bullet \mathbf{t} = 1 \cdot 0 + (-2)(-1) + 3 \cdot 2 = 8$$
$$\mathbf{s} \bullet \mathbf{t} = \|\mathbf{s}\| \|\mathbf{t}\| \cos(\theta)$$
$$8 = \sqrt{14} \cdot \sqrt{5} \cos(\theta)$$
$$\cos(\theta) = \frac{8}{\sqrt{70}}$$
$$\theta = 0.2971 = 17°$$

tip

In Maple, the dot product between two vectors **s** and **t** can be computed with a period like so: **s . t**.

The geometrical interpretation comes from the equation. Take the previous equation and divide each side by the product of the norms. What you get is that the dot product of two normal vectors equals the cosine of the angle between them. Figure 2.4 illustrates what this means geometrically when **s** and **t** are normal. The result of the normal dot product is called a *projection*—in this case, an imaginary line that goes from **s**'s head to **t** by hitting **t** such that the imaginary line and **t** are perpendicular (that is, separated by an angle of 90 degrees). There is no real reason to normalize **s**; as long as **t** is normalized, the projection still works out perfectly. Therefore, if you look at the dot product where only **t** is normal, what you get is the projection of s upon the unit vector **t**.

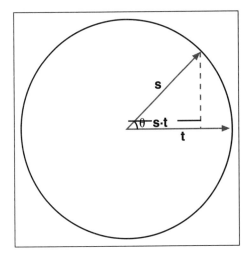

Figure 2.4
Projection of a normal vector on a normal vector

You can easily see in Figure 2.4 that if you extend s such that it goes outside the unit circle, you can still apply a proper projection of s upon **t**. This still follows the definition of cosine, as shown by the following equations:

$$\cos(\theta) = \frac{\text{Proj}}{\|\mathbf{s}\|}$$

$$\text{Proj} = \|\mathbf{s}\| \cos(\theta)$$

Unfortunately, this does not work if **t**'s norm is not 1.

You can deduce a few more things from the dot product given its geometrical interpretation and equation:

- If two vectors are perpendicular, geometrically, you can see that the result of the dot product should be 0 because the projection of the first vector upon the second one is 0.

- The dot product is in fact a good test for determining whether two vectors are orthogonal. (Orthogonal is another way of saying perpendicular, but without the geometrical undertones.) As usual, do not restrict yourself to a mere 3D world. This definition is valid for an n-vector, so it can determine orthogonality for a 4D world if you can visualize such a thing. (If you figure out how, e-mail me!)

- You can quickly determine whether two vectors are separated by less than 90 degrees by simply looking at the sign of the dot product. When the sign is positive, it means that the two vectors are separated by less than 90 degrees. (You can verify this by taking two normal vectors and substituting theta with a value of less than 90 degrees.)

One more thing of note: This function gives some form of "length" to a pair of vectors. This sounds an awful lot like a norm, except that this function allows for negative lengths and two vectors. To fix this, you can take the dot product of the vector upon the vector itself and it will always yield a value greater than 0 given a non-zero vector. Interestingly enough, if you do this, you will quickly realize that the square root of the dot product is in fact the 2-norm, as shown here:

$$\sqrt{\mathbf{v} \bullet \mathbf{v}} = \sqrt{\sum_{i=1}^{n} v_i^2} = \|\mathbf{v}\|_2$$

Projection of a Vector Upon a Vector

You have already seen that the dot product of **s** on **t** with **t** normal has the geometrical interpretation of being the scalar projection of **s** on **t**. One point of particular interest would be to project an arbitrary vector on another arbitrary vector as opposed to simply placing scalar lengths together. Shadows are a great example of projective geometry. You can easily deduce the equation for a general scalar projection by simply normalizing your vector **t** as done here:

$$\left|\text{Proj}(\mathbf{s})\right| = \frac{\mathbf{s} \bullet \mathbf{t}}{\|\mathbf{t}\|_2}$$

Because you are projecting a vector upon another vector, you should logically get back a vector. If you look back at Figure 2.4, you will notice that the projected length is actually along the vector **t**. This makes sense because if you are projecting **s** on **t**, then your vector should be a multiple of **t**. In order to compute the vectorial projection of a vector upon another, you simply need to change **t**'s length from whatever it may be to the projection length determined in the preceding equation. Simply put, start by normalizing the vector, thus giving it a length of 1 followed by a multiplication of the desired projection length, which you computed above. This yields the final equation for a projection of **s** on **t**:

$$\text{Proj}_t(\mathbf{s}) = \frac{\mathbf{s} \bullet \mathbf{t}}{\|\mathbf{t}\|_2^2} \mathbf{t}$$

$$= \frac{\mathbf{s} \bullet \mathbf{t}}{\mathbf{t} \bullet \mathbf{t}} \mathbf{t}$$

As an example, take the same values chosen above for **s** and **t**. The projection of **s** upon **t** is computed as such:

$$\text{Proj}_t(\mathbf{s}) = \frac{\mathbf{s} \bullet \mathbf{t}}{\mathbf{t} \bullet \mathbf{t}} \mathbf{t}$$

$$= \frac{8}{5} \mathbf{t}$$

$$= \left\langle 0, -\frac{8}{5}, \frac{16}{5} \right\rangle$$

Cross Product

The cross product, sometimes called the vector product, is another very important function to master. It is defined only for 3D vectors, but you could also use it in 2D with 3D vectors by simply setting the last component of the 3D vector to 0. The cross product is represented with a cross. Its equation operating on two vectors, **s** and **t**, is as follows:

$$\mathbf{s} \times \mathbf{t} = \left\langle s_y t_z - s_z t_y, s_z t_x - s_x t_z, s_x t_y - s_y t_z \right\rangle$$

This is in fact one of the most cumbersome ways to remember the equation; in Chapter 3, "Meet the Matrices," you will revisit the cross product by looking at it from a different angle. In that chapter, you'll see equations that make its computation much easier to remember.

One very interesting property of the cross product is that the dot product of it with any of its original vectors yields 0. Put in terms of equations, you have the following:

$$(s\times t)\bullet s = (s\times t)\bullet t = 0$$

If you recall what it means to have the dot product of two vectors equal to 0, you probably also recall that it implies that the two vectors are in fact perpendicular to each other. Thus, the cross product of s and t can geometrically be seen as a function that generates a vector orthogonal to both s and t. Another way to have the dot product yield 0 is if one of the two vectors is 0. What does it mean for the cross product of s and t to be 0? The trivial solution is where s and t are 0, but this is not really interesting. Alternatively, if s and t are linearly dependent (that is, parallel), the result of the cross product will be 0. This should come as no surprise because if you think about the geometrical implications, given two parallel vectors, you can generate an infinite number of perpendicular vectors, as shown in Figure 2.5.

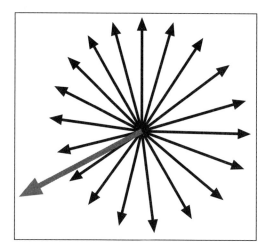

Figure 2.5
Cross product of two perpendicular vectors

So far, every operation you have seen could be handled using the same basic laws you are accustomed to using with real numbers. This, however, is where it all ends. Specifically, the cross product is not commutative. That means s • t is not the same as t • s. (You can easily verify this by expanding the equation on each side.) Thus, the cross product can yield two perpendicular vectors.

If you think about the geometrical implications of this, it makes sense because you can select a vector and invert its direction to yield a new vector, which is also perpendicular to the other two and parallel to the previous. This is somewhat problematic, however, because you do not know which direction the new vector will go when you compute this.

A very simple way to determine the new vector's direction is to use the right hand rule. First, open your right hand and let your thumb make a 90-degree angle with your fingers. Next, point your fingers at the first vector of the cross product. Then, if possible, curl your fingers such that they point in the direction of the second vector. If you can curl your fingers in this way, then the resulting vector will be dictated by your thumb's position. If you cannot curl your fingers because doing so would require you to bend them backward, rotate your hand such that your thumb points downwards. This should enable you to curl your fingers in the right direction, thus implying that the resulting vector would be pointing downwards.

The right hand rule is a visual technique to determine the direction of the resulting vector, but there is also a geometrical way to look at the problem. If going from **s** to **t** requires you to move in a counterclockwise fashion, then the vector points upwards. If the motion is clockwise, you are looking at a downward vector. Trigonometry offers yet another view of the problem. If the angle between **s** and **t** is smaller than π rad, the vector will point upwards. If not, it will point downwards. Here, when the angle is computed, you should be looking at an angle range that increases in a counterclockwise fashion. Do not simply take the smaller of the two angles between the vectors. Figures 2.6 and 2.7 illustrate the concept.

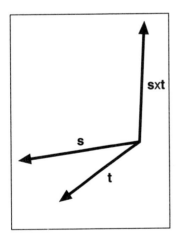

Figure 2.6
s • t resulting in a upward vector

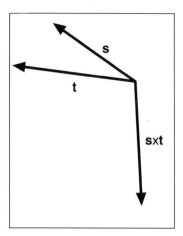

Figure 2.7
s · t resulting in a downward vector

Taking back our traditional values **s** = <1, −2, 3> and **t** = <0 −1, 2>, you can compute their cross product as follows:

$$s \bullet t = \langle (-2) \cdot 2 - 3(-1), 3 \cdot 0 - 1 \cdot 2, 1(-1) - (-2)0 \rangle$$
$$= \langle -4 + 3, 0 - 2, -1 + 0 \rangle$$
$$= \langle -1, -2, -1 \rangle$$

In a 2D world, you can use the cross product to determine the "side" of a vertex given a vector. In other words, if you have a vector, you can determine whether a particular point is to the right or to the left of the vector. To compute this, simply consider the cross product of the boundary vector (call it **st**) and consider the vector from point s to your point **p sp**. You know that the cross product's direction can tell you whether the vectors are separated by less than π. At this point, the deduction should be fairly straightforward; compute the cross product of **st** with **sp**, and if the z component is positive, you know that the counterclockwise angle between the two vectors is less than π and hence **sp** is on the left side of the vector **st**. Conversely, if the sign is negative, it implies an angle greater than π and thus that **sp** is on the right side of **st** as shown in Figure 2.8.

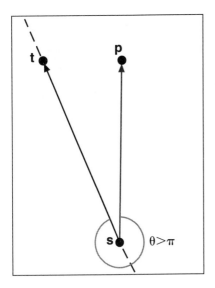

Figure 2.8
Using the cross product to determine on
which side of a vector a given point exists

This should not go without an example, so take **s** = <0, 0>, **t** = <-1, 1>, and **t** = <0, 1>, similar to what Figure 2.8 illustrates. By computing its cross product, you get exactly what you might expect from the geometrical point of view:

$$\mathbf{st} = \langle -1, 1 \rangle$$
$$\mathbf{sp} = \langle 0, 1 \rangle$$
$$\mathbf{st} \bullet \mathbf{sp} = \langle -1, 1, 0 \rangle \bullet \langle 0, 1, 0 \rangle$$
$$= \langle 0, 0, -1 \rangle$$

note

The *z* component of the cross product is also called the determinant, and can be generalized to greater dimensions—a topic you will dive into in the next chapter.

You have studied the cross product's direction quite a bit, but recall that vectors are elements determined by both direction and magnitude. Not much has been said thus far about the magnitude of the cross product, but there is a reasonably easy formula to determine it (the proof for this one is a rather long and boring algebraic manipulation involving the definition of the norm combined with the definition of the dot product and one trigonometric identity, so I'll skip that here):

$$\|\mathbf{s} \times \mathbf{t}\| = \|\mathbf{s}\| \|\mathbf{t}\| \sin(\theta)$$

This formula should come as no surprise because it is quite similar to the one for the dot product. You already observed that the direction of the vector generated by the formula was sensitive to angles greater to π, and this formula clearly states this fact by inverting the sign for such angles. This also brings up an interesting fact. If you take the cross product of s and t, you get a given vector. If you invert the order of s and t, you are basically changing the angle θ to $(2\pi - \theta)$; plugging this value into the equation will make you realize that all this does is invert the sign of the vector. In other words:

$$\|s \times t\| = -\|t \times s\|$$

There is also a geometrical explanation for the cross product's length. First, put the two vectors such that their tails match and rotate them equally such that one vector is horizontal. Then, add s at the head of t and t at the head of s to generate a parallelogram. Finally, cut off one of the sides' small triangles and paste it to the other end; you will notice that you have basically built a square. You probably already know how to compute the area of a square (height • width). You already have the width (it is given by the norm of t); you can compute the height because by using the sine identity, you know that it's $\sin(\theta)$ times the norm of s, as illustrated in Figure 2.9. To sum things up, the length of the cross product is actually the area of the parallelogram generated by the vectors s and t.

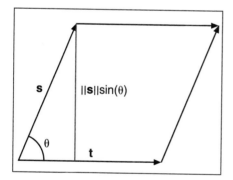

Figure 2.9
Computing the area of a parallelogram

Vector Spaces

The concept of vector spaces is rather interesting because it links vectors with the coordinate systems. A vector space is defined as a set of vectors s, t, u, which have the following properties given any scalar a, b:

a) $s + t = t + s$

b) $(s + t) + v = s + (t + v)$

c) $0 + v = v + 0 = v$

d) $v + (-v) = v + 0 = v$

e) $a(bv) = (ab)v$

f) $(a + b)v = av + bv$

g) $a(s + t)$

h) $1v = v$

This set of properties may very well sound quite ridiculous, but believe it or not, there are many other spaces that do not abide by some of these rules. Until now, you have implicitly used a vector space of $\{<1, 0, 0>, <0, 1, 0>, <0, 0, 1>\}$.

Independence Day

If you were expecting to read a few lines about the movie *Independence Day*, the short answer is that you are not. Rather, this section discusses linear dependency between the vectors.

As you work with vector spaces, it is useless to carry out the same information. Having two equal vectors does not really provide much information to you. As you work with vectors, you'll want to make sure that you do not have the same information twice.

It was previously noted that two vectors are linearly independent if they are not parallel. One way to state the opposite is to say that two vectors are linearly dependent if one vector is a multiple of the other. This stems from the fact that two parallel vectors must share the same direction, and therefore only the magnitude may change between them. You can also generalize this to say that a set of vectors is linearly dependent if there exists one vector that can be expressed as a linear combination of the others.

The odd term here is "linear combination." You know that for two vectors to be linearly dependent, one must be a scalar multiple of the other. In the general sense, a linear combination is nothing more than the sum of vectors individually multiplied by a scalar. If you think about it for a second, you used linear combinations when you learned about the addition of vectors. An addition is in fact a linear combination. The only trick here is that the vectors were always multiplied by the constant scalar value 1. This definition, however, is not that restrictive. Put in terms of an equation, a linearly dependent set of vectors $\mathbf{v}_i$ adhere to the following condition for one vector $\mathbf{v}_k$ and with at least one coefficient a_i non-zero:

$$\sum_{i=1}^{n} a_i \mathbf{v}_i = \mathbf{v}_k, i \neq k$$

This fact is important because, as was mentioned previously, if a vector is linearly dependent on others in the same set, then it does not bring any new information to the table, and you need not carry it around. For example, take the vector set $\{<1, 2, 3>, <4, 7, 10>, <1, 1, 1>\}$. You can obtain the middle vector by multiplying the first one by 3 and adding the last one to it. This means that the set of vectors is linearly dependent. The set of vectors that can be generated by a linear combination of a set of vectors is called a span. For example, you can say that in 3D, span$\{<1, 0, 0>, <0, 1, 0>, <0, 0, 1>\}$ is the set of all vectors in 3D space. This should be obvious; if you simply multiply the first vector by x, the second by y, and the third by z, you can generate any coordinate $<x, y, z>$.

When you talk about a span, redundancy becomes useless; you can discard any vector that is a linear combination of the others. In other words, the span for the first example of a vector set is no different than if you were to omit the last vector of the set. In fact, you could omit any of the three vectors because any vectors in that set can be expressed as a linear combination of the other two.

Basis

A basis can easily be defined as a minimal set of vectors that can span the entire space. The last example you saw is a basis. A more sophisticated example of a basis would be {<1, 2, 0>, <0, 1, 2>, <1, 0, 2>}. You can verify that this does indeed form a basis by trying to find non-zero scalars a, b, and c such that the linear combination of these vectors is the vector $\mathbf{0}$. Finding such a possibility implies that at least one vector can be written as a linear combination of the others. Note that this is exactly the same as the linear independence equation stated in the preceding section, in which every term was grouped on the same side of the equation. The equation is as follows:

$$\mathbf{0} = a\langle 1,2,0\rangle + b\langle 0,1,2\rangle + c\langle 1,0,2\rangle$$
$$\langle 0,0,0\rangle = \langle a+c, 2a+b, 2b+2c\rangle$$

$$0 = a+c$$
$$0 = 2a+b$$
$$0 = b+2c$$

$$a = -c$$
$$b = -2c = 2a$$

$$0 = 2a+b = 2a+2a = 4a$$

$$a = b = c = 0$$

You can juggle the equations as much as you like, but you will never find a non-trivial solution to this problem. Everything comes down to the trivial solution; hence, the set is linearly independent.

So you know that the vectors are independent, but you do not actually know if they are sufficient and minimal enough to describe the entire space. It turns out that they are. A theorem states that in n-space, a basis will have n vectors. One way to see this is that every linearly independent vector can control one single axis in a coordinate system. For example, the trivial base {<1, 0, 0>, <0, 1, 0>, <0, 0, 1>} controls three separate axes: x, y, and z, respectively. But what if the vectors are not trivial? To visualize this, you can simply think of it as a rotated set of axes in space, where each axis is defined by a vector. If you have fewer than n vectors, at least one axis will not be determined, and thus you will not be able to address every vector in space. If you have more than n vectors, at least one vector will be a linear combination of the others and therefore will not provide new information.

For obvious reasons, it is much easier to deal with vectors that affect only trivial axes than it is to deal with vectors that affect more than one component at a time for one scalar value. For example, try to find the scalar values {x, y, z} for the coordinate <1, 2, 3> in the two bases given so far, and you will quickly realize that {<1, 0, 0>, <0, 1, 0>, <0, 0, 1>} is a much nicer set to work with. This is because the first vector can be multiplied by 1, the second by 2, and the third by 3. This would clearly be harder with another basis (which, recall, still spans every coordinate in space).

One thing that makes this set so nice to work with is that it is orthogonal. That is, each vector taken two by two is orthogonal. This property enables you to control given axes separately. Such a basis is called an orthogonal basis.

Another very nice property is that the vectors all have a norm of 1. This makes the task of finding the scalar values much easier than if the values were more obscure. A basis whose vectors all have a norm of 1 is called a normal basis; a basis whose vectors are orthogonal and whose vectors have a norm of 1 is called an orthonormal basis.

Don't be confused by the preceding definition. There is an infinite set of vectors that form an orthonormal basis in 3D. Simply take the orthonormal basis you know and let it rotate freely around any axis, and you will still have an orthonormal basis. The reason you might want to build another orthonormal basis is to simplify your life by building another coordinate system, as you saw in Chapter 1, "Equation Manipulation and Representation." Besides, there is another reason why studying these concepts is important, as you will see in Chapter 3, where you will transform coordinates by using bases.

Orthogonalization

The word "orthogonalization" pretty much spells out what it does. Orthogonalization is the process of building an orthogonal basis out of a set of linearly independent vectors. This is useful not only for coordinate systems, but also for numerical reasons.

The IEEE floating points format, which is supported in all decent PCs today, has many numerical issues. For example, if you rotate three orthonormal vectors freely around in 3D space, eventually the precision gets bad enough that the vectors won't be orthonormal anymore. This can become an issue if you are using these vectors to transform shapes on the screen, because you will start to notice some weird deformations. Clearly, a process is required in order to re-orthogonalize these vectors.

Now that you understand the why, let's look at the how. It was previously shown that a projection of a vector **s** upon another vector **t** yields a new vector that is parallel to **t**, but with the projected magnitude of **s**. You can also look at the perpendicular component of **s** instead of looking at its component with regards to **t**. To compute this, you simply need to subtract the projected component from **s**. This is the same as saying that you have a coordinate $<x, y>$ and that you will subtract $<0, y>$ from it. What is left is the component in x, as shown in Figure 2.10.

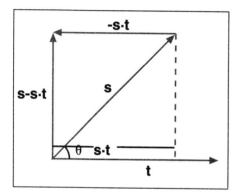

Figure 2.10
Perpendicular component of a projection

Mathematically, the perpendicular component of a vector is

$$\text{Perp}_s\left(\mathbf{t}\right) = \mathbf{s} - \frac{\mathbf{s} \bullet \mathbf{t}}{\mathbf{t} \bullet \mathbf{t}}\mathbf{t}$$

This works correctly for two vectors. Given two vectors, you can find a vector that is orthogonal to the other vector. If you think about the geometrical view of the problem, you can quite easily deduce that this process can be applied to more than one vector. For example, if you have three vectors, choose one vector to be the projective vector and another vector to be the projected vector. Compute the perpendicular vector for the projected vector, and you should now have two orthogonal vectors. For the third vector, you can subtract its projection from the first vector and its projection from the second vector and, for the exact same reasons, obtain a vector that is orthogonal to both the first and second vector. Put in terms of equations, what you get is the following:

$$\mathbf{v}_i\,'= \mathbf{v}_i - \sum_{j=1}^{i-1} \frac{\mathbf{v}_i \bullet \mathbf{v}_j}{\mathbf{v}_j \bullet \mathbf{v}_j} \mathbf{v}_j$$

Simply apply this process to your $n-1$ vectors, and you will successfully yield an orthogonal basis. You can easily compute an orthonormal basis if you simply normalize the end result vectors. Let's illustrate this with an example. Take the previous basis {<1, 2, 0>, <0, 1, 2>, <1, 0, 2>} and generate an orthogonal basis out of it:

$$v_1\,'=\langle 1,2,0\rangle$$

$$v_2\,'=\langle 0,1,2\rangle - \frac{\langle 0,1,2\rangle \bullet \langle 1,2,0\rangle}{\langle 1,2,0\rangle \bullet \langle 1,2,0\rangle}\langle 1,2,0\rangle$$

$$=\langle 0,1,2\rangle - \frac{2}{5}\langle 1,2,0\rangle$$

$$=\left\langle -\frac{2}{5},\frac{1}{5},2\right\rangle$$

$$v_2\,'=\langle 1,0,2\rangle - \frac{\langle 1,0,2\rangle \bullet \langle 1,2,0\rangle}{\langle 1,2,0\rangle \bullet \langle 1,2,0\rangle}\langle 1,2,0\rangle - \frac{\langle 1,2,0\rangle \bullet \left\langle -\frac{2}{5},\frac{1}{5},2\right\rangle}{\left\langle -\frac{2}{5},\frac{1}{5},2\right\rangle \bullet \left\langle -\frac{2}{5},\frac{1}{5},2\right\rangle}\left\langle -\frac{2}{5},\frac{1}{5},2\right\rangle$$

$$=\langle 1,0,2\rangle - \frac{1}{5}\langle 1,2,0\rangle - \frac{18}{21}\left\langle -\frac{2}{5},\frac{1}{5},2\right\rangle$$

$$=\langle 1.1429,-0.5714,0.2857\rangle$$

You can verify that these vectors are indeed orthogonal by computing the dot product on each possible pair of vectors. They therefore form an orthogonal basis in 3D. In 3D, if you know that two of these vectors are orthogonal, there is a much easier way to compute the third vector. Recall that the cross product is actually a vector that is orthogonal to both original vectors. Therefore, you should not waste time computing the Gram-Schmidt orthogonal vector as shown in the preceding equation, and instead should simply resort to using the cross product, which is much simpler to compute. For the second vector, the method presented in the preceding equation is pretty much as simple as it can get. It's important to remember the other things (such as the cross product) that are more specific than the general cases, but also more efficient.

Thinking Outside the Box

The vector spaces you have defined operate on real elements, but there is no law that states that vector spaces need to be composed of real vectors. One short and useful way to represent polynomials is by creating a vector space with polynomials as a basis. For example, suppose that you wanted to consider every third-degree polynomial. In that case, you could define a vector space $\{<1, 0, 0, 0>, <0, x, 0, 0>, <0, 0, x^2, 0>, <0, 0, 0, x^3>\}$. It doesn't give much geometrically, but mathematically, it is a very nice way to represent polynomials. If you wanted to represent the polynomial $1 + 4x^2 - 3x^3$ in this vector space, you could simply use vectors and refer to it as $<1, 0, 4, -3>$. This is the exact same thing you have seen in real vector spaces except that you are not working with real numbers.

You can also observe that the addition remains well defined for this vector space. In fact, every property stated previously for a vector space is well defined by the very definition of a vector space. This is a much more convenient way to work with polynomials because the representation is that much simpler. The rules about orthogonality are also still valid; you can verify this by computing the dot product of each vector, which build the vector space, which is also still valid. The cross product is a very specific case both in terms of dimensions and in terms of components, so this one is not well defined in this space. However, you can also define another set of operations in this space if you wish.

Vectors have thus far been defined mainly as a form of coordinate representation, but in the world of, say, SIMD and vertex shaders, you can think of a vector more as an array than as a mathematical coordinate. For instance, color can be represented in a 4-vector of the form <Alpha, Red, Green, Blue>. You can actually perform a set of operations on this vector, very similarly to what you saw above. Addition and dot product are the most appealing examples that come to mind when you want to blend colors together (more on this in Chapter 13, "Exploring Curvy Bodies"). Approximations and computations can also be applied more efficiently by computing four elements at a time in the SIMD scenario. As usual, think outside the box.

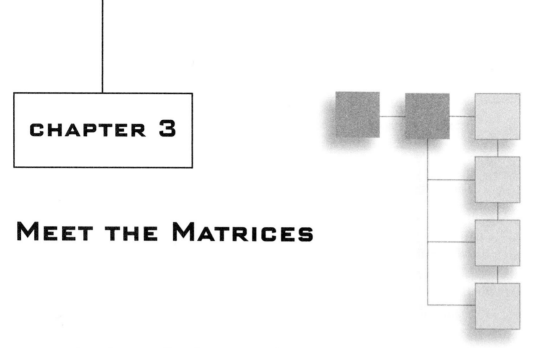

CHAPTER 3

MEET THE MATRICES

Sometimes the generality of a concept is obscured by the examples used to explain the concept. For example, in Chapter 2, "Baby Steps: Introduction to Vectors," you saw vectors as elements carrying real numbers, but how many were expressed in terms of, say, polynomials? Interestingly enough, the definition of a vector does not restrict vectors to real numbers in any way. You need not look at them as heads and tails, as in Chapter 2. Most of the material in Chapter 2 dealt with real elements, but what happens if you choose another type of element that is not a real number? For example, you saw how vectors could be used to represent such things as color channels by merely considering the vector as an array of elements.

Matrices and vectors share a very close relationship. In fact, a matrix is actually a vector at its base with some even more interesting operations added to it. This chapter goes beyond the basic material by examining some fairly advanced concepts you might use in a game's perspective. If you are thinking about skipping this chapter, I strongly advise against doing so; this chapter may well contain material that you have not seen before, or may describe some relationships that make certain concepts easier to remember.

tip

For most of its matrix operations, Maple requires that you load the linear algebra library: with(LinearAlgebra).

This chapter covers the following:

- Defining matrices
- Vector revision

Meat, the Matrices

The title is not a typo; it's a pun. Matrices are the real meat of math because they can be used to represent single numbers, vectors, and more. You know that vectors can carry pretty much any type of element. But what happens if the elements you choose are real vectors? In that case, what you get is a matrix. Simply put, a matrix is a vector of real vectors.

All in all, matrices are very powerful objects, which, like vectors, are there to simplify your life in terms of representation and computation. They are extremely helpful when dealing with linear transformations you will deal with in games, and they are one of the key data structures used to represent cumulative transformations efficiently. A matrix can thus represent a transformation that is applied (multiplied) with a vector.

There are many ways to write a matrix on paper. One such method is to use the very definition of it and to write the matrix as $<<\ldots>, <\ldots>, <\ldots>>$. Although this is a valid way to write a matrix (and it's how some mathematical applications will ask you to input matrices), it is not a very nice way to *see* matrices. A nicer way to write matrices is to have everything align correctly in an *nxm* table. For example, suppose you wanted to have a matrix that was a 3-vector carrying 4-vectors—which is, by definition, a 3×4 matrix. Such a matrix **M** can be written as follows:

$$\mathbf{M} = \begin{bmatrix} a_{11} & a_{12} & a_{13} & a_{14} \\ a_{21} & a_{22} & a_{23} & a_{24} \\ a_{31} & a_{32} & a_{33} & a_{34} \end{bmatrix}$$

Although this is the most common way to look at matrices, it is not always the easiest. As an alternative, if you consider your real vectors as atomic elements, you can let $\mathbf{r}_i$ refer to row *i* and then write your matrix in this form:

$$\mathbf{M} = \begin{bmatrix} \mathbf{r}_1 \\ \mathbf{r}_2 \\ \mathbf{r}_3 \end{bmatrix}$$

When expanded, this is in fact a 3×4 matrix. If you consider the rows as elements, however, you can also say that this is a 3×1 matrix because in reality, you are only carrying one element, which is a vector. An *n*×1 matrix is called a column matrix due to its column form.

There is yet another way to look at this matrix: by looking at it as having elements in the form of columns. So if you take the columns of matrix **M** and generate a vector for each of the four columns, what you get is another valid matrix representation:

$$\mathbf{M} = \begin{bmatrix} \mathbf{c}_1 & \mathbf{c}_2 & \mathbf{c}_3 & \mathbf{c}_4 \end{bmatrix}$$

This is beginning to look very much like a vector, but don't be fooled. Vectors throughout this book are written with pointy brackets, while matrices use square brackets. This form of $1 \times n$ matrix is called a row matrix, for obvious reasons.

When working with matrices, it is sometimes advantageous to look at them in a more abstract sense, such as a set of rows or columns. For this reason, these various representations offer some very good tools for working with matrices.

tip

In Maple, matrices can be defined with brackets, such as A := Matrix([[1, 2], [3, 4]]);

Basic Operations and Properties

A vector in real space is defined as a set of real values. As you move over to matrices, however, the same concept applies, but for vectors of reals instead of just reals. With matrices, you are working with a new element (a vector of real), so the rules for using them will be different—although similar. Have no fear; there are plenty of operations you can perform with matrices that you cannot perform with vectors of real elements. Matrices' usefulness has simply multiplied.

Just to give you an *avant-gout* of what is to come, you can take a set of linear equations and convert them into matrix form:

$$2x + 3y = 4$$
$$6x - y = 3$$

$$\begin{bmatrix} 2 & 3 & 4 \\ 6 & -1 & 3 \end{bmatrix}$$

Of course, to solve the actual problem, you will have to wait until you understand the basics about matrices and the laws that govern their usage.

Matrix Addition

As with vectors, the addition operation for matrices is well defined. All you need to do is add the individual elements of the matrix, which in turn implies the addition of two real vectors. Put in terms of equations, an addition operation is just as you might expect for two matrices **A** and **B**:

$$\mathbf{A} = \begin{bmatrix} a_{11} & \cdots & a_{1m} \\ \vdots & \ddots & \vdots \\ a_{n1} & \cdots & a_{nm} \end{bmatrix}, \mathbf{B} = \begin{bmatrix} b_{11} & \cdots & b_{1m} \\ \vdots & \ddots & \vdots \\ b_{n1} & \cdots & b_{nm} \end{bmatrix}$$

$$\mathbf{A} + \mathbf{B} = \begin{bmatrix} a_{11} + b_{11} & \cdots & a_{1m} + b_{1m} \\ \vdots & \ddots & \vdots \\ a_{n1} + b_{n1} & \cdots & a_{nm} + b_{nm} \end{bmatrix}$$

For obvious reasons, matrices can be added together only if they have the same dimension. This was no different with vectors, which also must be of the same dimension and type in order be added together.

Similarly, subtraction of matrices can be performed exactly as you would expect it:

$$\mathbf{A} - \mathbf{B} = \begin{bmatrix} a_{11} - b_{11} & \cdots & a_{1m} - b_{1m} \\ \vdots & \ddots & \vdots \\ a_{n1} - b_{n1} & \cdots & a_{nm} - b_{nm} \end{bmatrix}$$

All in all, the addition and subtraction operations for matrices are bound by the same rules as for vectors. You merely need to add sets of two vectors. As an example, let's take two matrices **A** and **B** and add them together:

$$\mathbf{A} = \begin{bmatrix} 1 & 2 & 3 \\ 4 & 5 & 6 \\ 7 & 8 & 9 \end{bmatrix}, \mathbf{B} = \begin{bmatrix} 3 & 4 & 9 \\ 2 & 5 & 8 \\ 1 & 6 & 7 \end{bmatrix}$$

$$\mathbf{A} + \mathbf{B} = \begin{bmatrix} 1+3 & 2+4 & 3+9 \\ 4+2 & 5+5 & 6+8 \\ 7+1 & 8+6 & 9+7 \end{bmatrix}$$

tip

In Maple, matrices can be added like numbers—for example, **A** + **B**.

Scalar Multiplication

With vectors, you saw scalar multiplication as a means to scale the magnitude of a vector. This is also true with matrices because they have a norm. If you recall the root definition of a matrix, you can again deduce that a scalar multiplication is performed exactly as expected. With vectors, the scalar multiplied every single element in the vector. With matrices, if you apply the recursive rule, you get the following:

$$k\mathbf{M} = \begin{bmatrix} k\mathbf{r}_1 \\ \vdots \\ k\mathbf{r}_n \end{bmatrix} = \begin{bmatrix} ka_{11} & \cdots & ka_{1m} \\ \vdots & \ddots & \vdots \\ ka_{n1} & \cdots & ka_{nm} \end{bmatrix}$$

If you understand how a matrix came about, it is very easy to see that the scalar multiplication of a matrix is nothing but a matter of multiplying every single element of the matrix by that same scalar k, as shown in the following example:

$$\mathbf{M} = \begin{bmatrix} 1 & 2 & 3 \\ 4 & 5 & 6 \\ 7 & 8 & 9 \end{bmatrix}, k = 2$$

$$k\mathbf{M} = \begin{bmatrix} 2 \cdot 1 & 2 \cdot 2 & 2 \cdot 3 \\ 2 \cdot 4 & 2 \cdot 5 & 2 \cdot 6 \\ 2 \cdot 7 & 2 \cdot 8 & 2 \cdot 9 \end{bmatrix}$$

$$= \begin{bmatrix} 2 & 4 & 6 \\ 8 & 10 & 12 \\ 14 & 16 & 18 \end{bmatrix}$$

tip

In Maple, a matrix can be multiplied with the dot command '.', as in A . B;.

Matrix Transposition

True or false: A matrix is typically written as a $n \times m$ table—that is, a table with n rows and m columns.

False. There are two types of matrices:

- **Row-major matrices**—You build a row-major matrix by considering its elements as rows. Row-major matrices are the types of matrices you have seen so far and are the type that will be used throughout this chapter.

- **Column-major matrices**—When building a column major matrix, you need to consider the vector elements as columns. For example, if you were to write the previous 3×4 matrix in column-major format, you would get the following:

$$M = \begin{bmatrix} a_{11} & a_{12} & a_{13} \\ a_{21} & a_{22} & a_{23} \\ a_{31} & a_{32} & a_{33} \\ a_{41} & a_{42} & a_{43} \end{bmatrix}$$

Notice what really happened here: Every element sitting at index ij got switched with the element at index ji. In contrast with row-major matrices, the first index in a column-major matrix refers to the column, and the second one refers to the row—hence, again, the name "column-major."

note

> The reason why this is important is because your favorite 3D library may use one format or the other. For instance, OpenGL uses column-major matrices, while Direct3D opted to go row-major. Long live standardization!

It may be useful to convert a matrix from one format to another from time to time from a performance point of view, as will be seen in Chapter 21, "Kicking the Turtle: Approximating Common and Slow Functions." So, one of the operations you may want to achieve is to transpose a matrix—that is, convert a matrix from one mode to the other. The definition of a transposition was already given, but in a more rigorous fashion, a matrix M's transposition can be written as follows:

$$M = \begin{bmatrix} a_{11} & \cdots & a_{1j} & \cdots & a_{1m} \\ \vdots & \ddots & a_{ji} & \cdots & \vdots \\ a_{i1} & a_{ij} & a_{jj} & \cdots & a_{im} \\ \vdots & \vdots & \vdots & \ddots & \vdots \\ a_{n1} & \cdots & a_{nj} & \cdots & a_{nm} \end{bmatrix}$$

$$M^T = \begin{bmatrix} a_{11} & \cdots & a_{i1} & \cdots & a_{1m} \\ \vdots & \ddots & a_{ij} & \cdots & \vdots \\ a_{1j} & a_{ji} & a_{jj} & \cdots & a_{nj} \\ \vdots & \vdots & \vdots & \ddots & \vdots \\ a_{n1} & \cdots & a_{im} & \cdots & a_{nm} \end{bmatrix}$$

In short, you can say that element $a_{ij} = a_{ji}$.

As noted in the preceding equation, a transposition is written with a capital T as super-script. It does not mean M to the power of T. Note that the T is not in italics, which implies that it is not a scalar value. For example, you can take the same matrix as the one used in the preceding equation, **M**, and compute its transposition to yield the following:

$$\mathbf{M} = \begin{bmatrix} 1 & 2 & 3 \\ 4 & 5 & 6 \\ 7 & 8 & 9 \end{bmatrix}$$

$$\mathbf{M}^\mathrm{T} = \begin{bmatrix} 1 & 4 & 7 \\ 2 & 5 & 8 \\ 3 & 6 & 9 \end{bmatrix}$$

tip

In Maple, a matrix is transposed using the Transpose command from the linear algebra package—for example, Transpose(Matrix);.

Matrix Multiplication

In Chapter 2, two types of multiplication were presented: dot product and cross product. The cross product is too specific to vectors to apply to matrices, but you will see a cousin of that operation a little later in this chapter. The dot product, on the other hand, has a future with matrices.

Let's start slowly and look at the dot product (multiplication) of a matrix and a vector (or a column-matrix if you prefer). The following logic ensues:

$$\mathbf{A} = \begin{bmatrix} a_{11} & a_{12} & a_{13} & a_{14} \\ a_{21} & a_{22} & a_{23} & a_{24} \\ a_{31} & a_{32} & a_{33} & a_{34} \end{bmatrix}, \mathbf{B} = \begin{bmatrix} b_1 \\ b_2 \\ b_3 \\ b_4 \end{bmatrix}$$

$$\mathbf{AB} = \begin{bmatrix} \mathbf{r}_1 \\ \mathbf{r}_2 \\ \mathbf{r}_3 \end{bmatrix} \bullet \mathbf{B}$$

$$= \begin{bmatrix} \mathbf{r}_1 \bullet \mathbf{B} \\ \mathbf{r}_2 \bullet \mathbf{B} \\ \mathbf{r}_3 \bullet \mathbf{B} \end{bmatrix}$$

$$= \begin{bmatrix} a_{11} \cdot b_1 & a_{12} \cdot b_2 & a_{13} \cdot b_3 & a_{14} \cdot b_4 \\ a_{21} \cdot b_1 & a_{22} \cdot b_2 & a_{23} \cdot b_3 & a_{24} \cdot b_4 \\ a_{31} \cdot b_1 & a_{32} \cdot b_2 & a_{33} \cdot b_3 & a_{34} \cdot b_4 \end{bmatrix}$$

This brings up a few interesting facts. For starters, the sizes of the matrices clearly need not be equal. The first matrix is a 3×4 while the second is a 4×1. By the very definition of the dot product, however, the number of elements of the two vectors to which the dot product is applied must be equal. Translation: The number of columns in the first matrix must match the number of rows in the second matrix, or else the multiplication is not defined. Thus, matrix multiplication can be expressed as the summed multiplication of the first matrix's row by the second matrix's column. (Obviously, the dot product does not restrict the matrix **B** to being a column-matrix. You could easily make **B** a matrix with more than one column.)

Let's put this concept into action. When you are dealing with two matrices **A** and **B** and you want to determine whether the two can be multiplied together, first determine whether the first matrix's column size matches the second matrix's row size. So if **A** was an $n×i$ matrix and **B** was an $i×m$ matrix, this would in fact be a well-defined multiplication because the column of the first (i), matches the row of the second (i).

The question is, then, "What is the size of the resulting matrix?" Because the dot product ends up canceling out the middle terms—or more appropriately, combining them—you can see that for matrices **A** and **B**, the resulting matrix becomes a matrix of size $n×m$.

In general, an element of a matrix product can be computed with the following equation:

$$\left(\mathbf{AB}\right)_{ij} = \sum_{k=1}^{n} a_{ik} b_{kj}$$

This is just another way to express the multiplication of two matrices. It is a little more cumbersome to remember than the dot product of a row and a column, but it does work.

One very important thing you need to observe here is that **AB** is not the same thing as **BA**. Although real numbers are commutative, matrices are not. This should be clear in the preceding equation; **BA** is not even defined, given the size of the matrices.

Although you are somewhat restricted in terms of algebraic operations, you can still find a few properties remaining for matrix multiplication:

$$\mathbf{ABC} = \left(\mathbf{AB}\right)\mathbf{C} = \mathbf{A}\left(\mathbf{BC}\right)$$
$$\mathbf{A}\left(\mathbf{B}+\mathbf{C}\right) = \mathbf{AB} + \mathbf{AC}$$
$$\left(\mathbf{AB}\right)^{\mathrm{T}} = \mathbf{B}^{\mathrm{T}}\mathbf{A}^{\mathrm{T}}$$
$$\left(a\mathbf{A}\right)\mathbf{B} = a\left(\mathbf{AB}\right)$$

Matrix multiplication is also often called matrix concatenation because in reality, it allows you to concatenate two transformations or to substitute one linear system into another. As an example, multiply two transformation matrices **A** and **B**:

$$\mathbf{A} = \begin{bmatrix} 1 & 2 & 2 & 4 \\ 5 & 0 & 1 & 0 \\ 2 & 3 & 0 & 2 \end{bmatrix}, \mathbf{B} = \begin{bmatrix} 1 & 0 \\ 4 & 2 \\ 0 & 3 \\ 1 & 2 \end{bmatrix}$$

$$\mathbf{AB} = \begin{bmatrix} 1 & 2 & 2 & 4 \\ 5 & 0 & 1 & 0 \\ 2 & 3 & 0 & 2 \end{bmatrix} \begin{bmatrix} 1 & 0 \\ 4 & 2 \\ 0 & 3 \\ 1 & 2 \end{bmatrix}$$

$$= \begin{bmatrix} 1\cdot1+2\cdot4+2\cdot0+4\cdot1 & 1\cdot0+2\cdot2+2\cdot3+4\cdot2 \\ 5\cdot1+0\cdot4+1\cdot0+0\cdot1 & 5\cdot0+0\cdot2+1\cdot3+0\cdot2 \\ 2\cdot1+3\cdot4+0\cdot0+2\cdot1 & 2\cdot0+3\cdot2+0\cdot3+2\cdot2 \end{bmatrix}$$

$$= \begin{bmatrix} 13 & 18 \\ 5 & 3 \\ 16 & 10 \end{bmatrix}$$

The Identity Matrix

In the world of real numbers, there is a single number that can be multiplied by any number without actually changing that number. That's right, it's the number 1. If you multiply 1 by any other number, you always get that same number back. For matrices, you have an equivalent: the identity matrix $\mathbf{I}$ (the equivalent of 1 in the real world), which does not change any other arbitrary matrix $\mathbf{M}$ under multiplication. Expressed mathematically:

$$\mathbf{IM} = \mathbf{M} = \mathbf{MI}$$

Here, $\mathbf{M}$ is an arbitrary square matrix, meaning it is a matrix of size $n \times n$, and $\mathbf{I}$ is the identity matrix, also a square matrix of the same size.

To solve this one, you can come back to vector spaces. In vector spaces, one space basis was such that it did not modify the values you passed to it. It was simply placing the values {x, y, z, ...} that were given to it in their corresponding positions. If you build a matrix that has the same set of vectors, then you can achieve the same effect. This basis in 3×3 was of the form <<1, 0, 0>, <0, 1, 0>, <0, 0, 1>>, which means that this would in fact build a matrix as follows:

$$\mathbf{I} = \begin{bmatrix} 1 & 0 & 0 \\ 0 & 1 & 0 \\ 0 & 0 & 1 \end{bmatrix}$$

You can verify that this matrix multiplied by any 3×3 matrix does yield the original matrix. You can also verify that commuting the two matrices still yields the original matrix. In a more general sense, the identity matrix is an $n \times n$ matrix for which the elements at the diagonals are ones and for which all the other elements are zeros. In terms of equations, you get the following:

$$\mathbf{I}_n = \begin{bmatrix} 1 & \leftarrow & 0 \\ \uparrow & 1 & \downarrow \\ 0 & \rightarrow & 1 \end{bmatrix}$$

Matrix Norm

Matrices are built out of vectors, so it should come as no surprise that they, too, carry a norm. For a real vector-norm, a length is attributed; for a matrix, however, you cannot really attribute a length in a geometrical sense. In this case, the term *norm* or *magnitude* is more appropriate. In addition, the same principles of normalization apply to both vectors and matrices, and thus a normal matrix is a matrix with norm 1.

The matrix norm is a clear indicator of the quality of the linear system. As you will discover in the upcoming sections on linear systems, life in computerland is quite different from the theoretical world. You thus need some way to identify which matrices will yield the results you expect and which won't. For instance, if you use a matrix to compute the intersection of a set of planes, you would indeed expect the result to be pretty close to the real solution if not the exact real solution. To be three units off is often not acceptable. Just try to recall the last time you shot someone in your favorite 3D shooter but the game did not detect a collision. Sometimes, you may be entirely right (that is, mathematically, you should have hit the other player), but because the developers opted for speed before accuracy, you're dead wrong. Before you take a deeper look at the problem, let's start by looking at how we can compute a norm.

tip
_____
In Maple, the norm of a matrix is computed like the norm of a vector (that is, norm(Matrix, norm);).
_____

Frobenius Norm

The Frobenius norm is one of the easiest norms to compute because the equation gives you the answer without requiring the application of iterative methods or something more involved. The Frobenius norm is also sometimes called the Euclidian norm, and is defined as the square root of the sum of the absolute square of its elements. For real numbers, the absolute value adds nothing new to the equation, so you can write the Frobenius norm for a real $n \times m$ matrix $\mathbf{M}$ as follows:

$$\|\mathbf{M}\|_F = \sqrt{\sum_{i=0}^{n}\sum_{j=0}^{m} m_{ij}^{2}}$$

Matrix p-norm

Of course, if the p-norm was defined for vectors, it ought to be defined for matrices. The problem with the p-norm is that the equation does not directly give you the answer. The norm is not computed as easily at it may appear. The p-norm of a real $n \times m$ matrix $\mathbf{M}$ can be written as follows:

$$\|\mathbf{M}\|_p = \max_{\|\mathbf{x}\|_p = 1} \|\mathbf{Mx}\|_p$$

As you can see, the p-norm is rather tricky to compute because it is in fact the maximum of the p-norm of $\mathbf{Mx}$ for any given vector $\mathbf{x}$ that has a p-norm of 1. This should not really be a problem, however, because matrix norms are mostly useful in your case for determining the numerical stability of a matrix. You can compute the numerical stability of a matrix by computing the norm of $\mathbf{M}$ multiplied by the norm of its inverse.

Of course, if you are looking at the 1-norm or the ∞-norm, you can get a much more manageable equation, as shown here:

$$\|\mathbf{M}\|_1 = \max \|\mathbf{c}_i\|_1$$
$$\|\mathbf{M}\|_\infty = \max \|\mathbf{r}_i\|_1$$

Table 3.1 shows a few examples of norm calculations for a given matrix $\mathbf{M}$:

$$\mathbf{M} = \begin{bmatrix} 1 & 2 & 3 \\ 4 & 5 & 6 \\ 7 & 8 & 9 \end{bmatrix}$$

Table 3.1 Norm Values for **M**

Norm	Expression	Value
F	$1^2 + 2^2 + 3^2 + 4^2 + 5^2 + 6^2 + 7^2 + 8^2 + 9^2$	285
$p = 1$	$3 + 6 + 9$	18
$p = 2$		16.8481
$p = \infty$	$7 + 8 + 9$	24

The computation details of the 2-norm are not given, mainly because you have yet to see the necessary information to maximize a multi-variable function.

Advanced Operations and Properties

Matrices are such a convenient way of representing things that they have found their way into many problems. Because a horde of problems can be expressed by using matrices, the need for operations that are similar to those you have come to enjoy with real numbers has grown. Other types of matrix operations are more similar to the cross product operation you saw in the last chapter; these have a more specialized use and thus solve only a limited set of problems. In this section, you will see both types of operations.

Linear Systems

One very important use of matrices is to represent linear systems of equations. A linear system of equations is a family of equations with n linear equations and k variables. For instance, the following set of equations forms a linear system:

$$2x - 3y + z = 3$$
$$4x + 2z = 2$$
$$3x + 2y - z = 1$$

From a game's perspective, such a linear system could represent the collision between a set of objects, and the solution to the linear system would thus be the intersection point of the objects. Matrices offer a very convenient way to represent these types of systems because they enable you to easily isolate the variables' coefficients by simply creating a variable vector $<x, y, z>$ and multiplying it by a matrix. The following matrix notation is equivalent to the linear system above:

$$\begin{bmatrix} 2 & -3 & 1 \\ 4 & 0 & 2 \\ 3 & 2 & -1 \end{bmatrix} \begin{bmatrix} x \\ y \\ z \end{bmatrix} = \begin{bmatrix} 3 \\ 2 \\ 1 \end{bmatrix}$$

You can verify that this form does indeed represent the preceding set of equations by simply multiplying the matrices together and by looking at each row as an equation.

There are many good approaches to solving a linear system. One such technique is substitution. The idea here is to isolate one variable in one equation and then substitute that variable in the remaining equations. If you apply this process iteratively for every variable, you eventually end up with one variable associated directly with one number (assuming you have enough linearly independent equations to solve the problem).

Another approach is to add or subtract equations. For instance, if you add together the first and last equation, you will successfully come up with an equation with one less variable: z. You can keep doing this until you reach a point where only one variable remains, at which point you can again solve the linear system correctly.

Combined with this operation is the fact that you can also multiply an equation by a scalar k without actually modifying anything in the system. For example, if you wanted to get rid of the variable x with the first and second equation, you could not do so with a single addition. Instead, you could add the second equation twice, or if you prefer, multiply the second equation by -2 and add it to the first. This is the principle you will use to solve this linear system.

tip

Maple can solve linear systems with the linsolve(Matrix, Vector); command.

The Gauss Method

Because carrying all those variables around is a bit cumbersome, you can define a new way to write linear systems. Instead of writing the variable vector and the equal sign, you can replace all that with a line splitting the coefficient from the values. In this way, the equation in the preceding section can be rewritten as follows:

$$\begin{bmatrix} 2 & -3 & 1 & | & 3 \\ 4 & 0 & 2 & | & 2 \\ 3 & 2 & -1 & | & 1 \end{bmatrix}$$

If you stick to using scalar multiplication of rows combined with additions and subtractions of rows, you can solve the linear system in this format quite easily. Such is the idea behind the Gauss method. It is a method that helps you solve linear systems of equations. To do so, you must first get rid of one variable. In the preceding section you learned how to get rid of x or z, but you can get rid of any variable you like by simply scaling both rows such that the variable you want to get rid of has a coefficient of 1. (Make sure that the sign of each equation is such that that variable cancels out.)

Another operation that can be pretty useful is to reposition the rows. This is obviously legal because in the original set of three equations, you can swap the order of the equations without modifying anything. Therefore, to solve a linear system, you first need to make sure that the first row has a non-zero coefficient for the first component. With it, you can get rid of the same component for the remaining equations below it. You can apply this process recursively on the smaller matrix to finally yield a system where the lower triangle of the matrix is set to 0. (This type of matrix is called an upper triangular matrix.) Let's see how this is done on the matrix given previously:

$$\begin{bmatrix} 2 & -3 & 1 & 3 \\ 4 & 0 & 2 & 2 \\ 3 & 2 & -1 & 1 \end{bmatrix}$$

$$\xrightarrow[\text{Scale down } r_2 \text{ by } 2]{\text{Scale down } r_1 \text{ by } 2} \begin{bmatrix} 1 & -\dfrac{3}{2} & \dfrac{1}{2} & \dfrac{3}{2} \\ 2 & 0 & 1 & 1 \\ 3 & 2 & -1 & 1 \end{bmatrix}$$

$$\xrightarrow[\text{Subtract } 3r_1 \text{ by } r_3]{\text{Subtract } 2r_1 \text{ by } r_2} \begin{bmatrix} 1 & -\dfrac{3}{2} & \dfrac{1}{2} & \dfrac{3}{2} \\ 0 & 3 & 0 & -2 \\ 0 & \dfrac{13}{2} & -\dfrac{5}{2} & -\dfrac{7}{2} \end{bmatrix}$$

$$\xrightarrow[\text{Scale up } r_3 \text{ by } 2]{\text{Scale down } r_2 \text{ by } 3} \begin{bmatrix} 1 & -\dfrac{3}{2} & \dfrac{1}{2} & \dfrac{3}{2} \\ 0 & 1 & 0 & -\dfrac{2}{3} \\ 0 & 13 & -5 & -7 \end{bmatrix}$$

$$\xrightarrow{\text{Subtract } 13r_2 \text{ from } r_3} \begin{bmatrix} 1 & -\dfrac{3}{2} & \dfrac{1}{2} & \dfrac{3}{2} \\ 0 & 1 & 0 & -\dfrac{2}{3} \\ 0 & 0 & -5 & \dfrac{5}{3} \end{bmatrix}$$

$$\xrightarrow{\text{Scale down } r_2 \text{ by -5}} \begin{bmatrix} 1 & -\dfrac{3}{2} & \dfrac{1}{2} & \dfrac{3}{2} \\ 0 & 1 & 0 & -\dfrac{2}{3} \\ 0 & 0 & 1 & -\dfrac{1}{3} \end{bmatrix}$$

Now you can solve the system by backward-substitution. You have a direct solution for z and, in this case, it so happens that you also have a direct solution for y. In order to solve for x, you can substitute y and z, so let's complete the task:

$$z = -\frac{1}{3}$$

$$y = -\frac{2}{3}$$

$$x - \frac{2}{3}y + \frac{1}{2}z = \frac{3}{2}$$

$$x = \frac{3}{2} + \frac{3}{2}\left(-\frac{2}{3}\right) - \frac{1}{2}\left(-\frac{2}{3}\right)$$

$$= \frac{3}{2} - 1 + \frac{1}{6}$$

$$= \frac{2}{3}$$

Thus, the final solution to the problem is <x, y, z> = <2, -2, -1>/3. When it comes time to actually implement this algorithm, it's much trickier because row reduction sometimes has to be done in a specific order.

```
// Simple definitions to make things more readable
#define M00 Matrix[0][0]
#define M01 Matrix[0][1]
#define M02 Matrix[0][2]
#define M03 Matrix[0][3]
#define M10 Matrix[1][0]
#define M11 Matrix[1][1]
#define M12 Matrix[1][2]
#define M13 Matrix[1][3]
#define M20 Matrix[2][0]
#define M21 Matrix[2][1]
#define M22 Matrix[2][2]
#define M23 Matrix[2][3]


Vector3D Gauss(float Matrix[3][4])
{
    // Let's make sure that the co-efficient we will multiply with are
    // non-zero or else we are destroying our matrix
    if (M00 <= THREASHOLD) {
        if (abs(M10> THREASHOLD)
            SwapRows(Matrix, 0, 1);
        else if (abs(M20 > THREASHOLD)
            SwapRows(Matrix, 0, 2);
        else
            return false;
    }
```

```
    // Now we know that A is satisfied, we have to make sure both vectors are
    if (abs(matrix[1][1]) <= THREASHOLD) {
        if (M21 > THREASHOLD)
            SwapRows(Matrix, 2, 3);
        else if ((M01 > THREASHOLD) &&
                        (abs(M11 > THREASHOLD))
            SwapRows(Matrix, 1, 2);
        else
            return false;
    }

    if (abs(M22 <= THREASHOLD) {
        if ((abs(matrix[0][2]) > THREASHOLD) &&
                        (abs(M02) > THREASHOLD))
            SwapRows(Matrix, 1, 2);
        else if ((abs(M12) > THREASHOLD) &&
                        (abs(matrix[2][1]) > THREASHOLD))
            SwapRows(Matrix, 2, 3);
        else
            return false;
    }

    // Here, we just factored a few things which were common
    CrossY    = M00 * M11 - M01 * M10;    // AF - BE
    CrossZ    = M00 * M21 - M01 * M20;    // AJ - BI
    Val       = M03 * M10 - M00 * M13;    // DE - AH
    ValZ      = M00 * M12 - M02 * M10;    // AG - CE

    float Z = ((CrossY * (M03 * M20 - M00 * M23) - Val * CrossZ) /                 (CrossY
* (M00 * M22 - M02 * M20) - ValZ* CrossZ));
    float Y =  ((Val - Z * ValZ) / CrossY);
    float X = ((-M02 * Z - M01 * Y - M03) / M00);

        return Vector3D(X, Y, Z);
}
```

Unfortunately, this is far from being the holy grail to finding the solution to a linear system. It is a pretty efficient method because it does not require that much computation, but it is very unstable numerically. If you test this code with a few sample values for the matrix and verify the accuracy of the method by substituting the solution back into the equations, you will notice that the precision is terrible. If you substitute the solution into the equations, you should mathematically get 0 on both sides of the equation.

The greater the value, the greater the error. With this method, I have computed errors of up to 10 virtual units with a normalized matrix. Thus if speed is a must and precision has little importance, this may be your ticket out. The error is notoriously bad because you end up multiplying the error. In other words, the error you had in X is multiplied to compute the error in Y and is again multiplied for the error in X, thus yielding a potentially pretty accurate Z, a so-so accurate Y, and a completely off X. For a bit more computational power, can you get more precision for Y and X?

The Gauss-Jordan Method

The Gauss-Jordan method is highly inspired by the Gauss method. The idea behind this method is to completely remove the requirement of applying the backward substitution. The approach to this problem is in fact very simple; you simply keep doing what you did in with the Gauss method—but to the upper triangle of the matrix. If you remove every coefficient in the upper and lower triangles and all you are left with is a coefficient matrix matching the identity matrix plus a column of values to the right, you will basically get a one-to-one match where one variable will be directly assigned to one value.

To look at this from another angle, what you get is an equation of the form $I<x, y, z> = <a, b, c>$, which is the same as $<x, y, z> = <a, b, c>$.

Let's take the previous example and finish the job by using the Gauss-Jordan method:

$$\left[\begin{array}{ccc|c} 1 & -\dfrac{3}{2} & \dfrac{1}{2} & \dfrac{3}{2} \\ 0 & 1 & 0 & -\dfrac{2}{3} \\ 0 & 0 & 1 & -\dfrac{1}{3} \end{array}\right]$$

$$\xrightarrow{\text{Subtract } \frac{r_3}{2} \text{ from } r_1} \left[\begin{array}{ccc|c} 1 & -\dfrac{3}{2} & 0 & \dfrac{5}{3} \\ 0 & 1 & 0 & -\dfrac{2}{3} \\ 0 & 0 & 1 & -\dfrac{1}{3} \end{array}\right]$$

$$\xrightarrow{\text{Subtract } \frac{3r_2}{2} \text{ from } r_1} \left[\begin{array}{ccc|c} 1 & 0 & 0 & \dfrac{2}{3} \\ 0 & 1 & 0 & -\dfrac{2}{3} \\ 0 & 0 & 1 & -\dfrac{1}{3} \end{array}\right]$$

This equation yields the same values as the ones obtained with backward substitution, but instead uses additions and scaling, which is simply another way of doing things. The added benefit here is that you don't cumulate the error from the previous solutions, but of course, you do so at the additional price of complexity and CPU time.

Linear Systems with an Infinite Number of Solutions

Not all linear systems yield one uniquely determined solution. Some linear systems have an infinite number of solutions, in which case there are no specific values for each variable involved. Even so, you might still be interested in finding out the values that you can generate to satisfy the equations. For example, consider the following linear system:

$$\begin{bmatrix} 2 & 4 & 2 & | & 10 \\ 0 & 1 & 1 & | & 3 \\ 1 & 3 & 2 & | & 8 \end{bmatrix}$$

$$\xrightarrow{\text{Scale down } r_i \text{ by } 2} \begin{bmatrix} 1 & 2 & 1 & | & 5 \\ 0 & 1 & 1 & | & 3 \\ 1 & 3 & 2 & | & 8 \end{bmatrix}$$

$$\xrightarrow{\text{Subtract } r_1 \text{ from } r_3} \begin{bmatrix} 1 & 2 & 1 & | & 5 \\ 0 & 1 & 1 & | & 3 \\ 0 & 1 & 1 & | & 3 \end{bmatrix}$$

$$\xrightarrow[\text{Subtract } 2r_2 \text{ from } r_1]{\text{Subtract } r_2 \text{ from } r_3} \begin{bmatrix} 1 & 0 & 1 & | & -1 \\ 0 & 1 & 1 & | & 3 \\ 0 & 1 & 1 & | & 3 \end{bmatrix}$$

You end up with the following set of equations:

$$x + z = -1$$
$$y + z = 3$$

Let $z = t$, a parameter
$$x = -t - 1$$
$$y = -t + 3$$
$$\begin{bmatrix} x \\ y \\ z \end{bmatrix} = t \begin{bmatrix} -1 \\ -1 \\ 1 \end{bmatrix} + \begin{bmatrix} -1 \\ 3 \\ 0 \end{bmatrix}$$

What you end up doing is redefining the variable that is in excess as a parameter, and consequently expressing the equations in a parametric form. In this case, your only option was to parameterize z because z was the only variable in excess. You cannot isolate for z uniquely, so this makes z a perfect choice for a parameter. If two objects were colliding with one another, you would compute an infinite number of collisions (because one section of a polygon would intersect with a section of another polygon). If you are planning to make a cool, entirely deformable world, this could be of interest to you, because you may want to dent the ground when a heavy object falls on it.

You may sometimes encounter systems in which a variable does not appear more than once. In such cases, you can isolate for any variable in the equations carrying more than two unknowns, and every solution will be a good solution for the system. This is guaranteed to happen if the system is underdetermined. In other words, if you have fewer equations than unknowns, you are guaranteed to be in this situation.

In the previous example, you can let t be any real value, and it will satisfy the set of equations that have been put forward. The reason this system of three equations and three unknowns did not yield a unique solution is because the equations are not linearly independent. The third equation can be expressed as a linear combination of the first two and thereby does not add any new information to the system. You can see that it does not add any new information because one of the rows nullifies, leaving only the linearly independent equations.

When a matrix has no linear dependencies, we say that the matrix is a *full-rank matrix*. On the contrary, when a matrix has n non-null rows, we say that the matrix is of rank n. The rank of the matrix can actually determine the number of parameters required to express the equation. A matrix with m rows and of rank n will have $m - n$ parameters. Another way to look at the rank is that it's the number of rows that are linearly independent. Generally, for collision detection like this, it is more efficient to compute the equation that is specific to the objects you are dealing with than to opt with a generic method such as this one. This one may be useful if you are using something "out of this world," but generally, the specific versions you will see in Chapters 4, "Basic Geometric Elements," and 5, "Transformations," will be more useful and faster.

Where Is My Solution?

It is also possible to have a system for which a solution does not exist. If, for example, a player shoots a projectile parallel to the ground, without gravity or any such force, the projectile will never actually hit the ground. In this case, there would be no solution to the system.

You have not yet seen how collisions and their building blocks work, so in the meantime, consider the preceding equations, which are actually planes in 3D. Given three planes, you will generally have a unique intersection. In other words, there will be a point in space that all three planes will share, as shown in Figure 3.1, so there is a unique solution to the system.

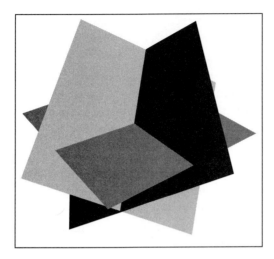

Figure 3.1
A linear system with a unique solution

The second possible scenario is if the planes are aligned like open pages in a book. In this case, they will share a line of intersection, which you can think of as the binding of a book. This is shown in Figure 3.2, where we have an infinite number of solutions to the system.

Figure 3.2
A linear system with an infinite number of solutions

The last possible case is one in which either the planes do not intersect because they are parallel, or they intersect two-by-two without actually having a common point of intersection, as shown in Figure 3.3, where the system has no solution.

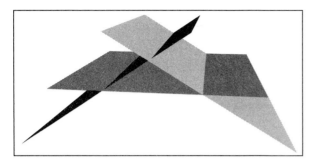

Figure 3.3
A linear system with no solutions at all

Mathematically, receiving no solutions means that you get an inconsistency in your equations. For example, you might get something along the lines of $0x + 0y + 0z = 3$, which is clearly not possible.

Determinant

The determinant can be seen as the cousin of the cross product. Granted, it does not yield a vector or a matrix, but it does yield similar results to what you have seen with the cross product. The determinant has the geometrical interpretation of being the signed area of the parallelepiped—a hyper volume created with parallelograms as faces. Therefore, in 2D, the determinant actually equals the 2-norm of the cross product.

The determinant is written in the form of an absolute value. For a 2×2 matrix, it is defined as follows:

$$|\mathbf{M}| = \begin{vmatrix} a & b \\ c & d \end{vmatrix}$$
$$= ad - bc$$

If you recall what was happening when you computed the cross product for a 2D vector, you may remember that this is in fact the equation of the z component when all the other components were zeroed out.

More generally, for an $n \times n$ matrix with n greater than 2, the determinant is defined by the following, where k is an integer constant anywhere from 1 to n and where $\mathbf{M}_{kj}$ is the minor matrix:

$$|\mathbf{M}| = \sum_{i=1}^{n} m_{ki} (-1)^{i+k} |\mathbf{M}_{ki}|$$

The minor matrix is the matrix obtained by eliminating row k and column j, as shown in Figure 3.4.

$$\mathbf{M}_{12} = \begin{bmatrix} a_{11} & a_{12} & a_{13} & a_{14} \\ a_{21} & a_{22} & a_{23} & a_{24} \\ a_{31} & a_{32} & a_{33} & a_{34} \\ a_{41} & a_{42} & a_{43} & a_{44} \end{bmatrix}$$

$$= \begin{bmatrix} a_{21} & a_{23} & a_{24} \\ a_{31} & a_{33} & a_{34} \\ a_{41} & a_{43} & a_{44} \end{bmatrix}$$

Figure 3.4
Minor matrix example

Another formula that works for computing the determinant is defined by the following:

$$|\mathbf{M}| = \sum_{i=1}^{n} m_{ik} (-1)^{i+k} |\mathbf{M}_{ik}|$$

Most implementations simply choose a value of $k = 1$ and use the first equation, but any value for k will do the trick here, and either equation can be used.

Let's carry on with an example:

$$\begin{vmatrix} 1 & 2 & 3 \\ 4 & 5 & 6 \\ 7 & 8 & 9 \end{vmatrix} = 1 \begin{vmatrix} 5 & 6 \\ 8 & 9 \end{vmatrix} - 2 \begin{vmatrix} 4 & 6 \\ 7 & 9 \end{vmatrix} + 3 \begin{vmatrix} 4 & 5 \\ 7 & 8 \end{vmatrix}$$

$$= 1(5 \cdot 9 - 8 \cdot 6) - 2(4 \cdot 9 - 7 \cdot 6) + 3(4 \cdot 8 - 7 \cdot 5)$$

$$= 1(-3) - 2(-6) + 3(-3)$$

$$= -3 + 12 - 9$$

$$= 0$$

Notice how this example, using the first formula, proceeds on a row, while the second formula proceeds on a column. This implies that the determinant of a matrix is the exact same as the determinant of its transpose. In symbols, you get the following:

$$|\mathbf{M}| = |\mathbf{M}^{\mathsf{T}}|$$

The determinant is a very important operation because it can enable you to express many things, such as cross products, volumetric area, the state of a linear system, and more. It is therefore useful to see what happens to the determinant when you shuffle the values of the matrix. All these operations can be proven rigorously, but for the most part, a simple look at the equations and a quick expansion will attest to the truthfulness of these corollaries:

- Exchanging two rows changes the sign.
- Exchanging two columns changes the sign.
- Multiples of rows can be added together without changing the determinant.
- Multiples of columns can be added together without changing the determinant.
- Scalar multiplication of a row by k multiplies the determinant by k.

The determinant has a few additional interesting properties:

- If one of its rows or columns is filled with zeros, the entire determinant is zero. This is clear from the very definition of the determinant. Simply choose the row or column that is zero for k, and it follows that everything is multiplied by zero.
- The determinant is invariant throughout the Gauss-Jordan method, except when exchanging rows where the determinant is negated and when an entire row is scaled. In the latter case, you would have to scale the determinant by the factor, as mentioned previously. If you recall, it was possible to determine whether a linear system is linearly dependent or not by looking at the rank of the matrix. A linearly dependent matrix had a full row of zeroes when it was written in reduced form using the Gauss method. This means that if any of the rows or columns in the matrix are linearly dependent, the determinant will be zero. This makes sense if you think about the determinant geometrically. If every plane was parallel in 3D, how could you compute the volume of the parallelepiped?
- The determinant of two matrices $\mathbf{A}$ and $\mathbf{B}$ multiplied together is the exact same as the determinant of $\mathbf{A}$ multiplied by that of $\mathbf{B}$. In mathematical lingo, this is expressed as follows:

$$|\mathbf{AB}| = |\mathbf{A}||\mathbf{B}|$$

With the Gauss method, the technique that was shown scaled down rows such that the first non-zero element was set to 1 to easily multiply and subtract against the other row. If you do this with the determinant, you must keep track of the scale factor, which you pulled out. Another way to approach this is to simply include the scale factor as part of the row multiplication. You know that this does not factor the determinant in any way because it is still a multiple of a row added to another. For example, suppose the pivot row (that is, the row that will be used to eliminate some elements) has a value of 2 and the row you want to reduce has a value of 3. In that case, you can multiply the first row by [3/2] and subtract the product of that operation from the second. You already know that adding a multiple of a row to another does not affect the determinant; this means the only change you may have to make to the determinant of the final matrix is to change the sign if you swap rows.

The following illustrates how the Gauss method can be applied to a matrix when computing the determinant of that matrix:

$$\begin{vmatrix} 2 & -3 & 1 \\ 4 & 0 & 2 \\ 3 & 2 & -1 \end{vmatrix}$$

$$\xrightarrow[\text{Subtract } \frac{3}{2}r_1 \text{ from } r_3]{\text{Subtract } 2r_1 \text{ from } r_2}} \begin{vmatrix} 2 & -3 & 1 \\ 0 & 6 & 0 \\ 0 & \dfrac{13}{2} & -\dfrac{5}{2} \end{vmatrix}$$

$$\xrightarrow[]{\text{Subtract } \frac{13}{12}r_2 \text{ from } r_3}} \begin{vmatrix} 2 & -3 & 1 \\ 0 & 6 & 0 \\ 0 & 0 & -\dfrac{5}{2} \end{vmatrix}$$

So the determinant of the initial matrix is exactly the same as the determinant of the second matrix. But something really nice happens when you put the matrix in this format. For instance, when computing the determinant, always choose k such that the last row of the matrix is processed. Because the last row will always have only one non-zero element, the determinant becomes easy to compute. It is the only non-zero term multiplied by the minor matrix. Recursively, if you apply this logic, you will notice that all that is required to compute the determinant, given a matrix in the augmented form, is to multiply every element of the matrix sitting on the diagonal together. Thus, for the preceding example, the determinant would be $2 \cdot 6 \cdot (-5) / 2 = -30$. As expected, this yields exactly the same value you obtain if you compute the determinant of the initial matrix.

Mathematically speaking, for a lower or upper triangular matrix (that is, a matrix for which every non-zero element sits in the upper or lower triangle, respectively), you get a much simpler equation to compute the determinant:

$$|\mathbf{M}| = \prod_{i=0}^{n} m_{ii}$$

The Inverse

When you speak of inverses in terms of real numbers, finding the answer is easy. If you are looking at a number r, its inverse can easily be obtained by dividing 1 by r. Finding the inverse of a matrix, however, is a little more complicated.

For instance, the identity element $\mathbf{I}$ (that is, 1) is a diagonal matrix of 1. To really understand what the inverse is, you have to go back to its definition. The inverse of $\mathbf{A}$ in general is a matrix $\mathbf{B}$ such that $\mathbf{AB} = \mathbf{I}$ where $\mathbf{I}$ is the unit matrix of the set, which for matrices is the identity matrix. You represent the inverse with a power of -1. This is the same convention used for real numbers. Therefore, for a matrix $\mathbf{M}$, you have the following:

$$\mathbf{MM}^{-1} = \mathbf{I}$$

This identity also provides another useful identity that you can use when you are dealing with the inverse of many matrices:

$$\left(\mathbf{AB}\right)^{-1} = \mathbf{B}^{-1}\mathbf{A}^{-1}$$

This last bit is quite easy to prove. You do so by using the preceding identity. In other words, you show that $\mathbf{B}^{-1}\mathbf{A}^{-1}$ multiplied by $\mathbf{AB}$ is the identity. Simply put the brackets at the correct positions, and you should easily be able to deduce this fact.

tip

Maple can compute the inverse of a matrix with the inverse command: inverse(Matrix);.

The Gauss-Jordan Inversion Method

The Gauss-Jordan inversion method is easier said than done. Finding the inverse of a matrix $\mathbf{A}$ requires a fair number of computations, as you might expect. There are many methods to achieve this. The simplest one is based on the Gauss-Jordan method. You will not see why it works here in detail, but the next section coupled with the following hint should put you in the right frame of mind. The idea is that if you can construct a matrix $\mathbf{B}$ such that $(\mathbf{BA}) = \mathbf{I}$, you can multiply each side of the equation by $\mathbf{B}$ and thus obtain the following equation:

$$\left(\mathbf{BA}\right)\mathbf{A}^{-1} = \mathbf{BI}$$
$$\mathbf{IA}^{-1} = \mathbf{B}$$
$$\mathbf{A}^{-1} = \mathbf{B}$$

The only question is, how do you create the matrix $\mathbf{B}$? You will see in more detail why this works in the next section, but for now, take it for granted that this method does yield the inverse. The idea is to start with a matrix $\mathbf{A}|\mathbf{I}$. You already used the separator symbol to split the coefficient of a matrix with the values; here, you are doing the same thing. The idea is to run the Gauss-Jordan algorithm on this set of rows. If the inverse does exist, the left side of the separator will hold the identity matrix, while the other side will hold the inverse.

Let's illustrate the algorithm with an example:

$$\left[\begin{array}{ccc|ccc} 2 & -3 & 1 & 1 & 0 & 0 \\ 4 & 0 & 2 & 0 & 1 & 0 \\ 3 & 2 & -1 & 0 & 0 & 1 \end{array}\right]$$

$$\xrightarrow[\text{Scale down } r_2 \text{ by 2}]{\text{Scale down } r_1 \text{ by 2}} \left[\begin{array}{ccc|ccc} 1 & -\dfrac{3}{2} & \dfrac{1}{2} & \dfrac{1}{2} & 0 & 0 \\ 2 & 0 & 1 & 0 & \dfrac{1}{2} & 0 \\ 3 & 2 & -1 & 0 & 0 & 1 \end{array}\right]$$

$$\xrightarrow[\text{Subtract } 3r_1 \text{ by } r_3]{\text{Subtract } 2r_1 \text{ by } r_2} \left[\begin{array}{ccc|ccc} 1 & -\dfrac{3}{2} & \dfrac{1}{2} & \dfrac{1}{2} & 0 & 0 \\ 0 & 3 & 0 & -1 & \dfrac{1}{2} & 0 \\ 0 & \dfrac{13}{2} & -\dfrac{5}{2} & -\dfrac{3}{2} & 0 & 1 \end{array}\right]$$

$$\xrightarrow[\text{Scale up } r_3 \text{ by 2}]{\text{Scale down } r_2 \text{ by 3}} \left[\begin{array}{ccc|ccc} 1 & -\dfrac{3}{2} & \dfrac{1}{2} & \dfrac{1}{2} & 0 & 0 \\ 0 & 1 & 0 & -\dfrac{1}{3} & \dfrac{1}{6} & 0 \\ 0 & 13 & -5 & -3 & 0 & 2 \end{array}\right]$$

$$\xrightarrow{\text{Subtract } 13r_2 \text{ from } r_3} \left[\begin{array}{ccc|ccc} 1 & -\dfrac{3}{2} & \dfrac{1}{2} & \dfrac{1}{2} & 0 & 0 \\ 0 & 1 & 0 & -\dfrac{1}{3} & \dfrac{1}{6} & 0 \\ 0 & 0 & -5 & -\dfrac{4}{3} & -\dfrac{13}{6} & 2 \end{array}\right]$$

$$\xrightarrow{\text{Scale down } r_3 \text{ by -5}} \left[\begin{array}{ccc|ccc} 1 & -\dfrac{3}{2} & \dfrac{1}{2} & \dfrac{1}{2} & 0 & 0 \\ 0 & 1 & 0 & -\dfrac{1}{3} & \dfrac{1}{6} & 0 \\ 0 & 0 & 1 & -\dfrac{4}{15} & \dfrac{13}{30} & -\dfrac{2}{5} \end{array}\right]$$

$$\xrightarrow{\text{Subtract } \frac{r_3}{2} \text{ from } r_1} \left[\begin{array}{ccc|ccc} 1 & -\dfrac{3}{2} & 0 & \dfrac{19}{30} & -\dfrac{13}{60} & \dfrac{1}{5} \\ 0 & 1 & 0 & -\dfrac{1}{3} & \dfrac{1}{6} & 0 \\ 0 & 0 & 1 & -\dfrac{4}{15} & \dfrac{13}{30} & -\dfrac{2}{5} \end{array}\right]$$

$$\xrightarrow{\text{Subtract } \frac{3r_2}{2} \text{ from } r_1} \left[\begin{array}{ccc|ccc} 1 & 0 & 0 & \dfrac{2}{15} & \dfrac{1}{30} & \dfrac{1}{5} \\ 0 & 1 & 0 & -\dfrac{1}{3} & \dfrac{1}{6} & 0 \\ 0 & 0 & 1 & -\dfrac{4}{15} & \dfrac{13}{30} & -\dfrac{2}{5} \end{array}\right]$$

You can verify that this matrix is the inverse of the original one by simply multiplying the inverse by the original matrix. Given this method, it should be obvious that a matrix that contains linearly dependent rows does not posses an inverse; otherwise, how could you build the identity matrix on the left side? Another way to put it is that, as you saw in the last section, a matrix possesses an inverse if and only if the determinant of the matrix is non-zero. This again comes back to lacking unique data, and thus would generate an infinite number of inverses, which makes no sense.

For matrices greater than 4×4, this is the way to go. It offers a pretty efficient way of dealing with things, but it does have stability issues, as noted before. In a game, we are mostly interested in 4×4 matrices, so you shouldn't need to bother yourself with this unless you are working with an esoteric case.

The Determinant Method

The Gauss-Jordan inversion method is somewhat cumbersome when computing the inverse because it requires you to operate on many elements at the same time. There is, however, another method that you can use to compute the inverse: via the determinant. On paper, this method actually takes longer to compute than the Gauss-Jordan method, but computationally speaking, it is the most attractive option if everything is factored such that computations are kept to a minimum. The technique relies on one simple fact:

$$b_{ij} = (-1)^{i+j} \frac{|\mathbf{A}_{ji}|}{|\mathbf{A}|}$$

You can verify that this formula is indeed true by computing the multiplication of matrix **A** with matrix **B** with index ij. What you should end up with is that when $i = j$, you get 1; when it doesn't, you get 0 because the final matrix will have identical rows. The end result should be the identity matrix. What this means for you is that you can actually write the inverse of a matrix element by element by replacing the coefficient with the preceding formula. A general equation for the inverse can written as follows:

$$\mathbf{M}^{-1} = \frac{\left(\mathbf{M}^*\right)^{\mathrm{T}}}{|\mathbf{M}|}$$

Where $\mathbf{M}^*$ is called the adjoint matrix of $\mathbf{M}$, the first being a matrix in which the values at ij carry the determinant of the minor matrix ij. In general:

$$\mathbf{M}^* = \begin{bmatrix} |\mathbf{M}_{11}| & \cdots & (-1)^{i+1}|\mathbf{M}_{1i}| & \cdots & (-1)^{n+1}|\mathbf{M}_{1n}| \\ \vdots & \ddots & \vdots & \ddots & \vdots \\ (-1)^{i+1}|\mathbf{M}_{i1}| & \cdots & |\mathbf{M}_{ii}| & \cdots & (-1)^{n+i}|\mathbf{M}_{in}| \\ \vdots & \ddots & \vdots & \ddots & \vdots \\ (-1)^{n+1}|\mathbf{M}_{n1}| & \cdots & (-1)^{n+i}|\mathbf{M}_{ni}| & \cdots & |\mathbf{M}_{nn}| \end{bmatrix}$$

Let's return to our previous example and apply this technique to it:

$$\mathbf{M} = \begin{bmatrix} 2 & -3 & 1 \\ 4 & 0 & 2 \\ 3 & 2 & -1 \end{bmatrix}$$

$$\mathbf{M}^* = \begin{bmatrix} \begin{vmatrix} 0 & 2 \\ 2 & -1 \end{vmatrix} & -\begin{vmatrix} 4 & 2 \\ 3 & -1 \end{vmatrix} & \begin{vmatrix} 4 & 0 \\ 3 & 2 \end{vmatrix} \\ -\begin{vmatrix} -3 & 1 \\ 2 & -1 \end{vmatrix} & \begin{vmatrix} 2 & 1 \\ 3 & -1 \end{vmatrix} & -\begin{vmatrix} 2 & -3 \\ 3 & 2 \end{vmatrix} \\ \begin{vmatrix} -3 & 1 \\ 0 & 2 \end{vmatrix} & -\begin{vmatrix} 2 & 1 \\ 4 & 2 \end{vmatrix} & \begin{vmatrix} 2 & -3 \\ 4 & 0 \end{vmatrix} \end{bmatrix}$$

$$= \begin{bmatrix} 0(-1) - 2 \cdot 2 & -(4(-1) - 3 \cdot 2) & 4 \cdot 2 - 3 \cdot 0 \\ -((-3)(-1) - 2 \cdot 1) & 2(-1) - 3 \cdot 1 & -(2 \cdot 2 - 3(-3)) \\ (-3)2 - 0 \cdot 1 & -(2 \cdot 2 - 4 \cdot 1) & 2 \cdot 0 - 4(-3) \end{bmatrix}$$

$$= \begin{bmatrix} -4 & 10 & 8 \\ -1 & -5 & -13 \\ -6 & 0 & 12 \end{bmatrix}$$

$$\mathbf{M}^{-1} = \frac{\left(\mathbf{M}^*\right)^{\mathrm{T}}}{|\mathbf{M}|}$$

$$= \begin{bmatrix} \dfrac{4}{30} & -\dfrac{1}{30} & \dfrac{6}{30} \\ -\dfrac{10}{30} & \dfrac{5}{30} & -\dfrac{0}{30} \\ -\dfrac{8}{30} & \dfrac{13}{30} & -\dfrac{12}{30} \end{bmatrix}$$

$$= \begin{bmatrix} \dfrac{2}{15} & -\dfrac{1}{30} & \dfrac{1}{5} \\ -\dfrac{1}{3} & \dfrac{1}{6} & 0 \\ -\dfrac{4}{15} & \dfrac{13}{30} & -\dfrac{6}{15} \end{bmatrix}$$

tip

The determinant can be computed using Maple if you issue the det command such as det(Matrix);.

Matrix Decomposition

You have already seen how much simpler some calculations—such as the determinant—can be when you have the right type of matrix. In the case of the determinant, you saw that a lower triangular or upper triangular matrix was a breeze to compute when compared to a matrix where you cannot do any assumptions.

Sometimes, when you compute functions such as inverses or determinants on a matrix multiplication **ABC**. . . , it can be a significant advantage to compute the function on each individual matrix. By using the properties explained previously, you can compute the function for the product of all matrices by computing them individually.

Unfortunately, however, there may be times you start with a matrix that does not yield a very nice computation for the function you want to compute. In such situations, there is an answer: matrix decomposition. This is not really about cutting down the computational time; rather, it's about increasing the precision.

Suppose you have a linear system and you have decided to run a few cycles of Gauss-Jordan iteration on a matrix. If you were to compute the error over random values for your matrix, you would quickly come to the conclusion that there is a bug in your code. In fact, there is probably not a bug in your code; the problem is that floating points do not carry the full-blown precision that a real number does in theory. As you crunch numbers, precision is being lost for just about every mathematical operation performed—some more than others. In general, you could easily get an error as large as, say, 2.5 screens for particles close to the camera.

This is clearly not acceptable. If, for example, you were computing the intersection of these equations with the linear system, you would be completely wrong about the intersection point. This can become a huge issue. Many of the problems do have a solutions that take the general equation but add a little bit of redundancy in order to reduce the error, but in the general case, you are stuck.

LU Decomposition

The "LU" in "LU decomposition" stands for "Lower triangular" and "Upper triangular." The idea with LU decomposition is to decompose an $n \times n$ (thus, a square) matrix into the product of two matrices: one lower triangular **L** and one upper triangular **U**. Triangular matrices are great to work with because they are much easier to play with—not only for the computation of the determinant and the inverse, but also for solving a linear system in a stable fashion, as mentioned previously. Before we tackle the myriad uses of LU decomposition, you should first look at how you can obtain these two matrices.

The idea is simple, and as an added bonus will also help you understand why the first inverse method works using the Gauss method. Every Gaussian operation (or, if you pre-fer, every step) can be expressed in the form of a matrix multiplied by your original matrix. This is in fact the proper mathematical way to apply the Gauss method on a matrix, and was shown when linear systems were introduced.

The Gauss method is interesting because applying it yields an upper triangular matrix (that is, a matrix where the non-zero terms are in the upper triangle of the matrix). For the lower triangular matrix, you have to work a little bit harder, but not by much. As you apply the Gauss method, you simply need to place the signed factor in the correct posi-tion of the identity matrix in order to add or subtract a multiple of one entire row.

A simple observation of the matrix multiplication will quickly reveal the position in which the factor should be placed. Specifically, it should always be placed at the spot where you want the factor of the original matrix to nullify. Following is an example that shows how the first term of the third row can be suppressed by a linear combination of the first row and the third row using the Gauss method:

$$A = \begin{bmatrix} 1 & 2 & 3 \\ 4 & 5 & 6 \\ 7 & 8 & 9 \end{bmatrix}$$

$$\begin{bmatrix} 1 & 0 & 0 \\ 0 & 1 & 0 \\ -7 & 1 & 1 \end{bmatrix} \begin{bmatrix} 1 & 2 & 3 \\ 4 & 5 & 6 \\ 7 & 8 & 9 \end{bmatrix} = \begin{bmatrix} 1 & 2 & 3 \\ 4 & 5 & 6 \\ 0 & -6 & -12 \end{bmatrix}$$

The following pseudo-code shows how to implement this technique:

```
for (k = 1 ; k < n - 1 ; k++) {
    if (Matrix[k][k] == 0) exit;    // Matrix does not have an inverse
    Swap with row 1 which is such that Matrix[1][k] is the element with the
greatest norm for column k
    for (i = k + 1 ; i < n - 1 ; i++) {
        Matrix[i][k] /= Matrix[k][k];
        for (j = k + 1 ; j < n - 1 ; j++)
            matrix[i][j] -= Matrix[i][k] * Matrix[k][j];
    }
}
```

Notice that every single multiplicative matrix that you use to reduce the matrix will be lower triangular. This is where it really becomes interesting because you have a bunch of lower triangular matrices at the left and one upper triangular matrix at the right. In terms of equations, after having applied all the steps for the Gauss method with associated matrices $\mathbf{A}_i$, on a matrix $\mathbf{M}$, you get the following:

$$\left(\prod_{i=1}^{\frac{n^2-n}{2}} \mathbf{A}_i \right) \mathbf{M} = \mathbf{U}$$

$$\left(\prod_{i=1}^{\frac{n^2-n}{2}} \mathbf{A}_i \right)^{-1} \left(\prod_{i=1}^{\frac{n^2-n}{2}} \mathbf{A}_i \right) \mathbf{M} = \left(\prod_{i=1}^{\frac{n^2-n}{2}} \mathbf{A}_i \right)^{-1} \mathbf{U}$$

$$\mathbf{M} = \mathbf{LU}$$

As mentioned, triangular matrices are that much nicer to work with. One property that they possess is the following, which can be generalized to matrices of dimension $n \times n$:

$$\begin{bmatrix} 1 & 0 & 0 \\ a & 1 & 0 \\ 0 & 0 & 1 \end{bmatrix} \begin{bmatrix} 1 & 0 & 0 \\ 0 & 1 & 0 \\ b & 0 & 1 \end{bmatrix} \begin{bmatrix} 1 & 0 & 0 \\ 0 & 1 & 0 \\ 0 & c & 1 \end{bmatrix} = \begin{bmatrix} 1 & 0 & 0 \\ a & 1 & 0 \\ b & c & 1 \end{bmatrix}$$

You can also verify that the inverse of triangular matrices is extremely easy to compute, and gives the following equation:

$$\begin{bmatrix} 1 & 0 & 0 & 0 \\ a_{12} & 1 & 0 & 0 \\ \vdots & \ddots & 1 & 0 \\ a_{1n} & \cdots & a_{(n-1)n} & 1 \end{bmatrix}^{-1} = \begin{bmatrix} 1 & 0 & 0 & 0 \\ -a_{12} & 1 & 0 & 0 \\ \vdots & \ddots & 1 & 0 \\ -a_{1n} & \cdots & -a_{(n-1)n} & 1 \end{bmatrix}$$

Thanks to both of these properties, the inverse product of the Gauss step matrices, referred to above as $\mathbf{L}$, will be a lower triangular matrix. You could easily skip the step of computing the inverse and multiplying the step matrices together and simply build $\mathbf{L}$ directly, but to be a little more rigorous, the following example shows the process by applying it the long way:

$$\mathbf{M} = \begin{bmatrix} 2 & -3 & 1 \\ 4 & 0 & 2 \\ 3 & 2 & -1 \end{bmatrix}$$

$$\begin{bmatrix} 1 & 0 & 0 \\ -2 & 1 & 0 \\ 0 & 0 & 1 \end{bmatrix}\begin{bmatrix} 2 & -3 & 1 \\ 4 & 0 & 2 \\ 3 & 2 & -1 \end{bmatrix} = \begin{bmatrix} 2 & -3 & 1 \\ 0 & 6 & 0 \\ 3 & 2 & -1 \end{bmatrix}$$

$$\begin{bmatrix} 1 & 0 & 0 \\ 0 & 1 & 0 \\ -\dfrac{3}{2} & 0 & 1 \end{bmatrix}\begin{bmatrix} 1 & 0 & 0 \\ -2 & 1 & 0 \\ 0 & 0 & 1 \end{bmatrix}\begin{bmatrix} 2 & -3 & 1 \\ 4 & 0 & 2 \\ 3 & 2 & -1 \end{bmatrix} = \begin{bmatrix} 2 & -3 & 1 \\ 0 & 6 & 0 \\ 0 & \dfrac{13}{2} & -\dfrac{5}{2} \end{bmatrix}$$

$$\begin{bmatrix} 1 & 0 & 0 \\ 0 & 1 & 0 \\ 0 & -\dfrac{13}{12} & 1 \end{bmatrix}\begin{bmatrix} 1 & 0 & 0 \\ -2 & 1 & 0 \\ -\dfrac{3}{2} & 0 & 1 \end{bmatrix}\begin{bmatrix} 2 & -3 & 1 \\ 4 & 0 & 2 \\ 3 & 2 & -1 \end{bmatrix} = \begin{bmatrix} 2 & -3 & 1 \\ 0 & 6 & 0 \\ 0 & 0 & -\dfrac{5}{2} \end{bmatrix}$$

$$\begin{bmatrix} 2 & -3 & 1 \\ 4 & 0 & 2 \\ 3 & 2 & -1 \end{bmatrix} = \begin{bmatrix} 1 & 0 & 0 \\ 2 & 1 & 0 \\ \dfrac{3}{2} & 0 & 1 \end{bmatrix}\begin{bmatrix} 1 & 0 & 0 \\ 0 & 1 & 0 \\ 0 & \dfrac{13}{12} & 1 \end{bmatrix}\begin{bmatrix} 2 & -3 & 1 \\ 0 & 6 & 0 \\ 0 & 0 & -\dfrac{5}{2} \end{bmatrix}$$

$$= \begin{bmatrix} 1 & 0 & 0 \\ 2 & 1 & 0 \\ \dfrac{3}{2} & \dfrac{13}{12} & 1 \end{bmatrix}\begin{bmatrix} 2 & -3 & 1 \\ 0 & 6 & 0 \\ 0 & 0 & -\dfrac{5}{2} \end{bmatrix}$$

This all comes back down to the example of matrix stability that was given initially. In other words, do you want your collisions to be dead-on or half a screen off? If you think that moving on to doubles will fix the problem, you are dead wrong. Doubles will help a little, but you will still have some numerical instability in your equation, which could hurt you. The amount of precision you require is really up to you. Generally, most games will settle down for the determinant method. This becomes attractive when you can afford to have various levels of precision. For instance, if you run a dedicated server, it may well be able to afford this type of decomposition and can notify the clients when a collision occurred and wasn't well computed on the clients. Meanwhile, the clients can run the faster, less-accurate version.

Cholesky Decomposition

LU decomposition is excellent for square matrices, but there is another method that is faster to compute if you are dealing with symmetric matrices that are positive definite: Cholesky decomposition. A matrix is positive definite if $\mathbf{x}^T\mathbf{M}\mathbf{x} > 0$ for all vectors $\mathbf{x}$.

Determining whether a matrix is positive definite is no easy feat. The easiest way to tackle this problem is to try to see whether the Cholesky decomposition exists by applying the Cholesky decomposition method. If you end up being forced to compute the square root of a negative value, then you know for sure that the matrix is not positive definite.

tip

If you are planning to implement this technique for many matrices for which you cannot control the values, then you are better off using LU decomposition.

Like LU decomposition, Cholesky decomposition also builds one upper triangular matrix and one lower triangular matrix. Thanks to the symmetry, it can make a pretty efficient decomposition. In order to obtain the Cholesky decomposition, simply take two matrices, one lower triangular and one upper triangular, where the first matrix is the transpose of the second. To get the coefficient, you merely have to express the equations of the unknowns with the knowns and isolate for each one of them as shown by the following general equation:

$$
\begin{bmatrix}
b_{11} & 0 & \cdots & \cdots & 0 \\
\vdots & \ddots & \ddots & \ddots & \vdots \\
b_{i1} & \cdots & b_{ii} & \ddots & \vdots \\
\vdots & \ddots & \vdots & \ddots & 0 \\
b_{n1} & \cdots & b_{ni} & \cdots & b_{nm}
\end{bmatrix}
\begin{bmatrix}
b_{11} & \cdots & b_{i1} & \cdots & b_{n1} \\
0 & \ddots & \vdots & \ddots & \vdots \\
0 & \ddots & b_{ii} & \cdots & b_{ni} \\
\vdots & \ddots & \ddots & \ddots & \vdots \\
0 & \cdots & \cdots & 0 & b_{nm}
\end{bmatrix}
=
\begin{bmatrix}
a_{11} & \cdots & a_{1n} \\
\vdots & \ddots & \vdots \\
a_{n1} & \cdots & a_{nn}
\end{bmatrix}
$$

Simply expand and isolate for each b_{ij}, and you should be able to get the equations and, thereafter, the values for the decomposition.

This decomposition is quite easy to process, but in the interest of being thorough, I've shown how it is done with an example:

$$\mathbf{M} = \begin{bmatrix} 4 & 0 & 2 \\ 0 & 1 & 2 \\ 2 & 2 & 14 \end{bmatrix}$$

$$\begin{bmatrix} a & 0 & 0 \\ b & c & 0 \\ d & e & f \end{bmatrix} \begin{bmatrix} a & b & d \\ 0 & c & e \\ 0 & 0 & f \end{bmatrix} = \begin{bmatrix} 4 & 0 & 2 \\ 0 & 1 & 2 \\ 2 & 2 & 14 \end{bmatrix}$$

$$\begin{bmatrix} a^2 & ab & ad \\ ab & b^2+c^2 & db+ec \\ ad & db+ec & d^2+e^2+f^2 \end{bmatrix} = \begin{bmatrix} 4 & 0 & 2 \\ 0 & 1 & 2 \\ 2 & 2 & 14 \end{bmatrix}$$

$$a^2 = 4$$
$$a = 2$$

$$ab = 0$$
$$b = 0$$

$$b^2 + c^2 = 1$$
$$c = 1$$

$$ad = 2$$
$$d = 1$$

$$db + ec = 2$$
$$d = 1$$

$$db + ex = 2$$
$$e = 2$$

$$d^2 + e^2 + f^2 = 14$$
$$f = 3$$

$$\begin{bmatrix} 2 & 0 & 0 \\ 0 & 1 & 0 \\ 1 & 2 & 3 \end{bmatrix} \begin{bmatrix} 2 & 0 & 1 \\ 0 & 1 & 2 \\ 0 & 0 & 3 \end{bmatrix} = \begin{bmatrix} 4 & 0 & 2 \\ 0 & 1 & 2 \\ 2 & 2 & 14 \end{bmatrix}$$

Solving Linear Systems More Precisely

These decompositions can be very helpful in finding the solution to $\mathbf{Ax} = \mathbf{b}$, a linear system. The logic simply uses the properties of matrices. The following logic ensues:

$$\mathbf{Ax = b}$$

$$(\mathbf{LU})\mathbf{x = b}$$

$$\mathbf{Uy = b}$$

$$\mathbf{Lx = y}$$

The steps are not complicated. You first solve for **y** in the equation **Uy = b**. This is something you can easily do with backward substitution because **U** is upper triangular. Next, you solve for **x** in the equation **Lx = y**. This is also pretty easy to compute because it can be done by forward substitution. The following example shows how you can solve a linear system with the Cholesky decomposition:

$$\begin{bmatrix} 4 & 0 & 2 \\ 0 & 1 & 2 \\ 2 & 2 & 14 \end{bmatrix} \begin{bmatrix} x \\ y \\ z \end{bmatrix} = \begin{bmatrix} 1 \\ 0 \\ 9 \end{bmatrix}$$

$$\begin{bmatrix} 2 & 0 & 0 \\ 0 & 1 & 0 \\ 1 & 2 & 3 \end{bmatrix} \begin{bmatrix} 2 & 0 & 1 \\ 0 & 1 & 2 \\ 0 & 0 & 3 \end{bmatrix} \begin{bmatrix} x \\ y \\ z \end{bmatrix} = \begin{bmatrix} 1 \\ 0 \\ 9 \end{bmatrix}$$

$$\begin{bmatrix} 2 & 0 & 1 \\ 0 & 1 & 2 \\ 0 & 0 & 3 \end{bmatrix} \begin{bmatrix} a \\ b \\ c \end{bmatrix} = \begin{bmatrix} 1 \\ 0 \\ 9 \end{bmatrix}$$

$$3x = 9$$

$$c = 3$$

$$b + 2c = 0$$

$$b = -6$$

$$2a + c = 1$$

$$a = -1$$

$$\begin{bmatrix} 2 & 0 & 1 \\ 0 & 1 & 2 \\ 0 & 0 & 3 \end{bmatrix} \begin{bmatrix} x \\ y \\ z \end{bmatrix} = \begin{bmatrix} -1 \\ -6 \\ 3 \end{bmatrix}$$

$$2x = -1$$

$$x = -\frac{1}{2}$$

$$y = -6$$

$$x + 2y + 3z = 3$$

$$z = \frac{31}{6}$$

This is necessarily longer to compute than the other methods, or computing the inverse and then multiplying it by the vector, but it has been proven to be much more stable. In the end, it all depends how much precision you need and can afford.

In addition, other techniques can be applied to aid in precision, such as scaling the matrix and arranging the rows such that the biggest numbers are on the diagonal. But in general, you do not need that much precision when it comes to linear systems.

As you write your game, it's important to determine whether you should use a decomposition of another method. You can verify this by computing the condition number of the matrix. This scalar indicates the numerical stability of the matrix and is a number that is relative to the norm of the matrix. A very large number indicates a very unstable matrix. The condition number is computed as such for square matrices:

$$k = \left\| \mathbf{A} \right\| \left\| \mathbf{A}^{-1} \right\|$$

The logarithm base 2 of k for the matrix A is an estimate of the number of bits lost when solving a linear system. Let's follow with some examples:

$$\mathbf{A} = \begin{bmatrix} 0.45 & -0.89 & 0 \\ 0.89 & 0.45 & 0 \\ 0 & 0 & 1 \end{bmatrix}, \mathbf{A}^{-1} = \begin{bmatrix} 0.45 & 0.89 & 0 \\ -0.89 & 0.45 & 0 \\ 0 & 0 & 1 \end{bmatrix}$$

$$\left\| \mathbf{A} \right\|_F \left\| \mathbf{A}^{-1} \right\|_F = 1.72 \cdot 1.72$$

$$= 2.98$$

$$\approx 2 \text{ bit of lost precision (Reasonable)}$$

$$\mathbf{B} = \begin{bmatrix} 10000 & 10 & 0 \\ 1 & 100 & 0 \\ 0 & 0 & 2 \end{bmatrix}, \mathbf{B}^{-1} = \begin{bmatrix} \dfrac{10}{99999} & \dfrac{-1}{99999} & 0 \\ \dfrac{-1}{99999} & \dfrac{10}{99999} & 0 \\ \dfrac{1}{199998} & \dfrac{-500}{99999} & \dfrac{1}{2} \end{bmatrix}$$

$$\left\| \mathbf{B} \right\|_F \left\| \mathbf{B}^{-1} \right\|_F = 10000.5 \cdot 0.5$$

$$= 5001.5$$

$$\approx 13 \text{ bit of lost precision (barely anything left)}$$

When such things happen, you may wish to consider renormalizing rows. For instance, the first row could be divided by 10,000. As long as you keep track of the factor so as to reapply it at the end, you should have no problem. Doing this enables you to stabilize the matrix by working with numbers that are within the same relative range. That's really the key to having a stable matrix.

Eigenvectors

Eigenvectors and eigenvalues are concepts that are barely useful for games, but they have a use nonetheless. As you'll see in Chapter 11, "Educated Guessing with Statistics and Probability," they're the key to determining the orientation of various bounding volumes. For any invertible matrix $\mathbf{M}$, there's a set of vectors $\mathbf{v}_i$, called eigenvectors, which only change in norm and not in direction. Mathematically, this is expressed as follows:

$$\mathbf{M}\mathbf{v}_i = \lambda_i \mathbf{v}_i$$

Here, $[\lambda]_i$ is defined as an eigenvalue and is the multiplier of the eigenvector. Reorganizing the equation, you get the following:

$$(\mathbf{M} - \lambda \mathbf{I})\mathbf{v}_i = 0$$

This implies that the determinant of the first part has to be 0. You can thus find the eigenvalues with this detail in mind:

$$\det(\mathbf{M} - \lambda \mathbf{I}) = |\mathbf{M} - \lambda \mathbf{I}| = 0$$

The remainder of this problem is best explained with an example. Take a 2×2 matrix. You can find the eigenvalues as follows by simply computing the determinant of the matrix:

$$\mathbf{M} = \begin{bmatrix} 1 & 2 \\ 2 & -1 \end{bmatrix}$$

$$|\mathbf{M} - \lambda \mathbf{I}| = 0$$

$$= \left| \begin{bmatrix} 1 & 2 \\ 2 & -1 \end{bmatrix} - \lambda \begin{bmatrix} 1 & 0 \\ 0 & 1 \end{bmatrix} \right|$$

$$= \left| \begin{bmatrix} 1-\lambda & 2 \\ 2 & -1-\lambda \end{bmatrix} \right|$$

$$= (1-\lambda)(-1-\lambda) - 2^2$$

$$= \lambda^2 - 5$$

$$\lambda = \pm\sqrt{5}$$

In short, to compute the determinant, you must use the technique shown in this chapter. The determinant will always give you a polynomial of degree, which is at most the degree of the matrix. You can abstractly compute the determinant of a matrix in order to obtain the general equation for the determinant given a 2×2 matrix. This will be necessary when it comes time to implement this. Once you know what the polynomial looks like, you must use the technique from Chapter 1, "Equation Manipulation and Representation," to solve the quadratic equations. Similarly, if you want to find the eigenvectors/eigenvalues of a 3×3 matrix, you would have to find the root of a cubic polynomial. Generally, these computations can be done at boot-up time, so you shouldn't really care about the speed too much.

Once you have the eigenvalues, you need to find the eigenvectors. Given the preceding definition, all you have to do is solve the linear system:

$$(\mathbf{M} - \lambda\mathbf{I})\mathbf{v}_i = \mathbf{0}$$

The tricky part about this linear system is that it will always give an underdetermined system. More specifically, it will give a system with an infinite number of solutions. The technique to solve this type of problem is also in this chapter. Pursuing the previous example, you have the following:

$$(\mathbf{M} - \lambda\mathbf{I})\mathbf{v}_i = \begin{bmatrix} 0 \\ 0 \end{bmatrix}$$

$$\begin{bmatrix} 1-\sqrt{5} & 2 \\ 2 & -1-\sqrt{5} \end{bmatrix}\mathbf{v}_i = \begin{bmatrix} 0 \\ 0 \end{bmatrix}$$

$$\begin{bmatrix} 1-\sqrt{5} & 2 \\ 0 & 0 \end{bmatrix}\mathbf{v}_i = \begin{bmatrix} 0 \\ 0 \end{bmatrix}$$

As expected, it's a system with an infinite number of solutions. Now you need to find the general solution to this system. As shown earlier, you should get the following:

$$\begin{bmatrix} x \\ y \end{bmatrix} = t\begin{bmatrix} -2 \\ 1-\sqrt{5} \end{bmatrix}$$

Thus, you've found your first eigenvector. If you do the same thing for the second root of the polynomial, you can get the second eigenvector:

$$(\mathbf{M} - \lambda \mathbf{I})\mathbf{v}_i = \begin{bmatrix} 0 \\ 0 \end{bmatrix}$$

$$\begin{bmatrix} 1+\sqrt{5} & 2 \\ 2 & -1+\sqrt{5} \end{bmatrix} \mathbf{v}_i = \begin{bmatrix} 0 \\ 0 \end{bmatrix}$$

$$\begin{bmatrix} 1+\sqrt{5} & 2 \\ 0 & 0 \end{bmatrix} \mathbf{v}_i = \begin{bmatrix} 0 \\ 0 \end{bmatrix}$$

$$v_2 = \begin{bmatrix} x \\ y \end{bmatrix} = t \begin{bmatrix} -2 \\ 1+\sqrt{5} \end{bmatrix}$$

Consequently, your two eigenvectors are

$$\mathbf{v}_i = \left\{ \begin{bmatrix} -2 \\ 1+\sqrt{5} \end{bmatrix}, \begin{bmatrix} -2 \\ 1-\sqrt{5} \end{bmatrix} \right\}$$

Curiously enough, you may also notice that these two vectors are orthogonal. This is always true for eigenvectors. They always form a basis.

Diagonalization

There's one area where eigenvectors are useful. When you have a matrix $\mathbf{M}$, it can be useful to diagonalize the matrix. This is the process of taking a matrix $\mathbf{M}$ and converting it via a set of operations into a simple diagonal matrix where only the diagonal elements are non-zero. In essence, you might be tempted to call the Gauss-Jordan method a diagonalizing process, but the term *diagonalization* only applies to an $n \times n$ matrix. There's no sense in proving this theorem because it's a rare case, but it can be shown that the row-vector of the eigenvectors $\mathbf{V}$ form a matrix for which the following holds:

$$\mathbf{V}^{-1}\mathbf{M}\mathbf{V} = \begin{bmatrix} \lambda_1 & 0 & \cdots & \cdots & 0 \\ 0 & \ddots & \ddots & \ddots & \vdots \\ \vdots & \ddots & \lambda_i & \ddots & \vdots \\ \vdots & \ddots & \ddots & \ddots & 0 \\ 0 & \cdots & \cdots & 0 & \lambda_n \end{bmatrix}$$

You can prove this by multiplying it the long way.

Typically, diagonalizing a matrix for games isn't useful. What *is* useful is that the matrix **V** can diagonalize a matrix. Thus far in the industry, the actual computation hasn't been proven useful for our purposes. In Chapter 17, "Filling the Gaps with Rendering Techniques," this is used to find bounding volumes.

Vector Revision

Matrices are obviously very powerful objects with which you can do many things. One thing that matrices can be used for is to write vectors. You can easily use a matrix convention when writing vectors. This changes some equations because the matrix can also be used to represent any other linear transformation. This section encompasses everything you have seen so far, but tries to show those ideas using different angles. A quick expansion of each formula should easily show you that the equations are indeed equivalent.

Dot Product

The vector form is 1D; thus, it does not have any sense of 2D placement of vectors. When you write a vector, little importance is placed on whether you write it as a column or as a row; after all, a vector is a vector. This is not true at all, however, for matrices. When multiplying matrices, the rows of the first matrix are multiplied with the column of the second matrix. Therefore, in matrix notation, you can represent the dot product of two vectors **A**, **B** in matrix notation with the following formula:

$$\mathbf{A}\mathbf{B}^{\mathrm{T}} = \begin{bmatrix} a_1 & \cdots & a_n \end{bmatrix} \begin{bmatrix} b_1 \\ \vdots \\ b_n \end{bmatrix}$$

This is useful when it's time to work with transformations, because it enables you to work with apples only (that is, matrices). Given the original definition of a matrix, it's clear that you can represent a vector by using a matrix notation. A matrix was defined as a vector of a vector. If you only choose a single vector, you get a single vector.

Projection of a Vector Upon a Vector

The projection of one vector upon another, interestingly enough, can be expressed in matrix notation. The matrix here simply takes advantage of the fact that it is possible to do a linear transformation in a slightly less cumbersome notation. The formula to compute the projection of a vector **A** on **B** is given by the following:

$$\text{Proj}_{\mathbf{B}}\left(\mathbf{A}\right)=\frac{1}{\left\|\mathbf{B}\right\|^{2}}\begin{bmatrix} b_1^2 & \cdots & b_1 b_i & \cdots & b_1 b_n \\ \vdots & \ddots & \vdots & \ddots & \vdots \\ b_1 b_i & \cdots & b_i^2 & \cdots & b_i b_n \\ \vdots & \ddots & \vdots & \ddots & \vdots \\ b_1 b_n & \cdots & b_i b_n & \cdots & b_n^2 \end{bmatrix}$$

This may seem like a much more cumbersome formula to work with—and in fact, it is. But if you are working on hardware that accelerates matrix computations, then it could very well be worth it to express your projection using this formula.

Cross Product

This one should come as no surprise because a lot was said in this chapter about its relationship with the determinant. Suppose we define three vectors **i**, **j**, and **k** as normal unit vectors parallel to the x, y, and z axis, respectively. Given this notation, the cross product of two vectors **a** and **b** can actually be computed using the following determinant form:

$$\mathbf{a}\times\mathbf{b}=\begin{vmatrix} \mathbf{i} & \mathbf{j} & \mathbf{k} \\ a_x & a_y & a_z \\ b_x & b_y & b_z \end{vmatrix}$$

Interestingly enough, this also introduces another way to represent vectors. Any real number multiplied by **i** becomes the component in x, **j** is associated with y, and **k** is associated with z. So in other words, a vector of the form $1\mathbf{i} + 2\mathbf{j} - 3\mathbf{k}$ is actually the same as the vector $<1, 2, -3>$. This is a neat way of representing the cross product, but it's not the only way (besides the gruesome formula given earlier). In matrix notation, you can also express the cross product as follows:

$$\mathbf{a}\times\mathbf{b}=\begin{bmatrix} 0 & -a_z & a_y \\ a_z & 0 & -a_x \\ -a_y & a_x & 0 \end{bmatrix}\begin{bmatrix} b_x \\ b_y \\ b_z \end{bmatrix}$$

You can also compute the determinant of a 3×3 matrix using the cross and dot product. The answer was already mostly given with the first method to compute the determinant. Computing the determinant can also be done with three vectors **a**, **b**, and **c** as follows:

$$\begin{vmatrix} a_x & a_y & a_z \\ b_x & b_y & b_z \\ c_x & c_y & c_z \end{vmatrix}=\left(\mathbf{a}\times\mathbf{b}\right)\bullet\mathbf{c}$$

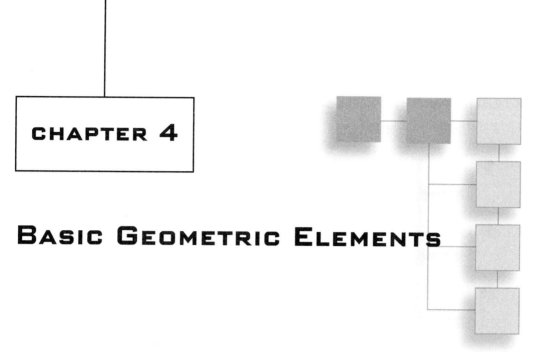

CHAPTER 4

BASIC GEOMETRIC ELEMENTS

I haven't conducted any surveys on the matter, but I believe that geometry is one of the most fun and well-loved area of mathematics. Geometry is so visual that it makes things easier to play with. Even so, geometry can also be pretty complicated, as you will see in Chapter 12, "Closing the Gap for Numerical Approximation." Perhaps Coxter and Greitzer put it best when they said, "With a literature much vaster than those of algebra and arithmetic combined, and at least as extensive as that of analysis, geometry is a richer treasure house of more interesting and half-forgotten things, which a hurried generation has no leisure to enjoy, than any other division of mathematics."

The fact is, geometry is one of those fields that will always be useful regardless of new things you learn. At some point, science may find something to replace matrices and may eliminate the use of vectors altogether, but geometry will still be there for games because it describes what you see on the screen. This chapter concentrates on the equations used to create various geometrical objects and the relationships between the various geometries. Understanding how the various geometries are created is important because they form the basis of many more advanced shapes. In addition, because you can't really do without an object loader these days, you will also look at the general structures used by popular object file formats. (If you are interested in a particular format—such as 3DS, M3D, and the like—you should be able to easily grab model loaders off of the Internet.) Also, included in the source code of this chapter is a preliminary 3DS model loader.

This chapter covers the following:

- Lines, planes, and spheres
- Intersections between two elements (vertex, line, plane)
- Shortest distance between two elements (vertex, line, plane)
- 3D structure file format

Creating Lines

You have already looked at the simplest 3D geometry object you can ever create—the vertex—so we'll skip to the second simplest one here: the line. Chances are, you already know the equation for a 2D line: $y = mx + b$, as illustrated in Figure 4.1. Although this formula is a good start, it is quite restrictive and offers very little when you move to 3D or higher-degree spaces. In this version of the equation, m is called the slope, and it defines the steepness of the line. A value of 0 yields a horizontal line, while a value that tends toward infinity yields a vertical line. This version of the equation can also be seen as a first-order polynomial equation.

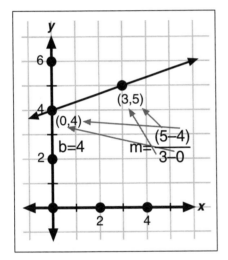

Figure 4.1
A simple line

This definition of a line is somewhat cumbersome because it defines an infinite line. When it comes time to define a finite line, it becomes more practical to bound your variable. It is also more practical to write the line as an interpolation or, if you prefer, as a straight positional change from one vertex to the other. You can write the equation of a finite line with endpoints $\mathbf{p}_1$ and $\mathbf{p}_0$ and with t, as illustrated in Figure 4.2, with the percentage of how close you are from $\mathbf{p}_1$ starting at $\mathbf{p}_0$, as follows:

$$\mathbf{p}(t) = t\mathbf{p}_1 + (t-1)\mathbf{p}_0$$

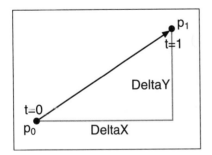

Figure 4.2
A finite line

This equation might seem like it comes out of the blue, but in reality, it is the parametric form of a line. Observe the following deduction:

$$y = mx + b$$

$$y = \frac{\Delta yx}{\Delta x} + b$$

$$f(t) = \left\{ \begin{array}{l} x = t \\ y = \dfrac{\Delta yt}{\Delta x} + b \end{array} \right\}$$

$$f(t\Delta x) = \left\{ \begin{array}{l} x = \Delta xt \\ y = \Delta yt + b \end{array} \right\}$$

$$f(t') = \langle 0, b \rangle + t \langle \Delta x, \Delta y \rangle$$

$$= \langle p_{0x}, p_{0y} \rangle + t \langle p_{1x} - p_{0x}, p_{1y} - p_{0y} \rangle$$

$$= \mathbf{p_0} + t(\mathbf{p_1} - \mathbf{p_0})$$

$$= t\mathbf{p_1} + (1-t)\mathbf{p_0}$$

As seen in Chapter 1, "Equation Manipulation and Representation," converting a function to a parametric equation is very easy. Where it gets more interesting is when it comes time to make the equation a little more friendly and meaningful. Because the general equation of a line is not bounded between two vertices, you can scale or translate your parameter t without actually changing the graph of the equation. The interesting thing is that if you scale t by delta x, you find that the equation can actually be written as one point on your line <0, b>, plus a linear combination of the slope in x and y. Because you can again substitute t with anything, if you substitute it with $(t + a)$, given that a is an arbitrary scalar, the result is still a point on the line and you can simply factor the equation such that it looks like $c + td$. Consequently, the second term does not actually change, but the first one does. Because this equation still yields a vertex on the line, c is thus itself a point on the line, which means that you can actually choose any point on the line for c. Because you do not want to deal with three vertices to build a line, you simply choose d to be $\mathbf{p_1}$ (one of your two endpoints) and you compute the value for the deltas as the difference between $\mathbf{p_1}$ and your second endpoint, $\mathbf{p_0}$. All in all, this makes for a much easier equation to work with.

In addition to being an easier equation to work with, it's easy to see how this equation works in 3D. Also, this equation ranges from one vertex to the other with t as a percentage (that is, of range [0, 1]). You can easily see that when $t = 0$, one vertex is the result; when $t = 1$, the other vertex is the output.

The second-to-last equation, shown here, is also extremely interesting for infinite lines:

$$f(t) = \mathbf{p_0} + t(\mathbf{p_1} - \mathbf{p_0})$$

This is so partly because it only has one multiplication, but also because it offers a comprehensive geometrical interpretation. Of course, it's nice to know the formulas, but it's also nice to see why they work outside of the algebra. Basically, the vector obtained by subtracting the two vertices is the component of the slope (DeltaX and DeltaY) of the line. In a nutshell, for such a vector $<a, b, c>$, this equation is telling you that for one abstract unit (which is $t = 1$), the x component moves of a, the y component moves of b, and the z component moves of c. The same process can be deduced for 2D lines. Thus, you can easily see how changing one of $\{a, b, c\}$ affects the slope of the line. On the other hand, you can generate an infinite number of lines with any given slope. In order to uniquely identify this line, you need to anchor the line; this is done by the addition of $\mathbf{p_0}$, as shown in Figure 4.3.

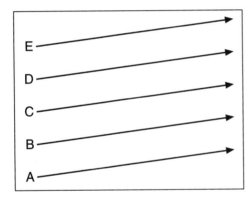

Figure 4.3
The effect of changing $\mathbf{p_0}$ = {A, B, C, D, E} on a line

Generating Planes

In the last section, you saw that lines can be expressed as parametric equations of order 1 (that is, where the highest power of t is 1). If an equation can be expressed with one parameter, you could easily envisage that an equation could be written using two parameters. A plane is exactly what this is. Due to the fact that there are two parameters, the equation is much less restrictive; and because the equation is still a linear combination, it has to be linear in nature. As illustrated in Figure 4.4, a plane can be seen geometrically as a sheet of paper in 3D space with the parametric equation $f(s, t)$ for three unique vertices—$\mathbf{p_0}$, $\mathbf{p_1}$, and $\mathbf{P_2}$—and two parameters s and t:

$$f(s,t) = \mathbf{p_0} + s(\mathbf{p_1} - \mathbf{p_0}) + t(\mathbf{p_2} - \mathbf{p_0})$$

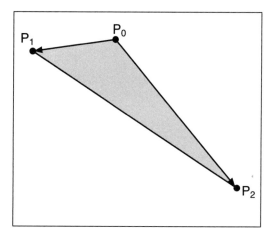

Figure 4.4
A plane defined by three vertices

If you choose a value for $<s, t>$ such as $<0, 1>$ or $<1, 0>$ from $<0, 0>$, you can see that you get the equation of two different lines. Assuming that $\mathbf{P_2}$ isn't equal to $\mathbf{p_1}$, you get the lines described by the vectors $\mathbf{p_1} - \mathbf{p_0}$ and $\mathbf{P_2} - \mathbf{p_0}$ and both anchored at $\mathbf{p_0}$. If the two lines are not different, then you really only have the equation of a line, not a plane. Because this is the equation of a plane, every other vertex on the plane not covered by either line is nothing but a linear combination of the vertices on these lines. If you remember that a line is a linear combination of two vertices, you can probably guess what this all means. In a nutshell, this implies that a plane is a linear combination of two lines. Another way to look at it is to take two pens and place a sheet of paper such that it touches both pens at all points. From then on, it should be easy to see every vertex that you can generate on that plane. Figure 4.5 illustrates the concept.

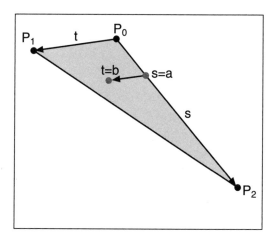

Figure 4.5
Finding a vertex on a plane

Unfortunately, this equation is not very convenient because it carries a total of three vertices. There is, however, another approach you can take. Computer scientists always try to keep the amount of redundancy as low as possible when it's not required, and that is exactly the plan here. Minimally, you could represent the equation with two vectors and one coordinate (one vector for t, and another for s with $\mathbf{p_0}$ as anchor). This is a good time to see whether you really remember the things you learned in the previous chapters. How can you convert the two-directional vectors into one single vector that will, in this case, contain as much information? By using the cross product, of course. If you take any sheet of paper, the orientation of the plane is uniquely identified by its normal vector (perpendicular vector to the plane). Of course, there exists a bunch of vectors that are parallel to the plane, but if you also keep track of one coordinate, you can therefore represent a plane with one normal vector and any one coordinate that sits on the plane, as illustrated in Figure 4.6.

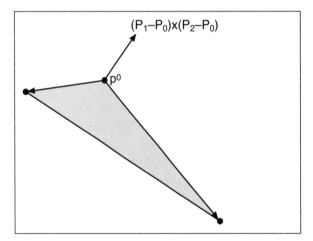

Figure 4.6
Plane represented by one normal vector and one anchor point

So what about the equation? Well, you can convert your parametric equation into a function (but it's cumbersome), or you could simply think outside the box. Because the normal vector is perpendicular to any line you have on your plane, it follows that given any point on the line generated by the plane normal $\mathbf{n}$, $\mathbf{p_0} = <x, y, z, 1>$:

$$\mathbf{n}\bullet\left(\mathbf{p_1}-\mathbf{p_0}\right)=0$$

Expand this equation for a point $\mathbf{p_1}$ that is known to be on the plane, and you should get something extremely similar to the following:

$$n_x x + n_y y + n_z z + D = 0$$

$$D = -\left(n_x p_x + n_y p_y + n_z p_z\right)$$

So what does D mean geometrically? Well, this is akin to matrices. This will come back to haunt you in Chapter 6, "Moving to Hyperspace Vectors: Quaternions," but the basic idea is that the value serves as a form of displacement for the plane along the normal vector, as illustrated in Figure 4.7. A value of $D = 0$ means that the plane passes through the origin. In fact, you can test that <0, 0, 0> does indeed satisfy the equation if $D = 0$. Typically, you will want to normalize the normal vector simply because it makes the plane's translation easier to manipulate. When this is the case, the value of D actually expresses the Euclidian distance (recall Pythagoras' theorem?) by which the plane is translated in the direction of the normal vector from the origin. In short, every plane can be expressed as a vector <x, y, z, d>—which is a much more convenient representation than the one previously posted.

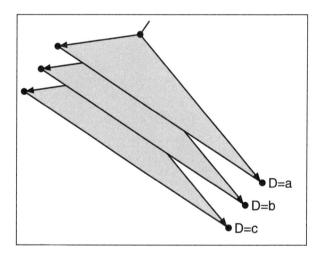

Figure 4.7
A plane translated along the normal vector by changing the value of D

A thinking mind would likely ask what happens if you choose to build an equation using three parameters instead of one or two. This would give a linear combination of three vectors. If you are still in a 3D world, you are basically looking at the span of the entire world (that is, a vector space). It's funny how all the concepts are actually intertwining now, isn't it?

Constructing Spheres

A sphere is another very important geometric object, but before you look at spheres, you should first look at circles. As usual, there are several different approaches you could use to find the equation for a circle. For instance, you could think about the Pythagoras theorem.

The approach I would like to take puts the purely algebraic techniques aside and looks at things from a different angle: by switching over to polar coordinates. In polar coordinates, a circle can be easily expressed because you can fix the radius variable to a fixed value while you let the angle roam freely around. Thus, you can express the equation of a circle with the equation of a radius r fixed at R:

$$r = R$$

There is absolutely no restriction on the angle, so you can let the angle be any value, and you will still satisfy the above condition. Pull out the algebra and convert this equation over to Cartesian coordinates, and you get the following:

$$x = R\cos(\theta)$$
$$y = R\sin(\theta)$$

$$x^2 = R^2 \cos^2(\theta)$$
$$y^2 = R^2 \sin^2(\theta)$$

$$x^2 + y^2 = R^2 \cos^2(\theta) + R^2 \sin^2(\theta)$$
$$= R^2 \left(\cos^2(\theta) + \sin^2(\theta)\right)$$

$$x^2 + y^2 = r^2$$

Normally, this would not make a very interesting proof, but this one *is* interesting because it converts a parametric equation into a function. This can be done because there is only one single variable and the technique used here is to simply add the squares of the two equations together. Clearly, you can apply the same idea of fixing the radius to a single value while letting the other variables roam freely in 3D to deduce the Cartesian equation of a sphere, as illustrated in Figure 4.8:

$$x^2 + y^2 + z^2 = r^2$$

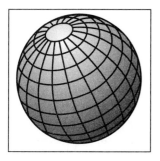

Figure 4.8
A typical sphere

Another way to look at a sphere, which the equation clearly defines, is that a sphere is a shape for which the distance of any point from the center is a constant. It is but a pure application of Pythagoras' theorem in 3D. If you think about the implications of this in spherical coordinates, you get that a sphere in spherical coordinates simply leaves the radii as a constant and allows the angles to roam freely. Unfortunately, these two circular shapes are always centered about the origin, but with some help from the next chapter, you should be able to deduce the equation that moves these shapes around.

When Elements Collide

The first section of this chapter looked at the equations of primitives; this section examines the intersections between various primitives. Intersections are interesting in games not only for Boolean collision problems, but also to simulate various interesting effects such as bullet holes in walls, denting the polygonal surface, and so on. Before you can understand how you can achieve these cool effects, however, you first need to understand how to compute the actual location of the intersection.

Intersection of Two Planes

The first thing you should ask yourself when dealing with two planes is whether they intersect. The only case where the planes may not intersect is when they are parallel. This implies that you would get a linear system, which has no solution. Thus the form:

$$\begin{bmatrix} x & y & z & a \\ 0 & 0 & 0 & b \end{bmatrix}$$

Is it necessary to compute this? Not really. Because you are only dealing with two vectors, the directional vector of any one plane has to be a linear combination of the other plane's vector. If both vectors are normalized, it means that they are in fact equal. Thus, if both normals are equal, the planes do not intersect. This is a really boring case because it serves little purpose. The real meat of the problem is when there really is an intersection. Due to the fact that you have an undetermined system (that is, you have more unknowns than you have equations), you will find an equation that describes all the possible solutions. In the case of two planes intersecting, this is a line. You can use the method presented in Chapter 3, "Meet the Matrices," but here you'll take a more geometrical approach.

If you place two independent planes in space and you think about the planes in terms of their normal vector, the direction of the intersection line is parallel with the cross product of the two planes' normal. If you think about this in a geometrical sense, it all makes sense. So now you have the direction of the line but are still lacking an anchor point for it. There are ways to solve this problem without having to check some preconditions (such as the Gauss-Jordan inverse method versus the determinant method), but the amount of computation they require makes them unattractive options. Instead, let's just go with pure algebraic observation given two planes $<n_1, d_1>$ and $<n_2, d_2>$ and their intersection $\mathbf{x}$:

$$\mathbf{n}_1 \bullet \mathbf{x} = d_1$$
$$\mathbf{n}_2 \bullet \mathbf{x} = d_2$$

There are a bunch of points that satisfy this equation. You could set any one value to 0 and isolate for the remaining components of the vector x. The only tricky thing is that if you choose to zero out the x component and the line is parallel to the x axis, you will never actually get any intersection. Thus all you have to do is to set one component to 0 provided that the same component for the direction vector is non-zero. The rest of the trick is mere problem-solving for two equations and two unknowns. It's not that hard. The following illustrates this:

$$\langle 1,2,3 \rangle \bullet \mathbf{x} = 4$$
$$\langle 5,1,3 \rangle \bullet \mathbf{x} = 2$$

$$Direction = \langle 1,2,3 \rangle \times \langle 5,1,3 \rangle$$
$$= \langle 3,12,-9 \rangle$$
$$= \langle 1,4,-3 \rangle$$

$$\begin{bmatrix} 1 & 2 & 3 \\ 5 & 1 & 3 \end{bmatrix} \begin{bmatrix} x \\ y \\ z \end{bmatrix} = \begin{bmatrix} 4 \\ 2 \end{bmatrix}$$

$$\begin{bmatrix} 1 & 2 & 4 \\ 5 & 1 & 2 \end{bmatrix} \begin{bmatrix} x \\ y \\ z=0 \end{bmatrix} = \begin{bmatrix} 4 \\ 2 \end{bmatrix}$$

$$\begin{bmatrix} 1 & 2 \\ 5 & 1 \end{bmatrix} \begin{bmatrix} x \\ y \end{bmatrix} = \begin{bmatrix} 4 \\ 2 \end{bmatrix}$$
$$\vdots$$
$$\begin{bmatrix} x \\ y \end{bmatrix} = \begin{bmatrix} 0 \\ 2 \end{bmatrix}$$

Thus, the solution is the line of the form $f(t) = <0, 2, 0> + <1, 4, -3>t$. You can verify that this point is indeed on both planes by substituting it back into the plane's equations. In this case, I chose z as the component to be nullified; this was possible because the direction vector had a non-zero value for its z component.

Intersection of Three Planes

The intersection of three planes is a problem that has many outcomes. Fortunately, this should be no news to you because you already know the equation of a plane, and you also know that three planes form a linear system. In mathematical terms, what you have is the following set of equations for three planes $<\mathbf{n}_i, D_i>$ and an arbitrary unknown vector $<\mathbf{v}, 1> = <x, y, z, 1>$:

$$\langle \mathbf{n}_1, D_1 \rangle \bullet \langle \mathbf{v}, 1 \rangle = 0$$
$$\langle \mathbf{n}_2, D_2 \rangle \bullet \langle \mathbf{v}, 1 \rangle = 0$$
$$\langle \mathbf{n}_3, D_3 \rangle \bullet \langle \mathbf{v}, 1 \rangle = 0$$

$$\left[\begin{array}{ccc|c} N_{1x} & N_{1y} & N_{1z} & D_1 \\ N_{2x} & N_{2y} & N_{2z} & D_2 \\ N_{2x} & N_{2y} & N_{3z} & D_3 \end{array} \right]$$

$$\begin{bmatrix} N_{1x} & N_{1y} & N_{1z} \\ N_{2x} & N_{2y} & N_{2z} \\ N_{2x} & N_{2y} & N_{3z} \end{bmatrix} \begin{bmatrix} x \\ y \\ z \end{bmatrix} = \begin{bmatrix} -D_1 \\ -D_2 \\ -D_3 \end{bmatrix}$$

$$\mathbf{Nv} = \mathbf{d}$$

Maybe it looks more familiar in this form. Nonetheless, as you have seen before, a linear system can have many solutions, all of which depend on the rank of the matrix. Geometrically, if two rows are linearly dependent, it implies that the two planes are in fact parallel. Your skills from Chapter 3 will come in very handy here. You may also notice how three planes may not actually possess an intersection. In this case, you get something impossible, in the form of 4 = 0, for example.

From Chapter 3, you should already know that the Gauss-Jordan decomposition is not ideally suited to finding the solution to this linear system. Another solution you should also be familiar with is the LU decomposition, which can be a great tool in many cases. In this case, however, for a 3×3 matrix, there exists a more direct solution that is also numerically stable. The idea comes in the simplest form of matrix algebra you know: the inverse. If you take the inverse on each side of the equation, you can effectively solve this problem. In fact, the Gauss-Jordan method and consequently the LU decomposition are intricately related to the inverse, as you saw in Chapter 3. The solution you should be looking at is something along these lines for a matrix $\mathbf{N}$ built with the normal vectors, a vector $\mathbf{v} = <x, y, z>$, and a displacement vector $\mathbf{d}$:

$$\mathbf{Nv} = \mathbf{d}$$
$$\mathbf{N}^{-1}\mathbf{Nv} = \mathbf{N}^{-1}\mathbf{d}$$
$$\mathbf{v} = \mathbf{N}^{-1}\mathbf{d}$$

You should also know that the Gauss-Jordan method is not well suited for computing the inverse of a matrix. A solution that was proposed at that point was to compute the inverse with the determinants. This method is much more numerically stable and, in the particular case of a 3×3 matrix, it offers a very short, sweet, and interesting formula to compute the intersection of three equations—and, more specifically in this case, of three planes. The thinking process involved here is interesting because it ties knowledge from Chapter 2, "Baby Steps: Introduction to Vectors," with knowledge from Chapter 3. The following shows how you can solve a linear system for a 3×3 matrix:

$$\mathbf{Bx} = \mathbf{a} \quad \text{First transformation}$$

$$\mathbf{Aa} = \mathbf{b} \quad \text{Second transformation}$$

Substituting yields the following:

$$\mathbf{ABx=b}$$

$$\mathbf{Cx} = \mathbf{b}, \mathbf{C} = \mathbf{AB}$$

Because it does not matter to you whether the vectors are column-vectors or row-vectors, you can completely forget about the transposition and come up with a simple and direct equation to compute the intersection of three planes:

$$\mathbf{v} = \frac{-D_1\left(\mathbf{n}_2 \times \mathbf{n}_3\right) + D_2\left(\mathbf{n}_3 \times \mathbf{n}_1\right) - D_3\left(\mathbf{n}_1 \times \mathbf{n}_2\right)}{\mathbf{n}_1 \bullet \left(\mathbf{n}_2 \times \mathbf{n}_3\right)}$$

Now that you have seen all of this, you may be wondering what exactly makes an equation numerically stable. The answer to this question is really not an easy one. Generally, an equation is numerically stable if it does not use the result of another computation. This is not a theorem, thus is not necessarily always true, but in almost every case it is. What happens is that every time you compute something, you lose precision. Thus, if you compute a nested number of calculations, you end up accumulating the error to a point where it may produce false or less accurate results. This is not the only way to lose stability in an equation. For example, let's say you are adding two numbers. If one number is significantly larger than the other number, the precision will take a serious hit.

There are two viable solutions to this problem. The first is to minimize the number of nested calculations, and the second is to introduce some redundancy to the equation in order to stabilize the values. When you compute the Gauss-Jordan method, you do a lot of nested computation; thus, this method is not numerically stable. In comparison, the inverse method shown here is much more stable because it does not nest the values very much. When solving a linear system using Gauss's method and backward substitution, you lose even more precision because of the backward substitution, which nests the equations even more.

note
Chapter 12, "Closing the Gap for Numerical Approximation," will give you a good start in understanding how you can iteratively improve the solution to an equation. Generally speaking, however, the equation mentioned here is sufficient.

For instance, consider the following planes <1, 2, 3, 4>, <3, 2, 4, 1>, <5, 1, 1, 3>:

$$v = \frac{-4\left(\langle 3,2,4\rangle \times \langle 5,1,1\rangle\right) + 1\left(\langle 5,1,1\rangle \times \langle 1,2,3\rangle\right) + 3\left(\langle 1,2,3\rangle \times \langle 3,2,4\rangle\right)}{\langle 1,2,3\rangle \bullet \left(\langle 3,2,4\rangle \times \langle 5,1,1\rangle\right)}$$

$$= \frac{-4\langle -2,17,4\rangle + 1\langle 1,-14,9\rangle + 3\langle 2,5,-4\rangle}{\langle 1,2,3\rangle \bullet \langle -2,17,4\rangle}$$

$$= \frac{\langle 15,-67,-19\rangle}{44}$$

$$= \left\langle \frac{201}{22}, -\frac{3593}{43}, -\frac{80}{11} \right\rangle$$

The three planes intersect at one unique location, which has been computed here.

Intersection of a Line and a Plane

Imagine that a massive meteor is hurtling toward Earth, falling at incredible speeds, finally landing on a hill. Unfortunately, without knowing exactly where the meteor will land on the plane, you will not be able to do much in the way of special effects, let alone affect the terrain. Fortunately, this section should get you up to speed when it comes to solving this problem. In fact, this is a pretty trivial problem. Given the equations of a plane and a line (which you already have), pretty much anyone with a grade-school education will be able to find where they intersect. Because you are more educated, you can represent things with vectors, thereby coming up with sleeker equations. Basically, for a plane with variable vector $\mathbf{x}$, and a normal vector $\mathbf{n}$ giving an equation of $\mathbf{n} \cdot \mathbf{x} + D = 0$ with a line $\mathbf{x} = \mathbf{l}(t) = \mathbf{p} + t\mathbf{v}$, you can combine both equations and isolate for t to yield the following:

$$\mathbf{n} \bullet \mathbf{x} + D = 0$$
$$\mathbf{x} = \mathbf{p} + t\mathbf{v}$$

$$\mathbf{n} \bullet (\mathbf{p} + t\mathbf{v}) + D = 0$$
$$\mathbf{n} \bullet \mathbf{p} + t(\mathbf{n} \bullet \mathbf{v}) + D = 0$$
$$t(\mathbf{n} \bullet \mathbf{v}) = -(\mathbf{n} \bullet \mathbf{p} + D)$$
$$t = -\frac{(\mathbf{n} \bullet \mathbf{p} + D)}{\mathbf{n} \bullet \mathbf{v}}$$

Send t back into the line equation to yield the final solution <x, y, z>, which is the intersection of the line and plane. Now do you see how much easier it is to represent this equation as vectors instead of using scalars? The final equation is thus:

$$x = p - \frac{(n \bullet p + D)}{n \bullet v} v$$

All right, we're down to an example. Suppose that you choose a plane with n = <1, 2, 3> and a displacement of $D = 4$, with line <1, 2, 3> + t<1, 1, 1>:

$$x = \langle 1,2,3 \rangle - \frac{(\langle 1,2,3 \rangle \bullet \langle 1,2,3 \rangle + 4)}{\langle 1,2,3 \rangle \bullet \langle 1,1,1 \rangle} \langle 1,1,1 \rangle$$

$$= \langle 1,2,3 \rangle - \frac{18}{6} \langle 1,1,1 \rangle$$

$$= \langle -2,-1,0 \rangle$$

Intersection of a Line Segment and a Triangle

Some game-programming situations deal with infinite lines. For example, if you are planning to add a rail gun, you may be considering an infinite line. If, however, you are planning to add a rocket launcher, it is highly likely that the rocket will not travel at a speed that is seemingly instantaneous. In that situation, you could compute the intersection between a triangle (because the world is rarely of an infinite nature, like a plane) and a line segment, as illustrated in Figure 4.9, which would be the path your rocket follows for a frame.

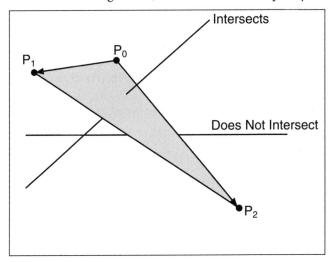

Figure 4.9
Intersection of a triangle and a line

This problem is similar to a line intersecting with a plane, as described in the previous section, because a plane can actually be seen as an infinite triangle while a line can be seen as an infinite line segment. Fortunately, you can solve this problem in two steps. First, make sure that the line is long enough that it can cross both sides of the triangle; second, make sure that the line is within the bounds of the triangle. Once you know that this is true, you can consider the triangle as a plane and compute the intersection of the two components as was done previously. In this section, you are particularly interested in knowing whether there is an intersection because the actual position of the intersection can be computed with the method shown previously.

For starters, you can approximate the triangle with a plane and test to see whether each end point of the line segment is on a different side of the plane. This will tell you whether the line is long enough to traverse the triangle. The problem is thus reduced to determining the side of the point given a plane. (This problem is actually simple and applies to many other shapes and primitives.) What you have to do is express the equation you have as a homogeneous equation—in other words, express the equation such that each side of the equation equals zero. This is easy to do for a plane because it is already homogeneous. What this means at this point is that zero is the turning point for the equation. Thus, if substituting $\mathbf{x}$ in the equation of the plane yields 0, $\mathbf{x}$ is on the plane because it verifies the equality. If $\mathbf{x}$ is not on the plane, the equation will be non-zero. In other words:

$$\mathbf{n} \bullet \mathbf{x} + D = a$$

where a is a non-zero scalar.

You can determine which side of the equation the vertex is on by merely looking at the sign of a. If you think of a in terms of an offset for D, you can see that geometrically, a is the amount by which you would need to offset the plane such that $\mathbf{x}$ is on that plane. If a is positive, you have to go on one side; if it is negative, the other direction must be chosen. As illustrated in Figure 4.10, a positive value implies that the vertex lies in the half that is pointed to by the normal vector of the equation. Conversely, a negative value implies that the vertex sits on the half of the plane that is in opposition to the normal vector. This is similar to what you saw with the cross product. If you inverted the two vectors, the sign of the normal vector changed; the same can be said about a homogeneous equation.

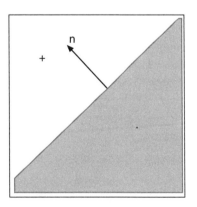

Figure 4.10
Signed half-plane dictated by the orientation of the normal $\mathbf{n}$

Generally, you would have to complete a good number of computations to know which side is which for a general shape, but in this case, you are not really concerned about the side in which the point resides as much as the fact that one resides on the other side of the first vertex. Recall that for the first step, you want to make sure that the segment traverses the plane. It this test fails, there can be no collision between the two elements; it needs one vertex on each side of the plane to work, as shown in Figure 4.11. To make things short, you are basically looking for a negative value for one vertex and for a positive value with the other vertex. Consequently, the homogeneous equation for a plane $<\mathbf{n}, D>$ and a vertex $\mathbf{p}$ that determine the side is

$$f(x, y, z) = \mathbf{n} \bullet \mathbf{p} + D$$

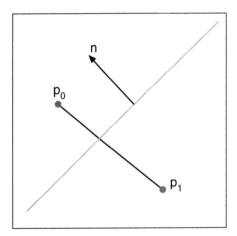

Figure 4.11
Line crossing a plane needs one vertex per half-plane

This equation has to be applied to the two endpoints of the segment. Thus, if you want to be extra lean, you can use an xor in order to differentiate between the two cases. An *xor* basically requires that both conditions not be equal for it to be true. Consequently, the following expression validates the fact that each vertex lies on a different side of the plane:

$$\left(\mathbf{n} \bullet \mathbf{p}_0 + D > 0\right) \mathrm{xor} \left(\mathbf{n} \bullet \mathbf{p}_1 + D > 0\right)$$

If this test passes, you are halfway there. (If it fails, you can discard the idea that an intersection exists at all, because a failure indicates that your segment is not long enough or is parallel to your triangle.)

note

If you were dealing with a line instead of a segment, you would not have to go through this test at all, because a line is infinite while a segment is finite.

Next, check whether the intersection of the line with the plane is actually within the triangle. To do so, you must first compute the intersection of the line with the plane. This will put the intersection vertex on the plane of the triangle. This makes things a little more interesting because it makes one coordinate unnecessary. For example, if you rotate the entire world such that the plane is aligned with the plane generated by two axes, the remaining third axis is actually useless, because every vertex in this new world will have the same value for the third component. As a result, you can forget about any one component of your choice. This slightly reduces the complexity because you only need to deal with two components instead of three. Figures 4.12 and 4.13 show the rotated version of the world, where there is no need for the z component once the intersection between the plane and the line is computed. Every coordinate will have an equal value for z because they reside on the same plane.

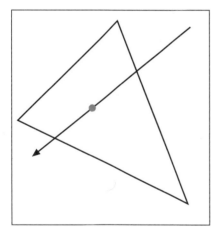

Figure 4.12
Line segment intersecting the plane of the triangle

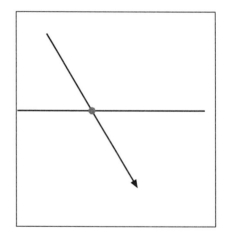

Figure 4.13
Side view of the triangle in Figure 4.12

You should already know how to compute the intersection of a line on a plane, so the next thing to look at is how you can determine whether a vertex is inside the triangle. You could use the same trick you used to determine the side of the vertex by computing the equation for a line and thereafter comparing the sign of the equation with a vertex that you know is inside the triangle (that is, the third vertex, which is not used to find the equation of the line). This method is doable but not very direct. Instead, you can use the cross product to achieve the same thing. The cross product can tell you whether a vertex is on one side of a line or the other by looking at the determinant (third component) of a 2D vector $<x, y, 1>$ as illustrated in Figure 4.14.

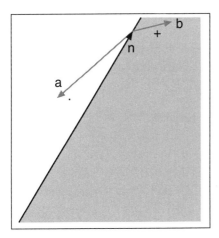

Figure 4.14
Cross product yields negative or positive depending on the
orientation of the vector **a** and **b** along the vector **n**.

There is yet another technique that is interesting only for 2D vectors, which is what you are dealing with here after you remove one of the components. For the remainder of this section, assume that the z component was removed.

You know that the cross product is sign-sensitive at π. In other words, given a vector **v**, you can determine the side on which a vertex resides by computing the cross product of the vector generated by a point of **v** and the vertex you are processing to check whether it lies inside the triangle. To check this, you simply need to look at the determinant's sign. But you also saw that the dot product carries a similar property. In this case, an angle of $\pi/2$ is the sign-sensitive angle. The dot product is faster to compute than the cross product because it requires you to compute only half the number of multiplications. A very swift solution is to simply rotate the vector of $\pi/2$, thereby enabling you to use the dot product's sign as a cross product's determinant's sign.

In a 2D world, such a rotation is extremely easy to apply. Given a vector $<x, y>$ after a rotation of $\pi/2$, the vector becomes $<-y, x>$. With this, the same idea as with the cross product is used. You can take a vertex that you know lies inside the triangle and check that the sign of its dot product with the triangle's side vector rotated by $\pi/2$ matches that of the dot product of the vertex you are verifying with the side vector rotated by $\pi/2$. Simply apply this process iteratively to each side vector of the triangle. If all tests pass, then you can safely say that the vertex lies within the rectangle and thus the line segment intersects the triangle.

The mathematical expression for the last check is as follows for a triangle with vertices {**a**, **b**, **c**} and with a vertex **v** where an exponent of S actually means a rotation of $\pi/2$ for the given vector:

$$\left((\mathbf{a}-\mathbf{b})^S \bullet \mathbf{c} > 0\right) \operatorname{xor}\left((\mathbf{a}\text{-}\mathbf{b})^S \bullet \mathbf{v} > 0\right)$$

$$\left((\mathbf{b}-\mathbf{c})^S \bullet \mathbf{a} > 0\right) \operatorname{xor}\left((\mathbf{b}\text{-}\mathbf{c})^S \bullet \mathbf{v} > 0\right)$$

$$\left((\mathbf{c}-\mathbf{a})^S \bullet \mathbf{b} > 0\right) \operatorname{xor}\left((\mathbf{c}\text{-}\mathbf{a})^S \bullet \mathbf{v} > 0\right)$$

Take a triangle with vertices <−3, −3, 1>, <3, −3, −1>, <−3, 3, 0> and a line with end-points <0, 5, 0> and <1, −6, 0>. You can verify that the normal vector for this triangle is <−12, −6, −36, −18> and that the intersection on the plane is <8, −43, 0>/9. Given **v**, you can compute whether there exists an intersection on the triangle. Because you are only concerned with the sign of the calculation, you can multiply each side of the equation, which carries **v** by 9, so that you can get rid of the ugly fractions:

$$\left((\langle\text{-}3,\text{-}3\rangle-\langle 3,\text{-}3\rangle)^S \bullet \langle -3,3\rangle > 0\right) \operatorname{xor}\left((\langle\text{-}3,\text{-}3\rangle-\langle 3,\text{-}3\rangle)^S \bullet \langle 8,-43\rangle > 0\right)$$

$$=\left(\langle 0,\text{-}6\rangle \bullet \langle -3,3\rangle > 0\right) \operatorname{xor}\left(\langle 0,\text{-}6\rangle \bullet \langle 8,-43\rangle > 0\right)$$

$$=(\text{-}18 > 0)\operatorname{xor}(258 > 0)$$

$$= 0\operatorname{xor}1$$

$$= 1$$

$$\left((\langle 3,-3\rangle-\langle -3,3\rangle)^S \bullet \langle -3,-3\rangle > 0\right) \operatorname{xor}\left((\langle 3,-3\rangle-\langle -3,3\rangle)^S \bullet \langle 8,-43\rangle > 0\right)$$

$$=\left(\langle 6,6\rangle \bullet \langle -3,-3\rangle > 0\right) \operatorname{xor}\left(\langle 6,6\rangle \bullet \langle 8,-43\rangle > 0\right)$$

$$=(\text{-}32 > 0)\operatorname{xor}(\text{-}210 > 0)$$

$$= 0\operatorname{xor}0$$

$$= 0$$

$$\left((\langle -3,3\rangle-\langle -3,-3\rangle)^S \bullet \langle -3,-3\rangle > 0\right) \operatorname{xor}\left((\langle -3,3\rangle-\langle -3,-3\rangle)^S \bullet \langle 8,-43\rangle > 0\right)$$

$$=\left(\langle 0,6\rangle \bullet \langle -3,-3\rangle > 0\right) \operatorname{xor}\left(\langle 0,6\rangle \bullet \langle 8,-43\rangle > 0\right)$$

$$=(\text{-}18 > 0)\operatorname{xor}(\text{-}258 > 0)$$

$$= 0\operatorname{xor}0$$

$$= 0$$

Easily, you could have stopped at the second step when you received a result of 0. It seems that only one test passes, which means that the vertex is on the "inside" half of one single line. For the two other lines, it is outside. You should always get at least one numeral 1 because no matter how you place your vertex, you should always be on the "good half" of at least one line. You can convince yourself by trying to prove the opposite with a small sketch. Also note that in this specific case, it was obvious that the vertex was not inside the triangle only because its second coordinate, y, was out of bounds with any of the other points. In other words, $-43/9 < -3$, which is the lowest point of the triangle. I will come back to similar concepts in later chapters.

Intersection Between a Box and a Line Segment

As you will see later on, it can be pretty convenient to represent a group of objects as a box, so it's pretty important to also look at the intersection between a line segment and a box. In this case, you assume that the box is axis-aligned, which means that the box has an $<x, y, z>$ range of $<[a, b], [c, d], [e, f]>$ exclusively. There is nothing especially hard here because the truth is that you already know all the material to achieve this. In short, you know how to check whether the line segment is long enough to go through the plane. Here, you could be a little more optimal and simply ensure that the component that corresponds to the plane you are checking matches the range.

For instance, if you had a plane defined by $x = 3$ (that is, a plane for which x is always equal to 3 and where z and y have no restrictions whatsoever) with a line segment $<4, 5, 6>$ and $<7, 8, 9>$, it's clear that the line does not go through the plane because no x is smaller than three. So if that plane ends up being the leftmost plane (with the greatest x value), there will be no intersections. You can apply a similar process to the other five planes. The next step, as mentioned previously, is to compute the intersection between the line and the plane. Again, you should take advantage of the fact that the plane is axis-aligned in your calculations to make the equation a little easier to compute. I'll leave the details and result of the calculation as an exercise for you to complete. After you have found the point of intersection, you simply check that the point fits within the domain defined by the box $<[a, b], [c, d], [e, f]>$. With regard to optimizations, see Chapter 19, "The Quick Mind: Computational Optimizations," for some nifty tricks to reduce the plane checks to three planes instead of six.

Know Your Distances

Knowing the equations of various shapes is a good thing, but it's also important to know a few of their properties. In this section, you are mostly concerned with computing the minimal space between two shapes. This type of information will become extremely handy when it comes time to determine whether two objects have collided. Although you have yet to learn the material necessary to fully understand collisions, this does not mean that you cannot get a head start on understanding how you can compute the distance between various objects.

note

There is an entire chapter dedicated to collisions later on, so don't be too worried if this section doesn't cover the more complex cases you may encounter. Chapter 10, "And Then It Hits You: You Need Collision Detection," should fill this gap.

Determining the Distance Between Two Spheres

Computing the distance between two spheres, as illustrated in Figure 4.15, is actually amazingly simple. Start by considering the spheres as two vertices, which you already know how to compute the distance between. This is a simple application of Pythagoras' theorem when you know the length (deltas) for each coordinate:

$$d = \sqrt{\Delta x^2 + \Delta y^2 + \Delta z^2}$$

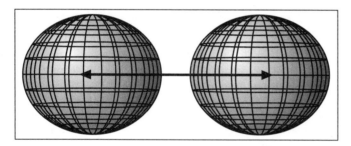

Figure 4.15
Distance between two spheres

This value, d, actually represents the length of an imaginary line going from the center of the first sphere to the center of the second sphere. If you forget about everything around the space and only consider what is in the vicinity of that line, you will notice that the two spheres intersect that line. More precisely, they intersect the line at a length that is equal to their radii from their respective endpoint; this is according to the very definition of a sphere (all vertices are at an equal distance from the center). If you have two spheres of radii r_1 and r_2, for which the centers are separated by d, the distance that separates them is as follows:

$$D = d - r_1 - r_2$$

Now that you understand how a sphere relates to a vertex, you can consider a sphere as a vertex for all remaining problems as long as you do not forget to subtract the radius of the sphere from the distance. In fact, if you wanted to be mathematically precise, you could define a vertex as a sphere with an infinitely small radius or, as you will see a little later in this book, a sphere with radii that tend toward 0. Don't worry if you don't understand the meaning of this sentence just yet; Chapter 7, "Accelerated Vector Calculus for the Uninitiated," will clarify all this for you.

For example, consider the two spheres centered at <0, 0, 0> and <3, 4, 5> with radii 1 and 2. The distance between both of them is defined by the following:

$$D = \sqrt{3^2 + 4^2 + 5^2} - 1 - 2$$
$$= \sqrt{50} - 1 - 2$$
$$= 4.0710$$

Determining the Distance Between a Vertex and a Line

Computing the distance between a line and a point is not as simple as computing the distance between two spheres. In fact, even saying that you want to compute the distance between a vertex and a line is rather imprecise. What you are truly interested in is computing the shortest distance between a vertex and a line. You could compute an infinite number of distances from a line $\mathbf{p} + t\mathbf{l}$ and a vertex $\mathbf{v}$ because there are an infinite number of points on a line. As you will discover in Chapter 7, the shortest imaginary line you can create between a line and any other object is perpendicular to the other line, as shown in Figure 4.16. Because this imaginary line is perpendicular to the other line, you can establish a triangle relationship with any given point on the original line in order to use Pythagoras' theorem to finally find the distance d. The following ensues:

$$d^2 = \left\| (\mathbf{v} - \mathbf{p}) \right\|_2^2 - \mathrm{proj}_l^2 (\mathbf{v} - \mathbf{p})$$

$$= \left(\sqrt{(v_x - p_x)^2 + (v_y - p_y)^2 + (v_z - p_z)^2} \right)^2 - \frac{\left((\mathbf{v} - \mathbf{p}) \bullet \mathbf{l} \right)^2}{\left\| \mathbf{l} \right\|_2^2}$$

$$d = \sqrt{(v_x - p_x)^2 + (v_y - p_y)^2 + (v_z - p_z)^2 - \frac{\left((\mathbf{v} - \mathbf{p}) \bullet \mathbf{l} \right)^2}{\left\| \mathbf{l} \right\|_2^2}}$$

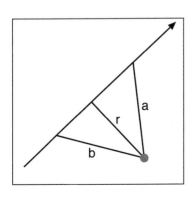

Of course, if you are planning to do a comparison with the distance, see whether you can't do a comparison with the square of the distance. This will save you a computationally costly function. This is in fact a nice proof of how to use the concepts about vectors that you saw in Chapter 2. This is not a complicated proof; you just need to think about the relationship between the vector and the elements that are in the universe.

Figure 4.16
Shortest distance between a line and point is perpendicular ($r < a$) and ($r < b$)

Thus, given a line <1, 2, 3> + t<1, 1, 1> and a point in space, <4, 2, 1>, you can compute the shortest distance between the line and the point as done here:

$$d = \sqrt{\left\|\langle 4,2,1\rangle - \langle 1,2,3\rangle\right\|_2^2 - \frac{\left(\left(\langle 4,2,1\rangle - \langle 1,2,3\rangle\right)\bullet\langle 1,1,1\rangle\right)}{\left\|\langle 1,1,1\rangle\right\|_2^2}}$$

$$= \sqrt{\left\|\langle 3,0,-2\rangle\right\|_2^2 - \frac{\langle 3,0,-2\rangle\bullet\langle 1,1,1\rangle}{\left\|\langle 1,1,1\rangle\right\|_2^2}}$$

$$= \sqrt{13-\frac{1}{3}}$$

$$= \sqrt{\frac{38}{3}}$$

Determining the Distance Between Two Lines

Imagine you have two objects, each moving along its own linear path. Will they intersect? This sounds like a line distance problem! Determining the minimal distance between two lines combines results from a line/vertex minimal distance problem. A line can actually be thought of as an infinite set of points, where the relationship between each point is a linear combination. What this means for you is that you can actually consider one of the lines to be an infinite set of points. To illustrate, take two lines, l_1 and l_2. From the last section, you know that you can compute the minimal distance between a line and a point by simply forcing the distance vector to be orthogonal to the line and passing through the point. Similarly, if you do this for both lines, you can conclude that the distance vector that separates each line is actually perpendicular to both l_1 and l_2. But how can you actually generate a vector that is perpendicular to both lines, as illustrated in Figure 4.17?

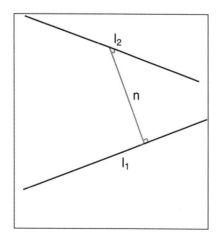

If you do not know the answer to this, consider flipping back to Chapter 2. If you do know the answer, then you must have known that I was talking about the cross product. This is exactly how you can obtain the directional vector of the line.

At this point, you have a good idea of the equation of the distance line, but you still need the anchor point, which fixes the line to a given position. If the directional vector of the distance vector is normalized, and the anchor point of the equation is on one of the two lines, the parameter will represent the Euclidian distance (along the vector) if you also let the equation equal the point on the other line of the equation. Mathematically, what you are looking at is

Figure 4.17
Minimal distance between two lines

the following for the two lines $f(s)$ and $g(t)$, each with directional vector DeltaG and DeltaG and with anchor points F and G:

$$\mathbf{f}(s) = \mathbf{f} + s(\Delta\mathbf{f})$$

$$\mathbf{g}(t) = \mathbf{g} + t(\Delta\mathbf{g})$$

$$\mathbf{n}(x) = \mathbf{n} + x(\Delta\mathbf{f} \times \Delta\mathbf{g})$$

$$\mathbf{f} + s(\Delta\mathbf{f}) = \mathbf{g} + t(\Delta\mathbf{g}) + x\frac{(\Delta\mathbf{f} \times \Delta\mathbf{g})}{\|\Delta\mathbf{f} \times \Delta\mathbf{g}\|_2}$$

$$\mathbf{f} - \mathbf{g} = t(\Delta\mathbf{g}) - s(\Delta\mathbf{f}) + x\frac{(\Delta\mathbf{f} \times \Delta\mathbf{g})}{\|\Delta\mathbf{f} \times \Delta\mathbf{g}\|_2}$$

$$\begin{bmatrix} f_x - g_x \\ f_y - g_y \\ f_z - g_z \end{bmatrix} = t\begin{bmatrix} \Delta g_x \\ \Delta g_y \\ \Delta g_z \end{bmatrix} - s\begin{bmatrix} \Delta f_x \\ \Delta f_y \\ \Delta f_z \end{bmatrix} + x\begin{bmatrix} \dfrac{(\Delta\mathbf{f} \times \Delta\mathbf{g})_x}{\|\Delta\mathbf{f} \times \Delta\mathbf{g}\|_2} \\ \dfrac{(\Delta\mathbf{f} \times \Delta\mathbf{g})_y}{\|\Delta\mathbf{f} \times \Delta\mathbf{g}\|_2} \\ \dfrac{(\Delta\mathbf{f} \times \Delta\mathbf{g})_z}{\|\Delta\mathbf{f} \times \Delta\mathbf{g}\|_2} \end{bmatrix}$$

$$\begin{bmatrix} \dfrac{(\Delta f \times \Delta\mathbf{g})_x}{\|\Delta f \times \Delta\mathbf{g}\|_2} & \dfrac{(\Delta\mathbf{f} \times \Delta\mathbf{g})_y}{\|\Delta\mathbf{f} \times \Delta\mathbf{g}\|_2} & \dfrac{(\Delta\mathbf{f} \times \Delta\mathbf{g})_z}{\|\Delta\mathbf{f} \times \Delta\mathbf{g}\|_2} \end{bmatrix}\begin{bmatrix} f_x - g_x \\ f_y - g_y \\ f_z - g_z \end{bmatrix} = t\begin{bmatrix} \dfrac{(\Delta\mathbf{f} \times \Delta\mathbf{g})_x}{\|\Delta\mathbf{f} \times \Delta\mathbf{g}\|_2} & \dfrac{(\Delta\mathbf{f} \times \Delta\mathbf{g})_y}{\|\Delta\mathbf{f} \times \Delta\mathbf{g}\|_2} & \dfrac{(\Delta\mathbf{f} \times \Delta\mathbf{g})_z}{\|\Delta\mathbf{f} \times \Delta\mathbf{g}\|_2} \end{bmatrix}\begin{bmatrix} \Delta g_x \\ \Delta g_y \\ \Delta g_z \end{bmatrix}$$

$$-s\begin{bmatrix} \dfrac{(\Delta\mathbf{f} \times \Delta\mathbf{g})_x}{\|\Delta\mathbf{f} \times \Delta\mathbf{g}\|_2} & \dfrac{(\Delta\mathbf{f} \times \Delta\mathbf{g})_y}{\|\Delta\mathbf{f} \times \Delta\mathbf{g}\|_2} & \dfrac{(\Delta\mathbf{f} \times \Delta\mathbf{g})_z}{\|\Delta\mathbf{f} \times \Delta\mathbf{g}\|_2} \end{bmatrix}\begin{bmatrix} \Delta f_x \\ \Delta f_y \\ \Delta f_z \end{bmatrix} +$$

$$x\begin{bmatrix} \dfrac{(\Delta\mathbf{f} \times \Delta\mathbf{g})_x}{\|\Delta\mathbf{f} \times \Delta\mathbf{g}\|_2} & \dfrac{(\Delta\mathbf{f} \times \Delta\mathbf{g})_y}{\|\Delta\mathbf{f} \times \Delta\mathbf{g}\|_2} & \dfrac{(\Delta\mathbf{f} \times \Delta\mathbf{g})_z}{\|\Delta\mathbf{f} \times \Delta\mathbf{g}\|_2} \end{bmatrix}\begin{bmatrix} \dfrac{(\Delta\mathbf{f} \times \Delta\mathbf{g})_x}{\|\Delta\mathbf{f} \times \Delta\mathbf{g}\|_2} \\ \dfrac{(\Delta\mathbf{f} \times \Delta\mathbf{g})_y}{\|\Delta\mathbf{f} \times \Delta\mathbf{g}\|_2} \\ \dfrac{(\Delta\mathbf{f} \times \Delta\mathbf{g})_z}{\|\Delta\mathbf{f} \times \Delta\mathbf{g}\|_2} \end{bmatrix}$$

$$\begin{bmatrix} \dfrac{(\Delta\mathbf{f} \times \Delta\mathbf{g})_x}{\|\Delta\mathbf{f} \times \Delta\mathbf{g}\|_2} & \dfrac{(\Delta\mathbf{f} \times \Delta\mathbf{g})_y}{\|\Delta\mathbf{f} \times \Delta\mathbf{g}\|_2} & \dfrac{(\Delta\mathbf{f} \times \Delta\mathbf{g})_z}{\|\Delta\mathbf{f} \times \Delta\mathbf{g}\|_2} \end{bmatrix}\begin{bmatrix} f_x - g_x \\ f_y - g_y \\ f_z - g_z \end{bmatrix} = [0]t - [0]s + x[1]$$

$$x = \frac{\begin{bmatrix} \dfrac{(\Delta\mathbf{f} \times \Delta\mathbf{g})_x}{\|\Delta\mathbf{f} \times \Delta\mathbf{g}\|_2} \\ \dfrac{(\Delta\mathbf{f} \times \Delta\mathbf{g})_y}{\|\Delta\mathbf{f} \times \Delta\mathbf{g}\|_2} \\ \dfrac{(\Delta\mathbf{f} \times \Delta\mathbf{g})_z}{\|\Delta\mathbf{f} \times \Delta\mathbf{g}\|_2} \end{bmatrix} \bullet \begin{bmatrix} f_x - g_x \\ f_y - g_y \\ f_z - g_z \end{bmatrix}}{}$$

This proof is a great example of how understanding the previous principles is extremely important; otherwise, you may find yourself computing numerous things that are in fact constant. Of importance in this proof is the fact that the original vectors delta F and delta G are perpendicular to the normal vector generated by both of them. Consequently, the dot product of any of these two vectors multiplied by the cross product will equal zero.

note

When it comes time to deal with light vectors and similar, much more complex cases, you should be familiar enough with the basic concepts to be able to simplify your equations as much as possible. This can make the difference between a wicked lighting model and yet another pathetic ambient lighting scheme. The power is in your hands.

Consider the two lines described by the equations <1, 2, 3> + t<1, 1, 1> and <1, 1, 1> + s<1, 2, 3>. What is the shortest distance between these two lines?

$$\Delta f \times \Delta g = \langle 1,1,1 \rangle \times \langle 1,2,3 \rangle$$
$$= \langle 1,-2,1 \rangle$$

$$\|\Delta f \times \Delta g\|_2 = \sqrt{1^2 + (-2)^2 + 1^1}$$
$$= \sqrt{6}$$

$$F - G = \langle 1,2,3 \rangle - \langle 1,1,1 \rangle$$
$$= \langle 0,1,2 \rangle$$

$$x = \begin{bmatrix} \dfrac{1}{\sqrt{6}} \\ \dfrac{-2}{\sqrt{6}} \\ \dfrac{1}{\sqrt{6}} \end{bmatrix} \bullet \begin{bmatrix} 0 \\ 1 \\ 2 \end{bmatrix}$$
$$= 0$$

Ouch, what happened here? Actually, this is correct. This implies that the two lines actually intersect. In other words, the shortest distance between them is 0. You can verify that this is indeed true by substituting $t = -1$ and $s = 1$.

Determining the Distance Between a Point and a Plane

I've seen some of the most complicated and obscure methods for obtaining the equation to compute a distance. Indeed, the method does not always have to be complicated or purely algebraic. If you are inclined to work visually, it may be easier to deal with a problem geometrically, as illustrated in Figure 4.18.

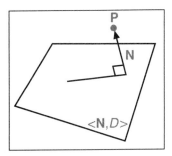

Figure 4.18
Minimal distance between a plane and a point

You have already seen that you can express the equation of a plane by its normal vector and with a value D, which represents the distance of the plane from the origin along the normal vector. The key to solving this problem is D. If you have a normalized plane, D becomes the Euclidian distance between the origin and the plane. If you translate everything such that the origin is the point you are dealing with, D will indeed equal the shortest distance between the plane and the origin (which will then be the vertex, by this hypothesis).

Normalizing a plane is an easy task. You know how to normalize a vector, right? Recall that you merely need to divide every component by the 2-norm of the vector. This is slightly different for a plane because you have an extra component D. Previously, it was mentioned that the plane needed to be normalized in order for D to represent the distance between the origin and the plane. This means that you have to divide the entire equation by the length of the normal vector. Thus, you should not count D as part of this normalization process. It's true that you represent the plane as a 4D vector where the fourth component is D, but the rule is that the normal must have a length of 1 and not that the plane's vector including D must have a length of 1 (normalized). Consequently, if you want to normalize a plane, you should observe the following equation for a vector $\mathbf{n} = <N_x, N_y, N_z, D>$:

$$\frac{N_x x + N_y y + N_z z + D}{\sqrt{N_x^2 + N_y^2 + N_z^2}} = 0$$

Now you would like to translate the world such that the origin becomes the position of the vertex. What, then, is the equation $f(x, y, z)$ that will take the world and translate it to the vertex? You will see the principles of translations in greater depth in the next chapter, but just so you know, the following trivial equation solves your problem:

$$\mathbf{0} + \mathbf{P} = \mathbf{P}$$

All you have to do is add the point to all <x, y, z> variables (and other points), as illustrated in Figures 4.19 and 4.20. So for any given point <x, y, z>, you should compute <x [ps] p_x, y [ps] p_y, z − [ps] p_z>. All you have to do at this point is add the vertex **P** from every other point/variable, and you will be able to obtain the distance between a point and a plane by simply isolating for D. Assuming that the vector **n** is already normalized, the following logic ensues:

$$N_x\left(x + P_x\right) + N_y\left(y + P_y\right) + N_z\left(z + P_z\right) + D = 0$$

$$N_x x + N_y y + N_z z + \left(D + N_x P_x + N_y P_y + N_z P_z\right) = 0$$

$$\mathbf{n} \bullet \langle x, y, z \rangle + \left(D + \mathbf{n} \bullet P\right) = 0$$

$$\mathbf{n} \bullet \langle x, y, z \rangle + d = 0$$

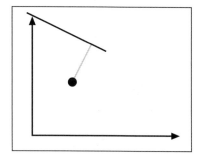

Figure 4.19
Shortest distance between a point and a plane

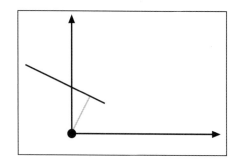

Figure 4.20
Figure 4.19 after the translation; it corresponds to the normal and the offset D

Combine all the terms to compute the final value for d, the distance between your vertex **p** and your plane:

$$d = D + \mathbf{n} \bullet \mathbf{p}$$

Consider the plane <1, 2, 3, 4> and the point <3, 2, 1>. Let's compute the smallest distance between the two elements (don't forget to normalize):

$$d = \frac{4 + \langle 1,2,3 \rangle \bullet \langle 3,2,1 \rangle}{\left\| \langle 1,2,3 \rangle \right\|_2}$$

$$= \frac{4+3+4+3}{\sqrt{14}}$$

$$= \frac{21}{\sqrt{14}}$$

3D File Formats

Last but not least, I promised a look at a 3D file format's general structure. Unfortunately, it's not very useful to go through one specific format because most contain a lot of details that are not worth looking at. In addition, there is a plethora of free object model loaders out there that you can pick up and use in your own source code, making it pretty useless to rewrite one here. What is worth looking at is the general structure they employ because what may work best is to create your very own file format that is more tailored toward your specific needs. For example, you might need to keep some additional information for each vertex.

A typical model file format has the following:

- **A list of vertices.** Some formats prefer to give every single detail about a vertex, while others prefer to build one large array of vertices that will be referenced later.

- **A texture coordinates array.** The two common implementations are to give this information right after the vertex or to simply have one large array that will be indexed later on.

- **A normal element.** The normal becomes extremely useful when it comes time to decide whether a polygon is visible, or when it's time to render the polygon with lighting.

note

A normal can be associated with every polygon, but typically it's much more convenient to have one normal per vertex. It may be hard to see how a vertex can have a normal, but it's not that complicated. You already know that a normal for a plane is basically the vector that is perpendicular to the plane. Similarly, a normal for a vertex is the normal that points outward from the shape. For instance, you could average every normalized normal vector that is related to the faces containing that point. Obviously, you can't really say "orthogonal" here because that is not truly the case, but you get the idea.

Thus far, every vertex has come with two additional chunks of information: the texture coordinates and the normal. It's not very common, but you can also include other information with the vertices. For example, if you are looking at a very foggy world, you may be interested in keeping the percentage of fog at every vertex. For example, it may be much more foggy in a small valley than in the mountains, so you could attribute a value of 70 percent to the bottom of the valley while gradually moving toward 0 percent at the top of the mountains.

- **An array of triangles.** Most models are composed of triangles, which are the simplest form of 3D polygon. As a result, using triangles makes all the calculations easier on you. Take, for example, the intersection of a pentagon with a line segment; you should clearly see how many more calculations it would require to determine this as compared to determining the intersection of a triangle with a line segment. For simplicity's sake, a typical object is composed of a bunch of triangles, and most file models describe these triangles by including three vertices. Typically, it's easier to simply use the offset of the vertex, but some file formats prefer to attribute an index into the vertex array, the texture array, and the normal array separately, simply because they can reuse some values. For instance, suppose you have a vertex that is shared by two triangles; they may have different texture coordinates if one triangle is the arm of the character while the other is part of his t-shirt. It can also be convenient to carry around the normal of triangle. That way, you do not have to recompute the normal every time you want to do something similar to an intersection between a line and a triangle. This is just something to keep in mind as you build your own format.

- **An array of groups of triangles.** Some file formats also like to build groups. For instance, you may wish to group together all of the triangles that comprise the head, while separating the ones dealing with the arm. That way, it's much easier to identify whether a rail gun has hit the character's head or his arm. This also makes it easier to move the head independently of the rest of the character's body, because every triangle related to the head is grouped together. Generally speaking, if you use a file format, you will also have to store everything in memory; the best way to proceed with this is to make arrays and to reference the objects via indices. It so happens that this is well suited for vertex lists and similar advanced concepts that the 3D APIs put at your disposal.

To sum things up, a general data format to store models is to store five arrays: One array of vertex, one array of texture coordinates, one of normal vectors, one of triangles, and one of groups of triangles. The triangles will typically index the vertices, the textures and the normals, while the group will index the triangles. As always, be smart about your data structures. If something makes more sense for your API or operations, do it. As you will see later on, some formats are particularly interesting for certain operations. Unfortunately, there's almost never a solution that fits all of them.

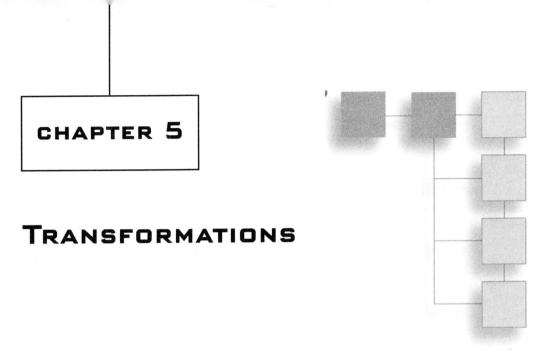

CHAPTER 5

TRANSFORMATIONS

Everyone goes through puberty; why should your objects be exempt from transformations? This may sound like a silly question, but it is serious. A static object is boring. To give life to any of your scenes, you need to make them mutate or transform, at least a little. Of course, when a person goes through puberty, he or she does not change from a male to a female or vice versa (unless some sort of operation is involved), and objects are no different. While being transformed, they should still be recognizable. They may grow, shrink, stretch, or even swell in certain areas, but the relationships between various pieces should remain. In other words, just as your head does not switch places with your legs (again, unless some sort of operation is involved), your objects should remain relatively intact.

note

As you will soon see, not all transformations modify what an object looks like. A translation, for example, does not actually modify the object, nor does a rotation.

In this chapter, you will tackle the general aspects of transformations and the components surrounding it. More precisely, you will look at the following:

- Point of view
- Linear transformations, such as translations, scaling, skewing, and rotations
- Multilinear transformations, including rotations about an arbitrary axis
- 3D projections
- Non-linear transformation

It's All About the Viewpoint

It's the year 3000, and you're planning for the next attack on a remote solar system. Space stations are a common thing, and many rotate freely around a mother planet. Rather than computing a lot of transformations to show the rotation of a space station about an arbitrary axis, the trick is to apply each one once and then store it. For example, if you were to pre-rotate the space station such that its rotation axis was already aligned with the z axis, all you would have to do is rotate around the z axis by θ and apply the inverse rotations, which sets the rotational vector back to its original position. This is the idea behind the creation of various spaces. When you design a game, you should store/load your objects in the most convenient space for your needs. Sometimes this may simply mean translating the object by a fixed amount or, as in your space station's case, it could mean applying a pre-rotation to it. Although you can easily create your own spaces, a few of them, covered here, are quite common.

Notably, you have the viewpoint of the object, the world as a container of objects, and finally the camera, which is your eye on the world. Before you begin studying the core of transformations, let's first look at the content in which they can be applied. In other words, let's look at the points of view you can take to transform your objects: object space, world space, and camera space.

Object Space

Some time ago, many religious scholars, philosophers, and scientists fancied the idea of a geocentric planetary system—that is, a solar system in which the Earth is the center of everything, and also a system in which every object rotates around the Earth. Scientists of the day devised a set of complicated equations to describe their understanding of the movement of the planets in space. With time, scientists proved that the geocentric theory, advanced by the Christian church, was faulty and that in reality, the sun was the center of our solar system. That is, rather than being geocentric, our planetary system was heliocentric. Given this new optic, the movement of the planets about our point of view was drastically easier to perceive. This by no means implies that it is not possible to describe the movement of the other planets from a heliocentric point of view; it simply means that it is much harder to think of the movement from our point of view than it is from the sun's point of view. That's what this section is all about: choosing the appropriate point of view to express your transformations in the most natural fashion.

In object space, you are mostly concerned about the object's point of view, hence the term "object space." The center of the space is located at the center of the object. (The center of the object does not have to be the *true* center of the object; it should be what you consider to be the center from the point of view of the object.) Using this point of view is extremely useful when rotating an object about itself or an arbitrary axis.

In object space, you look at the world from the object's point of view. This enables you to define a unique transformation for every object that is easily computable, such as rotations of the object about itself. Just try to imagine describing the movement of the moon around the Earth as a rotation and translation around the sun; you will understand what I mean by simplicity. Thus, all coordinates given in object space describe the object without accounting for its rotations, translations, or anything in between. These transformations are applied from another point of view. On Earth, it does not really matter that the Earth is rotating, now does it? This is true if you take only Earth into consideration without thinking about the sun and moon surrounding it.

The transformation matrix that is applied to coordinates in object space is called the *object transformation matrix*. Consequently, the rotation of the space station about an arbitrary axis would indeed be deemed an object space transformation. If you wanted to precompute the first rotation such that the rotation vector aligns with the z axis, you would have to create a second object space (more on this later). Thus, the fact that Earth rotates is represented here in the object space transformation matrix.

World Space

As the term suggests, world space looks at the world from its own point of view. The center of the space is actually the center of the world, and every transformation applied to this space (as with every space) is applied from its center. Consequently, every object in the world will experience the exact same transformations.

For example, suppose you have a space station rotating around a planet at $<x, y, z>$. With rotation in world space, the space station would rotate around the world's center, not around the planet. If you want the space station to rotate about the planet, you must create two separate object spaces. The space station transformation matrix should first rotate the space station and then translate it. You would first need to rotate the space station about itself (by using object space transformations); for simplicity, call it "space station space." The remaining question is, where should it be translated? The next step is to create yet another object space, which, for simplicity, you can call "planet space." In this object space, the center of the planet is the center of the space. Thus, after the rotation, you should translate the space station space such that the center of that space sits at the center of where you would like the space station to sit relative to the planet.

If you want to have your planet at position $<x, y, z>$, you would simply need to create another object transformation matrix (call it "planet transformation matrix"), which would simply need to translate planet space such that the center of the planet (and thus the space) sits exactly where you want the planet to be (that is, $<x, y, z>$). Because in that space, $<0, 0, 0>$ is the center of the world, you would finally have coordinates in world space. Quickly, a world transformation matrix is a matrix akin to an object matrix, but that is applied to the entire set of objects (that is, the world). Therefore, any world matrix needs to take its coordinates in world space exactly like an object transformation matrix needs object coordinates as input.

Camera Space

Unless you are planning to see everything from a world's point of view, you should probably start to think about having a mobile point of view in your world: a camera. Camera space is simple. The center of the camera is the center of the space. Consequently, when you receive coordinates in camera space, you are receiving coordinates that are from the camera's point of view, which is exactly what you want.

The same principles as before apply to this space. In order to convert from world space to camera space, you simply need to create a camera transformation matrix, which will first rotate the world accordingly, followed by a translation to the position you are looking for. A camera transformation matrix is really a world transformation matrix because the matrix actually operates on every single object, but to make the distinction clear between the two, I prefer to call them as such.

At this point, you may be wondering what a world transformation matrix may be used for because the object matrix takes care of the object and the camera matrix takes care of the world, but *Quake 3* actually found an interesting way to use a world transformation matrix. If you sink into the water in *Quake 3* and stop moving, you should see that the world around you seems to distort slightly. In fact, what the folks at ID have done is apply a wavy scaling factor to the world to give you the impression that you are under water. An interesting effect could have also been built with skews.

To make things crystal clear, take a look at Figure 5.1, which illustrates the steps you need to go through if you want to correctly and easily transform objects around the world.

Some 3D APIs, such as GL and Direct3D, already possess hardware support for some of these transformations. For example, GL combines an object/world/camera matrix into a single matrix, which means that you have to cut it down yourself if you want to work in another space.

Linear Transformations

There are many types of transformations, but one of the most important is the linear transformation. Transformations by themselves have no meaning; in order to have meaning, they must be applied to something. With respect to games, you typically want to transform an object that is composed of vertices or coordinates in the space in which you are working.

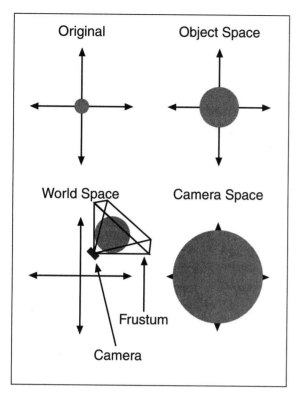

Figure 5.1
Changing the point of view of an object

There are a few different types of linear transformations, including the following:

- Translations
- Scaling
- Skewing
- Rotations

This type of transformation is called linear because for every resulting coordinate, the equation is a linear combination. In 3D, every linear combination can be drawn as a set of planes centered at the origin or as lines. For example, consider a square function x^2; as you learned in Chapter 4, "Basic Geometric Elements," a plane cannot be used to accurately portray this equation.

Because linear transformations are linear combinations, they can all be expressed in matrix notation as $\mathbf{x'} = \mathbf{Ax}$, where $\mathbf{A}$ is the transformation's matrix and $\mathbf{x}$ is the coordinate vector.

A matrix can be used as a data placeholder for transformations. The beauty of doing so is that each transformation can be contained within a 4×4 matrix. To concatenate transformations, you merely need to multiply the matrices together, which makes them very simple to work with. The other nice thing about it, as you saw in Chapter 3, "Meet the Matrices," is that the product of two matrices can be expressed in a single matrix, which means that a set of transformations can actually be described by a single matrix instead of requiring you to compute a long, windy set of matrix multiplication, every time you want to transform an element. As you saw, to transform a vector with the help of a transformation matrix, you merely need to multiply the vector to be transformed by the transformation matrix.

Translations

As shown in Figure 5.2, translations are easy to compute in a simple equation model. For example, if you wanted to translate x by 3, you would simply use the equation $x = x - 3$. In matrix form, however, this generates a problem because -3 is not a linear combination of x, y, or z. The solution is to add another component in order to be able to apply linear combinations. Choose x, y, z, and 1. If you want to do a linear combination for the translation, you simply need to write a linear combination choosing the coordinate <1, 0, 0, -3> for the space <x, y, z, 1>, and you will get the aforementioned equation. You can verify that this is indeed true by computing the dot product of both vectors. Translations can also be applied to x, y, z and theoretically to 1 (which makes absolutely no sense at this point). Thus, in matrix notation, you get the following:

$$\begin{bmatrix} x' \\ y' \\ z' \\ 1' \end{bmatrix} = \begin{bmatrix} 1 & 0 & 0 & \Delta x \\ 0 & 1 & 0 & \Delta y \\ 0 & 0 & 1 & \Delta z \\ 0 & 0 & 0 & 1 \end{bmatrix} \begin{bmatrix} x \\ y \\ z \\ 1 \end{bmatrix}$$

Figure 5.2
Translation of an object

Historically speaking, delta is typically used to mean "difference." Thus, in this case, delta x actually means "the difference in x" and consequently represents the translation to which x will be subject. Similarly, you can say the same thing about y and z. You can verify that this matrix multiplication does indeed yield a translation by multiplying the right side of the equation. For example, if you want to translate every vertex in your world of $<3, -4, 2>$, you would generate the following matrix:

$$\begin{bmatrix} 1 & 0 & 0 & 3 \\ 0 & 1 & 0 & -4 \\ 0 & 0 & 1 & 2 \\ 0 & 0 & 0 & 1 \end{bmatrix}$$

If you choose a vertex $<1, 2, 3>$, which in 4D becomes $<1, 2, 3, 1>$, you get what you'd expect:

$$\begin{bmatrix} 1 & 0 & 0 & 3 \\ 0 & 1 & 0 & -4 \\ 0 & 0 & 1 & 2 \\ 0 & 0 & 0 & 1 \end{bmatrix} \begin{bmatrix} 1 \\ 2 \\ 3 \\ 1 \end{bmatrix} = \begin{bmatrix} 1+3 \\ 2-4 \\ 3+2 \\ 1 \end{bmatrix} = \begin{bmatrix} 4 \\ -2 \\ 5 \\ 1 \end{bmatrix}$$

Note that it would indeed be impossible to translate a coordinate if you were working only with a 3×3 matrix in 3D $<x, y, z>$. Because of this, all 3D transformations will have to be defined as 4×4 matrices. If the matrices were not 4×4, then we wouldn't be able to multiply the matrices together, let alone compute the inverse that is required if we want to undo a transformation.

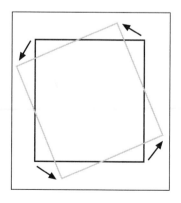

Scaling

The definition for scaling is actually in the word itself; scaling is the process of having something "scale"—that is, grow or shrink—as illustrated in Figure 5.3. You can do this by multiplying every component of your coordinate by a scale factor (which you can call s). Hence, the equation to scale a coordinate x would look something like x' = sx.

Figure 5.3
Scaling of an object

note

Because you have used a 4×4 matrix to do your transformations thus far, every subsequent transformation will have to be presented in a 4×4 matrix in order for any matrix operation to be defined
properly.

This definition is somewhat restrictive because every component of the coordinate is
scaled by the same factor. If you wanted to, you could, for example, scale your object only
in x or only in y. This broader definition suggests that each component should have its
own scale factor. Granted, if you want your object to keep the same proportions, you
should have all scale factors equal each other. So for the component in x, the vector $<x, y,
z, 1>$ should be multiplied by $<s_x, 0, 0, 0>$. If you think about every respective component
of the coordinate for s, in matrix form, you get the following:

$$
\begin{bmatrix} x' \\ y' \\ z' \\ 1' \end{bmatrix} = \begin{bmatrix} s_x & 0 & 0 & 0 \\ 0 & s_y & 0 & 0 \\ 0 & 0 & s_z & 0 \\ 0 & 0 & 0 & 1 \end{bmatrix} \begin{bmatrix} x \\ y \\ z \\ 1 \end{bmatrix}
$$

So far, this should be pretty easy stuff. If, for example, you wanted to scale $<1, 2, 3>$ by $<2,
2, -2>$, you would get the following result:

$$
\begin{bmatrix} 2 & 0 & 0 & 0 \\ 0 & 2 & 0 & 0 \\ 0 & 0 & -2 & 0 \\ 0 & 0 & 0 & 1 \end{bmatrix} \begin{bmatrix} 1 \\ 2 \\ 3 \\ 1 \end{bmatrix} = \begin{bmatrix} 1 \cdot 2 \\ 2 \cdot 2 \\ -2 \cdot 3 \\ 1 \end{bmatrix} = \begin{bmatrix} 2 \\ 4 \\ -6 \\ 1 \end{bmatrix}
$$

This example brings up an interesting observation. You can also mirror your object from
one of the three axes by choosing a scale factor of -1 in that axis. Thus, scaling can serve
two purposes: It can help scale objects, and it can be used to mirror objects.

Skewing

Although skewing is rarely mentioned in programming books, it is an interesting operation, and is the key to one of the most important linear transformations: rotation.
Skewing, as illustrated in Figure 5.4, can be seen as a progressive translation, which means
that it depends on the value of another axis.

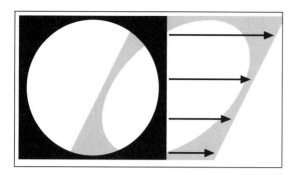

Figure 5.4
Skewing an object

It's important to note that skewing is not the same as stretching, which is attributable to scaling. When you stretch a shape, you increase its area. When you skew an object, you are not changing its area in any way because you are translating infinitely small pieces of it. It's as if you were to cut a single piece of paper into two separate pieces. Move the top piece a little to the left, and that's effectively a form of skewing. Repeat the process by cutting one of the two pieces in half, and you now have a more accurate skew. Repeat this process infinitely, and you can clearly see that the area of the paper has not changed. You've neither removed nor added any paper. Moving a piece to the left or right like you just did is simply a skew in y for x. In other words, the x coordinates have been modified in y. The theorem about the area is always true if it is aligned with an axis, but not necessarily true if the skew is done on two axes at the same time.

Another way to look at skewing is that, given any value x and a height y, the value x' is always translated by the same amount for the same y. Thus, because of the dependency, the equation to skew in x looks something like $x' = x + k_x y$. A similar deduction can be obtained for y. In 3D, the idea is exactly the same. Given a coordinate (such as x), you can either skew (that is, translate) for changing values of y or you can skew for changing values of z.

Because of this dependency on another variable, skews must be applied one by one. In the previous cases, you saw that you could scale or translate every axis independently. This is not the case for skewing. You can multiply two skew matrices together to show that they are not equal. In 3D, the following skew matrices can be used:

$$\begin{bmatrix} x' \\ y' \\ z' \\ 1 \end{bmatrix} = \begin{bmatrix} 1 & k_{xy} & k_{xz} & 0 \\ 0 & 1 & 0 & 0 \\ 0 & 0 & 1 & 0 \\ 0 & 0 & 0 & 1 \end{bmatrix} \begin{bmatrix} x \\ y \\ z \\ 1 \end{bmatrix} \qquad \text{Skew in } x$$

$$\begin{bmatrix} x' \\ y' \\ z' \\ 1 \end{bmatrix} = \begin{bmatrix} 1 & 0 & 0 & 0 \\ k_{yx} & 1 & k_{yz} & 0 \\ 0 & 0 & 1 & 0 \\ 0 & 0 & 0 & 1 \end{bmatrix} \begin{bmatrix} x \\ y \\ z \\ 1 \end{bmatrix} \qquad \text{Skew in } y$$

$$\begin{bmatrix} x' \\ y' \\ z' \\ 1 \end{bmatrix} = \begin{bmatrix} 1 & 0 & 0 & 0 \\ 0 & 1 & 0 & 0 \\ k_{zx} & k_{zy} & 1 & 0 \\ 0 & 0 & 0 & 1 \end{bmatrix} \begin{bmatrix} x \\ y \\ z \\ 1 \end{bmatrix} \qquad \text{Skew in } z$$

All in all, these are the steps you need to take to skew in each respective axis, but this does not by any means imply that you cannot skew simultaneously in, say, x and y. Just know that skewing in xy is not the same as skewing in x and then in y or vice versa. When you skew in such a fashion, you are skewing on an axis that is not purely in x or y or z. For example, suppose you want to skew on the line $x = y$. In that case, you would have to choose a skew in x that is equal to the skew in y; such a skew would look similar to Figure 5.5. These types of skews actually do change the area of the shape because they are not combinations of axis-aligned skews. You can verify this easily by looking again at Figure 5.5. If you were to cut the black triangles and try to patch them in order to fill the area, you would not be able to do so.

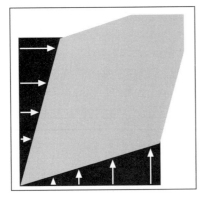

Figure 5.5
xy skew

Let's follow through with an example of a skew in xy for y and x along the line $3y = 2x$. The following example shows:

$$\begin{bmatrix} 1 & 3-1 & 0 & 0 \\ 2-1 & 1 & 0 & 0 \\ 0 & 0 & 1 & 0 \\ 0 & 0 & 0 & 1 \end{bmatrix}\begin{bmatrix} 1 \\ 1 \\ 1 \\ 1 \end{bmatrix} = \begin{bmatrix} 1 & 2 & 0 & 0 \\ 1 & 1 & 0 & 0 \\ 0 & 0 & 1 & 0 \\ 0 & 0 & 0 & 1 \end{bmatrix}\begin{bmatrix} 1 \\ 1 \\ 1 \\ 1 \end{bmatrix} = \begin{bmatrix} 1+2\cdot 1 \\ 1\cdot 1 \\ 1 \\ 1 \end{bmatrix} = \begin{bmatrix} 3 \\ 2 \\ 1 \\ 1 \end{bmatrix}$$

You may be wondering why you subtract 1 from 2 and 3 in the matrix. The reason is actually simple. You want the coordinate <1, 1> to move over to <3, 2>. Simply write your matrix as a linear system with the skews as unknown, and then isolate for the unknowns, and you will notice that this is indeed how things go.

Rotations

Rotations, illustrated in Figure 5.6, are often abstractly defined in books. Just as a test, try to define a rotation mathematically without using words like "turning," which in reality is just the product of a rotation. Obviously, it is not a trivial thing to define, but it can be defined in more rigorous terms to yield a much simpler proof of the equations. Not only is the more rigorous definition easier to process, it also reveals an extremely interesting relationship between skewing and rotation. The properties required for a rotation can actually be described in one single word: orthonormal. A rotation can be described as an orthonormal transformation. This bizarre-sounding word is easily decomposable into two separate words: ortho and normal (or, if you prefer, orthogonal and normal).

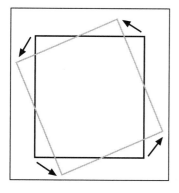

You already know what orthogonal means. Specifically, for a set of vectors, the vectors are orthogonal if the dot product of any vectors in the set chosen two by two is zero. An orthogonal transformation uses the same idea. An orthogonal transformation is such that if you choose any two orthogonal vectors, and you apply the transformation on these vectors, the two resulting vectors will also be orthogonal. Obviously, a rotation requires the object to retain its form, and thus it cannot suffer deformations like the ones that occur with skews. Hence the requirement for an orthogonal transformation.

Figure 5.6
Rotation of a square

A quick way to check whether a matrix is orthogonal is to multiply it by its transpose and see whether the resulting matrix is diagonal. This is a direct consequence of the very definition of orthogonal. When two different vectors (or rows, in this case) are multiplied together, you should get zero by definition. If you multiply the same vector twice, which only happens for the elements on the diagonal, you get an undefined value, and thus a diagonal matrix.

You also need the vectors to be normal. If you recall, a normal vector is a normal that has a norm of 1, also often called a unit-vector. Similarly, a transformation matrix is normal if, given any vector, the resulting transformed vector is also normal. This is also a requirement for a rotation. Just imagine what would happen if, while rotating, your object would scale. You obviously cannot allow this. Put the two concepts together, and you get an orthonormal transformation—a transformation for which every row and column vector has a 2-norm of 1 and a transformation matrix $\mathbf{M}$, where $\mathbf{MM^T}$ is a diagonal matrix. You can combine the first and second result to come up with the conclusion that $\mathbf{MM^T}$ should be the identity matrix. Let's first start by tackling the 2D version of a rotation.

Start with the identity matrix. The trick to rotating is to choose the skewing components such that the first vector is orthogonal to the second vector every time. The following matrix T can do this, as shown:

$$\mathbf{T} = \begin{bmatrix} 1 & a \\ -a & 1 \end{bmatrix}$$

$$\mathbf{T}\begin{bmatrix} 1 \\ 0 \end{bmatrix} = \begin{bmatrix} 1 & a \\ -a & 1 \end{bmatrix}\begin{bmatrix} 1 \\ 0 \end{bmatrix} = \begin{bmatrix} 1 \\ -a \end{bmatrix}$$

$$\mathbf{T}\begin{bmatrix} 0 \\ 1 \end{bmatrix} = \begin{bmatrix} 1 & a \\ -a & 1 \end{bmatrix}\begin{bmatrix} 0 \\ 1 \end{bmatrix} = \begin{bmatrix} a \\ 1 \end{bmatrix}$$

$$\begin{bmatrix} 1 \\ -a \end{bmatrix} \bullet \begin{bmatrix} a \\ 1 \end{bmatrix} = a - a = 0$$

These types of matrices actually have their own name: skew-symmetric matrices or anti-symmetric matrices. This is because the skew component of the matrix is the negative of the other skew component on the other side of the diagonal. This transformation matrix has been shown to be orthogonal but it is clearly not normal (yet). It is much more natural if you think of rotations in terms of polar coordinates. Thus, replace your unknown a with polar coordinates and, because you want a normalized value, choose a radius of 1:

$$\begin{bmatrix} 1 & 1 \cdot \sin(\theta) \\ -1 \cdot \sin(\theta) & 1 \end{bmatrix}$$

The fact that sine was chosen over cosine is absolutely irrelevant; it simply changes the reference angle's position in the rotation. At this point, you have a transformation that is not normal. The norm of the columns or the norm of the rows should be 1 in order for the matrix to be a normal transformation matrix. This means that the matrix you currently have is orthogonal but not of the right size, so you only need to scale down your object such that its size remains unchanged. You can verify that scaling by cos(ϕ) does the trick by computing the determinant of the matrix. Thus, the final matrix to apply a rotation of ϕ is as follows:

$$\begin{bmatrix} \cos(\phi) & \sin(\phi) \\ -\sin(\phi) & \cos(\phi) \end{bmatrix}$$

If you had chosen cosine instead of sine, every cosine would have swapped with a sine, but you would still have a very valid rotation matrix. The only problem is that the angle would have a bias, whereas this one rotates as expected. Thus, a rotation is actually nothing but a scaled skew-symmetric matrix.

This covers how rotations are done in 2D, but what about 3D? It just so happens that a rotation in 2D is the same as a rotation around the z axis. If you think of x and y as a sheet of paper and of the z axis as the axis sticking out of the paper, you can see that rotating the paper actually rotates around the z axis. Thus, the rotation matrix for this transformation is the following:

$$\begin{bmatrix} \cos(\phi) & \sin(\phi) & 0 & 0 \\ -\sin(\phi) & \cos(\phi) & 0 & 0 \\ 0 & 0 & 1 & 0 \\ 0 & 0 & 0 & 1 \end{bmatrix}$$

You already have two vectors that are orthonormal, so why not use them to build the rotations around the other axes? You simply have to note that a rotation around an axis is always such that the coordinate for that axis remains unchanged. Consequently, you simply need to position your factors accordingly. To rotate around the y axis, the matrix to use is as follows:

$$\begin{bmatrix} \cos(\phi) & 0 & -\sin(\phi) & 0 \\ 0 & 1 & 0 & 0 \\ \sin(\phi) & 0 & \cos(\phi) & 0 \\ 0 & 0 & 0 & 1 \end{bmatrix}$$

You will notice that the sign has actually been repositioned. It is in fact a fully valid rotation to keep the sign as was done previously, but this form of rotation is a little more practical because of its rotation orientation. The fact that the sign is changed only changes the orientation of the rotation and nothing else.

Finally, a rotation around the x axis can be performed with the following matrix:

$$\begin{bmatrix} 1 & 0 & 0 & 0 \\ 0 & \cos(\phi) & \sin(\phi) & 0 \\ 0 & -\sin(\phi) & \cos(\phi) & 0 \\ 0 & 0 & 0 & 1 \end{bmatrix}$$

Again, as with skews, this does not mean that you cannot perform a rotation in, say, xy. As long as your matrix is an orthonormal transformation, your matrix is still, technically speaking, a rotation. The only problem is that it can become pretty confusing. The following example shows how to compute the rotation of a coordinate around the x axis:

$$\begin{bmatrix} 1 & 0 & 0 & 0 \\ 0 & \cos\left(\dfrac{\pi}{4}\right) & \sin\left(\dfrac{\pi}{4}\right) & 0 \\ 0 & -\sin\left(\dfrac{\pi}{4}\right) & \cos\left(\dfrac{\pi}{4}\right) & 0 \\ 0 & 0 & 0 & 1 \end{bmatrix} \begin{bmatrix} 1 \\ 2 \\ 3 \\ 1 \end{bmatrix} = \frac{1}{\sqrt{2}} \begin{bmatrix} 1 & 0 & 0 & 0 \\ 0 & 1 & 1 & 0 \\ 0 & -1 & 1 & 0 \\ 0 & 0 & 0 & 1 \end{bmatrix} \begin{bmatrix} 1 \\ 2 \\ 3 \\ 1 \end{bmatrix} = \frac{1}{\sqrt{2}} \begin{bmatrix} 1 \\ 2+3 \\ -2+3 \\ 1 \end{bmatrix} = \frac{1}{\sqrt{2}} \begin{bmatrix} 1 \\ 5 \\ 1 \\ 1 \end{bmatrix}$$

Multiple Linear Transformations

You have seen how you can apply many operations on a vector, but clearly, it may be useful to apply a set of operations on a vector. For instance, suppose you want to rotate a vector, translate it, and then rotate it in another direction. Matrices are helpful here because they allow you to compute one single transformation matrix containing all the linear transformations you want. In fact, the operation is really simple. All you have to do is operate on matrices like a stack.

For example, suppose you have two transformations, **A** and **B**, and you want to apply **B** followed by **A** (remember, matrices—and, consequently, transformations—are not commutative; generally speaking, you cannot swap them). Given a vector **x**, what you get for the first transformation is as follows:

$$\mathbf{Bx} = \mathbf{a} \quad \text{First transformation}$$

$$\mathbf{Aa} = \mathbf{b} \quad \text{Second transformation}$$

Substituting yields;

$$\mathbf{ABx} = \mathbf{b}$$

$$\mathbf{Cx} = \mathbf{b}, \mathbf{C} = \mathbf{AB}$$

Consequently, given a set of linear transformations, you can apply the ordered set of transformations to a vector by simply computing the reversed multiplication of the matrices. Thus, instead of computing two or more matrix multiplications for every vector, you simply need to compute the product of the transformations once and thereafter compute one multiplication per vector. That is quite an advantage.

As was previously mentioned, matrices are not commutative. That is, the order of the matrices is important and cannot be disregarded. You cannot switch matrices around as you multiply them. In other words, translating an object followed by a scale transformation is not equivalent to scaling first and then translating. For example, if you translate and then scale, the equation you would get for a single component would resemble $x = (x' + t) * s$. On the flip side, if you start by scaling and then translate, what you get is something along the lines of $x = x' \cdot s + t$, which is drastically different. Similarly, rotation matrices also depend on order. Rotating in x followed by a rotation in y is not the same as first rotating in y followed by a rotation in x. All of this means that it can be pretty confusing to figure out the order in which the rotation should be applied.

If your favorite 3D library enables you to handle this automatically, then by all means use it. That being said, it is useful to understand what goes on underneath because, as you will see in upcoming chapters such as Chapter 10, "And Then It Hits You: You Need Collision Detection," rotating an object by hand is sometimes the only way to go. Also, libraries only go so far. They won't allow you to innovate. If you don't understand how the basics work, how can you come up with, say, an equation that rotates around a vector?

Rotation About an Arbitrary Axis

You have already learned how to rotate an object around one of the three axes in 3D, as illustrated in Figure 5.7. But what happens if you want to rotate the object around an arbitrary axis in 3D? At first, this problem looks like an algebraic monster, but the easiest way to solve any problem is to think at a higher level. You already know how to rotate an object about the z axis, so here you can rotate your arbitrary axis such that it aligns with the z axis, rotate your object about the z axis, and, when you are finished, simply undo the rotation you have applied to your rotation axis. Easier said than done, but in matrix terms, what you have is the following for a coordinate vector $\mathbf{x}$ where $\mathbf{R}$ is the rotation matrix, which rotates the object such that the rotation axis aligns with the z axis, and $\mathbf{M}$ is the actual rotation matrix to rotate the object of ϕ:

$$\mathbf{R}^{-1}\mathbf{MRx}$$

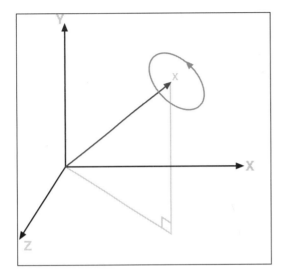

Figure 5.7
Rotation around an arbitrary axis **x**

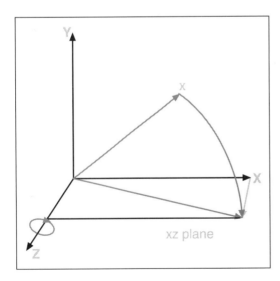

Figure 5.8
Rotation of a rotation vector on the *xz* plane

M is simply a rotation about the *z* axis, and is pretty easy. The tricky part is to know how to obtain **R**. There are many ways to do this; one is to first rotate around the *z* axis such that the rotation vector sits on the *xz* plane, as illustrated in Figure 5.8. When this is done, you lose the component in *y* for the rotation vector, and you can finish the task by rotating the vector around the *y* axis such that it matches the *z* axis, as shown in Figure 5.8. Now all that remains is to find the value for $\cos(\phi)$ and $\sin(\phi)$ for each of the rotations. You can look at the problem geometrically, but in this case, it is easier and less error prone to figure it out algebraically. All you have to do is make sure the first rotation you apply to your rotation vector **v** yields a 0 in the *y* component.

For a rotation around the *z* axis such that the rotation vector lands on the *xz* plane, the following applies:

$$\mathbf{R}_z \mathbf{c} = \begin{bmatrix} ? \\ 0 \\ z \\ 1 \end{bmatrix}$$

$$\begin{bmatrix} a & b & 0 & 0 \\ -b & a & 0 & 0 \\ 0 & 0 & 1 & 0 \\ 0 & 0 & 0 & 1 \end{bmatrix} \begin{bmatrix} x \\ y \\ z \\ 1 \end{bmatrix} = \begin{bmatrix} ? \\ 0 \\ z \\ 1 \end{bmatrix}$$

To solve the system, take the two equations $-bx + ya = 0$ and the known fact about cosines and sines $b^2 + a^2 = 1$, and you should be able to isolate for both *a* and *b* to yield the following:

$$a = \frac{x}{\sqrt{x^2 + y^2}}$$

$$b = \frac{y}{\sqrt{x^2 + y^2}}$$

The exact same idea can be used to obtain the rotation matrix around the y axis, as illustrated in Figure 5.9 with $\mathbf{R}_z\mathbf{c}$, yielding the two rotation matrices:

$$\mathbf{R}_z = \begin{bmatrix} \dfrac{x}{\sqrt{x^2 + y^2}} & \dfrac{y}{\sqrt{x^2 + y^2}} & 0 & 0 \\[2ex] -\dfrac{y}{\sqrt{x^2 + y^2}} & \dfrac{x}{\sqrt{x^2 + y^2}} & 0 & 0 \\[2ex] 0 & 0 & 1 & 0 \\[1ex] 0 & 0 & 0 & 1 \end{bmatrix}$$

$$\mathbf{R}_y = \begin{bmatrix} \dfrac{z}{\sqrt{x^2 + y^2 + z^2}} & 0 & -\dfrac{\sqrt{x^2 + y^2}}{\sqrt{x^2 + y^2 + z^2}} & 0 \\[2ex] 0 & 1 & 0 & 0 \\[2ex] \dfrac{\sqrt{x^2 + y^2}}{\sqrt{x^2 + y^2 + z^2}} & 0 & \dfrac{z}{\sqrt{x^2 + y^2 + z^2}} & 0 \\[2ex] 0 & 0 & 0 & 1 \end{bmatrix}$$

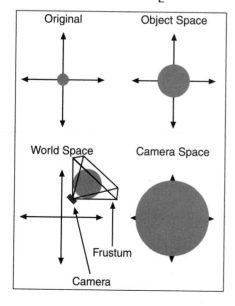

Figure 5.9
Rotation of a rotation vector on the z axis

If you combine both matrices to get the matrix **R**, which will rotate your space such that the rotation vector is aligned with the z axis, and if you assume that the rotation axis is normal, you get the following rotation matrix:

$$\mathbf{R} = \mathbf{R}_y\mathbf{R}_z = \begin{vmatrix} \dfrac{z}{\sqrt{x^2+y^2+z^2}} & 0 & -\dfrac{\sqrt{x^2+y^2}}{\sqrt{x^2+y^2+z^2}} & 0 \\[3mm] 0 & 1 & 0 & 0 \\[3mm] \dfrac{\sqrt{x^2+y^2}}{\sqrt{x^2+y^2+z^2}} & 0 & \dfrac{z}{\sqrt{x^2+y^2+z^2}} & 0 \\[3mm] 0 & 0 & 0 & 1 \end{vmatrix} \begin{bmatrix} \dfrac{x}{\sqrt{x^2+y^2}} & \dfrac{y}{\sqrt{x^2+y^2}} & 0 & 0 \\[3mm] -\dfrac{y}{\sqrt{x^2+y^2}} & \dfrac{x}{\sqrt{x^2+y^2}} & 0 & 0 \\[3mm] 0 & 0 & 1 & 0 \\[3mm] 0 & 0 & 0 & 1 \end{bmatrix}$$

$$= \begin{bmatrix} \dfrac{zx}{\sqrt{x^2+y^2+z^2}\sqrt{x^2+y^2}} & \dfrac{zy}{\sqrt{x^2+y^2+z^2}\sqrt{x^2+y^2}} & \dfrac{-\sqrt{x^2+y^2}}{\sqrt{x^2+y^2+z^2}} & 0 \\[3mm] -\dfrac{y}{\sqrt{x^2+y^2}} & \dfrac{x}{\sqrt{x^2+y^2}} & 0 & 0 \\[3mm] \dfrac{x}{\sqrt{x^2+y^2+z^2}} & \dfrac{y}{\sqrt{x^2+y^2+z^2}} & \dfrac{z}{\sqrt{x^2+y^2+z^2}} & 0 \\[3mm] 0 & 0 & 0 & 1 \end{bmatrix}$$

The last step of the process is to compute the rotation about the z axis and to undo the rotation **R** by transforming the object with its inverse. The following reasoning applies:

R⁻¹MR =

$$
=\begin{bmatrix}
\dfrac{z\cdot x}{\sqrt{x^2+y^2+z^2}\,\sqrt{x^2+y^2}} & -\dfrac{y}{\sqrt{x^2+y^2}} & \dfrac{x}{\sqrt{x^2+y^2+z^2}} & 0 \\[3mm]
\dfrac{zy}{\sqrt{x^2+y^2+z^2}\,\sqrt{x^2+y^2}} & \dfrac{x}{\sqrt{x^2+y^2}} & \dfrac{y}{\sqrt{x^2+y^2+z^2}} & 0 \\[3mm]
\dfrac{-\sqrt{x^2+y^2}}{\sqrt{x^2+y^2+z^2}} & 0 & \dfrac{z}{\sqrt{x^2+y^2+z^2}} & 0 \\[3mm]
0 & 0 & 0 & 1
\end{bmatrix}
\begin{bmatrix}
\cos(\theta) & \sin(\theta) & 0 & 0 \\
-\sin(\theta) & \cos(\theta) & 0 & 0 \\
0 & 0 & 1 & 0 \\
0 & 0 & 0 & 1
\end{bmatrix}
$$

$$
\begin{bmatrix}
\dfrac{z\cdot x}{\sqrt{x^2+y^2+z^2}\,\sqrt{x^2+y^2}} & \dfrac{z\cdot y}{\sqrt{x^2+y^2+z^2}\,\sqrt{x^2+y^2}} & \dfrac{-\sqrt{x^2+y^2}}{\sqrt{x^2+y^2+z^2}} & 0 \\[3mm]
-\dfrac{y}{\sqrt{x^2+y^2}} & \dfrac{x}{\sqrt{x^2+y^2}} & 0 & 0 \\[3mm]
\dfrac{x}{\sqrt{x^2+y^2+z^2}} & \dfrac{y}{\sqrt{x^2+y^2+z^2}} & \dfrac{z}{\sqrt{x^2+y^2+z^2}} & 0 \\[3mm]
0 & 0 & 0 & 1
\end{bmatrix}
$$

$$
=\begin{bmatrix}
\dfrac{x^2+\left(y^2+z^2\right)\cos(\theta)}{x^2+y^2+z^2} & \dfrac{x\left(1-\cos(\theta)\right)y+z\sin(\theta)\sqrt{x^2+y^2+z^2}}{x^2+y^2+z^2} \\[4mm]
\dfrac{x\left(1-\cos(\theta)\right)y-z\sin(\theta)\sqrt{x^2+y^2+z^2}}{x^2+y^2+z^2} & \dfrac{\left(x^2+z^2\right)\cos(\theta)+y^2}{x^2+y^2+z^2} \\[4mm]
\dfrac{z\sqrt{x^2+y^2+z^2}\left(1-\cos(\theta)\right)x+y\sin(\theta)\left(x^2+y^2+z^2\right)}{\left(x^2+y^2+z^2\right)^{\frac{3}{2}}} & \dfrac{z\sqrt{x^2+y^2+z^2}\left(1-\cos(\theta)\right)y-x\sin(\theta)\left(x^2+y^2+z^2\right)}{\left(x^2+y^2+z^2\right)^{\frac{3}{2}}} \\[4mm]
0 & 0
\end{bmatrix}
$$

$$
\begin{bmatrix}
\dfrac{zx\left(1-\cos(\theta)\right)+y\sin(\theta)\sqrt{x^2+y^2+z^2}}{x^2+y^2+z^2} & 0 \\[4mm]
\dfrac{zy\left(1-\cos(\theta)\right)+x\sin(\theta)\sqrt{x^2+y^2+z^2}}{x^2+y^2+z^2} & 0 \\[4mm]
\dfrac{\left(x^2+y\right)\cos(\theta)+z^2}{x^2+y^2+z^2} & 0 \\[4mm]
0 & 1
\end{bmatrix}
$$

Notice how the inverse of a rotation is actually the transpose of the original matrix. This is always true for rotation matrices and it greatly simplifies some computations. To simplify the equations in the matrix, simply choose a rotation vector v, which is already normalized, and use the Pythagorean identity. This simplifies the rotation matrix to the following:

$$\mathbf{R^{-1}MR} = \begin{bmatrix} x^2(1-\cos(\theta))+\cos(\theta) & x(1-\cos(\theta))y+z\sin(\theta) & zx(1-\cos(\theta))-y\sin(\theta) & 0 \\ x(1-\cos(\theta))y-z\sin(\theta) & y^2(1-\cos(\theta))+\cos(\theta) & zy(1-\cos(\theta))+x\sin(\theta) & 0 \\ z(1-\cos(\theta))x+y\sin(\theta) & z(1-\cos(\theta))y-x\sin(\theta) & z^2(1-\cos(\theta))+\cos(\theta) & 0 \\ 0 & 0 & 0 & 1 \end{bmatrix}$$

Thus, if you wanted to rotate the coordinate <3, 3, 3> around the un-normalized axis <1, 2, 3> at 30 degrees, you would compute the new coordinate as follows:

$$\left(\mathbf{R^{-1}MR}\right)\mathbf{v} = \begin{bmatrix} \dfrac{1}{14}+\dfrac{13\sqrt{3}}{28} & \dfrac{1}{7}-\dfrac{\sqrt{3}}{14}+\dfrac{3\sqrt{14}}{28} & \dfrac{3}{14}-\dfrac{3\sqrt{3}}{28}-\dfrac{1}{\sqrt{14}} & 0 \\ \dfrac{1}{7}-\dfrac{\sqrt{3}}{14}+\dfrac{3\sqrt{14}}{28} & \dfrac{2}{7}+\dfrac{5\sqrt{3}}{14} & \dfrac{3}{7}-\dfrac{3\sqrt{3}}{14}+\dfrac{\sqrt{14}}{28} & 0 \\ \dfrac{3}{14}-\dfrac{3\sqrt{3}}{28}+\dfrac{1}{\sqrt{14}} & \dfrac{3}{7}-\dfrac{3\sqrt{3}}{14}-\dfrac{\sqrt{14}}{28} & \dfrac{9}{14}+\dfrac{5\sqrt{3}}{28} & 0 \\ 0 & 0 & 0 & 1 \end{bmatrix}\begin{bmatrix} 3 \\ 3 \\ 3 \\ 1 \end{bmatrix}$$

$$= \begin{bmatrix} 3.1712 \\ 2.1407 \\ 3.5157 \\ 1 \end{bmatrix}$$

Projections

How can a topic like projections come back to the table? As it turns out, we have coordinates in 2D, but for some reason, my computer refuses to show me 3D images. It must have something to do with the fact that my screen is flat. (Sigh.) If you don't have a brand new 3D monitor, you will also need to convert 3D coordinates to 2D. It sounds like an awfully complicated task, but it really is very simple. There are various ways to do this—some better than others—all based upon the principle of projection, which you learned about in Chapter 2, "Baby Steps: Introduction to Vectors." The two main types of projection I cover here are orthographic projection, useful for 3D games, and perspective projection, which is great for isometric games.

Orthographic Projection

An orthogonal projection is one of many ways to project 3D coordinates on a 2D surface. The idea is to simply project the z component orthogonally on the xy plane, as shown in

Figure 5.10. In short, it is as though you are completely forgetting about the z component of the $<x, y, z>$ coordinates. It's not the most interesting projection, but it is the type of view that was widely used in older games such as *Sim City* and many others that used a 45-degree top view.

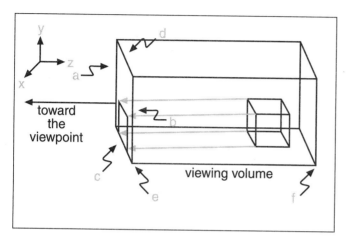

Figure 5.10
Orthogonal projection

For reasons you will soon see, it is very practical to map every coordinate in the range $[-1, 1]$ for each component. All you have to do to make this happen is scale the coordinates and translate them such that the camera can see everything bounded by $[-1, 1]$. The same process is applied to x, y, and z. So without loss of generality, suppose you choose to start with x, for which you have decided that every coordinate will have range $[a, b]$. To map x such that it fits the range $[-1, 1]$, you can first translate the coordinate such that the first half of it is negative and the other half is positive. You can do this by subtracting the average of the extremes. After the translation is applied, you merely need to rescale the coordinate by using the following:

$$x' = \frac{NewSpaceLength \cdot (x - CenterTranslation)}{OldSpaceLength}$$

$$= \frac{\left(1 - (-1)\right)\left(x - \frac{b+a}{2}\right)}{b-a}$$

$$= \frac{2x - (b+a)}{b-a}$$

$$= \frac{2x}{b-a} - \frac{b+a}{b-a}$$

This means that the orthogonal projection can actually be expressed as a linear combination. For each coordinate, the result is a scale followed by a translation (which is exactly what you would expect). Consequently, the matrix that can apply an orthogonal projection to a coordinate $<x, y, z, 1>$ with bounds $<[a, b], [c, d], [e, f], 1>$ is as follows:

$$
\begin{bmatrix}
\dfrac{2}{b-a} & 0 & 0 & 0 \\[2ex]
0 & \dfrac{2}{d-c} & 0 & 0 \\[2ex]
0 & 0 & \dfrac{2}{f-e} & 0 \\[2ex]
-\dfrac{b+a}{b-a} & -\dfrac{d+c}{d-c} & -\dfrac{f+e}{f-e} & 1
\end{bmatrix}
$$

Perspective Projection

An orthogonal projection is interesting, but it has its flaws. Notably, if you assume that a cylinder is defined between a range $[-1, 1]$, the matrix simplifies to the identity, meaning that $<x, y, z, 1>$ maps to itself. So if you were to look inside the cylinder of an orthogonal projection from the origin, you would only see the side edge of the cylinder and nothing at all inside the cylinder. The reality of our world is that the farther away objects are, the smaller they should appear. For this reason, you need a different type of frustum—one that takes this fact into account.

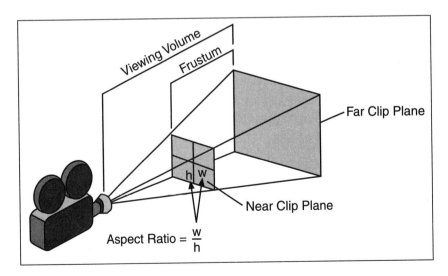

Figure 5.11
Viewing frustum

We can start by defining a frustum as the shape that describes the region inside which every vertex is viewable on the screen, as illustrated in Figure 5.11. Geometrically, you can represent the frustum as a box. If you were to place your eye (that is, the camera) in front of the box, given an orthographic projection, the box would appear as a square simply because the ranges for all the components form a box. On the other hand, with the perspective projection, the plane at the back should have more area than the plane at the front. This may lead to a bit of confusion because it was previously mentioned that objects that are farther away should appear smaller, but if you think about it for a second, this is really what is happening here. The objects at the back visually take a smaller percentage of the back plane if you apply an orthogonal projection on it. Consequently, they are smaller (percentage wise).

This idea leaves you with a frustum that looks like a cut-off pyramid in which the peak is the position of the camera, as shown in Figure 5.12. The tricky part is to figure out the transformation required to yield such a shape.

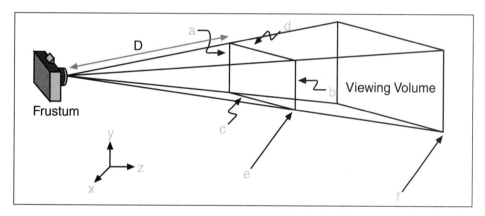

Figure 5.12
Perspective projection

This transformation should transform such a frustum into a box. Because you already know that a box is the same as an orthogonal projection, all you have to do is apply the projection to the transformation. A perspective projection of this type might look really complicated, but in reality, it comes back to math you most likely saw in your first year of high school. The projection works exactly like an acetate projector in reverse. (I'm sure this brings back some *really* exciting memories for you!)

If you look at the pyramidal frustum from the side only, you can reduce the problem to a simpler one. Every beam of light has to come down to the camera, so no matter where the object may sit, one of its vertices has to land on the camera's point. To determine where on your "screen plane" the vertex will be landing, all you have to do is cast a line in 3D from the vertex all the way down to the camera. Then, simply compute the intersection between the line and the plane. Of course, you could go about computing everything as you did in Chapter 4, but that would not be very wise because it is much easier to see this by looking at a 2D side view of the 3D view. It basically boils down to a relation between a triangle and any smaller triangle that possesses the same proportions. The equation to convert from 3D coordinates to 2D is as follows:

$$x' = \frac{D \cdot x}{z}$$

$$y' = \frac{D \cdot y}{z}$$

Because this transforms your pyramidal frustum into a box, you can simply finish everything off by applying an orthogonal projection. Because both x and y are the same, let's apply the logic on x only:

$$x'' = \frac{D \cdot x'}{z}$$

$$-\text{Proj}_{px} = \frac{-2x''}{b-a} - \frac{b+a}{b-a}$$

$$\text{Proj}_{px} = \frac{2Dx}{z(b-a)} + \frac{z(b+a)}{z(b-a)}$$

$$= \frac{1}{z}\left(\frac{2x}{b-a} + \frac{z(b+a)}{b-a}\right)$$

Normally, this is not a very interesting algebraic manipulation, but what makes this expansion worthwhile is that 1 over z has been factored out. The inverse of z has to be factored out because it does not fit the definition of a linear combination. If the function is not a linear combination, it cannot be expressed by using a matrix and therefore becomes extremely cumbersome for you. To fix this, you factor out z and you omit the division by z as part of the matrix. When it comes time to compute the actual 2D coordinates of the transformation, you simply divide back by z. It's cumbersome, but at least it works. The remaining question is, what becomes of z? You still need z to have a complete matrix, so how does z behave with the aforementioned transformation? The biggest mistake you could make is to think that it simply does the same thing it did with the previous projection. The easiest way to see it is to establish two equations (one for each boundary as seen in the orthogonal projection) and to solve for the two unknowns, $\{A, B\}$:

$$1 = \frac{A}{e} + B$$

$$-1 = \frac{A}{f} + B$$

At this point, it's boring algebraic work, which yields

$$A = \frac{-2ef}{f-e}$$

$$B = \frac{-f-e}{f-e}$$

Up to now, we've been rather careless about the fourth member of every coordinate (1), mainly because it was not affected. In this specific case, however, it is. The plan with the matrix is to apply the division by z after the matrix has been applied. To make things a little simpler, you can multiply the entire coordinate by the scalar z. Because you will divide the coordinate by the scalar identified by the inverse of z, you have to take into account that the fourth component (which is usually a 1) has to be 1 after the division. Because $z/z = 1$, it's easy to see that the only thing you need to do to make this happen is to make sure that the fourth component has the value z. All this yields the following projection matrix:

$$\begin{bmatrix} \dfrac{2D}{b-a} & 0 & 0 & 0 \\[2ex] 0 & \dfrac{2D}{d-c} & 0 & 0 \\[2ex] \dfrac{b+a}{b-a} & \dfrac{d+c}{d-c} & \dfrac{-f-e}{f-e} & -1 \\[2ex] 0 & 0 & \dfrac{-2ef}{f-e} & 0 \end{bmatrix}$$

When you physically render everything on the screen, you only need the x and y component, so what's the deal with computing the value of z or even w, the fourth coordinate? All these questions will be answered in Chapter 6, "Moving to Hyperspace Vectors: Quaternions."

You may have noticed in your favorite FPS that you can "zoom" into a scene. The zooming factor is tightly coupled with the principle of perspective projection. Your intuitive guess would probably be to zoom the scene such that an area would appear larger, but this simply doesn't look very good. The best way to achieve this is by changing the angle of the projection. Most games use a field of view angle of about 90 degrees, which yields pretty good results. For example, if you want to zoom in with a sniper rifle, then you may be looking at an angle of 15 degrees. It really all depends on how much zooming you would like to happen.

Screen Projection

Let's recap. First, you apply an object transformation, which is local to the object. Then, you apply world transformations to the entire set of objects, followed by the transformations required by the camera. This gives you the coordinates from the camera's perspective. The next step is to project these coordinates such that you could render the objects on a 2D screen. The coordinates you created with the latest transformations have a range of $[-1, 1]$, but unless your screen is three pixels wide, this won't work. Thus, the very last transformation matrix you need to apply is to fill the entire screen up. Call this matrix the "screen transformation matrix."

As an example, suppose you are running on a resolution of 800×600. In this case, the screen transformation matrix would be responsible for converting every coordinate from $[-1, 1]$ to 800×600. Furthermore, the screen geometry is such that <0, 0> is at the top-left corner while the fullest extent is at the bottom-right corner. Consequently, this matrix is also responsible for possibly inverting or mirroring the scene such that it satisfies this condition. All in all, this matrix is of little interest for our purposes because it is typically hidden by the hardware layers.

Bounding Frustum Planes

As you will see later in this book, it can be extremely useful to know the equation of the planes that bound your frustum. If you understood everything in this chapter so far, you should have absolutely no problem figuring this out. As you saw in Chapter 4, every plane can be expressed as a 4-vector. Because the resulting frustum (after transformation) is always box shaped, you can expect the resulting plane to be one of six axis-aligned planes forming your box. The following logic for a projection matrix $\mathbf{M}$ and a plane vector $\mathbf{P}$ where the prime stands for the translated unit planes, ensues:

$$\mathbf{MP} = \mathbf{P'}$$

$$\mathbf{M}^{-1}\mathbf{MP} = \mathbf{M}^{-1}\mathbf{P'}$$

$$\mathbf{P} = \mathbf{M}^{T}\mathbf{P'}$$

Nothing really new should come out of this one. Given the six planes, the information in Table 5.1 is the result.

Table 5.1 Finding the Bounding Frustum's Plane

Plane	Vector	Frustum Plane Vector
Near	<0, 0, 1, 1>	$(c_4 + c_3)$
Far	<0, 0, −1, 1>	$(c_4 − c_3)$
Left	<1, 0, 0, 1>	$(c_4 + c_1)$
Right	<−1, 0, 0, 1>	$(c_4 − c_1)$
Bottom	<0, 1, 0, 1>	$(c_4 + c_2)$
Top	<0, −1, 0, 1>	$(c_4 − c_2)$

Non-Linear Transformations

Thus far, this chapter has dealt only with linear transformations (with the noted exception of the perspective projection). Linear transformations can account for a great number of common transformations, but not all of them. Unfortunately, if you want to create non-linear transformations, you must create your own vector space, which means that you will not be able to use the video hardware's capability.

That said, you could generate some really cool effects with non-linear transformations. For example, I mentioned earlier how *Quake 3* handled the water effect by using linear transformations. If you have ever played *Quake 1*, you may remember that the water in that game was actually much fancier than what is displayed in *Quake 3*. The water in *Quake 1* made waves in sinusoidal motion, giving the impression of fluid moving around. To achieve this, *Quake 1* used a nonlinear transformation (because sine functions are not linear functions). To achieve this effect, Carmack most likely rendered the entire image to a buffer and thereafter rendered the image to the screen by displacing the pixels in a sinusoidal motion. Another approach you could take in 3D is to have the vertices move in a sinusoidal motion. The only drawback is that you would have to transform them yourself instead of having the hardware do all this for you. If you have enough CPU power, this may well be worth it.

Suppose you want to achieve this wavy water effect. You would first need to implement the entire transformation stack yourself. Unfortunately, the 3D APIs available today do not allow you to intercept transformations in the middle, so you will have to set the transformations to the identity and compute everything yourself. You should already know how to do this (thanks to the previous section), so let's skip right to the good stuff. To achieve this, add another transformation right between the projection transformation and the screen transformation. At that point, every coordinate has a range of $[-1, 1]$, which is well suited for sine curves. What you want to do is slightly displace the vertices in a sinusoidal motion. Therefore, you can guess that the equation you're actually looking at is something along the lines of

$$x' = x + Factor_x \sin(ax + by)$$
$$y' = y + Factor_y \sin(cx + dy)$$

The only thing you have to do at this point is choose visually pleasing values for a, b, c, d, and the two factors. Most likely, you will want factors a, b, c, and d to be pretty small numbers so that you can get many waves on the screen. Furthermore, you probably want the factors to be small numbers so that you get more than one wave on the screen. Finally, you probably want some animation, which means that you have to insert a timer variable somewhere in the sine wave; you can add a factor of the time to achieve this.

This type of intuitive method of figuring out equations actually has no defined steps. You basically need to think about the function you are trying to achieve and which variables will change the equation. It's not an easy task at first, but with time, it becomes very natural—especially with the help of the remaining chapters of this book, most notably Chapter 21, "Kicking the Turtle: Approximating Common and Slow Functions."

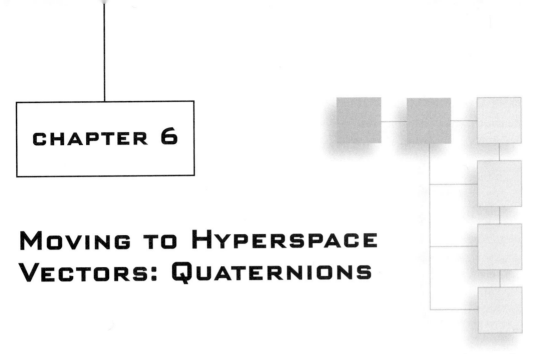

CHAPTER 6

MOVING TO HYPERSPACE VECTORS: QUATERNIONS

Using vectors presents its own set of problems. One of the most notorious problems related to rotations and vectors is called "gimbal lock," which is a result of Euler angles. (You know that a problem is *really* a problem when it has its own name.) As you learned in Chapter 1, "Equation Manipulation and Representation," any position in 3D can be uniquely determined by using two angles and one distance. In a rotation, the distance is fixed from the origin, thus any rotation in 3D can be done through two angles. In 3D space, however, Euler angles come in three distinct forms: x, y, and z rotation angles. The big problem with Euler angles, then, is the order of the rotation and its three rotation axes. That's because a rotation about one of the axes can actually be represented as a linear combination of a rotation around the two other axes, creating a linear dependency.

If you do not yet see the problem referred to as gimbal lock, suppose you have chosen to rotate in the order z, y, x. Then suppose you rotate 90 degrees in the y axis. The rotation in z and y is performed as desired, but the rotation around the third axis creates a problem: any rotation in the x axis really rotates on the z axis. Quaternions to the rescue! Quaternions are actually extensions of complex numbers. You can look at them as a 2×2 complex matrix or as vectors. The second option is more attractive and adaptable to games, thus so it shall be.

As part of this chapter, you will see the basics of complex math and how they extend to quaternions. You will see the basic operations you can perform with quaternions and how you can convert from a quaternion to a matrix to use its results as you did in previous chapters. In a more formal manner, the topics for this chapter are as follows:

- Complex number operations
- Basic quaternion operations
- Revisiting the vector operations with quaternions

153

Complex Numbers

Generally speaking, complex numbers are not used very much for gaming purposes. Most applications of complex numbers are in more advanced engineering work and in purely mathematical applications. Nonetheless, they are the foundation for quaternions, and as such they deserve a special place here.

If you remember how to solve quadratic equations from Chapter 1, you probably recall that not all equations actually have two real solutions. In these cases, the solution is complex. Any real number can actually be written by using a complex number. The main problem with solving such equations is that a negative square root is not actually defined. The trick to solving this enigma is to actually define a number, or more precisely, a complex number, which is exactly that. Therefore, you can define the value i as the square root of -1:

$$i = \sqrt{-1}$$

Thereafter, if you have a negative number that you would like to write as a complex number, all you have to do is to rewrite the number such that it uses the definition of i. The rest of the work is entirely based on this simple definition. For example, if you want to express the negative square root of 16, you would write the following:

$$\sqrt{-16} = \sqrt{16 \cdot (-1)}$$
$$= \sqrt{16} \cdot \sqrt{-1}$$
$$= 4\sqrt{-1}$$
$$= 4i$$

When a complex number is entirely referred to as a linear combination of i alone, that number is said to be imaginary. Furthermore, you can also say that the imaginary part of the complex number is 4. Complex numbers are generally written in the following form, where both a and b are real numbers:

$$a + bi$$

With this definition, a would be referred to as the real part of the complex number, while b would be the imaginary part as mentioned previously.

One last bit of important information about complex numbers is as follows:

$$i^2 = -1$$

This obvious deduction goes by the very definition of i.

Lastly, you probably want to know how to represent complex numbers on a graph. For vectors, you saw that there is an easy correlation. For matrices, although it was not shown, the correlation is similar because a matrix is defined as a vector of vectors (think of an array of vectors), so it still makes perfect sense. So what about complex numbers? What lies in the imaginary world? As it turns out, it is very simple. You can plot any complex number on a 2D plane by moving along the horizontal axis for the real component while leaving the vertical axis for the imaginary component, as illustrated in Figure 6.1. In a nutshell, if you know how to plot 2D coordinates, you should be able to plot a complex number, because the real portion of the number is treated like an x axis while the imaginary portion of the number is treated as the y axis. It's as easy as that.

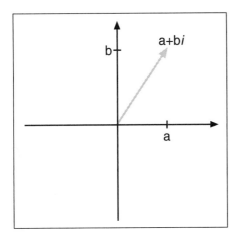

Figure 6.1
Plotting complex numbers

Now that you understand the basic representation and terminology of quaternions, let's take a deeper look at the basic operations you can apply to them.

Norm

As you have seen, vectors and matrices both have norms; likewise, quaternions should have norms. Interestingly enough, a real number also has a norm. In fact, because a real value is the same as a vector with one single value, the definition thus becomes pretty easy. When applying the p-norm on any real number, you will notice that, in fact, you are computing the xth power of an absolute value followed by the xth square root. Doing so, however, is pretty pointless because the operation actually comes down to what is well known as an absolute value. Formally, for a real number r, the following holds:

$$|r| = \|r\|_p = \sqrt[p]{|r|^p}$$

In other words, the absolute value of this real number is the same as its norm. If you think about it, it does make perfect sense. The norm was defined as the magnitude of the element, and obviously, the greater the number, the more magnitude it possesses.

This is interesting, but how does it apply to complex numbers? Well, the idea is exactly the same. If you simply consider the imaginary and real components of the number as two separate components, you can apply the same 2-norm to it. For a complex number $c = a + bi$, the following holds:

$$|c| = \|c\|_2 = \sqrt{a^2 + b^2}$$

Addition/Subtraction

These two operations are the easiest ones in the group. If you simply think of i as a variable, you should have no problem finding the equation for most of the basic operations. If you look at the addition first, you can easily see that you can factor out i. After this is done, you are basically working with two pairs of real numbers. The following shows the addition of two complex numbers p and q:

$$p = a + bi$$
$$q = c + di$$

$$p + q = (a + bi) + (c + di)$$
$$= (a + c) + (b + d)i$$

Applying a subtraction involves the exact same process, with the noted exception that the plus sign between the parentheses is changed with a minus sign. For example, if you had two complex numbers $(1 + 2i)$ and $(3 + 4i)$, you would add them as follows:

$$(1 + 2i) + (3 + 4i) = (1 + 3) + (2 + 4)i$$
$$= 4 + 6i$$

Multiplication

Addition and subtraction were almost too simple; what about multiplication? If you keep considering i as a variable, things become extremely easy. The last thing you need to keep in mind is the last identity noted about i. Otherwise, the equation is not necessarily wrong, but it becomes extremely cumbersome to write a complex number as a function with squares and cubes of i. If you can keep things shorter and easier, as always, do it. This also helps you to always write complex numbers using the same notation, therefore not adding any unnecessary complexity. If you still do not see how you can go about multiplying two complex numbers p and q together, observe the following:

$$p = a + bi$$
$$q = c + di$$

$$
\begin{aligned}
p \cdot q &= (a + bi)(c + di) \\
&= ac + adi + bci + bdi^2 \\
&= ac + (ad + bc)i - bd \\
&= (ac - bd) + (ad + bc)i
\end{aligned}
$$

Observe what happens geometrically to the phase (angle) and the length of the vector in Figure 6.2 when you multiply two complex numbers.

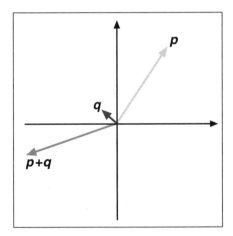

Figure 6.2
Geometrical interpretation of the multiplication of two complex numbers

Division (Inverses)

As always, division is the bad boy in town. You have seen how ugly such a simple operation for real numbers in matrices can be. It is not as involved for complex numbers, but it still requires a certain level of thinking.

An inverse is, as always, defined as a number for which a number p, multiplied by its inverse q, equals the identity (the real number 1 for a complex number). You can in fact look at the division of two complex numbers with simple algebraic manipulations. Alternatively, use a simpler, easier, more direct equation to obtain what you want:

$$\frac{p}{q} = \frac{a+bi}{c+di}$$

$$= \frac{a+bi}{c+di} \cdot \frac{c-di}{c-di}$$

$$= \frac{u \cdot \overline{v}}{c^2+d^2}$$

$$= \frac{p \cdot \overline{q}}{|q|^2}$$

Where v bar is called the conjugate of v and is defined as proposed previously, by the complex number v in which the sign for the imaginary part is inverted. Because you want to find the inverse, you can let u be the identity and simplify the equation as follows:

$$v^{-1} = \frac{1}{v}$$

$$= \frac{\overline{v}}{|v|^2}$$

DeMoivre Formulas

Because of the geometrical interpretation given to complex numbers, a series of properties also arises from this very definition. This is the basic idea behind the DeMoivre formulas. You have previously seen that a complex number can be written in the form $c = a + bi$, but as you will soon see, there are other ways of writing these tricky numbers. Two concepts are key to this: the geometrical aspect of a complex number and the relationship between c and its norm. By a mere geometrical observation and a simple trigonometric identity, you can easily find that the following formula stands:

$$c = |c|\cos(\theta) + |c|\sin(\theta)i$$

$$= |c|(\cos(\theta) + i\sin(\theta))$$

This and the previous expression are not the only two ways to write a complex number. There is yet another way to express such numbers. The details of the proof refer to series (yet to be covered in this book); thus, it shall promptly be omitted. (It is not an extremely interesting manipulation anyhow.) The equation, which also stands, is the following:

$$z = e^{i\theta}$$

Basic Quaternions

Quaternions were previously defined as extensions of complex numbers. Perhaps an easier way to visualize this extension is to look at quaternions graphically. In a complex number, the real component is positioned on the horizontal axis and the imaginary is positioned on the vertical axis. If you extend this concept into a higher dimensional space, the second imaginary component can be drawn as the z axis in 3D. Clearly, you can extend this concept for hyperdimensions to yield hyper-complex numbers. This is the simple yet powerful idea behind quaternions. Unfortunately, because they are 4D elements, they aren't quite as easy to illustrate.

note

> In my opinion, quaternions are not necessary in a game engine because, as you saw in earlier chapters, there are better ways to achieve the same results. Even so, it's a good idea to examine quaternions so that you'll know what they are, how they work, and in which cases they may be useful.

Specifically, quaternions can be written as four-dimensional vectors $<x, y, z, w>$. Similarly, previously you could have written complex numbers as vectors of the form $<a, b>$, as long as you knew that the vector space was actually $<<1, 0>, <0, i>>$. Consequently, you can write the equation of a quaternion c as follows, where i, j, and k are the imaginary components:

$$c = xi + yj + zk + w$$

If you prefer, you can also write this in vectorial notation:

$$c = \langle x, y, z \rangle \bullet \langle i, j, k \rangle + w$$

Or as follows:

$$c = \mathbf{x} + w$$

Is it just me, or does this equation look awfully similar to a plane's equation when $c = 0$? If you thought the same thing, then you are not far off. For planes, this notation was used because it offered a method that required less space to represent the equation, and also a much smoother way to apply a transformation upon a plane. It would be a hassle to transform the plane with two directional vectors, for example. Quaternions yield the same benefits.

This is the basic idea behind quaternions; now let's take a look at the math involved. For starters, quaternions follow the same rules for the imaginary components:

$$i^2 = j^2 = k^2 = ijk = -1$$

You also have properties, which are defined to be akin to vector cross products:

$$ij = -ji = k$$
$$jk = -kj = i$$
$$ki = -ik = j$$

Consequently, you can deduce that quaternions are not commutative. Conversely, they are negatively commutative.

Basic Addition All Over Again

Adding two quaternions is simple. If you understand how two complex numbers are added together, adding quaternions is nothing but an extension of this into higher degrees. Given two quaternions $a = s + u$ and $b = t + v$, you can add them as shown:

$$a + b = (s + u) + (t + v)$$
$$= (s + t) + (u + v)$$

Why get complicated when things are this simple? For example, if you have two quaternions $a = 1i + 2j + 3k + 4$ and $b = 4i + 3j + 2k + 1$, you would get the following result:

$$a + b = (1i + 2j + 3k + 4) + (3i + 4j + 1k + 1)$$
$$= 4i + 6j + 4k + 5$$

Multiplying Like Bunnies

Multiplication of quaternions is subject to the same logic and hula hoops as discussed in previous sections, but it also comes with a twist. As you multiply quaternions, not only do you have to keep in mind that a square of the imaginary components is -1, but also that the product of two imaginary components follows the rules as described for complex numbers. This makes things a little more tricky, but not too much. With a careful look at the algebra, you should be able to find the equation that dictates the multiplication between two quaternions $q_1 = x_1 i + y_1 j + z_1 k + w_1$ and $q_2 = x_2 i + y_2 j + z_2 k + w_2$:

$$q_1 \cdot q_2 = (x_1 i + y_1 j + z_1 k + w_1)(x_2 i + y_2 j + z_2 k + w_2)$$
$$= (w_1 w_2 - x_1 x_2 - y_1 y_2 - z_1 z_2)$$
$$+ (w_1 x_2 + x_1 w_2 + y_1 z_2 - z_1 y_2) i$$
$$+ (w_1 y_2 - x_1 z_2 + y_1 w_2 + z_1 x_2) j$$
$$+ (w_1 z_2 + x_1 y_2 - y_1 x_2 + z_1 w_2) k$$

The Norm

Just as vectors extend reals to define the norm, quaternions extend complex numbers to do so. Consequently, the definition is exactly as you would expect. For example, the norm of a quaternion $q = xi + yj + zk + w$ is defined by this equation:

$$|q| = \sqrt{x^2 + y^2 + z^2 + w^2}$$

The Inverse

For complex numbers, the conjugate was defined as the complex number with an inverse polarity in the imaginary space. Quaternions are, of course, no different. The conjugate of a quaternion is nothing but the negated value of its imaginary values. So for a quaternion $q = ai + bj + ck + w$, the conjugate can be written as follows:

$$\bar{q} = -ai - bj - ck + w$$

Thereafter, you can also write the formula for the inverse of q because the formula given for complex numbers does not have any regard for dimension. Thus, the inverse of a quaternion q is given by the following:

$$q^{-1} = \frac{1}{q}$$

$$= \frac{\bar{q}}{|q|^2}$$

Advanced Operations on Quaternions

So you have vectors, and you have quaternions. The question is, how do they relate to each other? After all, in 3D, coordinates have three components, while a quaternion has four. If you were paying careful attention when reading previous chapters, you already possess the answer to this question. The coordinates you dealt with before were indeed quaternions because they were required in order to translate with matrices. Consequently, to convert a 3D coordinate to a quaternion, all you need to do is to set the fourth component to 1. Thus $<x, y, z>$ becomes $<x, y, z, 1>$.

What about vectors? A vector is defined as the difference between two points. In other words, if you take two points and subtract one from the other, you get the 3D vector you would have expected from doing the same to 3D coordinates with an additional component set to 0. Now things are finally starting to fall into place.

By now, you may be wondering if that's all there is to quaternions. The answer is, of course not. Quaternions are so much more than the operations may seem to portray here. With quaternions, you can completely forget about the huge 4×4 matrix that you had to compute and instead focus on a transformation quaternion that is only a 4-vector. That makes for considerably less data to carry around. Even so, what you have seen so far is not really interesting in itself; it is simply the foundation required in order to really solve the problems that quaternions are good at solving, which involve multi-angle rotations.

Quaternion Rotations

A rotation is fairly easy to think about geometrically. Unfortunately, however, when you move toward more abstract groups and fields such as quaternions, things are not as simple as they may seem. As usual, the best way to resolve a problem is to stick to the basic definitions or properties—in this case, of a rotation. In 3D, a rotation is a function that maps a 3D vector in 3D space. For our purposes, however, the rotation must be performed in 4D (so to speak). A rotation was previously defined as an orthonormal transformation. If you were to decouple this word, you could claim that a rotation preserves the distance from the origin (thus the length, or the norm if you prefer), the angles' order, and the handedness of the axes (the "ortho" part of "orthonormal"). What you end up with is three constraints related to a coordinate p and with function Omega:

$$\left\|\theta(p)\right\|_2 = \left\|p\right\|_2 \qquad \text{Norm Preservation}$$

$$\theta(p_1) \bullet \theta(p_2) = p_1 \bullet p_2 \qquad \text{Angle Preservation}$$

$$\theta(p_1) \times \theta(p_2) = \theta(p_1 \times p_2) \qquad \text{Handedness Preservation}$$

Specifically, for quaternions, you can write the second equation in a quaternion form and combine it with the last equation to obtain the following relationship:

$$\theta(p_1)\theta(p_2) = \theta(p_1 p_2)$$

These types of functions are a well-known class of mathematical equalities called homomorphism. At this point, all you need to do to satisfy the rotation requirements is make sure that the length is preserved. You can do this if you multiply a rotation quaternion r with p and multiply the result with the inverse of the rotation. Because you are multiplying by a rotation vector and its inverse, the net product of the norms is that of the norm of p, thus satisfying the constraints. The final equation that can rotate a coordinate p specified by a rotation quaternion r is as follows:

$$\theta_r(p) = rpr^{-1}$$

For Euler angles, you first found a formula that described the rotation, and thereafter gave it a more meaningful sense by looking at polar coordinates and thereby expressing the equations in terms of angles. Here, you know that this equation generates a rotation, but no geometrical sense has yet been given to it. In other words, how does r rotate p, geometrically speaking? The details here are extremely algebraic and boring. The idea is to substitute the quaternion r for its componentized version $(s + \mathbf{t})$. Multiply everything out, apply some cross-product identities, and eventually you end up with the result that r can actually be written akin to a rotation in 2D as you know it. At that point, you only need to solve for both w values and you are finished. What you get is something along the lines of the following, where $\mathbf{a}$ is the rotation axis:

$$r = \cos\left(\frac{\theta}{2}\right) + \mathbf{a}\sin\left(\frac{\theta}{2}\right)$$

That means there is more than one way to rotate around an arbitrary axis, which is what quaternions are all about. This solves the gimbal lock problem because you are not accumulating a bunch of axis-aligned rotations.

Rightfully, you may wonder why I didn't use the matrix presented earlier. The truth is, nothing stops you from doing so, and this would in fact prevent you from requiring quaternions. If you look at the math required to compute a rotation around a vector, you will notice that you can actually eliminate a considerable number of multiplications if you use a vector for which the fourth component is 0. This is really what the quaternion proposition is all about: smaller memory footprint and speed.

note

It would in fact be more efficient to convert a quaternion to a matrix if you had more than one coordinate to transform. It would not, however, be more efficient to use a matrix if you wanted to accumulate a bunch of rotations. Therefore, quaternions are well-suited for camera rotations. For example, *Tomb Raider* uses quaternions for its camera.

Converting from Quaternions to Matrices and Vice Versa

Just how does 3D hardware deal with quaternions? It just so happens that there is indeed a way to convert from quaternions to a matrix. The proof of this equation, however, would result in an overall diminution of the forestry mass in the region. Given this fact, I would rather stick to the practical side of things. The basic idea behind the proof is to use the cosine rule combined with intermediate results from the proof in the previous section, which was also omitted. (If you desperately want the proof, you should be able to find it by searching Google with keywords such as "quaternion," "matrix," "conversion," and "proof.") The matrix that represents the rotation applied by the quaternion $<x, y, z, w>$ is as follows:

$$\mathbf{R} = \begin{bmatrix} 1-2y^2-2z^2 & 2xy-2wz & 2xz+2wy & 0 \\ 2xy+wz & 1-2x^2-2z^2 & 2yz-2wz & 0 \\ 2xz-2wy & 2yz+2wx & 1-2x^2-2y^2 & 0 \\ 0 & 0 & 0 & 1 \end{bmatrix}$$

Conversely, to convert from quaternions to matrices (here, to convert to a matrix $\mathbf{R}$):

$$q = \begin{bmatrix} \dfrac{R_{32} - R_{23}}{2\sqrt{R_{11} + R_{22} + R_{33} + R_{44}}} \\[2ex] \dfrac{R_{31} - R_{13}}{2\sqrt{R_{11} + R_{22} + R_{33} + R_{44}}} \\[2ex] \dfrac{R_{21} - R_{12}}{2\sqrt{R_{11} + R_{22} + R_{33} + R_{44}}} \\[2ex] \dfrac{1}{2}\sqrt{R_{11} + R_{22} + R_{33} + R_{44}} \end{bmatrix}$$

Spherical Linear Interpolation (SLERP)

Previously, with the equation of the line, you saw what a linear interpolation was. In a nutshell, that function shifts the weight from one vertex to the other. That equation was not really discussed in this context, but if you look at it, you will quickly come to realize that this is really what is happening. Initially, the entire weight is set on the first vertex. At the end, for $t = 1$, the weight is entirely shifted to the second vertex. Because this is a linear transformation, the weight is transferred linearly from one vertex to the other. In the middle, for example, the weight is evenly distributed between both vertices. This is just another interesting way to look at the function: as a weighting function.

Of interest at this point is the application of the same idea to a normal vector. In short, you want to interpolate linearly on a sphere. Why? Consider the case where you are using a vector to represent the camera. In this case, you may want to interpolate from one viewing vector to the other in a linear fashion. This will yield a smooth transition from one direction to the other. Figure 6.3 illustrates the idea.

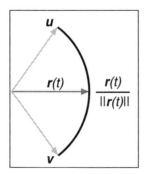

Figure 6.3
Spherical interpolation from one direction to another

The first thing that usually comes to mind is to simply apply the same process as was done before. This is an excellent start, but it is not the answer. Consider two positions in 2D to simplify the problem. Because you are dealing with camera vectors, they should ideally be normal. Therefore, the distance between the center of rotation and the two vertices should both equal 1. So far so good. If you were to interpolate the components linearly from one vertex to the other, your vector would not be normal during the transition. This may not be the solution. Even worse, consider the case where the two view vectors are parallel but of opposite directions. In this case, interpolating linearly would be such that you would be passing through the origin; if you pass through the origin, the vector is <0, 0, 0> and thus is directionless. This is complete nonsense in our case. A deeper thinking process is thus required.

Our first problem is that the norm of the vector does not equal 1, but that's easy to fix. If you simply normalize the vector, you can achieve this. So if you consider the linear interpolation equation of the two vectors, the equation you would be looking at would have two viewing vectors $\mathbf{u}$ and $\mathbf{v}$ and a rotation function $\mathbf{r}$ with t as a parameter, like so:

$$\mathbf{r}(t) = \frac{\mathbf{u}t + (1-t)\mathbf{v}}{\left\| \mathbf{u}t + (1-t)\mathbf{v} \right\|_2}$$

Is this sufficient for a linear spherical interpolation? If you look at the graph generated by this function (illustrated in Figure 6.3), you'll see that it does perform a circular arc by going from $\mathbf{u}$ to $\mathbf{v}$. There is still a problem, however, if you look at the angular rate of the equation (that is, how much the angles change per unit). In doing so, you will quickly come to notice that the interpolation is indeed not linear. The angle needs to change linearly for this to make any sense at all, so you still have some work to do.

If you think about the problem carefully, the conclusion you should draw from the preceding statement is that the angle between the two vectors ϕ has to change at a linear rate and thus its value at time t should be something along the lines of ϕt. Another way to look at it is to say that the angle between the current vector and the first one, $\mathbf{u}$, is ϕt, while the angle between the current vector and the last vector $\mathbf{v}$ is $\phi(1 - t)$. If you write the equation in terms of the arcs' lengths, this will respect the "true" spherical distance (or circular in 2D) from one position to another. Thus, write the following, where a and b are two functions that give the distance from $\mathbf{u}$ to the current position and from $\mathbf{v}$ to the current position respectively along the directions of $\mathbf{u}$ and $\mathbf{v}$:

$$\mathbf{r}(t) = a(t)\mathbf{u} + b(t)\mathbf{v}$$

You can find the distances for each of them by a mere observation of the similar triangles law coupled with a few identities. The equations you find are therefore as follows:

$$\frac{a(t)}{\|\mathbf{u}\|_2} = \frac{\|r(t)\|_2 \sin(, (1-t))}{\|\mathbf{u}\|_2 \sin(,)}$$

$$\frac{b(t)}{\|\mathbf{v}\|_2} = \frac{\|r(t)\|_2 \sin(, t)}{\|\mathbf{v}\|_2 \sin(,)}$$

Because the vectors are already normalized, you can write the equation in its shorter form:

$$a(t) = \frac{\sin(\theta(1-t))}{\sin(\theta)}$$

$$b(t) = \frac{\sin(\theta t)}{\sin(\theta)}$$

The angle gives birth to trigonometric functions and the like. If you wish, you can, for the most part, convert them to non-trigonometric equations:

$$\theta = \cos^{-1}(\mathbf{u} \bullet \mathbf{v})$$

Thus:

$$\sin(\theta) = \sqrt{1 - (\mathbf{u} \bullet \mathbf{v})^2}$$

To sum things up, you can interpolate spherically with the following equation:

$$\mathbf{r}(t) = \frac{\sin(\theta(1-t))\mathbf{u} + \sin(\theta t)\mathbf{v}}{\sin(\theta)}$$

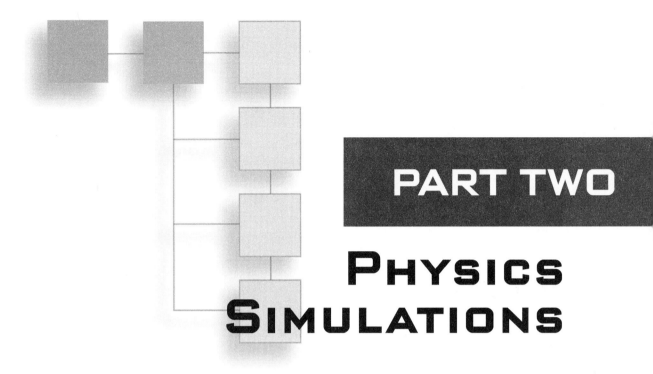

PART TWO

PHYSICS SIMULATIONS

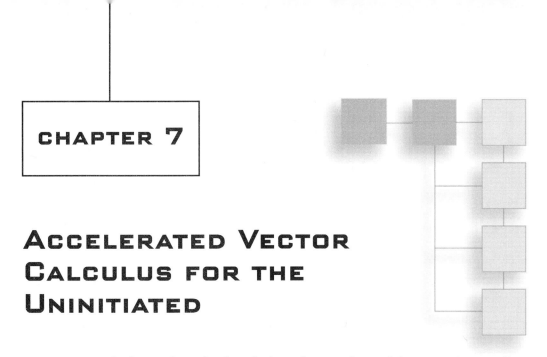

CHAPTER 7

ACCELERATED VECTOR CALCULUS FOR THE UNINITIATED

Because calculus—a branch of math that takes a stab at solving many intermediate problems concerning minimizing, maximizing, area calculation, speed calculation, and more—comes in many complex forms and shapes, it tends to scare a lot of people away. If you are a calculusphobe, you'll be pleased to learn that the goal of this chapter is not to turn you into a calculus guru who can apply calculus to every possible equation. Maple will do that for you. Instead, the goal here is to help you understand the basic idea behind calculus theory and how the basic functions work (not only in 2D but also in 3D), as well as to look at various methods to help you solve certain problems. Maple is a very complex piece of software, but it's not bulletproof; it can help you do a lot, but sometimes *you* have to help *it* in order to obtain the equation you are looking for. For example, there may be times when you have to give it a modified equation in order for it to be able to understand and process the equation, which is why it is quite important that you understand the tricks and techniques that can help you resolve key problems in calculus.

This book makes ample use of calculus, which is why it's important that you understand the basic concepts behind it. Calculus is not an end per se; rather, it offers a way to solve problems more or less in the same way addition enables you to solve problems such as translations. In more esoteric cases, calculus can help you solve the problems iterated in the preceding paragraph. Often, a problem in a game will simply end up being a problem of minimizing a path, minimizing a distance from one point to another, or computing the area of an object for visibility purposes.

All in all, this chapter discusses the following topics:

- The concept of limits
- Basic numerical differentiation
- Basic analytic differentiation

- Basic numerical integration
- Basic analytic integration
- Various integration techniques
- Integration/differentiation in 3D

The Concept of Limits

Oddly, a limit in math does not refer to the boundary of a span. Rather, defined loosely, the limit for a k-D function $f(\mathbf{x})$ as $\mathbf{x}$ tends toward $\mathbf{y}$ is the point p if and only if $\mathbf{y}$ gets in the vicinity of $\mathbf{x}$, $f(\mathbf{y}) = p$. In other words, if you go as close as possible to $\mathbf{y}$ in any given direction without actually reaching $\mathbf{y}$, you will get as close as possible to p. Intuitively, you can think of the limit as the value you would expect the function to return if you looked only at the values of that function minus the value of the function at the limit you want to compute. To clear things up, consider a polynomial function $f(x) = 2x + 3$, as illustrated in Figure 7.1. The limit of this function for $x = 3$ is 9. You can write it as follows:

$$\lim_{x \to 3} f(x) = 9$$

note

If you have taken calculus, you may have discussed limits in a different way. Generally speaking, the definition of a limit in calculus is very, er, limited. In calculus, the concept of limits can be quite a beast to understand, but for our purposes, the intuitive method described here will suffice.

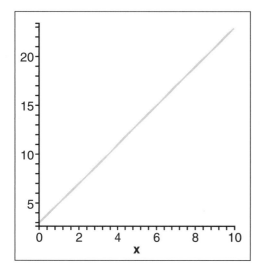

Figure 7.1
Plot of $2x + 3$

If you substitute $x = 3$ in the equation, you can verify that you get 9, but always doing so is incorrect, as you will soon see. If you stay strictly with the definition, you can verify that the closer to $x = 3$ you get, the closer you get to 9. Table 7.1 illustrates the idea. If you look at the function without looking at its value for $x=3$, you can easily see that the value will "tend toward" 3. This "tend toward" idea is important because the concept of a limit is also defined for functions that do not define a strict value. If the function is not defined at a given value, the limit could still exist as long as the values in the neighborhood of that value tend toward a value. Surprisingly, a function that can have a result of 3 may well end up with a result of -2 as a limit if, for example, the function is broken at that value.

Table 7.1 Substituting x

x	Result
2	7
2.5	8
2.9	8.8
2.999	8.998
3.001	9.002

In Table 7.1, the solution is quite obvious. But if you look at it carefully, you'll notice that as x gets closer to 3 from the smaller numbers, the result tends toward 9. If you choose the only other possible path, which is from the higher numbers (3.001 and above), you can also see that it converges toward 9. As a general rule, if the function is continuous, the limit of the function is equal to the result of the function. This is the very definition of continuity in mathematics. Unfortunately, not all functions are nice and continuous, especially if you want to do some fancy water effects in a game.

When you compute the limit, recall that the definition states that the point p is the limit as **x** tends toward **y** *if and only if **y** gets in the vicinity of* **x**, not *if and only if **y** gets in the vicinity and the actual position of* **x**. Consequently, you cannot claim that the limit is $f(\mathbf{y})$. As a proof, consider the equation plotted in Figure 7.2:

$$f(x) = \begin{cases} 1 & x \neq 0 \\ 0 & x = 0 \end{cases}$$

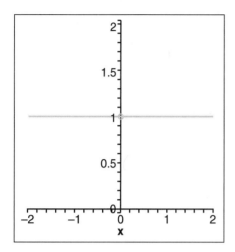

Figure 7.2
Plot of f(x)

In Figure 7.2, an empty circle implies that one specific point is not included in the curve. On the other hand, plotting a filled point indicates that a single point exists at that location. This is to clearly show the discontinuity that exists at $x = 0$. This is a pretty useless equation, but it does illustrate how the limit differs from the valued function. Here, if you were asked to compute the limit as x tends toward 0, the answer would be 0. You can easily verify this because as the x gets extremely close to 0, the value is still 0. At the precise point $x = 0$, it is true that the function is 1, but that is the only exception. There is not an infinite number of inputs that are discontinuous. It is also possible that the limit does not exist at all. Consider the following equation:

$$f(x) = \begin{cases} -1 & x > 0 \\ 1 & x \le 0 \end{cases}$$

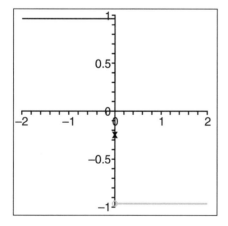

The graph of this equation, as shown in Figure 7.3, demonstrates that the function is representative of a graph for a broken line or, if you prefer, two distinct lines.

Figure 7.3
Plot of f(x)

If you were to compute the limit at $x = 0$, you would not be able to come up with a single solution. As you test for the limit around the vicinity of the negative numbers, you find that the value that seems likely is 1. On the flip side, if you take a look from the positive number's perspective, you find out that -1 is the value. You get two distinct values by approaching the limit from two different paths; therefore, the limit does not exist. The limit at any point should always be unique. If it is not, then it should be clear that the equation cannot converge toward a single number.

Although there are very rigorous methods that can be used to determine whether a given equation does have a limit, there are a few tricks you can use to determine this in advance. One is to consider that any continuous function possesses a limit at any point. For example, a function such as cosine or sine is continuous; neither function has any breaks, so a limit exists on each. Polynomial functions are yet another example of continuous functions.

As the previous example clearly illustrates, a function need not be continuous in order to possess a limit at all locations. In fact, if a function is continuous, the following property holds:

$$\lim_{x \to y} f(\mathbf{x}) = f(\mathbf{y})$$

If you look back at the first example, this was exactly the case. The function was a polynomial, thus it is continuous; and because it is continuous, the limit exists everywhere on it. In addition, because it is continuous, its limit actually equals the valued function at $\mathbf{y}$.

It is not always this easy to deal with limits. Many cases in calculus are such that the function is divided by 0 when $\mathbf{x} = 0$, and thus you cannot easily see what is happening. For example, consider the following equation, which could represent a hill as illustrated in Figure 7.4:

$$f(x) = \frac{x^2}{x^2 + y^2}$$

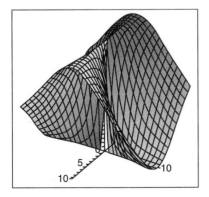

Figure 7.4
Plot of $f(x)$

If you were to compute the limit at <0, 0>, you would have a tough time determining if it exists or not. As it turns out, you can go by the intuitive method and try a few values around the vicinity but this will not actually guarantee that the limit does really exist. Especially if you are dealing with 3D equations, there are so many paths you can take to converge toward y that it is hard to say with very good certainty. Specifically, the preceding equation does not actually have a limit. The quick way to determine that is the fact that the numerator's equation converges more slowly than the denominator's equation. Obviously, x^2 converges faster than x plus some positive number.

Limit Properties

In addition to understanding limits in a general sense, it is also important to look at the properties of limits. These are the types of identities that will save you time at the end of the day. This book doesn't go to the trouble of proving these identities, but you should easily be able to do so yourself because they are mere algebraic manipulations.

Intuitively, these properties are quite clear. The first claims that a scaled limit is equal to the same scale on the limit of the function. In mathematical terms, this is conveyed as follows:

$$\text{If } \lim_{x \to y} f(x) = a,$$

$$\lim_{x \to y} \left(kf(x) \right) = ka$$

The second important property claims that the sum of the limits equals the limit of the functions' sum. In mathematical terms, this is conveyed as follows:

$$\text{If } \lim_{x \to y} f(x) = a \text{ and } \lim_{x \to y} g(x) = b$$

$$\lim_{x \to y} (f + g)(x) = \lim_{x \to y} f(x) + \lim_{x \to y} g(x) = a + b$$

The next property pertains to multiplication. It basically states that the multiplication of the limits is equal to the limit of multiplication of the functions. Again, in terms of math, this is conveyed as follows:

$$\text{If } \lim_{x \to y} f(x) = a \text{ and } \lim_{x \to y} g(x) = b$$

$$\lim_{x \to y} (f \cdot g)(x) = \left(\lim_{x \to y} f(x) \right) \cdot \left(\lim_{x \to y} g(x) \right) = a \cdot b$$

Similarly, you can deduce the same thing for the inverse of the function. Using a mathematical notation, you have the following:

$$\text{If } \lim_{x \to y} f(x) = a \neq 0 \text{ and } f(x) \neq 0 \ \forall x$$

$$\lim_{x \to y} \left(\frac{1}{f(x)} \right) = \frac{1}{b}$$

Derivatives (The Result of Differentiation)

The idea of the derivative encapsulates the concept of rate. For example, consider a car that moves linearly and that goes from the initial position $x = 0$ to its final position $x = 3$ in three seconds. How could you determine how quickly the car is going? If you look at the problem carefully, you will notice that the car performs three units of movement in three seconds or, put another way, the speed at which the car goes is 3/3s or 1 unit per second. It's a function of time. Geometrically, if you were to draw the position of the car as a function of the time, you would draw a straight line from one point to the other. The slope in this case actually represents the rate of change.

On the other hand, consider an object that moves in a parabolic motion, and suppose that the equation describing the object's motion is as follows:

$$x(t) = t^2 - 1$$

To compute the average rate for the range t = $[-1, 0]$, you would apply the same concept. In short, you would compute the slope of the line generated from the first point to the second point, as illustrated in Figure 7.5:

$$\frac{x(-1) - x(0)}{(-1) - 0} = \frac{\left((-1)^2 - 1\right) - \left(0^2 - 1\right)}{-1}$$

$$= -1$$

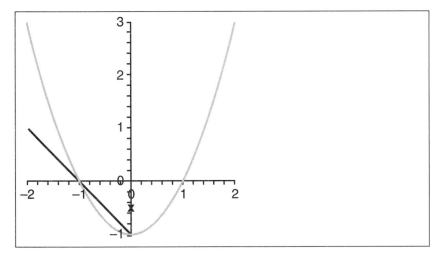

Figure 7.5
Plot of $x^2 - 1$ with its average rate of change for the range $[-1, 0]$

The average rate given a range of [a, b] is easily computed by the following, where m is the slope of the line from b to a:

$$m = \frac{x(b) - x(a)}{b - a}$$

So far so good. Consider what happens, however, if you shrink the range by half, as illustrated in Figure 7.6:

$$\frac{x(-1) - x\left(-\frac{1}{2}\right)}{(-1) - \left(-\frac{1}{2}\right)} = \frac{\left((-1)^2 - 1\right) - \left(\left(-\frac{1}{2}\right)^2 - 1\right)}{-\frac{1}{2}}$$

$$= \frac{\dfrac{3}{4}}{-\dfrac{1}{2}}$$

$$= -\frac{3}{2}$$

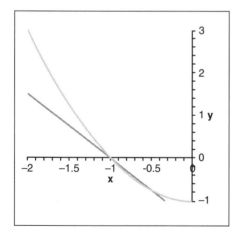

Figure 7.6
Plot of $x^2 - 1$ with its average speed for the range $[-1, -1/2]$

The slope is obviously steeper. Clearly, if you kept reducing the interval as such, you would iteratively get the rate for a smaller range of the curve to a point where you could say that you have computed the instantaneous rate of change for a given point in time merely because your range is so small that it is for all practical purposes instantaneous. This is the same thing that may happen as you drive a car. If you are accelerating in your car, you can look at your current speed (or instantaneous speed).

Of extreme importance is figuring out the instantaneous speed at a given point in time. For instance, given the position of an object, you might be interested in knowing the initial speed or rate of change of the object, or if you prefer, the slope at that point in time given a graph. As was observed previously, this corresponds to the slope at this instantaneous point in time, but more precisely, the slope at this instantaneous point in time is really the slope of the tangent line on this curve at the time t (that is, for *Time* = t in $f(Time)$). You will look at this in greater depth later on, but for now, let's look at the math involved in continuously reducing the interval:

$$m = \frac{x(b) - x(a)}{b - a}$$

$$= \frac{x(b) - x(b-h)}{h}, h = b - a$$

If $h = 0$, it is clear that this function equals infinity. Any function divided by 0, except 0 itself, is infinity. You can verify this by dividing any number by increasingly small numbers that are close to 0. In the interval problem, you do not actually require a strict equality to 0 for h. What happens with this equation is that as the value of h becomes smaller and smaller, the division makes the numerator increase considerably. On the other hand, the numerator also gets extremely small as h gets extremely small. This sure smells like a limit problem.

The derivative of a function $f(x)$ can thus be defined as follows:

$$f'(x) = \lim_{h \to 0} \frac{f(x) - f(x-h)}{h}$$

You write the derivative by adding one small stitch beside the function, so let's solve for the sample equation:

$$f'(x) = \lim_{h \to 0} \frac{(x^2 - 1) - ((x - h)^2 - 1)}{h}$$

$$= \lim_{h \to 0} \frac{(x^2 - 1) - (x^2 - 2xh + h^2 - 1)}{h}$$

$$= \lim_{h \to 0} \frac{2xh + h^2}{h}$$

$$= \lim_{h \to 0} 2x + h$$

$$= 2x$$

The graph of this function is plotted in Figure 7.7. Basically, for $x = -1$, you have that the instantaneous slope is -2, as shown in Figure 7.8. (Feel free to verify this.)

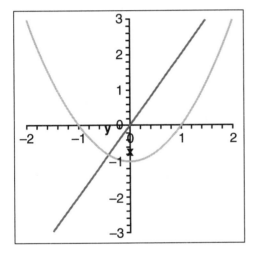

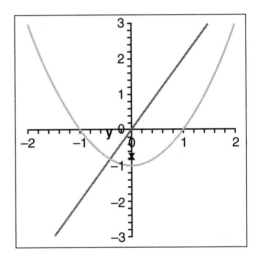

Figure 7.7
Plot of $x^2 - 1$ with its instantaneous speed, $2x$

Figure 7.8
Plot of $x^2 - 1$ and its tangent vector of slope -2 at $x = -1$

Next thing, let's look at the derivatives for more general and well-known functions. The concept of limits is important here because limits are the keys to solving problems that have no predetermined analytic solution. Alternatively, you can compute the numerical value of the limit by plugging in values extremely close to your solution and deducing the end value. Just make sure that you understand one thing: Not all functions have a derivative. If the limit of the function does not exist, it clearly cannot posses a derivative.

It is preferred to represent the derivative of a function $f(x)$ where the variable in the function is x. Notice how there was no mention of a convergence toward a specific value here. What you are particularly interested in is a general function where y converges toward x

in general. In short, you want the equation of the derivative and not the value of the derivative at a specific given point. You can write this with the following notation:

$$f'(x) = \frac{d(f(x))}{dx}$$

Polynomial Derivatives

Polynomials are very popular for many problems. Consequently, it can be pretty useful to generalize the derivative of a polynomial so that you can easily compute one. If you use the definition of the derivative as the limit of a function, you can easily find the limit of a polynomial:

$$\frac{d(x^n)}{dx} = \lim_{h \to 0} \frac{x^n - (x-h)^n}{h}$$

$$= \lim_{h \to 0} \frac{x^n - x^n + nx^{n-1}h + h^2(\ldots)}{h}$$

$$= \lim_{h \to 0} \left(nx^{n-1} + h^2(\ldots) \right)$$

$$= nx^{n-1}$$

It is a bit too early to get into the details of the expansion of a polynomial $(x + a)^n$, but the idea here is that if you multiply a binomial n times, you will get only one value in which a is not multiplied by x. This happens if you multiply the first term (that is, x) for every parenthesis.

If you look at how many terms have a power of 1 for h, you will notice that there are n of them and that all of them are the same value: x^{n-1}. As for the remaining terms, each has at least a power of h squared. Therefore, you can divide the entire thing by h and, because there is still a leading h coefficient for each of these terms, as h tends toward 0, the equation equals 0. Thus, you have the remaining term (the one that cumulates all the powers of 1 for h). After you have that, chances are that you will have multiplication by h, which is intuitively 0.

note

If you do not fully understand this, do not worry. The trick to find a limit is always the same. Try to algebraically work the equation such that you can cancel the division by h.

Thanks to the properties of the limit, this formula generalizes even more because you can apply the same thing to sums of polynomials and to scalar multiplications of polynomials. In a nutshell, you can apply this technique to solve the equation of any ordinary real polynomials.

The Mysterious Power

Polynomials cover a broad spectrum of problems, but they are not the only kids on the block. Another common function is the power function. Although this function is quite similar to polynomial functions in representation, the function itself is quite different and in general increases/decreases much more quickly than a polynomial. We want to find the equation for a general power function, so let's start with the basics:

$$\frac{d\left(e^x\right)}{dx} = \lim_{h \to 0} \frac{e^x - e^{x-h}}{h}$$

$$= e^x \lim_{h \to 0} \frac{1 - \dfrac{1}{e^b}}{h}$$

Here is where it gets a little trickier. Offhand, it seems like this function cannot be converted to get rid of the division by h, but a mere substitution of a few values in the vicinity of 0 does suggest that a limit might exist. With a stronger definition of the limit (called "epsilon delta"), it can be shown that the last limit here converges toward 1. Numerically, you can verify that this is so by trying very small values. The implication of this is as follows:

$$\frac{d\left(e^x\right)}{dx} = e^x$$

Furthermore, with the properties of the derivatives, which will be tackled shortly, you can also say that in general for any power a, the following holds:

$$\frac{d\left(a^x\right)}{dx} = \ln\left(a\right)e^x$$

Sine Function Derivatives

Dealing with the derivatives of trigonometric functions are an entirely different beast. The basic concept of limits is easy; it's the little tricks that you have to perform to rid your equation of nonsense such as divisions by 0 that make it hard. To illustrate the workings of sine function derivatives, I've elected to take a geometrical approach, because solving these functions algebraically can be difficult. The trick is to make a small sketch and to see what relationships exist. For example, draw a circle with the following points on it: the origin, **o**; the point at $\sin(x)$, **p**; and the point at $\sin(x + h)$, **q**. Further define the point **a** as the inner corner of the right triangle formed by **p** and **q**, as illustrated in Figure 7.9. Mathematically, you have the following:

$$\frac{d\left(\sin\left(x\right)\right)}{dx} = \lim_{h \to 0} \frac{\sin\left(x\right) - \sin\left(x - h\right)}{h}$$

$$= \frac{aq}{\text{arc } pq}$$

$$\approx \frac{aq}{pq}$$

$$= \cos\left(x\right)$$

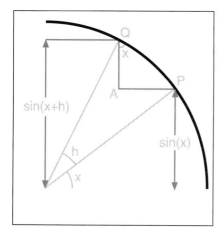

Figure 7.9
Informal proof that the derivative of sine is a cosine

It's a pretty tricky juggling act. In radians, the length of the arc for a unit circle matches with the angle's value. That's why a unit circle has a circumference of 2π, which accounts for all 360 degrees. That should clarify the first/second line. On the third line, an approximation is made. The logic at that point is that as h tends toward 0, the arc pq will tend toward a straight line. Basically, if you zoom to infinity on a circle, it will appear like a straight line. This is in fact why, in the old days, they believed that Earth was flat and not spherical (that and a little Biblical pressure, of course). The two last lines basically contain the definition of the cosine and itself; at that point, it's a mere definition.

note

There are plenty more functions that you can take a stab at. Most of the work from this point on, however, is algebraic, making it more appropriate for tables (for more information, see Appendix C, "Integral and Derivative Table").

Derivatives in 3D and Beyond

So far, you've seen functions that deal with only a single variable, and thus were equations that could be seen as 2D functions. You might have thought it odd, then, that the title of this chapter is "Accelerated Vector Calculus for the Uninitiated"; well, ponder no more. All the preceding equations can be written as vectors, and doing so makes it that much simpler for the higher-dimension equation to be manipulated.

After you have grasped the concept of 2D derivatives, one of the easiest concepts to understand is that of partial derivatives. The idea behind them is to apply a derivative to the entire function relative to a given variable. In other words, if you have a function f(x, y, z), the partial derivative would differentiate the function for x by considering all the other variables as constants. It would thereafter do the same thing for y and z. (This is not very different from what you have seen previously.) Mathematically, you can say the following about partial derivatives:

$$\frac{d\left(f\left(\mathbf{x}\right)\right)}{dx_i} = \lim_{h \to 0} \frac{f\left(\mathbf{x}\right) - f\left(\mathbf{x} - \mathbf{h}\right)}{h}, \mathbf{h} = \left\langle \begin{matrix} 0 & i = j \\ h & i \neq j \end{matrix} \right\rangle = \left\langle 0, \ldots, h \ldots, 0 \right\rangle$$

In short, you must generate $\mathbf{h}$ such that the ith component equals h and all the other components equal 0. Consider the following as an example, illustrated in Figure 7.10:

$$f\left(x, y\right) = 2x^2 - 2xy$$

$$\frac{d\left(f\left(x, y\right)\right)}{dx} = 4x - 2y$$

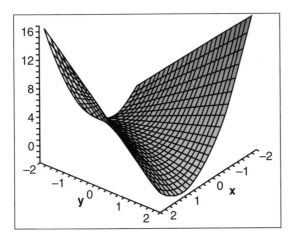

How does that help you to extend things up to 3D? Well, in 2D, the derivative represented the tangent line at x. In 3D, a derivative that takes two variables and outputs a single one should logically yield a tangent plane to the surface described by the function, as shown in Figure 7.11. Logically, the derivative in x should represent the slope in x; ditto the derivative and slope

Figure 7.10
Plot of $2x^2 - 2xy$

in y. Consequently, the <x, y, z> slope for the tangent plane can be written by using the partial derivatives as follows:

$$\mathbf{m} = \nabla f(\mathbf{x}) = \left\langle \frac{df(\mathbf{x})}{dx}, \frac{df(\mathbf{x})}{dy}, \frac{df(\mathbf{x})}{dz} \right\rangle$$

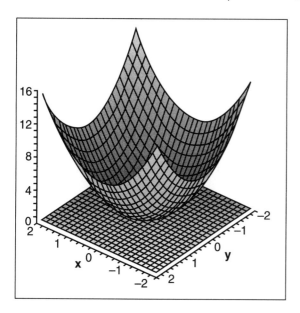

Figure 7.11
Plot of $2x^2 + 2y^2$ and its tangent surface <0, 0, 1, 0> at <0, 0>

You may be wondering how you can compute the normal vector of this surface if there is no z in the equation, but there really is a z. If you take the example of Figure 7.11, the equation $f(x, y) = 2x^2 + 2y^2$ is really the same thing as $z = 2x^2 + 2y^2$ or $0 = 2x^2 + 2y^2 - z$, which means that the normal vector would in fact be <$4x$, $4y$, -1>. Computing the normal vector can be very handy when it comes time to light up your scene.

This is often referred to as the gradient of the function. You can think of the gradient as a slope associated with each component. To determine the equation of the plane at this point, you can simply substitute a point that you know is on the plane (such as x) into the plane's equation. In short, you get the following:

$$z = f(x_0, y_0) + \left(\frac{df(x_0, y_0)}{dx} \right)(x - x_0) + \left(\frac{df(x_0, y_0)}{dy} \right)(y - y_0)$$

An astute person would also come up with the observation that this is the equation of a plane using a quaternion or, if you prefer to look at it this way, a vector and a displacement. You can indeed express the equation of the tangent plane by a quaternion here. As it turns out, the gradient is the normal that represents the normal vector to the plane. This equation should come as no surprise because it is extremely close to the equation of the tangent line, which is given below:

$$y = f(x_0) + \left(\frac{df(x_0, y_0)}{dx} \right)(x - x_0)$$

What happens if the equation does not map into one single real number? For instance, suppose you want to compute the derivative of a rotation. A rotation maps a coordinate into another coordinate, not a single value. One solution is to cut it down into a parametric form and do it from there. Here, I merely provide a better way to represent all this, using a familiar matrix notation. If your function has parametric equations, the following matrix will help you compute the derivative:

$$\mathbf{D}f(\mathbf{x}) = \begin{bmatrix} \dfrac{df_1(\mathbf{x})}{dx_1} & \cdots & \dfrac{df_1(\mathbf{x})}{dx_n} \\ \vdots & \ddots & \vdots \\ \dfrac{df_m(\mathbf{x})}{dx_1} & \cdots & \dfrac{df_m(\mathbf{x})}{dx_n} \end{bmatrix}$$

For any linear transformation, this is extremely simple, because linear transformation can be written in the form of a matrix $\mathbf{Ax}$. If you compute the derivative of this, $\mathbf{x} = <1,\ldots1>$, so the answer is $\mathbf{A}$. You can also compute the derivative for more complex transformations, as shown in the following example:

$$f(x, y) = \langle 2x + 3y, 2x^2 y \rangle$$

$$\mathbf{D}(f(x, y)) = \begin{bmatrix} \dfrac{f(x, y)}{dx} & \dfrac{f(x, y)}{dy} \end{bmatrix}$$

$$= \begin{bmatrix} d\dfrac{2x + 3y}{dx} & d\dfrac{2x + 3y}{dy} \\ d\dfrac{2x^2 y}{dx} & d\dfrac{2x^2 y}{dy} \end{bmatrix}$$

$$= \begin{bmatrix} 2 & 3 \\ 4xy & 2x^2 \end{bmatrix}$$

Properties and Rules of the Derivative

Like the limit, the derivative also has a set of properties that you can use to simplify your task. Some are obvious, others not as much. All are algebraic manipulations, meaning that their proofs are boring in most cases, and they can sometimes be nasty because they use the proper definition of the limit in terms of epsilon delta, which is not useful for games anyway. On the other hand, these properties are pretty important and useful for solving equations that would typically be pretty hard to compute, so let's get right to them.

The Chain Rule

The first one is commonly called the chain rule, and is extremely useful because it allows you to compute equations into other equations. The combination of an equation in an equation is written using an empty dot, as shown here:

$$f\big(g(x)\big) = (f \circ g)(x)$$

The chain rule states that the derivative of a chained equation equals the derivative of the function multiplied by the derivative of its internal function. Mathematically, this is expressed as follows:

$$\mathbf{D}(f \circ g)(x) = \mathbf{D}f\big(g(x)\big)\,\mathbf{D}g(x)$$

This may seem a little complex, so let's take a look at a 2D version of this function:

$$f(y) = 2y^2 + 3$$
$$g(x) = y = -4x$$

$$(f \circ g)(x) = \frac{d\left(2(-4x)^2 + 3\right)}{dx} \cdot \frac{d(-4x)}{dx}$$
$$= (-16x) \cdot (-4)$$
$$= 64x$$

It sounds pretty scary, but as you can see, it is not that bad. You can verify that this is indeed the correct solution by first substituting g into f and then computing the derivative from there. You should obtain the exact same solution.

The Product Rule

The chain rule can help you solve a lot of problems, but not all of them. Consider how you would find the derivative of a product of functions. The chain rule cannot help you here; unless the function can be easily expressed in one of the other types of derivatives, you will have a hard time solving this problem. This obviously calls for a rule that can help you figure out the product of two functions. Fortunately, just such a rule exists: the product rule. Mathematically, this rule is expressed as follows:

$$\mathbf{D}(f(\mathbf{x}) \cdot g(\mathbf{x})) = \mathbf{D}(f(\mathbf{x})) g(\mathbf{x}) + f(\mathbf{x}) \mathbf{D}(g(\mathbf{x}))$$

To understand this, take a look at the following:

$$f(x) = 2x^2 + 3$$
$$g(x) = -4x$$

$$\frac{d((2x^2 + 3)(-4x))}{dx} = \frac{d(2x^2 + 3)}{dx}(-4x) + (2x^2 + 3)\frac{d(-4x)}{dx}$$
$$= (4x)(-4x) + (2x^2 + 3)(-4)$$
$$= -16x^2 - 8x^2 - 12$$
$$= -24x^2 - 12$$

Basically, the chain rule simplifies your life. One way to approach the issue would be to compute the final equation. So, for example, suppose you have two equations: one to generate some terrain and a second to translate the terrain. The second equation is really a function of a function, and thus is perfectly suited to the chain rule. The terrain's equation would be f(x) and the translation would be g(x), which is the last transformation applied. Of course, you can apply this idea recursively. Thus if you had a scaling transformation applied after the translation, you would go through the same process.

The Quotient Rule

The last important property that can be exploited is the quotient rule. This is expressed as follows:

$$\mathbf{D}\!\left(\frac{f(\mathbf{x})}{g(\mathbf{x})}\right) = \frac{\mathbf{D}(f(\mathbf{x})) g(\mathbf{x}) - f(\mathbf{x}) \mathbf{D}(g(\mathbf{x}))}{g^2(\mathbf{x})}$$

Because the chain rule and the product rule were explained only in the context of 2D functions, and because the product rule is pretty similar to the quotient rule, let's use an example in a higher dimension here:

$$f(x,y,z) = x^2 + y^2 + z^2$$
$$g(x,y,z) = 3x^2 - 1$$

$$\mathbf{D}\left(\frac{f(x,y,z)}{g(x,y,z)}\right) = \frac{g(x,y,z)\,\mathbf{D}(f(x,y,z)) - f(x,y,z)\,\mathbf{D}g(x,y,z)}{g^2(x,y,z)}$$

$$= \frac{(3x^2-1)\langle 2x, 2y, 2z\rangle - (x^2+y^2+z^2)\langle 6x, 0, 0\rangle}{(3x^2-1)^2}$$

$$= \frac{\langle 6x^3 - 2x - (x^2+y^2+z^2)6x, 6yx^2 - 2y, 6zx^2 - 2z\rangle}{(3x^2-1)^2}$$

$$= \frac{\langle -2x - 6xy^2 - 6xz^2, 6yx^2 - 2y, 6zx^2 - 2z\rangle}{(3x^2-1)^2}$$

There you have it. Not the prettiest equation you could hope for, but that's what it all comes down to.

These three important properties coupled with a few basic derivatives should help you solve most of the calculus-related problems you'll encounter when programming games. Consider theses various rules as shortcuts when computing the derivative of an equation. Don't forget to look at Appendix C for at another set of interesting derivatives that can help you solve various problems. On the other hand, if you have a copy of Maple handy, you can always go with that to get the derivatives of the basic equations.

Resolving Problems Expressed with 3D Functions and Beyond

You have seen that the derivative represents the tangent hyperplane on a function. How does that relate to game programming? The derivative is a tool that you can use to solve more complex problems because it enables you to compute minima and maxima. (Together, these two sets of coordinates are referred to as *extrema*.) You will have plenty of opportunities to use calculus later on, so let's take a look at how this can be done.

Let's start with 2D functions before moving on to higher levels. Consider a simple 2D graph—say, a polynomial $y = 2x^2$. What is special about the minimum on this curve? For one, it is the lowest point, but the really interesting fact is that the tangent line at that point is horizontal. Technically, this means that the slope is 0, and golly, you know how to compute the slope! Solving for the equation $y = 2x^2$, you find the following:

$$y = 2x^2$$
$$y' = 4x$$
$$0 = 4x$$
$$x = 0$$

You find that the maximum is located at $x = 0$, which is further evidenced by the graph. In fact, the graph in Figure 7.5 is somewhat similar to the one generated here. Note how a translation in y does not actually change the position of the lowest point in x. This is great, but it can get pretty nasty.

To illustrate, suppose you have a polynomial with a pretty high degree. After you have computed its derivative, you must solve for the equation's zeroes. For example, suppose you have a more complex equation, such as a cosine function, in which it is not clear whether a null slope is a maximum or a minimum. Both have a slope of 0, so you need some way of differentiating between the two. It should not be too hard to do that if you look at the graph of the derivative, as shown in Figure 7.12. There, notice that from left to right, the value changes from positive to negative when you have a max and inversely when you have a min. An even more attractive property is that the tangent line at a minimum is such that the tangent line's slope is greater than 0. Conversely, for a maximum, the tangent line has a slope smaller than 0 . Consequently, you can deduce from this that the following property holds:

$$f'(\mathbf{x}) = 0, \text{then} f''(\mathbf{x}) = \begin{cases} < 0 & \text{local minimum} \\ > 0 & \text{local maximum} \end{cases}$$

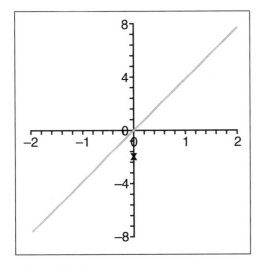

Figure 7.12
Plot of 4x

note

This brings us back to Chapter 1, "Equation Manipulation and Representation," which discusses solving equations—specifically, homogeneous equations (that is, of the form 0 = ...). You might also want to check out Chapter 12, "Closing the Gap for Numerical Approximation"; a few good tricks are presented there to solve equations iteratively.

Basically, you are looking at the derivative of the derivative, commonly called the second-order derivative. You can think of it as the slope function of the slope function of a function. If you prefer, you can simply look at it as the acceleration of the original function. Yet another way to look at it is as the change *in change* of a variable. For a car, this would be the acceleration, which is really the rate of change of the speed or, more precisely, the rate of change of the rate of change of the position.

What if the second-order derivative is 0? Should it be a maximum, a minimum, or something else? You can observe this with the equation $f(x) = x^3$; this happens at $x = 0$, shown in Figure 7.13. This location is called an *inflection point*, and it's the exact point where the slope changes from positive to negative. This is due to the fact that the acceleration equals 0.

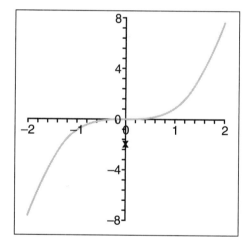

Figure 7.13
Plot of x^3

As an example, consider a case in which you want to find the minimum of a function—for example, to optimize an AI's *SimCity* cash-flow usage:

$$f(x,y) = x^2 + 3y^2 + 2xy$$

$$\mathbf{D}(f(x,y)) = [2x+2y \quad 2x+6y]$$

$$\mathbf{D}(f(0,0)) = [x+y \quad x+3y]$$

$$x+y = 0$$

$$x+3y = 0$$

$$\begin{bmatrix} 1 & 1 \\ 1 & 3 \end{bmatrix} \begin{bmatrix} x \\ y \end{bmatrix} = \begin{bmatrix} 0 \\ 0 \end{bmatrix}$$

$$\begin{bmatrix} 1 & 0 \\ 0 & 1 \end{bmatrix} \begin{bmatrix} x \\ y \end{bmatrix} = \begin{bmatrix} 0 \\ 0 \end{bmatrix}$$

$$\begin{bmatrix} x \\ y \end{bmatrix} = \begin{bmatrix} 0 \\ 0 \end{bmatrix}$$

$$\mathbf{D}(\mathbf{D}(f(x,y))) = \begin{bmatrix} \dfrac{d(2x+2y)}{dx} & \dfrac{d(2x+2y)}{dy} \\ \dfrac{d(2x+6y)}{dx} & \dfrac{d(2x+6y)}{dy} \end{bmatrix}$$

$$\mathbf{D}(\mathbf{D}(f(0,0))) = \begin{bmatrix} 2 & 2 \\ 2 & 6 \end{bmatrix}$$

The second-order derivatives are all positive, and the matrix is diagonally dominant (that is, the terms on the diagonal {2, 6} are greater than the other terms in the same row and column), thus the point <0, 0> is a maximum. (You can forget about this description, though, because a better one will be given shortly.) I pulled a quick one here and went straight to 3D to illustrate that the concept also extends to 3D. The only catch when you do this is that you can quickly get a lot of equations. At each pass, you multiply the number of equations by the number of variables, so things can quickly get out of hand, but it works. This is a good example where a matrix of a matrix could be useful.

Alas, the visual representation of such a concept is not very good on paper. Somehow, something looks wrong in the last equation. During the last step, you get four equations (because of the 2×2 matrix), but the test you have for the maximum/minimum is only applicable to a single real value. To complete the problem correctly, you must compute the matrix of the Hessian. In a nutshell, the same differentiation rules you saw previously apply, but the way you compute the second-order derivative real number is different. The same logic stands if the matrix is positive definite. (This was briefly mentioned in Chapter 3, "Meet the Matrices," but now it has come back to haunt you.) You can write the Hessian as follows:

$$H\left(f\left(x,y\right)\right)\left(\mathbf{h}\right)=\frac{1}{2}\begin{bmatrix} h_1 & h_2 \end{bmatrix}\begin{bmatrix} \dfrac{d^2 f}{dx^2} & \dfrac{d^2 f}{dydx} \\ \dfrac{d^2 f}{dxdy} & \dfrac{d^2 f}{dy^2} \end{bmatrix}\begin{bmatrix} h_1 \\ h_2 \end{bmatrix}$$

Ouch. No wonder I did not expand on this in Chapter 3! There is a lot of mathematical background behind this, which is not necessary for our purposes, but in short, you only care about the matrix itself because that is what will dictate the sign. So let's only consider the Hessian's matrix. It is positive definite if

$$\mathbf{H}=\begin{bmatrix} a & b \\ c & d \end{bmatrix}$$

$$\det \mathbf{H} = ad - bc > 0$$

Thus, if you return to the example, $2 \cdot 6 - 2 \cdot 2 > 0$, you can say that the matrix is positive definite. Consequently, you can also say that $<0, 0>$ is a maximum because $a > 0$. If a were < 0, you would claim a minimum. Now perhaps you can understand why, if you have a diagonally dominant matrix, the matrix is positive definite. Equipped with this knowledge, you'll be able to find the peak of a mountain on a terrain. Just remember (and please remind your AI as well) that this is a strategic location for just about any troop-based game.

Function Class

Functions can be categorized in classes. A function of class C^0 is a function for which every piece's ends meet. If you prefer, it is a function that is continuous. Likewise, a function of class C^1 is a function whose derivative is continuous, and so forth and so on. By extension, you can define a function of class C^n for which the nth derivative is continuous.

Reversing: Integration

When you look at a function, it's also good to take a look at its inverse—in this case, the integral of a function. The inverse, as always, is a beast to be reckoned with. The integral is indeed the inverse of the derivative. Geometrically, the derivative is the slope or instantaneous speed of the slope at a given location. Conversely, the integral is geometrically defined as the area under the curve. So for example, if you had a function that gave you the speed as a function of time, you could compute the acceleration by differentiating the equation, but you could also compute the total distance by integrating.

Numeric Computation of Integrals

It can become pretty tricky to compute the integral, mainly because the curves can become pretty complex. Also, there may be times when you simply don't have the full set of values readily at hand. For example, think of an auto-racing game. You're in your stolen car, which guzzles gas as fast as Homer consumes donuts. You need to keep track of the gas consumption, but all you have is the amount of gas that you are burning as a function of the mileage and speed. This obviously calls for integrating a rate. Let's start with a numerical approach. Suppose you were given a curve and you wanted to compute the area under the curve:

$$f(x) = 2x$$

$$Area = \sum_{i=1}^{n-1} f(x_i)\Delta x$$

To compute the area, you can break the curve into n rectangles, each with a width of delta x and a height such that it reaches the top of the curve. From there, you sum the area of the rectangles. Obviously, this is an approximation because if you decided to use only two rectangles, your approximation would not be too good. On the other hand, if you used a lot of rectangles, you would get a pretty precise result. (And yes, if you think in terms of limits and you let n tend toward infinity, you have an analytic solution for an integral.)

Before we take a look at analytic solutions, let's refine the numerical solution because not all functions can be analytically computed, and because there is a good deal of work you can do numerically to improve the approximation. One of the easiest ones to understand and compute is the trapezoid sum. The key to the trapezoid sum is the edge for which you choose the height of the rectangle. If you choose the right edge to be the height of the horizontal, you may get a higher value than if you choose the left edge, and vice versa. Thus, the trick is to compute the average of the two. Mathematically, the following holds:

$$\text{Riemann Sum} \approx Area = \frac{1}{2}\left(\sum_{i=0}^{n-1} f(x_i)\Delta x + \sum_{i=1}^{n} f(x_i)\Delta x \right)$$

Not a bad idea, and a simple one at that. For example, calculate the area of the function $1/t$ with $n = 10$ and range $[1, 2]$. Because you have 10 intervals, each will have a width of 0.1. Computing the sum for the left (Figure 7.14), the right (Figure 7.15) and the average of the edges (Figure 7.16) yields the following:

$$\text{Left Edge} = \left(1 + \frac{1}{1.1} + \frac{1}{1.2} + \cdots + \frac{1}{1.9}\right)0.1 \approx 0.7188$$

$$\text{Right Edge} = \left(\frac{1}{1.1} + \frac{1}{1.2} + \cdots + \frac{1}{1.9} + \frac{1}{2}\right)0.1 \approx 0.6688$$

$$\text{Trapezoid Area} = \frac{1}{2}\left(0.7188 + 0.6688\right)$$

$$= 0.6938$$

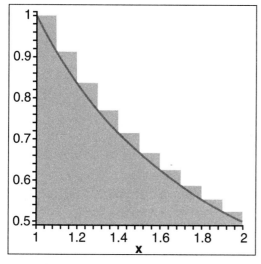

Figure 7.14
Area for the left edge

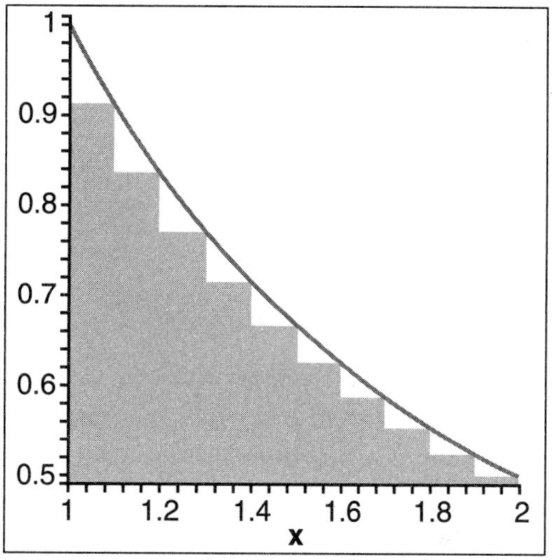

Figure 7.15
Area for the right edge

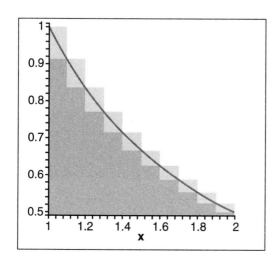

Figure 7.16
Area of the trapezoid

As you can see, depending on the function, the left or right method will generally overestimate, which means that you're giving more gas to the gamer than he really needs. Another worthy method is the Riemann sum (also called the *midpoint method*), which takes another approach. Instead of averaging (or computing the area of the trapezoid), it selects the middle of the interval as illustrated in Figure 7.17 and extends by half the interval on the left and right side, thereby reducing the respective left and right error by at least half. For this technique, computing the area is also pretty simple. Keeping the same example in mind, the following applies:

$$\text{Midpoint Area} = \left(\frac{1}{1.05} + \frac{1}{1.15} + \cdots \frac{1}{1.85} + \frac{1}{1.95} \right) 0.1 \approx 0.6928$$

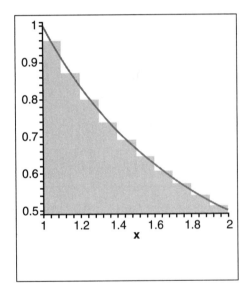

Figure 7.17
Area by the midpoint rule

This method, on the other hand, underestimates, which means that you are actually cheating the gamer out of gas without his knowledge. Once he figures it out, he'll surely want to get back at you for that. Is that the best we can do? Not quite. One of the most numerically accurate methods known is Simpson's method. A careful analysis of the two methods will show that the trapezoid method is generally twice as inaccurate at as the Riemann sum but with the opposite sign from the "true" value. That is, when one overestimates, the other underestimates. This is interesting because you can reuse the midpoint method by simply averaging the two methods out. Because the trapezoid is typically about twice as inaccurate, however, you do a weighted average by attributing twice the importance to the other method as compared to the trapezoid method. All in all, the following formula applies:

$$\text{Simpson Area} = \frac{2\text{Midpoint} + \text{Trapezoid}}{3}$$

Notice also that the area is signed. If you go under the horizontal axis, you will accumulate a negative area, while the opposite accumulates a positive area. This is actually a desired effect because you can easily compute the area under two curves by simply subtracting the signed area between the two curves—something you could not do without a signed area. On the other hand, if you are really looking at the sign-less area, nothing stops you from throwing an absolute value in there.

Analytic Integrals

Inverting an equation can become extremely nasty if you think about combining the chain rule, the product rule, and similar functions. Likewise, integrating can become a nightmare. If you can do it numerically, then do so; if you need an analytical solution for real-time purposes, then read on. If you can come up with an analytic equation that precisely defines the amount of gas used, then you can integrate the integral function and completely forget about computing the total gas usage with samples.

The integral is the anti-derivative (inverse). Suppose, then, that you graph a function and its derivative. In the second graph (the derivative), the height represents the slope at that very location. Because this graph gives you the speed, you know that for an infinitely small period of time, you have cumulated that speed times the amount of time you were in this position. Geometrically, this is nothing but computing the area. Previously, the function to compute the area was given in terms of a finite number of elements, but you can also define it by using a limit. With this notation, you can define the integral as follows:

$$\int f(x) = \lim_{n \to \infty} \sum_{i=1}^{n-1} f(x)$$

The curvy bar in front of $f(x)$ is the symbol used to represent the integral of the function $f(x)$. Previously, you have seen the limit as a simple function; now you see it as an infinite function. You do not actually need to go that path, however. Instead, if you simply think of the integral as the inverse of the derivative, you can solve a lot of problems.

There is one last thing you have to be careful about: Previously, when you computed the derivative of a function, you did not keep the information about any point on the tangent line. You only kept its slope. This becomes a problem when you invert simply because it means that when you integrate a function, you need more information in order to restitute the equation. The following illustrates this point:

$$f(x) = x^3 + 1$$
$$f'(x) = 3x^2$$
$$\int f'(x) = x^3$$

Notice that we lost the information on the +1. The only way to restitute the information that was lost is to have an initial condition that can help you plug a value into the equation and solve for it. For instance, if you know that $f(0) = 1$, you could easily reconstruct the equation.

Because integrals are defined as limits, the properties of the limits for a continuous function do stand for integrals. Thus, the process of adding integrals, as with derivatives, can be easily split up in pieces and multiplication by constants. As mentioned previously, if you want to use an integral to compute the area under two curves, you do not actually need the constant because it will cancel out. Observe:

$$\int_{a}^{b} f'(x) = f(b) - f(a)$$
$$= \left(b^3 + c\right) - \left(a^3 + c\right)$$
$$= b^3 - a^3$$

This notation, which basically states that the integral is computed with range [a, b], is what you will be using most of the time with respect to integrals. If it makes things easier for you, you can also split your integral into many smaller pieces. If, for example, the function was defined piece-wise, you could compute the integral on the first piece and the integral on the second piece, each with its own set of ranges, and it would be the equivalent of computing everything in one integral for the entire range (except if the curve was defined piece-wise, in which case you have to split the curve up).

The Intuitive Method

"The intuitive method" is quite a fancy name for the word "guess." Using this technique, you can intuitively find the equation with the knowledge of the derivative of a set of functions. Here's an example:

$$\int x^3 \sqrt{x^4 + 3} \, dx$$

The first thing that should come to mind is that the power of x inside the square root is only one degree less than the power inside the square root. This is a good hint that it probably comes from the product rule. To reconstruct the initial equation with this in mind, you basically need to find an equation that, when derived, will equal what you have up there. Let's continue:

$$\frac{d\left(\sqrt{x^4+3}\right)}{dx} = \frac{d\left(x^4+3\right)^{\frac{1}{2}}}{dx}$$

$$= \frac{4x^3\left(x^4+3\right)^{-\frac{1}{2}}}{2}$$

$$= 2x^3\left(x^4+3\right)^{-\frac{1}{2}}$$

Not quite it, but it is starting to look a bit like the previous equation. The power is obviously wrong, so the first step would be to rectify that. If you think in reverse, you actually need a power of 3/2 so that you can get a power of 1/2 when you derive. Let's plug and play again:

$$\frac{d\left(x^4+3\right)^{\frac{3}{2}}}{dx} = \frac{3}{2}4x^3\left(x^4+3\right)^{\frac{1}{2}}$$

$$= 6x^3\sqrt{x^4+3}$$

It smells like victory already. You are only missing the initial equation by a factor of six. All you need to do is add the inverse of a multiple of six in front of the equation to cancel it out:

$$\frac{d\,\frac{1}{6}\left(x^4+3\right)^{\frac{3}{2}}}{dx} = \frac{1}{6}\frac{3}{2}4x^3\left(x^4+3\right)^{\frac{1}{2}}$$

$$= x^3\sqrt{x^4+3}$$

$$\int x^3\sqrt{x^4+3}\,dx = \frac{1}{6}\sqrt[3]{x^4+3}+C$$

Got it! This method is nice, but unfortunately is not very direct; as a result, it can quickly get out of hand. Fortunately, there are other methods available for solving the harder integrals.

Integration by Substitution

This method is similar to what was done in the previous section, but is a little more formal. The idea is to substitute an expression with another expression. If you carefully keep track of everything, you can use the guessing method on the integral and obtain an easier equation to play with. Once you have the final solution, you can simply re-substitute the equations and you will be done. The only tricky part with this one is that you need to keep track of *dx*. Let's follow through with an example:

$$\int \tan(x)\, dx = \int \frac{\sin(x)}{\cos(x)}\, dx$$

This is where the tricky part begins. The substitution method is basically a process-driven guess-and-check method. It still requires some level of intuitiveness in order to solve the equation. By now, I hope you've had a chance to look at Appendix C. Specifically of interest here is the *ln* function. To achieve this task, substitute as shown:

$$w = \cos(x)$$

$$dw = \frac{d(\cos(x))}{dx}$$

$$= -\sin(x)$$

$$\int \tan = \int -\frac{dw}{w}$$

$$= -\ln|w| + C$$

$$= -\ln|\cos(x)| + C$$

Of course, this supposes that you know that the derivative of *ln* is 1 over *x*. When you know that, it becomes a piece of cake to play with algebraically. As you can see, this is basically the same method as the guess-and-check method, except that you define a function, test it against the integral, and, when you reach a point at which you have something that is familiar to you, you integrate it.

note

This can seem tricky, but practice makes perfect. If you grab a set of exercises and try them out, you should be able to do this type of thing like you can do additions now. Maple can help you a lot here if you want to practice. A Google search with keywords such as "exercise calculus" will quickly yield thousands of hits.

Integration by Part

It can be pretty hard to decrypt a formula when a product is involved in the initial derivative; it would be nice to have a formula that can help you with things like these. This is the idea behind the integration-by-part method. Observe the following logic:

$$\frac{d(uv)}{dx} = u\,'v + uv\,'$$

$$uv\,' = \frac{d(uv)}{dx} - u\,'v$$

$$\int uv\,' = \int \frac{d(uv)}{dx} - \int u\,'v$$

$$= uv - \int u\,'v$$

This looks like a mere algebraic juggling act, but this last expression can actually help you solve some problems. For starters, it enables you to look at the problem by looking at a smaller problem (also known as the "divide and conquer" technique); that is, it splits the function into two separate components and looks at each of them. One of the components is considered as another function, while the other is considered as the derivative of a function. Consequently, no matter which function you designate as being $v\,'$, it should be quite easy to integrate because you will need that in the expansion. Furthermore, if $u\,'$ is simpler than u, this will help you when calculating the integral. The same can be said about v toward $v\,'$. To illustrate, let's tackle a problem that is not obvious at first:

$$\int \cos^2(x)\,dx$$

Choose $u = v\,' = \cos(x)$

$$u\,' = \frac{d(\cos(x))}{dx} = -\sin(x)$$

$$v = \int \cos(x)\,dx = \sin(x)$$

$$\int uv\,'dx = uv - \int u\,'v$$

$$\int \cos^2(x)\,dx = \cos(x)\sin(x) + \int \sin^2(x)\,dx$$

$$= \cos(x)\sin(x) + \int 1 - \cos^2(x)\,dx$$

$$= \cos(x)\sin(x) + \int 1\,dx - \int \cos^2(x)\,dx$$

$$= \frac{\cos(x)\sin(x) + x + C}{2}$$

In this case, you were able to use an identity to convert the integral into the same thing as what you were looking for. Once you have that, you simply combine these terms on one side of the equation. Overall, the trick for this one is not so complicated; v must be easy to integrate and u must be easy to differentiate (that's usually not a problem). Finally, it helps if $u'v$ is easy to integrate. The key here is that if you can reduce the complexity of the integral of $u'v$, then you can apply this concept recursively until you reach something that is basic enough to integrate. Practicing is paramount here. Unfortunately, this is the type of thing that Maple may not be able to pick up on, so knowing these things can help a great deal.

Double and Triple Integrals

In 2D, the integral can be thought of as the signed area under a curve. In 3D, the same concept applies. Whereas you were integrating over a region $[a, b]$, you are now integrating over a rectangular region $[a, b] \times [c, d]$. But how does the math extend to higher dimensions? The idea is extremely easy. It sounds exactly like the idea that a matrix is a vector of vector. If you wanted to approximate the area of a 3D function, you could split the depth in m intervals. You can then compute the area of the curve in 2D and multiply that by the length of the depth interval. Sum over these small areas, and you now have a numerical approach. Apply the previous numerical integration method, but instead of computing the height of the function and multiplying that by the interval size, calculate the area of the curve (which you should know how to calculate by now) and multiply that by the interval size. It is a mere extension. The following illustrates this:

$$\mathrm{Volume} = \sum_{i=0}^{m} \mathrm{Area}\left(f(x)\right)\Delta z$$

$$= \sum_{i=0}^{m} \left(\int f(x)dx\right)\Delta z$$

As m tends toward infinity, what do you get? Drum roll… Another integral! Thus, the final equation looks something more like this:

$$\int_{a}^{b}\int_{c}^{d} f(x,y)\,dy\,dx$$

This type of integral is often called a *double integral,* which is simply an integral of an integral. (Obviously, you can extend this concept to 4D and beyond by using triple integrals and hyper-integrals.) In the preceding notation, the first (inner) integral is done with respect to y and then followed by x. For a square region, you can interchange the order without any worry provided they are continuous functions. As a result, whether you start by integrating in x or y really only depends on which of the two integrals is easier to compute. Let's follow through with a simple example:

$$z = x^2 + y^2 \text{ on the region } [-1,1] \times [1,1]$$

$$\int_{-1}^{1} \int_{-1}^{1} x^2 + y^2 \, dx \, dy = \int_{-1}^{1} \left(\int_{-1}^{1} x^2 + y^2 \, dx \right) dy$$

$$= \int_{-1}^{1} \left(\frac{x^3}{3} + xy^2 \right]_{-1}^{1} \right) dy$$

$$= \int_{-1}^{1} \left(\frac{1^3}{3} + 1y^2 - \left(\frac{(-1)^3}{3} - 1y^2 \right) \right) dy$$

$$= \int_{-1}^{1} \left(\frac{2}{3} + 2y^2 \right) dy$$

$$= \frac{2y}{3} + \frac{2y^3}{3} \right]_{-1}^{1}$$

$$= \frac{2 \cdot 1}{3} + \frac{2 \cdot 1^3}{3} - \left(\frac{2(-1)}{3} + \frac{2(-1)^3}{3} \right)$$

$$= \frac{4}{3} - \left(-\frac{4}{3} \right)$$

$$= \frac{8}{3}$$

Double Integrals Over Non-Rectangular Regions

Some problems may arise as you try to compute the integral on regions that are not rectangular in nature. For example, if you wanted to compute the area of a cylinder, you would probably have a hard time doing so using the techniques you have learned so far. If you already know the area of any slice on the shape following a straight line, however, you can compute the integral of the region by simply summing these slices using an integral—that is, by using a double integral. For example, you know that the area of a circle is $2\pi r^2$. To compute the area of a cylinder, you would simply sum these slices (that is, the many circles that compose a cylinder) over the height:

$$\int_{0}^{Height} 2\pi r^2 \, dx = 2\pi r^2 x \Big]_{0}^{Height}$$

$$= 2\pi r^2 Height - 2\pi r^2 0$$

$$= 2\pi r^2 Height$$

Multiply the area of the circle by its height, and you have it.

In physics, it can be pretty useful to relate the object's volume to its mass with its volumetric mass, so knowing the volume of the objects you create can be useful, not to mention knowing the advanced math, which you can apply to similar concepts. If, for example, you did not know the equation for the area of the circle, then you would need to do some real work to determine what it is. The trick in that case would be to write the equation of the boundary parametrically. Once you have this, you can plug these values/equations into the integration boundaries.

Let's see how this is done with the circle, where you can let x be linear and compute y as a function of x:

$$x^2 + y^2 = r^2$$
$$y = \sqrt{r^2 - x^2}$$

Consequently, you can integrate on the range

$$\left[-r, r\right] \times \left[-\sqrt{r^2 - x^2}, \sqrt{r^2 - x^2}\right]$$

This changes the boundary of y by taking the value of x into account. Obviously, the first range must be linear for you to get a numerical value. The other ranges can depend on any previous boundary value.

Now let's finish the problem of computing the area of the circle. (Note that there is a lot of funny business, which will be explained shortly after the example.)

$$\text{Area} = \int_{-r}^{r} \int_{-\sqrt{r^2-y^2}}^{\sqrt{r^2-y^2}} 1\, dx\, dy$$

$$= \int_{-r}^{r} y \Big]_{-\sqrt{r^2-y^2}}^{\sqrt{r^2-y^2}} dy$$

$$= \int_{-r}^{r} 2\sqrt{r^2 - y^2}\, dy$$

$$y = r \cdot \sin(\theta)$$

(continued on next page)

(continued from previous page)

$$\text{Area} = \int_{-\frac{\pi}{2}}^{\frac{\pi}{2}} 2\sqrt{r^2 - r^2 \sin(\theta)} r \, d\theta$$

$$= \int_{-\frac{\pi}{2}}^{\frac{\pi}{2}} 2r^2 \sqrt{1 - \sin^2(\theta)} \, d\theta$$

$$= \int_{-\frac{\pi}{2}}^{\frac{\pi}{2}} 2r^2 \sqrt{\cos^2(\theta)} \, d\theta$$

$$= \int_{-\frac{\pi}{2}}^{\frac{\pi}{2}} 2r^2 \cos(\theta) \, d\theta$$

$$= 2r^2 \sin\theta \Big]_{-\frac{\pi}{2}}^{\frac{\pi}{2}}$$

$$= 2\pi r^2$$

The first thing you should notice is the new way to compute the area of a circle. Yes, you can compute the area of a circle with a single integral, but you can also look at it as a double integral where all the pieces are small "pixels," if you will. The advantage of this method over the other is that it can also easily compute a function in 3D. For instance, to compute the area of a sphere, you simply need to replace 1 with the value for z. All in all, this methodology is more of a religious matter than anything else, so choose the one you prefer and get on with it.

The idea behind this section should be clear now. When computing the area, one variable ranges linearly, while the other variable depends on the previous one. When you compute the integral, you compute it as expected by substituting the function of y into the integrated variable. The part that may surprise you is the substitution being applied. You have seen the substitution method before, but here, the value was not re-substituted. Instead, a parasitic r appeared out of nowhere and you kept everything as is. In fact, this method is a mapping method and not a substitution method. It is simply another tool to add to your toolkit.

Integration by Mapping

As mentioned previously, mapping is different from substitution because nothing is substituted back into the equation. For instance, in the last example, a mapping was made from Cartesian coordinates to polar coordinates. Because you are not planning to substitute, it's important to look at the changes that your equation will suffer through this transformation. The first step for a mapping is to write out the parametric equation of mapping. Keeping the preceding example in mind, you have the following:

$$x = r\cos(\theta)$$
$$y = r\sin(\theta)$$

Accordingly, for this transformation to be valid, you need to change the integration bounds accordingly. To do this, you can invert the mapping and plug in the boundary values to see what they should be set to. In our specific case, we had the following:

$$y = r\sin(\theta)$$

$$\theta = \arcsin\left(\frac{y}{r}\right)$$

$$\theta_r = \arcsin\left(\frac{r}{r}\right)$$

$$= \arcsin(1)$$

$$= \frac{\pi}{2}$$

$$\theta_{-r} = \arcsin\left(\frac{-r}{r}\right)$$

$$= \arcsin(-1)$$

$$= -\frac{\pi}{2}$$

So far so good. Now the only thing you have left to explain is the fact that a parasitic r has surfaced. A mapping is truly a function of a function. In other words, the mapping function $g(x)$ on the function $f(x)$ is $f(g(x))$. Expand the formula all the way through, jump through a few math hoops, and you will get the following, where $\mathbf{x}$ is the original variable vector, $\mathbf{u}$ is the mapping vector, and R is a boundary region for integration with R*, the new boundary region for integration:

$$\int_{R^*} f(g(\mathbf{x}))\left|\frac{d\mathbf{x}}{d\mathbf{u}}\right| du = \int_R f(x)\, dx$$

This is basically what you saw during the discussion of the derivative matrix (also called the Jacobian). The Jacobian matrix you are looking at here is the matrix of the transformation. Pursuing the example established so far, you have the following:

$$\mathbf{B} = \begin{bmatrix} \dfrac{d\left(r\cos(\theta)\right)}{dr} & \dfrac{d\left(r\cos(\theta)\right)}{d\theta} \\[3mm] \dfrac{d\left(r\sin(\theta)\right)}{dr} & \dfrac{d\left(r\sin(\theta)\right)}{d\theta} \end{bmatrix}$$

$$= \begin{bmatrix} \cos(\theta) & -r\sin(\theta) \\ \sin(\theta) & r\cos(\theta) \end{bmatrix}$$

$$|\mathbf{B}| = r\cos^2(\theta) + r\sin^2(\theta)$$

$$= r\left(\cos^2(\theta) + \sin^2(\theta)\right)$$

$$= r$$

Now, when you revisit the example given in the previous section, you should be able to fully understand what was done. This is a pretty powerful integration tool, and it applies to spherical coordinate systems, cylindrical mapping, or any other form of mapping you can think of.

Using Integration to Compute the Arc Length

How might you find the circumference of a circle? If you were thinking about relationships between radians and the circle, take a stab at finding the circumference of an ellipse. The circumference of a circle is really the length of the arc of which the circle is comprised (a circle is really just an arc, after all). Fortunately, integrals can be pretty useful when it comes time to compute the length of an arc. It's always useful to know distances, especially when dealing with AI, which need to find optimal paths. The idea is based on an infinite sum of distances. If you cut your curves into a set of intervals and you cumulate the distance between two points on these intervals, you will obtain the length of the arc. This is the idea behind Figure 7.18, and following is the math behind it:

$$\text{Length} = \sum \text{Distance}$$

$$= \int \sqrt{\Delta^2 x + \Delta^2 y}$$

$$\approx \int \sqrt{\Delta^2 x + \left(f'(x) \cdot \Delta x\right)^2}$$

$$= \int \Delta x \sqrt{1 + f'(x)^2}$$

$$= \int \sqrt{1 + f'(x)^2}\, dx$$

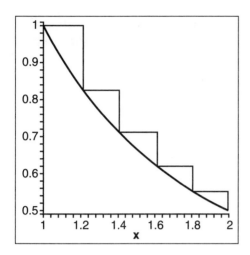

Figure 7.18
Computing the arc length for 1/x with range [1, 2]

If your function is defined parametrically, it becomes much easier to express as shown by the following equation:

$$\text{Length} = \int \sqrt{\left(x\,'(t)\right)^2 + \left(y\,'(t)\right)^2 + \left(z\,'(t)\right)^2}\, dt$$

The trick to solving this problem is to observe that as the deltas become really small, the arc actually looks like a straight line. This is similar to the Earth example mentioned previously in this chapter. As you zoom in, you can approximate delta y as a straight line by using the slope of delta x and x itself (that is, the equation of a line).

How is this useful? Well, suppose you wanted to draw a parabola with the equation $y = x^2 - 4$. You want to draw this curve with range $[-10, 10]$ by sampling a set of coordinates on the curve and joining these vertices with lines, but you want to determine how many samples you should take on the curve in order for it to look good. If you take too few samples, your curve will look ugly; taking too many will uselessly overload the CPU. If you know the length of the curve, then you can simply figure roughly how many points you would like per length and get the number of samples you should be doing. For instance, say you want an average ratio of two vertices per unit of length. How many vertices would you need for the aforementioned curve? Let's get down to the math:

$$\text{Length} = \int_{-10}^{10} \sqrt{1 + \frac{d^2\left(x^2 - 4\right)}{dx}}\,dx$$

$$= \int_{-10}^{10} \sqrt{1 + 4x^2}\,dx$$

$$= \int_{-10}^{10} \left(1 + 4x^2\right)^{\frac{1}{2}}\,dx$$

$$= \frac{x\sqrt{1 + 4x^2}}{2} + \frac{\operatorname{arcsinh}\left(2x\right)}{4}\Bigg]_{-10}^{10}$$

$$= 202.0946$$

At that rate, you would need 202 / 2 = 101 samples to get the required precision. Now you can see how complicated such a simple-looking integral may become. Try to see if you can find the path that was taken from the start to the finish. You may want to take a look at the integral tables in Appendix C to do so.

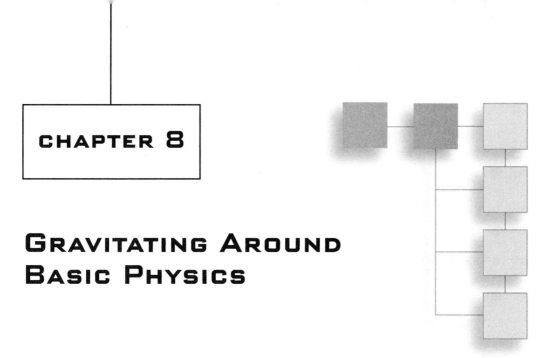

CHAPTER 8

GRAVITATING AROUND BASIC PHYSICS

Physics is not so much a field of mathematics as it is an application of mathematics; indeed, physics is drastically different from math because it is a science. Witness: Mathematicians typically build a branch by establishing a set of definitions and rules, which they use to deduce various conclusions. On the flipside, science introduces a branch by postulating a theory. Typically, for this theory to be considered good, it needs to be backed up by various examples of how it goes about solving various problems; even so, these theories need not be complete in order to be called theories. They are, in fact, speculative pieces of work that attempt to explain physical phenomena that we experience in our universe. Consequently, you should not expect the formulas you encounter in physics to be provable beyond a doubt. In fact, time has proven that some formulas are but approximations of the "true formulas" and sometimes even make a few assumptions.

But you know what? It doesn't matter! Your games need not be 100-percent physically correct in order for them to be killer fun. You just need something that looks reasonable. For instance, consider the old versions of *Mario Brothers* on the Nintendo. The gravity was totally out of whack, but that didn't stop it from being one of the top games for quite a while. *Duke3D* is another killer game with an unrealistic physical model; it did not matter, though, because the game was fun.

This chapter, the first of two in this book that focus on physics, concentrates on Newtonian physics and on what is typically referred to as linear physics. These branches of physics enable you to solve a good range of problems such as projectiles and collisions. Specifically, this chapter discusses the following:

- The concept of movement
- Gravitational force
- The theory of force and momentum
- The theory of conservation of energy

Move That Body...

A static game is pretty dull. Unless you plan to make a *Tetris*-type game with limited (read: systematic) movement, you need to know the equations that make things move.

Fortunately, it's pretty simple to make things move, but first you must define a few things—most notably, speed. Speed is defined as the distance traveled per second. When you drive a car, you typically drive at a roughly constant speed. When you accelerate, you are increasing or decreasing the speed.

note

> If you really want to be fancy, you can start thinking about speeding up acceleration, but it's not really worth it. In fact, the common physical model of movement only goes as far as acceleration.

If you were in space, where there is no friction or gravity, you could push an object and it would never stop. If you give a certain speed to a given object in space, it will, in a perfect world, keep that speed unless it collides with something else. On Earth, when you push an object horizontally, the same idea applies. Unfortunately, if you push the object on a rug, it will eventually stop because the rug creates friction, a concept we'll discuss later on. On the flipside, if you push an object horizontally off the top of a building, it would, in a simplistic model (that is, one that doesn't account for gravity), keep its speed. Keeping the speed constant yields the following equation, where v is the speed and v_0 is the initial speed:

$$v(t) = v_o$$

note

> You may wonder why the value is not marked s for speed instead of v. The truth is that in physics, you are more concerned with velocity (directional speed) than with speed itself, which is only a scalar. Throughout this chapter and the next, this convention will be used.

The speed can actually be seen as an instantaneous difference of distance over time, as you saw in the last chapter. Definitions aside, if you integrate the equation, you get a formula as a function of the position x and its initial position as follows:

$$x(t) = \int v(t) = v_o t + x_o$$

Therefore, if you have an object at $x = 0$ with a speed of $v_0 = 1$, for every integer value of t for the time, the distance increases by 1. So you have a function that, given the time, an initial position, and a velocity, can get you the projectile's position. That's interesting, but you may want to create something a little more involved—perhaps minimally 2D.

In such a case, you are looking at two variables. Let the x axis be horizontal and the y axis be the height. The x axis can behave as shown previously because this is exactly how it was defined. On the other hand, the y axis is pulled down by gravity. Gravity is a concept that is not very well understood even today. It was, in fact, Einstein's next great field of study, which he was unable to complete before he died. In the most simplistic models, gravity is considered a fixed acceleration, which for Earth is valued at 9.81 m/s² downwards. The value of the acceleration does not matter because your game will most likely not exhibit the same units unless you match OpenGL/Direct3D world units to meters, but doing so would be silly because things would move way too fast.

Having the acceleration as a constant has a few implications. For one, you can integrate this function to get the equation of the velocity as a function of time. Not only that, you can integrate once more in order to obtain the equation of the position as a function of time. The following illustrates this for a static acceleration a_0:

$$a(t) = a_0$$
$$v(t) = \int a(t) = v_0 + a_0 t$$
$$y(t) = \int v(t) = y_0 + v_0 t + \frac{a_0 t^2}{2}$$

As usual, it may be more convenient to express everything in the form of a matrix where $p(t)$ is the position $<x, y, z>$ of the projectile through time, t:

$$p(t) = \begin{bmatrix} 0 & v_x & x_0 \\ a_0 & v_y & y_0 \\ 0 & v_z & z_0 \end{bmatrix} \begin{bmatrix} \dfrac{t^2}{2} \\ t \\ 1 \end{bmatrix}$$

Notice how the velocity is split into three separate components. One is used for the horizontal axis and another for the vertical axis. While I was at it, I also added the z component. Obviously, the gravity only operates in one dimension, thus only the y axis has acceleration. (If you wanted to build something funky, you could set accelerations for the x and z, but if you do, you should first make sure that your game has such acceleration for a reason.)

For the sake of example, suppose your game features a tank sitting on a straight line, shooting out toward other tanks. Your game also has a cherry bomb that is set to explode at the maximal height of your projectile. To make this work, it is much easier for the user to describe the projectile's movement with a speed and an angle. Is it me, or does that sound like a polar coordinate? Well, it depends. If you were thinking in 3D, then you should have two angles—one for the height and the other for the sides—making a spherical coordinate. Suppose you restrict yourself to 2D, however. Given an initial speed and an angle, you should be able to compute the speed in x and the speed in y. Two down, three to go. The acceleration is set to a fixed value designed to make your game look good (if not physically perfect). All you have left to do is to set the initial position of your tank, and you have completed the equation. For example, suppose the speed is 5 with an angle of 45 degrees, an acceleration of 10, and an initial position of <0, 0>. The position of the projectile at time $t = 2$ is as follows:

$$p(t) = \begin{bmatrix} 0 & 5\cos\left(\dfrac{\pi}{4}\right) & 0 \\ 10 & 5\sin\left(\dfrac{\pi}{4}\right) & 0 \end{bmatrix} \begin{bmatrix} \dfrac{2^2}{2} \\ 2 \\ 1 \end{bmatrix}$$

$$= \begin{bmatrix} 0 & \dfrac{5}{\sqrt{2}} & 0 \\ 10 & \dfrac{5}{\sqrt{2}} & 0 \end{bmatrix} \begin{bmatrix} 2 \\ 2 \\ 1 \end{bmatrix}$$

$$= \begin{bmatrix} \dfrac{10}{\sqrt{2}} \\ 20 + \dfrac{10}{\sqrt{2}} \end{bmatrix}$$

This works, but it hasn't solved the problem of finding the maximum height. Fortunately, however, that's pretty easy. If you look at the problem carefully, the word "maximum" comes into play. The maximum for this function height is the maximum of the y function, which is the point at which the speed is null. By working on these equations, the following holds:

$$v(t) = \begin{bmatrix} 10 & \dfrac{5}{\sqrt{2}} & 0 \end{bmatrix} \begin{bmatrix} \dfrac{t^2}{2} \\ t \\ 1 \end{bmatrix} dt$$

$$= \begin{bmatrix} 10 & \dfrac{5}{\sqrt{2}} & 0 \end{bmatrix} \begin{bmatrix} t \\ 1 \\ 0 \end{bmatrix}$$

$$0 = \begin{bmatrix} 10 & \dfrac{5}{\sqrt{2}} \end{bmatrix} \begin{bmatrix} t \\ 1 \end{bmatrix}$$

$$t = -\dfrac{1}{2\sqrt{2}}$$

Something looks drastically wrong in this equation. According to these computations, the time at which the projectile hits a maximum is in the past. This doesn't make sense. The problem is that the signs of the axes have not been respected. In physics, everything is relative to something else. The sign and the side must be defined when you establish the problem. Before you tackle a problem in physics, the first step you should take is to define which side of the axis is positive and which side is negative. The same should be done for rotations. For example, if you choose the typical Cartesian coordinate system in which the positive values sit in the upper-right quadrants, your acceleration is completely wrong. The acceleration of Earth should pull the object downward, not upward. Consequently, you should reverse the sign of the acceleration. If you do so, however, you will notice that the equation *still* does not make sense. The time is positive, and thus represents an action in the future.

In order to obtain the position at the maximal point, you simply need to substitute t within the position equation. Given this, can you think of a technique to find the distance in x that the projectile will travel before it hits the ground at the same level? Hint: Recall that because a parabola is symmetrical, the point at which the object reaches a maximal height given a flat surface is the point where half the maximum distance in x has been traversed. This will be left as an exercise. The graph of the position of the projectile is plotted in Figure 8.1.

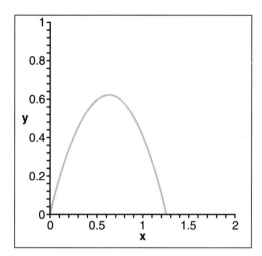

Figure 8.1
Graph of a projectile

Resisted Motion

As mentioned previously, the medium in which an object travels has some effect on the object. For example, if the object travels in air, it should be able to travel much faster than it would in water. All in all, it depends on the intensity of the damping force in which the object is traveling.

The equation that addresses this concept can be derived from an equation you will see later on. I've shown it here simply because the derivation is beyond the material covered in this book, and it would make for a rather long, boring proof. The equation to calculate the movement of an object at initial position x_0, and initial speed v_0, with acceleration a_0, and with a damping factor k, is as follows:

$$x(t) = x_0 + \frac{a_0}{k}t + \frac{kv_0 - a_0}{k^2}\left(1 - e^{-kt}\right)$$

This equation, whose graph is shown in Figure 8.2, is slightly different from the previous one and brings up an interesting fact. Often, the exponential function with a negative variable can be used in order to generate an asymptote. Notice what happens when t tends toward infinity for the last term. The exponential value tends toward 0 and the last term's value barely increases. This means that the equation actually tends toward something as t tends toward infinity plus the constant speed. For your purposes, it also means that there exists a terminal velocity, which is a boundary for the speed. In short, the actual speed should never reach the terminal velocity, but it should tend toward it.

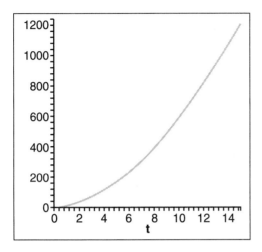

Figure 8.2
Graph of a resisted motion with $x_0 = 2$, $v_0 = 10$, $a_0 = 10$, $k = 0.01$

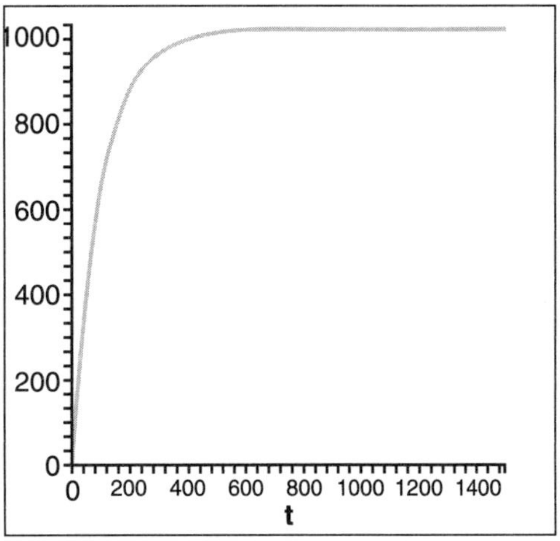

Figure 8.3
Graph of a resisted motion's speed with $x_0 = 2$, $v_0 = 10$, $a_0 = 10$, $k = 0.01$

How do you know what the terminal velocity is? You may want to choose k such that the equation has a given terminal velocity, which is a simple task. Simply compute the derivative of the function to see the equation of the speed, and you have what you are looking for if you set t such that it tends toward infinity. Figure 8.3 illustrates what the following equation proposes:

$$v(t) = x'(t) = \left(x_0 + \frac{a_0}{k}t + \frac{kv_0 - a_0}{k^2}\left(1 - e^{-kt}\right) \right)dt$$

$$= \lim_{t \to \infty} \frac{a_0}{k} - \frac{kv_0 - a_0}{k} e^{-kt}$$

$$= \frac{a_0}{k}$$

In a nutshell, you can choose the maximum speed your object should ever reach in the given medium and compute the value for k accordingly. After you have k, use the position equation in order to determine where the object is at a given point in time; that will give you the position of the object in time where the speed never actually goes past the terminal velocity.

Physical Force

In physics, there are many ways to go about solving a problem. Some optics are better suited for a specific problem than others. The equations presented earlier are great for solving simple problems, but they aren't much help when it comes to solving more complex problems. For example, if you roll a ball on a rug, the ball will eventually stop. The model of movement discussed previously does not take this into account.

The model of this section, which is force, is expressed in Newton (m/s²). (Incidentally, I'm sorry to be the one to break it to you, but the story about the apple hitting Newton on the head is pure myth, although Newton did come up with the equations for the force of gravity.) The interesting thing about force is that it can be described as a massacceleration. This being said, the force F for an object of mass m and acceleration a can be written as follows:

$$F = m \cdot a$$

In short, this model considers the object as a single point in space, and it looks at the various forces that are applied to the point representing the object. Because the object is represented as a point, it's not possible to solve every problem with this technique; even so, for a more complex model, it remains pretty simple to understand.

For example, returning to the tank game discussed earlier in this chapter, you would start out by considering the tank as one point in space (choose its center for the sake of convenience). If you look at the tank as is, two forces are applied to it:

▪ **Gravitational force.** Gravitational force pulls the tank downward toward Earth. That is, gravity is a force that applies a gravitational acceleration g to an object of mass m. The equation for gravity follows, where g is the acceleration due to gravity:

$$F = m \cdot g$$

▪ In essence, the more an object weighs, the greater its force of impact on the ground.

note

Acceleration itself does not depend on weight. That is, it doesn't matter whether you weigh 100 lbs or 1,000 lbs; you will always fall at the same speed after a given time. Well, this is almost true; it is, in fact, an approximation, but it's a fairly reasonable one. It's also partly false at the micro level because air creates a form of friction around an object as it falls, and the larger the object's surface area, the higher the resistance will be. This explains why a feather falls more slowly than a pin, even if both are the same weight.

▪ **Normal force.** Normal force is the force that is applied to the tank that prevents the tank from moving. Put another way, the normal force is the force of Earth against gravity. Remove this force (that is, remove the ground from under the tank), and the object will start to move toward Earth's center.

You can draw a diagram of the forces in order to help you see what is happening, as shown in Figure 8.4. Because forces are vectors, you can add them geometrically in order to more easily view what is happening. The norm of the vector should dictate the force's relative strength, as illustrated in Figure 8.5, where the normal and gravitational forces cancel each other out.

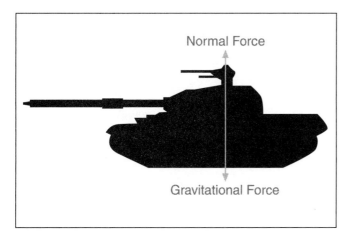

Figure 8.4
Graph of a set of forces applied to a tank

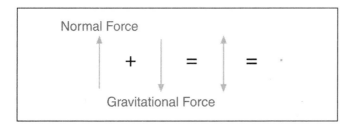

Figure 8.5
The addition of the forces applied to the tank

In addition to the gravitational and normal forces, several other forces come into play. Each has its own use, and will be discussed in the ensuing sections.

Friction

A world without friction would be a rather annoying world because nothing would ever stop moving. That wouldn't be so bad if you were building, say, a space game, but it would be really bad if you wanted to make a car-racing game.

Friction occurs when an object slides across a material. The rougher the material, the less easily the object will be able to slide across it. On the other hand, slide an object across ice, and it will travel much farther than if you roll the object. Clearly, though, if you slide a shovel across ice, chances are it will not go as far as, say, a skate sliding across ice because friction depends on two factors:

- The surface upon which you are sliding
- The object that is sliding

Most physical models take care of only the first factor, but in reality, both count.

note

Note here that there's a difference between sliding and rolling. When you try to turn a car while driving too fast, you slide. When your car slows down because you have released the gas pedal, the car is fact rolling. Generally speaking, you can roll much longer than you can slide.

Because the friction factor is dependent on the materials involved, it is pointless for a game to use the "real life" values for the friction coefficient, primarily because your favorite 3D libraries don't work in meters or feet or anything remotely familiar. It makes a difference only if you want one material to be relative to another. All in all, I suggest that you instead go by what looks and feels right. If you really want to be extra-realistic, you can grab tables of coefficients off the Net.

In addition to depending on the materials involved, friction also factors in the weight of the object that's doing the sliding. For example, it takes significantly more force to move a keg than it does to move a can of pop, even if both are made of the same material. More precisely, gravitational force plays a role; not only does the mass makes a difference, but gravity does too. If the gravitational force were really high, you could not move an object easily.

Mathematically speaking, the equation we are getting to for the force F_k, given the coefficient of friction μ ranging from $[0, 1]$ and the mass m for a gravitational acceleration g, is as follows:

$$F_k = \mu m g$$

If you were to make a force diagram to include the friction force, where would you put it? Friction does not help the object move forward, nor does it make it move in y. The only option is to have the friction go against the movement, as shown in Figure 8.6. In other words, if a tank in neutral was sliding off a roof, the friction would pull the tank backward (up toward the roof).

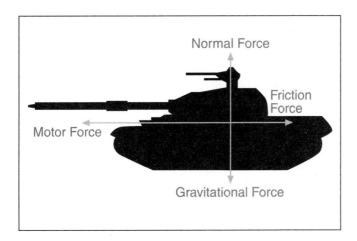

Figure 8.6
Diagram of forces on a tank, including friction and the motor's force

Of course, it does not make any sense for a tank to climb the roof. At best, friction should stabilize the tank such that it does not move at all. This fact forces you to introduce two new concepts:

- **Static friction.** The static force sets the threshold with regard to how much force is required for the object to start moving at all. Typically, it takes a much greater force to move a static object than it does to keep an object in motion. Consequently, you should expect the static friction coefficient to be greater than the kinetic friction coefficient.

- **Kinetic or dynamic (non-static) friction.** This refers to the coefficient of friction while the object is moving. It gauges the amount of force that is being wasted by friction. The fraction of the force that remains is used to accelerate the object, while the rest dissipates into heat or other form of energy, which is not of interest to you.

Let's return to our tank example. Suppose that a projectile has landed near the tank and that the tank has received a force of 10 units. The tank weighs 2 units of mass and has a static coefficient of 0.5, with a kinetic coefficient of 0.2. As an exercise, let's determine whether the tank will move and, if it does, the distance it will travel. It sounds like an easy problem, but it could get tricky, so let's take a look at the reasoning:

$$F_s = \mu_s mg$$

$$= \frac{1}{2} \cdot 2 \cdot 9.81$$

$$= 9.81$$

Because the force of friction is less than the force applied to the tank, the tank will in fact accelerate away from the winds generated by the blast. Now you need to determine the value of the acceleration by which the tank will be moved and to plug that value into the equations you saw in the first section. This is basic algebra work:

$$\sum F = ma = F_{blast} - F_k$$
$$2a = 10 - \mu_k mg$$
$$a = 5 - \frac{1}{5} \cdot 2 \cdot 9.81$$
$$= 1.076$$

This equation does not make much sense. It basically says that the tank will be continuously accelerated up to infinity, whereas in reality, the tank should stop moving at some point. The flaw is actually in the model. In reality, a blast generates a force that is radial; the effect of the force on an object depends on the object's distance from the blast. The farther away the object, the smaller the force. As an approximation, you can say that after one second, the effects of the blast have faded and all that is left is the speed that the object has accumulated and the force of friction. Given that, let's put everything together to see how far the tank has really moved:

$$x(t) = x_0 + v_0 t + \frac{a_0 t^2}{2}$$
$$x(1) = \frac{1.076}{2}$$
$$= 0.538$$

$$v(t) = v_0 + a_0 t$$
$$v(1) = 0 + 1.076$$
$$= 1.076$$

After one second, the blast's force fades away, thus

$$\sum F = ma = -F_k$$
$$a = -\mu_k \cdot g$$
$$= -\frac{1}{5} \cdot 9.81$$
$$= -1.962$$

When the speed is null, friction takes over. It follows that

$$v(t) = v_0 + a_0 t$$
$$0 = 1.076 - 1.962t$$
$$t = 0.548$$

Now compute where the tank is after t seconds:

$$x(t) = x_0 + v_0 t + \frac{a_0 t^2}{2}$$
$$= 0.538 + 1.076 \cdot 0.548 - 0.981 \cdot 0.548^2$$
$$= 0.833$$

There is yet another problem that is worth examining with regard to friction: the case of an object falling down from an inclined slope. Finding the acceleration on this one is pretty easy, but you have to know the trick or else the math can become pretty long. The idea is that you can rotate everything such that your axes are aligned with the slope. If you do that, things become much simpler, as illustrated in Figure 8.7. The math becomes as follows:

$$\sum F = -\mu_k mg \cos(\theta) + mg \sin(\theta)$$

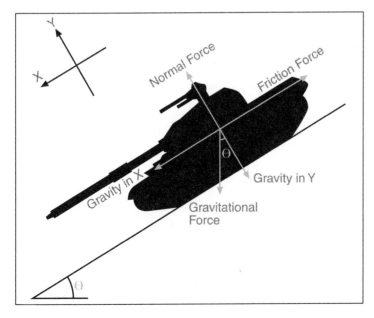

Figure 8.7
Diagram of forces on an inclined tank

Electrical and Gravitational Force Fields

Just when you thought you understood gravity, you find out there's more to it. The equation you saw for gravity was an approximation that is pretty close to the real solution when you are dealing with both a massive object and a very small object, such as Earth and a football. The reality of gravity is that mass does in fact matter.

Magnetism, electricity, and gravity follow very similar rules. Magnetism and electricity operate on the micro while gravity operates on the macro. In fact, these concepts are so similar that they actually share the same equation, just not quite the same constants. All of these concepts can be easily visualized as force fields. A force field, in turn, can be visualized as a vector field. A vector field is a mapping that assigns a vector to a coordinate.

Because vectors have a direction and a length, you can graphically represent a vector field by plotting the vector at the given input position. The resulting image gives a sense of flow. For instance, you could think of the field as water and the vectors would in fact give you the direction and strength of the current. This can be a pretty useful function. In our specific case, the vector field represents the gravitational or electromagnetic force.

The equation takes two electric charges (or masses), m_1 and m_2, as well as a constant k. The equation of the force going from m_1 to m_2 is as follows:

$$F_e(x, y, z) = \frac{km_1 m_2}{\sqrt{x^2 + y^2 + z^2}}$$

This equation can generate some pretty cool effects, such as a force field that can shield a player (or some other game element) from an object. If you were to draw a diagram of force, you would in fact draw a radial force because the force depends on the distance between any point in space and the reference point from which the force comes. A sample force diagram is illustrated in Figure 8.8.

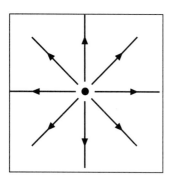

Figure 8.8
Diagram of forces on a charged particle

The interesting thing about this equation is that it yields an acceleration, which means that if, for example, a projectile was shot into a force field, the greater its initial speed, the farther into the force field it goes. That means you could have a *Quake*-style game with force fields around the characters; then, in order to kill a character, you would have to get close enough to them such that the speed of any projectile you shoot at the character is fast enough to penetrate the force field. The unfortunate thing about this equation is that it cannot provide the acceleration of the projectile over time. That is, there is currently no solution to this equation that can give you the flow (or lines of traversal) of a projectile in a force field over time. This is unfortunate because it somewhat limits what you can do with the equation.

For example, suppose that the network on which you are playing your game starts to lag. Your game starts off by computing the acceleration of a projectile from its current position $<x, y, z>$ and computes the position of the projectile after a given time t. Because the network is lagging, your projectile could actually go as far as the center of the force (which is assumed to be static and at the origin noted in the aforementioned equation). So what happens when the projectile is at $<0, 0, 0>$? The force results in a value of infinity. Alternatively, if the projectile is very close to the center, the equation yields a very large value; your projectile will go crazy in one direction in the next frame. On the other hand, if you always compute such that the difference in time is a very small number, you should be pretty close to the actual flow.

The other problem with this equation is that there is no easy way to synchronize every player such that they all obtain the same values. If one player has a faster computer, he'll expect to see more frames, but if you compute more frames, you do not follow the exact same path as you would if you were to compute fewer frames. The only way to rectify this is to set fixed frames and to move linearly from one sample position to the next through time. It's not the most elegant solution, but it works, and it doesn't look too bad.

Impulse

The general model you have seen thus far is one in which force is applied constantly to an object over time. Although this may represent a good number of forces, such as gravity, electricity, and such, there is another set of forces that are based on an impulse. Generally speaking, an impulse can be defined as an average force applied through time. For instance, suppose you want to fire two projectiles with the same cannon. Shouldn't it make a difference if one cannonball weighs twice as much as the other? Not a single model you've seen so far solves this problem because each one assumes that the speed was given initially. The idea behind an impulse, however, is that for a given period of time t, a constant force is applied.

The equation to compute the impulse, given the object's mass, its final speed v, and the two times between which the force F is applied, is as follows:

$$Impulse = F \cdot (t_2 - t_1) = m \cdot v$$

This is an extremely useful formula to find the initial speed of a projectile given a force and the projectile's weight. For instance, if you apply a force of 10N for 2 seconds on a mass of 2kg, you should get the following:

$$F \cdot (t_2 - t_1) = m \cdot v$$
$$10 \cdot 2 = 2v$$
$$v = 10 m/s$$

You can also use this formula to account for many other types of impulses. Indeed, most of the problems for which you would normally expect to receive an initial speed can take advantage of the impulse formula in order to account for the object's mass. Something as simple as a character jumping can be done with this model. Provide the force of the character's legs and the length of the impulse, and you get the vertical speed of the jump. Of course, you could also take into account that some characters are stronger than others, and thus the force could also change.

Buoyancy

This is not a problem you'll encounter as frequently as, say, dealing with projectiles, but it is pretty interesting and can yield some pretty cool effects. For example, suppose you are planning to make a 3D *Super Mario Brothers* game, and you have decided to create a level in which the character has to jump from one crate to another. The catch is that the crates are sitting on water and they move slowly due to the current that is applied in the pond. You have already simulated the current by giving the crates a static speed, but now you would like to simulate the additional weight of the character on the various crates in the level. This calls for a study of buoyancy and fluids.

Fluids can be an extremely complex field to study, but this particular problem can be solved easily using just a few basic concepts. The first thing you should be aware of is that all objects have a density. The mass density ρ is nothing but the calculation of how much mass, m, there is per unit of volume, V:

$$\rho = \frac{m}{V}$$

Take concrete, for example. Concrete is fairly dense, meaning that it contains a lot of mass per unit of volume. That's why even a small block of concrete is very heavy. On the flip-side, consider an empty crate that is the same size as the concrete block. Because a crate of that size weighs much less than a concrete block, it is less dense. Another example is water versus air. Water is much denser than air.

In addition to understanding fluids, you must be able to grasp the concept of pressure. Pressure can be defined as the amount of force applied per unit of area. For instance, even as you sit and read this book, air exerts a pressure upon your body, thereby squeezing it inward. Because water is denser, it applies an even greater amount of pressure to your body, which is why your skin wrinkles when you stay in water for too long. Mathematically, pressure P is defined with the force F and area A, as follows:

PACKING SLIP:
Amazon Marketplace Item: Mathematics for Game Developers (Game Development)
[Paperback] by Christopher
Listing ID: 0419T762134
SKU:
Quantity: 1

Purchased on: 03-Jun-2005
Shipped by: **alanreprah@hotmail.com**
Shipping address:

Ship to: David Marsh
Address Line 1: Wyeth Europa Ltd
Address Line 2: Vanwall Road
City: Maidenhead
State/Province/Region: Berkshire
Zip/Postal Code: SL6 4UB
Country: United Kingdom

Buyer Name: D W C MARSH

$$P = \frac{F}{A}$$

How does this all fit together? If you have ever been deep-sea diving, you may have noticed that as you swam deeper, your ears began to hurt. That pain is due to the increase of pressure on your ears; the deeper you go, the higher the pressure becomes. Why, though, does the pressure increase? As you swim, all the water above you exerts pressure on your body. The deeper you go, the more water there is above you, and the higher the pressure is. How does that relate to the crates in your game, though? If you were to draw the force diagram for your crate, you would find out that there are actually two main forces acting on the crate: gravity, which is pulling your crate toward the bottom, and pressure, which accumulates all around the crate.

If you look at the force on the side of the crate, you will notice that the pressure on the left side of the crate is the same as the pressure on the right, simply because the depth is the same. The forces on the crate's top and bottom panel, however, are different; specifically, the top panel will suffer a force of smaller magnitude than the bottom panel. Consequently, the crate should normally be moving upward unless it weighs so much that gravity pulls it completely under water. Now for the real question: How do you determine the force that goes against gravity, also know as the buoyancy force?

The last piece you need is the equation to give you the pressure of water given a height h. You can do this if you use the two preceding equations like so:

$$F = mg$$

$$= \left(\frac{m}{V} Ah \right) g$$

$$= \rho Ahg$$

Then, substituting into the equation of the pressure yields the following:

$$P = \frac{F}{A}$$

$$= \frac{\rho Ahg}{A}$$

$$= \rho hg$$

Thus, the buoyancy force is the difference between the force at the top of the crate and the force at the bottom of the crate. The following logic, illustrated in Figure 8.9, ensues for a volume of V:

$$F_b = F_{bottom} - F_{top}$$
$$= P_{bottom}A - P_{top}A$$
$$= \rho h_{bottom}gA - \rho h_{top}gA$$
$$= \rho gA\left(h_{bottom} - h_{top}\right)$$
$$= \rho gV$$

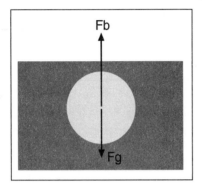

Figure 8.9
Diagram of the buoyancy force

As you saw in the previous chapter, every volume can be expressed as an infinite sum of infinitely small cubes; therefore, this formula stands for any type of volume. So you want to determine the acceleration of the crate in the water? Simply compute the sum of the force and find the acceleration. It's that simple. That said, be careful; the preceding equation assumes that the crate is completely submerged in water. If you want to handle a case where the crate is *not* completely submerged, you'll need to use one density for air and another for water. (Just so you know, air is typically about 775 times less dense than water. You can easily find these types of numbers on the Internet.)

To complete the simulation of your character jumping on the crates, you simply need to plug in some numbers. Suppose, for example, that the mass of the character is 60, the crate is a cube with unit 10 and mass 10, and the density of the water in which the crate is floating is 1. The following holds:

$$\sum F = 0$$
$$F_b - F_g = 0$$
$$0 = \rho_{water}gV_{water} - mg - Mg$$
$$= \rho_{water}V_{water} - m - M$$
$$= \rho_{water}A_{water}\Delta h - m - M$$
$$\Delta h = \frac{m + M}{\rho_{water}A_{water}}$$
$$= \frac{60 + 10}{1 \cdot 10^2}$$
$$= 7$$

Thus, the crate should be submerged 7 units instead of 1. If you want to be extra fancy, you can have the motion oscillate from 1 to 7 to really give the impression that the water is wavy.

You'll explore a slew of other forces in the next chapter. For now, let's stick to the ones you've seen so far. You can do some pretty cool stuff with them if you use them right.

Energy

Energy, which is expressed in Joules (which are, in fact, Newtons times meters), is based on an extremely simple theorem that states that energy is always conserved or, put another way, is never lost, but merely changes form. Though simple, this theorem has great consequences. For instance, suppose you used a lot of energy to throw a ball against a window. The energy starts in you and is transferred to the ball, enabling the ball to move forward, hit the window, and ultimately shatter the glass. Put another way, the energy that was transferred to the ball was transformed into another form of energy, which served to deform the glass and the ball a little bit. The energy you transferred to the ball was not really lost; rather, it was transformed into another form—heat, friction, and so on—and a little bit of that force was also used to thrust the ball further into the window.

note

> Interestingly enough, Einstein's most famous formula, $E = mc^2$, relates to energy. In fact, this equation expresses the energy of a relativistic particle where m is the mass and c is the speed of light. Unfortunately, this equation is not very useful for games.

There are many forms of energy—gravitational potential energy, kinetic energy, momentum—so without any further delay, let's take a look at the possible variations that could be of interest to you.

Energy, like force, is relative to a given point in space. When you are trying to solve a problem using the energy model, you have to set the baselines similarly to how you defined the baselines with forces. This is like choosing where the origin is within a system. Sometimes, choosing the right origin (or perspective, as was seen in Chapter 5, "Transformations") can be quite beneficial.

Potential Energy

Potential energy expresses the energy that a given object can potentially gain. It defines its potential in terms of energy. In general, potential energy U is defined relative to the force F over time t:

$$U = -\int_c F \cdot dt$$

Potential energy can be seen as energy that can potentially arise if something allows it to. For example, a water balloon contains potential energy because it can explode if it hits a wall. Think of it as dormant energy.

Gravitational Potential Energy

U, the potential, is defined as the path integral of the force. In our case, the path is simply a horizontal line because we are only concerned with the gravitational force. Thus, if you compute the equation specifically for gravity, you come up with the following formula, which is expressed in terms of the mass m, the acceleration due to gravity g, and h, the height of the object from the reference point.

$$U = mgh$$

Thus, if an object of mass 2 is thrown in the air at a specific time and reaches a height of 10 on Earth, its potential energy would be

$$U = 2 \cdot 9.81 \cdot 10$$
$$= 196.2 J$$

Kinetic Energy

Potential energy by itself is not that useful. Remember, the energy theorem states that energy is never actually lost. If you look at potential energy alone, you could easily claim that energy is lost as the object decreases in height. This is almost true, but not quite. The reality is that potential energy is lost simply because the object has less "potential" for going down. On the other hand, the potential energy is converted into another form of energy: kinetic energy that expresses the energy of motion. In a nutshell, the faster you move, the higher your kinetic energy should be, and the lower your potential energy should be. Put another way, potential energy complements kinetic energy. When one goes down, the other goes up, and vice versa.

You can determine the equation of kinetic energy with a bit of juggling with derivatives. It is done with concepts that look deeper into calculus, so I'll skip the proof, but in essence, kinetic energy is defined as the integral of the force for a path (not to be confused with a path integral). It basically gives the work it takes to get the particle moving at a velocity v:

$$K = \frac{1}{2}mv^2$$

How can this help you solve a problem? Consider a typical textbook problem in which a ball of mass $m = 2$ is dropped from a building of height $h = 1$, and suppose that you want to determine the speed of the object when it hits the ground. With this new tool, the problem becomes much easier to solve. Initially, the speed is 0, thus:

$$\sum Energy = U + K$$

$$= mgh + \frac{1}{2}mv^2$$

$$= 2 \cdot 9.81 \cdot 1 + 0$$

$$= 19.62 J$$

At the bottom, the energy is the same, but at the top, it equals 0, thus:

$$\sum Energy = U + K$$

$$19.62 = mgh + \frac{1}{2}mv^2$$

$$v = \sqrt{\frac{2 \cdot 19.62}{2}}$$

$$= 4.429 m/s$$

Momentum

Suppose you are writing another *Grand Theft Auto 3*, and you have the basic car movement, position, speed, and acceleration down, but something seems wrong when you hit another car—specifically, the other car acts like a static wall rather than a moving object. The prescription for such a problem is to revisit the formulas you use to account for the collision. Fortunately, such a problem can be expressed in terms of conservation of energy, and can be easily solved.

When a car hits another car, and both are of the same weight and are traveling at the same speed, you could expect them to just collapse one into another. On the other hand, if, say, a Mini Cooper were to hit a bus, you could expect the bus to crush the Mini simply because the bus has more mass. Alternatively, if you are driving a bumper car at the same time as your over-weight Uncle Sam, chances are that when he collides with you, you will rebound much more than he does—although he may still rebound to some degree because, after all, he did hit you.

Why is this so? Because of momentum, defined as the amount of weight carried over a given speed. Thus, if Uncle Sam were to hop into a bumper car, it might take him some time to get the vehicle up to speed, mainly because weight is the predominant factor of momentum. Likewise, when Uncle Sam hits you, it feels like you've been mowed down by a bus, yet he barely moves. That's because he has accumulated a lot of momentum. Because you have much less momentum than he does, his momentum absorbs your momentum and thereafter pushes you in the opposite direction. If the two momentums were the same, both you and Uncle Sam would simply stop moving in the event of a frontal collision.

Mathematically, the momentum p of an object is defined as follows:

$$p = mv$$

As you've seen, the more mass you have, the more momentum you build. The same is true of speed. If, for example, you were to gather tremendous speed before colliding with Uncle Sam, and if he was running at turtle speed, you would likely have generated adequate momentum to push him away even if he was slightly off the scale.

Elastic Collisions

An elastic collision is a collision in which the two objects that collide rebound with different velocities. You see a lot of elastic collisions in pinball machines, where the ball bounces all over creation.

We've talked about momentum and about conservation of energy, but not about how these concepts are useful to you for gaming purposes. The missing piece relates to momentum. Just as energy is conserved throughout a system, momentum is also conserved when the forces are constant. So suppose that you have two cars that are colliding a lá *GTA*, and you want to determine the resulting speed of each car. Thus, you have the mass of the two cars, m_1 and m_2, and the speed of the cars at the time they collide, v_1 and v_2. What you get is the following:

$$\frac{1}{2}m_1v_1^2 + \frac{1}{2}m_2v_2^2 = \frac{1}{2}m_1v_{1f}^2 + \frac{1}{2}m_2v_{2f}^2$$
$$m_1v_1 + m_2v_2 = m_1v_{1f} + m_2v_{2f}$$

$$m_1v_1^2 + m_2v_2^2 = m_1v_{1f}^2 + m_2v_{2f}^2$$
$$m_1v_1 + m_2v_2 = m_1v_{1f} + m_2v_{2f}$$

Isolate for values for the final speed of v_1 and v_2 and you get the following:

$$v_{1f} = \frac{(m_1 - m_2)v_1 + 2m_2v_2}{m_1 + m_2}$$

$$v_{2f} = \frac{(m_2 - m_1)v_2 + 2m_1v_1}{m_1 + m_2}$$

Because the two equations are quadratic, you really get two answers, but the answer basically states that nothing changes. This makes sense if the two masses are not colliding with each other, but having two masses *not* collide is not a really interesting problem, so these equations will do.

Let's look at what happens when various values are plugged into the equations. For starters, if one of the two masses is huge, you can verify with these equations that the small mass will rebound off the larger one as if the larger one were a brick wall. On the flipside, the heavy object will barely be affected. Secondly, if both masses and velocities are equal but of the opposite direction, what results is a perfectly symmetric collision that throws each object back to where it came from. But wait—there's something wrong with this picture. Do you really think that if a collision occurred between two identical cars, both would simply rebound to their starting positions? It's unlikely.

The cars rebound rather than crumpling on impact because this scenario uses a model called the elastic model, so called because it works very well for elastic objects that do not lose any energy upon collision. In reality, as mentioned previously, some energy is dispersed through objects upon impact in form of heat, deformation, or other similar forms of energy. But even though elastic collisions don't apply in a gaming scenario like the one described here, they are not to be discarded completely. They can still be used in other types of games, such as video pinball and the like.

Let's illustrate the use of the elastic model with a semi-complicated example. Suppose you have two super-balls, one large and one small, and they collide, as illustrated in Figure 8.10. The following process follows for balls of mass 2 and 1, respectively:

$$\mathbf{v}_1 = \langle 3, 4 \rangle$$
$$\mathbf{v}_2 = \langle -3, -2 \rangle$$

$$v_{1f} = \frac{(2-1)4 + 2 \cdot 1 \cdot (-2)}{2+1}$$
$$= \frac{4-4}{3}$$
$$= 0$$

$$v_{2f} = \frac{(1-2)(-2) + 2 \cdot 2 \cdot 4}{2+1}$$
$$= \frac{18}{3}$$
$$= 6$$

note

This problem is slightly more difficult, mainly because it deals with two dimensions. If you are careful with your angles, however, you should be fine.

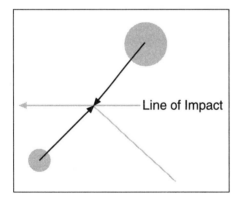

Figure 8.10
Collision between two spheres, showing the line of impact

You may have a hard time figuring out how to convert these equations to 2D, but doing so isn't terribly complicated. All you have to figure out is the angle of collision. When two objects collide, draw an imaginary line between the centers of both objects; this imaginary line indicates the point where the impact is propagated. If the two objects are spherical, it becomes pretty easy to see where the two objects will rebound. To tackle a problem like this, first determine this line of impulse.

The problem outlined above supposes that the balls collide vertically while moving toward each other horizontally. The line of impact in this case is 100 percent horizontal, which simplifies the problem. Here, the second ball goes flying downward while the other ball stops moving completely in y. It is not true, however, that any two spheres will collide horizontally. You could easily roll two marbles toward each other such that they would hit at an angle; it is this angle that you need to find. It depends on the position of the object as well as its form. (This type of problem will be discussed in more detail in Chapter 10, "And Then It Hits You: You Need Collision Detection.")

Inelastic Collisions

In an inelastic collision, the complete opposite of an elastic collision occurs. In such a case, the objects are glued together at the end. For example, if you were to shoot a player with a rocket, it is highly unlikely that the rocket would rebound even if the player was moving toward you. A more appropriate model would simply be to have the rocket "stick" to the player, or lodge itself into the other player's body. In an inelastic collision, the momentum is preserved (after all, mass does not disappear in Newtonian physics), but you do get a loss of kinetic energy, which is transformed into heat, sound, or other forms of energy.

The formula for this problem can be easily written:

$$m_1 v_1 + m_2 v_2 = (m_1 + m_2) v$$

Isolate for the final speed, v, and you have solved this problem.

$$v = \frac{m_1 v_1 + m_2 v_2}{m_1 + m_2}$$

Take, for instance, the collision of a bullet with an alien's body. In this case, the bullet is virtually weightless and the alien is initially motionless and massive. The following shows how much the alien of mass 1000 and the bullet of mass 0.001 with speed 500 would move after the gunshot:

$$v = \frac{1000 \cdot 0 + 0.001 \cdot 500}{1000 + 0.001}$$

$$= \frac{0.5}{1000.001}$$

$$= \frac{1}{200.0002}$$

As you can see, the alien barely moves. In fact, static friction is likely to cancel this effect completely.

Non-Conservative Energy

For the most part, the types of energy discussed so far have been conservative energies. Conservative forms of energy change from one type to another—for example, from kinetic to potential and vice versa—but do not dissipate into other forms, such as heat.

An alternative energy model involves non-conservative energies—for example, friction. Friction causes energy to dissipate into heat, but because heat is not part of your model (you don't compute heat inside or outside the system), it is considered external to your system and is thus defined as *non-conservative*. (On the flipside, if you keep track of heat inside whatever system you are using, you would indeed deal with friction as a conservative form of energy because it is conserved within the system.)

As a matter of fact, this is simpler than it may seem. The energy lost with friction is nothing but the friction force times the distance traveled. This is akin to potential energy, where the force is simply the gravitational force times the distance. Mathematically, the non-conservative W energy loss by friction is as follows:

$$W = F_k d$$
$$= \mu mgd$$

The easiest way to express the law of conservation of energy is to say that the sum of the differences between the energy before and after the event you study is 0. In other words, if some form of energy released X, then in a two-energy model, the second energy received X (obviously, you can generalize this to handle any number of levels of energy). This is represented mathematically as follows:

$$\Delta U + \Delta K = 0$$

When the energy is not conserved, some of the energy is released external to the set of equations. For instance, if you were to compute the sum of the differences of the potential and kinetic energy, you would find out that you are missing x Joules. If you subtract x Joules from each side of the equation, you get a more general equation expressing the non-conservation of energy:

$$\Delta U + \Delta K = W$$

In a more realistic *GTA* game, when you hit a car, chances are that the car has some friction with the tires. If you hit the car from the side, the wheels cannot roll, and thus you are slowed down considerably by friction. With the preceding equation and with the conservation of momentum equation, you can now compute a more realistic speed for the two cars after the crash. If you use the preceding equation to try to find the final velocity of each car, you'll find that they depend on the distance you have traveled. The farther you travel, the slower you get. What is happening here is that the friction is slowing you down to a crawl. If you want to maintain the same speed, you need an acceleration to compensate for that.

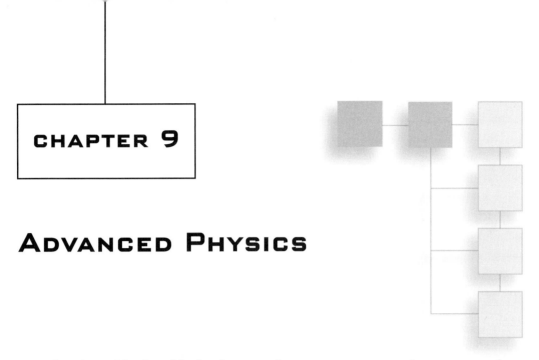

CHAPTER 9

ADVANCED PHYSICS

In keeping with the old-school approach to game programming, games such as Nintendo's *Super Mario Brothers* used hard-coded tables to simulate such aspects of physics as gravity. Similarly, in the first two versions of *Doom*, characters were rendered using sprites, which are precalculated rendered images taken at different key frames and angles. By the time *Quake* arrived, computers were fast enough that they could tackle polygonal characters, and the degree of realism was pushed well beyond the limits of the games at the time, but its animations were precomputed. For example, a character's arm could only move from one range to another in a linear fashion. Finally, more advanced techniques started to consider a character as a bony model—that is, its bones could move, which could then dictate the placement of the character's skin and cartilage. This development yielded models that enabled characters to move more freely and realistically.

Just like the "models" that games use to render a world, physics, too, is simply a model of the real world. In fact, just as the models used in a game are only accurate up to a point, so, too, is physics. For example, to account for all factors that affect the way an object falls, you have to think about, among other things, wind, viscosity, gravity, and one factor that wreaks havoc with the accuracy of physics: chaos. Low-level particles move in chaotic fashion, making it nigh-impossible to predict their movement. Physics models that are considered "accurate" are generally models whose chaotic behaviors are statistically averaged.

To illustrate, suppose you wanted to simulate air resistance under gravity. To do so, you could simply average out the resistance of air and claim that the resistance yields a factor of x, while in reality, a more accurate model would account for every air particle in space and how each one interacts with the falling object. Even that wouldn't be a perfect model, however, because you can break down the air molecule into various atoms, the atoms into quark particles, the quark particles into energy, and so on. Obviously, such a micro-level model is useless in game programming because the slight difference in accuracy is insignificant in a macro world.

Chapter 8, "Gravitating Around Basic Physics," provided you with the information you need to move objects linearly. In the real world, however, not everything moves in a straight line. In fact, many theories in physics claim that everything—even objects that are traveling in a straight line—oscillates. Controversial theories even go as far as to claim that an object is never really at a single defined position in time; instead, it can be said that an object is positioned in the vicinity of an area although we may perceive it as motionless.

One point you do have to keep in mind is that regardless of what kind of game you are planning to create, there is always a more accurate physic model available to you. Anyone claiming that a game's bottleneck is generally the GPU (Graphical Processing Unit) is seriously under-using the CPU. Ideally, the CPU and the GPU should both be maximized. If this is not the case, you should be able to use the CPU to help the GPU, or to increase a game's realism. Of course, don't go crazy on a single part of the simulation. For instance, if you simulated gravity through complex force field equations, you wouldn't yield a much nicer model than if you were to use the equations seen in the last chapter. But what you could do instead is use the CPU to add some cooler effects (that is, more realism) to the scene.

In the large realm of oscillatory motion, the following topics are of interest to this book:

- Angular movement
- Pendulum motion
- Spring motion
- Center of mass

Angular Movement

Suppose you are working on a 3D shooter in which players can throw hammers at each other. The only problem is, the hammer you have implemented using the knowledge you gained in Chapter 8—that is, effecting linear movement in Cartesian coordinates—simply translates from A to B. Instead, you would like to have it rotate while moving forward. If you swapped from using Cartesian coordinates to using polar or spherical coordinates, you could easily establish the equations for rotational movement linearly. This is exactly what you'll do in this chapter.

note

I only discuss polar coordinates here, but you should easily be able to see how this applies to spherical coordinates in 3D.

Rotational Movement

To program the hammer to not only move from A to B, but to rotate while doing so, requires a little more thinking. First, think about the order you will use to render this effect. For starters, you should work in an object model where the centroid of the object matches with the origin. This will enable you to perform the rotations first. Then, you can translate everything in world space where the hammer will move from A to B.

That's all nice, but what is the math behind this? Using what you've learned in previous chapters, you should be able to come up with the equations yourself. You start by setting your constants. For example, let's suppose that the object's velocity is constant—that is, you have thrown the object in a rotational manner, and it rotates constantly. You can write the equations by letting w be the angular speed (that is, the derivative of the angle over time), letting w_0 be the initial angular speed, and letting ϕ_0 be the initial angle:

$$w = \frac{d\theta}{dt} = w_0$$

$$\theta = \int w dt$$

$$= \int w_0 dt$$

$$= w_0 t + \theta_0$$

Surprise! The equations for rotation are the same as the equations for linear movement. The only difference is that here, the speed is circular and not linear. This makes a huge difference, which means you cannot convert from one to other that easily.

note

Just as the equations for rotations are identical to the equations for linear movement given a constant speed, so, too, are they identical given a constant acceleration.

Here, the speed and the angle's position, omega, is the angular position and angular speed. So for example, if you specify that the hammer starts at an initial angle of 0 and that it spins at a speed of 0.01 rad/sec, you could compute the equation for its angular rotation as a function of time:

$$\theta = 0.01t$$

Rotation is rather special mainly because the event is repeated through time, as illustrated in Figure 9.1. That is, as an object spins around a center, it will return to the same location after a specified time. For this reason, it can be useful to look at rotational movement in terms of period and frequency. The period p of the rotation is the duration of one full cycle, or if you prefer, it's the time the particle will take to make one full cycle around the center. On the other hand, the frequency f is the inverse of that. It tells you how many cycles you can do per unit of time. So how do both these concepts relate to the angular speed? The following equations describe it:

$$f = \frac{2\pi}{p}$$

$$w = 2\pi f$$

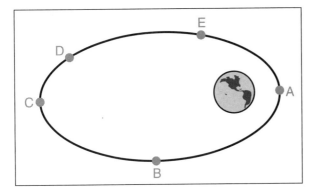

Figure 9.1
A satellite rotating around Earth

Thus, you can see that f is the inverse of p:

$$f = \frac{1}{p}$$

Velocity: Linear or Angular?

As you deal with rotations, it can be pretty useful to convert from linear velocity to angular velocity. Linear velocity is what you saw in the previous chapter, while angular velocity deals with velocity due to a rotational movement. For example, consider a car traveling down a slope. Unless your car is a vintage jalopy, it will not be dragged down the slope; instead, its wheels should roll nicely downward. Rolling is completely different from dragging because with rolling, you lose very little momentum; friction is less of a factor. If you were to model the tires spinning on this car, you would already have the car's speed, but not the speed at which the wheels are rotating. You would need that information to give the wheels the correct rotation.

To tackle this problem, look at it with the period and frequency in mind (recall that the frequency tells you how many rotations occur per unit of time). To determine the frequency with which the car's tires are rotating, start by using the equation $2\pi r$ to compute the circumference of a circle. Why? Because the car's tires are, in effect, circles. If you cut one of the tires and flatten it into a line, the line's length would be $2\pi r$. In other words, in one full tire rotation, the car will have traveled a distance of $2\pi r$.

To express all this as a function of the frequency, you need to determine how many rotations will occur in a given lapse of time. If you know the car has traveled a distance of x in a span of time dt, and that the tires have a radius of r, you can then divide the total distance x (that is, by the length of the tire) by the time to get the frequency:

$$f = \frac{x}{2\pi r dt}$$

$$= \frac{v}{2\pi r}$$

With the observation that the derivative of x over time is really the speed of the particle, you have found a relatively simple relationship between the frequency and the speed of a particle given the radii. If you plug this equation into the angular speed, you can finally convert from angular speeds to linear speeds:

$$w = 2\pi f$$

$$= \frac{2\pi v}{2\pi r}$$

$$w = \frac{v}{r}$$

Assuming the car's speed is 60 miles per hour, and that the car's tires have a radius of 0.0002367 miles (a whopping monster truck with 15-inch wheels), you get an angular speed of

$$w = \frac{60m/hr}{0.0002367m}$$

$$= 253485.4245/hr$$

$$= 4224.7570/min$$

$$= 70.4126/sec$$

That's 70 rad per second, or roughly 11 rotations per second—pretty fast indeed. Moreover, it brings up an interesting point: how does one determine the direction of velocity when the rotation is angular? To answer this, you simply need to consider the definition of velocity. In calculus, velocity is interpreted as the tangent slope of the curve at that point, and this definition applies here. In 2D, it is easy to obtain the direction, which is orthogonal to a point. In 3D, you can use the cross product to find the velocity, as illustrated in Figure 9.2:

$$\mathbf{v}(t) = \mathbf{w}(t) \times \mathbf{r}(t)$$

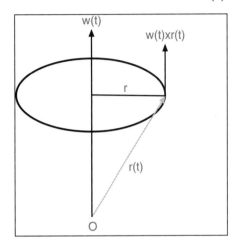

Figure 9.2
Computing the velocity of a rotational movement

In this equation, $\mathbf{v}$ is the velocity, $\mathbf{w}$ is the angular velocity, and $\mathbf{r}$ is the coordinate vector (that is, the vector that starts at the origin and goes to the point $\mathbf{r}$ on the circle). The beauty of writing this equation in this form is that it allows you to move the rotation axis around freely. Thus, if you saw someone waving a flare, you could easily determine the position of the object by integrating the aforementioned equation.

Acceleration

How hard is it to compute a rotation's acceleration? As it turns out, not that hard. You already have an equation describing the speed of the object as a function; all you need to do is to differentiate this function.

The equation is defined as the product of two functions, which should ring a bell: It's the same as with the product rule in calculus. It may not be obvious at first that the cross product also abides by this rule, but if you like, you can expand the equation the long way to see that it is really the case. This conclusion follows:

$$\mathbf{a}(t) = \mathbf{v}'(t)$$
$$= \frac{d\left(\mathbf{w}(t) \times \mathbf{r}(t)\right)}{dt}$$
$$= \mathbf{w}'(t) \times \mathbf{r}(t) + \mathbf{w}(t) \times \mathbf{r}'(t)$$
$$= \mathbf{w}'(t) \times \mathbf{r}(t) + \mathbf{w}(t) \times \left(\mathbf{w}(t) \times \mathbf{r}(t)\right)$$

Finally, if the angular velocity $\mathbf{w}(t)$ is constant, its derivative is 0. Thus, you get the following simplified equation:

$$\mathbf{a}(t) = \mathbf{w}(t) \times \big(\mathbf{w}(t) \times \mathbf{r}(t)\big)$$

A simpler form—and, if you're familiar with physics, a more familiar form—is the case where the rotation axis is perpendicular to the movement axis (this is the case in 2D, for example) and is described by the following scalar:

$$a = \frac{v^2}{r}$$

What does this mean to you? Graphically speaking, the higher-ordered function is always defined as the tangent (orthogonal) of the other function. Returning to the example of the person waving the flare, you know that the velocity is perpendicular to the rotation circle, or ellipse, or even sphere, depending on the choice of shape you made for $\mathbf{r}(t)$. The acceleration must be perpendicular to the velocity, so the only way to achieve this is to have the acceleration point toward the rotation axis. Because an acceleration is involved with a mass (the flare) at the end of the stick, there must necessarily be some forces involved. If you take such a weapon yourself and spin it around, you will quickly come to the conclusion that if you spin the thing quickly enough, it will pull your arm out, and that if you ever let it go, the object will fly at the velocity at which you have released it. Thus, the equation for the centrifugal force applied to the object is defined by the following:

$$F_c = -m\big(\mathbf{w}(t) \times \mathbf{r}(t)\big)$$

If you take Earth as another example, there is a good reason why it is not continuously pulled toward the sun by gravity. Take a close look at the direction of the centrifugal force, and you will notice that its force's sign suggests a force against the rotation axis, as shown in Figure 9.3. Thus, if you take an object, swing it around for a bit, and release it, it will probably fly away from you. The force required to keep the object in your hand as you swing it is the centripetal force, which is equal to the centrifugal force but with the opposite direction.

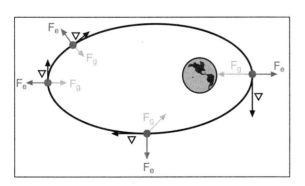

Figure 9.3
The centrifugal force applied to a satellite running around Earth

Oscillations

So you're building the next *Street Fighter* game, and you have great plans for wicked weapons. There are lightning spears, katana blades, shirukens, maces, and flails. Unfortunately, however, you're having some trouble rendering your flail. When the character holds the flail horizontally, the flail's chain, too, is horizontal. Ideally, the metal spiked ball should dangle due to gravity, but obviously, you don't want the ball to hit the floor (recall that there is a chain there to hold the ball in place). As it turns out, this case is similar to that of a pendulum.

Pendulum Motion

Suppose you want to render a pendulum composed of a weightless/frictionless string and attached to a static point. If you draw the force diagram of the pendulum such that the string is aligned with the axes as shown in Figure 9.4, you come up with a set of equations—in particular, one that can enable you to compute the linear acceleration of the mass (which really serves as a recall force such that the string ends up aligned vertically as compared with the ground):

$$T = mg \cos(\theta)$$

$$ma = -mg \sin(\theta)$$

$$0 = a + g \sin(\theta)$$

$$0 = \frac{d^2 s}{dt} + g \sin(\theta)$$

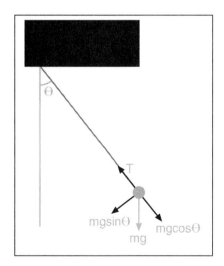

Figure 9.4
Force diagram for a simple pendulum

The first equation establishes the fact that the component of the force along the string cancels out. This makes sense, or else it would be the string is weaker or stronger than gravity, which would mean that the mass would either fall or move toward the ceiling—neither of which makes sense if the string is strong enough to support the mass. The second equation is the interesting one. It allows you to get the acceleration in the second direction. In these equations, s is defined as the arc distance that the mass will travel from its current point down until it becomes aligned vertically.

These two equations yield a linear function, which is great, except that this type of movement is frequency based. For this reason, it would be nice to have a function as a *rotational* movement. You can further reduce the equation if you note the simple fact that s can be expressed by a length via the angle, yielding the following:

$$s = L\theta$$

$$0 = L\frac{d^2\theta}{dt^2} + g\sin(\theta)$$

The only problem is that you have reached a point where the acceleration is defined by the gravity and the sine of the angle. This is an ugly equation, mainly because you define the equation with values that are dependent on lower-ordered differential values. You saw this in Chapter 8 in the section about force fields; the acceleration (from the force) was defined as a function of the distance of the object from the center. These types of equations are called ordinary differential equations (ODEs), and their goal is to find the original equation that makes this equation true.

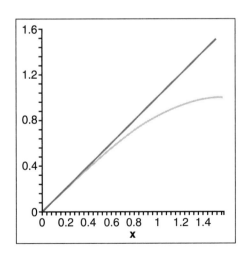

Figure 9.5
Graph of sin(x) and x

In a nutshell, you want to solve the preceding equation in order to find the angular function $\phi(t)$ (ϕ at time t, which is represented by ϕ alone above), which verifies the equation. These types of problems can be seen as more complex root-finding problems. Although this book does not cover these types of equations, it doesn't mean you can't find a solution to this specific problem in this case. Even with all the math knowledge in the world, however, there is no known analytic solution to this equation. Instead, what physicists have done is an approximation. The sine function is really the problem here, and thus it is replaced by ϕ. If you draw the graphs of these two functions, you will notice that they are fairly close to one another for small angles, as shown in Figure 9.5.

Now that you have a simple ODE, you can find the solution $\phi(t)$ for the problem, which yields the following:

$$\theta(t) = A\sin(ft + \phi)$$

with

$$f = \sqrt{\frac{g}{L}}$$

From here, you may wonder what A stands for and how you compute it. Fortunately, this is not too difficult. A is the amplitude or, if you prefer, the biggest absolute value ϕ will ever hold. ϕ, on the other hand, tells you the bias of the angle. This is also determined by the initial conditions, as will be shown shortly. Thus, if the mass of the character was initially in a horizontal position, the amplitude of the angle would be 90 degrees, or $\pi/2$ rad.

Let's follow through with an example. Consider a flail with a mass of 10 virtual masses under a gravitational acceleration of 9.81 units, and with a length of 2 virtual length units from the stick. At the last point where the character applied a force to the object, the flail was swung such that it ended up at an angle of $\pi / 4$. In this situation, the position of the mass at time t is $\pi/4$. So this is the value for the amplitude because gravity will only pull the mass downward, forming smaller angles only. As for ϕ, you need to find the value with your knowledge of the initial values. Initially, you know that at time $t = 0$, the angle is at a maximum. That said, if you plug the values $t = 0$ and $\phi(t) = A$ in the preceding equation, you will eventually come to the following conclusion:

$$A = A\sin(0 + \phi)$$
$$\sin^{-1}(1) = \phi$$
$$\phi = \frac{\pi}{2}$$

Another way to put this equation is to simply use the identity between sine and cosine, and to change the sine for a cosine while letting ϕ equal 0. The equation you eventually end up with is as follows:

$$\theta(t) = \frac{\pi\cos\left(\sqrt{\frac{9.81}{2}}\right)}{4}$$

$$= \frac{\pi\cos\left(\sqrt{\frac{9.81}{2}}t\right)}{4}$$

$$= \frac{\pi\cos(2.2147 \cdot t)}{4}$$

This type of equation can also be tremendously useful if you are planning to make a game like *Spider-Man* or the old Nintendo *Commando*, where the character swings from place to place. In this situation, the character is the mass, and the amplitude is always the angle at which the character is throwing his hooking device. In addition, ϕ is always 0 in this case, which makes things simple (relatively speaking).

n o t e

These types of functions are extremely CPU-intensive. Keep your eyes open in this book's last four chapters for tips on optimizing such operations.

t i p

In Maple, you can compute the solution to an ODE with the command dsolve(<ODE equation>, <function>);, and you can represent differentials of values by using the diff(<function>, <parameter>); function.

Springs

In game programming, there are some pretty interesting problems that can be solved using springs—with relatively simple equations, to boot. In fact, there are so many cases where springs can be used in games that whole books could be written about them. Indeed, one of the great things about springs is that you can use them to generate effects that go beyond their obvious form (that is, a metal spring). For example, you can use a string effect in the following scenarios:

- Strings
- Springy damping force
- Cloth simulation
- Jelly

In addition, you can apply various forces to springs to create some interesting effects. Before I get into the details of the various effects you can create with springs, however, let's see how you can determine the equation that gives the position of a spring with time.

First, note that the behavior of the spring depends on the distance of compression or decompression. That is, the more you compress a spring, the higher it will bounce when you release it—unless, of course, you compress it so much that it becomes deformed or is completely destroyed. Put in more scientific terms, the harder you push down on a spring, the greater the force the spring exerts on your fingers. Similarly, if you were to stretch the spring, you would notice that the more it is stretched, the harder it is to stretch it. Again, in more scientific terms, the more you stretch the spring, the greater the force that pulls the spring back to its original position becomes. (Of course, this is only partially true because the spring typically reaches a point where if it is squeezed or stretched too much, it will either break or be reduced to an open cylinder.) With this simple deduction, it should not be too hard to see that the force of restoration for the spring is a function of the squeezing/stretching distance d. Because of this, the natural resting position of the spring should not have any restoration force—or, put a different way, the force should be null. You can thus say that the force of restoration is defined as follows for a spring of constant restoration factor k:

$$F_r = kd$$

note

Depending on how you define k, you may sometimes see a negative in front of this equation.

This function is yet another ODE. If you expand it, you notice that the acceleration is given as a function of the distance:

$$ma = kd$$

This equation is slightly different from the preceding one but is still an oscillatory equation when written as a function of the spring's position.

If you compute the solution of the ODE, you get that the equation is actually the exact same at the higher level, but that the frequency and amplitude are different. The equation that defines the position of a mass attached to the end of a spring, then, is as follows:

$$x(t) = A \sin(wt + \phi)$$

$$A = \sqrt{\frac{mv_0^2}{k} + x_0^2}$$

$$w = \sqrt{\frac{k}{m}}$$

$$\phi = \sin^{-1}\left(\frac{x_0}{A}\right)$$

In this scenario, x_0 is the initial stretch (negative implies a compression) and v_0 is the initial speed. For example, suppose that Super Mario jumps on a spring and flies through the air. Given that $k = 500$ and that Mario weights 200 mass units, how much will he compress the spring by? If you draw the force diagram, you'll see that you have two forces at play: the restoration force of the spring and the force of gravity. If you sum both of them, you can isolate the acceleration:

$$\sum F_y = 0$$
$$0 = -mg + kx$$
$$x = \frac{mg}{k}$$
$$= \frac{200 \cdot 9.81}{500}$$
$$= -3.9$$

The first step is to determine how much the spring will be compressed. You know that when Mario sits on the spring, there will be a point at which the gravity he exerts equals the restoration force of the spring.

What about rebounding? Wouldn't a person being launched from a spring—say, a trampoline—end up with a higher acceleration in the opposite direction? Put another way, wouldn't that person fly higher than the height at which he or she started? Well, it depends. When a person jumps on a trampoline, he typically exerts a downward force by extending and straightening his knees during the course of the jump. If that person were to keep his knees straight, however, he would *not* go higher than the height from which he fell. What really makes the person launch upward is the simple fact that he pushes downward, which further compresses the spring. Thus, in this case, the acceleration the person gains is that of gravity plus the extra force he has exerted by bending and straightening his knees.

If you plan to use springs in your game, you could hard-code a jumping force for your characters and add that to gravity to compute the acceleration. This is not a great model, however, because it does not take speed into account. After all, as the character falls from higher buildings, he should obviously rebound higher, right? To solve such problems, you are better off using the energy model. In this case, the potential energy is simply the integral of the force, and the kinetic energy is the same as what you have seen before. In short, the equation for potential energy U and kinetic energy K is as follows:

$$U = \frac{1}{2}kx^2 = \frac{1}{2}kA^2 \sin^2\left(wt + \phi\right)$$
$$K = \frac{1}{2}mv^2 = \frac{1}{2}mw^2 A^2 \cos^2\left(wt + \phi\right)$$

If you understand the relationship between x and v (hint: v is really the derivative of x), this should be a pretty simple deduction. Now you can actually do something with this. Given the speed of Mario when $x = 0$, you can compute the total energy of the system because the potential energy is nada at that point. You can thereafter compute the maximum compression x when the speed v is 0 by using the kinetic energy's equation.

Knowing the compression, you can substitute x into the force equation in order to determine what the acceleration at that point will be. It should come as no surprise that the spring will launch Mario back to his original height. To account for the jump done by Mario, you would simply need to add an impulse, as was seen in Chapter 8. This would indeed take care of the problem. The impulse applied compresses the spring even more, which will make Mario go higher.

Strings

In Pennsylvania, where bats fly low and transform into gruesome vampires, a brave man steps in with whip at hand to defeat the vampire known as Dracula. Sound familiar? This is the setting for the well-known game series *Castlevania*. This particular game is of interest here mainly due to the whip. If you are planning to make a 3D game that involves a whip, then you'll need some way to make the whip look realistic. Enter the use of strings, which are also handy for the simulation of such objects as tails, wooden-plank bridges, and similar objects.

Of course, by virtue of the fact that you are dealing with physics, there are many models to choose from to create this effect, but the easiest one is without a doubt the string-mass model. The idea here is to create a string by modeling it with a set of masses separated by a distance x and connected together with springs, as illustrated in Figure 9.6. The model is pretty simple because it is nothing more than a set of springs connected together. The only major problem is that the computational cost of a reasonably long string will be very high. Cosine and sine functions are pretty costly, and you need to get rid of them presto.

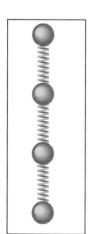

Initially, the equation for the force of restoration applied by a spring was pretty simple. The problem came when you solved the ODE and obtained a transcendental function (sine). Thankfully, there is another integration method to which you can refer: the *Euler forward differentiation method*, which is typically used in optimization. Chapter 12, "Closing the Gap for Numerical Approximation," uses a specialized version of this function to optimize polynomials without loss of accuracy, but in this situation, no polynomials are present. Instead, you have the acceleration and the distance from the spring's natural distance. The method is impressively simple, cutting everything into fixed-length steps and rewriting an equation as shown here:

$$\mathbf{x}_{n+1} = \mathbf{x}_n + \Delta t f\,'(\mathbf{x}_n)$$

Figure 9.6
String simulated with a mass-spring model

Does this equation make sense? As it turns out, it does. If you remember the section on numerical integration methods in Chapter 7, "Accelerated Vector Calculus for the Uninitiated," you recall that all the methods were pretty much based on the same principle: Compute the area under the curve by summing the area of squares whose heights were given by the function $f(\mathbf{x})$ and whose lengths were defined by the number of intervals taken. This method actually says the same thing. If you have a value x_n, the next value of interval delta t is really the current value plus the integral of the velocity function from x_n plus delta t.

Take the line illustrated in Figure 9.7. You can easily see that this equation does indeed make sense for the line. Given any point, you can add the step multiplied by the slope to get the x at the location $(x + step)$. You can also apply this logic recursively. In other words, apply the equation to the acceleration, then the speed, followed by the position. You should also be able to see that this works not only for polynomials but also for sine, cosine, and pretty much any other function. The only thing you need to be careful about is that the time step is not too large; otherwise, the equation is numerically unstable. As with the numerical-integration problems, you can end up with cases in which the approximation being performed is just too coarse. For example, if the time step is such that it makes x swing from -3 to 5, in the next step, it would likely go from 5 to a number smaller than 3. It follows, then, that the string ends up self-destructing. In reality, with a small time step, the string would oscillate.

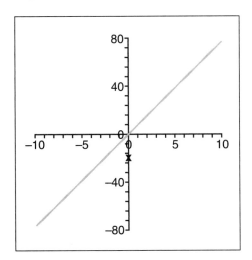

So how do you apply this technique to your equation? Simple, really; you have a basic equation, thus all you have to do is differentiate that equation using the forward Euler method. The following shows the idea:

Figure 9.7
A simple line

$$F_p = F_a + F_b$$
$$ma = k(x+y)$$
$$a = \frac{k(x+y)}{m}$$

The first step is to write the equation as a function of the acceleration, because this is the highest-ordered differential you have. In this equation, the point p is defined as the point you wish to compute. Because you only consider the force applied between the two adjacent points (a and b), you compute the force applied on p as the sum of the force coming from a and b, each with p. The next step is to compute the velocity of the mass. This is indeed the first step of the Euler forward differentiation. The following shows this:

$$v = v_0 + \Delta t \cdot v_0{}'$$
$$= v_0 + \Delta t \cdot a$$
$$= v_0 + \frac{\Delta t \cdot k}{m}(x+y)$$

Now you know the speed of the mass. The final step is yet another forward differentiation in order to compute the displacement from which the particle suffers:

$$x = x_0 + \Delta t \cdot x_0{}'$$
$$= x_0 + \Delta t \cdot v$$
$$= x_0 + \Delta t \cdot v_0 + \frac{\Delta t^2 \cdot k}{m}(x+y)$$

You have successfully converted an ugly equation with a sine into a fairly simple equation. Remember that the values for x here are not absolute values; rather, they are relative to the spring's natural position. If you want to look at them in a more ordered fashion, the values for x are really in "spring space."

There is one remaining flaw in this model: In an ideal world, where there is no friction, a spring will bounce indefinitely. Realistically, however, air in the environment will create friction against the spring, causing it to slow down. To rectify this flaw in the model, you need to introduce to it the concept of a damping force, as you will soon see. The stiffness of the whip can be simulated with a cleverer positioning of springs, as the next section proposes.

Strings can be used for your characters' hair. If you want to give more depth to the hair, you can simply consider each strand of hair as the center of a flexible cylinder, and you can thus compute the rings at various fixed-intervals. Strings are also useful for grass simulation.

Cloth

A line is akin to a string in that it involves only a single parameter (which you can call t). Likewise, a plane, which has two parameters, can be akin to a cloth, which, like a string, can be used to create some pretty interesting effects. For example, you can use cloth to simulate a character's skin; simply place the cloth on a mesh and pinpoint it such that some key areas stay in place. That way, you can make the character smile, frown, laugh, and so on merely by moving some key points of the cloth. And, because skin is rubbery in nature, the spring nature of cloth should enable you to make the face move correctly. Cloth is also great for making clothes for your characters, and for making flags.

Whereas a plane is a set of lines repeated infinitely, one next to the other, a cloth can be seen as a finite set of strings placed one beside the other, as illustrated in Figure 9.8.

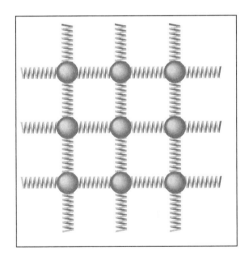

Figure 9.8
Cloth model using four neighboring springs

As you can see in Figure 9.8, the springs in a cloth are "woven"—that is, placed on both the horizontal axis and the vertical axis between the masses. If they weren't, the model would simply behave like a bunch of unattached strings. You'll need to keep this in mind as you compute the force between the springs. Specifically, you need to compute the force operating on the vertical axis and the force operating on the horizontal axis. If you understood strings correctly, then you'll see that cloth is but an extension of that. Where previously, when working with strings, you only had x and y, you now have four neighboring springs. You still need to componentize your string into the three axes x, y, and z.

If you implement this type of cloth in a game, however, you will notice that it does not fare very well. For example, if you skew a cloth, the natural distance of the springs in the cloth is not affected; it is merely skewed. The natural distance of the spring is the distance at which the spring is not compressed or stretched. Consequently, if you skew the strings in the cloth heavily, you will introduce a heavy distortion that will make the cloth seem unnatural. The solution is to introduce two new sets of springs to form an "X" between every small block of four masses, as shown in Figure 9.9.

note

In fact, a single diagonal spring would be sufficient to eliminate heavy skews, but I add two in order to program the cloth to behave symmetrically.

Figure 9.9
Cloth model using eight neighboring springs

Of course, you could improve the model by taking even more springs and particles into account. For example, you could consider the force applied to the 23 surrounding springs. This would indeed yield a more realistic model, but also a much slower model. In reality, every single spring in that model should affect the particle you are evaluating. In a game, however, you cannot afford such a high number of computations, and the simple model looks pretty good anyhow. The only remaining question is how many springs yield a good effect and what force should be applied to each of them. This is mainly a matter of trial and error because it really depends on the amount of CPU you can waste over this.

tip

To simulate facial deformation using cloths, you simply need to kill the anchor points on the skin. If a character's nose is blown away, for example, then you can simply omit the springs and anchor points related to the nose and you'll start to see everything droop downward where the nose was.

Jelly

You have seen the effects of springs on lines and planes; what about 3D objects? If you were to add one dimension, you would get a jelly-like form. Jelly models are extremely useful in games. For example, jelly models would be the way to go if you wanted to accurately model characters being squashed or thrown, suffering facial deformations, and whatnot. Jelly models are also pretty good for simulating any rubber-like objects that are thrown around.

For instance, *Hitman* used a jelly model. When the character was shot, a set of points was pushed backward and the entire set of mass followed. Because the designers did not want the overhead of having to compute the entire model as strings, they simply used a stick-man and attached various pieces of polygons around it. You can think of the stickman as the "bones" of the character upon which they added the "meat." Arguably, their model could be a better fit for cloth than jelly, but for realistic character models, jelly is the way to go if you want to simulate broken faces, shattered bones, and the like.

The idea behind creating jelly models is simple: Take the 2D cloth and extend the springs such that they fill a 3D shape. To illustrate, consider a cube of Jell-O, which has eight vertices. You need to add at least one spring for the frame of every square segment, another set of springs to account for skewing horizontally and vertically, and yet *another* set of springs to account for the depth skew. In short, to get a stable piece of Jell-O, you have to connect each of the eight vertices with the remaining seven vertices. As you deal with 3D objects that you would like to behave in a springy fashion, you must be pretty careful about the position of your springs.

When you design a jelly model, you have to think how the model will behave when you hold it from various viewpoints. As shown in the previous example, you have to add springs in the obvious joints, but because you also have to be careful about the object skewing under gravity, you have to add another set of springs in the diagonal to take care of that. Think of it as a stick model. If you were to create this pencil-based stick model, could you make it collapse by moving the pencils?

Applying Forces to Springs

Alone, a string, cloth, or glob of jelly is of limited use. To make them come to life, you must apply some forces to them—first and foremost, gravity. Doing so is simple; you simply add mg to the speed in y. It may sound weird to add a force to a speed, but this is what the Euler forward method tells us to do. The harder part is accounting for collisions between the particles and various objects that occur due to gravity.

Another force that can be interesting to work with is wind, which can be used to simulate flags as well as water. For example, if you consider the surface of a body as a cloth, you can apply wind to the cloth (water) in order to get it to move. It won't be as realistic as some hard-core fluid dynamics, but it'll do in a pinch for most games. You can use a similar strategy to simulate whirlwind effects; simply attach a bunch of leaves to invisible specific nodes and spin the cloth in a cylindrical motion (this is where cylindrical coordinate space can be useful). As long as you drag anywhere from two to four points on one edge of the cloth, the cloth will not collapse into a line, and it will instead look like a small whirlwind is making the leaves move. (This same technique can be applied to create the effect generated by an Apache helicopter near water.)

How, then, do you implement wind? First, it should be noted that the effect of wind depends on the angle at which it hits the surface. To illustrate, place a sheet of paper on your desk and blow at it from the side; notice that it moves considerably. If, on the other hand, you blow at it from directly overhead, it won't budge even if the force applied toward it is greater because the desk provides an equal force in opposite direction. Hmm. Do I smell a cosine?

Secondly, notice that the force applied to a patch is greater if the surface is greater. To illustrate, drop a piece of paper and a pen. Which would you expect to fall first? Probably the pen, because the paper will have a lot of resisted motion due to the air resistance. The problem of wind blowing on a surface is the same as that of air hitting a surface because the surface is moving.

Finally, you make a simplistic approximation as far as the force of the wind is concerned, which yields a pretty reasonable light-wind effect. This is not the best of models, but it works for something as simple as this. The idea is to move the surface along its normal vector. Note that a slanted figure is likely to receive less wind than a surface that is directly positioned into the wind (that is, perpendicular). In fact, what really matters is the projection of the surface perpendicular to the wind as illustrated in Figure 9.10.

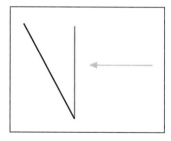

Figure 9.10
Impact of the wind on a sloped surface

Keeping track of the approximations done, as well as the observations, the following equation makes sense for this simulation:

$$F_w = \frac{\mathbf{n}}{\|\mathbf{n}\|_2}(\mathbf{n} \bullet \mathbf{w})$$

In English, the wind's force F_w equals the unit-normal vector of the cloth's surface being considered renormalized, such that its length is the projection. The dot product takes care of the angle and the normal vector takes cares of the direction. This type of wind is what would be called an *linear wind*—that is, it is basically equal across the board.

Of course, linear wind is only one type of wind. Other wind behaviors include

- Having a "wind source," such as a helicopter, that directs the wind toward a particular patch.

- Cylindrical wind, as is the case with wind whooshing through a jet engine. Within the cylinder, the wind speed is toward the bottom and equal across the board; outside the cylinder, you can establish an equation that describes the force and direction of the wind depending on the position $<x, y, z>$ of the patch.

- Spherical wind, in which the force applied to a patch is nothing but the vector created from the center of the sphere to the patch. Because the wind should decrease as you get farther from the center of the sphere, you will have to make sure that the force is inversely proportional. For instance, such an equation could do it, where $\mathbf{s}$ is the center of the sphere and $\mathbf{p}$ is the center of the patch (or triangle mesh):

$$\mathbf{w} = \frac{\mathbf{s} - \mathbf{p}}{\|\mathbf{s} - \mathbf{p}\|_2^2}$$

Damping Springs

An equation was presented in Chapter 8 to account for damping in an environment. If you recall, this was a complex exponential equation at the positional level. On the velocity level, it was determined that the damping factor was the acceleration divided by k. Why should it be any different here? (Because you already have a k here, let the damping factor be d in order to avoid confusion.) All you need to do to induce damping is to introduce a factor that spans between 1 and 0; then, simply multiply the factor by the original velocity v_0.

note

I prefer to use a multiplication instead of a division, mainly because multiplication occurs much more quickly on a PC. You can easily divide if you simply multiply by the opposite (that is, multiply by $1/x$).

The equation with the new damping factor d is thus:

$$v = v_0 \cdot d + \frac{\Delta t \cdot k}{m}(x + y)$$

$$x = x_0 + \Delta t \cdot v$$

The values you choose for d and k really depend on the type of object you wish to create. A damping value of 1 signifies that the string will move continuously, while a damping value of 0 will make the string really hard. So if, for example, you were designing a whip, you would probably choose a value that was close to but smaller than 1—say, 0.9—in order to make the whip adequately flexible, but not such that it moved constantly. The damping factor constantly decreases the speed of the object by a certain factor, which results in less chaotic behavior.

caution

If you choose a value greater than 1, the particles will *gain* energy, meaning that not only will they move continuously, they will actually *increase* in movement over time. This is obviously not the way to go because, as dictated by the law of conservation of energy, particles cannot gain energy without some other element losing energy. Besides, if you choose a value greater than 1, the particles will eventually have an infinite speed, which is not desirable.

You can also take advantage of the fact that the mass can vary at different points along the string. That way, if you were making a whip, you could set it up such that the handle would be much heavier than the tip. Then, all you would have to do to make the whip come into action would be to move one or two of the last particles according to the character's hand movement. Because of the stringy math behind all this, the entire whip should behave as a springy rubber string. Of course, this also means that the whip can collapse into two single points. To stop this, you must add more springs from, say, mass 0 to mass 2. That way, not only would mass i be tied to mass $i + 1$, it would also be tied to mass $i + 2$ and $i + 3$ and so forth until you feel that your whip feels natural enough. Of course, the factors would have to be adjusted such that the first mass doesn't affect the last mass that much because the distance is greater than the previous masses.

The equation thus far has been given only in two dimensions, but you can easily extend this concept to 3D. Simply use the preceding equation for x, y, and z, but compute each component separately. The only hitch is that x and y are really distances, which means you have to calculate the length of the distance in x, y, and z. Later on, you have to be careful to decompose the various axes. The following pseudo-code shows this:

```
Ax     = X[i - 1] - X[i];
Ay     = Y[i - 1] - Y[i];
ANorm  = sqrt(sqr(Ax) + sqr(Ay));
Ax     = Anorm - NaturalSpringLength;        // Spring's x in F = kx
```

```
Bx      = X[i + 1] — X[i];
By      = Y[i + 1] — Y[i];
BNorm   = sqrt(sqr(Bx) + sqr(By));
Bx      = Bnorm — NaturalSpringLength;          // Spring's x in F = kx

Vx      = (Ax * ax / ANorm) + (Bx * bx / BNorm);// These are only (x + y)
Vx      = (Ay * ax / ANorm) + (By * bx / BNorm);// as expressed in the equation
                                                 // V0 = vo*d + Dt*k*(x + y)/m
```

If you understand vectors correctly, this should be no problem. You can always check the source code included with this chapter if your understanding of this area is still vague, however.

Center of Mass

If you throw a hammer, you will notice that the point around which the hammer rotates is not really the center of the hammer. Because the hammer's head is much heavier than its handle, the handle seems to spin frantically around the head. Similarly, if you fill a ball with water and throw it, you will notice that the ball does not actually rotate from the center; instead, it seems to wobble in a harmonic motion while moving forward.

Initially, the way we solved a problem was by representing an object as an abstract point upon which forces were applied. Similarly, considering only a single point, we said that the object had velocities of a, accelerations of b, and so on. In reality, however, we were really only approximating the model—which, for a rotation, is not a very good one. A better model can be achieved if you study the center of mass.

The center of mass is a single point somewhere in space (it does not really have to be on the object itself) that represents a point at which you have as much mass on one side as you have on another side. (If this sounds familiar, it's because the center of mass is also the virtual point that you have been working with since Chapter 8.) In fact, if you could find the center of mass for any object with infinite precision, you could place the object on a thin nail and the object would be well balanced. If the object falls on one side or the other, it is simply because one of the two sides—specifically, the side the object is falling toward—has more mass than the other. This particular example works only in 2D, but the same goes for 3D. The center of mass in 3D is the point at which there is as much mass on any two sides of the shape if you were to split the shape in two.

The center of mass depends on the distance of the particles composing the object from the center of the object. Forcing equilibrium on the sides for two masses m_1 and m_2, at a distance of x and y, respectively, from the center of mass c, yields the following:

$$m_1(c-x) = m_2(c-y)$$

Given this simple equation, you can isolate for the center of mass to yield the following:

$$c = \frac{m_1 x + m_2 y}{m_1 + m_2}$$

More generally, if you have n objects, the center of mass is the sum of the objects' mass multiplied by their distance, the product of which is then divided by the sum of their masses. In short notation for distance x_i, the following holds:

$$c = \frac{\sum_{i=1}^{n} m_i x_i}{\sum_{i=1}^{n} m_i}$$

Returning to the hammer example, suppose your hammer consists of a head and handle, for which you know the weight and center. Specifically, the handle is centered at <0, 0> and has a mass of 1, and the head is centered at <0, 10> and has a mass of 10. To find the center of mass for this system, you would compute it as follows:

$$c_x = \frac{\langle 0,0 \rangle \cdot 1 + \langle 0,10 \rangle \cdot 10}{1+10}$$

$$= \left\langle 0, \frac{10}{11} \right\rangle$$

Notice how the formula is applied to both the x and the y component. This is because if you cut the object in two along the x, y, or any other component, the center of mass property still holds. To solve the problem, you need two equations to solve for two unknowns. You could really cut the object in two any way you wish along any axis, but because x and y are simple and natural, that is how it is done. This would work great with a jelly model.

Oddly enough, this is still an approximation of the center of mass. To be physically correct, you should compute this is to obtain the density of the material you are using and sum small cubes of mass multiplied by their density. In short, it's an integral of the position of the object from the center multiplied by the density:

$$c = \frac{1}{\int 1} \int \mathbf{x} \cdot dm$$

In layman's terms, the value is the infinite sum of the distance multiplied by the density, the product of which is then divided by the total mass represented by the integral of 1 over the entire region. For example, take a simple disc. You already know from simple logic and symmetry that the center of the circle is the center of mass, but just to make this clear in terms of integrals, the following example shows how this is obtained:

$$
c_x = \frac{\displaystyle\int_{-10}^{10}\int_{-\sqrt{10^2-y^2}}^{\sqrt{10^2-y^2}} p(x,y)\cdot x\cdot dx\cdot dy}{\displaystyle\int_{-10}^{10}\int_{-\sqrt{10^2-y^2}}^{\sqrt{10^2-y^2}} p(x,y)\cdot dx\cdot dy}
$$

$$
= \frac{\dfrac{p}{2}\displaystyle\int_{-10}^{10} x^2 \Big]_{-\sqrt{10^2-y^2}}^{\sqrt{10^2-y^2}}}{p\displaystyle\int_{-10}^{10} 2\sqrt{10^2-y^2}}
$$

$$
= \frac{\displaystyle\int_{-10}^{10}\left(10^2-y^2\right)-\left(10^2-y^2\right)}{2\cdots}
$$

$$
= 0
$$

You integrate in Cartesian coordinates. The major integration variable is y and you first integrate from $y = -10..10$, followed by an integration in x, which is the boundary of the circle in x. The function you integrate is the distance in x multiplied by the density function. In this case, you assume that the disc has a uniform density; thus, $p(x, y)$ is really constant and can be pulled out of the integral. At the bottom, you compute the total density of the disc by computing the integral of the density. Again, because the density is constant, this is the same thing as computing the area of the disc and then multiplying it by the density, thus the constant is pulled outside of the integral. The integration process goes on until you reach a point where the integral is 0 at the top, and consequently, the entire solution is 0.

Angular Forces

Previously, you saw how a force was linked to the translation of an object. Implicitly, the force was applied to the center of the mass of the object. To illustrate, imagine you've placed a book standing up; push the center of the book, and you will notice that it moves away from you. In contrast, take the same book and push it on its edge; you will notice that the book rotates around. This is in fact the link that binds the force and a new concept called torque. In this case, due to friction, the book rotates from the other side when you push it on one side, but in a frictionless world, it would rotate from its centroid.

If you apply a force outside of the center of mass to an object that has a fixed rotation axis, you generate torque. In short, torque is the analog of the force for rotations. In the book example, the book is not fixed along an axis such that it can rotate, but the force of friction partially simulates this effect. Similarly, if you drive your car into another car from the side and on its bumper, you will probably notice that the car is not simply plowed away from you. Instead, the car is likely to whirl around in circles while moving away from you. This is all due to torque.

The derivation of this formula is longwinded, so I'll get right to the point. The equation of the torque is given by the following:

$$\tau = I\dot{\alpha}$$

$$= \left(\sum_{i=1}^{n} m_i r_i^2 \right)\alpha$$

$$= \left(\int r^2 \cdot dm \right)\alpha$$

This is the equation that is akin to the force. I is the inertia tensor, and is given by an equation that resembles that of the center of mass, but that squares the distance instead for n connected elements. As you can see, there is a net relationship between the mass and the acceleration. Noteworthy is the fact that there is also a relationship between the distances from the axes of rotation given by r.

Obviously, this formula is very close to the center of mass; if you think about the problem for a second, it should become evident that the center of mass has something to do with it. The equation for the force supposes that you apply everything from the center of mass. This equation, on the other hand, supposes that the object cannot move and that the force that is applied is used completely for rotational purposes. Thus, the center of mass plays a big part because if you push an area where there is a lot of mass, you will need a greater force to move it.

The second part of the equation, which defines the torque, is given by the actual linear force **F** applied as a function of the distance **r** from the origin of the rotation:

$$t = \mathbf{r} \times \mathbf{F}$$

One thing you should quickly notice—primarily because it is defined as a cross product— is that the torque will actually be a vector oriented toward the axis of rotation. Its strength (or magnitude) depends on the force (that is, the greater the force, the greater the torque) and the distance, which is also greater as the distance increases. To verify this, consider a wrench. If you use a wrench to try to spin a nut into place, it will be much easier if you apply the force at the handle instead of closer to the nut. In fact, that's why you need a wrench in the first place; otherwise, you could simply use your fingers to do the job.

As a final exercise for this chapter, suppose you have a cylinder that is attached horizontally to a wall at one end, and Spider-Man is hanging on the very edge of that bar. Because he eats a lot between his movies, the bar breaks. Obviously, Spider-Man will fall downward, shoot a web, and survive, but the bar, which is released right after it breaks, will spin sporadically down the building. Compute the initial angular acceleration due to gravity for the bar.

The first thing you want to do is compute the inertia of the cylinder. This is easier said than done if you choose L as the length of the bar, m as the mass, and r as the radii:

$$dI = r^2 dm$$
$$= x^2 \left(\lambda dx \right)$$

$$\int_0^L dI = I$$

$$= \int_0^L x^2 \cdot \lambda \cdot dm$$

$$= \frac{\lambda \cdot x^3}{3} \Bigg]_0^L$$

$$= \frac{\lambda \cdot L^3}{3}$$

$$= \frac{m \cdot L^2}{3}$$

To solve the problem of finding the value for dm, you draw the bar as illustrated in Figure 9.11. dm is the amount of mass contained for a given distance, so if you multiply dx by the density lambda, you get dm. r is only replaced by x because x simply represents the distance from the rotation point. The rest is mere algebra. As long as you keep in mind that the total mass of the object is really the length of the bar times the density, you can simplify the equation at the very end.

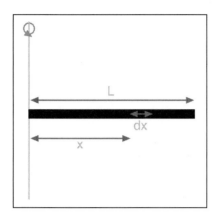

Figure 9.11
Computing the inertia on a bar

Now you have the inertia; you need to compute the angular acceleration with M as Spider-Man's mass. The following does exactly that:

$$\tau = I\alpha = \mathbf{r} \times \mathbf{p}$$

$$\alpha = \frac{\mathbf{r} \times \mathbf{p}}{I}$$

$$= \frac{1}{2} \frac{\langle L,0,0\rangle \times \langle 0,-mg,0\rangle}{\frac{m \cdot L^2}{3}}$$

$$= \frac{3\langle 0,0,-Lmg\rangle}{2m \cdot L^2}$$

$$= \left\langle 0,0,\frac{-3g}{L}\right\rangle$$

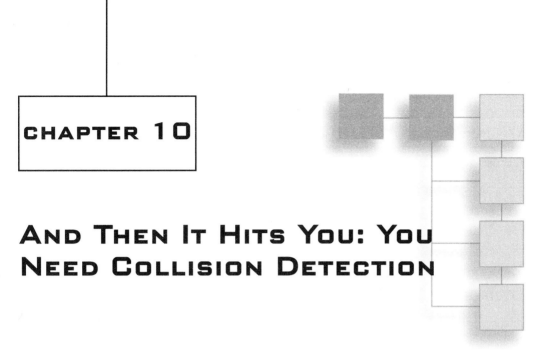

CHAPTER 10

AND THEN IT HITS YOU: YOU NEED COLLISION DETECTION

Very often, you believe that you've found the solution to a problem, only to realize that you forgot about something that makes it only a *partial* solution. Or sometimes, the solution you've found simply isn't a solution at all. I've done this a lot. Sometimes, you're so sure about the solution that you start to implement it, only to realize that you've merely changed the problem into yet another problem. Especially in graphics, you may often think that you have a perfect solution, when what you really have is something more of an approximation with ugly cases just waiting to surface.

At the very least, you're seeking solutions by yourself and not always referring to sites such as http://www.mathworld.com or textbooks. This shows that you have a good head on your shoulders and can think independently.

In Chapter 4, "Basic Geometric Elements," you learned the various definitions of some basic geometrical elements. You even learned how to find the existence of a collision between two elements, as well as a method to compute the precise location for the collision. But is all this really true? Did you really compute the precise location of the collision, or did you miss something there?

You have to keep in mind that the world is generally dynamic. Many things in the world tend to move, and this is where Chapter 4 is of little help. It dealt mainly with a static world and didn't take into account an object's movement through time. Unfortunately, if you shoot a rocket into space and merely check the collision of the rocket against sampled frames through time, you could miss some potential collisions.

For example, suppose that you shoot a rocket at a wall, and for some reason the frame rate drops such that the rocket moves from one side of the wall to the other in one frame, without actually touching the wall itself in either frame. Clearly, if you look at it from a physical standpoint, the rocket should have hit the wall and exploded at that point. But because you merely checked key frames, you didn't pick this up.

Clearly, this is an issue. In fact, it affects even the simplest cases of dynamic collision detection. In the more complex cases, both objects end up moving, and you must verify the collision between the two moving objects. That's where this chapter comes in handy. Whether you want to introduce time as a variable in your collision is entirely your choice. Again, it all comes back to creating a better model versus speed. All in all, the topics for this chapter are the following:

- Environmental collisions
- Collisions of objects among themselves
- Picking

Environmental Collisions

Let's start by taking it easy and looking at a problem where only one object moves and the other object is a plane. For practical reasons, typically it's easier to divide your world into a set of planes (as you'll see in Chapter 15, "Visibility Determination: The World of the Invisible"). For this reason, in this section you'll only see collisions between planes and other objects.

When it's time to move an object, mathematically the object may be moving in pretty complex ways! For instance, gravity may make the object move in a quadratic fashion (that is, second degree polynomial curve). As another example, a cloth's particles may move in a very complex way, as described by an ODE. In this case, the motion is extremely hard to analyze, and collision detection can quickly go haywire. Instead, a more practical approach must be used.

Rather than considering the "true trajectory" of an object, you can simply approximate its movement by looking at the linear trajectory of the object performed between frames. In other words, you approximate the movement of the object from frame $n - 1$ to frame n with a straight line, as shown in Figure 10.1. This simplifies things greatly, because every movement is treated as a straight line. A line is also a fairly easy geometry to work with and shouldn't complicate the equations too much. In some cases, even a simple linear movement can be quite a pain to deal with, compared to a case where nothing moves.

Let's look at our first case: sphere-plane collision through time. If you're looking for the plane-line collision test, see Chapter 4, which describes a triangle-line segment collision. This is in fact a more precise test, because it also verifies whether the collision is within the area of the triangle.

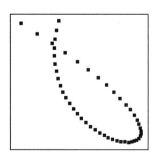

Figure 10.1
The approximate trajectory of an object through time

Sphere-Plane Collision

In Chapter 4, you saw a static version of this scenario. You learned how to compute the distance between a point in space and a plane. Specifically, the equation for the distance d between a plane $<\mathbf{n}, D>$ and a point $\mathbf{p}$ was

$$d = D + \mathbf{n} \bullet \mathbf{p}$$

Now you have to add the factor of time to that equation. Since you're dealing with a sphere, the distance between the sphere and the plane is $d - r$, where r is the radii of the sphere. This is illustrated in Figure 10.2. Thus, this is the equivalent of offsetting the plane by $-r$. Therefore, you can look at the problem not as a moving sphere, but as a moving point in space. The equation for a point moving along a line is

$$\mathbf{p}(t) = \mathbf{p}_0 + t(\mathbf{p}_0 - \mathbf{p}_1)$$

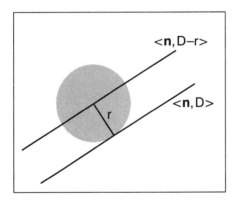

If you combine both equations (that is, the position of the point through time, $t = [0, 1]$) and the formula for the distance between the plane and the point, you get the equation for the distance between the point and the plane over time:

Figure 10.2
Plane-sphere collision

$$d = D + \mathbf{n} \bullet (\mathbf{p}_0 + t(\mathbf{p}_0 - \mathbf{p}_1))$$

A collision occurs with the plane if and only if the distance from the plane and the point is 0. Thus, you get the following:

$$-D - \mathbf{n} \bullet \mathbf{p}_1 = t \cdot \mathbf{n} \bullet (\mathbf{p}_0 - \mathbf{p}_1)$$

$$t = \frac{-D - \mathbf{n} \bullet \mathbf{p}_1}{\mathbf{n} \bullet (\mathbf{p}_0 - \mathbf{p}_1)}$$

Finally, expressing the equation such that it accounts for the radii of the sphere, $D' = (D - r)$, you have this:

$$t = \frac{r - D - \mathbf{n} \bullet \mathbf{p}_1}{\mathbf{n} \bullet (\mathbf{p}_0 - \mathbf{p}_1)}$$

Box-Plane Collision

In the last section, the approach was relatively simple. You took the equation describing the minimal distance between a point and a plane, and you simply made sure that the radius of the object was smaller than the distance available between the point and the plane.

What about when you're dealing with a box? It isn't realistic to think of a box with a radius... or is it? If you were to use the infinity norm on the box, you could indeed detect collisions between the box and an object. The only problem is that this doesn't permit the box to have any rotation at all, so it's not tremendously useful.

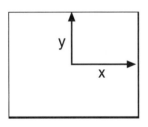

Figure 10.3
Box in 2D, described with two vector offsets, **x** and **y**

Instead, you can consider the box as a set of three planes, each coupled with its twin mirrored upon the center point of the box, as shown in Figure 10.3. Of course, this is applied to the z-axis also. Thus, the vectors **x**, **y**, and **z** shown in Figure 10.2 really represent the offset of the box from the center, and therefore give it its dimension. Notice that the offset doesn't need to be axis-aligned, so this notation can represent a box that isn't axis-aligned.

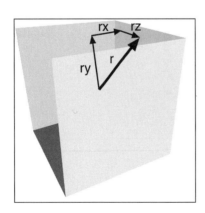

Figure 10.4
The effective radius of a box

How does that possibly help? The trick you'll use to attack this problem is the same used for the sphere. You'll end up computing the radius of the box. This may sound like a rather silly statement, but the radius isn't really what you would expect. It isn't the radius of a sphere, but rather the length of the box from its center to the plane. To make a distinction between this radius and that of a sphere, you'll call this one the *effective radius*. If you can successfully compute an effective radius for a box, you can then apply the same technique you've seen with a sphere, and at that point it all becomes mere algebraic details. Figure 10.4 shows the idea behind this.

One thing should be clear at this point: The vector of the effective radius, as illustrated in Figure 10.4, should have the same direction as the normal vector of the plane. In fact, you can look at this vector as the minimal distance vector between the plane and the box. Thus, it has to be perpendicular to the plane, and its tail must be set at the center of the box. What you need at this point is the length of this very vector. A tricky thing to compute, you think? Not really, if you understand how vectors work.

It all comes down to the dot product. Let's start by looking at the problem in 2D. It's always easier to visualize a problem in lower dimensions before tackling the higher end. You could compute the effective radius of a 2D box the hard way, by finding where the line cast from the center of the box outward intersects with the four faces. But that involves a hefty amount of computation, not to mention the complexity it adds.

Alternatively, you can solve this using the dot product. Take the two vectors that describe the box, x and y. If you look at the projection of x upon n, the effective radius's vector (and also the plane's normal vector), you get the distance of x along n. Typically, this doesn't cover the entire effective radius. The remaining portion is yet another projection on n, but by using the vector y, as shown in Figure 10.5. If you sum both of these lengths, what you get is the total length of the effective radius. In 3D, the concept is merely extended. If an additional dimension exists, it's merely a matter of dealing with an additional projection for the z vector on n.

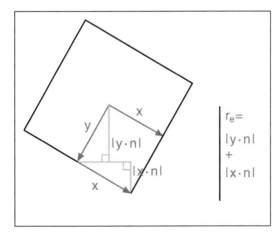

Figure 10.5
Computing the effective radius of a 2D box via added unsigned projections

Last but not least, you must recall that a projection is signed. In other words, it depends on the direction you're going. Thus, the distance could be positive, but it could also be negative. For instance, the normal vector n might be projected against one of the vectors, yet the length shouldn't change if you simply mirror the direction.

To fix this, you merely have to introduce an absolute value to the projected length, to make sure that the lengths are treated without regard to whether they're going toward or against the box's vectors, x, y, and z. This yields the following equation for the effective radius r_e:

$$r_e = |\mathbf{x} \bullet \mathbf{n}| + |\mathbf{y} \bullet \mathbf{n}| + |\mathbf{z} \bullet \mathbf{n}|$$

The equation to compute the time at which the intersection occurs is no different from the sphere's equation, provided that the radius is modified to reflect the changes. This is as proposed here for a plane $<\mathbf{n}, D>$ and a movement ranging from $\mathbf{p}_0$ to $\mathbf{p}_1$:

$$t = \frac{r_e - D - \mathbf{n} \bullet \mathbf{p}_0}{\mathbf{n} \bullet (\mathbf{p}_1 - \mathbf{p}_0)}$$

Clearly, computing the time of the collision isn't very complicated. What about computing the *position* of the collision? For a sphere, this is merely a matter of normalizing the normal vector such that its length fits the radius of the sphere. But here, it's a bit more complicated due to the uneven geometry of the object. The most common case is when none of the dot products are 0. Observe that the only way you could get a dot product between $\mathbf{n}$ and one of the box's defining vectors, $\{\mathbf{x}, \mathbf{y}, \mathbf{z}\}$, to be 0 is if the vector is perpendicular to $\mathbf{n}$. If none of the vectors are perpendicular to $\mathbf{n}$, the box will hit the plane via one of its corner vertices. All eight corners of the box, $\mathbf{w}$, are given by this equation:

$$\mathbf{w} = \mathbf{p}(t) \pm \mathbf{x} \pm \mathbf{y} \pm \mathbf{z}$$

The vertices that will collide with the plane are those whose distance from the plane is equal to or smaller than the distance between the plane and the other vertices. In other words, the vertices that collide with the plane are those that are the closest to the plane. Minimizing the distance implies that you need to minimize the dot product:

$$\mathbf{w} \bullet \mathbf{n} = (\mathbf{p}(t) \pm \mathbf{x} \pm \mathbf{y} \pm \mathbf{z}) \bullet \mathbf{n}$$
$$= (\mathbf{p}(t) \bullet \mathbf{n}) \pm (\mathbf{x} \bullet \mathbf{n}) \pm (\mathbf{y} \bullet \mathbf{n}) \pm (\mathbf{z} \bullet \mathbf{n})$$

The first term is a constant, because t is already determined and thus cannot be minimized. On the other hand, you can minimize the remaining terms. Quite clearly, the terms are minimized when the entire term, $\pm \mathbf{a} \bullet \mathbf{n}$, is minimized. This only happens when every one of these terms is negative. Thus, all you need to do is choose the sign such that the smallest value results from it. Given this, the corner, $\mathbf{c}$, that will intersect with the plane is given by

$$\mathbf{c} = \mathbf{p}(t) + \text{sgn}(\mathbf{x} \bullet \mathbf{n})\mathbf{x} + \text{sgn}(\mathbf{y} \bullet \mathbf{n})\mathbf{y} + \text{sgn}(\mathbf{z} \bullet \mathbf{n})\mathbf{z}$$

$$\text{sgn}(i) = \begin{cases} -1 & i > 0 \\ 1 & i < 0 \end{cases}$$

Observe how the equation isn't actually defined for a dot product of 0. When the dot product is 0, the box collides with the plane with more than one vertex. Specifically, if one and only one dot product is 0, an edge of the box collides with the plane. You may find the two corners of this edge by allowing the chosen vertex to be one of positive or negative. In other words, the sign function, sgn, changes to the following:

$$\text{sgn}(i) = \begin{cases} -1 & i > 0 \\ 1 & i < 0 \\ \pm 1 & i = 0 \end{cases}$$

Notice how this mathematical definition also works when one of the box's surfaces collides with the plane. In this case, two dot products will be nullified, and both signs can be taken freely to yield the set of vertices that form the ones to collide with the plane. The only way you could possibly get three null dot products is if the box was a degenerate case. If you think about this problem geometrically, you can see that no more than four of the eight vertices of a box can collide with a plane, given any angle for the box and plane.

Collisions of Objects Among Themselves

All of this can get much more tricky and CPU-intensive in a hurry when you keep track of time. This is why many games tend to minimize interobject collision detection. Most of the time you can do without it, such as with sparks in a particle system. On the other hand, you probably want to have this detection if you have two animated characters, unless you're making a ghost game.

Similarly to the object-plane collision model for the environment, you'll only approximate the movement of the objects. This is done by looking at the movement they've performed between the previous frame and the current frame. This is a linear movement from one point to the other, which is easier to handle.

Now that you've seen some equations in the previous section, you can probably appreciate this approximation even more. If you were to introduce a second-degree polynomial, you would need a quadratic solver instead of a linear solver. Clearly, you don't want to put your hands in that type of dirty water.

Sphere-Sphere Collision

Ah... as usual, the sphere comes in first. It is indeed the easiest object to work with, so it's a pretty good candidate for an analysis of collision detection between two objects through time. The very first point is pretty simple. Let's keep track of the positions of the spheres through time. Define the following two equations, $\mathbf{u}$, $\mathbf{v}$, which define the movement of each sphere through time, t:

$$\mathbf{u}(t) = \mathbf{u}_1 + (\mathbf{u}_0 - \mathbf{u}_1)t$$
$$\mathbf{v}(t) = \mathbf{v}_1 + (\mathbf{v}_0 - \mathbf{v}_1)t$$

You can also easily define the distance, d, between these two spheres through time:

$$d = \left\| \mathbf{u}(t) - \mathbf{v}(t) \right\|_2$$
$$= \left\| \mathbf{u}_1 + (\mathbf{u}_0 - \mathbf{u}_1)t - \mathbf{v}_1 + (\mathbf{v}_0 - \mathbf{v}_1)t \right\|_2$$
$$= \left\| (\mathbf{u}_1 - \mathbf{v}_1) + (\mathbf{u}_0 - \mathbf{u}_1 + \mathbf{v}_0 - \mathbf{v}_1)t \right\|_2$$

There's a messy square root hidden in this equation, but you can get rid of it if you simply compute the square of the distance. When comparing distances, it's often an intelligent move to compare the square of the distance. This doesn't affect the actual comparison. In other words, the numerical order set forth by the initial equation is preserved. Fortunately, this simplifies your job decently.

To simplify things a little more here, allow me to define two extra variables:

$$\mathbf{a} = (\mathbf{u}_1 - \mathbf{v}_1)$$
$$\mathbf{b} = (\mathbf{u}_0 - \mathbf{u}_1 + \mathbf{v}_0 - \mathbf{v}_1)$$

$$d^2 = \left\| \mathbf{a} + \mathbf{b}t \right\|_2^2$$
$$= \mathbf{a} \bullet \mathbf{a} + 2\mathbf{a} \bullet \mathbf{b}t + \mathbf{b} \bullet \mathbf{b}t^2$$

One of the first things you may want to do is compute the existence of the collision. If there's no collision at all, there's no point in computing one. This is easy to do with your knowledge of calculus. You merely need to compute the derivative and set the distance's speed to 0. This has the following consequences:

$$d^2 = \mathbf{a} \bullet \mathbf{a} + 2\mathbf{a} \bullet \mathbf{b}t + \mathbf{b} \bullet \mathbf{b}t^2$$
$$d^2{}' = 2\mathbf{a} \bullet \mathbf{b} + 2\mathbf{b} \bullet \mathbf{b}t$$
$$0 = 2\mathbf{a} \bullet \mathbf{b} + 2\mathbf{b} \bullet \mathbf{b}t$$
$$t = -\frac{\mathbf{a} \bullet \mathbf{b}}{\mathbf{b} \bullet \mathbf{b}}$$

Now it's merely a matter of plugging t back into the equation:

$$d^2 = \mathbf{a} \bullet \mathbf{a} + 2(\mathbf{a} \bullet \mathbf{b})\left(-\frac{\mathbf{a} \bullet \mathbf{b}}{\mathbf{b} \bullet \mathbf{b}}\right) + (\mathbf{b} \bullet \mathbf{b})\left(-\frac{\mathbf{a} \bullet \mathbf{b}}{\mathbf{b} \bullet \mathbf{b}}\right)^2$$

$$= \mathbf{a} \bullet \mathbf{a} - \frac{2(\mathbf{a} \bullet \mathbf{b})^2}{\mathbf{b} \bullet \mathbf{b}} + \frac{(\mathbf{a} \bullet \mathbf{b})^2}{\mathbf{b} \bullet \mathbf{b}}$$

$$= \mathbf{a} \bullet \mathbf{a} - \frac{(\mathbf{a} \bullet \mathbf{b})^2}{\mathbf{b} \bullet \mathbf{b}}$$

But golly, you've computed this equation before, haven't you? That's right, in Chapter 4 you learned how to compute the minimal distance between two lines. This is the same equation, except that it's squared. The advantage of this equation is that the comparison is faster, because you don't have to compute the square root required by the normalization of the function. The other extremely important aspect is that this equation only works for infinite lines. In this case, you're dealing with a line that spans a given range.

It's important to note that the time computed in the preceding equation isn't the time at which the two spheres intersect. It's only the time at which the distance between the two lines is minimal. If the spheres total a radius that's equal to the minimal distance, the time will match, but this is rarely the case. Thus, you need to compute the time at which the spheres collide, now that you know that they may intersect.

Now that you actually know that such a collision can occur if time goes to infinity, the quadratic equation comes to the rescue to solve this problem. Isolating for *t* yields

$$t = \frac{-2\mathbf{a} \bullet \mathbf{b} \pm \sqrt{(2\mathbf{a} \bullet \mathbf{b})^2 - 4(\mathbf{b} \bullet \mathbf{b})(\mathbf{a} \bullet \mathbf{a} - d^2)}}{2(\mathbf{b} \bullet \mathbf{b})}$$

$$= \frac{-2\mathbf{a} \bullet \mathbf{b} \pm 2\sqrt{(\mathbf{a} \bullet \mathbf{b})^2 - (\mathbf{b} \bullet \mathbf{b})(\mathbf{a} \bullet \mathbf{a} - d^2)}}{2(\mathbf{b} \bullet \mathbf{b})}$$

$$= \frac{-\mathbf{a} \bullet \mathbf{b} \pm \sqrt{(\mathbf{a} \bullet \mathbf{b})^2 - (\mathbf{b} \bullet \mathbf{b})(\mathbf{a} \bullet \mathbf{a} - d^2)}}{(\mathbf{b} \bullet \mathbf{b})}$$

At this point, you have two possible values. Geometrically, this is also true. If an intersection exists, there will be two points at which the two spheres will have an equal distance. You're particularly interested in the first collision. You don't really care about the second one, since the first collision should make things rebound in some way, and thus the second collision (which isn't really a collision as much as an intersection) will never really happen. Thus, the smallest value from the preceding equation appears if you choose the negative square root.

The last thing you need to take note of is that d is the distance between the centers of the spheres. Thus, you need to make sure that the centers of the spheres are the sum of both radii, r_1, and r_2, as illustrated in Figure 10.6.

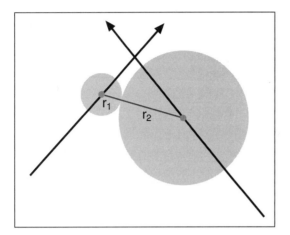

Figure 10.6
The intersection of two moving spheres

Consequently, the time of the collision is given by

$$t = \frac{-\mathbf{a}\bullet\mathbf{b} \pm \sqrt{(\mathbf{a}\bullet\mathbf{b})^2 - (\mathbf{b}\bullet\mathbf{b})\left(\mathbf{a}\bullet\mathbf{a} - (r_1 + r_2)^2\right)}}{\mathbf{b}\bullet\mathbf{b}}$$

Recall that the only valid time, by the definition of the sphere's movement, is $t = [0, 1]$. If the time is outside of this range, a collision doesn't occur, either because the event was in the past ($t < 0$) or has yet to come ($t > 1$). Alternatively, you could clip the value of t when you first do the test, to verify if the collision exists at all. If you clip the value of t at that point and compute the distance using t, you'll compute the minimal distance between the two lines for $t = [0, 1]$. Thus, you can filter the case where there are no intersections at all. And of course, you only need to compute the time of collision between the two spheres when you know that there's such a collision within your time frame.

Last but not least, you may be interested in finding the collision point. This could be useful for making the spheres rebound in opposite directions, for adding a decal, or for deformation purposes. This is pretty simple, if you take another quick look at Figure 10.6. Notice that this is the vector that describes the distance between the two spheres at time t. Consequently, if you want to find the intersection of the second sphere on the first sphere, you merely need to make sure that the length of the vector matches the length of the first sphere and idem for the second sphere. Thus, here's the equation that yields the position of the intersection $\{\mathbf{p_u} = \mathbf{p_v}\}$, relative to the origin of the world:

$$\mathbf{p_u} = \mathbf{u}(t) + r_u \frac{\mathbf{v}(t) - \mathbf{u}(t)}{\left\| \mathbf{u}(t) - \mathbf{v}(t) \right\|_2}$$

$$\mathbf{p_v} = \mathbf{v}(t) + r_v \frac{\mathbf{u}(t) - \mathbf{v}(t)}{\left\| \mathbf{u}(t) - \mathbf{v}(t) \right\|_2}$$

Sphere-Box Collision

This is all getting too easy for you, isn't it? There's a clear pattern throughout these solutions. This is where that trend ends, unfortunately. The first solution that comes to mind when you're computing a sphere-box collision is probably similar to the previous solutions: Compute the radius of the box and that of the sphere, and work the math as before. This doesn't work, though, because the collision isn't guaranteed to be along the vector between the two objects' centers. This is shown in Figure 10.7.

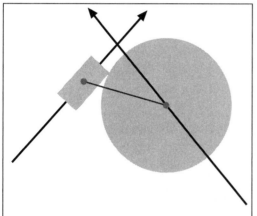

Obviously, this problem will require a little more thought. As a quick and dirty test, you could start by verifying that the sphere and a sphere encompassing the box do indeed intersect. This will significantly reduce the amount of computation you'll have to do. Finding the radius, r, of a sphere that can contain a box defined by the three offset vectors, $\mathbf{x}$, $\mathbf{y}$, and $\mathbf{z}$, merely requires an application of Pythagorea's theorem:

Figure 10.7
The intersection of a sphere and a box

$$r = \left\| \mathbf{x} + \mathbf{y} + \mathbf{z} \right\|_2$$

This partially solves your problem, but it doesn't really give you the answer you're looking for. Unfortunately, there's no elegant solution to this problem. The first trick you should employ is to change referential. When you computed the previous cases, you computed everything in world space. Nothing stops you from computing all of this in another space. This changes nothing for the existence of the collision. When it's time to compute the actual collision, you'll have to apply the inverse of that transformation in order to retrieve the correct collision point.

Of particular interest here is the box's referential. The box is really what causes the problems, because its orientation changes everything. The sphere isn't affected by the orientation. If you have two moving objects, each on a straight line, you can downgrade the problem to just one moving object if you consider the other object to be the referential, as illustrated in Figure 10.8. You merely need to subtract one object's movement vector from the other vector.

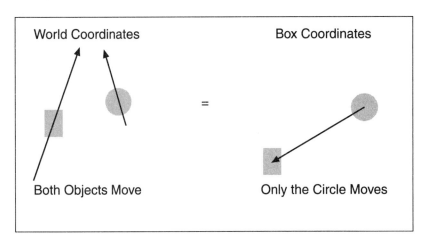

Figure 10.8
Changing the referential of the coordinates from world space to box space

An unaligned box is also painful to deal with, because you have to keep track of every axis. On the other hand, if the box is axis-aligned, its planes become equations of the form $x = a$, $y = b$, $z = c$, where a, b, and c are constants. Tests are easy to perform on these planes because you only need to worry about one axis. For instance, for any point $\mathbf{p}$, $\mathbf{p} - <a, 0, 0>$ would give you the distance between the point $\mathbf{p}$ and the plane $x = a$. Clearly, this is an attractive option. So how do you perform this rotation?

By definition, your box should be orthogonal. This implies that the vectors $\mathbf{x}$, $\mathbf{y}$, $\mathbf{z}$ that describe the box form a basis in 3D. If you think of the three vectors as the axes in the 3D world, you can redefine the basis of the Cartesian coordinate system such that every vector in this new coordinate system is a linear combination of the new basis. In short, you can treat the vectors $\mathbf{x}$, $\mathbf{y}$, and $\mathbf{z}$ as the new set of axes in the new space.

The last requirement for a rotation is that the transformation must be normal. Thus, you need to normalize every one of your vectors. Then you can generate the rotation matrix that takes any vector in Cartesian coordinate space and converts it to box-rotational coordinate space, as illustrated in Figure 10.9.

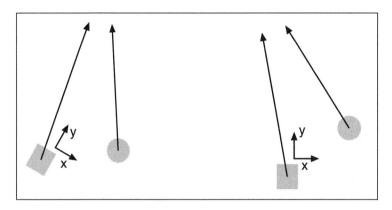

Figure 10.9
Rotating the world such that the box is axis-aligned

The matrix that achieves this is trivially computed as follows (assuming that $\mathbf{x}$, $\mathbf{y}$, and $\mathbf{z}$ are normalized):

$$\begin{bmatrix} \mathbf{x} \\ \mathbf{y} \\ \mathbf{z} \end{bmatrix} = \begin{bmatrix} x_x & x_y & x_z \\ y_x & y_y & y_z \\ z_x & z_y & z_z \end{bmatrix}$$

Last but not least, it may be easier to work with the box if it's centered about the origin. Thus, you should first apply a translation such that the box is the center of the universe, followed by a rotation such that the box is axis-aligned. Computing the composed matrix yields

$$\mathbf{M} = \begin{bmatrix} x_x & x_y & x_z & -\mathbf{x} \bullet \mathbf{p} \\ y_x & y_y & y_z & -\mathbf{y} \bullet \mathbf{p} \\ z_x & z_y & z_z & -\mathbf{z} \bullet \mathbf{p} \\ 0 & 0 & 0 & 1 \end{bmatrix}$$

Now you can test that the box's planes, $\{\mathbf{x}, \mathbf{y}, \mathbf{z}\}$, map to the basis, $\{<1, 0, 0>, <0, 1, 0>, <0, 0, 1>\}$, and that the center point of the box, $\mathbf{p}$, maps to the origin.

It would be much simpler if you could keep the box in its static position while only the sphere moved. To achieve this, you simply need to look at the equation for the movements of each object, $\mathbf{u}(t)$, $\mathbf{v}(t)$. If you subtract $\mathbf{u}(t)$, which is defined as the box's movement equation, from each of the other movement equations, you obtain the following:

$$\mathbf{u}'(t) = \mathbf{u}(t) - \mathbf{u}(t) = 0$$

$$\mathbf{v}'(t) = \mathbf{v}(t) - \mathbf{u}(t) = (\mathbf{v} - \mathbf{u})(t)$$
$$= \mathbf{v}_1 - \mathbf{u}_1 + (\mathbf{v}_0 - \mathbf{v}_1 - \mathbf{u}_0 + \mathbf{u}_1)t$$

You can do this because you are only interested in the distance between these two objects, and subtracting the same value for each object doesn't alter this distance. This is the same thing that would happen to two points in space. If you take two points in space and move them an equal amount in the same direction, the distance between the two points doesn't change. The same idea is applied here, except you subtract functions instead of subtracting a constant. In fact, you can verify that the transformation matrix doesn't alter distances by computing the determinant of the matrix (that is, the signed area of the axes), which will be equal to 1 by the very construction of the matrix.

Every object you'll work with in this new coordinate space must be transformed. Thus, the matrix $\mathbf{M}$ must transform the center of the sphere:

$$\mathbf{v}''(t) = \mathbf{M}\mathbf{v}'(t)$$

To make things simpler from here on, redefine $\mathbf{v}''(t)$ as $\mathbf{q}(t) = \mathbf{q}_0 + \delta\mathbf{q}$, and further define the length of the box as $\{a, b, c\}$. The length of the box is obviously the 2-norm of the vectors $\{\mathbf{x}, \mathbf{y}, \mathbf{z}\}$.

At this point, there's a well-known algorithm that can be used in a completely static world. This algorithm basically states the following, which is applied for every axis:

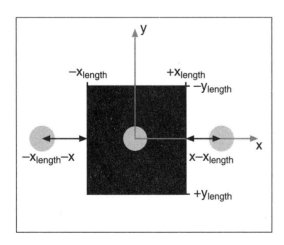

```
DistX = max(0, x - a, -a -x);
```

x is defined as the first component of the position of the sphere, while a represents the length of the box in x as defined above. This equation gives the distance between the point and the box in x only. If the sphere's x component is in the box, the result is 0. Otherwise, the distance is computed for each plane. The *max* here makes sure that the right plane gets chosen, and the 0 in the *max* makes sure that when the x value is between the two planes, the distance is 0. This is illustrated in Figure 10.10.

Figure 10.10
The relationship between the distance as a function of the position of the sphere and the box's length

You can repeat this for the *y*-axis and *z*-axis, to finally compute the square of the distance separating the sphere and the box, by simply computing the norm of that vector:

$$Dist^2 = DistX^2 + DistY^2 + DistZ^2$$

That wasn't too hard, but it still doesn't solve your problem. This equation doesn't take care of the time, and because of the absolute value, it isn't possible to isolate for the variable *t* if you apply the same trick as was used previously in the sphere-sphere collision-detection case. Here, you have to opt for a less elegant and general solution by splitting the absolute value into three distinct equations. The only issue is that this absolute value has to be applied for every coordinate. This means that you'll get 3 × 3 × 3 cases, yielding 27 different possibilities. In short, the box splits into 27 areas, as illustrated in Figure 10.11.

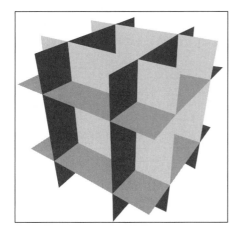

Figure 10.11
A box splitting the space into 27 areas

Because you assume that there's no intersection initially, you only have to compute 26 equations. (Whew, what a relief, you thought you had to compute 27, right?)

So what do these equations look like? Let's start by setting up a notation to make things easier. Any axis will be split into three sections, <+1, 0, −1>. Consequently, if the sphere's center was in the fully positive corner of the 27 areas, you would refer to the area as <+1, +1, +1>, which is the area where the component's values of the coordinate for the sphere **p** are all greater than the distance of the box. Let's start with this one as an example.

Computing the Box-Sphere Intersection for Corner Areas

In this case, you're trying to compute the distance between the corner of the box and the center of the sphere. The equation is pretty simple (and it works for all eight corners, for that matter). For notational sake, define *<a, b, c>* as **l**:

$$
\begin{aligned}
d^2 &= \left\| \mathbf{q}(t) - \langle a, b, c \rangle \right\|_2^2 \\
&= \left\| \mathbf{q}_0 + \Delta\mathbf{q}t - \mathbf{l} \right\|_2^2 \\
&= \left\| (\mathbf{q}_0 - \mathbf{l}) + \Delta\mathbf{q}t \right\|_2^2 \\
&= (\mathbf{q}_0 - \mathbf{l}) \bullet (\mathbf{q}_0 - \mathbf{l}) + 2(\mathbf{q}_0 - \mathbf{l}) \bullet \Delta\mathbf{q}t + \Delta\mathbf{q} \bullet \Delta\mathbf{q}t^2
\end{aligned}
$$

Doesn't that have a familiar ring? At this point, you proceed with the isolation of t:

$$t = \frac{-2(\mathbf{q}_0 - 1) \bullet \Delta\mathbf{q} \pm \sqrt{\left(2(\mathbf{q}_0 - 1) \bullet \Delta\mathbf{q}\right)^2 - 4(\Delta\mathbf{q} \bullet \Delta\mathbf{q})\left((\mathbf{q}_0 - 1) \bullet (\mathbf{q}_0 - 1)\right)}}{2\Delta\mathbf{q} \bullet \Delta\mathbf{q}}$$

$$= \frac{-(\mathbf{q}_0 - 1) \bullet \Delta\mathbf{q} - \sqrt{\left((\mathbf{q}_0 - 1) \bullet \Delta\mathbf{q}\right)^2 - (\Delta\mathbf{q} \bullet \Delta\mathbf{q})\left((\mathbf{q}_0 - 1) \bullet (\mathbf{q}_0 - 1)\right)}}{\Delta\mathbf{q} \bullet \Delta\mathbf{q}}$$

Obviously, not much optimization is possible here. Again, you take the smallest root and subtract the square root, for the same reasons mentioned earlier. If the square root is negative, there's no intersection. Furthermore, for an intersection to exist at all, the time must be within its span. For example, if the sphere remains in this area for its full duration, you would expect t to have a range of $[0, 1]$. If the sphere changes area in the middle, this is where you'll need to compute the new time span. You'll see this in greater depth very soon.

If an intersection did indeed occur, you simply need to compute the vector $\mathbf{l} - \mathbf{q}(t)$. This will give you a vector that goes from the center of the sphere to the box. Recall that this vector is now in box space. Thus, you need to convert the vector offset from box space to world space. This is where the inverse matrix comes in handy. You have to compute the inverse matrix of $\mathbf{M}$ and multiply it by the offset vector. Thankfully, since M is orthonormal, the inverse of $\mathbf{M}$ really is $\mathbf{M}^T$. Thus, the world space position of the collision $\mathbf{c}$ is

$$\mathbf{c} = \mathbf{v}(t) + r\mathbf{M}^T \left(\mathbf{l} - \mathbf{q}(t)\right)$$

Of course, this strategy will work for any corner of the box. You just need to change the signs of the components.

Computing the Box-Sphere Intersection for One or Two Edges

So what happens when you don't have a corner? Surprisingly, things start to get a little easier. It becomes much more difficult to express everything in terms of vectors, unfortunately, but the process is pretty much the same. The only difference is that one of the distances will be set to 0. For example, computing the time for the area $<+1, +1, 0>$ would imply that you should nullify the third variable. In other words, the computation becomes as follows:

$$d^2 = \left\| \left(\mathbf{q}(t) - 1\right) \& (1,1,0) \right\|_2^2$$

$$= \left\| \left\langle \mathbf{q}_x(t), \mathbf{q}_y(t) \right\rangle - \left\langle a, b \right\rangle \right\|_2^2$$

The length is fully described by only x and y, as described by the maximum equation stated previously. Basically, the same equation comes out of it. The only difference is that you completely omit the z component.

Last but not least, you may be interested in computing the actual position of the collision. In this case, you simply have to keep in mind which variable you had forgotten, and compute the difference between the box's extent, $\mathbf{l}$, and the position of the sphere when it collides, $\mathbf{q}(t)$. As for the variable you had masked out of the equation, it must remain as 0. Thus, for the preceding example, the offset vector from the sphere would be given by

$$\mathbf{c} = \mathbf{v}(t) + r\mathbf{M}^{\mathrm{T}}\left(\left(\mathbf{l} - \mathbf{q}(t)\right) \& \langle 1,1,0 \rangle\right)$$
$$= \mathbf{v}(t) + r\mathbf{M}^{\mathrm{T}}\langle \mathbf{l}_x - \mathbf{q}_x(t), \mathbf{l}_y - \mathbf{q}_y(t), 0 \rangle$$

Things are extremely similar when you have an intersection with a plane. In this case, your two components are masked out and only one component isn't. Consequently, the computations become pretty simple, because you need to mask two variables and only keep one. Thus, the vector generated by this type of intersection is always perpendicular to the plane (it's the plane's normal with the length of the sphere).

Knowing the Area

So now you know how to find the existence of a collision, but you still don't know how to determine the length of the 27 areas. This is pretty easy. You just need to verify that each component is smaller than a certain value, greater than a certain value, or in-between. Chapter 19, "The Quick Mind: Computational Optimizations," offers some very nifty tricks for quickly computing such an area. If you're clever enough, Ch. 20 also contains all the necessary information you'll need to make this step independent of the area vector's component case (-1, $+1$, or 0). This drastically simplifies and speeds up the code.

The first test you should do is to check if both endpoints of the sphere's movement are in the same area. If so, it becomes pretty clear and easy. The time, t, has range of $[0, 1]$, and you only have one check to apply. If that's not the case, it becomes a little nastier. For a general algorithm, you can go through all six planes and compute the time at which the line intersects with the plane (Chapter 4 has all the details required for this). Once you know the times for all six planes, you must choose the minimal time. Any time that's smaller than 0 or greater than 1 should be rejected right away, because it implies that the intersection will never be reached in this segment.

If you keep a sorted list of the times with the associated planes, you can determine the order through which you'll traverse the planes within the time $t = [0, 1]$. Once you've determined your first intersection with an area plane, you should first check if there's an intersection between the sphere and the box between time $t = [0, i]$, where i represents the time you've computed to be the intersection between the area planes.

The trickier part of this is to determine which area you're moving, given that you found an intersection and a plane. As it turns out, there's a really easy way to do this. If you place the initial center of the sphere into the equation of the plane, you can determine if the vertex is above or below the plane, as you've seen previously:

$$\mathbf{n} \bullet \mathbf{p} + D = s$$

Here, s is the sign of the point's position, $\mathbf{p}$, with regards to the plane, $<\mathbf{n}, D>$. If the result of s is positive, it means that you're in the same half-plane as that pointed to by the normal vector of the plane. Inversely, if the result is negative, you're in the other half-plane. Thus, you only have to make a convention out of this one. For instance, state that the upper top left direction is where the normal points for the plane will point toward when you compute the intersection. Consequently, if the center of the sphere was originally in a positive region (implying the same as that pointed to by the normal vector) and ends up in the negative after choosing a point past the time of collision, it means that you've moved one area to the right in that plane's component. Conversely, if you go from positive to negative, you've moved one area to the right. Figure 10.12 shows this idea in 2D.

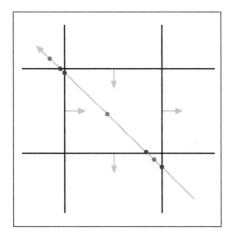

Figure 10.12
Determining the change of area of a box-sphere collision

In 3D, you could think of these planes as one 3×3 grid (let's say the middle one). Here, the plane's equations would be something similar to {<1, 0, 0, ||x||>, <1, 0, 0, -||x||>, <0, 1, 0, ||y||>, <0, 1, 0, -||y||>}. The sphere's center is located in the bottom-right area, which you assume to be the positive values. Computing this equation with the center would yield a value of $s = 1$ for every plane mentioned above. After the first intersection with the plane is detected, you can compute the average point between the second area's span to get a point that's in the new area, and place that point in the preceding equation to yield a negative value. Since you go from positive to negative, you deduce that the direction in x is to move one area above.

Similarly, the next intersection is in a plane sitting in y, and it goes from positive to negative, which means that the x value should be moved one unit to the left. If the opposite had happened, you would have to move one area in the opposite direction. If you keep track of the area using an area vector with potential values $\{-1, 0, +1\}$, it's very simple because you merely need to add 1 to or subtract 1 from the component's corresponding plane.

Obviously, this isn't the easy problem you saw earlier in this chapter, and a few faster but less precise tests should be performed ahead of this one to minimize computation. You should evaluate whether you really need to do this, or if a faster approximation is worth your while.

Box-Box Collision

Seeing how ugly the last case was, you probably can't wait to read this one. You've already found a test to verify if a box intersects with a plane. You can use this test to verify whether the boxes collide. As was done for the sphere-box collision detection, you can define the offset vector of box A as $\{x, y, z\}$. If you transform the coordinate space into box A's coordinate space, you get the same transformation matrix as you computed previously:

$$\mathbf{M} = \begin{bmatrix} x_x & x_y & x_z & -\mathbf{x} \bullet \mathbf{p} \\ y_x & y_y & y_z & -\mathbf{y} \bullet \mathbf{p} \\ z_x & z_y & z_z & -\mathbf{z} \bullet \mathbf{p} \\ 0 & 0 & 0 & 1 \end{bmatrix}$$

The first thing you should note is that you only need to check three planes against the box, not the entire set of six planes. In a nutshell, if you take any box and rotate it in any direction, you can't see more than three of its faces. Thus, the problem is identifying which faces are "visible." Chapter 16, "Space Partitioning: Cleaning Your Room," explains this and where it comes from.

Just for the purposes of this problem, given a normal for the plane $\mathbf{n}$ and the vector that's between $\mathbf{p_a}$ and $\mathbf{p_b}$, you can compute the visibility of the face by computing the dot product. The sign will signal if the face $<\mathbf{n}, D>$ is visible from the point of view of $\mathbf{p_b}$ looking towards $\mathbf{p_a}$.

$$\mathbf{n} \bullet (\mathbf{p}_A - \mathbf{p}_B) = s$$
$$\left\{ \begin{matrix} \text{Visible} & s > 0 \\ \text{Not Visible} & s <= 0 \end{matrix} \right\}$$

Once you've found the three planes that are visible, you can follow up by testing them for collision against box B. If you do find that a collision exists, it doesn't imply that a collision between the two boxes has truly occurred. You must first verify that the intersection of the plane and box B is indeed within the face of box A. The plane extends to infinity, while the face is finite in space. Thus, you must verify that the intersection point is within the bounds of its corresponding face by applying the following verification:

$$-\|\mathbf{x}\|_2 \le \mathbf{c}_x \le \|\mathbf{x}\|_2$$
$$-\|\mathbf{y}\|_2 \le \mathbf{c}_y \le \|\mathbf{y}\|_2$$
$$-\|\mathbf{z}\|_2 \le \mathbf{c}_z \le \|\mathbf{z}\|_2$$

Of course, one of the tests will be meaningless. The collision occurs with that very plane, so you know for a fact that it will pass. Therefore, only two of these tests are required per face. If you've tested against face **x**, you know that x will be within bounds, and consequently only need to test for **y** and **z**. If you do find a collision within the bounds, this collision is the first collision between the boxes and thereafter you can exit.

This test seems rather simple. Does it cover every possible collision? In other words, can you determine that in all other cases the two boxes don't collide?

Of course not, silly, that would be too easy. For example, let's say box B hits box A inside a face via one of its corner vertices. In this case, you can easily find the collision between the two boxes via the first step described before. But assume that the order of the boxes is inverted. In other words, you've chosen box B as the static box and box A as the moving box. In this case, box A approaches box B from a corner angle and from a flat direction, as illustrated in Figure 10.13.

Figure 10.13
Undetected case of intersection when considering three planes against a box test

The problem with this case is that you'll indeed find three collisions between the two boxes (one per plane), but for every plane, the collision you'll find will be out of bounds and won't pass the collision test, as shown in Figure 10.13. But fortunately, since inverting box A and B works, you can add another set of three tests by testing box B against box A. To recap, you need to test box A's three planes against box B, and you also need to test box B's three planes against box B.

That take care of this case, but does it cover every possible collision? What if two boxes intersect each other on an edge and none of their axes are equivalent, as illustrated in Figure 10.14? In this case, all six tests against the planes will find no valid intersection point. The tests that will find a collision won't detect an intersection between the two boxes, because the intersection won't be within the bounds of the plane. Houston, we have a problem!

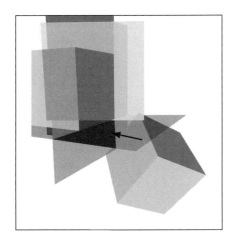

Figure 10.14
Undetected case of intersection when considering three planes against a box test in both directions

Obviously, this method has flaws. It can detect when two boxes collide in the majority of the cases, but not in every case. You could approach this problem from a similar angle to the previous section, but instead, you'll look at it from a completely different angle.

The first section (using the box-plane intersection test) uses a theorem called the *theorem of separating plane*. This very obvious theorem states that if you can find a plane in space that separates the two geometries such that every point of one geometry is on the positive side of the plane, while the points of the other geometry sit on the negative side of the plane, the two objects don't collide. This is pretty obvious. Geometrically, when the two objects collide, it means that there's no plane that can separate the two objects. This works pretty well when you can position the plane in space, and it works perfectly for the 2×3 plane-box tests you initially performed.

A lemma of this test is the *theorem of separating axis*. This theorem states that if there's a directional vector **l** for which the projection of the shapes on this vector doesn't intersect, the shapes don't intersect. This theorem exploits the same idea as the other theorem. If there's a gap between the two objects, by projecting the objects on the line (as you might do orthogonally for a shadow), the projection won't intersect either. The idea behind this theorem is illustrated in Figure 10.15.

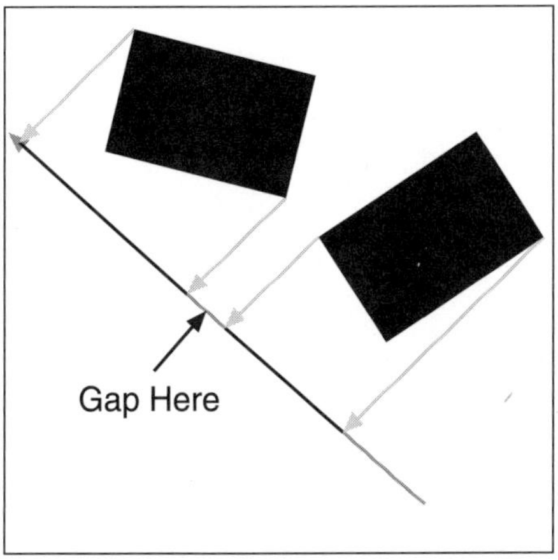

If you wanted to, you could choose the three normal vectors of the boxes as directional vectors. If you computed the projection of the shapes upon these vectors, you'd get the same result as you would with the plane-box intersection test. The plane-box intersection test is a little more helpful, in the sense that it directly provides you with the time of intersection and the position of the collision. Projecting the objects upon a line may seem like a daunting task, but it really isn't. In fact, you've already learned how to project a box upon a vector. Here's the equation that does so:

Figure 10.15
The separating axis theorem

$$r_e = |\mathbf{x} \bullet \mathbf{l}| + |\mathbf{y} \bullet \mathbf{l}| + |\mathbf{z} \bullet \mathbf{l}|$$

Look like a familiar equation? It should be. Testing for the projected intersection is pretty simple. If you can verify that the sum of the box's radii is smaller than the projected distance between the centers of the two boxes, you've proven that there's a gap between the two objects and they don't collide. Mathematically, what you're trying to find is the following for boxes of center $\mathbf{u}$ and $\mathbf{v}$, with respective radii r_{ea} and r_{ec} and a projection vector $\mathbf{l}$:

$$\mathbf{l} \bullet (\mathbf{u} - \mathbf{v}) \geq r_{ea} + r_{rb}$$

When you find that this test isn't true, that's when you must try to find another line segment $\mathbf{l}$ that will satisfy this inequality. A failure to find such a vector means that the objects intersect. To be decisive on this test, you have to find the complete set of projection vectors, $\mathbf{l}$, which will enable you to check every possible case of box intersections. The only case missed by the box-plane collision detection test is when two edges intersect. Interestingly enough, if you were to build a plane that was normal to both edges, you could determine if the two objects were intersecting that point or not. The only problem is finding the position of the plane. If you use the axis theorem's test instead, you don't need to position anything in space, because the projection is done on a direction vector and not an anchored position vector in space. That's the beauty of this test.

The tests also have an extremely tight relationship. Due to the orthogonality of the boxes, the normal of the plane, which is verified for the first test, can be used as a direction vector for another pair of edges. If you think in terms of edges, each box is equipped with three sets of edges. Each of the edges from one box can intersect any edge from the other box. This means that you must compute an additional nine edges, which are nothing but every possible cross product between the edges of the two boxes. If the boxes weren't orthogonal (and hence not boxes at all, but quadrilaterals), you would also have to add the cross product between every possible pair of independent edges.

To sum things up, the separating axis theorem must be verified on a total of 15 directional vectors if performed independently (that is, without the separating plane theorem). These planes are the six normals of the planes from the two boxes, and the unique cross product of each possibility between these six normals. Mathematically:

$$\mathbf{l} = \begin{cases} \mathbf{x}_a, \mathbf{y}_a, \mathbf{z}_a, \\ \mathbf{x}_b, \mathbf{y}_b, \mathbf{z}_b, \\ \mathbf{x}_a \times \mathbf{x}_b, \mathbf{x}_a \times \mathbf{y}_b, \mathbf{x}_a \times \mathbf{z}_b, \\ \mathbf{y}_a \times \mathbf{x}_b, \mathbf{y}_a \times \mathbf{y}_b, \mathbf{y}_a \times \mathbf{z}_b, \\ \mathbf{z}_a \times \mathbf{x}_b, \mathbf{z}_a \times \mathbf{y}_b, \mathbf{z}_a \times \mathbf{z}_b \end{cases}$$

This set is the complete set that's required for static boxes in space. Yes, the keyword here is *static*. All of this still doesn't take time into account. Given your non-intersection test, it isn't very complicated to add the concept of time to it. You can simply let $\mathbf{u}$ and $\mathbf{v}$ be a function of time and apply the test to the range $t = [0, 1]$:

$$\mathbf{l} \bullet \left(\mathbf{u}(t) - \mathbf{v}(t) \right) \geq r_{ea} + r_{rb}$$

Because the movement $(\mathbf{u}(t) - \mathbf{v}(t))$ is linear, you simply need to show that there is no intersection at the beginning or the end, and that the direction of the projection for the beginning and end did not change sign. For example, if a box starts off to the right of the other box, and at the end it moves to the left of the other box without intersecting at any point, this isn't a comprehensive test. The fact that the boxes should remain in the same relative positions to each another fixes this problem. Mathematically, the check comes down to the following:

$$\mathbf{l} \bullet \left(\mathbf{u}(0) - \mathbf{v}(0) \right) \geq r_{ea} + r_{rb}$$
$$\mathbf{l} \bullet \left(\mathbf{u}(1) - \mathbf{v}(1) \right) \geq r_{ea} + r_{rb}$$
$$\mathrm{sgn} \left(\mathbf{l} \bullet \left(\mathbf{u}(0) - \mathbf{v}(0) \right) \right) = \mathrm{sgn} \left(\mathbf{l} \bullet \left(\mathbf{u}(1) - \mathbf{v}(1) \right) \right)$$

This test should be applied to the 15 previous planes. If any of the tests pass, it means that the boxes don't actually collide. The motion complicates things a little bit here. In fact, the 15-plane test isn't comprehensive enough to claim a collision if all the tests fail.

Yep, you have to add yet more directional vector cases. The case that isn't covered by the movement through time is when the direction vector is chosen such that it's perpendicular to the movement between the two objects. To simplify the notation, you can define a vector $\mathbf{w}(t)$ as the vector of $\mathbf{u}(t) - \mathbf{v}(t)$. Thus:

$$\mathbf{u}(t) - \mathbf{v}(t) = \mathbf{u}_1 + (\mathbf{u}_0 - \mathbf{u}_1)t - \left(\mathbf{v}_1 + (\mathbf{v}_0 - \mathbf{v}_1)t \right)$$
$$= (\mathbf{u}_1 - \mathbf{v}_1) + (\mathbf{u}_0 - \mathbf{u}_1 - \mathbf{v}_0 + \mathbf{v}_1)t$$
$$\mathbf{w}(t) = \mathbf{w}_1 + \Delta \mathbf{w} t$$

For notational sake, let $\delta \mathbf{w} = \mathbf{d}$. To keep the same view as was proposed before, you can consider the movement $\mathbf{d}$ as another segment. Then you'll want to compute the cross product (that is, the perpendicular vector) between $\mathbf{d}$ and the normal vectors of the planes $\{\mathbf{x}, \mathbf{y}, \mathbf{z}\}$ for each box. Thus, you must add an additional six directional vectors for a total list of 21:

$$l = \begin{Bmatrix} \mathbf{x}_a, \mathbf{y}_a, \mathbf{z}_a, \\ \mathbf{x}_b, \mathbf{y}_b, \mathbf{z}_b, \\ \mathbf{x}_a \times \mathbf{x}_b, \mathbf{x}_a \times \mathbf{y}_b, \mathbf{x}_a \times \mathbf{z}_b, \\ \mathbf{y}_a \times \mathbf{x}_b, \mathbf{y}_a \times \mathbf{y}_b, \mathbf{y}_a \times \mathbf{z}_b, \\ \mathbf{z}_a \times \mathbf{x}_b, \mathbf{z}_a \times \mathbf{y}_b, \mathbf{z}_a \times \mathbf{z}_b, \\ \mathbf{d} \times \mathbf{x}_a, \mathbf{d} \times \mathbf{y}_a, \mathbf{d} \times \mathbf{z}_a, \\ \mathbf{d} \times \mathbf{x}_b, \mathbf{d} \times \mathbf{y}_b, \mathbf{d} \times \mathbf{z}_b \end{Bmatrix}$$

This list of vectors, on the other hand, represents a complete test. In other words, if all tests fail, you've detected an intersection, and if one test passes, you've detected a non-intersection. Only one problem remains. You don't know the time of intersection. This in itself isn't alarming, because you know that it's between frames. However, you may want to find the exact point of collision between the two objects. Of course, getting the time is the most appropriate method of achieving this. You can get the time if you simply isolate the equation you use as a test:

$$r_{ea} + r_{rb} = l \bullet w(t)$$
$$= l \bullet (w_1 + dt)$$
$$= l \bullet w_1 + l \bullet dt$$
$$t = \frac{r_{ea} + r_{rb} - l \bullet w_1}{l \bullet d}$$

The time you'll get out of this equation is the time at which the projection of the two objects from the point of view of the directional vector l intersect. It isn't implicitly the time at which the two objects intersect, per se. Thus, to get the true time of intersection, you also have to check the next directional vector. The intersection test necessarily needs to detect a collision, so you must again compute the time, but you must take the greatest time between the two. You must thereafter apply this process to every plane and consequently compute the maximum time of intersection. It may sound confusing to compute the maximum time in order to compute the first time at which the two objects collide, but this comes from the very definition of the separating axis theorem. As long as there's one existing separating axis, the objects don't intersect. Thus, you must continue until all planes do, and that can only happen at the maximum time between the collisions.

Now that you have the time, all that remains is to compute the actual intersection. This is easy to do if you keep track of the direction vector associated with the last time. This direction vector is the vector that gets the best view in the house for the collision. Since it's the last vector to see the projected lengths collide, it's the vector that sees the objects when their extents first intersect. Again, for this section, I'll take an approach that's slightly different from the previous approaches. Instead of trying to compute the position of the intersection, I'll try to find which vertices of the box are the ones that collide with the other box.

To do this, first you need to observe yet again the link between the theorem of separating plane and the theorem of separating axis. If you generate a plane by using the directional vector as normal vector, you can generate the last plane with which you intersect. Once you have the plane, the trick is simply to compute the set for vertices that have the minimal distance between the planes. Notice how the plural is used for "vertices" here. You must recall that two boxes may intersect in many ways. A single vertex may intersect, but two edges may also intersect. Alternatively, you may also get an intersection between two planes. This technique easily covers every case, because the distance between each of these vertices from the plane will be relatively equal. Relatively is used here, since floating-point precision may make it such that the distances aren't strictly equal in practice. Thus the need to compare using a threshold.

Because you compute the distance between the plane and the vertices at time t, it isn't really important where the plane sits, provided that the plane intersects with the object on the surface only. In other words, the vertices must all be on either side of the plane, or else the distance between the plane and the vertices has no meaning.

You know from the hypothesis that, initially, the boxes don't intersect. Consequently, you merely have to choose a point from the other box as an anchor point, and you'll be guaranteed that all of the vertices from the other box will be on one side of the plane. Thus, the plane in question, defined by the last directional vector $\mathbf{l}$ and any point $\mathbf{p}$ from box B when testing against box A, is

$$\langle \mathbf{l}, -\mathbf{l} \bullet \mathbf{p} \rangle$$

The separation axis theorem is pretty useful, because it enables you to work with various objects. It may not be as direct as some of the other methods shown in this chapter, but it does offer a solid base that works for any convex body (a body that doesn't have any dents). The specific example of a box-box collision was tackled because once you understand the idea behind the box-box collision detection using the separating axis theorem, you won't have any problem understanding the triangle-triangle, triangle-box, and many other similar types of intersection tests. The only difference, if you're working with a triangle, for example, is that the range on the plane will be slightly different, and you only have one plane to worry about instead of three.

Picking

When you run a game such as *Warcraft III*, it's essential to be able to select some of the units that move on the screen with the click of a mouse. Obviously, you cannot simply wave a magic wand and expect the game to know which object you want to pick.

Fortunately, picking in 3D games is a relatively simple task, and it doesn't have to deal with the concept of time. Thus, it doesn't have to delve too deeply into complex algorithms.

All picking problems can be reduced to an infinite line intersection with an object on the screen. To solve the picking problem as the user clicks the mouse at a specific location on the screen, you need to convert this $<x, y>$ coordinate in screen coordinates into a 3D vector that points from the camera down into the depth of the world. The first step is to understand how to retrieve such a vector.

Computing the Position and Direction of the Pick

Retrieving the direction and position of the pick is rather trivial. The position of the pick (or anchoring vertex) is simply the position of the camera. The vector passes through the center of the camera, so it's a point on your picking vector. What's a little trickier is retrieving the direction of the pick.

The process is pretty simple, since you only need to look at how a 3D coordinate can become a 2D coordinate to understand how the inverse of that process should work. Working your way backward, the last thing 3D APIs do is convert from transformed coordinates into screen coordinates. Consequently, the first operation you should do to your 2D vector is to scale it to a range $<x, y>$ from a range of $[-1, 1]$. This process may already be done, depending on the API you're using.

Once you have this, you must undo the work that was done by the projection matrix. Thus, you need to compute the inverse of the projection matrix. If you take the perspective matrix shown in Chapter 5, "Transformations," while keeping the exact values of the terms abstract, what you get is the following inverse matrix:

$$
\begin{bmatrix} a & 0 & 0 & 0 \\ 0 & b & 0 & 0 \\ c & d & e & -1 \\ 0 & 0 & f & 0 \end{bmatrix}^{-1} = \begin{bmatrix} \dfrac{1}{a} & 0 & 0 & 0 \\ 0 & \dfrac{1}{b} & 0 & 0 \\ 0 & 0 & 0 & \dfrac{1}{f} \\ \dfrac{c}{a} & \dfrac{d}{b} & -1 & \dfrac{e}{f} \end{bmatrix}
$$

Thus, it isn't necessary to go through a typical matrix inverse followed by a vector multiplication. Instead, you can simply divide x by a and divide y by b, followed by an assignment of $z = -1$.

The first step (omitting the object's transformation) is the camera and world transformation matrix, so your last step is inverting the process. If you let the matrix be **M**, all you need to do at this point is invert the matrix and compute the product of the matrix with the vector you've built thus far. For this to work, you have to be sure that the world matrix has been loaded into your API stack and retrieve that matrix. The world matrix shouldn't be coupled with the object matrix, because the picking should occur on a world scale and not in the perspective of the object.

Last but not least, you need to subtract the position of the camera from the vector such that you only get a direction. The position of the camera should be kept in a separate vector, so that you can easily express the equation of an infinite line $\mathbf{x}(t) = \mathbf{x}_0 + \mathbf{v}t$. If you understand the matrix stack of your 3D API, this shouldn't be a problem. They all work the same. Look at the source code to get a glimpse of the specifics for OpenGL.

This section covers some pretty trivial cases compared to what you've seen. Again, if you're looking for the ray-triangle or ray-plane intersection test, you should take closer look at Chapter 4, which contains all of the gritty details about such an implementation.

Ray-Sphere Intersection

Without a doubt, this is one of the easiest tests to perform. With the range of techniques you've learned thus far, this type of problem should be a no-brainer. All you have to do is compute the minimal distance between the point **p**, representing the center of the sphere, and test if the radius is smaller than or equal to that. Of course, you want to be somewhat more optimal than the test shown in Chapter 4, so you can compute the square of each side and verify that the inequality holds. Mathematically, this trivial test is applied to the center of the sphere **v** with radius r and to a ray of equation $\mathbf{p} + t\mathbf{l}$ as follows:

$$r^2 \le \left(v_x - p_x\right)^2 + \left(v_y - p_y\right)^2 + \left(v_z - p_z\right)^2 - \frac{\left(\left(\mathbf{v} - \mathbf{p}\right)\bullet\mathbf{l}\right)^2}{\|\mathbf{l}\|_2^2}$$

Ray-Box Intersection

The box, when dealing with a plane, was treated pretty similarly to the case of a plane and a sphere. This test is no exception. The only tricky aspect of this test is that you don't immediately have the vector upon which to project the box in order to compute the effective radii. But of course, you can compute this vector. As long as you remember that the vector must be normal, and that this normal vector goes from a point on the line to the vertex **v**, it all becomes simple:

$$0 = \mathbf{l} \bullet \mathbf{n}$$
$$= \mathbf{l} \bullet (\mathbf{p} + t\mathbf{l} - \mathbf{v})$$
$$= \mathbf{l} \bullet (\mathbf{p} - \mathbf{v}) + t\mathbf{l} \bullet \mathbf{l}$$
$$t = \frac{\mathbf{l} \bullet (\mathbf{p} - \mathbf{v})}{\mathbf{l} \bullet \mathbf{l}}$$

Once you have the time, you're done. You can substitute it back into the equation to find the value of $\mathbf{n}$, and thereafter you can compute the effective radius of the box. With the effective radius, you can apply the same test in order to verify for an intersection. The following equation shows this:

$$\mathbf{n} = \mathbf{p} - \mathbf{v} + \frac{\mathbf{l} \bullet (\mathbf{p} - \mathbf{v})}{\mathbf{l} \bullet \mathbf{l}} \mathbf{l}$$
$$r_e = |\mathbf{x} \bullet \mathbf{n}| + |\mathbf{y} \bullet \mathbf{n}| + |\mathbf{z} \bullet \mathbf{n}|$$
$$r_e^2 \le (v_x - p_x)^2 + (v_y - p_y)^2 + (v_z - p_z)^2 - \frac{((\mathbf{v} - \mathbf{p}) \bullet \mathbf{l})^2}{\|\mathbf{l}\|_2^2}$$

Ray-Capsule Intersection

Here's a new interesting shape you may not have seen before. A capsule is very similar to a cylinder and looks a bit like a pill. Mathematically, a capsule is an object for which every point on its surface is of an equal distance from a line. Consequently, on the axes orthogonal to the line, the object looks like a cylinder, but the ends are half-spheres, as illustrated in Figure 10.16.

Due to its rather nice mathematical definition, it's an object that isn't too hard to check for collisions. Let's start by defining the capsule as two vertices forming its line, $\mathbf{u}$, $\mathbf{v}$, and a radius r. Thus, the capsule's centerline has an equation with a range of $t = [0, 1]$:

Figure 10.16
A capsule

$$\mathbf{f}(t) = \mathbf{u} + t(\mathbf{v} - \mathbf{u})$$

The first easy test to perform is to compute the square of the distance between the line and the ray. You already learned how this is done in the section on sphere-sphere collision detection, so it's pointless to go through it again. You first compute the time of the intersection for two infinite lines:

$$\mathbf{a} = \mathbf{u} - \mathbf{p}$$
$$\mathbf{b} = \mathbf{v} - \mathbf{u} - \mathbf{w}$$
$$t = -\frac{\mathbf{a} \bullet \mathbf{b}}{\mathbf{b} \bullet \mathbf{b}}$$

Then, you must clip the time t such that it doesn't exceed its range of $[0, 1]$. Once you have that, you must substitute the time back into the equation for the distance, as shown in the sphere-sphere collision case, to yield the final test:

$$r^2 \leq \mathbf{a} \bullet \mathbf{a} + 2\mathbf{a} \bullet \mathbf{b}t + \mathbf{b} \bullet \mathbf{b}t^2$$

This chapter, like many others, could be expanded into an entire book. The cases you've studied here are specific, useful ones you'll encounter from a game's perspective. As always, it's very useful to know the thinking process behind them so that you can figure out your own tests.

For instance, let's say you have to perform a test that detects the collision between a plane and an ellipsoid. An ellipsoid is to a sphere what an ellipse is to a circle. Thus, the ellipsoid is described by three radii, and it's really nothing but an ellipse that's scaled differently in x, y, and z.

If you were to solve this problem in a smart way, you would simply apply a scaling transformation matrix to the sphere-plane such that the ellipsoid became a sphere. This would convert a problem that seemed pretty complex into another problem for which you already have the solution. If you convert a problem into one you know, you already have the solution as long as you invert the change you've done at the end so as not to change the inital problem. In this case, once you've computed the position of the collision, you should apply the inverse transformation matrix in order to convert from scaled coordinates to world coordinates.

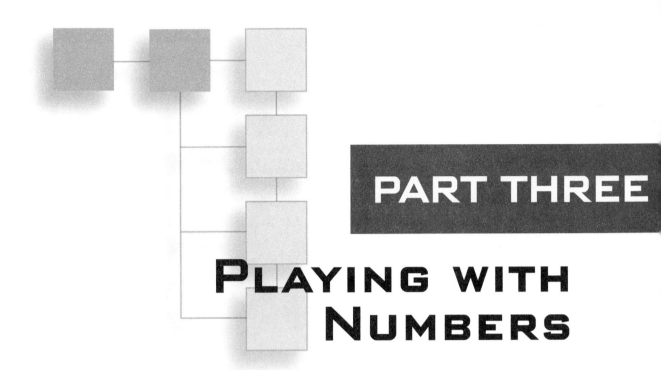

PART THREE

PLAYING WITH NUMBERS

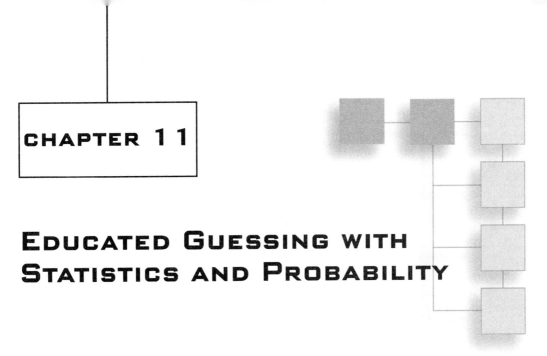

CHAPTER 11

EDUCATED GUESSING WITH STATISTICS AND PROBABILITY

Quake III is one of my favorite games. Thanks to my *Quake/Quake II* background, I was able to start at the second-highest level of bots the first time I played *Quake III*; eventually, I became confident enough to tackle the nightmare bots. Initially, those bots took me out pretty quickly (as soon as one got hold of that rail gun, I was in deep trouble).

Interestingly enough, by looking at the bot's point of view in *Quake III*, you can determine just how the bots aim at you. It appears that the game establishes the bots' degree of accuracy by randomly moving the camera around a small circle. For the beginner bots, this circle is huge, and as a result these bots rarely shoot where they should. The nightmare bots, on the other hand, have such a small circle that they hit you dead-on virtually every single time (which also explains why they sometimes miss you on a rail, but only rarely). This brings up one very interesting problem. Initially, when I began tackling *Quake III's* nightmare bots, I could hardly beat one. Now, on some levels, I can ramp up to six and *still* win. Somehow, I doubt that if I were playing against six humans I would win.

One of the biggest problems with artificial intelligence (AI) is that computers are either too smart or too dumb. In the case of *Quake III*, the bots' intelligence is everywhere on the map except where it needs to be. Wouldn't it be nice if a computer could be exactly at your skill level? That way, as your skills increased, so would the computer's. After all, playing against a computer should be a fair fight for both sides, not a situation where one side gets seriously whupped.

All told, there are two main types of AI:

- Omniscient AI, which knows the entire map and exactly what moves the computer should make in order to win. This type of AI is not particularly interesting from a mathematical point of view because it primarily involves min/max searches in structures or something along these lines.

295

■ Adaptive AI, which enables the computer to adapt to the environment. *Quake* is a good example of a game that uses this type of AI, because in *Quake*, the computer cannot possibly enumerate all the possible scenarios.

How, exactly, does AI work? AI works primarily though the use of probability and statistics, which are the focus of this chapter. Specifically, in this chapter, you'll explore the following:

- Probability
- Permutations
- Combinations
- Random number generation
- Distribution
- Genetic algorithms
- Fuzzy logic
- Neural networks

Basic Statistics Principles

Statistics is an interesting chapter in math because it deals with the unknown. The idea behind statistics is to be able to crunch of bunch of numbers in order to predict a future outcome. Oddly enough, the statistically correct output rarely if ever matches reality. For example, if a student has an average grade of 2.346, would you expect him to receive a grade of 2.346 in his next course? Probably not. But you could say with some degree of certainty that his grade will be roughly around that point value. The idea is that the answer in reality will not deviate wildly from the expected output.

The field of statistics relies on the following tools, each of which is discussed in ensuing sections:

- Probability
- Permutation
- Combinations

Probability

Probability is the evaluation of how likely it is that a particular event will occur. For instance, consider a chess game in which the computer must determine whether moving a knight from one position to another is a good move. In order to decide, the computer might look at its past experiences. If, in the past, making an identical move was successful, the computer might decide that repeating the same move would be a good idea. Put another way, the computer might decide that it is highly probable that this is a good move.

On the other hand, if moving this piece in the past led to the computer's queen or even king being taken, then the computer might decide to consider the alternatives. That is, the computer might decide that it is highly *improbable* that this is a good move.

One way to measure these abstract concepts—probable and improbable—is to use set theory, and to write them in terms of percentages. Again using the chess game as an example, suppose that, over time, the computer made the same move 100 times, and that it was successful 80 of those times. In that case, you'd say that the move has a success rate of 80%.

Another example comes from shoot-em-up games. Suppose, for example, that a bot keeps shooting at you during a game, and that the game has a tool you can use to keep track of how many shots were fired at you and how many of them actually hit you. If, at the end of the game, you determine that the bot shot at you 1,000 times, and hit you 300 times, you can compute a ratio—and, by extension, a percentage—to describe the probability of the bot hitting you in the future:

300/1000 = 0.3 = 30%

Mathematically, the probability $p(x)$ of an event x being met is as follows:

$$p(x) = \frac{\text{Successes for } x}{\text{Total Attempts for } x}$$

With this definition in hand, you can look at the range that p should exhibit. For starters, you know that the probability cannot be negative because neither the total number of attempts nor the total number of successes can be negative. In addition, you know that you cannot have more successes than attempts. The best possible scenario would be to have a situation in which all the attempts were successes. In such a case, you would get a probability of 1, or 100%. If, on the other hand, all the attempts were failures, you would get a probability of 0. Consequently, the range for $p(x)$ is [0, 1].

How would you compute the probability of *not* having a success for x, also known as computing the complement of the probability? You can find the complement by subtracting the successes from the total attempts, basically inverting the percentage:

$$p(\bar{x}) = 1 - p(x)$$

In set theory, a bar is used to represent the complement of a set. The complement can be thought of as "anything but." Returning to the bot example, you can determine the odds of the bot *not* hitting you as follows:

1 − 0.3 = 0.6 = 60%

Probability of Simultaneous Events

Suppose your game does not have bots, but instead has automated turrets that are shooting. Each turret has its own statistics. That is, for each one, you know how many shots it takes to hit its target. This is your first probability. Your second probability is whether, given a hit target, the shot is fatal. You may also be interested in determining the probability that a given turret shoots the fatal blow—put another way, the probability that the turret will both hit and kill its target. If the probability is low, you might want to consider having another turret aim for the object if it is within critical space.

Mathematically, this can be expressed as follows, where x represents the turret landing a hit and y represents the hit being fatal:

$$p(x \cap y)$$

If you think of this only in terms of the equation for the probability, you can see that the rate of success has in fact multiplied. For each case where x is a success, y also needs to be a success for the entire probability to be a success. So if you multiply the probability of success for x by the probability for y, you get the probability that both events occur at the same time. Mathematically, this is expressed as follows:

$$p\left(\bigcap_{i=1}^{n} x_i\right) = \prod_{i=1}^{n} p(x_i)$$

tip

> If you are not familiar with this notation, take a look at Appendix A, "Notation and Conventions."

If the odds of a given turret hitting a target were 0.2 and the odds of killing the target were 0.5, then the odds of both hitting and killing the target would be 0.1, or 10%. Thus, it could reasonably be predicted that one shot in 10 will kill the target. This does make sense when you consider that one shot out of five will hit the target and that it takes, on average, two hits to kill the target.

To complicate things, suppose that one turret is lagging, so you have decided to put two turrets on the same target. In this case, you want to compute the odds that either one of the two turrets will hit the target. Mathematically speaking, what you are looking for is as follows:

$$p(x \cup y)$$

At first, you might be seduced into thinking that the solution is extremely easy—all you need to do is add the odds of x and the odds of y to hit the target. Unfortunately, that's not always the case. For example, what happens if both turrets hit the target? Because you have added together the odds of the first turret hitting the target and the odds of the second turret hitting the target, you have accounted for the possibility that both turrets have a rate of success twice. Consequently, if you subtract the odds of both turrets hitting the target, you get the valid equation that computes the odds of either turret hitting the target:

$$p\left(\bigcup_{i=1}^{n} x_i\right) = \sum_{i=1}^{n} p(x_i) - \sum_{i=1}^{n}\sum_{j=2}^{n-1} p(x_i \cap x_j) + \cdots +/\!\!-\, p\left(\bigcap_{i=1}^{n} x_i\right)$$

If you apply this idea recursively, you will conclude that if you have three elements, you will need to compute the case in which each pair of turrets has a success. By doing so, however, you will have overcomputed the case in which all three turrets have a success. Consequently, in this case, you need to subtract from the previous subtraction or, if you prefer, you need to add back the probability of intersection of all three elements. Apply this logic to *n* simultaneous elements and you get the preceding equation. This is commonly referred to as the *principle of inclusion exclusion*. You can visualize what is happening by examining the intersection of circles (called a Venn diagram), as shown in Figure 11.1.

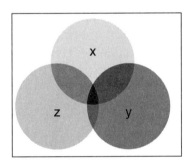

To help you better understand this idea, suppose that you have three turrets with success rates of 0.2, 0.4, and 0.6 respectively. You can calculate the odds that at least one turret will hit the target as follows:

Figure 11.1
Venn diagram of three events x, y, z

$$p(x \cup y \cup z) = p(x) + p(y) + p(z) - p(x \cap y) - p(x \cap z) - p(y \cap z) + p(x \cap y \cap z)$$
$$= 0.2 + 0.4 + 0.6 - 0.2 \cdot 0.4 - 0.2 \cdot 0.6 - 0.4 \cdot 0.6 + 0.2 \cdot 0.4 \cdot 0.6$$
$$= 0.808$$

Not bad! That's roughly 80%, which means that between the three turrets, the target will be killed four times out of five.

As an interesting twist, suppose that you know that a turret has hit and killed a target. Furthermore, you know the probability of death after a hit, but not the probability of a hit for the turret. Deducing this is basic algebra, and is read as "the probability of event *b* knowing that event *a* has occurred":

$$p(a \cap b) = p(a)\, p(b)$$

$$p(b \mid a) = \frac{p(a \cap b)}{p(a)}$$

Permutation

Permutation is a basic probability tool that helps you to count the ways in which objects can be ordered or picked. This can be useful when you want to compute a probability, but you need to know how many ways you can arrange your elements. It's also a good tool for calculating the complexity of a problem, as you will see when you get deeper into the AI portion of statistics.

To illustrate, suppose you have three objects—a, b, and c—and three boxes, and you want to determine the number of ways the objects and the boxes can be paired up. When choosing the object to be placed in the first box, you have three objects to choose from. When choosing the object to be placed in the second box, you have two objects to choose from, because one object has already been placed in a box and is therefore no longer among the choices. When choosing the object to be placed in the third box, you have only one object to choose from, because the other two objects are already in the box. Mathematically, then, you can determine that you have 3 • 2 • 1 = 6 ways, or permutations, of pairing the objects and the boxes. If you enumerate them, you will see that this is indeed the case: {a, b, c}, {a, c, b}, {b, a, c}, {b, c, a}, {c, a, b}, {c, b, a}.

What would happen if you only had two boxes, but still three objects? In that case, you would still have three objects to choose from when deciding which object would be placed in the first box, and two objects to choose from when deciding which object would be placed in the second box. Thus, you can use the equation 3 • 2 = 6 to determine that the number of permutations does not change. To verify this, simply look at the first two elements of the set of three; each is unique. This tells you that, in general, a permutation of *r* elements chosen out of *n* elements is as follows, in which *i*! for a given number *i* is defined as the product of *i*, *i* − 1, *i* − 2, all the way down to 1:

$$P(n, r) = \frac{n!}{(n-r)!}$$

This only works if the boxes are distinguishable. If you simply claim that a box is a box, the ordering is of no importance and you're actually looking at a combination problem. Mathematically, the following holds:

$$i! = \prod_{j=1}^{i} j$$

Combinations

Combinations are similar to permutations, but do not account for order. In other words, a combination is a permutation in which no two sets contain exactly the same elements. For example, suppose you're out to dinner, and you have the option of choosing two side dishes out of the four that are available. In that case, the order of the selection doesn't matter and you can verify that six possibilities exist. Returning to the object/box example from the preceding section, though, suppose you have as many objects as you do boxes. In this case, a combination equals a permutation, and similarly if you only chose one object out of the whole pack. This is obvious if you simply think about the definition of combinations in relation to permutations. Recall that combinations are really permutations in which the order does not matter. If you have to choose one out of n, then in that case, the order is irrelevant. Similarly, if you need to omit one object, the same logic applies, but in reverse. Omitting one object makes no sense out of order, because you are removing one object (or choosing $n - 1$ out of n).

But how can you solve a combination problem in general? It's really not that complicated. In a permutation $P(n, r)$, you have compute the number of ways to position r elements chosen out of a group of n. Then you need to remove the sets in the permutation that are the same, but ordered differently. Interestingly enough, you already know that r elements can be positioned in $r!$ ways. Thus, for each possibility, $r!$ ways exist to position the objects that have been chosen. Consequently, if you divide by this amount, you will remove all differently ordered sets:

$$C(n,r) = \binom{n}{r} = \frac{P(n,r)}{r!} = \frac{n!}{r!(n-r)!}$$

You can apply this idea recursively to get the multinomial formula, which is nothing but a generalized combination. For example, suppose you want to make four groups of air units for your game. You want to determine how many ways you can achieve this; of course, you don't care about the order of the choices because they are battle groups. If you do the math for 16 planes with groups of 5, 4, 3, and 2, you get the following:

$$\binom{16}{5}\binom{11}{4}\binom{7}{3}\binom{4}{2} = \frac{16!}{5!11!}\frac{11!}{4!7!}\frac{7!}{3!4!}\frac{4!}{2!2!}$$

$$= \frac{16!}{5!4!3!2!2!}$$

$$= \binom{16}{5,4,3,2}$$

Combinations also become a pretty powerful tool for computing the coefficient of a polynomial power. A polynomial's coefficient for a given set of power can be computed as follows:

$$\text{For } \left(x_1 + x_2 + x_3 + \cdots \right)^n$$

$$\text{the co-efficient of } x_1^{a_1} x_2^{a_2} x_3^{a_3} \cdots$$

$$\text{is } \begin{pmatrix} n! \\ a_1, a_2, a_3, \ldots, a_i \end{pmatrix}$$

This can be a pretty efficient problem-solver. For instance, the coefficient of the polynomial $(x + y + z)^8$ for $x^2 y^2 z^4$ is $8! / (2!2!4!)$. You can solve a plethora of problems with these types of tools, but because doing so is not always that useful in games, I've kept my coverage of them brief.

Random Number Generation (Uniform Deviates)

What, exactly, is randomness? The dictionary defines it as lacking a plan, purpose, or pattern. As a mathematician, I prefer to think of randomness as the lack of perceived order. I say *perceived* because many things that you believe to be random, such as the outcome of rolling dice, can be explained, calculated, and repeated. After all, is it so hard to believe that if someone positions, shakes, and releases a pair of dice in exactly the same fashion as the previous roll, he couldn't get the same result? Taking that a step further, couldn't that person repeat the drill multiple times, tabulate and evaluate the results, and use that information to predict the outcome of subsequent rolls? Of course, there are so many parameters and variables involved in rolling dice—force, speed, angle, and the like—that it would be almost impossible to position, shake, and release a pair of dice in *exactly* the same manner multiple times. The point here, though, is that there is no such thing as a true random number.

In a game context, you are not interested in obtaining a true random number generator as much as obtaining pseudo-random numbers (that is, numbers that *seem* random but in fact are not, the way the outcome of rolling dice seems random but isn't) within a given range and, most importantly, achieving this task quickly. The problem is, aging language standards do not take into account the full capabilities programmers now possess, and hence penalize the programmers. For example, the standard srand()/rand() functions are remnants that can only output 16-bit values. What happens when you need floats, doubles, 32-bit values, or even 64-bit values? You use uniform deviates—that is, random numbers with equal probability within a given range—which are the fastest-known way to generate a reasonable random set. In addition, if you know SIMD, you can take advantage of this knowledge to quadruple the speed of random number generation. In statistics, random number generation can be done on various distributions. A distribution defines how probable it is that a number will be chosen.

note

What happens when you need floats, doubles, 32-bit values, or even 64-bit values? Granted, there are ways around them, but I think of these techniques as hacks. They are anything but optimal, but the techniques mentioned in this book provide a well-deserved upgrade to the standard random number generator of C/C++ libraries.

Integer Standard Linear Congruential Method

As mentioned previously, uniform deviates are random numbers that are equally likely within a given range. There are other types of random numbers, but you don't care about them because their purpose is usually to bias some numbers with a mean and standard deviation such as the Gaussian distribution. There is a method, however, to generate pseudo-random numbers, called the *standard linear congruential method*. In short, *congruential* implies that a modulus operation is present; *linear* implies that each number is equally likely (uniform deviates). This method specifically deals with integers.

Just what makes a good random number generator in a game context?

- For starters, you want the numbers to seem, well, random. Put another way, you don't want the number generation to follow any obvious patterns.

- You also want the numbers to span entirely within a range. After all, a random number generator that can only output 10 numbers within a 10K range won't be much good for most projects.

- Of prime importance, you want the number to be generated quickly. There's nothing more frustrating than a game that pauses while the random explosion particles are being generated.

What, then, does the ANSI C standard—which suggests what most C/C++ libraries currently implement with regard to random number generation—recommend? The truth is, the committee doesn't recommend anything. It merely gives an example and notes that whatever function is implemented, it should produce a good random sequence. Their example was the upper 16-bit of the recurrence equation:

$$N_i = (1103515245N_{i-1} + 12345) \bmod 32768$$

In short, the modulus guarantees that the random number will be contained within the range [0, 32767]; its very simplistic form makes for a rather attractive option. Even so, it does beg a few questions. Why do you choose these numbers and why do they work? Without dwelling too much on the math, the random number always needs to be bounded; hence the modulus here is a clear choice because you know for sure that the remainder can't possibly be greater than the divisor. As for the linear function preceding the modulus, there's actually a plethora of functions that can be inserted here. One other popular choice, which is shown here, is the family of Fibonacci lagged series, which is nothing but a back-buffer sequence of additions. Nonetheless, all methods have the problem of not being as fast as the linear congruential for equal entropies.

$$N_i = (N_{i-10} + N_{i-7}) \bmod 24$$

The simplest (fastest) non-constant equation you could use is $(N_{i-1} + b)$ where b is a constant, but these terms yield a very predictable and continuous set, which is not desirable. The next logical step is to try $(aN_{i-1} + b)$, where a and b are constants. This function is still continuous and predictable, but if your variable a is large enough, it will be pulled back down by the modulus, which will yield a not-so-predictable set. Some theorists have shown that removing b altogether can also yield good results with a careful choice of a, but because the addition instruction is pretty cheap, you will keep it. It's important to note that due to the nature of the modulus, the terms in the sequence will eventually repeat and the length of the cycles will be smaller or equal to the divisor. The general form of a linear congruential random number generator is given here:

$$N_i = (aN_{i-1} + b) \bmod c$$

Coming back to the ANSI/C example and the actual values of $a=1103515245$ and $b=12345$, there are many other numbers from which you could choose, although you cannot choose any number you want. For example, in the 1960s, IBM distributed a well-known algorithm with the values $a = 65539$, $b = 0$, $c = 2^{31}$. In the case of the 1D distribution, everything looks fine. The 2D distribution also looks pretty good. Looking at the 3D distribution with a given angle, however, you quickly notice that a clear pattern emerges. The lesson: In order to obtain a good sequence, you need to comply with a few rules; even then, nothing guarantees that the numbers used will be good for any and all applications.

Because you work with PCs, your ideal numbers for c will always be a logical variable boundary (that is, 8-/16-/32-/64-/128-/... bit). What, then, is a good value for a and b? For starters, the value of a or b should be large or else a clear linear function will be noticeable. Proof: In 1961, Greenberger proved that the sequence has a maximal period of c for numbers 2^n if and only if:

- *b* is not odd
- $(a - 1)$ is a multiple of 4

Microsoft seems to use the following equation for its Visual C++ .NET `int rand()` function:

```
int rand() = ((Seed = (Seed * 214013) + 2531011) / 65536) mod 32768
```

This equation is perfectly in line with the preceding theorem given values of $a = 214013$, $b = 2531011$, and $c = 2^{15}$. The curious thing here is the added division. In any random sequence that uses a linear congruential equation, the lowest bits always tend to have the worst entropy. For this reason, the equation first divides the value by 65,356 before calculating the remainder of the equation. When fixing the random number to fit a range, dividing the number such that it fits the range instead of applying another modulo and retrieving the lower bits of the number is recommended. In a game scenario, however, you don't care much about producing better (that is, more random) random numbers, so you will happily let go of this extra division.

Now that you understand the theory behind it, let's turn to the problem at hand. Remember the hack I mentioned earlier that you can use to obtain 32-bit random numbers? The process involves nothing but a calculation of two random numbers; you assign the top 16 bits to the first number and the bottom 16 bits to the bottom number. This is bad for two reasons:

- You calculate two random numbers—two multiplications, two shift rights, and two ands in the Microsoft case
- You produce only 32,768 possible numbers, while a 32-bit integer should produce 2^{32} unique numbers

You now know how to create a linear congruential function, hence the only thing you need are values for *a* and *b* to plug into your equation for 32-bit values. For 32 bits, $c = 2^{32}$; if you follow Knuth's proposition that $a = 1,664,525$ and $b = 1,013,904,223$, you will have created a 32-bit random number generator. This sequence does rather well and has a full-cycle 2^{32} by the theorem above.

```
int rand() = Seed = (Seed * 1664525) + 1013904223
```

What you have done here is two-fold:

- You have created a function that has more possibilities.
- You have created a function that is faster than its 16-bit counterpart.

With regard to 64 bit, there doesn't seem to be any agreement or conjecture with respect to a good set of values for *a* and *b*. Therefore, for your purposes, I conjecture that $a = 49,948,198,753,856,273$ and $b = 7,478,206,353,254,095,475$ are good values. These have been analyzed with various well-known tests such as the spectral test, calculating the entropy, the serial correlation, the arithmetic mean, Chi-square, Monte Carlos, and compression, all of which yielded good-enough results for your purposes.

The most important test for games, however, is the spectral test, which seeks to determine how good the random distribution looks when plotted in *n* dimensions. To illustrate, let's assume the usage of random numbers to determine the location and speed for your particle system generator. Clearly, if all the vertices being generated by the particle system lie on parallel planes, it will look rather awkward. This is also where IBM's random number generator fails. Included with the book is a spectral rendering program. "Random" can render random sets in up to six dimensions without losing information by encoding information by changing the color of the pixels. Feel free to test your own set of parameters; if it works in your case, then that's all that matters. The test is pretty simple. It plots vertices for which the coordinates are randomly selected (which is quite similar to a particle system that generates random positions or random velocities).

Finally, let's finish this section by illustrating a few specters (see Figures 11.2, 11.3, and 11.4) with the random number generators presented in this section.

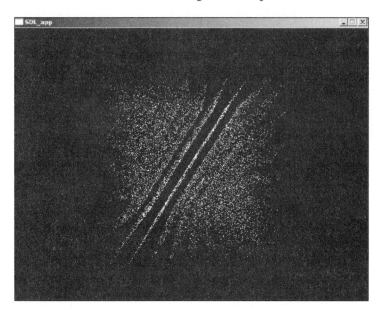

Figure 11.2
The specters of IBM in 3D

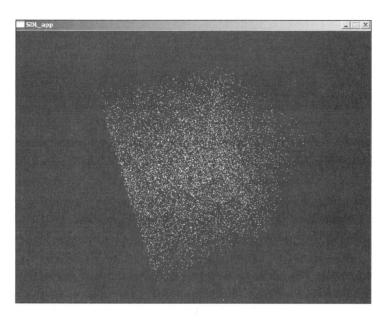

Figure 11.3
The specters of Microsoft C++ .NET

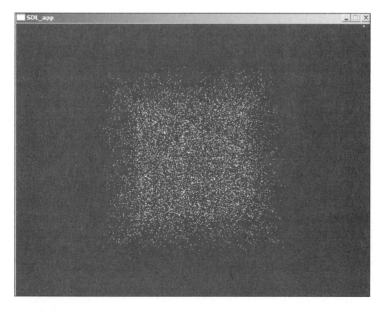

Figure 11.4
The specters of Knuth's method

Floating-Point Linear Congruential Method

Integers are nice, but not nice enough. If you're serious about games, then you know that a lot of the fancy graphics benefit greatly from floating-point values. The usual hack to achieve this is to pick a random integer number, divide the number by the maximum number you can generate (hence creating a range from 0 to 1), and then multiplying your number to fit your floating-point range. Needless to say, this leaves plenty of room for some optimizations. You already know what the linear congruential method is (at least for integers); now you need only apply a similar concept to floats. Or do you?

Optimization is one of the fields that requires deep knowledge about the machine you're working with. In this case, you are interested in the bit-wise representation of floating-point values on the PC. Luckily for you, this format is standardized and quite easy. In short, every floating-point number can be written in the following form:

$$\pm(1 + 2^{-mantisa}) * 2^{exponent-127}$$

note

Please see Chapter 19, "The Quick Mind: Computational Optimizations," for the gritty details on optimizing.

If you fix the exponent to 0 so that you end up multiplying your number by 1, you can randomize the mantissa to obtain a random number. That leaves only one little devil you have to exorcise before you can call this method complete. Recall that in the mantissa, the first bit is implicitly 1, which means that your numbers will be of the form 1.xxx. The value of xxx, which is the mantissa, will range from 0 to 1, but will never actually reach 1 because adding $1/2^i$ for all positive integers i will tend toward 1 but will never actually reach it. This shouldn't be an issue for you because any subsequent operation will most likely fix the infinitely small lack of precision. Because you generate a random number between 1.0 and ~2.0, you can simply subtract 1 to yield a range of [0, 1], as the following code shows:

```
unsigned long Result = (Seed & 0x007FFFFF) | 0x3F800000;
float RandomFloat = ((float)*(float *) & Result) - 1.0f;
```

It turns out there's one last surprise with this technique. Looking at the specter of these numbers with Knuth's values reveals that the fourth dimension of these values exposes a pattern, which implies that these values are not the best around. Figure 11.5, which has been digitally enhanced, illustrates this. (You'll be able to see much more clearly that the specter of this ordered set is not very good if you run the application yourself.)

Figure 11.5
The specters of Knuth's method for floats in 4D

I don't claim to have found a perfect solution because I don't believe that one exists. But at the very least, the specters of the values $a=85899573$ and $b = 101390421$ do not seem to generate any visible patterns. Does that mean you should change the values for a 32-bit integer random number generator? Not quite. The specter didn't reveal anything alarming when it dealt with 32-bit integers, but these values *might* be better.

Before you finish this section, let's take a look at double floating-point precision variables. The double floating points follow the same idea as the single floating points, but the number of bits allocated to the sections are different. In a double, the exponent has 11 bits, the mantissa 52, and the sign 1. If you are looking for a full-blown precision randomizer, then you have little choice but to compute in 64 bit and then apply the masks followed by a subtraction of 1. In most cases, you don't actually need 52 bits of decimal precision. 32 bits should be plenty in most—if not all—situations. Consequently, instead of generating random bits for all 52 bits, you can simply generate random bits for the first 32 bits and leave the remaining bits at 0. This is nothing but a 32-bit integer random number that is shifted to fit the required bit position. The following piece of code illustrates this:

```
unsigned long Result[2] = {
    ((unsigned long)Seed << 20),
    ((unsigned long)Seed >> 12) | 0x3FF00000,
};
double RandomDouble = (double)*(double *)Result - 1.0;
```

Generating Linearly Unpredictable Random Numbers

You may decide it is of interest to be able to generate a random number that is not linearly predictable. Why? Because hacking in multiplayer games has increased, and it only seems to be getting worse. Thus, in certain types of games, if a player can get his hands on the seed of the other player's random number, he can basically predict the number and use this information to his advantage.

One of the best techniques to generate linearly unpredictable random numbers is with a white noise generator. Examples of white noise include the snow that appears on your television on unoccupied channels, thermal capacitor noise, and so on. Of course, you don't have access to any such material on the PC, but you can use external devices in order to shift the seed once in a while. For instance, every second, you could read the mouse position and add the least significant bit of that value to the seed. Another source of randomness can come from the joystick or keyboard. Your imagination is the limit. Fight the hacks, though, because they really bring down the fun factor.

Distributions

Distribution is an important aspect of statistics, which looks at how the samples you have taken of an event are related. As you know, gathering statistics involves observation; to accumulate data, you need to take samples. Sometimes you'll be able to take every possible sample, yielding a complete model. For example, you could sample the grade of every student in a class and produce the distribution of these values, and then use a distribution graph to show relatively how many people have a particular grade. You can think of a distribution graph as a large *Connect 4*–type structure. In this case, the graph has five columns: A, B, C, D, and F. If the percentage of students who received an A was between 0 and 25%, add one "token" to the A column. If the percentage of students who received an A was between 25 and 50%, add two "tokens" to the A column. Then move to the B column and add tokens accordingly. When you're finished, you'll be able to see how the grades were distributed.

A distribution graph is not limited to four classifications (0–25%, 25–50%, 50–75%, 75–100%). In fact, you can plot a graph that has an infinite number of divisions. A distribution graph can thus be seen as the density of a value as a function of its possible values as illustrated in Figure 11.8 (see the section "Normal Distribution" later in this chapter). Such a graph is typically normalized such that the area under the graph is 1. By doing so, the integral from one boundary to the other gives you the percentage of samples in that span as illustrated in Figure 11.7 (see the section "Uniform Distribution" later in this chapter).

Distribution Properties

A distribution is typically attributed to a series of well-known factors that helps you to visualize what the distribution should look like:

- The mean
- The variance
- Standard deviation

The Mean

A *mean* is a weighted average of possible values, where the weight is the probability. In a typical average, all values have an equal weight/probability. In a weighted average, however, different weights are attributed to different values. For instance, suppose you had a set of numbers {1, 2, 2, 3}. The average could be computed using the equation (1 + 2 + 2 + 3) / 4. On the other hand, you could also represent the same thing in a more convenient way by using weights (1*1 + 2*2 + 1*3) / 4. In the second case, a weighted average is used in which the number 2 has a weight or, if you prefer, a probability that is twice as large as the other numbers.

For a continuous function, you can define the mean as such:

$$\mu = E(X) = \int_{-\infty}^{\infty} x \cdot p(x) \, dx$$

The Variance

The variance is a value that gives you an idea of how much the sample values in a set deviate from the mean. For example, if many students had the same grade, the variance would be low. On the other hand, if many students failed an exam and many others aced it, the variance would be high. One way to determine the variance is to compute the mean of the difference between an element x and μ, but this method can be problematic if the sign becomes an issue. Instead, simply square the difference to obtain a signless result. Consequently, the variance is defined as such:

$$\sigma^2 = E\left((X-\mu)^2\right)$$
$$= E(X^2) - \mu^2$$
$$= \left(\int_{-\infty}^{\infty} x^2 p(x)\right) - \mu^2$$

Standard Deviation

For your purposes, standard deviation can be defined as the square root of the variation. The standard deviation is, generally speaking, more useful than the variation, mainly because it works under the same scale as your data. The square root that is introduced in the variance changes the scale, but computing the square root of the final results helps you to reestablish everything on the same foot. In other words, it's like comparing oranges with oranges instead of comparing squared numbers with ordinary numbers.

Covariance

You've already seen what the variance is. The covariance is a very closely related principle that is simply more general. Given n sets $\{X_1\}, \ldots, \{X_n\}$, the covariance $[s]_{ij}$ of x_i and x_j is mathematically defined by

$$\sigma_{ij} = \overline{(x_i - \mu_i)(x_j - \mu_j)}$$

Here, μ_i represents the average of the ith set, and the overbar represents the average of all possible values. This type of analysis is very useful for determining the direction of a set of samples. For instance, if you wanted to determine the direction of the formulation for a group of tanks, you could build a covariance matrix. This is simply a matrix where every element ij represents the covariant value for ij. This matrix goes through every value of $[s]_{ij}$ as a table would. Generally, you can write the covariance matrix $\mathbf{C}$ as follows:

$$\mathbf{C} = \frac{1}{n}\sum_{i=1}^{n}(\mathbf{x}_i - \mu)(\mathbf{x}_i - \mu)^{\mathrm{T}}$$

If you write this matrix for a set of 3-vectors, you get the following matrix:

$$\mathbf{C} = \frac{1}{n}\begin{bmatrix} \sum_{i=1}^{n}(x_i - \mu_x)^2 & \sum_{i=1}^{n}(x_i - \mu_x)(y_i - \mu_y) & \sum_{i=1}^{n}(x_i - \mu_x)(z_i - \mu_z) \\ \sum_{i=1}^{n}(y_i - \mu_y)(x_i - \mu_x) & \sum_{i=1}^{n}(y_i - \mu_y)^2 & \sum_{i=1}^{n}(y_i - \mu_y)(z_i - \mu_z) \\ \sum_{i=1}^{n}(z_i - \mu_z)(x_i - \mu_x) & \sum_{i=1}^{n}(z_i - \mu_z)(y_i - \mu_y) & \sum_{i=1}^{n}(z_i - \mu_z)^2 \end{bmatrix}$$

The first thing you may notice is that the matrix is symmetric. Thus, only half of it needs to be computed. But how can you use this matrix to, say, determine the general direction of a bunch of tanks? Well, it should be pretty clear that the covariance is closely linked to the variance. In fact, the ith variance for the ith group consists of the elements in the diagonal of the matrix. Consequently, this matrix gives you a sense of the deltas between the components (or the offset, if you prefer). An offset is a vector, and thus it gives you a general direction toward which a group is heading. If you get a diagonal matrix, it implies that the values are evenly distributed on each axis, and thus the general direction is nothing but the axes. When any covariant is 0, it implies that there's no correlation between the two elements.

You still need to determine a basis (a set of three vectors) that will give you the general direction of the formation for tanks. The key to solving this problem is that a diagonal covariance matrix has its axes in a trivial basis {<1, 0, 0>, <0, 1, 0>, <0, 0, 1>}. Consequently, if you can find a basis **B** (a rotation matrix) that transforms the covariance matrix into a diagonal matrix, the basis **B** would be your set of directional vectors. This comes from the fact that a rotation is simply a linear combination of a set of vectors that redefine the axes of the space. If you apply this logic, you get the following:

$$\mathbf{C}' = \frac{1}{n}\sum_{i=1}^{n}\left(\mathbf{Bx}_i - \mathbf{B}\cdot_{,i}\right)\left(\mathbf{Bx}_i - \mathbf{B}\cdot_{,i}\right)^{\mathrm{T}}$$

$$= \frac{1}{n}\sum_{i=1}^{n}\mathbf{B}\left(\mathbf{x}_i - \cdot_{,i}\right)\left(\mathbf{x}_i - \cdot_{,i}\right)^{\mathrm{T}}\mathbf{B}^{\mathrm{T}}$$

$$= \mathbf{BCB}^{\mathrm{T}}$$

Now is a good time to recall what you learned in Chapter 3, "Meet the Matrices"—namely, about eigenvectors and the diagonalization process. This is exactly where you want to start using this technique. To solve the problem, all you have to do is find the eigenvector matrix B that satisfies the preceding statement; this matrix will be the basis for the direction of the set of units. This finding will be extremely important in Chapter 15, "Visibility Determination: The World of the Invisible," when you compute the bounding volume of various elements. At that point, you'll want to know the general direction of a set of vertices in order to determine the extent and direction of the volume.

Uniform Distribution

The methods that were previously shown to generate random numbers can generate a uniform distribution. A uniform distribution gives an equal probability to every sample. If you look at the graph of such a distribution, shown in Figure 11.7, you will notice that it is a straight line running from a to b, the two boundaries. This means that the odds of having one specific value out of an event is equally as likely as the odds of having another specific value out of that same event.

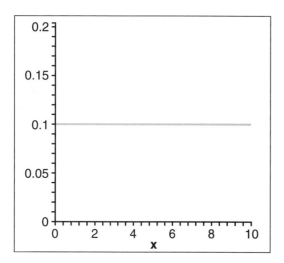

Figure 11.7
A uniform distribution [a, b] = [0, 10]

If you take a look at the random number generation, you can verify that this is the case. The generator will pass through every value from *a* to *b* before choosing any same value once more. Every possibility has an equal likelihood. In real life, if you were aiming for a bot, chances are that you would hit in the vicinity of the bot if you were to fire at it. Because you are more likely to hit one certain area more than another (the extreme sides, perhaps), this type of distribution would not be uniform.

Typically, when you look at a distribution, you are in fact looking at a function that gives the density of the probability. This comes back to the example of the *Connect 4* game. The more elements you have in one column, the denser that column becomes. If you take a look at the density function for this distribution, you will notice that it is a flat line. This should come as no surprise because any element *y* has the same probability. The likelihood that the result of the event is within range [*a*, *b*] is thus easy to compute. The only thing you have to determine is the height of the density function. If you force the area under the curve to equal 1, you get the following logic for the density *h*:

$$1 = p_u (a,b)$$
$$= hb - ha$$
$$h = \frac{1}{b-a}$$

It follows that the probability that the event's result falls within the range [c, d] is

$$p_u(a,b) = \frac{1}{b-a}(d-c)$$

Notice something interesting in this distribution (and for any continuous distribution). If $c = d$, you get 0. In other words, any single real number on a continuous function has a probability of 0. This makes sense if you think of the problem in real space. If you chose a single real number within the range $[a, b]$, there is an infinite number of values that you can build in that segment. Infinity compared to one single number is pretty dim, and 1 over infinity is obviously 0. On the other hand, if you chose a range $[c, d]$, you also have an infinite number of values within your range, so if you compute the ratio (in unorthodox math), the infinity symbol cancels and you get the percentage.

note

> The idea of dividing infinity symbols as such is not generally valid, however; it was used here only to demonstrate the idea that a single real value on an infinite range stands no chance of being picked.

For obvious reasons, the mean of this distribution is given by a typical average:

$$\mu = \frac{a+b}{2}$$

Similarly, you can look at the variation, which is a little more complex but given by the following:

$$\sigma^2 = \frac{(b-a)^2}{12}$$

Binomial Distribution

It is often useful to classify an event simply as successful or not. In such a case, you have two possible outcomes, and you can let the probability for each of them be p and q. It is generally the case that an event is repeated until success is met. Returning to the turret example, the turret will fire until it kills its target. One thing that the last model did not take into account is the fact that if the turret misses, it has better a chance of hitting its target the next time it fires. This makes sense because it has a 60% hit rate, which means that you would expect that in most cases, every three shots out of five will hit. If you know that it has missed a shot, then its chances of hitting the next shot are increased to three out of four. This idea, the probability of two outputs, or a repeated binomial event, is what the binomial distribution tries to model. You can, in fact, look at this as a binomial where n is the number of times the experiment is repeated:

$$(p+q)^n$$

The cool thing about this notation is that if you look at the coefficient of the expansion for which the power of p is equal to the amount of success for which you want to compute the probability, it represents the probability of having x successes out of n. For instance, if an AI hits you, his success would increase. The success is thus the percentage of success you expect from an event. With a more rigorous definition, the number of ways to get x successes out of n attempts for an event X is as follows:

$$p_b(X = x) = (\text{Number of ways to get } x \text{ successes out of n}) p^x q^{n-x}$$

$$= \binom{n}{x} p^x q^{n-x}$$

So in truth, this expansion is saying, "I want x successes (thus the p^x) and $(n - x)$ failures (thus the q^{n-x})." To illustrate, try computing the odds of the turret with a 60% accuracy rate getting five perfect shots in a row:

$$p_b(X = 5) = \binom{5}{5} 0.6^5 0.4^0$$

$$= 0.07776$$

$$= 7.7\%$$

Pretty slim odds, as you can see. Increase the number from 5 to something higher, and you will get even worse results. If, on the other hand, you wanted to calculate the odds of the 40% turret killing a target in five shots, you would really be trying to determine the probability of the event X having any value of $\{1, 2, 3, 4, 5\}$. Summing these terms will give you your answer:

$$p_b(X \leq 5) = P(X = 5) + P(X = 4) + P(X = 3) + P(X = 2) + P(X = 1)$$

$$= \binom{5}{5} 0.4^5 0.6^0 + \binom{5}{4} 0.4^4 0.6^1 + \binom{5}{3} 0.4^3 0.6^2 + \binom{5}{2} 0.4^2 0.6^3 + \binom{5}{1} 0.4^1 0.6^4$$

$$= 0.01024 + 0.0768 + 0.2304 + 0.3456 + 0.2592$$

$$= 0.92224 = 92.2\%$$

Thus, overall, even a target with only 40% accuracy has pretty good odds of killing a target within five shots.

A more intelligent way to solve this problem would have been to simply take its inverse. In other words, compute the probability that the turret missed all of its targets and then compute the inverse of that probability ($q = 1 - p$).

The binomial distribution is not a continuous distribution. Thus, instead of using integrals, you have to use finite sums. This should not be a problem. The probability of success is always the same for this distribution, so it is pretty easy to compute the mean and variance of the function—a process that will be left as an exercise:

$$\mu = np$$
$$\sigma^2 = npq$$

Poisson Distribution

The binomial distribution attributes a single probability to a single unit. Another approach is to take a lot of similar units and to look at probabilities regarding the group of units. This is the idea behind the Poisson distribution. For example, suppose you are running with a bunch of tanks in the night and, because you were cheap on materials and repairs, parts of the tanks begin to fail. Does a preconceived rate of 1.02 tank failures per battalion (comprised of 100 tanks) per battle implicitly mean that at least one tank per battalion will fail during a battle? No. This rate is no different from the probability rates discussed previously. A probability rate such as 60% is really just an average; it is quite possible to go through a battle without actually losing any tanks. On the other hand, you could lose three tanks or more during the course of a single battle. That's what probability is: a mere guess.

A lot of complex math is involved in the distribution (density function), so let's just jump right into it. The distribution of the Poisson process (Poisson distribution) for a rate $[L]$ verified for x units is as follows:

$$P_p(x) = \frac{\lambda^y e^{-\lambda}}{y!}$$

Let's come back to the tank example. What are the odds that at least one tank will fail during battle? The math is pretty simple:

$$P_p(X > 0) = 1 - P_p(X = 0)$$
$$= 1 - \frac{1.02^0 e^{-1.02}}{0!}$$
$$= 1 - e^{-1.02}$$
$$= 0.6394 = 63.94\%$$

If you recompute the formula to check the odds of more than one tank failing, you get a mere 0.72%. So if you can sacrifice a single tank, perhaps the choice to skimp on materials and repairs was worth it.

Because the rate is given as a precondition to the Poisson process, the mean of the function is thus the given rate. If you do the math for the variance, you will find that it, too, equals the rate. In mathematical terms the following holds:

$$\mu = \sigma^2 = \lambda$$

Normal Distribution

The normal distribution is commonly used in simulations because it follows many physical phenomena. Physicists sometimes call the normal distribution the Gaussian distribution, while sociologists prefer to call it the Bell curve.

This distribution is interesting in games because it offers a lot of flexibility in the simulation. The beauty of it is that you have control over the variation. For example, suppose you are playing a 3D shoot-em-up and your bots have a mean accuracy of 60%. If you write your code such that every six bullets out of ten hit the player, the player will soon realize what is going on and will quickly learn to hide during the harmful shots, therefore drastically reducing the bot's "true" accuracy. A more realistic approach is to give the bot a deviation. For instance, you could treat the distribution curve as a function of the distance of the shot from you. You can then say that the span [a, b] is the span that is considered a hit (success), while anything outside this range is a miss. From this point, you can write variously skilled bot shooters by simply changing the variance of the bots. The killer bots will have a very short variance, while the stupid bots will have a very long variance. The nice thing about this is that regardless of how good the bot is, the possibility that it will miss is always present. That means that rather than generating a super-bot, you are generating a more "human" bot.

The function for the normal distribution is nothing but a normalized continuous Poisson distribution ranging from $[-\infty, \infty]$, as depicted here and illustrated in Figure 11.8:

$$p_n(x) = \frac{e^{-\frac{(x-\mu)^2}{2\sigma^2}}}{\sqrt{2\pi\sigma^2}}$$

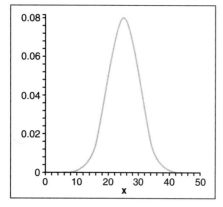

Figure 11.8
A normal distribution with mean 25 and variance 5

Intelligence Everywhere

The main goal behind statistics with respect to game programming is to be able to use it somehow for AI purposes. A few examples were already given on how you could go about doing this to make your units smarter and more efficient, but there is much more you can do with statistics to leverage AI. The following section looks at a few well-known AI techniques and how they fit into the statistical gaming model.

The Exponential Function

The problem with the previous probability methods is that they do not allow the mean to change much. A game is dynamic, however, in that it changes with time. Suppose, then, that you want to build an AI that will more or less match the player's own ability. For example, if you set the accuracy of the bot in *Quake* to a fixed value, the player will likely reach a point where he will be able to beat the bot at difficulty n, but will not actually be able to beat the bot at difficulty level $n + 1$. The solution, then, is simple: Why have any levels at all? Instead, you can simply match the bot's skill with that of the player by computing some statistics on the player and feeding that data to the bot. For example, suppose you have an accuracy rate of 20%. Ideally, the bot should try to match that accuracy to give you a decent challenge.

Simply computing a mean of the player's accuracy over time is an ineffective way to determine the skill level at which the computer should play. Why? Suppose a player switches to a certain gun that suddenly improves (or worsens) his play. If the player's accuracy is charted as a mean, then it may take some time for the altered accuracy to be translated into data that changes the computer's skill level. To illustrate, suppose you have an accuracy average of 8,000,000/10,000,000, or 80%. Suppose further that a new sample is generated on a per-100 basis. If you suddenly plummet down to 20% accuracy, the next evaluation of your accuracy will be 8,000,020/10,000,100, or 79.999%—a barely discernable difference. As a result, the bot's accuracy level will remain roughly static, even as yours plummets; it will be some time before the two even out.

Enter the exponential function. The idea behind this function is that you attribute a certain weight to the most recent approximation; the sum of all the older approximations combined is then allotted the remaining percentage. For example, to give a weight of 50% to your current approximation, you can simply run the following formula:

$$Size_n = \frac{NewSample}{2} + \frac{Size_{n-1}}{2}$$

To illustrate, assume your samples are described in the set {4, 7, 2, 6, 3, 7}. Given the preceding equation, your approximation would yield {4, 5.5, 3.75, 4.87, 3.93, 5.46}. If you want fewer perturbations, you can attribute a smaller percentage to the new value; conversely, if you want the approximation to skew more wildly, you can give more prevalence to the latest value. If the sampled value changes, a low percentage will take a long time to adapt (change), while a higher one won't. On the other hand, a higher percentage might change too quickly and may not be able to adequately absorb the perturbations. You know your software; you should know how much your samples should change over time and how quickly.

One problem with exponential functions is that they often predict a number smaller than your average maximum. In other words, if the player is getting better with time, the bot will never try an accuracy level that is greater than the player's. This becomes a problem because it does not force the player to get better; he can get some pretty easy wins because he is always fighting an inferior bot.

For example, if you refer to the two sets posted above, you will notice that the prediction is smaller than the real value of three times out of five. In your game, you can keep track of the minimum and the maximum. You want to tend more toward the maximum because you probably prefer to challenge the player somewhat. The other important fact is that if the player reaches a given accuracy at some point, it is likely that he can always return to that level of accuracy in the future, even if his accuracy level slides in the interim. To handle this, cheat a little bit. Instead of keeping track of the maximum, use an exponential function on the maximum itself, and you can then apply a weighted average with the maximum and the current accuracy value.

They may be a little confusing, so let's take a deeper look. Suppose you had the same streak of integer numbers as posted above—{4, 7, 2, 6, 3, 7}—for accuracy on a scale of ten. (By the way, you would obtain these numbers by computing the number of hits per total hits for a given fixed interval.) Thus, you could define that you will be checking how many hits are successful for every 10 shots. Every time the tenth shot is sent, the instant probability reverts to 0/0.

Obviously, the player may have some huge swings of accuracy over ten shots—behavior that you do not want the bot to adopt. To avoid this, use an exponential function such as the example given previously that yielded {4, 5.5, 3.75, 4.87, 3.93, 5.46}. In many cases, however, you can verify that the player can do better than that. Simultaneously, take note of the maximum. If the current probability is higher than the maximum, then you can set the new maximum. If the probability is lower, this is where you may want to run an exponential function on it. For example, if you assume that you use a percentage of 5% for the maximum, you would get {4, 7, 6.75, 6.71, 6.52, 7}.

Now that you have two sets of the probability, you can combine them one last time with a weighted average to yield the final accuracy of the bot. For example, if the current value is 80% and the maximum is 20%, you get {4, 5.8, 4.35, 5.23, 4.44, 5.76}. As you can see, this new method challenges the player to do better.

note

Of course, you could also apply a bias to the equation, but the problem with a bias is that it can mean a lot if the accuracy is pretty bad, and it can mean very little if the accuracy is already good. With the exponential function, however, you get a pretty good balance.

Fuzzy Logic/Neural Networks

Is there really such a thing as an absolute truth and absolute falsehood? Is there such a thing as never and always? Just about every rule has an exception. This is especially true with AI. A good AI typically evolves, refining itself, over time. The process by which this occurs is sometimes called *fuzzy logic*, and the idea behind it is that it accumulates a set of hypotheses, verifies them, and instead of saying that it is "true" or "false," it gives the set of hypotheses a probability of truthfulness.

For instance, consider a bot that keeps track of the player's high-level movements, such as jump&shoot. Instead of saying that the player always jumps before shooting, the bot computes an average or, even better, an exponential function (that way, if you suddenly stop jumping and shooting, the AI does not get confused). With this, the AI can keep track of the times you jumped before shooting and how many of those shots were successful. If the probability exceeds a certain threshold that you predefine, then the AI can look at countermeasures.

Here, you can insert yet another fuzzy statement. The bot can randomly try some combinations and, instead of finding one unique combination that it asserts to be the "ultimate truth," it can keep track of how effective its weapons are against the player, and it can start matching the player's attacks with the various defenses or counterattacks that the bot can perform. Because this system is dynamic (with an exponential or mean function), the bot will adapt to the new techniques you throw at it. This begs the next question: How do you figure out an effective attack or defense? The next section suggests one method.

Evolutionary Algorithms

Evolutionary algorithms are greatly inspired by the Darwinian way of thinking. Darwin asserted that life evolved by the law of survival the fittest. The strongest of the pack lived, while the weaker ones died. As a result, what you have today are some of the strongest species or, more precisely, the ones that have proven to adapt the best.

You can use the exact same idea on software. If you come back to the idea of a bot that is trying some new tactics, one good approach, if you do not want your bot to swing from one good tactic to one stupid tactic, is to use a mutation. Initially, you can generate a set of random tactics—(jump, strafe, shoot), (duck, hide), (strafe, shoot), and so on. You can thereafter evaluate the efficiency of these tactics. When you know which ones work best, you can discard the ones that were not successful and generate mutations of the ones that worked.

For example, if you figured that (strafe, shoot) was the best option, perhaps the next set of mutations would have ({strafe, shoot, duck}, {duck, strafe, shoot}, and {shoot, strafe}). The extent of the mutation is up to you. If you want drastic swings, this is the way to go, but if you prefer the more conservative approach, you can do smaller mutations over longer time intervals.

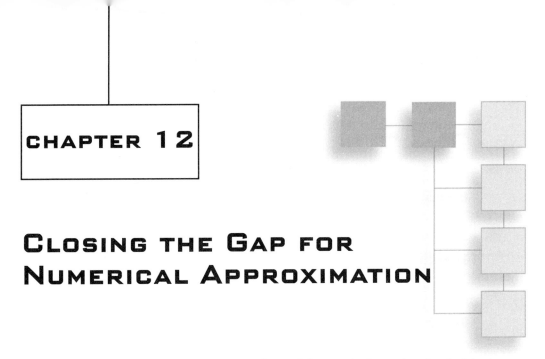

CHAPTER 12

CLOSING THE GAP FOR NUMERICAL APPROXIMATION

There's an old joke about π: For mathematicians, π is the ratio of a circle's circumference to its diameter $d = 2r$. For an engineer, π is about 22/7. For a physicist, π is 3.14159, give or take 0.000005. For a programmer, π is 3.141592653589. For a nutritionist, π is a misspelled dessert. (Ba-dum-*bum*.)

Okay, okay. It's a bad joke. But even so, I think each answer is correct in its context. For the engineer, the rough translation of 22/7 suffices. Similarly, the physicist is satisfied with his own approximation. Programmers profit from the maximum precision that a double can handle. And the nutritionist? Well, he couldn't care less about π, so he chooses what pleases him.

In truth, it really boils down to how much pie—or π—you want to have. If you prefer, it depends on the amount of precision you are willing to sacrifice. The functions provided with C/C++ libraries are mostly direct FPU calls, and are calculated to attain the best precision possible. For some geometric algorithms, you absolutely require utmost precision; otherwise, it could mean the difference between a missing polygon and getting it right. In numerous other cases, however, such precision is not required. This is especially true in games, which typically move quickly enough that the user will not perceive much difference between a fully accurate function and one that is a bit less precise.

This chapter attempts to open your eyes to the vast world of numerical approximations by presenting efficient methods to approximate functions and solutions at the cost of accuracy, with speed as its primary benefit. Specifically, you'll learn about

- Equation solution approximation using the Newton-Raphson method
- Equation solution approximation using Halley's method
- Function approximation using the Taylor series

323

- Function approximation using the least square method
- Function approximation using a Legendre polynomial
- Function approximation using a Chebyshev polynomial
- Function approximation using a Minimax polynomial
- Multivariable function approximation

tip

In Maple, you can load the approximation package with the command with(numapprox);.

Solution Approximation

One dilemma that approximation can resolve is that of solving an equation that seems impossible. For example, in Chapter 1, "Equation Manipulation and Representation," you learned about a few techniques for finding the roots of polynomials with a degree of up to 4. Clearly, however, there must be techniques for solving this type of problem for higher-degree polynomials.

Indeed there are: approximation techniques. The approximation techniques used to solve such equations come in the form of trial and error or, perhaps more appropriately put, test and fix methods. These typically recursive equations require an initial guess; with each iteration, they refine the answer, hence converging toward the solution. These techniques are interesting because the more recursive steps you take, the more precise your solution becomes.

The Newton-Raphson Method

The Newton-Raphson method is a very powerful method for finding the roots of an equation in a reasonable time frame. You start by taking a guess at the root you wish to find— for example, x_0. From there, you approximate a piece of the function with the tangent line at x_0. Of course, the approximation may be pretty rough, but most of the time, the little bit of information you require is given to you by this method.

For example, consider that it is quite trivial to find the root of a line. If the tangent line is the approximation of your initial curve, the root will, in most cases, also be an approximate root of your equation. Obviously, the tangent line could give you a value that is far from the real value, but the idea is that if you take the line's root, which you can call x_1, you can reapply the same logic by using the later value as your initial guess. The beauty of this sequence is that if the initial guess is good enough, the function will converge toward the root, as illustrated in Figure 12.1 for steps a, b, c, and d. Of course, the better your initial guess, the faster it will converge toward the real root.

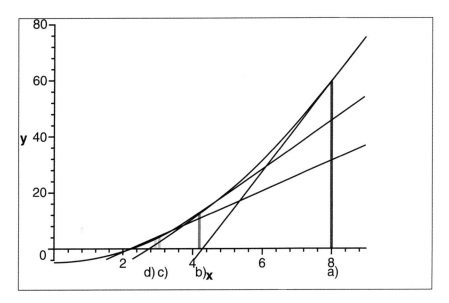

Figure 12.1
The Newton-Raphson root-finding method

Now that you understand this principle, let's look at the math behind it by starting with the tangent line's *x* intercept and its slope:

$$f'(x_n) = \frac{y - f(x_n)}{x - x_n}$$

$$= \frac{0 - f(x_n)}{x - x_n}$$

$$f'(x_n)(x_{n+1} - x_n) = -f(x_n)$$

$$x_{n+1} = -x_n - \frac{f(x_n)}{f'(x_n)}$$

This is a pretty straightforward method. For example, suppose you want to approximate the solution to the square root of 5. These are the steps you would take to compute this value with an initial guess of 8:

$$x^2 = 5$$
$$0 = x^2 - 5 = f(x)$$
$$f'(x) = 2x$$

$$x_{n+1} = x_n - \frac{x_n^2 - 5}{2x_n}$$

With this equation, you obtain the values rounded to the fourth digit {8, 4.3125, 2.7359, 2.2817, 2.2365, 2.2360}. With a calculator, you can then verify that the solution starts with 2.2360.

This is a nice technique for computing the roots of higher-order polynomials because there is no direct equation for most of them. Given the generality of the equation, this method also applies to other non-polynomial functions. Despite its practicality, however, this method is not bulletproof. If, for example, you take your initial guess to be a maximum on the curve, the tangent line will be horizontal and there will be no unique solution to this problem. Another problem may arise if you choose an initial guess that is too far from the root you are expecting to find. In that case, the tangent line may go farther down into the curve, and it may find a root other than the one you expected, as shown in Figure 12.2 for the two first steps.

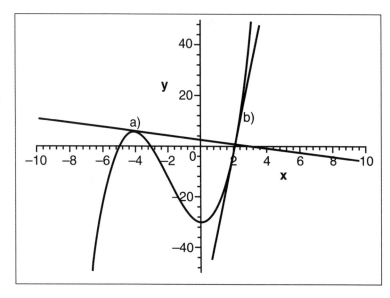

Figure 12.2
A problem with the Newton-Raphson root-finding method

Halley's Method

In Newton's method, a tangent line is used to approximate the original curve because you know that you could obtain an easy root with a line. As you will soon see, you can just as easily obtain a tangent parabola (from a Taylor series, which you will see shortly). A parabola is a more attractive approximation because it can better approximate any shape since parabolas can be used to represent lines and more. I have skipped the proof here because it is simply an algebraic manipulation with the tangent parabola and the identity you found in the preceding section—not very interesting. Halley's method converges faster than the Newton-Raphson method because of its higher degree. Its formula is given by the following:

$$x_{n+1} = x_n - \frac{2f(x_n)f'(x_n)}{2(f(x_n))^2 - f(x_n)f''(x_n)}$$

This method suffers from problems that are similar to those encountered with the Newton-Raphson method, but it is more robust. Besides, you generally need not compute these types of equations in real time, so you will likely be less concerned with their convergence speed than with their computational complexity.

2D Function Approximation

Function approximation becomes extremely useful when you want to insert a lot of eye candy without incurring the high computational cost associated with using complex functions in your game. For example, you might want to generate caustic waves, but you might not really care if the waves are following to the letter the laws of viscosity and density movement. You might simply want "some wavy function," in which case you don't care about the accuracy at all. (See Chapter 21, "Kicking the Turtle by Approximating Common and Slow Functions," for many applications of approximation.)

When you approximate a curve with another curve, one of the first questions you should ask is what function, which you can call $f(x)$, do you want to use to approximate the initial function? Some equations are much better approximations of curves than others. For example, a parabola is a better approximation than a line because you can also do a line with a parabola, which means that you can only increase the accuracy. There is no real limit to the target function you can choose, but whatever function you choose to approximate with, it should have some significant advantages over the other available functions. Otherwise, why approximate at all when you can get the real deal?

One of the most convenient functions to approximate with is the polynomial function. A polynomial is particularly interesting because if its parameters increase linearly, then you can convert every single multiplication into an addition. Furthermore, polynomials are generally decent approximations to most common functions. In addition, as you saw in Chapter 1, you can apply a substitution to reduce the polynomial's complexity by one multiplication to a subtraction. That being said, nothing stops you from using another function as the approximating function, but know that most instructions more complex than a multiplication or a division typically suck the FPU's cycles dry. As a last note on the choice of approximating function, you should not compute a polynomial in its tradition-al form $a_n x^n + \ldots + a_0$. Instead, you should use the Horner form, which factors out x for every power—in other words, of the form $a_0 + x(a_1 + x(a_2 + x(a_3 + \ldots)))$. This form is computationally less expensive because it carries fewer complex operations than comput-ing the equation with sums of factored powers.

tip

You can use Maple to convert an equation into the Horner form by issuing the convert command convert(<equation>, horner).

Forward Differentiation

I just mentioned that it is possible to convert a polynomial into additions when the poly-nomial has to be evaluated at fixed intervals. Suppose that the fixed interval is a. The ques-tion you must ask is, by how much does the function increase if you add a for every step? In other words, what is $f(x + a) - f(x)$?

$$f(x) = a + bx + cx^2 + \ldots$$

$$f(x+a) = a + b(x+a) + c(x+a)^2 + \ldots$$

$$f(x+a) - f(x) = \left(a + bx + ba + cx^2 + 2cax + ca^2 + \ldots\right) - \left(a + bx + cx^2 + \ldots\right)$$

$$f(x+a) - f(x) = \left(ba + 2cax + ca^2 + \ldots\right)$$

What are the implications of this? You have just determined that every time x increases by a, $f(x)$ increases by $(ba + 3cax + ca^2 + \ldots)$. So instead of computing $f(x)$ every time, all you need to do is keep track of the old value for $f(x)$ and, when you are ready to advance x with a, simply add this value to it. In other words, you successfully converted one level of mul-tiplication to an addition. How sweet is that?

If you take a look at the resulting equation, you can see that it still has a lot of multiplications, but you can apply the process recursively as much as you want in order to convert the entire polynomial into one single set of additions. You could always try this trick on other types of functions, but chances are that you will not be able to convert the function to the point where it becomes pure additions—or, for that matter, any simple operation.

Let's continue with an example, taking the third-degree polynomial $f(x) = 1 + 2x + 3x^2 + 4x^3$ and converting it to additions. Furthermore, let's suppose that the function starts at $x = 3$. The following process yields the stepped increments you need to compute the polynomial:

$$f'(x) = f(x+a) - f(x)$$
$$= a + 2(x+1) + 3(x+1)^2 + 4(x+1)^3 - (1 + 2x + 3x^2 + 4x^3)$$
$$= 2 + 6x + 3 + 12x^2 + 12x + 4$$
$$= 9 + 18x + 12x^2$$

$$f''(x) = f'(x+a) - f'(x)$$
$$= 9 + 18(x+1) + 12(x+1)^2 - (9 + 18x + 12x^2)$$
$$= 30x + 24x$$

$$f'''(x) = f''(x+1) - f''(x)$$
$$= 30 + 24(x+1) - (30 + 24x)$$
$$= 24$$

You can calculate the initial values for $x = 3$; Table 12.1 illustrates the steps taken to compute the values for $f(x)$ iteratively.

Table 12.1 Forward Differentiation of $1 + 2x + 3x^2 + 4x^3$

f(x)	f'(x)	f''(x)	f'''(x)
142	171	102	24
142+171 = 313	171 + 102 = 273	102 + 24 = 126	24
313 + 273 = 586	273 + 126 = 399	126 + 24 = 150	24
586 + 399 = 985	399 + 150 = 549	150 + 24 = 174	24

The Taylor Series

Now that you understand why polynomials are so useful, let's take a look at how you can actually achieve the task at hand. For example, let $g(x)$ be your reference curve (that is, the curve you want to approximate), and let $f(x)$ be the curve you are looking for. Let's start with a simple case, $f(x) = mx + b$, a first-order polynomial. The tangent line at a given point on the curve is not a terrible approximation. At least around the vicinity of the chosen point, which you can call x_0, the error is null to potentially increasing. From Chapter 7, "Accelerated Vector Calculus for the Uninitiated," you know that the slope of the tangent line at a point on a continuous line is its first derivative. You can then deduce the equation for your line as illustrated by the graph in Figure 12.3:

$$f(x) \approx f(a) + f'(a)(x-a)$$
$$\approx f'(a)x + f'(a) - f'(a)a$$

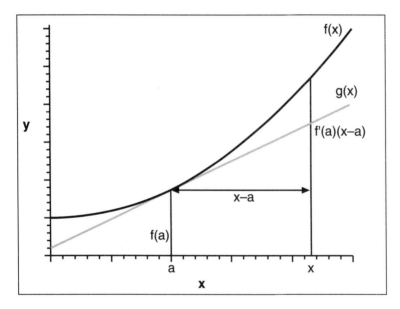

Figure 12.3
A tangent line roughly approximating a curve

This is the first-order Taylor series. A series can quickly be described as a sum of terms. For the sake of simplicity, let's consider only the case where $a = 0$. This particular series actually has a particular name: the MacLaurin series. The idea behind the Taylor polynomial is that if $f(x)$ at $x = a$ has the same value, speed, acceleration, and so forth as $g(x)$, then the approximation will be reasonable. What this implies on a calculus level is that the first derivative of your function should match the derivative of the original function and, similarly, should match all higher-order derivatives up to an arbitrary amount of precision, because some functions have an infinite number of non-zero derivatives. Mathematically speaking, you are looking for the coefficient of the polynomial $f(x)$ such that the derivatives equate your original function's derivatives. On mathematical grounds, the consequence of that logic is the following:

$$g(x) = a_0 + a_1 x + a_2 x^2 + \cdots + a_n x^n$$

$$
\begin{aligned}
f(0) &= g(0) &&= a_0 \\
f'(0) &= g'(0) &&= 1 \cdot a_2 = a_2 \\
f''(0) &= g''(0) &&= 2 \cdot 1 \cdot a_2 = 2a_2 \\
f'''(0) &= g'''(0) &&= 3 \cdot 2 \cdot 1 \cdot a_2 = 6a_2 \\
&\vdots &&\vdots \\
f^n(0) &= g^n(0) &&= n! a_n
\end{aligned}
$$

It follows, then, that the coefficient (a_i) for the MacLaurin series is

$$a_i = \frac{f^i(0)}{i!}$$

and its associated equations become

$$g(x) = \frac{f(0)}{0!} + \frac{f'(0)x}{1!} + \frac{f''(0)x^2}{2!} + \frac{f'''(0)x^3}{3!} + \cdots + \frac{f^n(0)x^n}{n!}$$

Let's come back to the original case, the Taylor series. You want to be able to handle any arbitrary value on a curve. You can apply the same process to $x_, = x + a$ to approximate around $x = a$. Isolating for x, you get $x = x_, - a$. Substituting that into the first equation and evaluating at $f(a)$ yields the Taylor polynomial approximation given by the following formula:

$$g(x) = \frac{f(a)}{0!} + \frac{f'(a)(x-a)}{1!} + \frac{f''(a)(x-a)^2}{2!} + \frac{f'''(a)(x-a)^3}{3!} + \cdots + \frac{f^n(a)(x-a)^n}{n!}$$

One interesting fact is that if $n \to \infty$, you can say that in practice, $g(x) = f(x)$. Table 12.2 shows some popular MacLaurin series.

Table 12.2 Popular MacLaurin Series

Function	MacLaurin Series
$\sin(x)$	$\dfrac{x}{1!} - \dfrac{x^3}{3!} + \dfrac{x^5}{5!} - \dfrac{x^7}{7!} + \dfrac{x^{2i+1}}{(2i+1)!}$
$\cos(x)$	$\dfrac{1}{0!} - \dfrac{x^2}{2!} + \dfrac{x^4}{4!} - \dfrac{x^6}{6!} + \dfrac{x^{2i}}{(2i)!}$
e^x	$\dfrac{1}{0!} + \dfrac{x}{1!} + \dfrac{x^2}{2!} + \dfrac{x^3}{3!} + \dfrac{x^i}{i!}$
$\dfrac{1}{1-x}$	$1 + x + x^2 + x^3 + x^i$
$(1 + x)^p$	$\dfrac{1}{0!} + \dfrac{px}{1!} + \dfrac{p(p-1)}{2!} + \dfrac{p(p-1)(p-2)}{3!} + \cdots$ $x = (-1,1)$

tip

In Maple, you can find the Taylor series for a given curve by issuing the taylor command coupled with the convert command to convert the function into a polynomial like so: convert(taylor(<function>(x), x=a, <degree>), polynom).

Error Analysis

One of the most important parts of an approximation is error analysis. This analysis is how you can determine how closely your solution matches the actual solution. Fortunately, in addition to being critical, error analysis is also rather simple. You just render the difference between the real curve and your approximation. Alternatively, you can compute the difference between the two curves, find the global maximum, and compute the value of the error at that location.

When doing an error analysis, you must always bound your analysis to a range in x. Otherwise, as x goes to infinity, most curves will diverge considerably from the original. Quite obviously, the smaller the error, the better off you are. For example, take a look at the plotted graphs of $\sin(x)$, $\tan(x)$, and $e(x)$ using dually increasing degrees of approximation for the Taylor series in Figures 12.4, 12.5, and 12.6, respectively. If you take a look at the error of the 10th degree Taylor polynomial, you get the graphs illustrated in Figures 12.7, 12.8, and 12.9, respectively. In all six figures, the increasing Roman numerals indicate increasing power approximation.

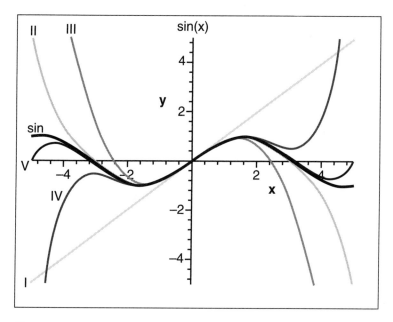

Figure 12.4
Graph of sin(x)

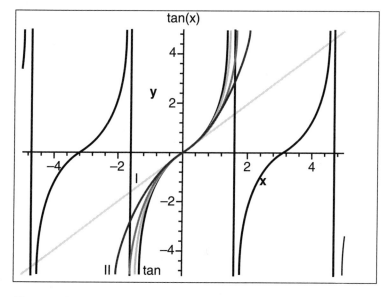

Figure 12.5
Graph of tan(x)

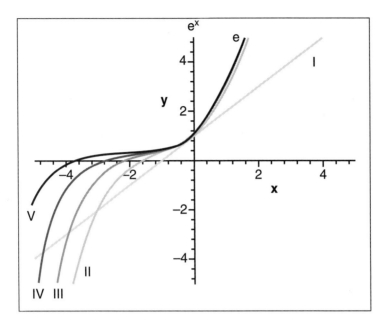

Figure 12.6
Graph of e^x

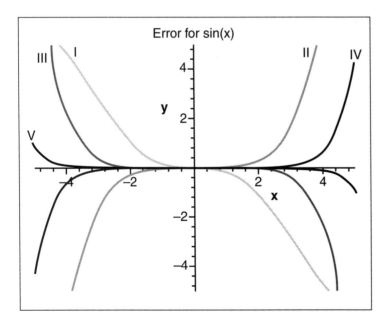

Figure 12.7
Graph of the MacLaurin series error for sin(x)

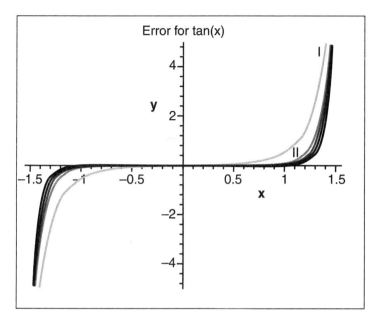

Figure 12.8
Graph of the MacLaurin series error for tan(*x*)

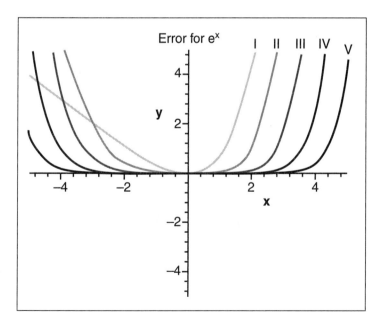

Figure 12.9
Graph of the MacLaurin series error for e^x

One thing is clear from the Taylor series: The approximation around a is extremely good, but the farther you sway from the curve, the worse your potential error becomes. Another point that may be interesting is to determine an optimal value for a. It's clear that if you take a to be in the center of your approximation, you will, in general, yield a better approximation than if you were to choose a at one of the curve's end-points. Many mathematicians consider the Taylor series a Mickey Mouse function, but the reality is that computationally speaking, the Taylor series can be as competitive if not more so than the most complex approximations. This all depends on the degree of the complexity of the Horner form. For example, take $\sin(x)$'s Horner form:

Let $y = x^2$

$$\sin(x) = x + y\left(-\frac{1}{6} + \left(\frac{1}{120} + \left(-\frac{1}{5040} + \frac{y}{362880}y\right)y\right)y\right)$$

This makes things a little more interesting because it suggests that any other series with a non-zero coefficient for all x_i will have to compete against the Taylor series at twice the power. Of course, not all functions have a nice Horner form, but when you optimize your equations, you should consider the possibility that a generally worse approximation may yield better results when you compare complexity against precision. This also means that if you can algebraically eliminate every odd or even power, you will obtain a nicer Horner form and consequently obtain a much more competitive function. This is where tricks like the substitution trick you saw in Chapter 1 can come in handy.

The Least Square Method

The Tayloristic approach was to choose a point and to mimic its derivatives. Let's take the example of a line approximating a square root function with range $x = [1, 2]$. With the Taylor approximation, you would first find out that the slope of the line should be 0.5. The problem with the Taylor function is that the error is large at the end of the range and null at the beginning, as illustrated in Figure 12.10. One approach is to translate the curve downwards such that the error at the beginning is the same as the error at the end. To solve this equation, you simply let the initial error at the left boundary of your range be equal to the final error at the right boundary of your range.

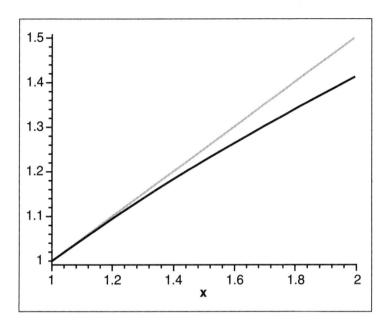

Figure 12.10
Graph of the MacLaurin series error for e(x)

This has the following effect:

$$\sqrt{x_i} - \left(\frac{(x_i+1)}{2} + a\right) = \sqrt{x_f} - \left(\frac{(x_f+1)}{2} - a\right)$$

$$\sqrt{1} - \frac{(1+1)}{2} - a = \sqrt{2} - \frac{(2+1)}{2} + a$$

$$-2a = \sqrt{2} - \frac{3}{2}$$

$$a = \frac{3}{4} - \frac{\sqrt{2}}{2}$$

This equation tells you that if you shift the line by $2 - \sqrt{2}$, the initial and final error will be equal. This becomes much more interesting because now, you can say that your error will be at most a for this specific equation, as shown in Figure 12.11.

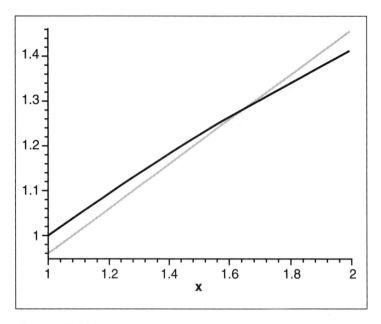

Figure 12.11
The translated Taylor approximation of the square root

This is a better approximation than the Taylor approximation, but is far from being a good approximation. One of the problems with this approximation is that the error is verified only at the start and end of the curve. What would happen if the curve was wavy and a large lump existed in the middle? You would indeed have a large error in the center, which would not be a good thing. Another issue is the slope. It is obvious by looking at the graph in Figure 12.11 that if you take the line such that it intersects at the same location and change the slope slightly such that the ends are again minimized, you obtain an even better approximation than any of the previously seen scenarios.

One heuristic you can use to distinguish a good approximation from a bad one is to find the approximation that minimizes the sum of the errors. What does it mean for the sum of the errors to be minimized? Because your equation is continuous, the infinite sum is the same thing as an integral, so in reality, you are looking at the integral of the errors. Before you consider the implications of this train of thought, however, there remains one problem. Notice how you negated the value of a on the other side for the line approximation of the square root. You did this because in the first case, a was going down, while at the other boundary, it was going up. This happens because the chosen function was $f(x) - g(x)$; clearly, however, the function $g(x) - f(x)$ is just as likely to yield the error. This causes problems because you don't know the sign of the distance. In this case, however, you care only about the distance, not the sign. One approach might be to figure the sum of the absolute values of the error, but this creates a rather cumbersome formula to integrate. Instead, you can take the square of the error. This will effectively nullify the sign, and will make your calculations much simpler.

Unfortunately, however, there is a drawback: When a number greater than 1 is squared, the number becomes greater; the greater the number, the greater the difference between the original value and its square. You can easily test this by squaring any number greater than 1. Similarly, if a number is smaller than 1, it will decrease the number; the smaller it is, the smaller its square will be. This is a double-edged sword because the error here is squared. The general formula you are looking at is the following:

$$error(x) = (f(x) - g(x))^2 = (g(x) - f(x))^2$$
$$ErrSum(x) = \int error(x) = \int (f(x) - g(x))^2 = \int (g(x) - f(x))^2$$

This equation is a function that gives you the squared sum of the errors. To yield a good approximation, you want to minimize this function, which implies that its derivative must be 0. The parameters of the errors' sum are the coefficient of $g(x)$, so in order to minimize the function, you need to minimize the partial derivatives of the errors' sum. Put in mathematical notation, this means the following:

$$\frac{dErrSum}{da} = 0$$

$$\frac{dErrSum}{db} = 0$$

$$\frac{dErrSum}{dc} = 0$$

The beauty of this equation is that there is a clean-cut solution if you simply look at the partial derivates. Take this example:

$$g(x, a, b, c) = ax^2 + bx + c$$
$$f(x) = e^x$$
$$x = [0,1]$$

Given the equation to approximate $g(x)$, its range, and the equation you will use to approximate $f(x)$, you can deduce the following:

$$error(x) = \left(g(x) - f(x)\right)^2$$

$$= \left(ax^2 + bx + c - e^x\right)^2$$

$$A(x,a,b,c) = \int_0^1 \left(ax^2 + bx + c - e^x\right)^2$$

$$= \left. \begin{array}{l} \dfrac{a^2 x^5}{5} + \dfrac{abx^4}{2} + \dfrac{2acx^3}{3} - 2a^x 2e^x + 4axe^x - 4ae^x + \\[2mm] \dfrac{b^2 x^3}{3} + bcx^2 - 2bxe^x - 2be^x + c^2 x - 2ce^x + \dfrac{e^{x^2}}{2} \end{array} \right|_0^1$$

$$= \dfrac{a^2}{5} + \dfrac{ba}{2} + \dfrac{b^2}{3}\dfrac{2ac}{3} + bx + c^2 + \dfrac{e^2}{2} - 2ce - 2ae - \dfrac{1}{2} + 4a - 2b + 2c$$

At this point, you can let the partial derivatives {da, db, dc} equal 0 to yield the following:

$$\frac{dA}{da} = 0$$

$$2e - 4 = \frac{2a}{5} + \frac{b}{2} + \frac{2c}{3}$$

$$2 - e = \frac{a}{5} + \frac{b}{4} + \frac{c}{3}$$

$$\frac{dA}{db} = 0$$

$$2 = \frac{a}{2} + \frac{2b}{3} + c$$

$$1 = \frac{a}{4} + \frac{b}{3} + \frac{c}{2}$$

$$\frac{dA}{db} = 0$$

$$2e - 2 = \frac{2a}{3} + b + 2c$$

$$e - 1 = \frac{a}{3} + \frac{b}{2} + \frac{c}{1}$$

You should notice one very interesting pattern throughout the equations. If you did not notice the patterns, observe the same set of equations written in matrix form:

$$
\begin{bmatrix} \dfrac{1}{5} & \dfrac{1}{4} & \dfrac{1}{3} \\[2mm] \dfrac{1}{4} & \dfrac{1}{3} & \dfrac{1}{2} \\[2mm] \dfrac{1}{3} & \dfrac{1}{2} & 1 \end{bmatrix} \begin{bmatrix} a \\ b \\ c \end{bmatrix} = \begin{bmatrix} e-2 \\ 1 \\ e-1 \end{bmatrix}
$$

This gives you three equations, three unknowns, and, if you isolate for $\{a, b, c\}$, your approximating polynomial. In this case, $a = 0.839183$, $b = 0.851125$, and $c = 1.012991$. The general solution to the least square method should become apparent at this point. For an approximation polynomial $f(x)$, and $g(x)$, the function being approximated, the general solution for the least square method is as follows:

$$
\begin{bmatrix}
\dfrac{1}{2n+1} & \dfrac{1}{2n} & \dfrac{1}{2n-1} & \cdots & \dfrac{1}{n+3} & \dfrac{1}{n+2} & \dfrac{1}{n+1} \\[2mm]
\dfrac{1}{2n} & \dfrac{1}{2n-1} & \ddots & & \dfrac{1}{n+3} & \dfrac{1}{n+2} & \dfrac{1}{n+1} & \dfrac{1}{n} \\[2mm]
\dfrac{1}{2n-1} & \ddots & \ddots & \ddots & & \dfrac{1}{n+1} & \dfrac{1}{n} & \vdots \\[2mm]
\vdots & \dfrac{1}{n+3} & \ddots & \ddots & \ddots & \ddots & \dfrac{1}{4} \\[2mm]
\dfrac{1}{n+3} & \dfrac{1}{n+2} & \dfrac{1}{n+1} & \ddots & \ddots & \dfrac{1}{4} & \dfrac{1}{3} \\[2mm]
\dfrac{1}{n+2} & \dfrac{1}{n+1} & \dfrac{1}{n} & \ddots & \dfrac{1}{4} & \dfrac{1}{3} & \dfrac{1}{2} \\[2mm]
\dfrac{1}{n+1} & \dfrac{1}{n} & \cdots & \dfrac{1}{4} & \dfrac{1}{3} & \dfrac{1}{2}
\end{bmatrix}
$$

Error Analysis

Plotting the graph and looking at the error's graph for the aforementioned equation shows just how good the approximation is when compared to graphs associated with the Taylor approximation. Figures 12.12 and 12.13 show the graphs related to the least square method, while Figures 12.14 and 12.15 show them for the Taylor approximation.

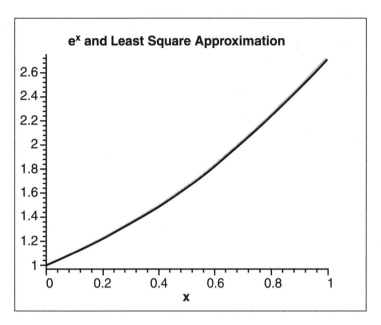

Figure 12.12
Least square approximation of the exponential function

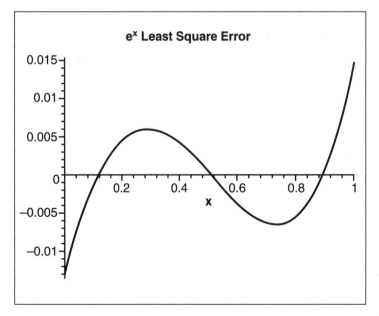

Figure 12.13
Least square approximation error of the exponential function

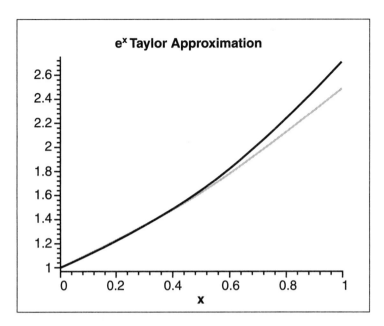

Figure 12.14
Taylor approximation of the exponential function

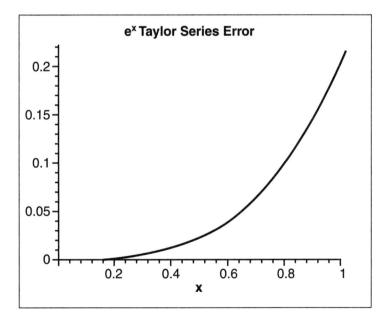

Figure 12.15
Taylor approximation error of the exponential function

Again, feel free to use the trick you saw in Chapter 1 to reduce this equation to the form $Ax^2 + C$, thereby reducing the computational complexity by removing one multiplication. This polynomial was constructed with the constraint that it must minimize the unsigned sum of errors. This means that you should not be able to find another polynomial with the same degree that has a smaller unsigned area under the real curve and the approximation. That does not mean, however, that this is the most practical approximation you can compute.

Legendre Polynomial

The least square method is pretty good, but you can significantly decrease the computations you must perform for a small price in precision, by using the Legendre polynomial. This can be especially useful if you have no access to mathematical software and when the function you want to approximate is very ugly to process with calculus.

Generally, a polynomial is written as a linear combination of powers of x. Although this offers a more efficient way to compute the polynomial, nothing stops you from writing it as a linear combination of yet more polynomials (for the sake of simplicity, I will call them *sub-polynomials*). If you expand such an equation, you should be able to come back to the traditional form of a polynomial (that is, a linear combination of powers).

The Legendre polynomial takes advantage of this. If you define π as the ith sub-polynomial of the Legendre polynomial, the general Legendre polynomial is therefore of the form:

$$aP_0(x) + bP_1(x) + cP_2(x) + \cdots$$

Its terms, which are graphed in Figure 12.16, are defined as follows:

$$P_n(x) = \frac{(-1)^n}{2^n n!} \frac{d}{d^n x}(1 - x^2)^n$$

$$P_0(x) = 1$$

$$P_1(x) = x$$

$$P_2(x) = \frac{3x^2 - 1}{2}$$

$$P_2(x) = \frac{5x^3 - 3x}{2}$$

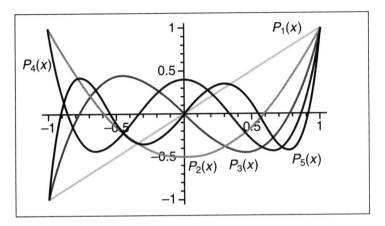

Figure 12.16
Graph of the Legendre polynomial terms

Now that you understand how to obtain such a polynomial, let's define a few things. First, define $w(x)$ as a weight function that attributes various weights to various values of x, and define $c(x)$ as the multiplicand for the Kronecker delta. The Kronecker delta's simplest form is a trivial function that returns 0 if $i \neq j$ and returns 1 if $i = j$. Furthermore, the Legendre polynomial is an orthogonal polynomial. You have already seen what orthogonal implies when vectors are concerned; the principle is very similar when dealing with polynomials. A polynomial is considered orthogonal if, when multiplying two type polynomials of different degrees within a range and a weight, you get the Kronecker delta's simplest form multiplied by a possible value. Mathematically put, a polynomial is orthogonal if it satisfies the following condition:

$$\int P_i(x) P_j(x) w(x) = \begin{cases} i = j & 1 \\ i \neq j & 0 \end{cases} c(x)$$

tip

With Maple, you can load the orthogonal polynomial package with the command with(orthopoly).

These types of polynomials are really interesting because of the Kronecker delta. Because you're multiplying two terms where $i \neq j$ returns a value of 0, you end up with a significantly easier formula to play with because a lot of terms end up canceling each other out. The Legendre polynomial has a weight function of 1 and is orthogonal in the range $[-1, 1]$.

You can easily verify that the Kronecker delta is true for each one of these polynomials and the general case. Obviously, this type of definition somewhat restricts your choice of coefficient for the general polynomial, but as you will soon see, you can obtain some very interesting results with it anyway.

Now that you know what the Legendre polynomial is, let's take a look at the implications of the least square method on the Legendre polynomial:

$$A(x) = \int_{-1}^{1} a_0^2 P_0^2(x) + a_1^2 P_1^2(x) + a_2^2 P_2^2(x) + \cdots + f^2(x) - 2f(x)\left(a_0 P_0(x) + a_1 P_1(x) + a_2 P_2(x) + \cdots\right)$$

$$\frac{dA}{da_i} = \int_{-1}^{1} \left(2a_i P_i^2(x) - 2f(x) P_i(x)\right) dx = 0$$

$$a_i \int_{-1}^{1} P_i^2(x) dx = \int_{-1}^{1} f(x) P_i(x) dx$$

$$a_i = \frac{\int_{-1}^{1} f(x) P_i(x) dx}{\int_{-1}^{1} P_i^2(x) dx}$$

This is pretty and, in fact, the solution stands for any orthogonal polynomial multiplied by its weight. You can simplify the coefficient's equation even more, however, if you look at what happens when you compute the $[-1, 1]$ integral of the square of any Legendre polynomial term. I will spare you the algebra; the coefficient of the Legendre polynomial can be expressed in its simpler form:

$$a_i = \frac{(2i+1)\int_{-1}^{1} f(x) P_i(x) dx}{2}$$

How is that for simplicity? Well, okay, you could have gotten something simpler, but when compared to the purist least square method, this sure beats resolving n equations with n unknowns.

Let's come back to the example from the least square method and see what happens when the exponential function is thrown to a third-degree Legendre polynomial as an approximation guinea pig. The first step is to change the range such that it fits the orthogonal polynomial's range. You want to approximate e^x with range $[0, 1]$, so you need to substitute a value t such that the input range $[-1, 1]$ becomes $[0, 1]$. If you substitute x with half of $t + 1$, you can achieve this. You can verify this by substituting -1 and 1 into t to yield the range $[0, 1]$. Now all that remains is to apply the substitution and to compute the three coefficients a, b, and c. The following logic ensues:

$$a = \frac{\displaystyle\int_{-1}^{1} e^{\frac{t+1}{2}}\,dt}{2} \qquad = \frac{2e^{\frac{t+1}{2}}\Big|_{-1}^{1}}{2} \qquad = e-1$$

$$b = \frac{\left(2(1)+1\right)\displaystyle\int_{-1}^{1} te^{\frac{t+1}{2}}\,dt}{2} \qquad = \frac{3\left(2te^{\frac{t+1}{2}} - 4e^{\frac{t+1}{2}}\right)\Big|_{-1}^{1}}{2} \qquad = 9-3e$$

$$c = \frac{\left(2(1)+1\right)\displaystyle\int_{-1}^{1}\left(3t^2-1\right)e^{\frac{t+1}{2}}\,dt}{2} \qquad = \frac{5\left(2e^{\frac{t+1}{2}}\left(3t^2-12t+23\right)\right)\Big|_{-1}^{1}}{2} \qquad = 95-35e$$

Finally, as usual, you need to apply the reverse substitution $t = 2x - 1$ in order to restore the order you have initially broken, and substitute a, b, c into the second degree Legendre polynomial to yield the final coefficient for your regular polynomial. The following shows this:

$$f(x) = aP_0 + bP_1 + cP_2$$

$$= (e-1)1 + (9-3e)t + (95-35e)\frac{3t^2-1}{2}$$

$$= (e-1)1 + (9-3e)(2x-1) + (95-35e)\frac{3(2x-1)^2-1}{2}$$

$$= (39e-105) + x(588-216e) + x^2(210e-570)$$

tip

Maple can compute the Legendre polynomial terms by issuing the P command P(<degree>, <variable>).

Error Analysis

Surprisingly, the Legendre polynomial has an error term pretty similar to the one obtained by the least square. This means that in general, the Legendre polynomial is an easier way to compute a least square on a polynomial with relatively the same error. If you plot the exponential function and the approximation, as well as the error, you will notice no perceptible difference on the graphs with the least square method, as shown in Figures 12.17 and 12.18.

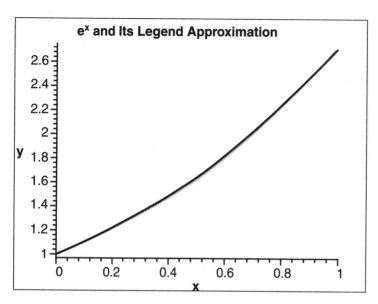

Figure 12.17
Least square Legendre approximation of the exponential function

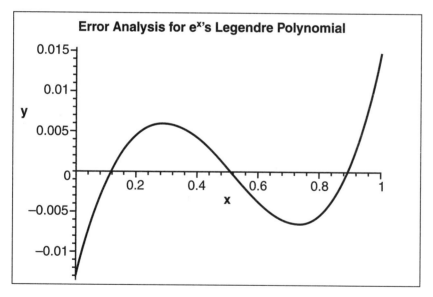

Figure 12.18
Least square Legendre approximation error of the exponential function

To get a better idea of the difference between the least square method and the Legendre polynomial, you can plot the graph of the difference between the two errors to yield the graph shown in Figure 12.19.

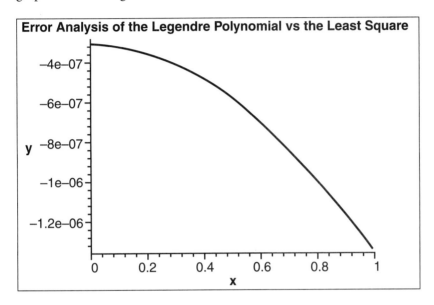

Figure 12.19
Least square error versus the Legendre approximation error for the exponential function

Because of the constraints set by its very creation, the purist least square method is a better approximation than the least square applied on the Legendre polynomial. In this specific case, the Legendre polynomial is at worst approximately 10^{-6} off from the purist least square method—which is not so bad for a second-degree curve. In practice, the Legendre polynomial's error behaves very similarly to the purist least square, and suffers from the same problems.

Chebyshev Polynomial

You could go through a good set of orthogonal polynomials such as the Hermite, Jacobi, and Laguerre polynomials before you reached the mother of all polynomials, the Chebyshev polynomial, but those polynomials just don't do much for game developers. The Chebyshev polynomial, on the other hand, although a beast to compute in most cases, is interesting because it defines its coefficient by using trigonometry. As you already know, trigonometry is very good with curves and circular motions, and with any motion that oscillates. The Chebyshev polynomial, which is another orthogonal polynomial in the range $x = [-1, 1]$, has the following characteristics, which are graphed in Figure 12.20:

$$P_n(x) = \cos(n\arccos(x))$$

$$w(x) = \frac{1}{\sqrt{1-x^2}}$$

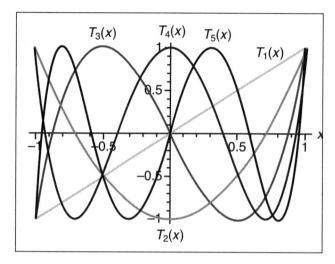

Figure 12.20
Graph of the Chebyshev polynomial terms

At this point, you may be wondering how a cosine and—even worse—an arccosine can help you determine a polynomial. The key is a really nice trigonometric identity that converts this trigonometric function into one simple and nice polynomial. You can find the identity in Appendix B, "Trigonometry." As for the terms, the following first few polynomial terms can be computed:

$$P_{n+1}(x) = 2xP_n(x) - P_{n-1}(x), x \geq 1$$

$$P_0(x) = 1$$
$$P_1(x) = x$$
$$P_2(x) = 2x^2 - 1$$
$$P_3(x) = 4x^2 - 3$$

You know that every coefficient can be computed using the general orthogonal polynomial coefficient as seen previously, but is there a simple function that multiplies the Kronecker delta? The answer is yes. As with the Legendre polynomial, you can verify that the Chebyshev polynomial has a rather nice function $c(x)$, which multiplies the Kronecker delta as shown here:

$$\int_{-1}^{1} \frac{P_i(x)P_j(x)}{\sqrt{1-x^2}} dx = \begin{bmatrix} 0 & i \ne j \\ \dfrac{\pi}{2} & i = j \ne 0 \\ \pi & i = j = 0 \end{bmatrix}$$

Now that you have this relationship, you can more easily compute the general solution for the Chebyshev polynomial coefficient:

$$a_i = \frac{\displaystyle\int_{-1}^{1} \frac{g(x)P_i(x)}{\sqrt{1-x^2}} dx}{\displaystyle\int_{-1}^{1} \frac{P_i^2(x)}{\sqrt{1-x^2}} dx}$$

$$a_i = \frac{2}{\pi} \int_{-1}^{1} \frac{g(x)P_i(x)}{\sqrt{1-x^2}} dx$$

$$= \frac{2}{\pi} \int_{0}^{\pi} g(\cos(\phi)) \cdot \cos(i\phi) d\phi, i > 0$$

The second version of the coefficient's definition is a little more useful because it does not have the cumbersome inverse square root. It can obviously be obtained with a substitution of $x = \cos(\phi)$. For the practical part, let's compute the Chebyshev approximation for e^x with range $[-1, 1]$. You have already determined the substitution required to convert to the appropriate range, so without further delay, let's compute the coefficient. (Note that the integral is so cumbersome that I prefer to integrate numerically at this point.) You can use the mathematics packages provided with the CD-ROM that accompanies this book, but you could also apply numerical integration methods such as a Riemann sum or Simpson's rule in order to compute this value.

$$a = \frac{1}{\pi} \int_{0}^{\pi} e^{\frac{\cos(t)+1}{2}} dt = 1.753387654$$

$$b = \frac{2}{\pi} \int_{0}^{\pi} e^{\frac{\cos(t)+1}{2}} \cos(t) dt = 0.8503916539$$

$$c = \frac{2}{\pi} \int_{0}^{\pi} e^{\frac{\cos(t)+1}{2}} \cos(2t) dt = 0.1052086936$$

Finally, as done previously, you must apply the reverse substitution $t = 2x - 1$ in order to restore the order you have initially broken, and you must substitute a, b, c into the second-degree Chebyshev polynomial to yield the final coefficient for your regular polynomial, as shown in the following:

$$f(x) = aP_0 + bP_1 + cP_1$$

$$= 1.753387654(1) + 0.8503916539t + 0.1052086936(2t^2 - 1)$$

$$= 1.753387654(1) + 0.8503916539(2x - 1) + 0.1052086936\left(2(2x-1)^2 - 1\right)$$

$$= 1.008204694 + 0.8591137592x + 0.8416695488x^2$$

tip

Maple can compute the Chebyshev polynomial terms by issuing the T command T(<degree>, <variable>).

tip

Maple can approximate the Chebyshev polynomial approximation by issuing the chebyshev command chebyshev(<function>, <variable>=a..b), where a..b is the range of approximation.

Error Analysis

As shown in Figures 12.21 and 12.22, the Chebyshev polynomial has a total error that is considerably worse than the two previous polynomial approximations. Compute the area under the error curve, and you'll see this right away. Yet one interesting fact about it is that although the error curve's distance from 0 is, in general, greater than that of the previous methods', the Chebyshev polynomial has a much better higher bound. Where the previous methods reached error values of up to 0.015 for the exponential function, the Chebyshev polynomial never does worse than a little more than 0.008 for the previous example, which is a quality you can appreciate in an approximation. It doesn't really matter if the polynomial has an extremely good approximation within the sub-range of the range. What you want is an approximation that yields a reasonably good approximation throughout the curve. For example, suppose the Taylor approximation for a given function is really good at the beginning, but at the end, for an extremely small fraction of time, the error increases one million-fold. Such an approximation is not very good because if you are approximating a sine wave, the approximation around the point a will be extremely good, but the approximation on the other edge will be a disaster.

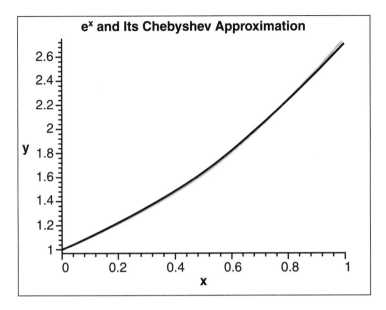

Figure 12.21
Least square Chebyshev approximation of the exponential
function

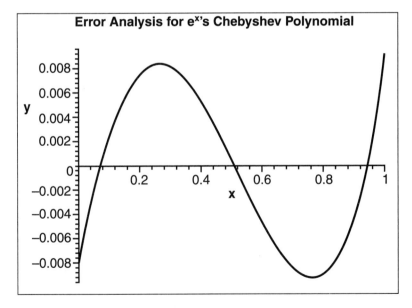

Figure 12.22
Least square Chebyshev approximation error of the exponential function

That means minimizing the area under the error curve does not yield the best numerical approximation. You have to look at the problem from another angle to solve it in a more acceptable way. The Chebyshev polynomial in practice has proven to be an extremely good approximation of the most optimal polynomial, which is why I've presented it here. Put another way, the Chebyshev polynomial is the simplest way to obtain the closest approximation to the best approximation.

Minimax Approximation

The Chebyshev approximation opened your eyes to the fact that minimizing the total sum of errors was not really the best metric. If you think about the error analysis on the Chebyshev polynomial, you could naturally conclude that an even better approximation technique would be to minimize the maximum error. This is the entire idea behind the Minimax approximation. If you can MINImize the MAXimum error, you will successfully find a polynomial for which you can say that the error is not larger than x and where this very maximal error x is as small as it can be throughout the curve.

The conditions you need to solve this enigma come from a theorem, one that Chebyshev himself put forward. This theorem states that when an approximation polynomial of degree n is such that the maximum error is minimized, its error function has $(n + 1)$ nodes with $(n + 2)$ local maximums, all of which share the same value. In other words, the maximum error on the polynomial appears $(n + 2)$ times on the error curve, and the maximums all express the same error. If you look at the last Chebyshev approximation, you can see that it isn't that far off from this approximation because all of its maximums appear pretty much at an equal height—but not exactly, because of the restrictions the polynomial terms impose on the final polynomial. You cannot obtain *the* best approximation with a Chebyshev polynomial, similar to what you saw with the difference between a purist least square method and the Legendre polynomial.

The only problem with the Minimax polynomial is that it is not easy to compute. With what has been put forward so far, you have enough information to write the entire set of equations you will then need to work with. Let's stick to the example of e^x. Geometrically speaking, you can easily see that there will be a maximum error both at the beginning of the range and at the end of the range. (This has been the case for every approximation you have done so far; a proof of this would not help you further understand anything important for game development, so simply take this fact as a given.) Because you are approximating with a second-degree polynomial, according to Chebyshev's theorem, you should have three nodes and four maximums. From your previous experience in approximation, you may also notice that the polynomials go from a maximum to a minimum; this also makes perfect sense if you think about distributions for a bit. Mathematically speaking, that means you have the following:

$$g(x) - f(x) = (-1)^i E$$

$$e^0 - \left(a(0)^2 + b(0) + c\right) = -E$$

$$e^x - \left(ax^2 + bx + c\right) = E$$

$$e^y - \left(ay^2 + by + c\right) = -E$$

$$e^1 - \left(a(1)^2 + b(1) + c\right) = E$$

Unfortunately, however, you won't get far with six unknowns and four equations; you need at least two extra equations. The equations you have written express the fact that at $\{0, x, y, 1\}$, your error function is leveled. It does not say that the error is an extremum, so if you add that extra information in there (derivative = 0), you get two additional equations:

$$0 = \frac{d\left(e^x - \left(ax^2 + bx + c\right)\right)}{dx} = e^x - 2ax - bx$$

$$0 = \frac{d\left(e^y - \left(ay^2 + by + c\right)\right)}{dy} = e^y - 2ay - by$$

Six linearly independent equations with six unknown $\{a, b, c, x, y, E\}$ suggest that you should have one unique solution. The problem at this point lies in determining the solution itself. You have seen how you can use iterative methods to solve an equation, and the Minimax polynomial is one good example of this.

The iterative steps to find the Minimax coefficient are somewhat of a pain to compute, and it's a rather long process—especially if you do it by hand. The Remez algorithm, which does the dirty work, is as follows:

1. Choose an initial guess for the maximum's locations, denoted x_i.
2. Find the values for the co-efficient denoted a_i for the linear system $g(x) - f(x) = (-1)^i E$.
3. If the error E is satisfactory, then stop. Otherwise, find the maximums x_{i+1}, and take that as your new guess and loop.

To illustrate this, I'll use the same example that was used previously. First off, you can choose $\{a, b, c\}$ from your Chebyshev approximation, jump right to step 3, and compute the extremums. Then you need to find the roots of the derivative of the general equation. You can do this with the techniques you saw in Chapter 1 or use the techniques you saw in this chapter to approximate the root of an equation. The choice is yours, but in this case, you are restricted by the fact that the equation is not a polynomial. So the iterative method it is. When you have these values, you can restart the loop until you reach a satis-factory level. Let's see what this implies mathematically:

$$e^x - (2ax + b) = 0 = f(x)$$

$$e^x - 3a = f'(x)$$

$$x_{n+1} = x_n - \frac{e^{x_n} - (2ax_n + b)}{e^{x_n} - 2a}$$

You know from previous experience that 0 and 1, the boundaries, will be two maximums, so it's pointless to compute their value. In fact, it is not even possible with this formula because they are maximums only when the function is bounded between [0, 1]. Suppose you start with an initial guess of 0 (which is not the most intelligent guess, since you already drew the curve for the primitive of this function and could put forward a better visual guess, but nonetheless, let's take 0). The values you obtain for x are {0.2061, 0.2563, 0.2604}. Because $f(x)$ is very close to a parabola, you can substitute the value 1 to obtain the second root. The values you obtain for x are {0.8301, 0.7693, 0.7606, 0.7604}. That means the extremums are located at x = {0, 0.2604, 0.7604, 1}. You can now substitute these values into your first equation to compute the new coefficient:

$$ax^2 + bx + c \pm E = e^x$$

$$\begin{bmatrix} 0 & 0 & 1 & -1 \\ 0.677 & 0.2604 & 1 & 1 \\ 0.5781 & 0.7604 & 1 & -1 \\ 1 & 1 & 1 & 1 \end{bmatrix} \begin{bmatrix} a \\ b \\ c \\ E \end{bmatrix} = \begin{bmatrix} 1 \\ 1.2974 \\ 2.1390 \\ e \end{bmatrix}$$

Solving the linear system gives you the solution {a, b, c, E} = {0.8460272118, 0.8547425724, 1.008756022, 0.008756022}. This quadruplet is still not the most optimal set of values; you will have to run through the algorithm a few more times before you can yield the most efficient coefficients, which are {a, b, c, E} = {0.8360273888, 0.8547499232, 1.008752258, 0.008752258}.

Error Analysis

If you compare the error with Chebyshev's maximum error, you will notice that you truly did improve upon the Chebyshev solution. All in all, however, you can also say that the Chebyshev approximation is pretty close to the most optimal case, the Minimax approx-imation, as shown in Figure 12.23, and the Minimax approximation error, shown in Figure 12.24.

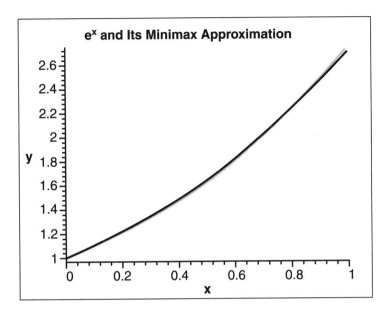

Figure 12.23
Minimax approximation of the exponential function

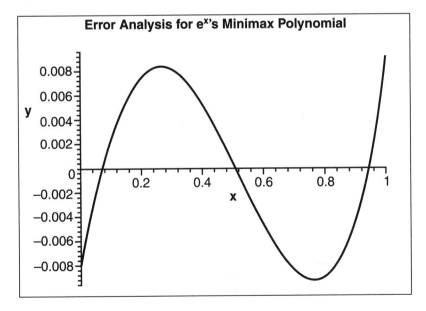

Figure 12.24
Minimax approximation error of the exponential function

The Minimax polynomial is known as the Holy Grail of polynomial approximation, and rightfully so. One thing you do have to keep in mind as you compute approximations, however, is that in your case, you are not interested in obtaining the best approximation for a given polynomial degree, but rather in obtaining the best polynomial possible for the least complex computation. So if any other polynomial's complexity (such as the Taylor series, for example) ends up being less computationally expensive than an equally precise, lower-degree Minimax polynomial, the Minimax approximation is not the best tool.

tip

Maple can approximate using a Minimax polynomial approximation by issuing the minimax command minimax(<function>, <variable>=a..b, <degree>), where *a..b* is the range of approximation.

Piece-Wise Approximation

As a general rule, the greater the approximation range is, the worst the approximation becomes. For this very reason, you should always do your best to find special relationships in your function, which makes the approximation range as small as possible. It may even be beneficial to sometimes cut the curve into two separate pieces and to approximate each of them individually. For more details, see Chapter 21, which looks at many common functions and attempts to approximate them in a piecewise fashion to yield the best and fastest approximations possible.

Multivariable Function Approximation

The previous functions you looked at dealt with only one variable. You might rightfully ask, then, what happens if you move to 3D and your equations now take two input parameters? It turns out you can still approximate a surface or any higher-order function in relatively the same way you have done for single-variable functions. The only difference is that you must now consider more coefficients and a slightly different polynomial function to integrate.

There are two types of polynomials that you can use, one of which is more accurate than the other but comes with a slightly bigger price. The first type of polynomial is nothing but the addition of two polynomials (one as a function of x and the other as a function of y), while the other considers x multiplied with y and similarly with higher-order functions. Expressed mathematically, the two types are as follows:

$$f(x,y) = ax^2 + bx + c + dy^2 + ey + f + \ldots$$
$$f(x,y) = ax^2 + bx + c + dy^2 + ey + gxy + \ldots$$

The second equation may be a little more cumbersome, but in general, if you use forward differentiation, you should be able to compute it reasonably quickly. Because you have two variables to play with, you must compute a double integral for x and y. Instead of minimizing an area, you are minimizing a volume. The last step is exactly the same; you must compute the derivatives of each factor in order to minimize the distance. Let's follow through with an example. Consider the 3D equation $f(x, y) = \sin(x) + \cos(y)$, illustrated in Figure 12.25, with the least square method applied to the range $[-\pi, \pi]$ and with the approximating polynomial $f(x, y) = a + bx + cy + dx^2 + ey^2 + fx^3 + gy^3 + hx^3 + iy^3$:

$$A(x) = \int_{-\pi}^{\pi} \int_{-\pi}^{\pi} \left(\sin(x) + \cos(x) - \left(a + bx + cy + dx^2 + ey^2 + fx^3 + gy^2 + hx^4 + iy^4 \right) \right)^2 dxdy$$

$$= \frac{4\pi^2}{1575} \begin{pmatrix} 1575 + 18900f - 75600i - 3150b + 12600i\pi^2 - 3150f\pi^2 + 525\pi^2 c^2 \\ +175\pi^8 i^2 + 525\pi^2 b^2 + 1050\pi^2 ae + 126\pi^8 hi + 450\pi^6 ei + 210\pi^6 di + \\ 630\pi^4 bf + 630\pi^4 ha + 210\pi^6 he + 350\pi^4 de + 1050\pi^2 da + 450\pi^6 dh + \\ 63 - \pi^4 cg + 630\pi^4 ai + 224\pi^6 f^2 + 315\pi^4 d^2 + 315\pi^4 e^2 + 225\pi^6 g^2 \\ +175\pi^8 h^2 + 6300e + 1575a^2 \end{pmatrix}$$

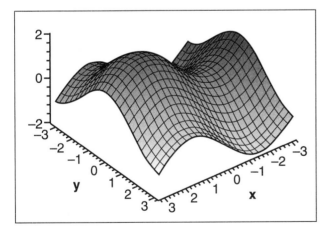

With the derivatives, you end up with a linear system of nine equations with nine unknowns, represented by the following matrix:

Figure 12.25
Graph of $\sin(x) + \cos(y)$

$$
\begin{bmatrix}
15 & 0 & 0 & 5\pi^2 & 5\pi^2 & 0 & 0 & 3\pi^2 & 3\pi^4 \\
0 & 5\pi^2 & 0 & 0 & 0 & 3\pi^4 & 0 & 0 & 0 \\
0 & 0 & 0 & 0 & 0 & 3\pi^2 & 0 & 0 \\
105 & 0 & 0 & 63\pi^2 & 35\pi^2 & 0 & 0 & 45\pi^4 & 21\pi^4 \\
105\pi^2 & 0 & 0 & 35\pi^4 & 63\pi^4 & 0 & 0 & 21\pi^6 & 45\pi^6 \\
0 & 7\pi^4 & 0 & 0 & 0 & 5\pi^6 & 0 & 0 & 0 \\
0 & 0 & 7 & 0 & 0 & 0 & 5\pi^2 & 0 & 0 \\
315 & 0 & 0 & 225\pi^2 & 105\pi^2 & 0 & 0 & 175\pi^4 & 63\pi^4 \\
315\pi^4 & 0 & 0 & 105\pi^6 & 225\pi^6 & 0 & 0 & 63\pi^8 & 175\pi^8
\end{bmatrix}
\begin{bmatrix}
a \\ b \\ c \\ d \\ e \\ f \\ g \\ h \\ i
\end{bmatrix}
=
\begin{bmatrix}
0 \\ 15 \\ 0 \\ 0 \\ -630 \\ 35(\pi^2-6) \\ 0 \\ 0 \\ 6300(6-\pi^2)
\end{bmatrix}
$$

Finally, the solution you get in alphabetic order of variable is $\{1.22815034433,$ $0.856983327795, 0, 0, -0.664912463546, -0.093387697283, 0, 0, 0.049242014837\}$, which is illustrated in Figure 12.26.

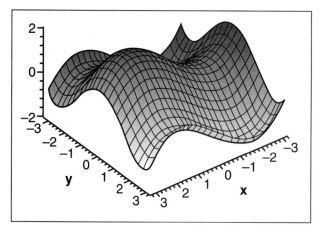

Figure 12.26
Least square approximation of sin(x) + cos(y)

Error Analysis

As should be expected, the error on a surface like the one shown in Figure 12.27 is many times greater than the error on a simple curve. This is because the span on a surface is that much greater than the span on a simple function. Generally, you can yield better approximations by using approximation within the calculations of the surface. So for example, you could approximate sin and cos separately instead of considering their combination as a surface. This will yield much more precise results, but it is not always that simple. Many times, you don't actually require dead-on precision for surfaces, and can likely accept a function with a large error. In this case, a surface approximation becomes much more interesting than a subfunction approximation as suggested above. It's the never-ending balancing act: Do you need a lot of accuracy, or do you need a lot of speed?

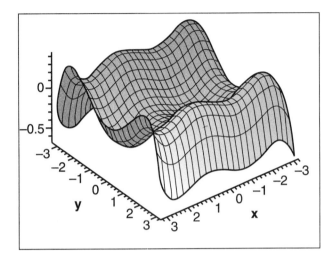

Figure 12.27
Least square approximation error of sin(x) + cos(y)

As a last note, you can also easily approximate parametric equations, because parametric equations are nothing but a set of functions, which means that these methods apply readily to this set of equations. The next chapter takes a thorough look at splines and curves, which are all parametric equations for which numerical approximation can be really handy.

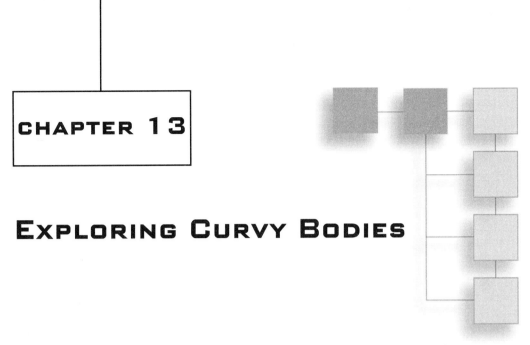

CHAPTER 13

EXPLORING CURVY BODIES

It's fair to say that a nice, smooth, curvy body is easier on the eyes than a body with rough edges. (Easy tiger, this is a math book, not one about human anatomy.) It's also fair to say that moving along a nice, smooth curve is generally preferable to moving in a jerky fashion.

Curves and motion possess various properties that you can examine, such as periodicity (repeated patterns) and uniformity. In this chapter, you'll look at a few curves that can be generated easily and quickly to yield very practical values. What makes these particular curves more important than general curves is that they can easily be manipulated. Such curves can be used to move the camera smoothly and comfortably around the screen; in addition, you can use these curves to generate smooth hill-like surfaces or other interesting shapes and geometries.

Specifically, the topics you'll tackle in this chapter are as follows:

- Bézier curves
- Knot vectors
- B-splines
- NURBs
- Surfaces

Splines

Curves, such as the one illustrated in Figure 13.1, come in various forms, shapes, and styles. Of particular interest in this section are 2D splines. In short, a *spline* is a piecewise simple polynomial function that is globally flexible and smooth. What gives splines this extreme flexibility is the fact that they are described via *control points*, which are vertices in space that serve to guide the curve. (You can think of control points as being like magnets, attracting the curve toward it.) The polygon generated by the set of control points is called the *control polygon*. Neither the control points nor the control polygon are implicitly a part of the curve. Rather, both serve as a guide to the curve's behavior.

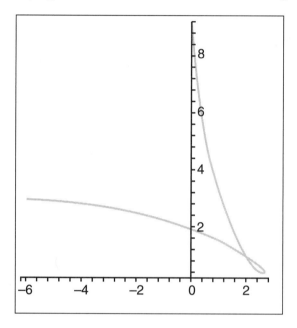

Figure 13.1
A sample curve

As mentioned previously, splines are piecewise polynomial functions, which, as you learned in Chapter 12, "Closing the Gap for Numerical Approximation," make for an interesting and useful form when you wish to determine the location of the polynomial in increments of fixed intervals. Because the splines have the requirement of flexibility, however, they cannot be functions; they have to be piecewise functions. After all, you saw in Chapter 1, "Equation Manipulation and Representation," that a function is limited to a monotone function of its parameters, thus a shape such as a circle cannot be expressed as a function. (Of course, you can use the dirty tricks shown in the first chapter and make my previous statement false, but in general, it's not true that you can convert any equation into a function.) Thus, because functions are too restrictive, you can use parametric equations. They offer the flexibility of all directions but remain manageable equations because they are actually a set of functions respective to the axes. Therefore, you shall write splines using parametric equations, which still allows for polynomial equations in each respective axis.

There are several types of splines, including the following:

- Bézier curves
- Cardinal splines
- B-splines
- NURBs

Each spline discussed in this chapter can be seen as a form of interpolation. You should already be familiar with a few forms of interpolation, such as linear, spherical, and inverse. All these interpolations are fixed increments of a parameter within a function, as shown in Figure 13.2. Typically, they are easier to deal with when they are expressed in terms of percentages, thus with parameters ranging from 0 to 1.

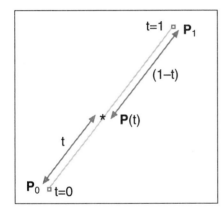

Figure 13.2
A simple linear interpolation

Bézier Curves

The Bézier curve is named after French mathematician Pierre Bézier, who, during the 1970s, worked for a well-known European car company, Renault. Bézier used these curves to easily describe a smooth surface, like you see on cars today. Of course, you are more interested in using these curves to generate things such as terrain or camera movement, or to represent other types of objects in 3D space. For example, *Tomb Raider* likely uses Bézier curves for its camera movement; this allows for a smooth position transition without forcing fixed camera positions.

Obtaining the equation of a Bézier curve is simple. A Bézier curve can actually be seen as a linear interpolation of two equal linear interpolations, as shown in Figure 13.3. This may sound like nonsense, but it isn't. For example, suppose you choose three vertices **a**, **b**, and **c**. Together, these vertices can be referred to as the control points of the curve. Furthermore, you can define the triangle generated by these three vertices as the control polygon. Because a Bézier curve is a linear interpolation of two linear interpolations, you must first determine what the first two linear interpolations are. Because you have three vertices, you can define your first interpolation as a linear interpolation from **a** to **b**, and the second linear interpolation as the one between **b** and **c**. On top of this, you can let their equations share a common parameter t. Thus, if you choose any value for t, you get two coordinates—or, if you prefer, two interpolations. From that point, you can simply interpolate from the first coordinate to the second by using the exact same parameter t; what you end up with is a Bézier curve. The math is as follows:

$$f(t) = t\mathbf{b} + (1-t)\mathbf{a}$$
$$g(t) = t\mathbf{c} + (1-t)\mathbf{b}$$

$$h(t) = t \cdot g(t) + (1-t) \cdot f(t)$$
$$= t\big(t\mathbf{c} + (1-t)\mathbf{b}\big) + (1-t)\big(t\mathbf{b} + (1-t)\mathbf{a}\big)$$
$$= \mathbf{c}t^2 + \mathbf{b}t - \mathbf{b}t^2 + t\mathbf{b} + \mathbf{a} - \mathbf{a}t - t^2\mathbf{b} - \mathbf{a}t + \mathbf{a}t^2$$
$$= t^2(\mathbf{a} - 2\mathbf{b} + \mathbf{c}) + t(-2\mathbf{a} + 2\mathbf{b}) + \mathbf{a}$$

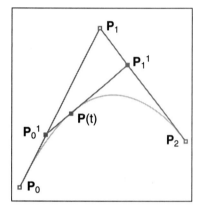

Figure 13.3
A linear interpolation of a linear interpolation

So far so good; you can now generate a curve that can be guided by three control points. Before you move on, let's first look at a few properties that this curve exhibits. For starters, if you set $t = 0$, you get the first vertex, which is **a**. Similarly, if you set $t = 1$, you get the other endpoint, which is **c**. If you try to isolate for **b**, however, you will quickly notice that it is impossible to do so. No matter what value you choose for t, **b** will generally not be on the curve, but it will still have some "pulling control" over the general aspect of the curve. I say "general" simply because you could have a Bézier curve that degenerated into a line; in this specific circumstance, you could indeed get a curve in which **b** is part of the line. With this noted exception, however, for a quadratic Bézier curve (that is, of the second degree), you cannot generate a curve for which **b** is a solution to the curve.

So you know to deal with three control points, but what about dealing with four of them? This, too, is easy. To obtain the equation of a cubic Bézier curve (that is, of the third degree), you simply take two cubic Bézier curves and linearly interpolate from one to the other. The process is as follows:

$$f(t) = t^2(\mathbf{a} - 2\mathbf{b} + \mathbf{c}) + t(-2\mathbf{a} + 2\mathbf{b}) + \mathbf{a}$$
$$g(t) = t^2(\mathbf{b} - 2\mathbf{c} + \mathbf{d}) + t(-2\mathbf{b} + 2\mathbf{c}) + \mathbf{b}$$

$$h(t) = t \cdot g(t) + (1-t) \cdot f(t)$$
$$= t\big(t^2(\mathbf{b} - 2\mathbf{c} + \mathbf{d}) + t(-2\mathbf{b} + 2\mathbf{c}) + \mathbf{b}\big) + (1-t)\big(t^2(\mathbf{a} - 2\mathbf{b} + \mathbf{c}) + t(-2\mathbf{a} + 2\mathbf{b}) + \mathbf{a}\big)$$
$$= t^3(-\mathbf{a} + 2\mathbf{b} - 2\mathbf{c} + \mathbf{d}) + t^2(3\mathbf{a} - 6\mathbf{b} + 3\mathbf{c}) + t(-3\mathbf{a} + 3\mathbf{b}) + \mathbf{c}$$

At this point, you should be able to see how this extends to higher-order Bézier curves, as shown in Figure 13.4. You simply need to take two curves of one lesser degree and linearly interpolate between them.

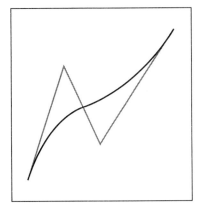

This type of definition can be pretty cumbersome to derive every time you want to use an equation of higher degree, however. Due to their form, the equation of a Bézier curve can be obtained in a much more direct method with the mere observation that the coefficient of the control points can actually be expressed by the following:

Figure 13.4
A third-degree Bézier curve

$$1 = 1 + t - t$$

$$= \left(t + (1-t)\right)^n$$

$$= \sum_{i=0}^{n} \binom{n}{i} t^i (1-t)^{n-i}$$

Because the Bézier curve is defined as an interpolation of an interpolation (recursively), you can write its equation as a product of a linear interpolation. If you expand this equation by using the binomial coefficient seen in Chapter 11, "Educated Guessing with Statistics and Probability," you can express the coefficient of ith vertex out of the n control points. Consequently, the factor of a control point i can be expressed as follows:

$$B_{i,n}(t) = \binom{n}{i} t^i (1-t)^{n-i}$$

Thus, the equation of a Bézier curve can be written as follows, where $\mathbf{p}_i$ is the ith control point:

$$p(t) = \sum_{i=0}^{n} B_{i,n}(t) \mathbf{p}_i$$

This gives you a quick and easy way to compute the various factors of the curve. If you wish to be a little more optimal at run-time, you can write the equation in the typical polynomial notation, or you can write it using the Horner form as mentioned in the previous chapter. In this form, the curve is expressed as a linear combination of the control points. You can look at this as a vector space where $B_{i,n}$ is the set of functions that form the vector space. You can also say that these functions are the basis functions for the Bézier curve, which can be plotted. If you do so, you will notice that the sum of the curve at any point is 1, which is a requirement set forth by the definition of a basis. Furthermore, you will notice that the functions have a range of 0 to 1. This later observation means that moving one of the control points will affect the entire length of the curve, where the change is proportional to the amplitude of the basis function. This should be clear if you simply lay out the math in these terms, something I will do next.

So far, you have looked at Bézier curves as linear interpolations of linear interpolations. This is a good optic for this curve, but it's not the only one. Another elegant way to write the equation of a Bézier curve is by writing it in matrix form. For the cubic Bézier curve, the resulting equation in matrix form looks like this:

$$p(t) = \begin{bmatrix} t^3 & t^2 & t & 1 \end{bmatrix} \begin{bmatrix} -1 & 3 & -3 & 1 \\ 3 & -6 & 3 & 0 \\ -3 & 3 & 0 & 0 \\ 1 & 0 & 0 & 0 \end{bmatrix} \begin{bmatrix} P_1 \\ P_2 \\ P_3 \\ P_4 \end{bmatrix}$$

This simple yet powerful method of writing the equation of a Bézier curve enlightens you to yet another way you can look at Bézier curves. If you simply consider the product of the two first matrices as one matrix, you have the multiplication of two matrices. More precisely, you have the product of one row matrix with one column matrix, the latter being the set of control points. Consequently, a Bézier curve can thus be expressed as a weighted sum of the control points. The control points are given different weights, a concept that, again, you can visualize as magnetic force. The stronger the magnet, the stronger the pull is, and the closer the curve will bend toward the control point. I will come back to this, but keep it in mind as you read the more advanced material in this chapter.

Matrices are not the only way to express the equation of a curve. In fact, as you will see in this chapter, all curves can be written using the following general equation (with one noted exception), where B is the set of basis functions and where P is the set of control points.

$$p(t) = \sum_{i=0}^{n} B_i(t) \cdot P_i$$

Evaluating a Bézier Curve

There are many ways you can go about evaluating a Bézier curve; the method you use depends on how you will use the curve. For instance, if you were planning to use a Bézier curve to move the camera smoothly around the world, you could simply choose your current character's position as the first control point. The last control point will be the position where your character will likely be in x milliseconds. Finally, choose the other points such that the control polygon does not intersect with anything in the world, and your camera will move from the first to last point by panning toward the other vertices.

In this situation, you probably want to select the parameter t as a function of the frame rate only. So if, for example, you wanted to go from point **a** to **z** in two seconds, you would simply scale the time such that it ranges from 0 to 1 in two seconds. Simply divide the time by 2 to achieve this.

If you were wondering about rendering a Bézier curve—for example, to create hills for a snowboarding game—then a few options exist. If you want a fixed number of intervals on the curve (or if you want to be lazy), you can simply forward-differentiate the equation to sample the Bézier curve. On the other hand, if you prefer to set the quality level dynamically, you can take advantage of the very definition of the Bézier curve in order to come up with a well-known algorithm.

Allow me to first introduce the idea for a quadratic Bézier curve. The concept can thereafter be extended similarly to what was done in the very definition of the Bézier curve. The algorithm is actually derived from the definition of the curve. The curve is an interpolation of two other interpolations, so the algorithm divides the problem in two. It first evaluates the middle point of the curve by evaluating the halfway interpolation on the first and second curve, and thereafter evaluating the halfway interpolation on the interpolation between the halfway interpolations. This is getting a little tricky, but all in all, what it basically does is evaluate the curve halfway.

After it has found this vertex, the algorithm verifies whether it should continue. This heuristic is typically based on two checks, the first being that it has generated a minimum number of vertices (usually at least greater than the total number of control points), and the second being to ensure that the two slopes between three adjacent vertices are roughly equal. (Of course, the slope should not be exactly equal, unless you are dealing with a line. But you need to set a tolerance level, which means that there should not be any difference of slope larger than x. This basically defines how smooth the curve will look.)

So far, you have only three vertices on the curve—the first vertex, the midpoint vertex, and the last vertex—which isn't very useful. To increase the number of vertices, you need to apply this process recursively, as shown in Figure 13.5, where two sets of four vertices can be reused to generate two new Bézier curves. Subdividing the curve as such yields four line segments. The two first segments can be used to determine another midpoint, while the two other line segments can be used to determine yet another midpoint vertex. As a result of this process, you should effectively have five vertices sampled on the line. Keep repeating this process until you reach a maximum or until the difference of slope between two adjacent vertices is satisfactory, and you are finished.

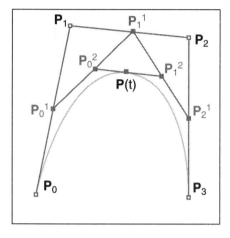

As previously mentioned, this is an interesting technique for rendering purposes mainly because you can dynamically set the slope tolerance, which in turn affects the smoothness of the curve. If you use a forward-differentiation technique, you can still yield a good-looking curve, but that curve may not look as good when it is heavily accelerated. That's mainly because the rate of change of the curve is very high in that region, whereas the region that is more or less linear does not need as many samples.

Figure 13.5
Rendering a third-degree Bézier curve

Intersections and the Convex Hull

If you use Bézier curves as a form of terrain, what you get is the ability to dynamically generate smooth terrain *and* the ability to easily compute the intersection of any object with the terrain. The other typical solution for terrain generation is a height map. In short, this is an even-square map that gives the height of the map given $<x, y>$. The problem with the height maps is that they do not give you any information between the sample values $<x, y>$ and they are also limited to a well-defined size. On the other hand, Bézier curves can generate a large piece of terrain with little data and can accurately give the intersection of something falling on it. Although you may already have a good idea how it is done, you have yet to see how to generate surfaces with Bézier, so let's stick to 2D curves for now.

For starters, you can calculate if an object is above or below the curve by using the trick given in Chapter 4, which suggested generating a homogeneous equation and plugging values for x and y to verify if the resulting equation is greater or smaller than zero. This will work fine if you only need an intersection test. The other more elaborate way is to actually compute the intersection by isolating for the parameter t and the set of equations that describe the movement of the object, as seen in Chapter 10. Another quick test that can be applied is that of the convex hull as seen in Chapter 12. Bézier curves have the interesting property that they are bounded by the convex hull of their control polygon, as illustrated in Figure 13.6. Meaning that at any point in time, the curve will never go outside the convex hull described by the ordered set of control points. This can be very interesting if you are thinking of using a Bézier curve to move the camera around, for example. It implies that if you choose vertices in the world such that the convex hull does not intersect with anything else in the world, the Bézier curve will never actually go "inside" any object. That is unless you prefer to have the gamer's camera go through the walls and see what lies on the other side. Who knows? It also means that if you choose the control polygon such that it is convex, you can generate an easy bounding box test. On the other hand, if you are playing with a lot of Bézier curves in one particular area, you can also generate a greater bounding convex body upon which you can test for collision. The sky's the limit.

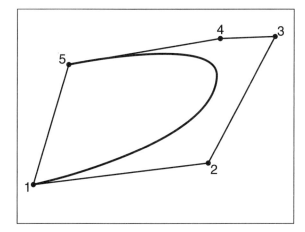

Cardinal Splines

What you have seen so far are not splines. If you take a close look at the definition of a spline given previously, you will notice that a spline is continuous, piecewise. The Bézier curve is continuous within range [0..1], but it is not continuous piecewise (that is, by connecting two Béziers). If you append two Bézier curves one after the other, there is nothing that guarantees that they will be continuous.

Figure 13.6
Convex hull of a Bézier curve

Minimally, you probably want your curve to be of class C^0. If not, you will get the impression of teleporting here and there in the world. You can easily achieve this with a Bézier curve by simply forcing the next Bézier curve to start at the first Bézier curve's endpoint. There's nothing to it. On the other hand, if you want your curve to be of class C^1, then you have a lot of work to do. Basically, you need to make sure that the derivative at $t = 1$ for the first curve equals the derivative at $t = 0$ for the second curve.

This does not sound like a major issue. If you isolate the equations coming out of this, you will come up with the solution that the second point of the second Bézier must be set to a very specific value. Namely, for a cubic Bézier curve, this value is twice the last vertex of the first Bézier, minus the third vertex of the first Bézier. The remaining two points can be chosen arbitrarily. This is cumbersome because you have to eliminate two degrees of freedom (you are losing the first and second point of every consecutive Bézier curve), but at least it gives you a G¹ curve. The difference is illustrated in Figure 13.7. For now, I shall only consider a cubic curve, but know that the same idea and process applies to any higher-order curve.

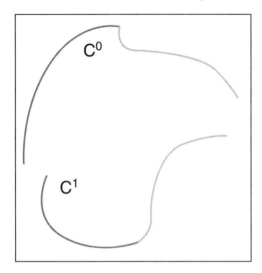

Figure 13.7
Two curves, one with C⁰ and the other of class C¹

A different approach is to do another interpolation by forcing a set of constraints that you would like to be applied to the system. One constraint you benefited from with the Bézier curve was that the curve started and ended at the first and last point of the piecewise curve. respectively. In other words, the curve in its simplest form spanned from a vertex P_k to P_{k+1}. Another property, which you can set to force G¹ continuity, is to force the derivative for the first and last point to each have its own constant value. For a point k, the chosen tangent vector is the one generated by the vector $P_{k+1}P_{k-1}$. In other words, the derivative at P_k is a linear combination of the vector generated by P_{k+1} and P_{k-1}. Similarly, for $t = 1$, the endpoint, P_{k+1}, you can define the derivative as the one generated by the vector P_kP_{k+2}. Put in mathematical terms, the constraints set forward for a parametric curve $C(t)$ are as follows:

$$C(0) = P_k$$
$$C(1) = P_{k+1}$$
$$C'(0) = s(P_{k+1} - P_{k-1})$$
$$C'(1) = s(P_{k+2} - P_k)$$

From this point on, you are basically dealing with algebra in order to find a coefficient matrix for the Cardinal spline. In more detail:

$$C(t) = \begin{bmatrix} t^3 & t^2 & t & 1 \end{bmatrix} \begin{bmatrix} a_x & a_y & a_z & a_w \\ b_x & b_y & b_z & b_w \\ c_x & c_y & c_z & c_w \\ d_x & d_y & d_z & d_w \end{bmatrix}$$

$$\begin{bmatrix} 0 & 0 & 0 & 1 \\ 1 & 1 & 1 & 1 \\ 0 & 0 & 1 & 0 \\ 3 & 2 & 1 & 0 \end{bmatrix} \begin{bmatrix} a_x & a_y & a_z & a_w \\ b_x & b_y & b_z & b_w \\ c_x & c_y & c_z & c_w \\ d_x & d_y & d_z & d_w \end{bmatrix} = \begin{bmatrix} P_k \\ P_{k+1} \\ s(P_{k+1} - P_{k-1}) \\ s(P_{k+2} - P_k) \end{bmatrix}$$

$$\begin{bmatrix} 0 & 0 & 0 & 1 \\ 1 & 1 & 1 & 1 \\ 0 & 0 & 1 & 0 \\ 3 & 2 & 1 & 0 \end{bmatrix}^{-1} \begin{bmatrix} 0 & 0 & 0 & 1 \\ 1 & 1 & 1 & 1 \\ 0 & 0 & 1 & 0 \\ 3 & 2 & 1 & 0 \end{bmatrix} \begin{bmatrix} a_x & a_y & a_z & a_w \\ b_x & b_y & b_z & b_w \\ c_x & c_y & c_z & c_w \\ d_x & d_y & d_z & d_w \end{bmatrix} = \begin{bmatrix} 0 & 0 & 0 & 1 \\ 1 & 1 & 1 & 1 \\ 0 & 0 & 1 & 0 \\ 3 & 2 & 1 & 0 \end{bmatrix}^{-1} \begin{bmatrix} P_k \\ P_{k+1} \\ s(P_{k+1} - P_{k-1}) \\ s(P_{k+2} - P_k) \end{bmatrix}$$

$$\begin{bmatrix} a_x & a_y & a_z & a_w \\ b_x & b_y & b_z & b_w \\ c_x & c_y & c_z & c_w \\ d_x & d_y & d_z & d_w \end{bmatrix} = \begin{bmatrix} 2 & -2 & 1 & 1 \\ -3 & 3 & -2 & -1 \\ 0 & 0 & 1 & 0 \\ 1 & 0 & 0 & 0 \end{bmatrix} \begin{bmatrix} 1 & 0 & 0 & 0 \\ 0 & 1 & 0 & 0 \\ 0 & s & -s & 0 \\ -s & 0 & 0 & s \end{bmatrix} \begin{bmatrix} P_k \\ P_{k+1} \\ P_{k-1} \\ P_{k+2} \end{bmatrix}$$

$$= \begin{bmatrix} 2-s & s-2 & -s & s \\ s-3 & 3-2s & 2s & -s \\ 0 & s & -s & 0 \\ 1 & 0 & 0 & 0 \end{bmatrix} \begin{bmatrix} P_k \\ P_{k+1} \\ P_{k-1} \\ P_{k+2} \end{bmatrix}$$

Consequently, the equation for the Cardinal spline is as follows:

$$C(t) = \begin{bmatrix} t^3 & t^2 & t & 1 \end{bmatrix} \begin{bmatrix} -s & 2-s & s-2 & s \\ 2s & s-3 & 3-2s & -s \\ -s & 0 & s & 0 \\ 0 & 1 & 0 & 0 \end{bmatrix} \begin{bmatrix} P_{k-1} \\ P_k \\ P_{k+1} \\ P_{k+2} \end{bmatrix}$$

You may be wondering what s stands for. s is nothing more than the un-normalized length of the tangent vector. The smaller s is, the closer the curve will be to the points. On the other hand, the bigger s is, the more the curve will diverge from the points and the funkier your path will look. You can choose any value for s here, and again, it serves as a form of magnetic pull toward the control polygon. Heck, if you wanted to, you could even choose different values for your two constraints. That's the beauty of *understanding* the math here rather than using plug-and-play equations.

This brings up an interesting concept. Recall that by definition, rendering this function for a range of $t = [0, 1]$ only renders from P_k to P_{k+1}. What you end up with is a bunch of cubic functions, each describing a piece of the entire spline, which in turn is described by a finite set of control points as shown in Figure 13.8. What makes this curve even better than the Bézier curve is that it is of class G_1, and that only the local vertices are affected by a change of vertex. If you remember the Bézier equation, its basis functions affected the entire span of the curve. The only way you could create a curve that was only locally affected was by constructing a piece-wise Bézier curve. By looking at the equation of this particular curve, you can see that given any point k, only four vertices will affect the segment of the curve. This is really neat because it means that if you change the value of P_k, the whole curve won't start to change. Instead, only three other vertices at most will be affected by this. This is really good because it means that you can move vertices around without changing the overall look of the curve.

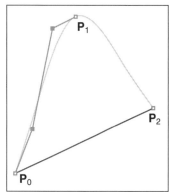

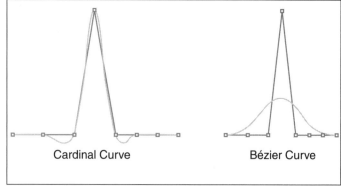

Cardinal Curve   Bézier Curve

Figure 13.8
The Cardinal curve as two separate Bézier curves

Figure 13.9
Difference between a Bézier and Cardinal curve

This equation was derived for a cubic curve. You could easily apply the same process by generating a new set of either more or fewer constraints to follow, establishing a linear system to solve, and, as done above, solving for the coefficient matrix. If you do so, you will end up with a larger or smaller square matrix, the size of which is the order of the polynomial minus one. If you take a look at what was done previously, four constraints were set. That means you required a polynomial of the third degree and, consequently, a 4×4 matrix. The difference between a normal Bézier curve and a Cardinal curve is illustrated in Figure 13.9.

B-Splines

So far you have seen the Bézier curve, which is excellent if you do not need a class C_1 curve. On the other hand, you have the Cardinal curve, which can be used for class G_1 curves, but which require three times the number of computations as the Bézier curve (recall that the average vertex is used four times in the matrix). Nothing actually forces the spline to be of class G_2, however. In fact, a function of class C_2 can be interesting if you want your movement's acceleration to stay the same. That's what B-splines are all about.

Before you take a deeper look into B-splines, let's examine things from a different angle: the basis functions. For a Bézier curve, the basis functions cover the entire range of the curve. This was noted to have the effect of a single vertex affecting the entire curve. Some basis functions for the Bézier curve have been rendered in Figure 13.10. The Cardinal curve, on the other hand, has basis functions that cover only a small range.

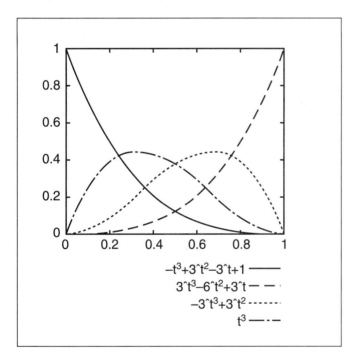

Figure 13.10
Basis functions for a Bézier curve

The basis functions for the B-spline have been rendered in Figure 13.11. In the previous section, you learned that a cubic Cardinal curve is such that every control vertex affects at most four control vertices away. In other words, a given control vertex only has an effect on the surrounding control vertices' curve section. It cannot affect the entire curve, as Bézier curves alone did. If you were to plot the basis functions, you would notice that this is actually represented in the plots. Every basis function spans at most four control vertices away. You may also notice that the sum of the functions' amplitude at any point in time is 1. The Bézier function also had this property, which was noted algebraically.

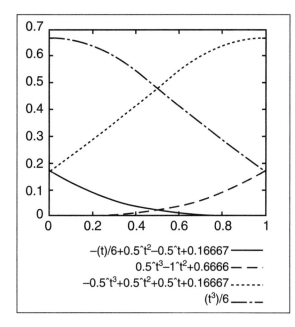

$-(t)/6+0.5\hat{\ }t^2-0.5\hat{\ }t+0.16667$ ———
$0.5\hat{\ }t^3-1\hat{\ }t^2+0.6666$ — —
$-0.5\hat{\ }t^3+0.5\hat{\ }t^2+0.5\hat{\ }t+0.16667$ ······
$(t^3)/6$ —·—

Figure 13.11
Basis functions for a B-spline curve

In order to get the equation for the B-spline, you can think of the vector space you will create in terms of basis functions. If you keep your mind on the cubic version of the curve, you can set a strict set of rules that must be met. A basis curve for a cubic spline is created by four basis polynomials, as shown in Figure 13.11. (It takes four points for each basis because of the degree.) For these four polynomials, it should be evident that the beginning and end of the curve should equal 0. Furthermore, the last value of the first polynomial should equal the first value of the second polynomial, and so forth for all of the polynomials. Again, this statement simply enforces C^0 continuity. You can apply the same idea to enforce C^1 and C^2 continuity; this will give you 15 equations, with 15 unknowns. But because you have a 4×4 basis matrix to fill, you are missing one more condition. You can pretty much choose any condition you wish, but the one that eventually proves the most useful is the fact that all polynomials add up to 1 at $t = 0$, as did the Bézier and the Cardinal curves. In fact, it will not be shown, but this is a requirement that enforces the convex hull rule. All in all, the set of equations you have are the following:

Positional Conditions	Slope Conditions	Curvature Conditions
$0 = a(0)$	$0 = a'(0)$	$0 = a''(0)$
$a(1) = b(0)$	$a'(1) = b'(0)$	$a''(1) = b''(0)$
$b(1) = c(0)$	$b'(1) = c'(0)$	$b''(1) = c''(0)$
$c(1) = d(0)$	$c'(1) = d'(0)$	$c''(1) = d''(0)$
$d(1) = 0$	$d'(1) = 0$	$d''(1) = 0$

and

$$1 = a(0) + b(0) + c(0) + d(0)$$

Sixteen equations with 16 unknowns. In short, this is one mean and ugly algebraic expression. I'll spare you the juggling act by getting right to the solution:

$$b(t) = \begin{bmatrix} t^3 & t^2 & t & 1 \end{bmatrix} \frac{1}{6} \begin{bmatrix} -1 & 3 & -3 & 1 \\ 3 & -6 & 3 & 0 \\ -3 & 0 & 3 & 0 \\ 1 & 4 & 1 & 0 \end{bmatrix} \begin{bmatrix} P_{i-2} \\ P_{i-1} \\ P_i \\ P_{i+1} \end{bmatrix}$$

One thing you should notice by simply plugging values into the equations is that it is not always possible to have any vertex P_i as a part of the curve. That is, the fact that you force the curvature to be equal between pieces of the spline comes at a price. Consequently, a B-spline cannot be called an interpolation simply because it does not go from *a* to *z* by going through a set of points. In fact, it might not even go through *a* and *z* at all! This can be a big drawback if you are planning on having an interpolating curve rather than one that is simply aesthetically pleasing. Of course, the vertices still act as a form of magnet toward the control points, but the curve does not necessarily go directly to them. Before you look at your options here, let's see how you can go about rendering such curves.

Converting B-Splines into Piecewise Béziers

Rendering B-splines can seem like a monumental task because there is no easy, obvious algorithm. Granted, you can use a form of subdivision algorithm, but you will not be able to use the efficient division speedups from which the Bézier curve benefits. But what if you could express the B-spline as a Bézier curve? Both the B-spline and the Bézier curve are linear transformations , so why not? The following logic ensues:

$$b(t) = \begin{bmatrix} t^3 & t^2 & t & 1 \end{bmatrix} \frac{1}{6} \begin{bmatrix} -1 & 3 & -3 & 1 \\ 3 & -6 & 3 & 0 \\ -3 & 0 & 3 & 0 \\ 1 & 4 & 1 & 0 \end{bmatrix} \begin{bmatrix} P_{i-2} \\ P_{i-1} \\ P_i \\ P_{i+1} \end{bmatrix}$$

$$= \begin{bmatrix} t^3 & t^2 & t & 1 \end{bmatrix} \left(\begin{bmatrix} -1 & 3 & -3 & 1 \\ 3 & -6 & 3 & 0 \\ -3 & 3 & 0 & 0 \\ 1 & 0 & 0 & 0 \end{bmatrix} \begin{bmatrix} -1 & 3 & -3 & 1 \\ 3 & -6 & 3 & 0 \\ -3 & 3 & 0 & 0 \\ 1 & 0 & 0 & 0 \end{bmatrix}^{-1} \right) \frac{1}{6} \begin{bmatrix} -1 & 3 & -3 & 1 \\ 3 & -6 & 3 & 0 \\ -3 & 0 & 3 & 0 \\ 1 & 4 & 1 & 0 \end{bmatrix} \begin{bmatrix} P_{i-2} \\ P_{i-1} \\ P_i \\ P_{i+1} \end{bmatrix}$$

$$= \begin{bmatrix} t^3 & t^2 & t & 1 \end{bmatrix} \begin{bmatrix} -1 & 3 & -3 & 1 \\ 3 & -6 & 3 & 0 \\ -3 & 3 & 0 & 0 \\ 1 & 0 & 0 & 0 \end{bmatrix} \left(\frac{1}{6} \begin{bmatrix} 0 & 0 & 0 & 1 \\ 0 & 0 & \frac{1}{3} & 1 \\ 0 & \frac{1}{3} & \frac{2}{3} & 1 \\ 1 & 1 & 1 & 1 \end{bmatrix} \begin{bmatrix} -1 & 3 & -3 & 1 \\ 3 & -6 & 3 & 0 \\ -3 & 0 & 3 & 0 \\ 1 & 4 & 1 & 0 \end{bmatrix} \begin{bmatrix} P_{i-2} \\ P_{i-1} \\ P_i \\ P_{i+1} \end{bmatrix} \right)$$

$$= \begin{bmatrix} t^3 & t^2 & t & 1 \end{bmatrix} \begin{bmatrix} -1 & 3 & -3 & 1 \\ 3 & -6 & 3 & 0 \\ -3 & 3 & 0 & 0 \\ 1 & 0 & 0 & 0 \end{bmatrix} \left(\frac{1}{6} \begin{bmatrix} 1 & 4 & 1 & 0 \\ 0 & 4 & 2 & 0 \\ 0 & 2 & 4 & 0 \\ 0 & 1 & 4 & 1 \end{bmatrix} \begin{bmatrix} P_{i-2} \\ P_{i-1} \\ P_i \\ P_{i+1} \end{bmatrix} \right)$$

Wasn't that simple? All you need to do to convert from B-spline points to Bézier points is to multiply the set of points by a linear transformation matrix. Consequently, this means that every B-spline is actually a concatenation of a set of Bézier curves. Thus, the B-spline form is actually nothing but a restriction that is applied to a set of Bézier points. The same can be said about the Cardinal spline. You can convert from B-spline points to Bézier points with the following formula:

$$
\begin{bmatrix} BezierPt_0 \\ BezierPt_1 \\ BezierPt_2 \\ BezierPt_3 \end{bmatrix} = \frac{1}{6} \begin{bmatrix} 1 & 4 & 1 & 0 \\ 0 & 4 & 2 & 0 \\ 0 & 2 & 4 & 0 \\ 0 & 1 & 4 & 1 \end{bmatrix} \begin{bmatrix} P_{i-2} \\ P_{i-1} \\ P_i \\ P_{i+1} \end{bmatrix}
$$

tip

You might have noticed that this chapter's section on Cardinal curves did not contain information about how to render these types of curves. Cardinal curves are rendered using the same technique as B-splines—although the math for a Cardinal curve is just a tad uglier because of the *s* variable.

The B-splines you have seen so far fit into a group called uniform B-splines. The next section is meant to expand on that "uniform" part.

The World Beyond: Extending the Concept of Locality with Knot Vectors

You have seen that you can create a function that has local control over the vertices. Specifically, the cubic function has control over four neighbor vertices. You can extend this concept such that you have control over five, six, or any number of vertices. To do so, simply list the set of constraints, as shown above in the B-spline section, and derive the corresponding matrix. This is a cumbersome task indeed. You will see another method of deriving the basis functions, but before you do, I'd like to take a stab at another concept: knot vectors.

A *knot vector* is a vector that gives the range of influence, and it can be used to create a B-spline curve that is not necessarily uniform. For a given point i, you can determine its range using the knot vector by looking at its lower bound v_i and its upper bound v_{i+k+1}. With the splines you have seen so far, you didn't really look at the influence range as a percentage [0..1], but as a range in terms of surrounding vertices affected. This is the equivalent of giving an equal distance to each vertex, which is why these types of splines are called "uniform" B-splines. That is, they are called "uniform" because their knot vector increases linearly.

Obviously, for a knot vector to make any sense at all, it must be increasing or else you get clear inconsistencies. Also, because your curve is defined on a range of [0, 1], the knot vector must also be bounded by [0, 1]. (With regards to the more general definition of a B-spline, this is not a requirement because the equation scales things down. For simplicity's sake, however, let's stick to the more practical approach—that is, [0, 1].) For example, if you wanted to represent the cubic B-spline you saw in the B-spline-to-Bézier conversion example as a knot vector, for six vertices, you would write the vector as follows:

$$\left[\frac{0}{9}, \frac{1}{9}, \frac{2}{9}, \frac{3}{9}, \frac{4}{9}, \frac{5}{9}, \frac{6}{9}, \frac{7}{9}, \frac{8}{9}, \frac{9}{9} \right]$$

The range for the first vertex is thus [0, 4/9], the second vertex has range [1/9, 5/9], and so forth, up to the sixth vertex with range [5/9, 1]. If you do the math, you will notice that the knot vector always has as many values as the number of vertices plus the degree. So for the preceding example, you had $4 + 6 - 1 = 9$ different values. Splitting ten values equally means that you have to increase by 1/9 each step by starting at 0. But here's a trick question: How do you represent Bézier curves using this notation? Fortunately, it's not that difficult. Recall that Bézier curves affected the entire curve with range [0, 1]. This implies that given a degree k, whichever range you chose should always have a range of [0, 1]. The only way to do this is to set half the value to 0 and the other half to 1. Thus, a cubic Bézier has a knot vector of

$$[0, 0, 0, 0, 1, 1, 1, 1]$$

These forms of knot vectors are called *open vectors* because they repeat the value of the range at the beginning and at the end. Open vectors are still considered uniform if and only if removing the duplicates at the beginning and the end yields a uniform knot vector.

tip

> You could optimize the calculations of your curve considerably if you simply considered the uniform (not open) subvectors of your vector as translations of the first occurrence. The uniform B-spline you have seen so far is an excellent example where translation could be used to save some time.

There are also knot vectors that are not uniform, but are still part of the B-spline family. The concept is exactly the same as the uniform version except that the range of influence is not equal from one interval to the other. I'll skip the complex algebra of conversion to and from recurrence relations and will present the equation to recursively compute the basis functions of a B-spline given its degree k and the number of control points n. The ith basis function of a k degree polynomial B-spline $B_{i,k}$ with knot vector elements x_i is as follows:

$$B_{i,1} = \begin{cases} 1 & x_i \le t < x_{i+1} \\ 0 & else \end{cases}$$

$$B_{i,k}(t) = \frac{(t - x_i) B_{i,k-1}(t)}{x_{i+k-1} - x_i} + \frac{(x_{i+k} - t) B_{i+1,k-1}(t)}{x_{i+k} - x_{i+1}}$$

At this point, it would probably be appropriate to look at the effect of the knot vector over the curve in general. For starters, with the Bézier curve, you can establish the generalization that you can force a spline of degree k to go through the initial and last control point if all of the k first and k last control points are such that their range affects the first/last control point. Put in simpler terms, a spline goes through its first and last control point if its knot vector starts with k zeros and finishes with k ones. Of course, as mentioned previously, you could have a range that is not [0, 1] and the definition would change accordingly. But because you only care about the [0, 1] range, you shouldn't bother much with the other cases, such as pure integers, which are sometimes used in literature to "simplify" things.

Closing the Gap

B-splines are great because they offer C² continuity, but they do not guarantee that any of the control points will be part of the final curve. (Of course, because you can express a Bézier curve as a B-spline, there is at least one curve that allows for this and you could probably come up with some other examples as well.) As a result, it can be difficult to close the shape. For instance, if you wanted to express the equation of a circle or something similar with B-splines, you would probably not find this to be an obvious problem initially. The solution, however, is surprisingly simple. All you have to do to close the shape is to add the first $k - 2$ vertices. It's that easy.

NURBs

The NURB, which is the last type of spline I'm going to cover, offers the most control, but is also the heaviest spline to compute. The idea behind the NURB (non-uniform rational B-spline) curve is to define weight factors for every vertex. In other words, for a control point P_i, the NURB spline redefines it as a new control point Q_i, shown:

$$P_i = \begin{bmatrix} x_i \\ y_i \\ z_i \end{bmatrix} \approx w_i \begin{bmatrix} x_i \\ y_i \\ z_i \\ 1 \end{bmatrix} = Q_i$$

Unfortunately, you cannot simply multiply a vertex like this without worrying about anything else. Your curve is defined for a range of [0..1], and applying random multiplications like this simply is not going to work. What you have to do in order to keep the same integrity and properties defined in previous sections is to renormalize the curve. Of course, if you had chosen Q_i such that they were already normalized, this would not be a problem. But like a vector, the general case assumes non-normalized weights; thus, you must divide by the perspective division in order to obtain the final equation. Put everything together, and you get the following:

$$f(t) = \frac{\displaystyle\sum_{i=1}^{n} P_i \cdot B_{i,k}(t) w_i}{\displaystyle\sum_{i=1}^{n} B_{i,k}(t) w_i}$$

But wait—didn't I say earlier that every curve/spline could be written in the form of a summed addition of the basis function multiplied by a control point? Well, not quite. If you remember, I added a parenthetical "with one noted exception." If, for example, you were to choose an open third-degree uniform B-spline, you could write it in matrix representation as shown here:

$$b_i(t) = \frac{\begin{bmatrix} t^3 & t^2 & t & 1 \end{bmatrix} \dfrac{1}{6} \begin{bmatrix} -1 & 3 & -3 & 1 \\ 3 & -6 & 3 & 0 \\ -3 & 0 & 3 & 0 \\ 1 & 4 & 1 & 0 \end{bmatrix} \begin{bmatrix} w_{i-2} & 0 & 0 & 0 \\ 0 & w_{i+1} & 0 & 0 \\ 0 & 0 & w_i & 0 \\ 0 & 0 & 0 & w_{i+1} \end{bmatrix} \begin{bmatrix} P_{i-2} \\ P_{i-1} \\ P_i \\ P_{i+1} \end{bmatrix}}{\begin{bmatrix} t^3 & t^2 & t & 1 \end{bmatrix} \dfrac{1}{6} \begin{bmatrix} -1 & 3 & -3 & 1 \\ 3 & -6 & 3 & 0 \\ -3 & 0 & 3 & 0 \\ 1 & 4 & 1 & 0 \end{bmatrix} \begin{bmatrix} w_{i-2} \\ w_{i+1} \\ w_i \\ w_{i+1} \end{bmatrix}}$$

In this form, you can probably understand a little more why NURBs are much more computationally expensive than B-splines. You could change the multiplication of the two upper matrices into a dot product, but that would not be a purist matrix representation. Of course, flexibility almost always comes at a price, and such is the price for NURBs. So the question you may well rightfully ask is, what can you do with NURBs that was not possible with the previous curves?

The nice thing about NURBs is that they can accurately represent conic sections and, by extension, circles, ellipses, hyperboles, and such. It's also much easier to think of a curve in terms of weighting factors than to think about increasing the order of the curve or changing the affected region by using the knot vector. The beauty of this function is that it can easily be converted into a B-spline equation if you consider the normalized weighted points as the input for the B-spline. Thus, you can also convert from B-spline to Bézier and consequently render the curve.

How do the various values of the weight affect the overall look of the curve? For starters, your curve is still bounded by the range you have set in the knot vector. If you look at this algebraically, you will notice that setting the weight to 0 is the same thing as simply forgetting about the vertex altogether. Thus, setting one of the weights to 0 would have the same effect as never specifying the control point at all. On the other hand, if you set the same weight to every other vertex, what you get is B-spline. Because every weight has the same value, the normalized weight is thus 1 and, as you saw in the B-spline section, the sum of the basis functions for any given value of t is 1 (set forth by the definition). From this point on, you can see how the values between 1 and 0 will behave. A value closer to 0 will give little importance to the control point, while a value that tends toward infinity basically ignores every other control vertex. If you prefer to look at it another way, a value of infinity basically lets the normalized weight of the other control vertices tend toward 0. Figures 13.12, 13.13, and 13.14 illustrate the effect of the weights on the curve.

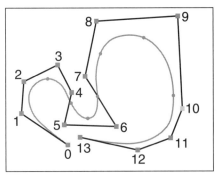

Figure 13.12
NURBs with weight of point 9 set to 1

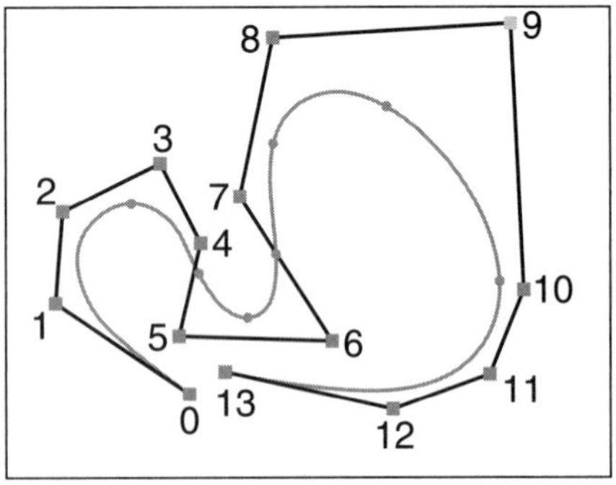

Figure 13.13
NURBs with weight of point 9 set to 0.5

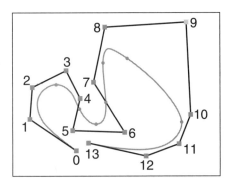

Figure 13.14
NURBs with weight of point 9 set to 0

Using NURBs to Represent Conic Sections

What makes NURBs particularly interesting is that by using them, you can combine the benefits of Cardinal and B-splines. In fact, if you think about it, you will probably notice that NURBs are actually a stricter version of B-splines, which in turn are a stricter version of a set of Bézier curves. The problem with B-splines and Cardinal splines, however, is that they cannot easily represent conic sections (ellipses, hyperboles, and so on). With NURBs, however, you can define a curve that passes through its first and last points by using an open knot, yet you can still use the weight factors to obtain better control over your curve. That is, with NURBs, you can have a curve going through a given set of points and still have a good level of control over the curvature of the curve—which is particularly effective for conic sections.

If you take a curve with only three vertices, chosen as the three points on an equilateral triangle (each side is of equal length), you can force the curve to go through the first and last vertex, and you can still change the curvature of the curve by simply changing the weight of the middle vertex while setting a weight of 1 on the ends. With such a curve, setting a middleweight value of 0 will draw a straight line from a to b. On the other hand, if you set a weight of 1, you will generate parabolic curves. Setting a weight value above 1 will yield a hyperbolic curve, while setting a value below 1 will yield an elliptical curve. You can verify this by plugging some values inside the curve and by computing its derivative. The hyperbolic curve tends toward a $[+/-]1$ slope, the elliptical one's slope is smaller than 1 in absolute value, and the parabola is the remaining values.

If you want to do a circle, you should expect to have a weight less than 1 because a circle is an elliptical arc. If you force the midpoint of the curve to be on a circle of radius r, you could determine the weight you would need in order to do so. This would imply that the circle should actually be composed of three separate curves with weight $[1\ w\ 1\ 1\ w\ 1\ 1\ w\ 1]$ and knot vector $[0\ 0\ 0\ 1\ 1\ 2\ 2\ 3\ 3\ 3]$. It's pointless to go through the details of this proof; just know that the equation you end up with is as follows:

$$w = \cos\left(\frac{\pi}{6}\right) = \frac{1}{2}$$

Obviously, this works, but it's not a very convenient form for your circle, mainly because you cannot stretch it easily to obtain an ellipse. On the other hand, if you had a square, you could simply translate the control points in order to obtain an ellipse. This now becomes much more attractive. Of course, you could also apply any transformation you like on these control points to rotate, translate, scale, and so on. As you do this, just make sure that you have not assumed anything while computing the weight factors; otherwise, everything will fall apart. For instance, you cannot scale in x a circle described using seven control points, primarily because this would break the rule you have set with regards to triangles being equilateral. So then, how do you go about computing the weight factors for a $k = 3$, nine-control-point NURBs?

Why do things always have to look more complicated than they really are? You can apply the exact same logic in order to determine the weight you need. All in all, you could do this in general for n vertices on a circle. The solution to this specific problem is $w = -1$. The general case will be left as an exercise. You can write some code to render such a curve if you want to verify that you have indeed done this correctly.

As always, the best way to tackle such a problem is to think about what you know about the problem. What inputs can you can use to solve the problem? After you have the inputs, you can look at the problem's relationships in order to find a solution. The last step is to test it out and try various inputs to see how it behaves. Sometimes you may come up with something that is more of an approximation than an exact solution, but this is not necessarily problematic—especially for gaming purposes, where accuracy can easily be put aside on the visual side for higher frame rates.

Using the Curves Wisely

It's one thing to know the math; it's another to know where it should be used. These curves can find their way into all kinds of things. Where they are used is entirely up to you. One popular choice is to use these curves to move the camera around. No one really likes jerky camera movement; it simply looks unprofessional. Fortunately, these types of movements do not really require that much precision, so in order to render them, you don't need a fancy curve. As long as you can choose the control points such that you won't hit a wall, you should be fine. As I mentioned earlier, you can use the convex hull property of the splines to guarantee this.

Of course, you can do much more with these types of curves than simple camera translations. After all, for the most part, these curves are interpolating curves. They differ from approximating curves because they go from one value to another in a well-defined manner. Of course, this doesn't mean you can't use both at the same time. For instance, you could use Bézier curves to render a circle if you wish. Simply apply an approximation on the parametric equation of the circle and you will be well on your way. Again, this does not only really relate to movement. Because these curves interpolate between various values, you can use the interpolation for yet more things. For instance, you could use such a curve to smooth out the camera's rotation—a definite "nice to have." If you would like your camera to point toward the direction in which you are going, then you should easily be able to do so by computing the tangent vector of the spline. This is one of the easiest derivative problems, so computing it should be a breeze for you. Terrain is also a very attractive option for such curves because it guarantees piecewise continuity and requires much less memory than conventional heightmaps.

Surfaces

Without a doubt, curves/splines are quite useful—and they can be made even more so by pushing them into higher dimensions by adding one extra parameter. Adding an extra parameter enables you to define a surface, which can thereafter be used in your world. The snowboarding game mentioned previously comes to mind. The beauty of splines is that you can use something such as an extremely long B-spline to basically describe the entire world.

In contrast with using a height map, you can use surfaces to render only the small portions of your game's world that are potentially visible according to your camera, thereby defining a very long world with little data, with the added benefits of continuity and collision accuracy. Surfaces can also be used as objects. *Quake III* comes to mind here; it uses surfaces to generate various world objects. These types of objects are actually quite easy to deform simply because moving a control point will affect a small defined region in accordance with your knot vectors. If you wanted to be extra fancy, you could even use a spline to move the control points of your surface to generate an interesting morphing effect.

There's no point in looking at the various possible surfaces independently, mainly because they are all extensions of their derivative curve/spline, and thus follow the same properties and rules. For example, consider a string that was bent in various directions that were defined by control points. Now, switch to second-dimension parameters by expanding the string into a sheet of paper. As with the string, you can bend the sheet of paper according to a set of control points, as illustrated in Figure 13.15.

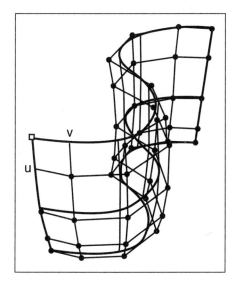

Figure 13.15
NURBs surface with two controlling axes
u, v

In fact, a sheet of paper can actually be defined with two strings. If you let the first string roam freely along the *x*-axis, you lock one of the parameters. From there, you can use the second string to define another curve orthogonal to the first one, which can be seen as the *y* or *z*-axis, depending on your point of view. Now you have two strings whose parameters are defined orthogonally. Beware: I did not say that the *curves* were orthogonal. Instead, I said that the strings' *parameters* are orthogonal. If you prefer, you could say that *t*, the first parameter, is not dependent in any way on *s*, which you can define as the second parameter and vice versa. You can also see this more or less like a basis where the parameter *t* moves in one direction while *s* enables you to move freely in another direction in 3D.

The idea for a surface is to combine the basis function $B_i(s)$ and $B_j(t)$. Consequently, the final basis function for the parameter i, j is

$$B_{i,j}(s,t) = B_i(s)B_j(t)$$

If you look at the formula closely, you will notice that it actually has the same properties as a one-parameter basis function. As you would expect, because both one-parameter basis functions have a range of $[0, 1]$, the multiplication of two such ranges will also yield a range of $[0, 1]$, which means that the curve will, again, satisfy the convex hull property. As far as the equations are concerned, they behave in the exactly same fashion as they used to except that you have to account for both parameters. Thus, the NURBs equation that was

$$f(t) = \frac{\displaystyle\sum_{i=1}^{n} P_i \cdot B_{i,k}(t) w_i}{\displaystyle\sum_{i=1}^{n} B_{i,k}(t) w_i}$$

now becomes

$$f(s,t) = \frac{\displaystyle\sum_{j=1}^{m}\sum_{i=1}^{n} P_{i,j} \cdot B_{j,l}(s) \cdot B_{i,k}(t) w_{i,j}}{\displaystyle\sum_{j=1}^{m}\sum_{i=1}^{n} B_{j,l}(s) \cdot B_{i,k}(t) w_{i,j}}$$

First, notice how the basis functions can actually have different polynomial powers. One has degree k while the other has degree l. This means that if you want to have more local control in one axis, you can easily do so. On the other hand, if you prefer to stay symmetrical, you can always let $k = l$. Next, notice that the weight and the control points have multiplied. Every point is associated with a weight, so that's nothing new, but the control points themselves have jumped an extra dimension. To understand why this is so, simply think about the difference between a plane and a line. A plane can actually be described as a set of lines along a line.

Similarly, here, the surface can be described with a set of a set of control points or, if you prefer, a set of curve control points. If you still have problems visualizing a surface, think of four Bézier curves in 2D separated by a fixed distance in 3D. In other words, you have four Bézier curves in 3D that are parallel to one of the axes in 3D, but that roam freely in the other two axes, which are separated from one to another by a fixed value. Now take the first control points of each of these Bézier curves and generate another Bézier curve with them. Do this for all sets of four control points, and you will in fact start to see a surface; that is pretty much what is happening here.

So what is the equation for a surface based on a B-spline, a Cardinal curve, or a Bézier? Well, it uses the same process as explained previously. Simply change the basis function and the fixed values such that they take care of the two parameters, and you are set. If you already have a shape in 2D, you can easily extend it in 3D by adding more details about its new dimension. For instance, you already know how to create a circle in 2D. If you wanted to create a tube in 3D, all you would have to do is specify the control points in the z axis. If you want the tube to have an even radius, you only need to copy the control points but to change the z value linearly. Alternatively, you can start to morph this shape by increasing the size of the circle at various values of z to yield something like, say, a pot. A pot is made of a small circle at the bottom and another slightly larger circle at the top. Meanwhile, it has a large circular waist, which means that the control points should be placed accordingly.

Rendering Surfaces

If you need to compute a surface's normal vector for lighting purposes and hidden surface removal, you should easily be able to do so by computing the tangent vector of the function in s and in t and by computing the cross product of both. This is something you should be quite familiar with by now.

Next, turn your attention to determining points along the curve. For simplicity's sake, let's consider a Bézier surface. Of course, you can use the previous analytic method that consisted of forward-differencing the formula and rendering fixed increases in parameter squares. The other technique is to use the subdivision algorithm presented previously. For surfaces, the algorithm has to work a little differently to account for the extra dimension of freedom. Basically, a surface is an interpolation of an interpolation in two directions (defined by s and t). Suppose you were working with a cubic surface (four control vertices with four rows). To render the cubic surface, you first need to apply the subdivision algorithm to every row. This will give you two new curves per row and thus two new surfaces. Rotate the two new surfaces 90 degrees and apply the same thing to both surfaces. This will give you four surfaces. Apply this process recursively; you may stop whenever the slope in both axes is satisfactory.

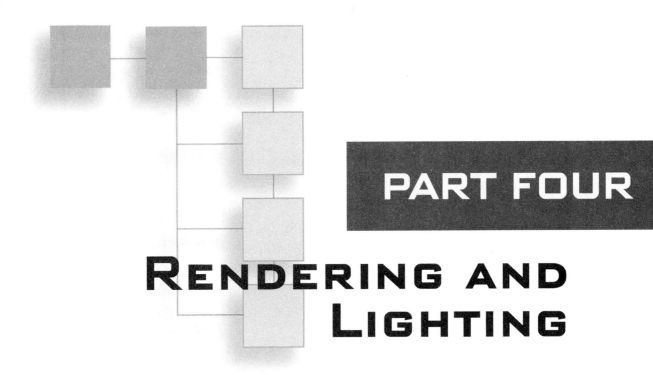

PART FOUR

RENDERING AND LIGHTING

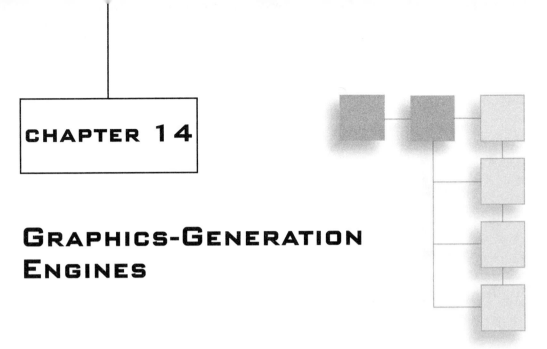

CHAPTER 14

GRAPHICS-GENERATION ENGINES

I f nothing moved in a game, that game would be very dull. Of course, you already know how to get the objects in your game moving using basic elements of physics and a bit of camera trickery. You know how to throw rockets around and can even align the rocket's direction with the slope of its movement. But although your rocket may move, it has no fire coming out of it. Worse, it simply disappears when it collides with a character. Your character might follow the rules of physics, rebounding and landing in water, but he sinks into the water without even making a splash.

These are the types of small but extremely important elements that make the difference between yet another 3D maze engine and *the* engine; they're what give your game spark. After all, the more special effects you can cram into your game, the more realistic it will look, and the more bonus points you get. Be aware, though, that "realistic" in this case does not mean physically realistic (that is, realistic in terms of our world). On the contrary, twisting the laws of physics usually makes for some great effects. The fact that a character can climb walls, or that a world you create has weird green gook falling from the sky, is all for the best—as long as it doesn't interfere with proper game play.

Because these types of elements are generally dynamic—that is, they come and go depending on the context of your game—they require a graphics generation structure or, if you prefer, a factory of particles. That's what this chapter is about. Specifically, this chapter discusses the following:

- Decals
- Billboards

Decals

Take an AK-47, shoot a few rounds into a piece of wood, and what happens? Chances are that anyone hiding behind the piece of wood will have been hit by a round or two, and that the wood itself will have splintered into many #2 pencils. Likewise, when a character in your game shoots wildly around in the world, he should be able to see the damage he has done.

Most of the time, the world is considered static for optimization reasons. That's because in general, the more dynamic the world is, the slower the game becomes because of partitioning/collision problems. You simply cannot precompute a lot of things as you could in a static world. For this reason, you want to modify the world only minimally such that speed is minimally affected, but realism—and that coolness factor—is still increased.

An object called a *decal* is often used in games to represent changes in the material of the world. A decal is, in effect, a masking polygon that is applied over the affected area. A decal might be designed to resemble a hole shot in the wall, a spatter of blood, a bomb's burn marks, or a footprint on a snowy mountain. It cannot generate a see-through effect since it's only a mask, but it can generate "destruction marks" as we all like to call them.

Decal Rendering Issues

The hard part about using a decal—that is, placing a masking polygon containing an image of, say, a bullet hole—is determining where the polygon should be placed. The most obvious solution is to take the plane upon which the decal is to be placed (a wall, for example) and to apply the decal polygon over that part of the wall. Doing so, however, can create problems because, ultimately, two polygons are placed on the same spot. How is the graphics card supposed to know which one should be on top? You could disable z buffering, but then how would you take care of the visibility? The solution is pretty simple. If you move the object forward (in the direction of the normal vector, off the wall) ever so slightly, then you could render the decal without changing much.

> **note**
>
> I have encountered some of the most complicated and obscure solutions to this problem, including computing a new projection matrix that shifts the decal forward without actually giving the impression that it has moved forward. This, however, is a great example of thinking outside the box, because it removes the z-buffering issue while giving the decal the same look by computing a new projection matrix for the object. It does require a hefty amount of math, however, which makes this solution unattractive.

OpenGL and Direct3D are equipped with something they call *depth value offset*. The idea is that you can call a function that will offset the depth values. The specific functions for

OpenGL and Direct3D are glPolygonOffset(1, Bias) and SetRenderState(D3DRS_ DEPTHBIAS, Bias), respectively, where Bias is the offset you wish to apply. Typically, a value of 1 will suffice, but if you have multiple decals, then you may want to increase the bias. The solution is thus quite simple. Simply offset the z-buffer such that you guarantee that the polygon will always pass the z-buffer test.

Generating the Decal

Now that you have set up your decal to sit above the object behind it (be it a wall, a floor, or any other object), you should be able to easily compute the collision point between the object and the projectile that was fired, but you have yet to actually position the texture correctly at that point. Let's start with a simplistic case by supposing that the collision only occurs with one single triangle. In other words, your bullet is endlessly small, and it will only hit one triangle at any point in time. Next, you have to generate a decal that is aligned with this triangle. Let $\mathbf{p}$ be the collision point, or the center of the decal if you prefer.

It may not always be necessary to orient the decal, but in some cases—take the snow footprint as an example—an orientation for the decal may be useful. In that case, let $\mathbf{u}$ be the direction for the decal, as illustrated in Figure 14.1; the orientation might, for example, correspond to the direction in which the character is walking. You should also have the normal vector for the triangle (compute it if necessary as shown in Chapter 2, "Baby Steps: Introduction to Vectors"); $\mathbf{u}$ defines the rotation of the decal around the normal vector. If you do not care about the direction, you can build a second vector by using the Gram-Schmidt orthogonolization process with $\mathbf{n}$, or you can generate your own vector by choosing a point $\mathbf{a}$ from the triangle generating the vector $\mathbf{ap} = \mathbf{a} - \mathbf{p}$. If you decide to choose your own, then you have to make sure that $\mathbf{u}$ is orthogonal to $\mathbf{n}$, or else your decal will not be aligned correctly.

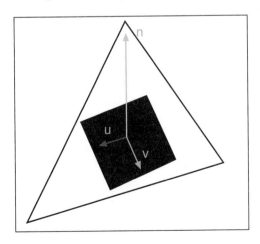

Figure 14.1
Decal's components

If your character is walking in a direction and you would like to add his footprint, then you have the character's direction $\mathbf{d}$. $\mathbf{d}$ is not necessarily aligned with the surface on which the character is walking, however. For example, suppose the character is climbing a hill. In that case, he may be walking straight ahead, but because of the hill, his direction is really straight and upward. For this reason, the orientation vector $\mathbf{u}$ needs to be aligned with the surface or else your decal will sink into the object behind it. You can easily solve this problem by computing the projection of the vector upon the plane. More precisely, this is the perpendicular component of the projection of **u** upon **n**.

Lastly, define **v** as the vector that completes the basis and thus is perpendicular to both **u** and **n**. Is it me, or does this sound like a cross product? If you examine Figure 14.1, you'll see that you already have the answer you are looking for. To find the endpoints of the surface, **u** and **v** are your keys. You first need to normalize, and then multiply half their width/height (half on each side from the center point yields a full length). After that, you can obtain the four corners of the decal by adding the vectors from the center point and by changing the signs. Thus, the four corners would be defined by the following pre-computed factors:

$$\mathbf{u}' = \frac{Height \cdot \mathbf{u}}{2\|\mathbf{u}\|_2}$$

$$\mathbf{v}' = \frac{Width \cdot \mathbf{v}}{2\|\mathbf{v}\|_2}$$

and defined by the following:

$$\mathbf{TopLeft} = \mathbf{p} - \mathbf{u} - \mathbf{v}$$

$$\mathbf{Top\,Right} = \mathbf{p} - \mathbf{u} + \mathbf{v}$$

$$\mathbf{LowerLeft} = \mathbf{p} + \mathbf{u} - \mathbf{v}$$

$$\mathbf{LowerRight} = \mathbf{p} + \mathbf{u} + \mathbf{v}$$

Triangle Clipping

Now that you know *where* to render a decal, it's time to look at clipping and beyond. For example, what happens if your character fires a bullet at the *edge* of a wall? According to the model established so far, the decal would be rendered on the edge of the wall, with part of the decal on the wall, and part of it beyond the wall. Put another way, the decal will appear as though someone stuck a piece of paper containing an image of a bullet hole on the edge of the wall, with part of the paper on the wall, and part of it dangling in the air. To fix this problem, you have to *clip* the decal such that only the portion that should appear on the wall, floor, or other surface shows up.

To use clipping, first assume that the game's world is composed of triangles, because in the end, this is how all polygons are converted anyway. Thus, you are looking at clipping a triangle on the edge of a wall. To help you visualize this, place a sticky note on the edge of a door. If you stuck the sticky note close enough to the edge of the door, it is probably sticking out. In other words, the sticky note isn't completely on the door; a part of it is sticking out in the air. That's exactly what you would like to clip. The idea behind clipping is based on the intersection between a line (the edge of the door) and a triangle (your sticky note, or decal). Mathematically speaking, if your systems were 100 percent precise, they would do this calculation without a problem; unfortunately, however, that's not the case. The line is on the same plane as the decal's triangle, which means that precision issues will make your calculations very hard in 3D. Instead, what you need to do is to replace the edge by a plane, which will cut the triangle with the same angle as the one cut by the edge.

There are a bunch of planes you can select. The only rule is that the plane needs to cut the triangle in the same fashion as the edge did. Thus, you could generate a plane with the edge's vector, the normal vector of the triangle, and one point of the edge. Another valid choice is to choose the plane described by one of the triangles that shares the same edge as the chosen edge. For instance, coming back to the door example, you could choose the face of the door that is perpendicular to the face upon which the sticky note is stuck. This would indeed cut the sticky note at the right position.

Lastly, you can't work on the triangle as a whole. Instead, you have to look at a series of smaller problems, the first of which involves finding the intersection between a line segment and a plane. Thus, given a triangle, you will have to look at all three of its edges and test them against a plane. More generally, the algorithm is as follows. You first need to pick one edge from the decal's triangle. Then, for every edge with endpoints $\mathbf{p}_1$ and $\mathbf{p}_2$, you do the following:

- If both points lie on the positive side of the plane, then add the last point ($\mathbf{p}_2$).
- If both points lie on the negative side of the plane, don't do anything.
- If you go from inside ($\mathbf{p}_1$) to outside ($\mathbf{p}_1$), you must add the intersection between the plane and the line.
- If you go from outside ($\mathbf{p}_1$) to inside ($\mathbf{p}_1$), you must add the intersection between the plane and the line *and* you must add the last point ($\mathbf{p}_2$).

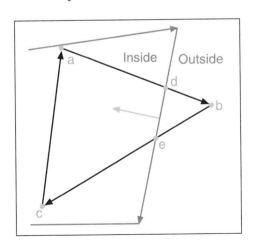

With this algorithm, you start with an empty list of vertices and insert them as prescribed by the algorithm. The step for one edge of the background with the decal is shown in Figure 14.2. You may end up with more vertices then a triangle requires. In this case, you can still render the shape but as a polygon instead of a triangle, or if you prefer, you can tessellate the polygon (that is, decompose the polygon into a set of triangles) by simply choosing a point from which all edges will be created.

Figure 14.2
Clipping a triangle to an edge

In Figure 14.2, assuming that you start with point **a**, you would categorize point **a** as inside by using the rules discussed in Chapter 4, "Basic Geometric Elements" (that is, by substituting the point inside the equation of the normal and checking the sign). Obviously, **c** would have the same result, while **b** would be flagged as outside. Because at the beginning you went from inside to outside (**a** to **b**), you add the intersection **d**. The next point is **c**; by checking on the previous point **b**, you notice that you now go from outside to inside, which means that you must add yet another vertex **e** and you must also add **c**. Finally, for the last edge, you go from **c** to **a**; because both are inside, you add **a**.

You already saw how to compute the intersection between a plane and a line in Chapter 4, so the only thing missing now is the method to compute the plane itself given the edge of the triangle. Luckily, this is easy. If you take the cross product of the decal's normal with the vector generated by the edge of the triangle, you get the normal's direction. Because a plane <**n** ,*D*> also has a displacement *D*, you simply need to substitute one of the background edge's points to compute the 4-vector for the plane. In math terms:

$$\mathbf{n'} = \left\langle \mathbf{n} \times (\mathbf{p}_1 - \mathbf{p}_2), -\left(\mathbf{n} \times (\mathbf{p}_1 - \mathbf{p}_2)\right) \bullet \mathbf{p} \right\rangle$$

The cross product is pretty picky with regard to the order of the vectors, so it is important to note that this formula works only if your polygons are defined in a clockwise fashion and if the normal vector points toward the camera. If not, then you must invert the order of the cross product to get a normal vector in the opposite direction. (If the normal does not point toward the camera, then why are you rendering the polygon to start with?) The rest should be a piece of cake.

A few words of advice about decals: Make sure you check the intersection of the decals with the surrounding polygons (not just the intersecting triangle) because the decal may actually span between two triangles. Lastly, be sure to correctly fix your texture coordinates as you cut the triangle into pieces. The texture coordinates should be interpolated in the exact same manner you interpolate vertices from one point to another. The only difference is that instead of interpolating <*x, y, z*>, you do so for <*u, v*>. Recall that computing the intersection between a plane and a line involves a parameter *t*. This value, if the vectors are normalized, represents the distance from the starting point to the end point. Thus you can interpolate your texture coordinates from one position to another by using this same *t*. The equation would look something like **a** + *t***b**, where **a** is the first texture point and **b** the second one for the edge (a linear system, which you should know how to solve by now). Thankfully, this process does not need to be applied to every single frame. You can simply compute this as it happens and keep the vertices as you go.

Most games put a limit to the number of decals that can be pasted on the screen; they typically use a form of queue in which newer decals erase older ones. Furthermore, they typically have the decal fade away with time by simply increasing its transparency up to a point where it is no longer visible and is then deleted. If you wanted to be extra-fancy, you could use a concept called *bumpmapping* to make these decals look even more real; you'll learn more about bumpmapping in upcoming chapters.

Another interesting trick is to permanently affect a texture by updating the texture itself. If, for example, you have shot a wall and you know for a fact that this bullet hole needs to remain there for the duration of the game, you can apply the decal on the texture itself. In other words, compute a new texture by rendering the texture and rendering the decal above it, and then storing this texture. The only catch with this is that you can't do it for every bullet hole, or else you will end up with more textures than you can account for. That said, it does speed up the game if you have the memory for it, and if you can guarantee that it needs to stay there.

Billboards

Have you ever wondered how cool effects such as lens flares, water splashes, blood explosions, or the smoke and fire burning behind a rocket are done? Billboards are what make all this happen.

Billboards operate in a manner that is similar to the moon. Have you ever noticed that the moon never changes? By that, I mean that no matter which side of the moon is lit, you always see the same holes, bumps, and such—even though the moon is a sphere that not only rotates around Earth but also about itself. That's basically because the moon spins in such a way that from Earth's point of view, the same side is always displayed. Billboards use the same principle to generate some surprisingly stunning effects from the gamer's point of view.

If you were to model smoke, fire, water, or any other type of particles using a 3D description, it would take a hefty amount of time to render every piece of the puzzle. Just imagine if you had to render the smoke behind a rocket using repeated and animated 3D models. The video card would surely die. Instead, what you can do is render the smoke once in a texture for use as a billboard, and show the sprite instead of a full-fledged 3D model when you want to draw it. This is clearly preferable with regard to speed, but obviously the quality is not the same since you can only see one side of it. For environmental effects such as smoke, fire, and water, this is perfect, because they generally do not have a very complex depth—if any.

note

If an object is really far away, it may be desirable to use billboards instead of rendering a complex object. This will significantly speed up your game and will hurt the quality only minimally.

Efficient Unconstrained Billboards

The only problem with billboards is that you can only see one side of the object rendered on the billboard. Back in the *Doom I/II* days, 3D engines used billboards to render the bad guys. At some point, John Carmack (of ID software fame) figured that PCs were fast enough to tolerate true 3D objects, and *Quake* came to life with stunning characters (in comparison to *Doom*'s). In some circumstances, such as when they are extremely far away, this is still the best way.

Just how do these work? For starters, you have to consider every object as a particle, one unique point in space. You can apply physics or whatever motion formula you desire to these points. The billboard itself must be like the moon, however, showing just one side of the object. To address this limitation, you can use a trick that is quite similar to what you used for decals. Given the center point of the particle, find the two offset vectors, which will construct a particle such that the normal vector of the billboard is aligned with that of the camera.

The model transformation matrix is the key here. The model transformation matrix is defined as the matrix that converts objects into camera coordinates. As such, it includes the object matrix, the world matrix, and the camera matrix all in one. If you had an identity model transformation matrix, the camera would be pointing down the z axis. You can thus create your billboard in the space before the matrix is applied, transform the coordinates, and then render normally. A billboard rendered on the xy plane is always normal to the camera before the transformation, so if you transform this billboard using the same matrix, you will necessarily get a billboard for which the normal of the camera after transformation is aligned with that of the billboard. To speed things up, you can transform two corners of the billboard (you could also do two orthogonal directions). For example, you might choose to transform the bottom-left and bottom-right corners, thus transforming the two vectors $<Width/2, Height/2, 0>$ and $<-Width/2, Height/2, 0>$.

These are the two vectors that can help you generate the four corners after transformation, as shown previously. Thus, you do not need to transform the four corners because the other two corners are a linear combination of the other two; they have a mere inversion of sign. After these two vectors are transformed, the beauty of this technique is that you can keep this offset, and it will be the same for every single particle you generate.

To recap, start by transforming the vectors $\mathbf{u} = <Width/2, Height/2, 0, 1>$ and $\mathbf{v} = <-Width/2, Height/2, 0, 1>$ with the model transformation matrix. Thereafter, for each particle, you need to draw the quad($<\mathbf{p} + \mathbf{u}, \mathbf{p} + \mathbf{v}, \mathbf{p} - \mathbf{y}, \mathbf{p} - \mathbf{v}>$).

Precise Unconstrained Billboard

The previous method is great because it is very efficient. Assuming that the offset has to be computed only once, the rest of the operations are mere additions and subtractions.

Unfortunately, it is not the most precise method. If you think of the camera as a frustum and not an actual vector, it is clear that the billboards in the center of the camera should be facing the camera directly. On the other hand, the billboards that are on the edge of the frustum should really be normal to the direction pointed to by the frustum (that is, the vector generated by the center of the particle and the position of the camera), as shown in Figure 14.3.

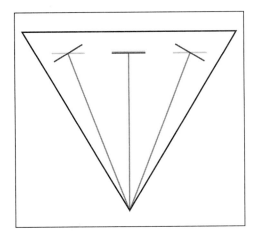

Figure 14.3
Precise and non-precise billboard orientation

The problem with this version is that it is position dependent, which means that the offset will have to be computed every single time you want to render a new particle. Such is the price for greater accuracy. You start by constructing the vector that goes from the camera to the billboard (**Billboard.Position − Cam.Position**) because the definition of this technique requires that the plane of the billboard be orthogonal to this very vector. Thus, let **q** be this vector and further define the vector **r** as the normal vector, which you used in the previous method. This vector can be obtained by transforming the vector $<0, 0, 1>$ with the transformation matrix. When you have these two vectors, solving merely involves a cross product for the height offset and yet another cross product for the width offset:

$$\mathbf{x} = \frac{\mathbf{r} \times \mathbf{q}}{\|\mathbf{r} \times \mathbf{q}\|_2}$$

$$\mathbf{y} = \mathbf{q} \times \mathbf{x}$$

Understanding vectors and their operations is key to understanding this. All you do here is build vectors that are orthogonal to two vectors, which you have. Where **x** and **y** are the offset vectors, you can build the two corner offset vectors by computing **x** + **y** and **x** − **y**, and by using the same technique listed previously to compute the four corners. The offsets in this case are only the vectors, which will get you to the nearest edge (either of the sides, or the top or bottom); thus, you need to add or subtract them to go through the corner. Now all you have to do is decide which technique suffices for your needs.

Constrained Billboards

Unconstrained quads are billboards that can move freely in space. No matter which direction your camera looks, the unconstrained quads are there, looking you straight in the eye. Although unconstrained quads may be useful for many things, they do not cover all types of possible billboards. For example, consider a torch. In this case, it could be practical to define the fire such that it changes direction as you rotate around the torch, but not when you look at the torch from above. In fact, it may be useful to display one billboard when you look at the torch from above and another when you look at it from the side. These types of billboards are special because they are locked upon an axis. The sideways torch, for example, is locked to the y axis, which goes up and down.

note

Although the equation will be deduced for billboards that rotate around the y axis, you could easily apply the same logic to find the equation for a rotation around any other axis.

The first thing you should notice is that the height of the billboard never changes regardless of the direction. Because the billboard only rotates around the y axis, its y component does not move. Consequently, the offset of the billboard in y can be easily expressed as half the height:

$$y = \left\langle 0, \frac{h}{2}, 0 \right\rangle$$

That was too easy; what about the x and z coordinates? You know that the plane of the billboard has to be parallel with the camera vector, and you already have a vector that is aligned with the plane <0, 0, 1>, which forces the billboard to be aligned with the y axis. Compute the cross product of these two vectors and voilà, you get the following, where q is defined as the vector that goes from the camera to the billboard:

$$x = \frac{w}{2} \cdot \frac{q \times \langle 0, 0, 1 \rangle}{\left\| q \times \langle 0, 0, 1 \rangle \right\|_2}$$

Once again, if you wanted to use the less precise method, you could use the camera's normal vector, which is obtained through the model transformation matrix and is the same for all billboards. The method you choose is a matter of speed versus image quality.

Shocking with Polylines

When I saw the lightning in *Return to Castle Wolfenstein* (*RTCW*), I was awed by its beauty and realism. Indeed, lightning has been used a lot in games, but never as beautifully as in *RTCW*. The main difference between the lightning in this game and the lightning that appeared in the others is that *RTCW* used some great colors and textures to achieve the effect.

Lightning can also be rendered by using a form of billboard, which is generated at run-time. The only hiccup there is building a billboard that is aligned with the camera and that moves through time. The idea is again pretty simple. If you consider the lightning bolt as a set of connected points that moves, you can easily see how this works. (By the way, you could also use this approach for something more esoteric such as a whip, a chain, or other similar elements that are string-based.)

The trick here is to build what is commonly referred to as a *polyline*. A polyline is nothing but a thick line. You could try to render it as a set of rectangles or thick lines, but it simply won't look good at the joins because you will be missing the joins altogether. For this reason, you need some method of generating a continuous thick line, including the joins.

Instead of using rectangles or thick lines, why not use quadrilaterals? That way, you could fill the connecting gaps since it needs not be a rectangle. You can construct such a shape by computing the offset of the join from the center point as shown in Figure 14.4.

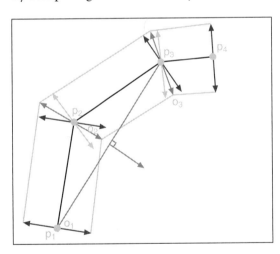

Figure 14.4
Precise and non-precise billboard orientation

Again, this is just playing with the properties of vectors. What you need is a vector that is perpendicular to the one formed by two continuous points defined by the string. This point has to be perpendicular to the camera and to the line segment, thus a cross product is used. You can use either the precise but slower technique or the fast but less accurate technique discussed previously in this chapter. If you choose the fast technique, then your camera vector is constant; if not, the camera vector depends on the position of the point you are currently evaluating, which was q (the vector from the camera to the particle) in the earlier section. If you consider the more precise and complicated case (the other one can be easily obtained by the same logic as stated previously), you have to define a vector $\mathbf{d}$ as the vector that goes from one point on the string to the next point on the string. Thus, the offset $\mathbf{o}$ from that point is defined as such, where t is defined as the orthogonal distance or, if you prefer, the width of the thick line:

$$\mathbf{o} = \frac{t(\mathbf{d} \times \mathbf{q})}{\|\mathbf{d} \times \mathbf{q}\|_2}$$

Therefore, the two vertices you want to add to the list for the current point **p** are **p** + **o** and **p** − **o**. There is one problem if you do this for every point, however. For example, suppose you have a very tight 90-degree turn. In this case, the extension of the particle would lie exactly on the next edge. This is clearly not desirable. If you take another look at Figure 14.4 and only consider the offsets, which are orthogonal to the previous line, it's obvious that this deforms the width of the line in some cases. For the 90-degree case, it collapses it completely on one end. As an alternative, you can compute the average between the current edge's offset and the next edge's offset. Another way to look at this is to generate the vector **d** such that it is the vector going from point $\mathbf{p}_{i+1}$ to $\mathbf{p}_i - 1$ as shown in Figure 14.4. Thus, with the noted exception of the first and last vertices, which are computed as shown previously, you can compute the offset of the polyline via the following method:

$$\mathbf{d} = \mathbf{p}_{i+1} - \mathbf{p}_{i-1}$$

Applications

So far, you have focused on the basics of how things work. Now you'll take a look at some neat things you can do with these concepts. You probably already have a good idea of how these concepts come into play; their uses are really only bound by your imagination.

The Explosion

What would be a game without explosions? When I wrote a small *Lemmings* game for the TI-86, what made gamers smirk was that it replicates the lemmings' self-destruct sequence. They start to swell and, eventually, every single one of them blows up.

Creating an explosion in 3D is a little more involved than creating the right sprites; it involves a particle system equipped with a physics engine and pushed by a billboard rendition engine. The idea behind an explosion is that initially, all the particles are centered about the same point in space. Before the explosion, the particles are given various normalized velocity vectors. Once the explosion starts, it forms a spherical cloud (due to the normalization) that falls according to gravitational rules. It is in fact pretty simple to make an explosion. The hardest part is to get the right physical constants and the right textures for the billboard to look real enough.

As a truly nice touch, consider setting up your game such that the walls onscreen are affected by the explosion. That way, if you compute the intersection of the particle with the world, you can detect whether any blood will squirt over a wall or even if it hits another character. This type of scheme can also be applied to water splashes, fireworks, gunshot smoke, and various other types of explosions.

SSSSssssssmokin'

A là Jim Carrey in *The Mask*, another neat effect is smoke. This is a pretty simple particle generator to implement. All you need is the position of the object that generates the smoke, and you can let the object generate one cloud of smoke every *x* milliseconds. To move the smoke around the world, you can again use something very similar to an explosion. What's a bit more interesting, though, is the fact that smoke dissipates with time. For example, when someone creates a puff of smoke with a cigarette, it expands up to a point where it blends completely with the ambient air. (Of course, if you do that too many times in a room, you end up with a room where you cannot see anything, but you get the idea.) In order to take this into account, you can be extra-fancy by having the billboard expand with time. *Quake* uses this strategy when firing rockets. Fire a rocket in *Quake III*, and you will notice that the smoke expands. In addition, you may want to set up the billboard to fade with time such that it eventually blends into the background. You can easily achieve this by decreasing the alpha value of the billboard over time, just as you can configure a decal to fade over time. (This is called giving the object "life.")

Lens Flare

Here's an effect that, in my opinion, is not very well implemented in many games. Lens flares can sometimes improve the visual quality of the game, but you have to make sure that they do not steal the whole scene. By that I mean that a flare should not be so obvious that it detracts from the actual game. Unfortunately, a lot of games tend to use some funky colors, which makes the flare quite obvious and thus not very attractive.

A lens flare is actually a physical phenomenon that happens only when a lens is used in a camera. There are physical representations if you really want to be physically correct, but in reality, you don't have to be in order for flares to look good—which is the whole reason to use flares anyway. A flare is generally seen as a set of circles and sparks aligned on a straight line, which coincides with the center of the screen and the position of the light source. Thus, if you have a sun located at a specific position on the screen, all the flare circles will be positioned along the infinite line that spans the area between the center of the screen and the sun. You have to make sure to distinguish between the two. (I'm actually talking about the center of the screen here and not the center of the world.)

When you create a flare, the textures used typically include a spark, a gradient circle (going from light to dark), another gradient circle (going from dark to light), and a halo. You can compose these images as you see fit. The only restriction is that you should give each image an interpolation value *t* that is fixed for the line generated between the light source and the center of the screen. This will guarantee that the flares will move correctly.

If the center of a flare is occluded by another object, you should not draw the flare at all. Let me reiterate: You should not clip the flare; you should not draw the flare at all. You can test these physical phenomena yourself. Look at a lamppost at night and hide the source of light with your hand. If you almost close one eye, you will notice that you no longer see the flare of the light.

This brings us to yet another topic. It may be very ugly to implement lens flare everywhere in your game (or at all). Although many would agree on this count, many would also agree that objects such as streetlights, for example, would benefit from a small contained spark at the position of the light source. *Flare* is perhaps not the right word here; perhaps *halo* is more appropriate. You are used to seeing a reasonably sized halo around lights, so it's not a bad idea to add them to your scenes. Then again, in your game, whether you add a halo may well depend on environmental conditions. For example, when it rains, a more pronounced halo becomes visible due to the increased refraction between the light and the rain. In fact, during the day, you would probably not notice a halo at all unless you are inside. Go with what looks good. These are implemented with billboards, so the only real work you have to do is to choose/create the right textures.

Fire

Fire is not an easy thing to reproduce. Some implementations tend to use constrained billboards, which works really well if you can afford a set of textures that, when animated, make the area look like a moving flame (as is the case with *Quake*). The other approach to fire is to simulate it with a bunch of particles. The idea it to fuse a bunch of small particles, each of which is simply a small, partially bright spot, such that the color goes from dark orange to bright yellow/white. To make these particles realistic, you need another particle generator, which generates particles with a given life because the particles eventually need to extinguish. This carefully simulates the edge of the flame. The tricky thing is when it comes down to getting a formula for the motion of the particles. If you operate under a rocket, it is not so hard because gravity takes the better part of it; you can simply let a lower gravitational acceleration pull the particles down. If that's not the case, then you can go the alternate route.

You can randomize the particles' velocity, but you have to make it such that they are generated in a sharp conic fashion. Using cylindrical coordinate space would help achieve this. In this case, the y coordinates would be randomized, as would the x and z coordinates within the ring of the cone at height y. If you leave it as such, the particles will only move within the cone, which will not look good. To insert the randomness that appears in fires, you need to make it possible for the particles to go slightly outside the cone. The final step, which makes this extra-realistic, is to increase the size of the particle when it is close to the center of the cone. That way, the particles that are closer to the source should have more energy than the ones that are farther away. Because the energy is mostly along the y axis of the cone, this is where the size should be the biggest. The farther the particle is from that point, the smaller it should be. Thus, the size of the particle should be affected by its life (the older the particle, the smaller it should be) and by its distance from the center (the closer to the center, the bigger it should be). If you play with numbers, you will eventually reach something that looks good.

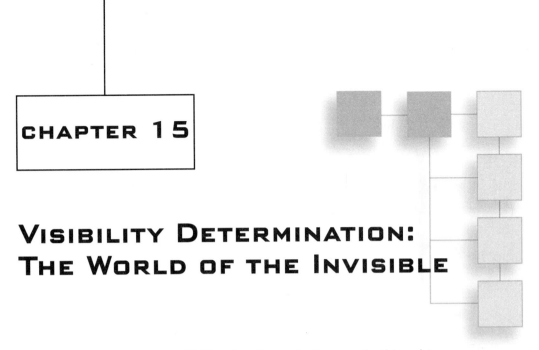

CHAPTER 15

VISIBILITY DETERMINATION: THE WORLD OF THE INVISIBLE

A lbert Einstein once said, "Any intelligent fool can make things bigger, more complex, and more violent. It takes a touch of genius—and a lot of courage—to move in the opposite direction." I cannot think of a better philosophy when designing game algorithms. Any fool can build a 3D engine, but it takes a genius to build a good, efficient 3D engine. The idea applies pretty well to collision detection as well. You can take the lazy way, implementing everything as spheres and forgetting about the concept of time, or you can choose the more accurate model, which takes time into account.

I do *not* want you to get the impression that the previous method is no good. On the contrary, it can be very good for some things. But it can yield disastrous results, such as if you wanted to represent a truck as a sphere. The collision would be off quite a lot at the top of the truck. A bounding box would be a much better choice there.

Visibility is a problem that also deserves some attention. You can choose the lazy way of doing things, which is to render every single object in the world, or you can choose the more intelligent way, which is to remove some pieces of the world that aren't visible to the user. That's the entire idea behind this chapter.

When you look at the 3D pipeline, you have three big segments that can slow down your game. The first is the CPU, where the processing is performed. The second is the geometry processing of the GPU. This unit is responsible for all of the transformations. The third and last is the rasterizer, which deals with the actual rendering of the triangles on the screen. This chapter looks at optimizing the second level by reducing the amount of geometry that the GPU has to process. There are broad classes of approaches to this problem:

- *z*-buffer
- Back-face culling
- Frustum culling

405

- ▪ Projection culling (bounding volume)
- ▪ Object culling

GPU-Level Visibility Determination

First things first. You should start by understanding how the GPU works before you look at the optimizations you can perform beforehand. The typical GPU has two visibility layers it uses to detect the visibility of a primitive: the *z-buffer* and back-face culling.

Z-Buffer

You might already know about the *z-buffer*, but there are probably things you don't know about it. The *z-buffer* is an on-GPU memory buffer that contains 16/32 bits of data on a per-pixel basis. This is the lowest level of culling you could ever do, because it sits at the pixel level. The *z-buffer* keeps track of the *z* value for every pixel and stores this value in the buffer corresponding to that specific pixel. As the GPU renders the elements, it verifies that the pixel that is to be drawn is in front or behind the pixel that was last written. If it is in front, the pixel is rendered, thereby removing the previous color. In today's 3D APIs, typically you can control the writing rule set by the *z-buffer*. You can ask it to render pixels only if the *z* component is smaller or greater. From a visibility point of view, the previous case is the most attractive option.

This type of test is pretty expensive in software, because every single pixel has to be tested in order to be plotted. Of course, it can be disabled, but there's no real way to determine the order that works for every possible case. Even the old painter-algorithm, which consists of painting the objects from back to front such that the things the farthest away are rendered first, suffers when two polygons intersect and parts of both are visible. In hardware implementations, on the other hand, *z-buffer* comes at a small cost. Sometimes it might come for free, depending on your hardware vendor and their implementation, making it a viable option, but overall, it is not the most optimal form of visibility determination because it requires that you send every single object down the card even if some objects need not be transformed.

The *z-buffer* does have issues, unfortunately. The first problem is that it's limited by the precision of floating points. For example, if you take two triangles and draw one on top of the other, mathematically the triangles are at the same position at any point along both of them. But because of the precision exhibited by the *z-buffer*, sometimes parts of the first triangle will show up while parts of the other triangle will surface. This illustrated in Figure 15.1.

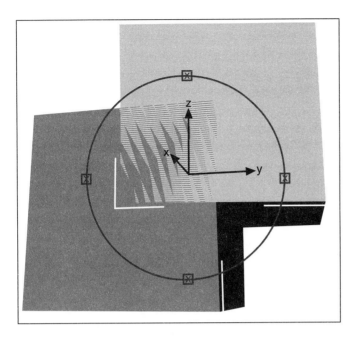

Figure 15.1
Translation of an object

There is one thing you should know about the *z*-buffer, however. It doesn't behave linearly. Objects that are closer to the camera won't suffer from the artifacts shown in Figure 15.1 as much as objects farther from the camera. In itself, this isn't a bad thing, but it does mean that your objects won't be consistent.

But why does this occur? It's pretty simple, really. If you recall how the projection matrix worked, you had to divide the components by *z* to project from 3D to 2D. The *z-buffer*'s value is computed as follows:

$$ZBuffer\left(z\right)=\frac{2^{n}\left(ZFar\cdot ZNear-ZFar\right)}{z\left(ZNear-ZFar\right)}$$

Here, *n* is the number of bits for the *z-buffer*, and *Zfar* and *Znear* are the two planes <0, 0, ±1, Z[Near/Far]>. As you can see, if *z* increases by 1, the value stored in the *z-buffer* obviously isn't going to increase by 1, because the relationship between the *Zbuffer* and *z* is that it is proportional to 1/*z*. The function 1/*z* provides more accuracy to the smaller values than it does to the greater values (thus, closest versus farthest). On the other hand, some cards provide a w-buffer, which stores values in a 1/*z* fashion instead of *z*, as this equation shows. Thus, you use an equation for the *z-buffer* where *z* is proportional to the *z-buffer*, and hence a linear mapping. With a w-buffer, the accuracy is linear.

What does all of this mean for your game? Well, basically it means that there's a lot of accuracy where it may not really be needed. It's nice to have more accuracy for the elements closer to you, but for a game that's mostly outdoor scenes, most of the objects are relatively far away. At that point, it's useful to have something that provides more precision for greater distances. What you can do is simply move the nearest frustum plane farther back. If you push back that frustum plane, you'll push back the *z-buffer* values so that objects that are farther away will have a little more accuracy. Of course, you should only do this up to a reasonable point, or else you'll be missing parts of the scene. Experimentation is the key here. This really is a per-game configuration.

Back-Face Culling

Back-face culling is one of the easiest and simplest forms of culling to implement. The idea is that most objects are closed, so you'll only see one side of the object's surface at any one time. Take a sphere, for example. You never actually see the interior of the sphere unless your collision detection system goes out of line.

But how is it done? Mainly, it relies on properties set forward by the cross product. Recall that the cross product is really sensitive about the order that you give to it. If you compute the cross product of two vectors, and then compute the cross product of these two vectors once more by inverting their order, you'll get the same vector but in the opposite direction.

This depends on the implementation of your hardware vendor, but the test in the GPU can be performed one level above the *z-buffer*. The *z-buffer* was performed at the rasterizer stage, and this test is performed at the geometry stage. More specifically, it's performed right after the triangle has been converted into a 2D triangle where you are only dealing with $<x, y>$ vertices. Some smarter hardware can perform back-face culling before transforming the object to 2D, as discussed later in this chapter.

If you state that every visible triangle will be stored in a clockwise fashion, computing the z component of the cross product $<x_1, y_1, 0>$, $<x_2, y_2, 0>$ will tell you if the polygon is clockwise or counterclockwise merely by looking at the sign of the component. Interestingly enough, when the polygon doesn't face the camera, its projection generates a counterclockwise triangle.

This makes perfect sense if you use the following trivial example: Take a triangle that is visible, and rotate it 180 degrees around any axis. Once you do this, the triangle shows its back-face. If you also look at the ordering of the vertices, you'll notice that the direction has changed from clockwise to counterclockwise. Again, this is easy to detect with the cross product by looking at the sign.

Frustum Clipping

Another form of clipping that the hardware performs is *frustum clipping*. This introduces another space, referred to as *clipping space*. A view of a perspective map transforms a box into a pyramid, as discussed in Chapter 5, "Transformations." Consequently, after the projection, a point should have a range of $<[-1, 1], [-1, 1], [-1, 1]>$. At that point, the hardware can clip a triangle if the triangle resides completely outside of the view frustum.

This test is very easy to perform because it is a simple addition to the 3D pipeline, which is already present. In addition, the test has a very low cost because it merely needs to test on an axis-aligned box. The only problem is that this is only performed on a per-triangle basis, which means that you are still working at a rather microscopic level.

CPU Culling

The back-face culling test is clearly better than the *z-buffer*, because it allows you to skip the rasterization pipeline for certain polygons. Similarly, the frustum-culling test is better than both previous ones because it clips at a higher level. But is this really enough? Sometimes, objects are completely invisible to the camera, in which case you're transforming the entire object only to notice at a rather low level that it is not visible piece-by-piece. The only solution is to take one more step back, and look at what can be done at the CPU stage to diminish the number of triangles sent down to the transformation stage. The faster you can find out if an object is visible or not, the better it is.

If you have to go all the way down to the *z-buffer* to figure it out, it takes that much more work and that much more wasted GPU bandwidth. The only thing you have to be careful about is that the CPU doesn't become the bottleneck. As always, you have to do a careful balancing act in order to minimize latency. If the CPU becomes the bottleneck, you may as well send more triangles down to the GPU and free the CPU a tad. Generally, though, this isn't the case. Let's look at the various ways you can achieve culling.

Frustum Culling

Without any doubt, the most obvious and simple test you can perform is to verify whether or not the objects are within the frustum. Recall that the frustum can be seen as a set of six planes that describe the visible area from the camera's point of view in the world. Consequently, if you want to check that an object is visible from the frustum's point of view, all you have to do is obtain the world coordinates of your object and test the world coordinates of the frustum, as shown in Chapter 5.

What's nice about visibility determination is that you can overestimate the visible region without any change in the result. In other words, you can claim that an object is visible even if it really isn't, and the result won't change. This doesn't mean that you should do a really coarse test, because it goes against the idea of optimizing the pipeline. Ideally, you're looking for a test that can be performed efficiently and that detects most of the invisible objects. This is in contrast with collision detection, where it's all about precision. Changing the precision in the collision detection could change the result, because nothing else will take care of the collision for you if you don't detect an existing one.

Plane-Frustum Test

Detecting the intersection between a plane and a frustum is easy if you use half-planes. In other words, you can verify that all corners of the frustum are on the same side of the plane. This is a good solution, but it's not a very lean one because it implies that eight vertices must be checked against the plane.

Instead, it's much better to transform the plane into clipping space. As it so happens, the projection matrix was defined as a matrix that converts an ordinary unitary box (in clipping space) into what you know as a 3D frustum (in screen space). The invert of this matrix does the opposite. It takes anything in screen space (or projected space) and converts the space such that the frustum becomes a box, and the transformation matrix changes all objects relative to the frustum accordingly.

If you recall how planes are transformed, you should have no problem accepting that the formula to convert the plane $\langle \mathbf{n}, D \rangle$ from projected to projection space is

$$\langle \mathbf{n}, D \rangle \, ' = \left(\left(\mathbf{PC} \right)^{-1} \right)^{\mathrm{T}} \langle \mathbf{n}, D \rangle$$

Here, $\mathbf{P}$ is defined as the projection matrix and $\mathbf{C}$ is defined as the camera matrix that converts an object from world space to camera space. Once you've done the conversion, you're dealing with a simple box and a new plane. From this point, you can compute the distance between the plane and the box. If there's an intersection, the plane is potentially visible. If not, you should forget about it.

Sphere-Frustum Test

Now that you understand the intersection tests that were elaborated in the previous chapter, such problems should be easy to solve. The frustum is described using six planes, all pointing toward the center of the frustum. The most obvious test you could perform is whether the center of the sphere is on the inner side of the plane. Recall that you can achieve this by simply computing the four-vector dot product between the plane and the position. A positive sign indicates that the vertex is on the correct side, while a negative sign indicates that the vertex isn't within the frustum. (This shouldn't be a new concept to you, because it was already used in Chapter 4, "Basic Geometric Elements.") If all six planes pass the test, your object is potentially visible and you should render it. The meaning of "potentially" will be explained later in this chapter.

Thus, the test is simple. Go through all six planes $\langle \mathbf{n}_i, D \rangle$ of the frustum and verify that the following test passes for the center of the sphere $\mathbf{p}$:

$$0 \leq \langle \mathbf{n}, D \rangle \bullet \langle \mathbf{p}, 1 \rangle$$

If you could use only that as your test, it would be great. Currently, though, this cannot be a comprehensive test. It misses some cases where the sphere is visible yet isn't detected, as illustrated in Figure 15.2.

The problem is that you're dealing with a sphere and not a point in space. To make this test comprehensive, you can push all six planes out from the frustum's center along the normal of the planes with a distance of the radius r. In short, you're extending the frustum such that every plane of it increases by r. This will indeed detect every case where the sphere is visible. The new equation to achieve this comes down to the following for a normalized normal $\mathbf{n}$:

$$-r \le \langle \mathbf{n}, D \rangle \bullet \langle \mathbf{p}, 1 \rangle$$

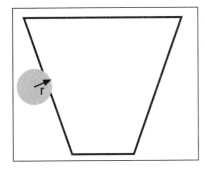

Figure 15.2
Frustum-sphere intersection test, done by using the center point of the sphere

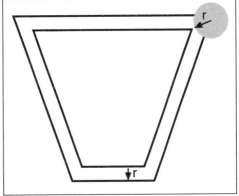

Figure 15.3
Frustum-sphere intersection test, done by extending the frustum's planes by r

As you go through all six planes, you exit as soon as the test fails.

This test is pretty simple and lean, but does it handle everything perfectly? Not really. It will detect every potentially visible object, and it will also flag objects that aren't visible, as shown in Figure 15.3.

To be mathematically correct, a perfect test would have to increase the frustum by the sphere's radius at every single point of the frustum. Here, the planes are simply extended by the frustum. This guarantees a "perfect" match along the edges of the planes, but it doesn't test correctly at the frustum's corners, which should be extended to spheres as shown in Figure 15.4.

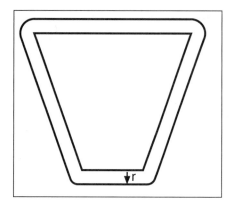

Figure 15.4
Frustum extended by a spherical radius of r

Fortunately, it isn't a big deal if you detect that some objects are visible when they really aren't. This won't happen very often, because the two extended frustums in Figures 15.3 and 15.4 only differ by eight little areas at the corners. For the speed you gain from this test, this is well worth it.

Box-Frustum Test

If you do a quick search on the Internet for a solution to this problem, the typical solution shows how developers don't think in terms of vectors (which is a bad thing). The typical solution is to consider each corner of the box as a separate vertex and to test if any of the box's vertices are on the positive side of the plane. If there's a vertex for every one of the frustum's planes, that satisfies this test and the box is visible. This involves a total of 36 tests for a single box, which means 36 dot products and an inefficient test.

Instead, turn to the solution that was proposed in the last chapter, which is to compute the effective radius of a box given a plane. This only requires six tests, such as was done with the sphere. The only extra computation is the radius of the box, which involves an extra dot product per test. You can reduce the computation power from 36 dot products to 12 dot products, and from 35 conditions to merely six.

When you work with vectors, you're working with geometrical elements. Typically, it's much easier to look at a problem from that point of view than in terms of Cartesian units $<x, y, z>$. To sum things up, the test goes as follows for each plane of the frustum $<\mathbf{n}, d>$ and a box with extent $\{\mathbf{x}, \mathbf{y}, \mathbf{z}\}$ and center $\mathbf{p}$:

$$-r_e = -\left|\mathbf{n}\bullet\mathbf{x}\right|-\left|\mathbf{n}\bullet\mathbf{y}\right|-\left|\mathbf{n}\bullet\mathbf{z}\right| \leq \langle\mathbf{n}, d\rangle \bullet \langle\mathbf{p}, 1\rangle$$

Again, this test suffers from the same problems illustrated by the sphere-frustum intersection test. Sometimes the box will be detected as visible when it really isn't. In this case, the box would extend the frustum. In the first case, the extended spherical frustum was obtained by "rolling the sphere" along the edge of the frustum. Here, the same applies. You can slide the box such that it maximizes the extent of the frustum to yield the "true" region where the test would be perfect in identifying which boxes are in the frustum.

Again, this short loss isn't very significant, and the speed of the test really outweighs the benefits of a 100% accurate solution. A large error can be accrued if one of the directional vectors of the box is significantly larger than the others. In that case, the error at the corners of the frustum gets greater. This is where it may be more interesting to approximate the shape with another one, such as a cylinder.

Ellipsoid-Frustum

In the previous chapter, it was quickly mentioned that you could do an ellipsoid-box test by transforming the space such that the ellipsoid becomes a sphere, and then unapply the transformation. This isn't a bad solution, and if you expand the math around the solution and apply it to a box-ellipsoid case, you'll get the exact same solution that will be obtained here. The only difference is that here, you take a different approach and look at the problem.

First things first, you should start by analyzing what was done for the box-plane intersection. The projection of the box upon the normal vector of the plane can actually be seen as the x, y, and z component of a vector. In other words, the length of the projection for vector x of the box could correspond to the x component, and similarly for y and z. After all, the box is described with three orthogonal axes, which means that the dot product of each box is zero. When you solve these problems, you basically map a vector $<x, y, z>$ into a length. Of course, this x, y, z vector is really the projected length:

$$\langle x, y, z \rangle = \langle \mathbf{n} \bullet \mathbf{x}, \mathbf{n} \bullet \mathbf{y}, \mathbf{n} \bullet \mathbf{z} \rangle$$

The mapping you will choose maps a vector into a distance such that every vector with equal norms form a shape. As you saw in Chapter 2, "Baby Steps: Introduction to Vectors," the vector 2-norm is such that every point from the center that has an equal Euclidian distance also has an equal 2-norm. If you take all vectors that have a norm of one for the 2-norm, you'll notice that the set of points that satisfy this condition forms a circle, as shown in Chapter 2. The interesting point is that if you choose the infinity-norm, you get a square. By golly, the infinity norm's equation is the same as that of the box's effective radius. What a coincidence. Unknowingly, the equation for the box-plan intersection really computes the infinity-norm of your projected vector. This norm is perfectly chosen to compute the radii of a box because of its abrupt square behavior.

This is all nice, and it shows the relationship between the box and the infinity norm, but how can it help you solve the problem for the ellipse? Well, the answer is already in front of you. Given a project length vector, if you can map every vector on the surface of a box (or a box, which is really like a sphere with infinity norm) into an equal length, you should be able to find a norm that maps every point on the surface of an ellipsoid to an equal length. This is nothing but the 2-norm. The 2-norm maps the Euclidian distance between a point and the center, and thus maps any point on the surface of an ellipsoidal into an equal length. Consequently, you can compute the effective radius of an ellipsoidal using the following formula:

$$r_e = \sqrt{(\mathbf{n} \bullet \mathbf{x})^2 + (\mathbf{n} \bullet \mathbf{y})^2 + (\mathbf{n} \bullet \mathbf{z})^2}$$

Cylinder-Frustum

If you're planning to approximate a character using a capsule or a cylinder, you should also know how to find if a player is visible or not. In the previous tests, the pattern was pretty much the same. You started by computing the radius of the object (if you didn't have it yet). Once you had the radius, you proceeded by extending the frustum by that radius. From that point on, you had successfully converted an object-frustum problem into a point-frustum problem, which is pretty simple.

Similarly with the cylinder, you can convert an object-frustum problem into a line-frustum problem. Thus, you define the cylinder with its two endpoints, $\mathbf{u}$ and $\mathbf{v}$, and with radius r. You can further define the vector $\mathbf{w}$ as the unit-vector, which goes from $\mathbf{u}$ to $\mathbf{v}$:

$$w = \frac{\mathbf{u} - \mathbf{v}}{\|\mathbf{u} - \mathbf{v}\|_2}$$

The first step to solving the problem is to find an effective radius. Figure 15.5 illustrates the relationship between the radius and the various components of the cylinder. After a careful examination and a simple trig relationship, you come up with the following formula for the effective radius:

$$r_e = r\sin(\theta)$$
$$= r\sqrt{1 - \cos^2(\theta)}$$
$$= r\sqrt{1 - (\mathbf{v} - \mathbf{u}) \bullet \mathbf{n}}$$

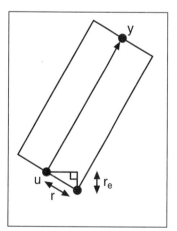

So now that you have an effective radius, you can extend the planes outward by this amount. The real problem now is to find out if there's an intersection between a line and a plane. This sounds familiar, doesn't it? It should! You first need to verify if each endpoint is on a different side of the plane, as was done in Chapter 4. Let's say both endpoints follow this condition:

Figure 15.5
The relationship between the radius and the various components

$$-r_e \geq \mathbf{n} \bullet \mathbf{a}$$

Here, $\mathbf{a}$ is an endpoint $\{\mathbf{u}, \mathbf{v}\}$ and $\mathbf{n}$ is the normal for the plane. You can deduce that the cylinder isn't visible at all. On the flipside, if you find that one or both endpoints don't satisfy the condition, you cannot deduce anything yet and must verify the next plane.

Bounding Volume Generation

So far, you've learned how to perform a lot of tests on spheres, cylinders, capsules, boxes, etc. In the real world, objects aren't made of spheres, cylinders, or capsules. Most of the time, they're made of triangles. So how useful are these tests?

As it turns out, generally you won't really do a triangle-triangle intersection test. Instead, what you end up doing is building a bounding region to which a set of vertices is guaranteed to be bounded. This significantly speeds up the calculations, because basically you compute the collision of many objects in one shot.

It does have a bad side, which is that if an intersection is detected with a bounding volume, the internal objects probably don't actually collide. In this case, you can either claim that there *is* a collision with the object, or get down and dirty to analyze exactly which triangle of the object has been affected. The next chapter will concentrate on things like this. For now, let's concentrate on the problem at hand, which is to generate the bounding volume in the first place.

Bounding Box Generation

If you take the simple case where the box is axis-aligned, it's very simple to determine the bounding box for the set of vertices. All you have to do is find the minimal and maximal value in $\{x, y, z\}$. The center of the box becomes the middle of that, and the extent of the box becomes half of the difference between the max and min $\{x, y, z\}$. It's quite obvious that this box bounds every vertex, because you've constructed it by taking the min/max in every axis.

Now, if you want to build a general box, things become a little more complicated. First you have to determine what orientation the box will have. Here, it doesn't really matter if this process takes a long time, because you only need to do this once. But once it's done, it should be done well.

First things first. Let's start by choosing a center for your box. Because the box isn't axis-aligned, it gets a little tricky. This is where all the seemingly useless stuff about diagonalization from Chapter 3, "Meet the Matrices," comes in handy. Every bounding volume requires the computation of the diagonalization basis, which is really the basis for the direction of the volume. As you've seen in this very chapter, there's not much difference between an ellipsoid, a box, and a diamond. It all depends on the norm you choose, so the process is very similar.

The basis that you find with the orthogonal process should be normalized. The actual length of the vectors forming the basis $\{\mathbf{x}, \mathbf{y}, \mathbf{z}\}$ is of no use to you. Since the length is meaningless, you have to compute the extent (the distance along the basis axes) yourself. This is easy if you project the vectors upon the basis vectors. This will give you the length of this point from the center, and choosing the minimum and maximum of the dot product will give you your planes. More rigorously, the eight planes that bound the box can be defined mathematically as follows:

$$\left\langle \mathbf{x}, -\min_{1 \le i \le n}\{\mathbf{v}_i \bullet \mathbf{x}\} \right\rangle \quad \left\langle -\mathbf{x}, \max_{1 \le i \le n}\{\mathbf{v}_i \bullet \mathbf{x}\} \right\rangle$$

$$\left\langle \mathbf{y}, -\min_{1 \le i \le n}\{\mathbf{v}_i \bullet \mathbf{y}\} \right\rangle \quad \left\langle -\mathbf{y}, \max_{1 \le i \le n}\{\mathbf{v}_i \bullet \mathbf{y}\} \right\rangle$$

$$\left\langle \mathbf{z}, -\min_{1 \le i \le n}\{\mathbf{v}_i \bullet \mathbf{z}\} \right\rangle \quad \left\langle -\mathbf{z}, \max_{1 \le i \le n}\{\mathbf{v}_i \bullet \mathbf{z}\} \right\rangle$$

This is great, but in the previous examples, you worked with extents and a box's center. It's pretty easy to convert from one to the other. To convert this set of planes into a center, you only have to take the average of the two planes. You know that the total extent of the box is really the max offset minus the min offset. That's how you compute a simple length. If you have two values and you want to know the norm, you take the bigger of the two values and subtract it from the smaller one. The same thing is done here. This offset gives the offset (or extent) for that specific directional vector. You want half of that total extent, because you compute the planes as one directional vector, where one plane is found by adding the center to that directional vector and the other by subtracting the directional vector from the center. Thus, you need half the total extent. Mathematically, the equation for the extents $\{|\mathbf{x}|, |\mathbf{y}|, |\mathbf{z}|\}$ is simply given as follows:

$$|\mathbf{x}| = \frac{\max_{1 \le i \le n}\{\mathbf{v}_i \bullet \mathbf{x}\} + \min_{1 \le i \le n}\{\mathbf{v}_i \bullet \mathbf{x}\}}{2}$$

$$|\mathbf{y}| = \frac{\max_{1 \le i \le n}\{\mathbf{v}_i \bullet \mathbf{y}\} + \min_{1 \le i \le n}\{\mathbf{v}_i \bullet \mathbf{y}\}}{2}$$

$$|\mathbf{z}| = \frac{\max_{1 \le i \le n}\{\mathbf{v}_i \bullet \mathbf{z}\} + \min_{1 \le i \le n}\{\mathbf{v}_i \bullet \mathbf{z}\}}{2}$$

Note that the absolute value is used here instead of the norm notation. This is mainly because the norm of $\mathbf{x}$ is the full extent, and here the absolute value of $\mathbf{x}$ is defined as the half-extent or the extent of the box from the center. Similarly for $\mathbf{y}$ and $\mathbf{z}$. Thus, all you have to do to find the center is move along the directional vector of the half-extent. The half-extents have already been computed above this, so it becomes pretty easy to compute the center of the box. Mathematically, you're looking at the following equation for the center of the box $\mathbf{c}$:

$$c = \frac{\max\limits_{1 \le i \le n}\{v_i \bullet x\} + \min\limits_{1 \le i \le n}\{v_i \bullet x\}}{2} x + \frac{\max\limits_{1 \le i \le n}\{v_i \bullet y\} + \min\limits_{1 \le i \le n}\{v_i \bullet y\}}{2} y + \frac{\max\limits_{1 \le i \le n}\{v_i \bullet z\} + \min\limits_{1 \le i \le n}\{v_i \bullet z\}}{2} z$$

Bounding Sphere Generation

As you've seen, spheres make for a pretty efficient way to compute a collision or apply a culling test, so let's look at how you can construct the bounding sphere for a set of vertices. The technique relies on the same principles that were elaborated above. Spheres are different than boxes, because you have no control over extents in three different directions.

With the box, you find the orientation of the vertices by computing the eigenvectors. This gives you the general direction of the box and a general sense of direction (a greater norm implies a greater extent toward that vertex), but it doesn't implicitly give the extent. You have to compute the extent yourself by finding the min and max vertex in that direction. Since this is a box, building a plane at the min and max guarantees that all the vertices are on one side of the plane. If this wasn't true, they wouldn't be the min and max, would they?

With a sphere, you cannot set a radius and guarantee that every vertex is within the sphere. An even bigger problem is that you have three axes, but the sphere has only one parameter besides its center: the radius. Thus, you have to choose the greatest of the three axes. The greatest extent (or principal axis) corresponds to the greatest eigenvalue obtained. As mentioned before, the eigenvalue gives you a sense of relative norm but doesn't actually give you the true extent. From now on, let the vector corresponding to the largest eigenvalue be q.

note

If a matrix M is symmetric, the greatest unsigned eigenvalue is equal to the 2-norm of M. More generally, the matrix 2-norm can be computed as the square root of the greater eigenvalue for MM^T.

Now that you know the most important direction for the set of points, you simply need to find the extent of the vertices in that direction. This is done exactly as before. If you compute the projection of every vertex on q, you can obtain the min and max values that form the extent in that direction. Thus, in terms of equations, you have the following:

$$u = \left\{ p_i \bullet q = \max\limits_{1 \le i \le n}\{p_i \bullet q\} \quad p_i \right\}$$

$$v = \left\{ p_i \bullet q = \min\limits_{1 \le i \le n}\{p_i \bullet q\} \quad p_i \right\}$$

And of course, the average between these two points, **u** and **v**, will give you the center **c** of the sphere. Meanwhile, the half-distance between these two vertices will give you the radius:

$$\mathbf{c} = \frac{\mathbf{u} + \mathbf{v}}{2}$$
$$r = \|\mathbf{u} - \mathbf{c}\|_2$$

Unfortunately, by the very nature of the box's construction, you're guaranteed that every vertex is enclosed within the box. This isn't true for a sphere. This is nothing but an approximation of the real deal. Generating bounding spheres (or even bounding circles, for that matter) isn't a trivial problem, and currently there's no clean, foolproof solution. This method gives you a pretty decent approximation without taking ages to run.

A bounding volume that doesn't bound its entire volume is pretty useless, so at the very least you should have a way to compute another bounding sphere that handles every vertex. One way this could be achieved is to verify that the distance between the vertex and the center of the sphere is smaller than or equal to the radius:

$$\|\mathbf{p}_i - \mathbf{c}\|^2 \le r^2$$

In short, you verify that the vertex is within the sphere. If this is not the case, you can change the radius such that the encompassing sphere includes the vertex. In itself, this isn't a bad solution, but it adds extra space at the other side of the sphere where there might not really be any vertices. This means that you would in fact compute a sphere that is larger than necessary. Instead, what you can do is expand the sphere by a radius that's smaller than the difference between the radius and the length, and translate the sphere ever so slightly toward the vertex to compensate for the smaller radius increment. This technique guarantees that every vertex that was inside the bounding volume is still inside the bounding sphere, and it also minimizes the size of the radius increase.

So what's the magic trick to do this? You need to find the position where you'll move the center of the sphere. If you move toward the vertex that wasn't bounded by the sphere, you can increase the radius just enough so that the sphere is guaranteed to bound the area that it bounded before. This is necessary, or else you'll just end chasing your tail. You can easily find the vertex at the other end of the sphere and in the opposite direction of $\mathbf{qp}_i$ (the vector going from **q** to $\mathbf{p}_i$). Since this point is on the sphere, it becomes pretty easy to find its position. Let this point be **w**:

$$\mathbf{w} = \mathbf{c} - r \frac{\mathbf{p}_i - \mathbf{c}}{\|\mathbf{p}_i - \mathbf{c}\|_2}$$

From this point on, it's pretty straightforward. You have two opposite extrema on a sphere, so the center of the sphere is located at the average of these two points, and the new radius is half of the distance between these two points. Mathematically:

$$\mathbf{c}' = \frac{\mathbf{w} + \mathbf{p}_i}{2}$$

$$r' = \left\| \mathbf{c}' - \mathbf{p}_i \right\|_2$$

If you repeat this process until every single vertex in your list is inside the bounding sphere, you'll construct a sphere that bounds every single vertex in your list. It's not the minimal bounding sphere, but it's very close.

Bounding Ellipsoid Generation

As noted, an ellipsoid is closely related to a sphere. It's nothing but a sphere that has been scaled unevenly on three different axes. If you keep this in mind, finding the bounding ellipsoid is just like finding the bounding sphere.

Again, the first step is to compute the direction vectors $\{\mathbf{x}, \mathbf{y}, \mathbf{z}\}$ for the set of vertices. Once you have that, you should also compute the extent as was done in the two previous methods. At this point, define the length of the extents as follows:

$$a = \max_{1 \le i \le n} \{\mathbf{p}_i \bullet \mathbf{x}\} - \min_{1 \le i \le n} \{\mathbf{p}_i \bullet \mathbf{x}\}$$

$$b = \max_{1 \le i \le n} \{\mathbf{p}_i \bullet \mathbf{y}\} - \min_{1 \le i \le n} \{\mathbf{p}_i \bullet \mathbf{y}\}$$

$$c = \max_{1 \le i \le n} \{\mathbf{p}_i \bullet \mathbf{z}\} - \min_{1 \le i \le n} \{\mathbf{p}_i \bullet \mathbf{z}\}$$

If you recall how you got the extent's direction in the first place, you understand how to convert every point into a space where the ellipsoid becomes a sphere. First, if you want to convert an axis-aligned ellipsoid into a sphere, all you have to do is scale the axis-aligned ellipsoid by the length of the radius of each respective axis. In other words, an ellipsoid with radius $\{a, b, c\}$ for $\{x, y, z\}$ simply needs to be scaled down by $\{1/a, 1/b, 1/c\}$, respectively. Thus, the matrix that scales this specific ellipsoid into a sphere is $\mathbf{K}$:

$$\mathbf{K} = \begin{bmatrix} \dfrac{1}{a} & 0 & 0 \\ 0 & \dfrac{1}{b} & 0 \\ 0 & 0 & \dfrac{1}{c} \end{bmatrix}$$

When the equation you've used to transform the points and get the directional axis for the bounding volume is applied to K, it gives the following:

$$\mathbf{M} = \begin{bmatrix} \mathbf{x} & \mathbf{y} & \mathbf{z} \end{bmatrix} \mathbf{K} \begin{bmatrix} \mathbf{x} & \mathbf{y} & \mathbf{z} \end{bmatrix}^{\mathrm{T}}$$

$$= \begin{bmatrix} \mathbf{x} & \mathbf{y} & \mathbf{z} \end{bmatrix} \begin{bmatrix} \dfrac{1}{a} & 0 & 0 \\ 0 & \dfrac{1}{b} & 0 \\ 0 & 0 & \dfrac{1}{c} \end{bmatrix} \begin{bmatrix} \mathbf{x} & \mathbf{y} & \mathbf{z} \end{bmatrix}^{\mathrm{T}}$$

So the idea is as follows: You must initially transform the points by using matrix **M**. Once you've transformed every single one of these points, you should perform the bounding sphere calculation to find the center of the sphere. Once you have the center of the sphere, you can remove the transformation by applying the inverse of **M,** which is easily obtained by observation of matrix rules:

$$\mathbf{M}^{-1} = \begin{bmatrix} \mathbf{x} & \mathbf{y} & \mathbf{z} \end{bmatrix} \begin{bmatrix} a & 0 & 0 \\ 0 & b & 0 \\ 0 & 0 & c \end{bmatrix} \begin{bmatrix} \mathbf{x} & \mathbf{y} & \mathbf{z} \end{bmatrix}^{\mathrm{T}}$$

The lengths themselves are obtained by transforming the radius with **K**. In other words, just multiply the radius r obtained by computing the sphere's bounding volume by the ellipsoid's extents $\{a, b, c\}$. The direction of the ellipsoid is given by the values of the directional vectors $\{\mathbf{x}, \mathbf{y}, \mathbf{z}\}$. In terms of equations:

$$a' = ra \quad \text{Along } \mathbf{x}$$
$$b' = rb \quad \text{Along } \mathbf{y}$$
$$c' = rc \quad \text{Along } \mathbf{z}$$

Again, it's merely a matter of knowing which space and coordinate system you're working in. Once you know that, you just need to convert one problem into a simpler problem that you know how to solve. Once you have the solution to that problem, you need to invert the conversion you've done to obtain the results you're looking for. This is a great way to solve many problems, but it only works if there's a way to uniquely reverse the change you've done to convert the problem to the one that you know how to solve.

3D Back-Face Culling

Generally, back-face culling isn't a popular method because the hardware already does something extremely close to this. However, back-face culling at the CPU level can be an attractive option if you're limited in terms of bandwidth (number of vertices sent to the

GPU). In that case, you might be interested in computing whether a triangle or quad is facing the camera or not. The only tricky thing is that you don't have the 2D coordinates of the triangle/quad.

However, there's another method that you can use to determine if a face is visible or not. In the spirit of specifying the polygon in a clockwise/counterclockwise fashion, you can compute the normal vector of the polygon. Once again, the normal vector can have one of two directions, both of which are dependent on the ordering of the vertices (clockwise or not). In 3D, there's no sense in simply looking at the sign of the z component, because nothing guarantees that you're axis-aligned. In fact, it's rare.

Instead, this approach looks at the angle between the camera's directional vector and the normal vector of the plane. If the angle between the two vectors is smaller than 90 degrees, the normal vector is pointing toward the camera, and thus the polygon that represents it is potentially visible. On the other hand, if the angle is greater than 90 degrees, the normal vector is facing in the same direction as the camera's vector. In that case, the polygon isn't visible.

Finally, which test from Chapter 2 can help you solve the mystery related to the 90-degree angle? It's the dot product, of course. The dot product of two vectors is positive when the angle between the two vectors is smaller than 90 degrees, and it's negative otherwise. Thus, the test is pretty simple. Given the directional vector of the camera $\mathbf{c}$ and the normal vector of the polygon $\mathbf{n}$, you can compute its visibility as follows:

$$\mathbf{c} \bullet \mathbf{n} = \begin{cases} \geq 0 & \text{Visible} \\ < 0 & \text{Not Visible} \end{cases}$$

Object Culling

So, you bounded your shapes so as to determine if they were visible on the screen, you removed the back-faces on the CPU, and yet you still need some extra GPU bandwidth and still have CPU bandwidth. When an object/polygon is detected as visible with the previous tests, it doesn't guarantee that it is *truly* visible. Thus, it's *potentially* visible. For example, if you look up at the ceiling of your house, can you see the sky? Not unless you have a sun roof. Yet the sky is still in your view frustum. If the roof wasn't there, you would see the sky. You don't see the sky because your roof obstructs it.

The idea behind object culling is to determine if some objects are hiding other objects, and if so, to completely remove the hidden objects. This means that you can remove entire objects without having to look at them in further depth. At this point, you should only have a set of objects that are within the frustum. For this test to be useful at all, there must be a set of good occluders in your world.

Let's define the term "good occluders." If you take a game such as *Quake 3*, most of which takes place indoors, there's no good candidate for occlusion. The game doesn't have many large objects that can obstruct the view of your character. (Walls don't count because they're composed of a more complex structure, which you'll see in the next chapter.) On the other hand, if you take a game such as *Grand Theft Auto 3*, where there are a lot of small buildings, high ground, low ground, cars, and similar objects, there are a lot of potentially good occluders. But again, the walls of a building don't really count. You're looking more at a big object that hides a lot of the world behind it.

Another thing you have to be careful about is that this method should be used only if there's always an occluder not too far away. If this isn't the case, a typical gamer would expect the game to be relatively fast at all times. If the game is only fast when you walk in front of a hill, it's pretty much useless to implement this method. Instead, you should look at a better division technique, as will be shown in the next chapter. So the ideal case for occlusion is when there are many large objects obstructing the view nearly all the time.

Another good example of this is a specific level in *Unreal Tournament*. This level has a lot of hills. Hills are large objects that are pretty much everywhere, so they're good occluders. If the character climbs a hill, you'll still need to have a respectable frame rate, which really depends on the type of game you are making. But if the character generally won't be at the top of a hill that resides at the top of the world (or that can see most of the world), you're safe.

So this tells you when to use the technique, but what actually *is* the technique? This field is pretty new, and not that much work has been done. Often, developers are afraid to implement such techniques because the speed gains aren't clear, but this one can be very beneficial in the right situation. On the other hand, if you implement this technique and there are few occluders, you'll be kicking yourself in the head.

There's no magic equation to find the best occluder. Use your judgment for your specific game. Generally, the distance of the camera from the occluder and the volume taken by the occluder play a big role in whether or not verifying occlusion against this object would be beneficial or not. Most of the time, you can probably get away with the area of the bounding volume for the object and the distance between the object and the camera. You can come up with an equation that gives you an acceptability range. For example, you can claim that any number in the range [0..1] implies that the object should be considered for occlusion, while anything larger than that shouldn't be considered. For instance, here's such a function:

$$p = \frac{Distance^2}{Area \cdot 10}$$

Three things can make this happen. First, the object needs to be really close, in which case *p* gets really small. Another possibility is that object is quite distant from the view, but it's so large that it still appears to be big. The last option is a well-balanced situation where the object is relatively close and of a reasonable size. Here, a factor of 1/10 is applied (this should be adjusted according to your specific game situation).

The other interesting part is that the distance is squared. This is because the distance has a pretty important effect on the area that the object occludes off the screen. For example, take a book and place it before your eyes so that you can't see anything else. Now move the book back until your arm is fully extended. Now that the book is farther away, it probably occludes 2–3 medium objects. While it was close, it hid almost everything.

Again, this is an equation you should come up with yourself. Chapter 13, "Exploring Curvy Bodies," can help you find a suitable solution. Now let's turn to the real problem, which is actually removing the occluded objects.

Convex Shadow Occlusion

This technique advances the idea that you can cull a set of objects if you can build the shadow of an occluding object. This makes perfect sense if you think about the solution in terms of the world. Take a light source and place it in the center of your world. Now take a few selected occluders, and observe how the shadows are cast on the various other objects behind the occluders. If an object is visible, light is shining directly on it. If the object isn't visible, light isn't cast upon it.

If you replace the light with the camera, a similar thing happens. The light only lights up what it can see directly from its source. If it cannot see an object, it cannot light it directly. Thus, everything that the camera sees is the equivalent of what a light source lights up. Consequently, if you can find the volume of the shadowed region, you can perform an intersection test to see if any object's bounding volume is completely shadowed. If so, the object shouldn't be drawn at all.

This is a pretty simple principle, but it's easier said than done. You should have enough background at this point to determine if an object is visible or not, given a set of planes. That part should be a walk in the park. What isn't so clear is how to construct the set of planes that make up the shadowed region.

The first thing you should do occurs at the graphics-design level. For every object that will be a potential occluder, you should generate two representations. The first representation is what the gamer will see on his screen. This is the full-fledged, textured, and detailed version of the object. The second representation is a convex version of the object, which is completely contained by the previous object. You need a convex body (a volume that doesn't have any internal dents), because it's much easier to test if an object is inside this volume or not.

There are 5–6 algorithms out there that can build convex bodies out of a set of vertices. The one I prefer is a gift-wrapping method that acts like wrapping a Christmas present. It constructs the set of vertices/planes that wrap the entire object. The problem with this type of algorithm for this specific solution is that it generates a volume equal to or larger than the previous object. You cannot use a larger volume, or else you'll cull some objects that are potentially visible.

Thus, you need to obtain a convex volume that's completely contained by the previous object. In short, if you superimpose the two objects onto each other, the original and the convex body, the convex body should disappear completely from view because it's contained within the original volume. You could generate such a volume algorithmically, of course, but it's easier and more optimal to generate it by hand. It's optimal because by doing this with a 3D modeler, you can also remove details in the object that are useless or insignificant for culling purposes. Again, this is provided that the object is completely contained within the other one and is convex.

For instance, if you want to get the contained convex body of a building, you can forget about the roof (which might stick out of the foundation), the step edges of the windows, and the fancy bricks by simply replacing the entire thing with a box. This will significantly reduce the required computation power. Once you have these two objects, the idea is to render the original "complex" object and use the simplified object for culling purposes.

Since the later volume is convex, you can easily test if anything is inside the volume by substituting the point into the plane's equation. As you learned in Chapter 4, you can determine on which side of the plane a given vertex lays by computing the following:

$$d = \langle \mathbf{n}, D \rangle \bullet \langle \mathbf{x}, 1 \rangle$$

This is given a plane <**n**, D> and a vertex **x**. The sign will be positive if you're in the same half-plane that the normal points toward, and conversely, a negative result means the vertex is positioned in the other half-plane. If every plane doesn't point toward the vertex ($d = 0$ for normals pointing outwards), you know that the vertex is inside the convex body.

Now you have a convex body, but you don't have any shadow. You don't want to test that the object is inside the potential culler, but that the object is *behind* it. Thus, you have to compute the shadow's convex body, which looks like a frustum. You can easily determine a set of planes that can help you test this. If you take the set of triangles that are visible from the camera's point of view, every one of these triangles is on the boundary of the convex body. Thus, they should all be part of the shadow's convex body. These triangles can be converted into planes for your point-is-inside-a-convex-body test, seen previously in this section. Although these planes are numerous, they aren't sufficient because they cap the objects on the boundary. They only cap the shadow's convex body at the front. You also need to take care of the sides.

To obtain the planes that build the shadow's extension, you must first determine which edge of the convex body defines the boundary of the convex body. If you can find every edge that defines the boundary of the convex body from the given viewpoint, you can generate a plane from the camera's center and the two vertices comprising the edge that corresponds to one part of the shadow's side plane.

There is a very easy way to obtain this list of edges. As you compute which triangles are visible, you should also keep track of the edges. Insert every edge for every visible triangle into a list. If the edge already exists in the list, remove it, because it means that there is another visible triangle that shares this edge. If two triangles share the same edge, that very same edge cannot possibly define the boundary of the shape from the camera's viewpoint. In the end, what remain are the edges that aren't shared by any two visible triangles. Once you have this set of edges, you can create the set of planes that, together with the visible triangle's planes, build a convex shadow volume.

To be technically correct, this bounding volume isn't truly convex because the far side of the object isn't closed. For your purposes, though, you don't need the object to be closed at that specific location. The inside-a-convex-body test will still work just fine.

Once you've built the set of planes to test with, you can simply test against the bounding box of the objects to determine if these objects should be culled or not. Recall that the object must be completely inside the shadow frustum for this to work. If a piece of an object is visible, it should be drawn. Consequently, you'll have to modify the intersection tests for the sphere/box/etc. to make sure that the entire object is inside the convex body. This is pretty easy if you determine everything by computing the signed distance between the plane and the bounding object.

Now, you can probably see why it's important to first create a convex body that doesn't have too many details. The more details you add to the convex body, the more detailed the shadow volume becomes and the more planes you have to test against.

Detail Culling

The idea behind detail culling is that objects that are relatively far from the camera don't really need as much detail as objects that are really close to the camera. This is pretty obvious. If you have an extremely detailed lion and look at its face close-up, it looks relatively good. If you take this same lion and move it a block away, you probably can't even tell what color its eyes are or if it even has whiskers. That's the entire idea behind detail culling. It's a function of distance. The farther away an object is, the fewer details you require. Furthermore, the larger the object is, the more details are important.

If you have a tiger and a small rock, both close to the camera, you probably don't care if the rock is detailed to death because the tiger takes up most of the onscreen space. The best solution here, again, is to implement various versions of your models for various depths. You can separate the depths in various intervals if you want, and these intervals will show less-detailed objects as the depth increases. The number of models you keep around will depend on how much memory and bandwidth you can afford.

There are also methods that attempt to remove triangles dynamically as the object moves away from the viewer. The unfortunate truth about these methods is that they're not very efficient and tend to generate results where the triangles seem to pop out of nowhere. Granted, this effect can happen if you generate many variously detailed models, but it can be controlled. There are also methods that attempt to completely remove this popping effect by gradually moving the vertices that have been added to their respective positions. However, this requires even more CPU power, and such methods are already CPU-hungry.

Depth Culling

You'll see this type of thing in racing games, mostly. For example, GTA3 uses this technique to reduce the number of polygons it needs to render. The idea is simply not to render the objects that are a certain distance from the camera. It's that simple. Surely you've noticed in racing games that buildings tend to appear at the horizon, which is the best indicator that this technique was used. Often, a developer will use something such as fog to mask the popping effect that a new object makes on the scene.

Another alternative I have seen in the past is to gradually reduce the transparency of an object as it moves toward the camera. This and the fog use pretty much the same idea, which is to diminish the abruptness in the visual flow. It's always nicer when things feel smooth and gradual.

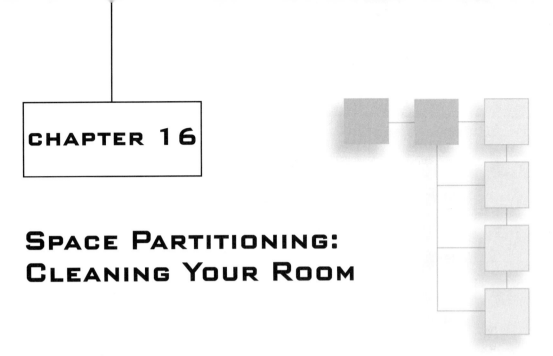

CHAPTER 16

SPACE PARTITIONING: CLEANING YOUR ROOM

At this point, you should be able to detect collisions and the visibility of a set of objects. It should now be a trivial task for you to verify a static intersection. In the previous chapter, some rather efficient techniques were given to achieve this task, but these alone won't help you to build a fast, commercial-quality game. The tests are fast, but you have to apply them to every single object in the world. It would be nice if you could group the objects together, similarly to what was done by using a bounding box, but generalized to the world and not just a simple object. Just imagine how slow your game would be if you had to take a game such as GTA3 and verify every possible object. Without a doubt, it would make a Pentium feel like an X86.

This chapter will show you how to divide the world and store this information in a data structure. This data structure can take days to generate (you don't really care, because it can be pregenerated for a static world), but it must have a killer run-time speed and must efficiently give you a small subset of objects to test against.

Specifically, you'll learn about the following:

- Grid division
- Quadtrees and octrees
- *k*-D trees
- Binary space partitioned (BSP) trees
- Portal subdivision

Grid Division

One of the simplest ways to divide your world is to split it into equal-sized quads, as illustrated in Figure 16.1. This simple yet valuable method can make a great difference.

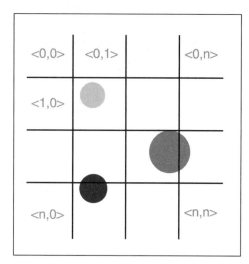

Figure 16.1
Grid world subdivision

The data structure for such a division is pretty simple. You just need to keep a 2D array where the index $<x, y>$ is the xth division block in x and the yth division block in the y axis. The 2D array should thus contain a pointer to a linked list (or a static array) giving you the list of objects contained within the division $<x, y>$. If your world is more 3D than 2D (for example, if it is a space game, as opposed to a game such as *GTA3*), you can still apply this structure. You can divide the world into a 3D array representing the subdivision $<x, y, z>$. Generally, the 2D version is more often used than the 3D version.

This world division can be pretty helpful in games such as GTA3, where every division has a fair number of elements inside. The intersection tests are simplified by forcing the fact that the grid must be axis-aligned with the world. As you've seen, such a subdivision yields significantly fewer complex problems than having no axis-alignment. The only problem with this type of structure is that, given a large world, you must still verify against a pretty large number of divisions. It's true that the test is very efficient due to the alignment of the divisions, but it's not worth the sheer number of tests you may have to do for a small frustum (in comparison with the world).

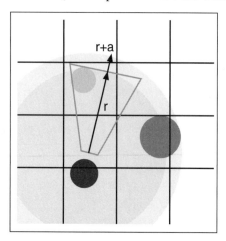

Figure 16.2
Divisions visible within a radius of *r* and (*r* + *a*) from the camera's center

This starts to become a little more attractive when you think outside the box. For instance, you can find the division where your camera is positioned. If the length of your division is 10, for example, you need only divide the position of the camera by 10 to yield the index. This division is almost guaranteed to be visible, because it's the first point of the frustum. What's nice is that you're guaranteed that the visible division is adjacent to that very division. Thus, you could verify every division that is within a given radius from the camera's center, as illustrated in Figure 16.2.

You can obtain a good approximation of the radius by computing the difference between the near and far plane. This is just an approximation, because the extent of the frustum (which goes sideways) generates a radius that's larger than this, but you can increase the radius slightly to compensate. After all, the radius of the frustum should be a constant for the most part. Once you have that constant, you can simply leave it as a constant radius. Of course, again, you'll have to convert your world-space radius into division-space, which is a mere division by 10 for your example.

If you wanted to be even leaner and meaner with a 2D division, you could project the frustum on the 2D plane forming the ground (assuming that your division is done on that plane) and verify every division that's within or touching the frustum's boundary. With this method, there's no visibility or collision test between the frustum and the subdivision. Instead, you get a 2D polygon containing the set of divisions that are visible. This is an extremely efficient technique, because it gives you the exact divisions that are potentially visible.

You can achieve this by computing the intersection of every plane of the frustum. (This will give you eight points in 3D.) Project the vertex orthogonally to the ground plane by discarding the y component of the coordinates, thus yielding $<x, z>$. Once you have these 2D vertices, you must compute a convex polygon that bounds this set of vertices. You can do this by finding one point in the set that you know to be a part of the convex body (the minimum or maximum), and you can find the next point by finding the vertex that generates a line with all vertices on one side of it. If you don't want to complicate the problem too much, you can also go with a technique that merely checks every division in a square fashion, where the length of the square is akin to the radius' length.

Offhand, this method doesn't look like it helps much, because it still has a lot of divisions to check against. But it does pretty well, if you look at the surrounding divisions from the camera's division. In fact, if the division size is well chosen, it can be one of the best division methods available. This method is really useful in cases where the world is pretty cluttered (GTA3 comes to mind). Otherwise, you'll end up with divisions containing no objects, and that's where it starts to be pretty expensive in terms of memory.

Memory is the main problem with this method. Choosing a small division will make things extremely fast, but it will leave a lot of empty divisions (thus, lost memory). On the other hand, if you choose large divisions, you may end up with one division carrying too many elements. It would thus be a division that was too big for the world. Balance is the key, and it's game-specific. This is probably where you want to run some statistical analysis and see which size is best suited to your specific problem.

The beauty of dividing your world is that doing so not only applies to visibility determination, but also to collision detection. It reduces the problem to a level that helps your entire game deal with fewer objects, which is a great thing overall. Specifically, grids are more useful for collision detection because the number of divisions to be tested is generally smaller.

You wouldn't need a very fine-grained grid if you were to use it for collision-detection purposes, whereas visibility would require a more fine-grained grid. This is true in general, but it always really depends more on the game you are creating than on anything else.

Quadtrees and Octrees

The previous method is great in terms of speed, but it's memory-hungry. There's not much you can do to change that without drastically changing the way the method works.

This drastic change of method is what the quadtree attempts propose. Specifically, the problem in the previous function was that one side of the world could have only one object, and yet you divided the space into equal intervals, which wasted memory. If you'd only divided the other half and kept this half intact, you would have saved a considerable amount of space.

This is where the quadtree comes in. Abstractly defined, a quadtree is a recursive grid. To simplify the problem and alleviate memory issues, it takes a grid that splits n spaces into two divisions per dimension. Thus, you get a total of 2^n divisions for one recursion step, as illustrated in Figure 16.3.

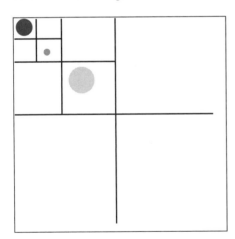

Figure 16.3
Quadtree division of a world

The data structure for such a division is obviously different from the grid division. Due to its recursive nature, the quadtree binds very well to a tree. The root of the tree should be a box that holds the entire world. This box should be divided in half for x and in half for y, thus yielding four new divisions and the four children of the root tree. If the divisions are empty, it's useless to apply the process recursively on the subdivision. In this case, you can set the children's pointers to NULL.

On the other hand, if there's more than one object in the division, you'll want to subdivide it once more. The rule of thumb while building the quadtree is that an object must be completely contained within the division. In other words, an object cannot span more than one division. With the previous method, if an object spanned more than one division, you would simply repeat the object in both divisions and make sure not to draw it twice (inserting the object into a renderable list). Here, you can't do this, because you don't know when to stop the recursion.

Of course, if you followed the preceding rule strictly, all shapes would fall into the root node. The proper rule is that the object should be assigned to the smallest subdivision in which it's completely contained. Thus, when you're inserting an object into the quadtree, you need to subdivide the quadtree recursively until it yields an intersection with the object. At that point, you must assign it to the last leaf (that is, that end node of a tree that is a division that is not subdivided in this case). You can see this in Figure 16.3. The biggest circle couldn't afford to have its space divided in half without yielding an intersection, while the two other circles could.

When it comes time to verify for an intersection or a collision, you start by verifying which of the four halves you're intersecting with—that is, by performing a simple box-object collision test. If one of the quarters doesn't intersect, you can skip that quarter of space. After you have determined which quarters intersect, you must keep verifying against the subdivision for each quarter until you reach a leaf, at which point you'll want to test the set of objects that are located in that leaf. Obviously, the data structure for each leaf of the quadtree division is a linked list of objects that are contained in this division (again, just as the grid method worked). In terms of speed, you don't really save as much as with the previous method because it could give you a pretty good approximation of the set of intersecting regions in one pass. This method requires a few recursive passes, but you save a great deal of memory by not subdividing the empty regions.

The quadtree is a 2D structure, and its sibling the octree is its 3D version. For an octree, you're not only dividing space in x and y, but also in z. This means that every node has up to eight children. The process itself remains the same as that of the quadtree, except that you have to account for the greater number of children.

k-D Trees

If you look at the quadtree/octree structure from a statistical data point of view, the tree isn't well-balanced in general. An ideal tree would always split the world in half for every axis. If half of the objects are split in x, half of them in y, and another half in z, you've split a division that had n objects into another four (or eight) divisions that have n/4 objects (or n/8 for the octree) each.

For instance, suppose that you have a world where 99% of the objects are cluttered in the same octree division. The octree is of little help because you always need to verify the intersections for this one division that has most of the objects. And of course, you have to verify against every one of these objects. If you have a balanced tree, on the other hand, half of these objects are in a separate division than the other half, and furthermore for all other axes. The tree is effectively balanced, because every object is split evenly.

A *k*-D tree is a *k*-dimensional tree that fixes this problem by dividing space unevenly, geometrically speaking. Where the space is divided evenly is in terms of object density. That is, there are as many objects in one half as there are in the other half.

In a way, you can define the *k*-D tree as a balanced octree. The *k*-D tree is the data structure that splits the world in half for every division. It doesn't split the world in half geometrically, but rather in density (the number of objects). For example, the first pass of a *k*-D tree counts the number of elements and splits the world in half according to the *x* coordinate. In other words, you would find the value x, which is such that half of the objects' *x* values are smaller than it and the other half are greater than or equal to it.

This is a much more efficient method than the octree. For every pass of the *k*-D tree, you're guaranteed to look at half the number of objects you looked at previously. Thus, if you have *n* objects, you should expect $\log_2(n)$ passes (plus tax, as you'll soon see).

The *k*-D tree operates in one direction at a time. The order of the direction is up to you, but here let's assume an $\{x, y, z\}$ split ordering. This means that you should first split in *x*. Once you've split the objects 50/50 in *x*, look at splitting the two subregions in *y*. Once this is done, look at splitting the subregions in *z*. Thereafter, this process is applied recursively.

One thing that you may have noticed is that this doesn't yield a nice symmetric model. The first split in *x* will give you two half-spaces. Because the density of objects is probably different on each side, the value in *y* that splits the right half probably won't be the same as that which splits the left half, as illustrated in Figure 16.4.

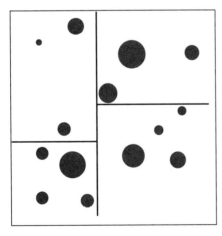

Figure 16.4
First steps of a *k*-D tree division on a world

This isn't a real problem per se, but it does mean that you'll have to keep track of the value where you perform the division. In other words, you'll have to keep track of the value where you've divided the *x* component for the first pass. Similarly, you'll have to keep track of the *y* value where you've divided the world in each subregion, and so forth. If you keep subdividing your tree as shown in Figure 16.5, eventually you'll hit a wall. That is, you'll reach a point where there's no such thing as a dividing line that can split two objects (or two sets of objects) in an equal fashion. If you stop the process here, as was done with the octree, you can't divide the set of objects in two. This means that the *k*-D tree basically becomes a linked list.

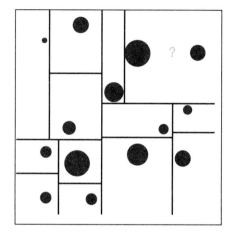

Figure 16.5
k-D tree division on a world after further
steps

Obviously, this is not a good solution. Instead, you can set aside the rule about having exactly the same number of objects on each side (or with one difference, in the case where the total number of objects is odd), and simply find the best fit. "The best fit" is defined as the split that minimizes the difference between the two sides. In the case of Figure 16.5, you would have to add a dummy horizontal line to finish everything off with a vertical line that would split the two objects correctly.

Finding the Best Axis-Aligned Split

This technique will almost always work if the two objects don't intersect. If they don't intersect, there must be an axis separating them (by the separating axis theorem seen in the previous chapter). The tricky part is that this structure only allows for axis-aligned cuts, so you might have two spheres close enough that the axis-aligned line can cut the space in half. In this crummy case, the two objects need to be enlisted in one division. Ideally, you would want to generate a tree where there's one object per division, at most. For reasons seen above, this isn't always possible, so you must also be able to cope with a division containing many elements.

Now you must turn to a newly arisen problem, which is finding the best line that splits the set of objects into two equal (or as close to equal as possible) sets. Because there's no real-time requirement for generating such a structure (you don't want to dynamically generate this structure; it's a one-time operation for a static world), you can use a method that takes a little more time but is easy to implement and understand. The technique is based on a divide-and-conquer method.

If you split the space in half geometrically, you can count how many objects are completely on one side of the line and how many are completely on the other side. Make sure to account for each object's effective radius. This is what makes it a harder task than it should be. If you get an equality there, you may not even be done, because there may be an intersection between an object and that line. If there's an intersection, you may have to continue with the algorithm. If you don't find an intersection and the space is split in half (with the exception of an odd number), you should stop.

The other situation where you should stop is if the space is divided in half (up to an odd number of objects) and objects on each side of the line intersect it. If you've found a line that balances the number of objects on each side and for which both sides intersect, you won't be able to find a line that splits that space in half that doesn't intersect.

On the other hand, if you find that objects from only one side intersect the line, there still might be a line where no intersection occurs at all and that splits the space equally. Thus, you must continue the algorithm. To apply the recursion, you must decide which half of the line you'll be recursing. The side with the greatest number of objects should be reduced in area so that some objects can be moved over to the other side. Consequently, you must add or subtract half of the total distance in x to the current x and reapply the calculations. Whether you add or subtract that value depends on whether the greatest number of objects is at the left (where you want to subtract) or the right (where you want to add). You must thereafter apply this process recursively, as Figure 16.6 illustrates. In the case where the objects are split equally but an intersection occurs on only one side of the line, you should move the line toward the side where there's no intersection. Thus, you must choose the addition or subtraction side wisely.

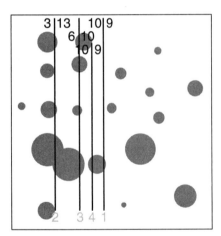

Figure 16.6
The process of finding the best separation line for a k-D tree

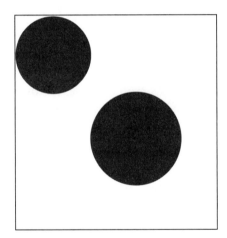

Figure 16.7
Problematic k-D tree cut

The only remaining problem is how to know when to end this process. What happens if you try to run this algorithm with the example in Figure 16.7? The algorithm will run like Forrest Gump, never to return to this world.

To fix this, you can apply a threshold. It runs forever, because the two circles don't really intersect given a vertical or horizontal line. Given any axis-aligned line, there will always be one object on the other side and one intersecting the line, but the two objects will never intersect the line at the same time. Basically, they're infinitely close one to one another. You can say that, once the value you add (or subtract) becomes something that's smaller than or equal to 0.0001, you stop and choose the current line as the separating line. This is the best approximation for a separating line that divides the space in half without actually separating it in half (due to impossibility).

Now to sum up the best axis-aligned line-searching algorithm:

```
Function (x = split line, T = Total Length of the axis, d = depth)
{
    for (every objects) {
        if (object center + effective radius < x)
            Left++;
        else if (object center - effective radius > x)
            Right++;
    }
    if (Left + OddNumberOfObjects < Right)
        Recurse(x - T/2, T/2, d++)
    else if (Left > Right + OddNumberOfObjects)
        Recurse(x + T / 2, T/2, d++);

    if (intersections on only one side)
        Recurse(x ± T/2, T/2, d++);

    // No Intersection, so return the split line
    return x;
}
```

Now you've just finished splitting space in half in x. You should have one tree with one root containing the value x, which is the splitting value $x = a$, which you found with the preceding algorithm. This node should have two children, one for the left and another for the right. The next step is to take the left set and to apply the same subdivision in y. Following is the right side, where you also apply a subdivision in y. After that, you may follow through by applying a subdivision in z for each four subdivisions (yielding eight children). At the end of the tree (for every leaf), you should have a linked list (or static array) containing the list of objects that are in this space. This linked list should be pretty small, because the odds of having many objects cut by one line (or plane in 3D) are pretty small.

This also brings up the one remaining problem that you've yet to solve: How do you determine when a division such as the one in Figure 16.7 isn't possible and bail out? If you applied this recursively, the space would be continuously divided by $x, y, z, x, y, z\ldots$ You need to find a condition that will stop this madness. In fact, it's pretty simple to detect. If all axes are such that the total number of objects that don't intersect the line is equal to 1 at most (in the case of an odd group), you should bail out of the division.

As always, because some objects could appear more than once, you should be careful not to apply the test twice for these objects. A simple flag would do the trick here.

Walking Through the Tree

In the last two methods, this section was omitted, mainly because it's pretty easy to determine which areas intersect with the frustum (for visibility testing) or how to find the area of a specific location (for collision testing). In the first method, you merely needed to scale the coordinates, while in the octree division, you had to recurse and do a box-frustum intersection test. You should have already seen these techniques by now. Thankfully, this structure isn't much trickier than the previous two. The areas are still defined as boxes, although they aren't axis-aligned. Finding the area, given a position, is pretty easy. You simply need to check if the object is on the positive or negative side of the line/plane. Apply this process recursively, and eventually you'll reach a point where no divisions occur. This means you've found the area that contains the coordinate you're looking for.

For the frustum, however, it's a much more painful process. You'll have to look back at the intersection between a frustum and a plane. The technique proposed in Chapter 15, "Visibility Determination: The World of the Invisible," was to transform the elements into frustum space, and this works very well here too. The only problem is that for your case, knowing whether or not the frustum intersects with a plane doesn't give you the full information. If you know that the plane splits the frustum into two areas, you know that both sides of the plane are potentially in the frustum. Thus, you have to go deeper into the tree on each side of the plane. If the frustum is fully contained on one side, you should go deeper into the tree on that side only. Because of the construction of this tree, no objects should lie on the other side (the one not containing the frustum). But you need to know which side this is before you can choose the left or right branch of your tree.

If you start by transforming the plane into frustum space, you'll generate a frustum for which the corners will be in the format $<\pm1, \pm1, \pm1>$. Consequently, if you compute the distance between the closest vertex and the plane, as well as the most distant vertex from the plane, you get that the min and max distance between the box and the plane. This is illustrated in Figure 16.8, and is given by the following formulas for a plane $<\mathbf{n}, D>$:

$$d_{max} = |\mathbf{n}_x| + |\mathbf{n}_y| + |\mathbf{n}_z| + D$$
$$d_{min} = -|\mathbf{n}_x| - |\mathbf{n}_y| - |\mathbf{n}_z| + D$$

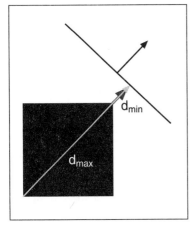

If these two values have different signs, the frustum intersects with the plane and thus both sides should be visited. If both values are negative, the frustum lies on the negative side of the plane. Conversely, if both values are positive, the frustum lies on the positive side of the plane (which is the half pointed to by the normal vector). With this method, you don't even need to compute the distance between the box and the plane, because this method also tells you if there was an intersection or not.

Figure 16.8
Min/max distance between a plane and a box

Binary Space Partitioned (BSP) Trees

Binary Space Partitioned trees were red-hot a few years ago. They were made popular by games such as *Doom*, and later on by *Quake*, which extended the concept to a true 3D world. BSPs are still pretty popular for indoor games. If you move to outdoor games, typically the previous methods are more efficient.

A BSP is the natural next step after the k-D tree. A BSP is a k-D tree whose planes need not actually be axis-aligned. In other words, a BSP tree enables you to cut space using a line (or a plane in 3D) without regard to its alignment. This obviously introduces more flexibility (thus a greater, more accurate culling method), which does indeed fix the problem you saw in Figure 16.7. In fact, as long as no two objects intersect in the world (something that you can force), by the theorem of the separating axis, there will always exist a line/plane that separates the two objects.

Using a BSP tree to perform culling or collision detection is the easy part. If you understand the k-D tree, you basically understand the BSP tree. Where it becomes much trickier is in the creation of the tree. Ideally, the tree would always split the current division in equal halves, thereby producing a logarithmic access tree. The method you use to create the BSP tree really depends on the uses you have for it, as well as the type of world you're dealing with. The construction given here is well suited to a world that's built with many bounded objects (as the previous cases were). For an indoor game such as Quake and Unreal, the walls and ceiling and floor would actually be the equivalents of the objects in this method. Of course, because they're walls, a finer tuning can be applied, but the general idea is still the same.

So how can you determine a good candidate plane? If you had an orientation, it would minimally lock one variable, and the position would be the only remaining one. The real problem here is the large number of planes that you can choose to separate the world. You could easily waste days trying to find the best matching plane. In order to save memory and simplify things, the *Quake/Unreal/Doom* approach is used. The cutting plane is chosen so that it matches with a wall (or a similar geometry for fully 3D worlds). Figure 16.9 illustrates what a BSP tree might look like in Doom. The lines in this figure represent the walls as you would see them from a top view. As you can see, line segment one separates the space in half. For the left and right halves, the space is divided by line segments 2 and 3, respectively.

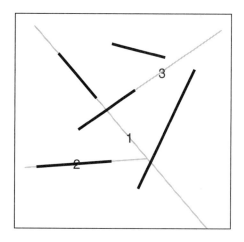

As you may have noticed, some splits cut another segment in two. In those cases, games such as Doom tend to split this wall/polygon in two pieces so that the two of them are mutually exclusive. This helps when it's time to render, because it means that you don't need to check if an object was already rendered. It's similar for collisions. For walls like this, it's pretty easy. You choose a wall and split space by this wall. Everything on one side goes on one side of the tree, and the rest goes on the other side of the tree. You apply this process recursively until the area has one element, at most. The difference between the BSP and the wall as it's applied here is that the BSP also contains information about the objects in the nodes.

Figure 16.9
BSP tree built by using the walls as cutting planes

Let's pull back a little from the *Doom* scenario and assume that you want to partition a set of objects (which could be bounded by a bounding volume). A wall would simply be seen as an infinitely thin bounded rectangle. Given an object, you should choose a plane that goes in the same general direction as that of the object. This principle of "general direction" merely means that you should choose the longest extent of the bounding volume as the direction for the plane. To be a little more specific, the plane that separates the world should be the plane for which the normal vector is the smallest extent so as to minimize the distance between the object's bounding volume and the plane, as illustrated in Figure 16.10.

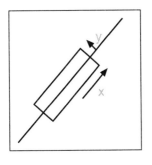

Figure 16.10
Choosing the plane that minimizes the distance to a bounding box

This plan is pretty easy to compute. If you have the vector of the smallest extent **v** (this could be the extent of an ellipsoid, a box, a cylinder...), you can compute the equation for the splitting plane s such as

$$s = \langle \mathbf{n}, -\mathbf{n} \bullet \mathbf{c} \rangle$$

Here, **c** is the center of the object. Along with the splitting plane, you should also store the object in the node of the tree (more on this later). Once you've written your first node, the objects that sit completely on the positive side of the plane go on the left branch, while the other elements go on the right branch. Obviously, you cannot always split an object in two pieces. If you can afford to do so, it will save you some time. If it's not an option or you don't want the bother for the extra speed gain, you'll have to store the object in both the positive and the negative side of the plane as was done with the previous methods.

Finally, let's look at the data structure in a bit more detail. The data structure is a binary tree (has two children). One child is for the object sitting on the positive half (the half pointed to by the normal vector), and the remaining child is in the other half. Initially, the world is divided in half by the first plane (or line). This plane is associated with an object that has its axis for the smallest extent in that direction. In the case of a sphere, where there really isn't a greatest or smallest extent, you may use the statistical method presented in Chapter 11, "Educated Guessing with Statistics and Probability," to determine which is the axis with the smallest extent. This object is stored in the tree alongside the splitting plane. Recursively, the set of objects for the children are partitioned.

As an example, look at Figure 16.9. Further define the two remaining lines, which aren't numbered as 4 and 5 from top to bottom. Assume that these lines represent objects that are sorted alphabetically (1 = a, 2 = b, and so on). The construction steps of the tree would be as shown in Figure 16.11. Of course, it would make no sense to build a tree if the positive and negative directions of the splitting elements weren't indicated. Consequently, the tree really reflects Figure 16.12, which indicates the direction of the planes (or lines for 2D).

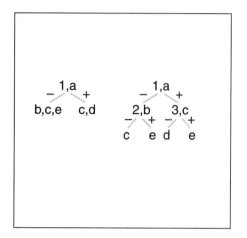

Figure 16.11
Step-by-step construction of the BSP tree

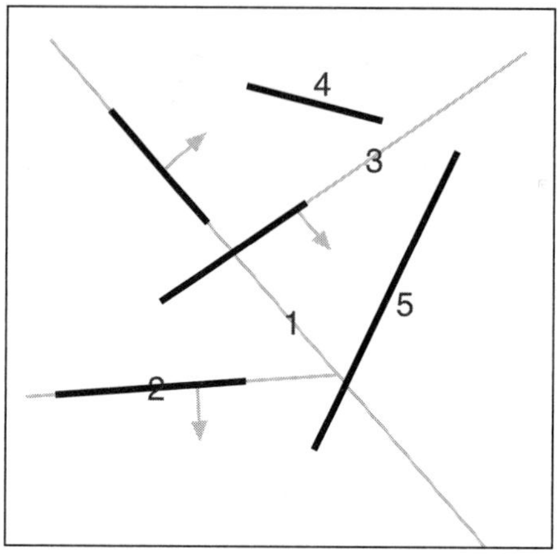

Figure 16.12
Binary Space Partitioned space

The last thing that needs to be addressed is the choice of plane. Many analyses have been done on BSP trees, and generally a random pick generates a pretty reasonable BSP tree. If you care to waste the extra cycles, you could implement a trial and error method that attempts to find the object that can split space into the most equal halves. Such a method isn't bad, but it isn't guaranteed to generate the most balanced tree possible.

Front to Back Rendering

In the *Doom* days, when hardware acceleration cards were available only on extremely expensive professional workstations, visibility and rendering techniques were different from what they are today. Since the z-buffer is an extremely expensive thing in software, games like Doom couldn't afford to use anything similar to that. Consequently, they still required a way to render a scene such that the visibility was maintained.

A BSP can give you the set of visible surfaces, but how about the order of the polygons? If you have no z-buffer (or something similar), the rendering order becomes important. If you render a close surface before a far surface, you won't respect the fact that the closer surface occludes the other one. Thus, the most commonly used technique was the painter's algorithm. This technique is as simple as it sounds. The idea is to render the polygons that are farthest away from the camera first. This way, the visibility is maintained.

With today's hardware, you can achieve this if you plan to disable the z-buffer, but why would you want to do that? Instead, you should optimize your rendering to take advantage of the z-buffer. If you can write the polygons in a reverse painter's algorithm—in other words, render the polygons from close to far—you could save a considerable amount of GPU. More specifically, you could save a lot in the rasterization pipeline, because every pixel that's found to be occluded in the z-buffer won't be displayed on the screen. On the other hand, if you were to draw using something similar to a painter's algorithm (rendering from far to close), you would effectively have a lot of overdraw, which isn't a good thing. As you will see in the next chapter, modern hardware does an early z-test to avoid expensive per-fragment operations like texturing for fragments that aren't visible anyway.

Why is this a topic for this chapter anyway? Well, BSP trees were used in *Doom* to render using the painter's algorithm. If you can render from back to front, surely you can render from front to back simply by inverting the process. BSP or any half-plane (a division that recursively differentiates between the positive and negative side of the plane) allows for such a technique. The trick is in the way you traverse the tree. You'll have to visit the set of objects that are closer to the camera than the other half. It's extremely simple. Assuming that you have a list of objects that are visible, the closer one half-plane is to the camera, the closer the set of objects described in it are to the camera. So assuming that both sides of a plane are visible, you just have to determine which of the two divisions is closer to the camera.

It's very simple to find out which half is closer to the camera. Just check if the camera itself is on the positive or negative side of the plane. The objects on the same side of the plane are closer to the camera than the objects on the other side of the plane. This test is no different than the test you would apply on any object. Because you already know how to determine if an object sits on the positive or negative side of the plane, you should choose the negative or positive child of the tree, depending on the following formula for a plane <**n**, *D*> and a 4D camera <**c**, 1>:

$$Side = \langle \mathbf{n}, d \rangle \bullet \langle \mathbf{c}, 1 \rangle$$

Side < 0 implies the negative half-plane, while *Side* > 0 implies the positive half-plane. Since you've standardized the tree such that one child holds the objects on the positive half and the rest on the negative, it's just a matter of knowing which comes first. When *Side* = 0, the object is on the actual plane. In this case, you have to arbitrarily determine whether you want objects that are on the plane to sit on the positive or negative side of the plane. It really makes no difference, but you need to make it a constant throughout the algorithm.

Portal Subdivision

BSP trees are used a lot for indoor worlds, but they also apply very well to outdoor worlds if you determine the correct separating plane that optimizes the tree. Some games, on the other hand, prefer to keep all of their skeletons in their closets and stay indoors. *Doom* is a pure indoor game, for example, and *Quake 1* and *2* also fit in this category. *Quake 3* is somewhat in the middle because it has both outdoor and indoor maps, but that's merely the combination of a few techniques that are given here.

Portal subdivision offers a completely new way of thinking. In the previous methods, the world was given as a raw world (that is, without any prior hierarchy), and you had to subdivide this world using planes so as to produce an efficient structure for comparison. The idea behind portals is simple. Each room is divided into a disjointed set of zones, all of which are connected to other zones through an entity that you refer to as a portal.

You can think of a portal as a dark mirror through which you can see another piece of the world, as illustrated in Figure 16.13. It's like looking through a window, where a zone defines each side of the window. This idea was best demonstrated in *Shadow Warrior*. This game wasn't as notorious as the game upon which its engine was based (*Duke Nukem 3D*), but the addition they made to the engine was pretty clever. Portals were already used in games like *Doom*, but what made *Shadow Warrior* stick out was that you could actually have a portal in the ceiling. This enabled developers to give the effect of having multiple levels for the same $<x, y>$ by simply attributing a portal to the ceiling. This was a pretty brilliant idea. If you remember *Doom* and *Doom II*, you probably remember that you couldn't be on two different levels at the same time. In other words, the map was really a 2D map with information on the height at each location, and you couldn't find a spot on the map that carried more than one height (one ceiling and one floor). The 3D Realms technique did allow for this by using portals, thereby keeping the speedy rendering of *Doom* and allowing for two levels of height.

The key to understanding portals is the portal itself and the frustum. The way the method works is that you initially need to isolate which zone the camera is in. Once you've determined this, you have to check which zones are connected to that zone and test if that zone is visible. If it is, you have to recurse until no more zones are visible. The key to

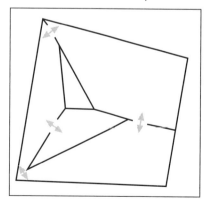

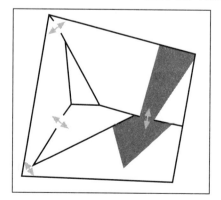

Figure 16.13
A portal applied to a world (the portals are the red arrows)

Figure 16.14
Frustum reduction due to a portal

determining if a zone is visible or not comes from the frustum itself, as was done previously, but the beauty of this method is that the frustum can be reduced in size for the next zone, as illustrated in Figure 16.14. This reduced frustum can significantly reduce the number of objects that need to be verified against. The only tricky part is that this new frustum may not be in the shape you would expect it to be in. In fact, it's easier to consider this frustum as a set of independent planes.

Frustum Clipping on the Portal

Before you clip your frustum to a portal, you should first look at the portal in closer detail. To make things simple, the portal should be defined as a convex polygon. In Chapter 15, you saw how nice it is to work with a convex frustum, because you can easily verify if an object is inside or outside of it. In fact, the convex shadow occlusion section of Ch. 11 will be very useful here, because the idea is pretty much the same. The convex portal itself should be stored in a well-defined order. To make matters simpler here, let's simply choose it as a counterclockwise ordering. It's important to choose an order for the convex portal, because you want to know which side of the portal contains the next zone to test. If you clip the frustum to a portal, you probably want to remove the frustum volume that was in the initial section, and only keep the frustum volume that's located in the next zone.

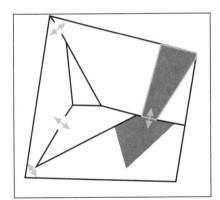

Recall that the frustum itself is composed of a set of eight planes: one near, one far, and four planes bounding the volume on each side. In a portal system, the far and near planes are the trivial planes to clip. If you move from one zone to another, the far plane shouldn't be changed. The near plane, on the other hand, will be pushed forward so as to match with the plane described by the convex polygon composing the portal, as illustrated in Figure 16.15.

Figure 16.15
Frustum clipping before (dark gray)
and after (light gray)

Thus, these two planes are pretty easy to handle. The tricky part is the handling of the side planes. These are the planes that are most likely to be clipped and transmogrified by the portal. Initially, this is the typical set of four planes that you've come to know very well. Eventually, this will likely become a set of planes, so you should hold a dynamic structure that allows you to keep track of a set of planes. Define the set of vertices that compose the portal as v_i. The idea here is to clip the polygon with each plane in the frustum set. The technique is the same as that described in Chapter 14, " Graphics-Generation Engines," where a triangle is clipped to a plane. Instead of applying the process to three vertices, you'll have to apply it to the set of vertices that compose the convex polygon of the portal. If you apply this clipping process to every single plane, you'll effectively clip the convex polygon on the set of planes that describe the frustum.

Once you've clipped the convex polygon of the portal, you've determined the new convex polygon that describes the window through which you can see the next zone. A window by itself isn't very useful; you need to construct a frustum. But you've already learned how to construct a frustum with the convex shadow culling method, so this process is a piece of cake. The clipping is done with the triangle clipping method from Chapter 14, and the frustum regeneration is done with the convex occlusion shadow method from Chapter 15. This will give you yet another set of planes (smaller than or equal in area to the previous frustum). At this point, you can apply the process recursively for the zones that are part of the new zone you're visiting. The obvious question is, when do you stop? Well, that's the easy part. You stop when the frustum is entirely clipped (no convex polygon vertices exist), or when no further zones are available.

Potentially Visible Set (PVS)

Typically, because your world is all connected in some way, you may well be verifying a host of portals that are technically impossible to view from a given zone. With the preceding algorithm, you would still need to go through each portal in the zone and verify that it's visible. This involves a lot of useless computation if you already know that a given set of zones will never be visible from a certain room, regardless of the angle.

Consequently, the idea behind PVS is to build a set of potentially visible zones given a certain zone. The idea is pretty simple. You should keep a list of zones that are potentially visible from any angle in a room, and when it's time to look for neighboring zones, just check against this list to determine which zones are visible. Sounds simple, doesn't it?

The tricky part is actually getting this list of zones. The easiest way is to do it manually. But it's often practical to set up an automated way to achieve this. There are many options for this, but the method that yields the best results is to build a frustum of 180 degrees (a box) and test the visibility from a given zone by putting the camera extremely close to the vertices of the portal. If you move the camera extremely close to the first vertex of the portal and have a frustum of 180 degrees, you'll be able to capture every other zone that's made available to you by going through the algorithm and verifying that you can go to the next room (that is, if the frustum is non-empty after clipping). Putting the camera at the portals' vertices is the key here, because this is the closest location in the first zone that can see into the second zone. Because it's the closest you can get to the second zone, it's the widest view you'll get of the room from that point. The frustum is forced to have an angle of 180 degrees, mainly because this simplifies the problem of finding the frustum's angle. If the frustum didn't have an angle of 180 degrees, thus generating a box, you would have to determine a set of angles to test against. But with 180 degrees, you cover all of the possible angles that can see inside the zone. All you have to do is make sure that the frustum's near plane is aligned with the portal plane; the rest is just an orthogonal extent of the frustum.

Ideally, you want to find a box such that if you rotate the frustum in any angle, the box will always contain the frustum. You can find this extent if you compute the intersection of three orthogonal planes from the frustum. For example, when computing the intersection of the far plane with any side plane and with the top/bottom plane, will yield a single point of intersection. If you compute the distance between this point and the center of the camera, you'll get the longest extent e the frustum ever reaches. At this point it's a simple matter of building a box aligned with the portal plane that extends e in every direction. You could build a sphere, but clipping to it would be a bigger pain than dealing with a set of planes. To obtain the two missing planes, you can simply build them with the Gram Schmidt orthogonalization process, as shown in Chapter 2, "Baby Steps: Introduction to Vectors." Figure 16.16 illustrates what is done here.

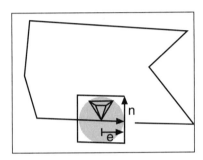

Figure 16.16
Frustum box built out of the frustum's extent e aligned with the portal normal **n**

Portals as a Large-Scale Division

In most implementations, portals are used to divide the world at a large scale factor. For instance, you could use portals to zone the various rooms in a game such as *Quake*. Typically, the rooms themselves are pretty complex. For instance, you may want to add a few objects to a room, render fancier walls, and generally give the place a little bit of style. This changes the geometry considerably, and it's not reasonable to separate all of these little details into portals where one complete large edge is the portal. In such cases, these rooms should be considered zones and should have an associated division structure (a BSP per room, for example). The beauty of portals is that they allow you to divide your rooms as you see fit. The "windows" through the other rooms are really where they can optimize things for you. In general, this is a great optimization. Typically, a room won't have that many occlusion objects, so another division structure is appropriate for objects at that level. Where you can really cull a lot of things is at the corridors leading to other rooms, and that's where portals excel.

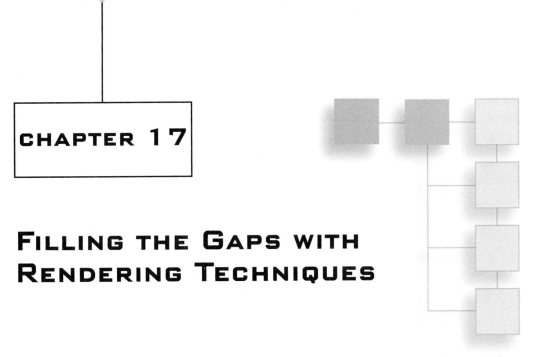

CHAPTER 17

FILLING THE GAPS WITH RENDERING TECHNIQUES

A few years ago, when DOS ruled the PC world and Windows was but an infant, developers had to write everything by hand. The Internet wasn't widely available, so you couldn't really log on to it to learn how to do cool things with your games. Bulletin boards (BBS) were the only resort. Someone in a small town wouldn't be able to reach out for many things.

I was lucky enough to grow up in a relatively big city, and gained access to many of these bulletin boards. At that point in time, the compilers didn't provide a very rich set of libraries, and accessing the mouse, the joystick, and even the keyboard for a game was ideally done in assembler. If you didn't know the inner workings of the algorithms and the PC's architecture, you were really restrained in terms of what you could do with a game. Libraries existed, but often the developers wouldn't provide the source code, and a few glitches in these libraries made them completely unusable (assuming you could gain access to them in the first place).

Today, things have changed drastically. No one thinks a lot about the problem of getting input from the mouse or keyboard (assuming you even dare call that a problem). Instead, you can focus more on game-related problems. Often enough, a game is like a marketing ad. It's filled with hype and B.S., and it looks twice as good as it really is. For the gamer, usually this is acceptable.

Typically, a game uses a lot of tweaks to fool the gamer into thinking that one thing really is something else. The first and most obvious example of this is 3D. Game programmers can easily fool someone into thinking that they're seeing a game in three dimensions, yet the monitor really is 2D. The same idea applies to techniques such as the billboards you've seen previously. The billboards fool you into thinking that an object has volume (3D), while in reality, the object is a mere screen-aligned texture.

447

As you'll see in this chapter, there are many dirty tricks you can use to fool the user into thinking that he sees something that isn't really there. These tricks are often used extensively in order to speed up the rendering process. As you'll see in the next chapter, lighting a model as it's physically done in real life can't be computed in real time.

Specifically, this chapter covers the following:

- Studying the 3D pipeline
- Texture transformations
- Cube map tricks
- Cel shading
- Shadows

Studying the 3D Pipeline

The next chapter will look at how you can carefully select the right color in a global and per-pixel fashion to rasterize some nice-looking scenes. This chapter mainly deals with the tricks that can be used at a higher level. You need to know which hardware is available to render things.

This section is particularly suited for the fragment operations. These are the operations that are performed after you've selected the color for the pixel but right before you render the pixels. The z-buffer is such an operation because it's done after the color has been selected but before the pixel is actually plotted. Figure 17.1 illustrates a general per-fragment pipeline. Depending on the manufacturer's implementation, some of these operations may come for free (without any difference in speed), while some may induce serious costs. Although this is true, if you understand how things are done under the hood, you'll be able to detect which operations are potentially free and which aren't.

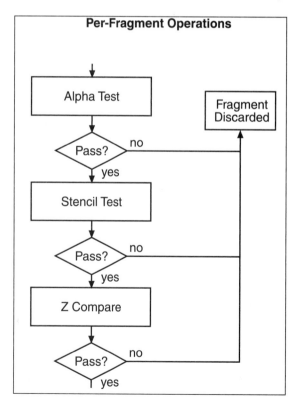

Figure 17.1
3D GPU fragment pipeline

For instance, if you enable backface culling and use an operation to do lighting, the backface culling comes for free because the lighting calculations depend on the triangle's normal vector (as you'll see in the next chapter). In other words, you need to do the calculations for both, so chances are the hardware vendor has optimized this path so as not to compute the normal vector twice for the same polygon.

Alpha Test

The alpha test is a good thing to perform when you want to reduce the rasterization cost of the rendering pipeline. The idea behind this test is that a general function is used, such as (*Alpha* > *Constant*), where *Alpha* represents the percentage of transparency of the pixel. If this test passes, you plot the pixel, but if it fails, you don't. Thus, if you have objects that have a nearly invisible alpha (say < 5%), you can refrain from rendering them at all, thereby reducing the rasterization latency. Typically, your favorite 3D API will allow you to use a set of functions (greater than, lesser than, or equal to) that will allow you to weed out a few pixels before they even go into the other per-fragment operations. This can be pretty useful if you are planning to render many billboards, which are typically composed of many completely invisible pixels; it can quickly remove the pixels that are invisible without actually going farther down the pipeline.

Stencil Test

As the name suggests, the stencil buffer works similarly to a stencil. The idea is to have a buffer that can mask the pixels, thus allowing pixels to be written only in the region described by the stencil buffer.

The stencil buffer is a little more powerful than a mere on/off test. It can accept a set of values whose maximum is hardware-dependent. This allows you to render only a portion of the screen. For example, for a portal, you could fill the pixels pertaining to the portal with 1 and the rest with 0. When it's time to render, you can set the function that states that only the pixels with 1 can be written to. Thus, even though you may ask to render the new zone, only the zone that's visible through the portal will be rendered.

As this chapter will illustrate, there are a lot of things that you can do with the stencil test. In any decent 3D API, the stencil buffer can be written into, and the test against it can be performed. Either of these two operations can be turned off or on, so you could refrain from writing into the stencil buffer and only check on it, or you could simply write into it without any regard to what was in it previously. When you write into the stencil buffer, any pixel that's written to can be incremented, decremented, inverted, zeroed…

For example, if you wanted to know how much overlap you had in your scene, you could have an incremental function and ask it to render only the pixels where the stencil value is greater than 1 (that is, where the pixel was written to more than once). Similarly, you could count the total amount of overlap (the depth of your scene) by doing this recursively until nothing was visible on the screen. As mentioned in the previous chapter, overlap isn't a good thing and should be minimized whenever possible. This gives you a way to visualize this overlap. You could also use the stencil buffer as a means of showing the scene through a gun's scope (which is circular) by masking the bits that aren't inside the circle.

The z-buffer will be skipped here, because it was already covered in Chapter 15, "Visibility Determination: The World of the Invisible." Thus, this concludes the per-pixel fragment pipeline. You're now ready to tackle some texturing tricks.

Texture Transformations

In the previous chapters, you've a seen a lot of methods that relied on transforming objects in 3D space. For the most part, these transformations were linear and thus were represented in a matrix form. These matrices typically transformed a 4D vector into another 4D vector, and operations such as rotation, translation, scaling, and skewing were demonstrated. Where it starts to become interesting, as you get closer and closer to the pixel renderer, is that the texture coordinates can also be transformed. Typically, when you render a textured triangle, one texture coordinate is given per vertex. This texture coordinate is then mapped to the texture, and the texels (texture's equivalent of a pixel) are mapped onto the screen pixels, as illustrated in Figure 17.2. This mapping is done per pair of edges, so you don't need to worry about it. The interesting part is when you can transform these coordinates.

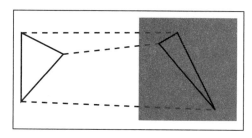

Figure 17.2
Mapping a 2D texture onto a triangle

Any decent 3D API is also equipped with a texture transformation matrix, which is all too often underused. It lies dormant mainly because most programmers don't really know how to use it well. You can do a lot with it if you take the time to think about its capabilities.

The texturing matrix transforms the texture coordinates in the same fashion that the transformation matrix of the camera/world transforms 3D coordinates. For instance, you could use the texture matrix to scale the texture by using the transformations you saw in Chapter 5, "Transformations." Alternatively, you could create a cheap moving-sky effect if you translated your texture over time and placed it at the ceiling. Now you simply need to know how to transform it correctly to achieve the desired effects.

Texture Coordinate Generators

Most 3D APIs are equipped with texture coordinate generators. Typically, these functions set the matrix for you to achieve commonly used tasks. They save you the trouble of setting the texture matrix for every triangle. Instead, you generate it either on the GPU or at the driver level (depending on implementations). It's a good thing to take a look at these generators, since not that many people actually know about them. Many developers tend to implement them the hard way, or simply forget about them.

Object Space Texture Coordinate Generation

The idea here is to generate texture coordinates that are in object space. This means that a texture is applied upon the entire object. For instance, if you have a teapot and it's made out of a certain material, that's given by a texture. You can precompute a bunch of texture coordinates so that the material "fits" the object, or you can simply use this technique to apply the texture to the entire object. It's as if you're wrapping a textured cloth around the object.

This can be useful for terrain. For example, assume that you want to give a certain color to the terrain depending on its height. You can use a 1D texture and apply it to the object (the terrain) along the height axis, y. To simplify the problem, let's say the object is axis-aligned and rotated so that it faces the direction you want to apply the texture on. If you had to determine the $<u, v, w>$ texture coordinate for each vertex, you would only have to assign the value of the vertex to be the texture coordinate, assuming that the object was in the positive octant. In other words, there would be a direct mapping from the vertex's location to the texture coordinate. Since most textures are in 2D, you would discard the information about the depth. Thus, for a vertex $<x, y, z>$, the texture coordinate would be $<x, y>$. It's that simple!

Things can be a little more complicated than that, though. Now you have to extend your thinking to include transformations. In the preceding situation, you looked at the object in object space. In most cases, object space will be conveniently placed so that the center of the object is the origin. This makes rotations about the object much easier. The problem is that the coordinates range from negative to positive in all axes. Ideally, the texture should fit the object exactly (unless you're thinking about applying a repeat mode to repeat the texture). Thus, the range of texture coordinates should be $[0, 1]$, but the vertices of the object probably don't have a range of $[0, 1]$.

The texture transformation matrix should handle this. You should scale the object's texture coordinates so that the extent of the object in all directions is 1 and the center of the object is at $<0.5, 0.5>$, which would finally yield texture coordinates between the range $[0, 1]$. Thus, the transformation matrix **T** for an object bounded by a box of extent $<x, y, z>$ should be as follows:

$$\mathbf{T} = \begin{bmatrix} \dfrac{1}{x} & 0 & 0 & 0.5 \\ 0 & \dfrac{1}{y} & 0 & 0.5 \\ 0 & 0 & \dfrac{1}{z} & 0.5 \\ 0 & 0 & 0 & 1 \end{bmatrix}$$

Because the coordinates you give are in object space, the texture coordinates should be given in object space too. This is what's done if you give $\mathbf{x}$ as texture coordinate for a vertex at position $\mathbf{x}$. Some 3D APIs allow you to specify a plane by which the texture is applied. In this situation, it's just a matter of determining the distance between the vertex and the plane. In this model, it's assumed that the length of the vector indicates how stretched-out the texture should be. In other words, the length of the plane's normal should dictate the extent of the bounding box. Once again, this guarantees that the texture's matrix is utilized correctly.

Think about the trivial case where you have three planes, $\mathbf{x} = <1, 0, 0>$, $\mathbf{y} = <0, 1, 0>$, $\mathbf{z} = <0, 0, 1>$. The distance between a point and a plane is trivially given by

$$d = \left| \langle \mathbf{n}, d \rangle \bullet \langle \mathbf{p}, 1 \rangle \right|$$

Here, <$\mathbf{n}$, d> is the plane and $\mathbf{p}$ is the vertex to be evaluated. This only works if the plane's normal vector is normalized. But in your case, if the normal vector has a length of 2, it will multiply (scale) every component by 2, which is the effect you want to achieve in order to bound the texture coordinates to a [0, 1] range.

The value of d is also important, because the object should lie completely on the positive side of the plane. This enables you to get rid of the absolute value, as well as to completely remove the translation by 0.5. If you choose d such that the plane <$\mathbf{n}$, d> is the closest plane for which every vertex is on the positive side of the plane, you'll effectively achieve this. Since this needs not be done at run-time, you can easily compute the plane that contains a given vertex $\mathbf{p}$ and test that all vertices are on the positive side of it or on it. If the test fails, choose another vertex $\mathbf{p}$ and apply the test again until it passes. As mentioned in the previous chapters, the equation that gives you the value of d is

$$d = -\mathbf{n} \bullet \mathbf{p}$$

The distances between the various planes that have been computed can be placed in a matrix notation, which sets the texturing matrix $\mathbf{P}$ to the following value:

$$\mathbf{P} = \begin{bmatrix} a_x & a_y & a_z & -\mathbf{a} \bullet \mathbf{p} \\ b_x & b_y & b_z & -\mathbf{b} \bullet \mathbf{p} \\ c_x & c_y & c_z & -\mathbf{c} \bullet \mathbf{p} \\ 0 & 0 & 0 & 1 \end{bmatrix}$$

Here, {*a*, *b*, *c*} are the three planes bounding the object with the aforementioned properties. All of this is done for you automatically if you use the texture generation functions of your 3D API. The only thing you have to give to it is the set of planes controlling this. You do need to make sure that the planes have the right length and the right offset, however, or else the generated texture coordinates won't work as you would expect them to.

To wrap things up, the texture coordinate **u** for a vertex **x** is given by this formula:

$$\mathbf{u} = \mathbf{Px}$$

Camera-Space Texture Coordinate Generation

The previous texturing method wrapped a texture around an object by taking the coordinates directly from object space and manipulating them so that they fit the range taken by the texturing unit. Another useful texturing technique is to generate texture coordinates in camera space, also called eye-space. Consequently, regardless of how the object rotates, the texture will always be applied in the same way. In fact, this texturing technique is like inserting a veil in front of a solid-colored object. If your object was a mountain that you were looking at from a top view, you could use this technique to texturize the mountain by having the shadow of a cloud move over it. The texture would need to be translated at regular intervals to simulate the wind in the clouds.

Of course, this would only work if you looked at the object from a top view. As soon as your angle changed, that same shadow would be projected on the mountain as if you were looking at it from a top view. Thus, this isn't the solution, but it's one good step forward.

After all transformations are applied, what you want is for the vertex **x** transformed by the world/camera transformation matrix **M** to be associated with the texture coordinate **t**. Mathematically:

$$\mathbf{t} = \mathbf{Mx}$$

$$\mathbf{x} = \mathbf{M}^{-1}\mathbf{t}$$

Thus, the coordinate **x**, which you've played with in the object-space texture coordinate section, should really be replaced by the equation given previously. **x** becomes **Mx** by using the notation of the object-space texture coordinate generator. Here's the end equation for the texture coordinate **u**:

$$\mathbf{P} = \begin{bmatrix} a_x & a_y & a_z & -\mathbf{a} \bullet \mathbf{p} \\ b_x & b_y & b_z & -\mathbf{b} \bullet \mathbf{p} \\ c_x & c_y & c_z & -\mathbf{c} \bullet \mathbf{p} \\ 0 & 0 & 0 & 1 \end{bmatrix}$$

$$\mathbf{u} = \mathbf{P}\mathbf{M}^{-1}\mathbf{x}$$

$$= \left(\mathbf{P}\mathbf{M}^{-1}\right)\mathbf{x}$$

P here is defined as the angle at which you want the texture to be applied. Regardless of the camera's rotation, the texture will always be applied at the same angle. If you want the texture to be applied in a top view, as in the terrain example, could you simply let this matrix be the identity? Not quite, because it doesn't fit the requirement that the textures must be between [0, 1]. Instead, you should use the matrix **T**, as defined in the next section. So setting the texture matrix to **PM**−1 should do the trick.

If you have a hard time visualizing this geometrically, think of **M** as a mere rotation. Assume that the texture is a piece of paper. Take this piece of paper and rotate it. Because you work in eye-space, the "texture" should still be that of the not-rotated piece of paper, but the paper itself should outline a rotated piece of paper. To find the texture coordinate, you need to remove the rotation in texture space, as the algebra suggests. In short, this is the same equation as in object space (and you can still choose the direction arbitrarily), except that the direction is static to the camera's point of view. That's where the inverse of the world/camera matrix comes in.

Projective Texture Coordinate Generation

The previous two methods were pretty similar. One applied an inverse camera/world matrix to cancel out the effect of the camera's movements, while the other kept it local to the object. Both of them can be considered orthogonal projectors. In other words, if you only use 2D coordinates for your texture, which is the most typical case, you simply ignore the third component. That's the characteristic of an orthogonal projection.

On the other hand, the projective texture coordinate generator uses a perspective projection. Thus, it distorts the scene so that the objects that are farther away from the near plane are scaled. Think of it like a frustum, where typically the near plane is smaller in area than the far plane because the frustum forms a type of pyramid in z. The idea behind this type of texture generator is to project a texture, more or less like you would project slides on a wall. The idea is shown in Figure 17.3.

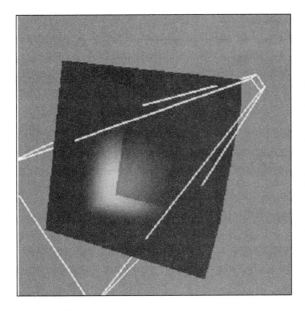

The beauty of this technique is that you can use it to light up your scene. If you combine the object's texture with the light's texture, you can achieve dynamic scene lighting very efficiently. How cool is that? Of course, if you want to be lame, you can project a Batman logo onto some clouds. This technique also enables you to implement the shadows of moving clouds on a mountain, as mentioned previously.

Figure 17.3
Projection of a light map upon a corner

Here, you aren't interested in keeping the texture relative to the eye, so you can forget about the inverse camera matrix. Consequently, you should probably start from the object texture coordinate generator. This enables you to set a static texture on an object from a given angle defined by three planes, and thus the matrix **P** as defined earlier.

$$\mathbf{P} = \begin{bmatrix} a_x & a_y & a_z & -\mathbf{a} \bullet \mathbf{p} \\ b_x & b_y & b_z & -\mathbf{b} \bullet \mathbf{p} \\ c_x & c_y & c_z & -\mathbf{c} \bullet \mathbf{p} \\ 0 & 0 & 0 & 1 \end{bmatrix}$$

$$\mathbf{u} = \mathbf{RPx}$$

R, as defined here, is the projection matrix you've seen before. To wrap things up, this method is the same as the object method, but it adds an extra projection to account for the effect of depth. To be more accurate, the previous method used an orthographic projection, which doesn't distort the values as the depth from the projection point increases, while this method does distort the values. Now you can effortlessly and efficiently achieve your shadow-on-mountain effect.

Omni-Spherical Texture Coordinate Generation

The previous texturing modes generated coordinates that were Cartesian in nature. In other words, the transformation generated textures with range $<[0, 1], [0, 1]>$ and was based on the vertex's position x. Another approach to texturing is to take the normal vector of that vertex. This implies that you're providing normal vectors per vertex. If not, you simply cannot use this technique. To bound the normal vector, you can normalize it. Thus, the normal vector will have a radius of one and two angles free to roam. You also need to make sure that the range of the textures is $[0, 1]$, so you can add 0.5 to the normal vector to make sure that all values are positive.

If you take this same vector and apply camera-space texture transformations on it, you get something really interesting. You get a function that chooses the texture coordinate depending on the angle of the vertex and consequently of the underlying triangle. Here is the matrix T for this transformation and the associated coordinate for the texture u:

$$T = \begin{bmatrix} 0.5 & 0 & 0 & 0.5 \\ 0 & 0.5 & 0 & 0.5 \\ 0 & 0 & 0.5 & 0.5 \\ 0 & 0 & 0 & 1 \end{bmatrix}$$

$$u = TM^{-1} \frac{n}{\|n\|_2}$$

Here, n is the normal vector of the vertex. The matrix T, as defined in the last section, is really the trivial basis. Sphere texture coordinate generators are only defined for the case where the planes are aligned with the camera. Thus, T becomes the identity matrix. Because you have to respect the length of the plane's normal vector and the position of the plane mentioned previously, you have to scale the direction by one half and add one half to guarantee that the coordinates will have a range of $<[0, 1], [0, 1]>$. Due to the construction, this will never generate coordinates outside of the range $[1, \phi]$ in polar coordinates. This means that your texture should always look like a circle (or more appropriately, a 2D representation of a sphere). So at any point, the texture generated is a function of the angle of that vector from the camera's point of view. This angle is really the byproduct of the normal vector, which gives you a sense of direction. The normal gives you more than an angle, because it tells you the length as well.

The texture should always look like a circle or a sphere, and the value at $<x, y>$ on the texture is really the color value for a normal of $<2[*]x - 0.5, 2[*]y - 0.5>$. This is nice, because it means that you can dictate one pixel for various angles. For example, assume that the world you're looking at is really far away from you, far enough that translating doesn't affect your view of it. The stars are a good example of this. If you walk one mile (assuming you can do so instantaneously), it doesn't seem like the stars have moved at all. In reality, the stars do move relative to you, but their movement is so small compared to their distance from you that you don't perceive the difference. Think of your eyes as a camera. When you compute the projection of the light (in 3D) to your eye (in 2D), there is little or no difference in what you perceive.

This can be verified by looking at the projection formulas from Chapter 4, "Basic Geometric Elements," where the projection matrix was first introduced. When simplified, they give the following approximate functions:

$$x' \approx \frac{x}{z}$$

$$y' \approx \frac{y}{z}$$

It's important to apply the projection, because you want your coordinates to be scaled as they go deeper (like a frustum grows larger as you go from the near plane to the far plane). As you can see, if the stars are really far away, z will be very large, and a relatively small change in x or y won't affect the final output very much. In these situations, what you see is independent of the position and purely dependent on the angle (or the direction from which it comes). Typically, this isn't implemented in the 3D APIs. Instead, what's implemented is known as *spherical texture coordinate generation*.

Spherical Texture Coordinate Generation

The details of why this is such will be seen in the next chapter, so don't worry too much if you don't understand where the equations come from yet. This method differs from the previous one in that the input vector, which is given, is the reflection vector from the vertex. A reflection is like a superball bouncing on the ground without the effect of gravity. When the superball hits the ground, it reflects (or rebounds) in a given direction. That direction is what this technique captures as a texture coordinate. Light has this same nature, and thus you can use spherical texturing coordinates to simulate shiny objects, for example. Shiny objects depend on only two things: The point of view of the eye and the normal to the vertex. The equation, which will be much clearer in the following chapter, is as defined here:

$$\mathbf{T} = \begin{bmatrix} 0.5 & 0 & 0 & 0.5 \\ 0 & 0.5 & 0 & 0.5 \\ 0 & 0 & 1 & 0 \\ 0 & 0 & 0 & 1 \end{bmatrix}$$

$$\mathbf{n'} = \mathbf{M}^{-1} \frac{\mathbf{n}}{\|\mathbf{n}\|_2}$$

$$\mathbf{v} = \left(\mathbf{e} - 2\mathbf{n'}(\mathbf{e} \bullet \mathbf{n'}) \right)$$

$$m = \sqrt{v_x^2 + v_y^2 + (v_z + 1)^2}$$

$$\mathbf{u} = \frac{\mathbf{Tv}}{2m}$$

As with the other method, this is only valid for 2D/1D textures. It doesn't make any sense for 3D textures because of the normalization. Here, $\mathbf{e}$ is the camera-pixel vector. At this point, you may wonder why you have to divide $\mathbf{v}$ by a very weird norm. This merely helps you generate the texture beforehand and introduces a nice spherical relationship in the texture by attributing a weight (that is, a pulling force, which makes it look like a sphere) to the various texels. If you look at a spherical map texture, all texels contained by the radius

$$r = \frac{1}{2\sqrt{2}}$$

represent the reflection vectors that sample the light in front of the shape, while the remainder of the radius represents the sample of the light behind the shape. If you take a plane and cut a sphere in half so that the plane is aligned with the view vector, what lies on the positive side of the plane (toward the viewer) is what lies in front of the sphere. So in short, it's possible to see the reflection of what's behind the sphere by looking at the radius greater than r. This may sound impossible, but the next chapter will fully explain this phenomenon.

The nice thing about this relationship is that there's as much area describing the pixels behind the sphere as there is describing the front half of the sphere. In short, each one is represented equally with this construction, and m is what makes this a reality. To be mathematically correct, m is the scalar that allows you to project the 3D normal vector to 2D.

The inner workings of this aren't really important in this chapter (although they will be in the next one). Here, you're particularly interested in how such textures can be generated and used. Because this technique takes the reflection vector into account and not just the normal vector, it can be used for any object that's reflective in nature. Pretty much any object built out of metallic coating, for example. The nice thing about reflection vectors is that they actually depend on the position of the object. If you take a spoon and move it, you'll see different things in the spoon as it moves. The previous technique didn't do this. It allowed you to see the same thing regardless of the object's position, but reflective objects don't work like this.

Thus, you can use spherical textures to simulate environment mapping. This technique is built on the idea that the environment reflects on the object. As with the previous method, this assumes that the environment is endlessly far from you for all practical purposes. In other words, it assumes that the object always stays relatively in the same position. (Remember the example of you walking on the Earth and looking up at the stars.) Obviously, if you generate a spherical texture and have a box very close to you, moving to the other side of the box should *show* you the other side of the box (in all good reflective theory). But with spherical textures, the texture is generated only on one side of the box, so you'll never actually see the other side even if you move over there. This is the shortcoming of these textures, but if your environment is reasonably far from the object, having the object move isn't a problem.

Another use for spherical texture coordinate generation is to add highlights to an object. The highlight discussed here is the reflection of the light source upon the object. For instance, this could be light from a bulb directly reflected on a plastic lamp. This generates a spherical highlight on the object, which is of course purely dependent on the angle and the viewing position. Consequently, you can generate a sphere map with a very strong highlight in the center and pure blackness around it. Using this on an object will generate this highlight without a problem.

Generating sphere maps with 3D authoring tools is very easy. All you have to do is create a sphere at the position from which you would like to see the world. Due to the construction of the texture generation, this sphere should be as small as possible so as not to occlude or touch any objects. The sphere should have complete reflectivity, and what you want to grab as a texture is the sphere itself. You can keep the world rendered around the sphere, but it's useless since it won't be used for sphere texture coordinate generation. Figure 17.4 shows an example of environment mapping applied to a gun; Figure 17.5 shows the same thing with added highlights, which can also be achieved with spherical environment mapping.

Figure 17.4
A gun rendered with environment mapping

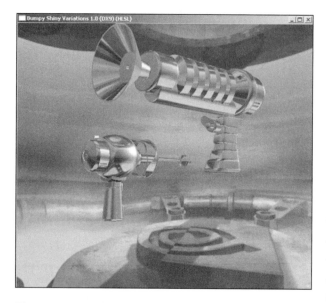

Figure 17.5
A gun rendered with highlights and environment mapping

Cube Texture Coordinate Generation

The spherical coordinate generator is great for things such as highlights and distant environments, but it does have a few annoying traits. For one, it doesn't have many samples. You would need a pretty large texture to represent the environment accurately. For things such as reflective metals and highlights, you don't really need that much detail, so it's perfectly suited for those cases. The other nuisance is that it's very hard to generate in real time. If you assume that the environment isn't far from the view, in an ideal world, you would have to generate the texture at every frame. This would work to some degree, even for spherical texgen. You could generate what the object should see from a given point by generating the texture, and then using this texture to render it upon the object. The only problem is that generating this texture isn't something you can do efficiently on hardware, due to the spherical nature of the texture.

To fix this issue, along comes cube texturing. Instead of using one texture to apply on the object spherically, you use six planes defining a cube. The input vector is still based on the reflective vector of the vertex, so this can still be used for environment mapping and highlights. This means the following still holds:

$$\mathbf{n}' = \mathbf{M}^{-1} \frac{\mathbf{n}}{\|\mathbf{n}\|_2}$$

$$\mathbf{v} = \left(\mathbf{e} - 2\mathbf{n}'(\mathbf{e} \bullet \mathbf{n}')\right)$$

What really changes is the way the vector **v** is projected onto the set of textures. Here, you have six textures, so the first thing that should be done is to isolate which texture your reflective vector really refers to. You decide the plane and the coordinate of the texture by looking at the sign of the component with the largest absolute value. There are many other ways to split it; this just happens to be one of them. Once you've identified the component with the largest absolute value, you've isolated the problem by finding two potential textures. If this corresponds to the x axis, for example, it means that the plane is either the right or left plane of the cube. Similarly, for y, it is the top or bottom plane of the cube and z stands for the near/far planes, the actual sign of that component will tell you which of the two planes it is.

For instance, if your coordinate system is such that the negative x component is at the left, having a negative component of x when the absolute value of x is greater than the absolute value of y and z means that the texture in question is the one at the left. If you apply a perspective projection, as shown in Chapter 4, you can keep the law of similar triangle in mind, and you can easily see how each vector gets projected upon the 2D texture map. Table 17.1 shows the matrices defining this.

Thus, if you had a vector <1, 2, 3> and wanted to compute the texture coordinate, the following is how you would achieve this:

$$\mathbf{x} = \langle 1, 2, 3 \rangle$$

$$|3| > 2 > 1 \rightarrow z$$

$$\mathbf{v} = \mathbf{T}\mathbf{x}$$

$$= \begin{bmatrix} \dfrac{0.5}{z} & 0 & 0 & 0.5 \\ 0 & \dfrac{-0.5}{z} & 0 & 0.5 \\ 0 & 0 & 1 & 0 \\ 0 & 0 & 0 & 1 \end{bmatrix} \begin{bmatrix} x \\ y \\ z \\ 1 \end{bmatrix}$$

$$\begin{bmatrix} v_x \\ v_y \end{bmatrix} = \begin{bmatrix} \dfrac{x}{2z} + 0.5 \\ -\dfrac{y}{2z} + 0.5 \end{bmatrix}$$

Table 17.1 Matrices Defining Vector Projection

Face	Matrix	Projection Variable
x < 0, -x > |y|, -x > |z|	$\begin{bmatrix} 0 & 0 & -0.5 & 0.5 \\ 0 & 0.5 & 0 & 0.5 \\ 0 & 0 & 1 & 0 \\ 0 & 0 & 0 & 1 \end{bmatrix}$	x
x > 0, x > |y|, x > |z|	$\begin{bmatrix} 0 & 0 & -0.5 & 0.5 \\ 0 & -0.5 & 0 & 0.5 \\ 0 & 0 & 1 & 0 \\ 0 & 0 & 0 & 1 \end{bmatrix}$	x
y < 0, -y > |x|, -y > |z|	$\begin{bmatrix} -0.5 & 0 & 0 & 0.5 \\ 0 & 0 & 0.5 & 0.5 \\ 0 & 0 & 1 & 0 \\ 0 & 0 & 0 & 1 \end{bmatrix}$	y
y > 0, y > |x|, y > |z|	$\begin{bmatrix} -0.5 & 0 & 0 & 0.5 \\ 0 & 0 & -0.5 & 0.5 \\ 0 & 0 & 1 & 0 \\ 0 & 0 & 0 & 1 \end{bmatrix}$	y
z < 0, -z > |x|, -z > |y|	$\begin{bmatrix} 0.5 & 0 & 0 & 0.5 \\ 0 & 0.5 & 0 & 0.5 \\ 0 & 0 & 1 & 0 \\ 0 & 0 & 0 & 1 \end{bmatrix}$	z
z > 0, z > |x|, z > |y|	$\begin{bmatrix} 0.5 & 0 & 0 & 0.5 \\ 0 & -0.5 & 0 & 0.5 \\ 0 & 0 & 1 & 0 \\ 0 & 0 & 0 & 1 \end{bmatrix}$	z

The projection in this case is in accordance with the projection you've seen in the previous chapter, where the distance between the eye and the plane is 1 (which is the case for a texture <[0, 1], [0, 1]>). That wasn't so hard, now, was it?

The generation of these texture coordinates is also pretty simple. Due to the cubic nature of cube mapping, it's possible from the fictitious textured cube's center to choose a frustum that looks purely at one texture. This is ideal for in-game cube map generation. You simply need to set the correct rotations and frustum size, and you should be able to render the world from a given view to generate one cube map texture. If you apply this for every one of the six textures, you can generate a cube map on the fly and use that as an environment.

You can look at this process from a mere angular level. Suppose you rotate around the z axis. There are 360 degrees in spherical coordinates for the camera to rotate and return to its original starting point. The cube map, on the other hand, has four textures if you rotate in z. Thus, you have 360 degrees for four textures, which is 90 degrees per texture. If you build a frustum that has an angle of 90 degrees or $\pi/2$ rad, you can generate all four side textures. You can then do the remaining two planes (top/bottom), and you'll have successfully generated all six textures for the cube map.

The only "gotcha" with this method is that you need to render the world six times from six different points of view. This means a considerably slower frame rate. If you can determine that some textures aren't needed, you can save yourself the generation of a few textures. Whenever possible, you should use display lists, because they will all precompile the required computations. You only need to add a rotation before calling the list at that point.

Another way to reduce bandwidth and increase frame rate is to render the scene at a slightly decreased quality. For instance, you may want to turn lighting off, use a cheaper texturing method, and omit objects that are remotely distant from the center of the cube map generation. This is especially true if you're planning to use this technique in real time with a good frame rate. In this case, the small details may not be that important in the reflection. You could add an extra texture on top of that to blur things a little bit (such as a dirty window), to diminish the effect of the loss in quality.

Cube Map Tricks

Interestingly enough, cube maps can be used for much more than may be apparent on the surface. As previously stated, what makes the cube map so appealing is that it can attribute up to four values for a given angle. In the previous example, cube maps were used to texture objects, and the four values attributed were the red, green, blue, and alpha channels.

The other thing that makes cube maps much more attractive than spherical maps is that they provide a good sampling of the angles. The spherical map has only one texture, and thus has a poor resolution. The cube map offers six textures, and also better resolution. As you'll see in the following subsections, cube maps can do some very helpful things.

Normalization Cube Map

Using an array of constants is nothing new in the gaming industry. In the early days, tables were used for cosine and sine functions. Even today, such tables would yield faster results than computing a function through the GPU's functions, but the lack of precision offered by these tables has made them unattractive for such operations. Normalizing a vector is quite an easy task, and it's even easier when the GPU generates it for you in an efficient manner.

As this book has shown, it's sometimes quite important to normalize vectors. The next chapter will stress this even more. Unfortunately, if you look at the normalization equation for the CPU to compute, it's anything but pretty:

$$\mathbf{n}' = \frac{\mathbf{n}}{\sqrt{\mathbf{n} \bullet \mathbf{n}}}$$

It involves one square root (how ugly), one division per component (unattractive), and one square per component (acceptable). Wouldn't it be nice if you could simply take this vector **n**, throw it into an index, and retrieve a normalized vector? You wouldn't have to compute anything, and you would just need to do a lookup.

All of this is possible, thanks to cube maps. The cube map, as you may recall, doesn't require a normalized vector as input. It takes an arbitrary vector **n**, indexes it into one of the six textures, and spits out another vector that has previously been used as a color component. In other words, the cube map enables you to map a vector's direction to another vector. Pretty powerful, no?

If the vector contained by the cube map is the normalized version of the input vector, you can get a cheap normalization function for your fragment shaders. Due to the nature of the cube map, the values that are encoded will have to be written so as to fit the range of the colors $[0, 1]$. Thus, a little work will be required to ensure this is respected. A normalized vector typically has a range of $[-1, 1]$ per component. Thus, if you divide the range by 2 and translate the values by one-half, you can safely store a normalized vector. The following equation shows this:

$$\mathbf{c}_n = \frac{\mathbf{n} + 1}{2}$$

Simple enough, right?

To retrieve the vector, obviously, you'll have to do the opposite. In that case, you'll have to multiply the resulting vector by 2 and subtract one. This will effectively give you the normalized vector that was encoded in the cube map. But remember, just because vectors are often used for real coordinates or colors, those aren't the only things you can do with them. Think outside the box.

Sky Boxes

If you've attempted to write an outdoor game, you've likely come upon the problem of rendering the far environment. Some games like to place a few clouds in the sky; others like to make it look like you're near a planet or in mountainous scenery. Whichever scenario inspires you, sky boxes can come to the rescue.

If you recall how cube maps are generated, basically you have the entire solution in front of you. Taking a snapshot of the surrounding world from six mutually exclusive angles generates the six textures for the cube map. The important part is that these sections are mutually exclusive. In other words, the scenery information absorbed by a texture is unique. If you see a ball in one of the textures, you shouldn't see the same ball at all in any of the remaining five textures (unless it spans two frustums). Furthermore, the cube map textures take a 3D environment and render it upon a cube, regardless of the complexity of this world.

What does that mean to you? Well, it means that instead of rendering an extremely complex world, you can render a cube where the six textures related to the six faces of the cube compose the cube map. The cube samples the entire world, so you'll see the entire world by rendering this cube map. Furthermore, because the snapshots are taken from mutually exclusive and adjacent angles, you'll generate a seemingly continuous 360-degree world with a mere box.

To render this effect, simply render a cube that is centered about the camera. In other words, rotation is the only transformation by which the cube should be affected. Of course, you should disable *z*-buffering, because you can assume that the scenery is infinitely far. The nice thing about it is that at any point in time, you should see at most three faces of the cube. Furthermore, you don't actually need to clear the screen at all, because the cube map will always overwrite whatever was there before. The size of the cube you render does not really matter. Because you are at the center of the cube, increasing its size will have no effect on the final visual appearance.

This is a great trick to use. A box is lightning-fast to render, and it gives a great depth to the scenery to have the environment rendered. The beauty of this technique is that it feels continuous. On a good rendering platform, you won't see the discontinuity in the cube map. If you associate the camera's rotational movement with the sky box's rotational movement, it will feel like you're truly in the environment. Of course, once again, this assumes that the scenery is relatively far from the viewer. If you rotate your head, you may see a slightly different angle on an object that is close. But try rotating your head all you want, and I bet that you'll always see the same angle of the moon. It's amazing how such a simple trick and a bit of math can make a big problem into a really small problem.

Cel Shading

Figure 17.6
Ship rendered as a toon

Cel shading is what is used to render cartoons. These elements are surprisingly easy to draw. There are two things that make an object look very realistic. The first one is the color depth. The fewer colors you have, the more cartoonish the drawing looks. In a cartoon, light is grossly approximated. In other words, sometimes a cartoon has a single fill color instead of having a really complex light color gradient. The nicer ones have 4–10 shades of a color, which are still grossly chosen. In other words, there isn't a nice progressive gradient from one color to the other. Typically, it appears more like patches of colors. The last observation that is necessary for rendering cartoons is that they're mostly bounded by black strokes. Figure 17.6 shows an example of a toon.

So at this point, you know what you want to achieve. Now you have to look at how you can achieve it. The most obvious thing is that lighting should be disabled. As soon as you use a form of hardware-provided default lighting in your scene, you inevitably introduce a color gradient (such as GL's lights, for example). You've already established that this isn't something you want for a cartoon. If you look at the way a cartoon is lit, there's always a more predominant color, and sometimes the darker colors are simply there to delimit things that stand out about the object. For instance, a character's neck might be delimited with a black stroke, and the neck itself might be darker than the face.

There are two types of cartoons. Some use a solid color and a black stroke to delimit the objects. The fancier ones use various shades of the predominant color inside the characters or objects. Let's try to understand the first and easiest type.

One way you can achieve this is by rendering the object in wireframe mode with a thick black color. This will render the entire object using thick lines. Once this is completed, you can render the solid fill into the object by rendering the triangles composing it. This will effectively render a solid object with a black border. The only problem is that it leaves the border as black. If you wanted to draw a round nose, for example, you wouldn't see a black border around the nose because it was overwritten by the fill. This can be good for some cases, but it doesn't work for most cases. Fortunately, you already know how to find the edges that compose the boundary of an object.

The last chapter detailed a visibility technique to determine the boundary edges of a convex object. As it turns out, this same algorithm can also be used for non-convex objects to find the edges of the contour. In fact, a contour is any edge where the triangle on one side of the edge is visible and the triangle on the other side of the edge isn't visible. If you keep track of this set of edges, you can determine exactly which ones should have a black outline.

Also observe how this takes care of the nose. If the nose is like a sphere (as it often is), some faces of the sphere will be hidden in a front view. This means that some contour edges will exist in that vicinity, and thus can be blackened by this technique. Due to this new rendering technique, you'll have to reverse the rendering order. By that, I mean that you should first fill the object and then draw the contour. At that point, you don't really need to have a thickness greater than 1, as in the previous situation. You can have lines as thick as you want, since the order forces the line to be visible anyway.

The only catch is that you have to be careful about occlusion. You shouldn't render black lines that lie underneath the cartoon. For this, you can introduce a polygon offset that will push the line toward the camera just enough that it will pass the z-buffer test. Alternatively, you could also apply the offset yourself if your 3D API didn't provide it, simply by moving the line toward the camera by a small value.

This covers the black contour of a cartoon, but it doesn't help you to shade it with more than one color. A cartoon is really nothing but a less detailed object. By that, I mean that whereas an object would have perhaps 100 million colors, a cartoon makes a gross approximation and may only have 10 colors. In other words, you can take any texture you have and reduce the number of colors to do the trick.

If you choose to have a non-textured cartoon that has a single color, you may still want to introduce some form of lighting effect on the cartoon. Most cartoons that take lighting into account also produce a gross approximation of it by adding ~4 shades of color for lighting purposes. Again, you can reproduce this effect by lighting the object grossly. Sphere mapping attributes a single color to various reflection vectors. For cartoons, the approximation is much more gross than that. Instead, you probably just want to attribute one color per angle. In other words, the fact that the light comes from the top, bottom, or left isn't that important. If it's all the same, you can use a 1D texture, which depends purely on the angle between the view and the normal of the triangles. In this case, you can compute the coordinate of the texture coordinate u yourself, with the following equation:

$$u = \mathbf{n} \bullet \mathbf{l}$$

Assuming that **n** and **l** are unitary, this will map the texture coordinate to a $[-1, 1]$ range, but the values within the range $[-1, 0]$ are really backfaces and thus are hidden. This gives you a function that maps the angle between the view and the normal into a 1D texture. To create the texture, you must choose which color should represent which angle. Generally, you'll want the color to drop off in a spherical fashion so that only the edges that are close or that compose the contour will be more heavily lit.

If you plan to implement this in a vertex shader, then you can use a normal lighting function such as those found in Chapter 18, "Building a Light Show," but add a simple function that converts the precise color into a 3- or 4-step color. The entire idea behind toon shading is simple. Take a gradient-shaded color and convert it into a function that allows only a limited amount of colors.

Shadows

There are numerous ways to add shadows to a game. Some solutions are geometric, others are purely based on rasterization, and yet others are based on texturing. In my opinion, right now there's only one decent shadowing technique, which is also the core of the new *Doom 3* engine.

Before you look at that solution, let's quickly take a look at what is still a clever technique. There's no point in going into this technique in any depth, because it has a drastic drawback that makes it useless for any decent-quality game.

Shadow Mapping

Shadow mapping is the idea of mapping a shadow texture upon the world. You can think of it as the projection of a texture as was done before, but with a tweak. If you simply project a shadow texture on the world, you won't respect the order of things. In other words, an object that occludes others will be shadowed as much as the object that causes the shadow. This obviously becomes a problem.

This technique requires various rendering passes in order to achieve the final image. The more complex the technique, typically the more passes you have to apply. Generally, you want to keep the number of passes pretty low, because it implies rendering the scene a few times. As you've seen in the cube map generation, this can be up to six times (seven times, if you include the actual scene from the eye's point of view). If you draw the scene from the light's point of view, you can get a function that maps a coordinate into a depth by the z-buffer. If you render the scene from the eye, the z-buffer will be a function that can map a vertex $<x, y>$ into a depth z. Thus, if you have a vertex $<x, y, z>$, you know according to the z-buffer that any value for z, given x and y, is shadowed beyond what the z-buffer contains. After you've rendered the scene from the light's point of view, if you take any coordinate in space $<x, y, z>$, the value is shadowed if the value for z is greater than the z-buffer's value.

This is true by the very construction of the z-buffer. The light's viewpoint is actually the only viewpoint in the entire scene where you can see the light, and in which the shadow is completely occluded by the object. This viewpoint makes it ideal for generating a depth reference map (which is the z-buffer). Obviously, you render the scene from the eye's point of view, so all you need to do is find the function that converts any coordinate in eye-space into a coordinate in light-space. If you do this, you merely need to compare the z value, and you'll be able to tell whether or not the pixel in eye-space is shadowed.

You won't actually go into the math for this technique, because it has a serious problem that makes it impractical or at least very ugly for games with omni-directional lights. It's pretty efficient, since the hardware supports these transformations, and that test can also be performed in hardware. But one of the big problems with this technique is that it's limited to the resolution of the z-buffer. In other words, the precision can only be as good as the precision offered in the z-buffer, and you've already determined that the z-buffer has a poor resolution. This may be satisfactory in some cases; it really depends how you set up your scene and how fast everything is moving, plus the resolution. Sometimes the z-buffer is not even good enough to depth-sort a mere scene, let alone a shadow map, but once again, it depends how deep your scene goes. As was seen in the visibility chapter, the z-buffer can generate artifacts. The biggest problem is that it's not possible to create omni-directional lights because this technique assumes a projective light model. Unfortunately, this restriction cannot be alleviated unless you want to render multiple depth-maps.

Stencil Shadows

Stencil shadows tackle the problem from a geometrical perspective. When using something such as the z-buffer or textures as references, you're inherently limited by the resolution of the z-buffer (24/32 bits). If you approach the problem geometrically, you need heavier computations, but the precision is as good as floats will allow you to have.

The stencil shadow technique is heavily based on the object occlusion technique. In fact, it can be shown that any occlusion problem really is a shadow problem, and vice versa. To be more precise, the shadow is the region of occlusion given an object and a point of view, which so happens to be the light source for shadows.

Interestingly enough, you have already taken a look at a method that can find the occlusion of bounded volumes given a convex object. The method given in the occlusion chapter first finds the boundary of the object, and then it generates a set of planes from the viewpoint of these edges, which ends up creating an occlusion volume. By the definition given previously, this occlusion volume is the "shadowed volume" of the object. This volume is illustrated in Figure 17.7, while the effect is illustrated in Figure 17.8.

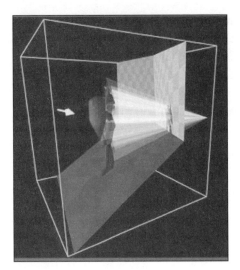

Figure 17.7
Shadow volume of a model

Figure 17.8
The shadow of a knight

What I'm getting at here is that you should already know a technique to generate the shadow volume of an object given a light point. The technique shown previously was only defined for a convex object that occludes a scene, but this same algorithm will work for a concave shape as well. The reason why the occlusion algorithm requires a convex body is that it's much easier to test for a point inside a convex body. It's not impossible to check this with a concave body, but it's significantly more involved. Fortunately, in this case it doesn't matter if the volume is convex or not.

Once you've identified the shadow region by keeping the set of shadow bounding planes, you still haven't solved the problem. You cannot render the volume as-is with alpha blending so as to darken the area. Well, you could, but it wouldn't generate the shadow as you would expect it to be. In other words, the shadow wouldn't be projected on the shapes. Instead, it would feel like there was a window in front of the screen, which darkens an area. If you still don't see it, think about a simple scenario where there's a light with an object blocking it. Assume that the ground is flat. What you should see is a shadow in the ground and not the actual frustum of the shadow. Thus, you need some way to mask out the pixels that aren't shadowed.

As the name of the technique suggests, the stencil buffer is your savior here. The technique relies on a simple observation. With a convex shadow frustum, if an object is shadowed, it's because at least one face of the object lies behind the frustum polygons that are visible from the eye's point of view, and in front of the polygons that are backfaced from the eye's point of view. This is simply another way of saying that the object is "inside" the shadow frustum.

The algorithm first requires you to render the actual scene as-is with the depth buffer toggled on. The trick is to find every vertex for which the front face of the frustum shadow is the frontmost polygon. This will give you a set of vertices that are contained in the frustum shadow and that are visible. It's pointless to shadow an area if there's already an object in front of it that occludes the entire scene. Given this set, remove all vertices for which the backface of the shadow frustum is visible, and this set of vertices will be the ones that should be shadowed.

This may sound a bit confusing, but it's really simple. It was previously mentioned that an object, and more precisely a pixel, should be shadowed if it lies behind the front faces of the frustum and in front of the backfaces of the frustum. In other words, the pixel is inside the shadow frustum. If you take all the vertices that are behind the shadow frustum and remove the vertices for which there's no pixel before the backfaces of the shadow frustum, you're left with the pixels that are inside the shadow frustum and thus must be shaded.

There is one little problem you still have to deal with. All this is only true for a convex shadow. What happens if the shadow isn't convex? The idea still works, because a concave polygon viewed from the side can really be seen as a set of convex polygons. In other words, if you take a line that goes from the camera out to infinity, the line may enter the shadow frustum, but it will necessarily exit it before potentially entering another part of the shadow frustum.

You can achieve the same effect if you keep track of how many times this virtual line crosses boundaries. Suppose you start by rendering the front faces of the shadow frustum. For a pixel $<x, y>$ on the screen, every time the shadow's polygon is above the value in the z-buffer (closer to the camera), you should increment the stencil buffer of one for $<x, y>$, implying that you've entered the frustum from the front once. Because you don't actually want the shadow frustum to be rendered as-is, you should render the frustum such as it only modifies the stencil buffer, and not the color or depth buffer.

For the second pass, you'll have to render the backfaces of the shadow, and in that case, you'll have to match the front faces with the backfaces. Thus, you should set the rules so that the stencil buffer decrements if the shadow frustum is visible. This would mean that this line has crossed both boundaries of the frustum and the pixel is not shaded. If an object was between the front and back shadow frustum, the backfaces of the frustum wouldn't decrement the shadow volume, because the depth of the object was above that of the frustum and therefore would leave a 1 in the frustum. Once you're done with this, you have a stencil buffer with values of zero where the pixels shouldn't be shadowed, and non-zero values when the pixels should be shadowed.

At that point, you can render a set of shadows using the same stencil buffer in order to save some rendering time. Once you've fully identified which pixels are shadowed with the stencil buffer, all you have to do is apply a solid alpha-blended polygon (a dark transparent polygon) to give the effect of shadowing. That's all there is to it.

This sounds almost too easy, and it is. If the camera is inside the shadow frustum, you have a problem. The stencil will only change one time, because some of the front faces might be hidden behind the camera. This is obviously a problem, but it can be fixed pretty easily. Instead of checking if the shadow frustum's polygons pass the z-buffer test, let's test the opposite. In other words, let's check if the test fails. If the test fails for the front faces, you can increment, and if the test fails for backfaces, you can decrement. What if the test never fails (the line goes in and out of the frustum, and the stencil buffer isn't actually touched)? This is nothing but the inverse of the previous test, which will obviously still work, so how does this help you? Well, suppose that the shadow frustum is a closed shape. Being inside that frustum will actually toggle the bit of the stencil's shadow polygon, but since the front face isn't visible, it won't untoggle it. So the test works perfectly both inside and outside the camera.

Now the only problem left is determining how to bound the shadow frustum. It's not very hard. The first step is to cap the frustum from the occluding object's triangles. You can simply use the object's frontface triangles to cap the volume. This cap is akin to the near plane, because it's the closest plane from the light's point of view. Now you need to find what is akin to the far plane. This is pretty tricky business, because you can run into very nasty cases. For instance, if the omnidirectional light is inside a pot that has holes in it, a plane won't do the job because two holes may be opposite one another. Instead, you can project the backfaces of the occlusion object to infinity. But exactly how can you project to infinity? Something doesn't seem right!

In the texture projection section, one thing was omitted. A typical projection matrix won't work very well in every case. That's because the projection matrix that you've seen actually clips everything to the frustum planes, and thus also clips to the z-plane. Obviously, if you project a texture on a wall, there really isn't any restriction on the length of the projection, thus making the typical projection matrix undesirable. Here is the typical perspective projection matrix $\mathbf{P}$:

$$\mathbf{P} = \begin{bmatrix} \dfrac{2e}{b-a} & 0 & 0 & 0 \\[2mm] 0 & \dfrac{2e}{d-c} & 0 & 0 \\[2mm] \dfrac{b+a}{b-a} & \dfrac{d+c}{d-c} & \dfrac{-f-e}{f-e} & -1 \\[2mm] 0 & 0 & \dfrac{-2ef}{f-e} & 0 \end{bmatrix}$$

Here, d is the distance from the eye to the near plane, and f is the distance to the far plane. If you evaluate what happens as the far plane tends towards infinity, you can effectively achieve what you're looking for:

$$\lim_{f \to \infty} \mathbf{P} = \begin{bmatrix} \dfrac{2e}{b-a} & 0 & 0 & 0 \\ 0 & \dfrac{2e}{d-c} & 0 & 0 \\ \dfrac{b+a}{b-a} & \dfrac{d+c}{d-c} & -1 & -1 \\ 0 & 0 & -2e & 0 \end{bmatrix}$$

Chapter 7, "Accelerated Vector Calculus for the Uninitiated," didn't take a very thorough look at the evaluation of a limit from an intuitive perspective. An intuitive method is always good for posing a decent guess, but it doesn't guarantee that it's the solution. You would indeed have to go through the rigorous math if you wanted to determine with certainty that your guess was correct. In this situation, you can see that as f tends towards extremely large numbers, e virtually becomes insignificant. If you substitute e with 0 to represent its insignificance, you get the ratio of -1. If you apply the same logic in the second case, you'll have a faulty guess, thus the importance of verifying your guess. In this specific case, you can divide both the top and bottom portion of the fraction by f. This will give you the following:

$$\lim_{f \to \infty} \frac{-2ef}{f-e} = \lim_{f \to \infty} \frac{-2e}{1 - \dfrac{e}{f}}$$

$$= \frac{-2e}{1-0}$$

$$= -2e$$

As a matter of fact, this method can also be used on the previous case, and you'll see yet again that the result is -1. Because of precision, unfortunately, this matrix can yield normalized coordinates with a z-component slightly larger than 1. Why should you care? Well, the hardware performs a transformation from eye-space to clip-space in order to clip the points. This normalizes the vector, and if your infinite projection has relatively bad precision, it may be detected as clipped when you don't want it to be clipped at all in z.

To fix this, you can add a small positive constant to the range. Thus, instead of having a range of $[-1, 1]$ for z, you can have a range that is slightly shifted $[-1, 1 + \varepsilon]$. If you work the math for it, you should get the final projection matrix:

$$\lim_{f \to \infty} \mathbf{P} = \begin{bmatrix} \dfrac{2e}{b-a} & 0 & 0 & 0 \\ 0 & \dfrac{2e}{d-c} & 0 & 0 \\ \dfrac{b+a}{b-a} & \dfrac{d+c}{d-c} & \varepsilon-1 & -1 \\ 0 & 0 & n(\varepsilon-2) & 0 \end{bmatrix}$$

Consequently, if you want to save yourself the trouble of building the matrix from scratch, you can load a typical projection matrix and modify the two parameters that are different from the typical perspective projection matrix. Namely, these are the ones including epsilon. Alternatively, some cards actually support a mode called depth clamping. This enables you to clamp the normalized vectors to the range of $[-1, 1]$. That way you don't need to worry about epsilon, but you still need to modify the matrix before it's modified with epsilon.

Another approach based on the same idea is to render the scene using different lighting models, covered in Chapter 18. The idea is pretty much the same, but instead of using a polygon to darken/shadow an area, you can render the scene once with ambient lighting—that is, light that is common to shadowed and non-shadowed regions. Then you should render the shadow volume in order to determine which region is shadowed using the stencil buffer, but without modifying the on-screen color. Finally, you can render the scene again by enabling all lights. Thanks to the stencil buffer, this should only render the objects that are not within the shadow, and thus should light them correctly. The unfortunate thing about this technique is that it does require you to render everything twice (or a little less with some optimizations), and it requires much more work than simply darkening an area. The added effect you get, however, is that the scene is lit correctly as far as the physical description of light is concerned.

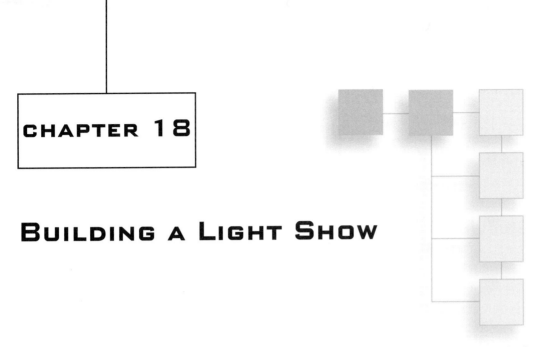

CHAPTER 18

BUILDING A LIGHT SHOW

The newest technological advance in games has been done on the graphical end of things. The initial PC architecture started out with a mere CPU. Later on, the FPU (floating-point unit) helped you accelerate lagging floating-point functions. Not too long after that, the concept of having the equivalent of two CPUs in one was invented. (This isn't two full CPUs running in parallel, but a single CPU with another partial CPU built-in, enabling you to run a partial set of instructions in parallel. The Pentium chips started this trend, which has since been put aside in favor of the out-of-order execution cache.) Finally, the latest processor step is the GPU, a fully programmable graphical processing unit. This is the dream of so many programmers since the beginning of time (or the invention of the PC, at least).

This means a few things for today's game programmers. It means that you need to balance the workload between the CPU and the GPU. The GPU is powerful enough to let you describe an algorithm that sets the color of the pixel and/or the location of that vertex. This is powerful, because you can do a lot of fancy things (dot products, cross product) naturally and accelerated by the GPU. The actual how-to of this isn't the purpose of this book. You should take a look at any book covering shaders for more on this topic.

Although this is a really nice thing, it's also very recent, so there are no helper libraries to help you implement the fancy stuff you may see in games today. In order to take full advantage of the GPU, it's crucial to understand the inner workings of light and how it interacts with the environment. Without this knowledge, you'll have a hard time deciding on the color a given pixel should hold.

Specifically, this chapter covers the following:

- The rasterization pipeline
- Lighting a ray-tracing model
- Light sources
- Lighting models

Studying the Rasterization Pipeline

In Chapter 13, "Exploring Curvy Bodies," you took a deep look at the fragment 3D pipeline, but you didn't actually look at the texturing/rasterization stage. This stage of the pipeline is responsible for sampling a texel (the equivalent of a pixel for a texture), applying a set of operations on it, and blitting it to the screen. It may sound like a really simple task, but it's much more involved than you may initially believe. Choosing the color of a single texture, even if you're only thinking about a simple texture without any form of light, still requires a little bit of sampling theory in order to produce a good-looking texture.

Sampling theory is the branch of math that looks at sampling values (in this case colors) out of a data source. It's important to understand this in order to understand the techniques used in today's hardware, and also to give you a sense of how slow one method can be when compared with another. Fortunately, a lot of the material here works very well with the information found in Chapter 13 because that chapter also dealt with sampling. It described a function that can be used for sampling purposes. The difference is that here, you are only interested in a particular sample and not really the entire function. Nonetheless, the next few sections should enlighten you on the techniques that are already implemented within most 3D APIs.

Texture Fetch

This is the unit that's responsible for retrieving the pixel color from the texture. This may sound like an easy task at first, but it does have its caveats. As specified by most 3D APIs, the texture data that's handed down to the 3D engine contains the coordinates of the texture. These coordinates can be 3D, 2D, or 1D. A 3D texture you can actually see as the description of the color in 3D. For example, it could be useful if you wanted to draw a rock and you could chip off pieces of it. What you can do is create a 3D texture that describes the color of the rock at $<x, y, z>$. As you remove pieces of the rock, the texture can map the values directly from the object's coordinate in object space to the texture coordinate.

A 1D texture, on the other hand, could be a texture that's dependent on something such as the curvature of the object. If you wanted to have various degrees of illumination depending on the angle, you could use a 1D texture where the values of texture $[0, 1]$ would get you a highly illuminated texture color down to pitch black, as was done for cel-shading in Chapter 17, "Filling the Gaps with Rendering Techniques."

Mipmapping

Mipmapping is a way to improve the quality of texture samples that are distant from the viewer. If you take a cloth texture and move it very far away from the viewer, a single pixel on the screen could represent a large piece of the texture. To be mathematically correct about it, you map the pixel to the texture. In other words, you transform the space defined by a single pixel into texture space, and you average every pixel contained in that shape. Consequently, if a single pixel represents an entire texture, the color of that pixel is ideally the average of every texel in the texture.

This is extremely expensive to do at run-time. Thus, the idea was introduced to precompute a set of averaged textures. Most implementations choose to generate a new mipmap if one pixel contains more than one or two texels. In other words, if you skip one texel for every texel you select, you should generate a new mipmap. Consequently, a texture with a resolution of 512×512 will likely have a set of textures generated for it (256×256, 128×128, 64×64, 32×32, 16×16, 8×8, 4×4, 2×2, 1×1). This process is not done on the fly; instead, it is typically done right after the GPU texture loading process. The number of mipmap levels generated depends on the hardware implementation, of course, and choosing which mipmap is selected is pretty simple and *is* done on the fly. To do so, you just look at how many texels/pixels are used. Since the generation of the texture changes when the ratio is two texels/pixels, it becomes a matter of computing the ratio in one direction. The integer of that ratio will tell you which mipmap should be chosen.

Affine Texture Mapping

There are two generally accepted ways to apply a texture to a triangle. The first is the most obvious method, which is typically referred to as plain old *texture mapping*. This simply takes the $<x, y>$ value of the texture for the 2D $<x, y>$ vertices of the triangle, and it interpolates the sampling linearly from one point to the other. This gives you two texture coordinates on the edge of the triangle. Once you have that, you simply fill the triangle by interpolating linearly yet again from the right texture coordinate to the left texture coordinate. The sampling for the line is interpolated in increments such that one increment moves one pixel in y for the triangle to be rendered. This process is referred to as *scan conversion*, because it converts a shape into a set of scan lines. In other words, the rendition engine computes how much t (for a line equation) increases if y increases by one (on the screen). The value of t is then scaled down to the length of the sampled texture, and the sample is then fetched.

So, given an onscreen position $<x, y>$, the rasterizer maps this value to an associated texture coordinate $<u, v>$ by two simultaneous interpolations in x and an interpolation between these two interpolations in y.

Perspective Correct Texture Mapping

But from your knowledge of the z-buffer, you know that this isn't the correct way of dealing with the problem. Depth isn't linear, so it's incorrect to linearly interpolate from one color value to the other. The correct function to interpolate by is $1/z$ due to the projection. To correctly interpolate from one texel to another, you need to interpolate the texel coordinate $<u, v>/z$ linearly, as well as $1/z$ linearly. When you want to obtain the coordinate of your texture at a given point in time, you simply take the texel coordinate $<u, v>/z$ and divide it by $1/z$. This may sound like the two z's cancel each other out, but this isn't the case because $1/z$ is interpolated linearly. Your function looks like this:

```
su = U/Z;
sv = V/Z;
sz = 1/Z;

for (x = startx ; x <= endx ; x++) {
    u = su / sz;
    v = sv / sz;
    PutPixel(x, y, texture[v][u]);
    su += deltasu;
    sv += deltasv;
    sz += deltasz;
}
```

This obviously isn't an efficient way to deal with it, but if you play with the equation enough, you can make the core loop of this renderer a linear mapping.

Nearest Sampling Method

Because the $<u, v>$ values are floats, you have to convert them into integers because the texture is made out of discrete samples. Truncating the texture coordinates is called the *nearest sampling method*, because it chooses the nearest sample texel. An alternative is to use the extra precision that you have. Floats give you sub-pixel information on the position of the sample for the texture. Use this to your advantage by doing yet another interpolation at the color level.

Bilinear Sampling Method

This stuff should be easy after you've read Chapter 13 regarding interpolating curves. When the coordinate of a texture is an integer, the color of a pixel at that location describes the color of that entire location with 100 percent accuracy. If you move halfway between this pixel and the next one, it's the equivalent of having half the weight of the first pixel and half of the weight of the second pixel. All you have to do is apply a linear interpolation of the color from one pixel to the next pixel. This interpolation should be the mantissa of a number, because you have determined that at an integer position, the pixel fully describes the value. The mantissa has a convenient range of [0, 1], which is perfectly suited to an interpolation.

If you apply the same idea as texture mapping (interpolating in x for two values, a pixel and the pixel below that) and interpolate these two values in y, you achieve what is commonly known as *bilinear interpolation*. If you have a texture coordinate $<u, v>$, you should choose the pixel at the location of the truncated coordinates. Let the remainder of that floating point coordinate be $<s, t>$. Computing the value of the color just requires an interpolation of the color, which is given by the following formula:

$$Color1 = (u,v) + s\big((u+1,v) - (u,v)\big)$$
$$Color2 = (u,v+1) + s\big((u+1,v+1) - (u,v+1)\big)$$
$$Color = Color1 + t\big(Color2 - Color1\big)$$

This technique is called *bilinear sampling* or *linear sampling*. It's nothing but a weighted average on the four closest texels. In fact, what you end up doing is building a function defined for a range $<[0, 1), [0, 1)>$, which describes the color value between four pixels. The shape of this interpolation is a plane, because it's built out of two linearly independent interpolations (or vectors).

Trilinear Sampling Method

Another way to sample is by using a *trilinear* technique. This simply extends bilinear sampling by looking at things from a mipmaps level. When you work with mipmaps, you can see drastic differences when the hardware changes from one mipmap to the other. A polygon starts out looking detailed, and suddenly looks fuzzy or blurry. This is due to mipmapping.

In order to fix this, you can interpolate between mipmaps, which is *trilinear sampling*. To do so, you first perform bilinear filtering on the two closest mipmaps, and then you interpolate linearly between these two samples. It's a mere additional level of linear interpolation, where the parameter of the interpolation is given by the texels/pixels remainder and the two closest mipmaps are the integers of this function (much like what was done with the colors). It's a weighted average between the eight closest texels (four each from the two closest mipmaps). It's a good way to deal with mipmap sampling, but it gives relatively blurry results at low angles.

Anisotropic Sampling Method

Another sampling method is known as *anisotropic*. This takes everything a step further and takes the angle into account. When you choose a mipmap, you compute the texel/pixel ratio in more than one direction (x and y, for example). If the two ratios don't match, you have a distortion, which is introduced by trilinear filtering that assumes linear weights. You must remember that the depth of the scene isn't linear, it's *inversely* linear ($1/z$). To fix this, additional samples are taken when the ratio between the directions is different. In short, you can see it as the pixel being projected into 3D texture space and the set of texels being averaged with weights. The implementations of anisotropic sampling are pretty drastically different from one vendor to the next, unfortunately.

Multitexturing

This specific area is pretty complex and takes up most of this chapter. This is the part that combines various textures together and adds proper lighting, fog, etc. It puts a bunch of textures together, coupled with a set of parameters, to produce the final pixel color. A color is composed of red, green, and blue channels, as well as an alpha (or transparency) channel. Generally, a few things describe what a pixel will look like: the color of the triangle, the level of fog for each vertex, the set of textures used to determine the color, and the function that combines everything together. Provided in most hardware implementations is a concept referred to as *multitexturing*. There are many ways to combine two textures together, and the function you choose depends on the effect you want to achieve. There's a plethora of effects you can achieve that are supported by the hardware, but two of them are particularly useful for your purposes: modulation and decal.

Modulation

Modulation is what is typically seen as a color combination between two texels. It multiplies the channels together. For two given color channels, a, b, with range $[0, 1]$, the resulting output is given by the following formula:

$$\mathbf{c} = \mathbf{c}_1 \cdot \mathbf{c}_2$$

For example, in Chapter 17, if you wanted to project a texture upon another texture, you could have used the modulation function to combine the two textures. This will indeed project one texture on another texture, just like light is projected. You can choose the level of transparency by giving a lower alpha component to the color of the second texture.

Decal

Decal is similar to modulation, but it permits you to define the merger of both textures with the alpha channel of one of the two textures. It's mathematically defined as a linear interpolation between the color of the first texture and that of the second texture, where the interpolation parameter is the alpha value of the first texture:

$$\mathbf{c} = \left(1 - c_{1\alpha}\right)\mathbf{c}_2 + c_{1\alpha} \cdot \mathbf{c}_1$$

In the first case, if you want to project a light to brighten the scene, and the center is white while the outside is black, the scene would in fact be pitch black for the black pixels. This is because the product of 0 and another color still yields 0, which is black. That does become a problem. On the other hand, if you use decal to achieve this effect, the color of the pixels can still remain black, but they should be completely transparent (that is, the alpha at that point should be 0).

Fog/Haze

The last piece that I want you to look at is the fog factor. In real life, fog is a liquid/gas that floats in the air. The reason fog obstructs your view is that the particles suspended in the air block the light from coming through. When you enter a foggy area, objects at a distance can be completely obscured by the fog. The thickness of the fog is a function of distance and density. The farther away you look, the more fog is between you and the distant objects, and the more occluded the objects are (less light comes through).

Due to its nature, fog is really a bunch of particles with an alpha value, but this is way too slow to implement if you want to render a realistic model. Instead, the hardware does a color bias on the final color right before it's rendered.

Linear Fog

Fog f can be treated as a linear function of the distance:

$$f = \frac{far - z}{far - near}$$

Here, the far and near values don't necessarily need to match the far/near frustum plane. If you factor out the numerator, you can see that this function is really a linear function (the function of a line) where the slope is $-1/(far - near)$. This slope is defined as the density of the fog, and the reminder or the bias is the initial density of the fog. Thus, f is used as a blending factor (transparency level). The fog color biases the computed color (without fog). The fog factor f is consequently clamped to the range $[0, 1]$, where 0 means that nothing is visible while 1 is the case where no fog is applied.

Exponential Fog

If you think about fog in terms of infinitely small particles suspended in the air, which are simulated with an alpha value, the linear fog model isn't precise. The infinitely precise model is that a bunch of particles are simulated with mere pixels, where the alpha dictates how much light goes through each particle. If you think about this model for a bit, you'll definitely have a bunch of particles overlapped at some point. If two particles overlap, the alpha blending operation is applied in order. To keep the correct order of transparency, you would normally have to render from back to front, and the alpha blending operation is applied for a color $\mathbf{c}$ and a transparency value α:

$$\mathbf{c} = (1-\alpha)\mathbf{c}_{dest} + \mathbf{c}_{src}\alpha$$

If you apply the alpha blending equation recursively, you get an exponential function (you apply a function to the last function). Replace the destination color a few times recursively and you'll see what I mean. It follows the definition given in Chapter 17. Because of that, the exponential model is the best model you can employ. It is the fastest model. The equation that defines an exponential fog is defined as such:

$$f = e^{-density \cdot z}$$

Once more, you get a fog factor that spans [0, 1] and applies a bias on the fog color. Some APIs also provide square exponential functions. In such a case, you simply need to square the exponent. This model is typically a bit too aggressive and inserts fog extremely quickly.

Volumetric Fog

If you've played games such as *Quake 3* and *Unreal*, you've noticed the interesting fog they've implemented. This fog is different than the fog from the previous methods, because they assumed that you were in an infinite area of fog. Volumetric fog, on the other hand, takes more properties of fog into account.

For instance, you may have noticed that fog tends to stay at the ground level. That's merely because the density of fog is lower than the density of air. Like the example of water vs. wooden crate given in Chapter 8, "Gravitating Around Basic Physics," the fog floats above the ground. When you enter a room in a game, it isn't necessary to have the entire room filled with fog. You may want to fog up just a section of the room. For this, most 3D APIs allow you to control fog with a host of parameters. For example, you can specify the distance of an object from the fog volume, or you can specify the coordinate of the fog relative to a point in space that is the center of the fog.

Thanks to these extensions, you can create fog pretty much as you would like. If you want to be really fancy, you can make the fog ooze through the air with a formula that simply looks good. If you play with the equations of cosine and sine functions and translate the fog, you can create a blob of fog that moves more or less like you would expect fog to move. Alternatively, you can simulate this by using a spring model to determine the boundary of the fog if you use a Jell-o blob maintained together by a set of springs. You need only stimulate the blob by having wind blow against it once in a while. This will generate the effect of a blob of smoke.

The slower the better for fog, since it looks more realistic. Achieving this is a matter of telling your GPU how distant a given vertex is from a source, either by giving it a coordinate or a depth. A coordinate is obviously easier, but it takes up more bandwidth on the GPU.

Light a Ray Tracing Model

So far, you've looked at light in a rather abstract way. You've mainly seen it as a component that modulates the color of objects (such as spotlight projection). Light itself is a phenomenon that needs to be studied because it's the key for shaders. Light must not be mixed with pigment. With pigmentation color, mixing all the colors together will yield black. You can take a bunch of things at home, mix them together, and if the result is homogeneous, chances are that it will be pretty dark. Light behaves differently, and it also has different primary colors.

As previously stated, light is composed of three colors that are recognized by the cones in the human eye. The eye has three color cones that discern the difference between red/green and blue colors. Some rare people actually have four cones and can differentiate between more colors. People who are color-blind are missing a cone and cannot tell the difference between certain colors. This is because each color has a different level of intensity. For example, red is much more intense than blue. If you take a black and white picture of a completely red object and another picture of a completely blue object, the red object appears darker than the blue object because of this. In fact, experimentally, converting an RGB color to an intensity (grayscale) is done via the following formula:

$$Intensity = 0.299Red + 0.587Green + 0.114Blue$$

Consequently, if you're planning to do a black and white scene, you should take this fact into account. Simply doing an average of the color component will not yield a really impressive result. In fact, it will lack information. If, for example, your image had red and blue, each full intensity, the colors would appear the same with an averaging calculation, yet they should not be because blue is less intense than red.

So, now, what about light itself? Light is really electromagnetic radiation with a wavelength that the eye can capture and categorize. In the range from 4,000 to about 7,700 angstroms, the eye decodes this information in the form of colors. So if light is really radiation, the question becomes, how does radiation actually behave? Well, there's a lot of debate on whether light is a particle or a frequency, and I will leave the speculation for the physicists. For your particular case, it's easier to consider light as a particle.

The Movement of Light

As discussed previously, light is captured in three components (red, green, blue). When you do an operation on a color, you must consider these components separately. In other words, you can't mix the blue color with the green color if you want the result to be a color and not intensity. Don't mix apples with oranges, basically.

Since you want to look at light as a particle, you have to start from a source location. Light is radiation, so the source sends a bunch of particles in just about every direction. A spotlight, for example, is really an omni light source inside a cone or a box shadowing a region that would normally be lit. Since light is a particle, it's subject to the same laws of physics related to movement. Einstein would likely disagree with this, but for your purposes, this is a reasonable way to simulate light.

Furthermore, if light interacts with anything, it must therefore have a speed. This speed has been estimated to be constant at 300,000 kilometers per second, or 186,000 miles per second. I guess you could say that's pretty fast.

Let's get back to your original model. You have a light source, which is spitting out virtually weightless light particles (call them photons) in all directions at an incredible speed. Due to this speed, light is instantaneous for all practical purposes. This means that in a scene that's lit, the particles of light collide with the surfaces and irradiate them. If you isolate this to look at a single photon, this photon ends up rebounding numerous times on various surfaces before it finally reaches your eye. Once the photon reaches your eye, you decode that radiation as a color. Because the mass is so tiny and the speed so high, the rebound of the photon can be seen as the simplest case: a purely elastic collision. Consequently, the "true" way to render a scene would be to cast a set of rays in all directions from the light source and capture them on the near plane. This is completely impractical, though, because it involves an infinite number of directional vectors.

Instead, what the 3D renderers do is called *ray tracing*. The process is simply reversed. Instead of casting rays from the light source, you can cast a ray for each pixel on the near plane and determine the color depending on the various objects the ray hits. For game purposes, this is impractical because it operates on a per-pixel level and requires a lot of collision detection. Instead of projecting single rays, you use approximations such as projecting a texture for the light spot. This works pretty well, as you've seen in previous chapters, but it doesn't account for many potential hits. For example, it wouldn't look realistic if you projected a light map on a glass object, because glass does two things: it distorts light, and it absorbs only a small amount of color intensity.

You'll understand this better later in the chapter. For now, let's look at the behavior of a single ray of light to understand how to choose the color for a given pixel.

Reflective Surfaces

When an object rebounds off a surface, it rebounds in the same direction, except that the direction perpendicular to the plane is inverted. Take the simplest example: a ball bouncing on the floor without gravity. Suppose that the floor is merely the *xz* plane. The ball will keep moving in the same direction for the *x, z* component. The component that's affected is *y*, which is in fact inverted.

This case is pretty simple because it deals with an axis-aligned situation, but it doesn't have to be so. You can choose any arbitrary plane for the object to rebound from. You have to look a little deeper into the problem and think in terms of vectors. The direction that's inverted is defined by the normal of the plane **n**. That much is pretty easy and obvious. If you take the direction of the object **d** and subtract the projection of **d** onto **n** from **d**, you end up with an object that's always on the plane regardless.

Once more, take the example of the ball with the plane *xz*. If you subtracted the normal component of the plane from the direction, *y* would be equal to zero if the lengths matched. You want your object to rebound and not to suffer an inelastic collision, so you need to subtract the normal vector once more. This only works if the directions are equal. If not, you need to compute the projected length of the direction upon the normal. This is the length of the vector you should subtract. As Regis might say, here's the final answer for a reflection vector **r**:

$$\mathbf{r} = \mathbf{d} - 2\mathbf{n}(\mathbf{d} \bullet \mathbf{n})$$

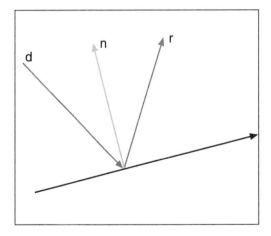

This should come as no surprise because it was already mentioned in the last chapter. Except here, everything probably makes more sense. If you still don't see it, try looking at Figure 18.1.

Of course, it only works if **n** is normalized, because this is how the projection and dot product was defined. It works for a single ray, but of course, you don't render in terms of single rays. If you want to render a reflective surface such as a mirror, one way is to use the stencil buffer.

Figure 18.1
r; a reflection of a vector **d** upon a surface with normal **n**

Planar Mirrors

The technique is done in two steps, just as the shadow in the last chapter was done. The first step consists of rendering the scene normally, and rendering the mirror such that it only toggles the stencil bits on. This delimits the region through which the objects are visible.

Start by taking the simplest case, a floor (the plane *xz*), as a reflective surface. One easy way to achieve this reflection is by rendering the scene such that it's mirrored to that very surface. In other words, render the scene with an additional transformation that simply inverts the *y* value:

$$\mathbf{M} = \begin{bmatrix} 1 & 0 & 0 & 0 \\ 0 & -1 & 0 & 0 \\ 0 & 0 & 1 & 0 \\ 0 & 0 & 0 & 1 \end{bmatrix}$$

The mirroring matrix **M** can be appended to the camera matrix, and it effectively inverts every object along the plane *xz*. Thanks to the stencil buffer, the objects that are above the *xz* surface are rendered below the surface such that they're mirrored. This does involve rendering the entire scene twice, but it sure beats rendering it six times, as required by cube mapping.

This is a little too easy because the plane is axis-aligned, but the idea isn't so different for an arbitrary plane. The process of obtaining this transformation matrix is exactly the same as obtaining the transformation matrix for a rotation about an arbitrary vector. It's a set of transformations that results in a single transformation matrix.

It's pointless to go through the entire derivation of the formula, because it's so similar to a rotation about an arbitrary vector. You already know intuitively how to perform a mirror upon the *z* axis, so it only makes sense to apply a set of transformations that will give you the plane *xz*, apply the mirror transformation, and follow through with the inverse of the initial transformation so as to restore the position and rotation of the object. Consequently, you need to do two things. First, you need to translate the plane to the origin, followed by a rotation that puts your plane co-planar to the *xz* plane. At that point, you can apply **M** and the inverse of the rotation/translation. The rotation part has already been covered in Chapter 5, "Transformations," with rotations about an arbitrary axis, so all you need to understand is how to obtain the translation that brings your plane to the origin.

Given any vertex on the plane **v** and the plane's normal **n**, the following matrix does the trick when applied to the camera matrix **M**:

$$\mathbf{M} = \begin{bmatrix} 1-2n_x^2 & -2n_x n_y & -2n_x n_z & 2(\mathbf{n} \bullet \mathbf{v})n_x \\ -2n_x n_y & 1-2n_y^2 & -2n_y n_z & 2(\mathbf{n} \bullet \mathbf{v})n_y \\ -2n_x n_z & -2n_y n_z & 1-2n_z^2 & 2(\mathbf{n} \bullet \mathbf{v})n_z \\ 0 & 0 & 0 & 1 \end{bmatrix}$$

Of course, you've already seen that it's possible to generate reflection via environment mapping, which is much more efficient because the entire world is precomputed into a texture. The only problem is that this assumes that the objects are infinitely far from the reflective surface, which can yield a significant image warp for a planar surface. Your eyes are pretty well trained for planar surfaces, so a slight deformation may feel like much more.

The advantage of this technique is that it allows any form of animation to happen in front of the reflective surface. A character moving in front of the mirror will also appear in the mirror, whereas this wouldn't happen in an environmental map unless you recomputed the map at each frame, making the overall performance worse than this method. Of course, you have to apply this technique recursively if two mirrors can see one another. It becomes extremely expensive to redraw the scene numerous times. But then again, how often do you see a game that has more than one adjacent mirror? In general, environment maps are better if you wish to render a really complex world because they encapsulate much more information into a few selected textures, which is much faster indeed.

In order to speed up calculations, you probably want to consider clipping the scene to the set of planes defined by the boundary of the mirror. When you look into a mirror, it's highly likely that some pieces of the scene aren't visible at all, so computing the set of planes for the convex volume of the object (as was done for shadows and object culling) isn't a bad idea. Since mirrors are often composed of two pairs of orthogonal edges, the convexity of the object is already guaranteed. On the other hand, you can also precompute the convex polygon of the mirror if you decide not to have a convex mirror. Granted, this means that you'll allow some objects that potentially aren't visible, but at least it will be faster.

Another approach you may want to consider is to use some form of visibility test, as was shown in the last chapter. For instance, perhaps you could give the objects a pure solid color, instead of coloring them with an expensive shader through the mirror.

Refractive Surfaces

Reflective surfaces take the light and bounce it back in the opposite direction from the surface normal. In a transparent material, a *refractive* property can also be observed. Refraction is the distortion of light induced by a change of the material it passes through. You can observe this effect by looking down into a pool of water. Notice that parts of the pool look like they're wobbling. If water was completely transparent, you wouldn't notice any distortion. But you do, because water is refractive. Water is also reflective, because shining light on a pool also yields a wobbling pattern. Another example is glass. You can see through it, but what you see is in fact distorted lightly. This is again the effect of refraction.

Light is a physical process that can be deduced only by observation. One such observation regarding refractive surfaces, often referred to as Snell's Law, observes the following relationship between two materials with respective refraction indices η_1 and η_2:

$$\eta_1 \sin\left(\theta_1\right) = \eta_2 \sin\left(\theta_2\right)$$

Here, the angle θ_1 is referred to as the angle of incidence, and θ_2 is the angle of refraction. The first angle describes how a ray of light leaves a material, and the second describes how the light penetrates the new material. Consequently, the material itself doesn't modify the direction of the light. It's really the transition from one material to another that does this. For example, the reason your pool looks like it wobbles is because light changes in its journey from air to water.

A vector of light initially has an angle θ_1, and this angle is transformed to θ_2 such that the preceding equation is satisfied for two refractive constants. The behavior of the ray is similar to that of reflection. For reflection on the xz plane, recall that only the y component changes. In this case, only the angle between the vector and the plane changes. In 2D, you can come up with this relationship:

$$\theta_2 = \arcsin\left(\frac{\eta_1}{\eta_2}\sin\left(\theta_1\right)\right)$$

Unfortunately, this notation does little to help you in 3D. The law in 3D is defined similarly, but to make any sense out of it, you should look at the problem in terms of vectors, which are scalable to higher dimensions. As a notational convention, let **s** be the incoming ray of light, and let **t** be the transformed ray of light. The vector **t** can be expressed as a combination of one vector along the normal of the surface **n** and another vector **m**, which is perpendicular to **n**. Thus, you have the following:

$$\mathbf{t} = -\mathbf{n}\cdot\cos\left(\theta_2\right) + \mathbf{m}\cdot\sin\left(\theta_2\right)$$

You have the normal vector of the surface, but you don't actually have **m**. If you keep in mind that the angle along the surface is the only thing that changes, and not the entire direction, **m** is defined as follows:

$$\mathbf{m} = \frac{\mathrm{perp}_{\mathbf{n}}\mathbf{s}}{\sin\left(\theta_1\right)}$$

$$= \frac{\mathbf{s} - \left(\mathbf{n}\bullet\mathbf{s}\right)\mathbf{n}}{\sin\left(\theta_1\right)}$$

Now, putting everything together yields the final answer:

$$t = -\mathbf{n} \cdot \cos(\theta_2) - \frac{\mathbf{s} - (\mathbf{n} \bullet \mathbf{s})\mathbf{n}}{\sin(\theta_1)} \cdot \sin(\theta_2)$$

$$= -\mathbf{n} \cdot \sqrt{1 - \sin^2(\theta_2)} - \frac{\sin(\theta_2)}{\sin(\theta_1)}(\mathbf{s} - (\mathbf{n} \bullet \mathbf{s})\mathbf{n})$$

$$= -\mathbf{n} \cdot \sqrt{1 - \frac{\eta_1^2}{\eta_2^2} \sin(\theta_1)} - \frac{\eta_1}{\eta_2}(\mathbf{s} - (\mathbf{n} \bullet \mathbf{s})\mathbf{n})$$

$$= -\mathbf{n}\left(\sqrt{1 - \frac{\eta_1^2}{\eta_2^2}\left(1 - (\mathbf{n} \bullet \mathbf{s})^2\right)} + \frac{\eta_1}{\eta_2}(\mathbf{n} \bullet \mathbf{s})\right) - \mathbf{s}\frac{\eta_1}{\eta_2}$$

It's not the prettiest equation you could hope for, but you can't really contradict math, can you? Notice that the function isn't defined for all values. It's possible to obtain a negative square root if your choice of coefficient isn't very good. Typically, everything is relative to air. Air is a factor of 1, while water is [4/3]. Physically speaking, if you get a negative square root, it implies that you're working with a material where total internal reflection occurs. Light is trapped within the material, and for your purposes it's completely useless.

Light Sources

If you study light in terms of a single ray reflecting on various surfaces, it's interesting, but it isn't very practical for games. You can't shoot an infinite number of light rays in order to create a light.

Instead, I prefer to look at the behavior that given sources of light exhibit. These models are based on physical observation you can do yourself. Typically there are equations that are cluttered with constants you must fine-tune for your specific needs. The equations force the general behavior of the light, but the details about it are fine-tuned with the constants.

Ambient Light

Ambient light is the accumulation of low-frequency light that comes from numerous reflections in the scene. When you turn on a light in a room, one particular area of the room is well-lit. The rest of the room is also lit up, because the rays of light bounce off virtually all surfaces. This is ambient light.

Consequently, ambient light can be seen as the base lighting level of a scene. It doesn't really depend on direction, because it's an approximation that accounts for light coming from reflections in all directions. Typically, ambient light is a constant describing the lowest level of light a region can attain, regardless of whether it's directly lit or shadowed. Take a look at Figure 18.2 for an example.

Figure 18.2
A gun rendered using ambient light

Directional Light

Directional light is akin to environment mapping, in that it also approximates light that comes from a very distant (read: infinitely distant) object. The sun, stars, or any other lights coming from far away emit directional light. For all practical purposes, this type of light doesn't diminish with distance. The light from the sun doesn't decrease in intensity by the time it reaches the Earth, for example. Directional lights have no position in space. They're purely defined by a direction, as the name suggests.

Point Light

Unlike a directional light, a point light has an anchor point. Thus, it also has attenuation. In other words, the intensity of the light is proportional, depending on the distance between the point light and the lit object. Turning on a lamp in a room has this effect. The farther the lamp is from a wall, the less intense the light hitting the wall is. If you wanted to mathematically describe the intensity i of the light as a function of the distance from the point light, you would write it as such:

$$i = \frac{1}{a + b \cdot d + c \cdot d^2}$$

The values of a, b, and c are constants that are defined per light. In fact, if you were to graph this equation, you could see how the intensity changes as a function of distance:

$$\frac{1}{a + b \cdot x + c \cdot x^2}$$

You can fine-tune the constants to generate a light that works for your world. There really isn't a magic number that works for all cases, simply because the size of the world really depends on the units and the size of the objects you use. Plug and play, and you should be able to come up with an equation that makes sense for your case.

The intensity itself describes how much light goes through a medium such as air. Consequently, if you want to compute the intensity of a white light, you have to multiply the intensity for each color channel of white ($<1, 1, 1>i$). If the light is red, you have to multiply the color red by the intensity of the light $<1, 0, 0>i$. It's pretty simple to handle the light's intensity. The only "gotcha" you may want to avoid is the point where $x = 0$. You have to make sure that when the distance is 0, the range of the intensity doesn't yield a number greater than 1. If it does, you can get a light color greater than 1, which makes no sense if each color channel has bound $[0, 1]$. Having $a = 1$ fixes this problem, but it may not yield the type of light you want, so be careful.

Spotlight

A spotlight is very similar to a point light, but enclosed on the sides. It can be round or square or any odd shape. Here, let's assume a rounded shape. The light source is really a point light inside a cylinder with one end open. Because you're still dealing with a point light, there will be an attenuation of the light's intensity with distance. But another phenomenon occurs too: The rays of light end up reflecting off the cylinder. If this wasn't true, a spotlight would produce a very hard shadow, but it doesn't. The light gradually degrades from the center of the spotlight. This is due to the various beams of light that reflect on the cone and end up on a surface, generating a nice elliptical gradient. The farther away the surface is from the center of the point light, the fewer beams hit it. In other words, there are far fewer beams of light outside the region that's directly visible from the point light inside the cylinder. The farther from the projection of the cylinder you are, the less light will accumulate.

You have to define a few additional things. The spotlight has a source defined by the position $\mathbf{p}$, and it's coupled with a direction $\mathbf{d}$, not to be confused with the distance from the point in space d. The equation defining the intensity of the light at a point $\mathbf{v}$, with the aforementioned parameters, is given by the following equation:

$$i = \frac{\max\left\{\mathbf{d} \bullet \dfrac{\mathbf{v} - \mathbf{p}}{\|\mathbf{v} - \mathbf{p}\|_2}, 0\right\}^p}{a + b \cdot d + c \cdot d^2}$$

As you can see, the equation is the same as the point light equation, except that it also takes into account the angle between the vector $\mathbf{vp}$ (the vector of the light's direction) and the vector $\mathbf{d}$ (the vector of the point relative to the light's source). Consequently, the larger the angle is, the smaller the value for the cosine of that angle and the less intensity. It all makes perfect sense if you take a few seconds to think about it.

The last mystery variable you may have noticed is the exponent p. This exponent defines how sensitive the angle is. For example, a value of 100 would yield a very solid light, while a value of 1 would yield a much smoother and more gradual light that goes much farther.

Lighting Models

Since you've already determined that light rebounds off surfaces, wouldn't it make sense to also study the surfaces that reflect the light? If all surfaces were straight, as was previously assumed, every material would be 100 percent reflective, like a mirror. Yet even mirrors absorb a little bit of the light that bounces off them. If you take two mirrors and place them opposite each other, what you see reflected in them gets greener and greener (the color of the glass itself) until it gets dark. You can simulate this with a mirror by adding a transparent greenish texture upon the scene seen through the mirror.

Similarly, in Chapter 8, you learned that some objects stay in place instead of sliding because of friction. Some objects are harder to push across some surfaces than other surfaces (sandpaper vs. ice, for example). This is because at the atomic level, the surface isn't as smooth as you may expect it to be. This effect also has large consequences on light. Because light rebounds from a surface defined by the equation seen previously, the orientation of a material's microsurfaces is important. If you take a piece of tissue paper, for example, many tiny threads have been pressed together to create it, and it would be unrealistic to compute the exact surface angle from which every ray of light rebounds. Consequently, you have to come up with models that approximate the way light interacts with specific materials as best as possible.

Diffuse Lighting

Diffuse lighting was popularized by early PC games, where image quality was really a luxury and software renderers ruled the Earth. A diffuse surface reflects light in a more or less random fashion. This means that a given area is lit relatively equally. For instance, turn on the nearest lamp. Now take a small rug and place it under the lamp. This should remove the spotlight effect, or at least diminish it quite a lot. This is also in accordance with the spotlight equations where the distance is a large number. In that position, the rug looks relatively equally lit. On the other hand, if you take a piece of plastic and look at it from behind the lamp, you'll probably notice a highlight in the center (which corresponds to the direct light). The difference is that the rug reflects the light in random fashion due to the nature and arrangement of the fibers. The plastic, on the other hand, offers a much more even surface and is not a diffuse surface.

Because the reflection is relatively uniform, lighting doesn't depend on the position of the object in a purely diffuse model. Intensity is really a value that computes how much light hits a given area. It's a ratio of lighting over area. If you look at light that comes from a direction **d** and assume a diffuse lighting model, computing the intensity is dependent on the area. As it turns out, the lit area of a surface really depends on the inclination of that surface. This effect can be seen if you take a piece of paper. Rotate the piece of paper so as to change the angle the light reflects on the paper, and you'll notice how the intensity of the light diminishes pretty quickly. The same thing happens to our planet, in fact. The reason it's warmer in California than in Iceland isn't because Iceland is farther from the sun (although it probably does contribute a very small amount). The real reason is that Iceland is at an angle such that the area that receives light is much greater than that of California, which is much more perpendicular to the light vector coming from the sun. It's also the same reason it gets colder at night. The sun is at a lower angle and its intensity diminishes.

In older games, polygons had only one color, which changed as the shape rotated. This form of lighting is called Lambert shading. The idea is simply to change the intensity of the color for a polygon depending on its orientation from the light source. It doesn't really yield good results, but it's a fundamental principle of light that can be used in combined lighting models. The cosine can be retrieved through the dot product, and the following equation expresses the light component added by diffuse lighting:

$$i_{\text{diff}} = i_{\text{source}} \left(\mathbf{n} \bullet \mathbf{d} \right)$$

Diffuse lighting has a direct effect on the intensity of the overall lighting model source defined by i_{source}. Obviously, if the dot product in the preceding equation is negative, it implies that the surface is hidden and should receive no light at all, causing the intensity to plummet to zero.

A fancier form of lighting that kicks Lambert shading's rear any day also arises from this technique. Since I've already established that you can compute a normal vector not only per triangle, but also per vertex, it means that you can actually compute one color per vertex. If you compute the diffuse light color on all three vertices for a given triangle, you get three colors (one per vertex). Given these colors, you can then render the triangle by interpolating the color from one vertex to another down the left and right edge, and interpolating once more from left to right. In fact, this is more or less the same process as bilinear sampling, except that the interpolation isn't orthogonal. Such triangles can be rendered with any decent 3D API by simply rendering a triangle with three different colors for each vertex. This form of shading is commonly referred to as Gouraud shading, and it's the technique in software that yields the best quality/speed ratio. But in a hardware world, who really cares?

You still care, because the concept is important. Commonly used through games are textures called *diffuse maps*. These textures have only one purpose, and that's to give the image a greater sense of depth. The goal of this texture is to change the intensity of various parts of a texture. For instance, if you render a world with plain textures, it will look

Figure 18.3
A gun rendered using diffuse and ambient light

very dull because you'll have no concept of light. If you create diffuse maps that are strategically placed within the scene to darken the corners of the room and apply similar lighting, these maps will greatly increase the depth of the scene. Of course, you could argue that if you want to shade a crate with a darker color, you could do so in the texture itself, but here the problem is memory. If you want to apply various spotlight-like halos around the map, you had better have a lot of memory to generate all possible combinations. Instead, you can use multitexturing with the modulation mode, which will generate what you would expect out of it. Take a look at Figure 18.3 for an example of a gun rendered using diffuse lighting.

Specular Lighting

If you take a very shiny opaque object, such as painted metal, you'll notice that it has a small halo. In fact, it looks more or less like a light bulb's reflection on an opaque surface. This property is exhibited by any surface that isn't too coarse. The curious thing about this halo is that it's very bright only in one specific region on the object, and this is the section where the light rays rebound directly from the source to your eyes. By definition, specular light depends on the position of the viewer. Again, you can test this yourself by moving around the object and moving the light.

With this observation, a simple formula can be used to approximate this effect reasonably. In fact, you could nearly claim that specular lighting is really a very sharp spotlight that depends on the angle of reflection and not the light's direction. Because they are so similar, the following equation does a decent approximation of specular lighting:

$$i_{spec} = \left(\mathbf{r} \bullet \frac{\mathbf{v} - \mathbf{p}}{\|\mathbf{v} - \mathbf{p}\|_2} \right)^m$$

Here, $\mathbf{v}$ is defined as the viewer's position in space, $\mathbf{p}$ is the light's position, and $\mathbf{r}$ is the reflective vector as previously defined. The specular exponent m is really only there to make sure that the intensity is really sharp. Giving a small value such as 1 to *m* will yield a very large highlight, virtually lighting the entire object. On the other hand, having an exponent of 50 will give you a very sharp (pun intended) highlight. If you don't mind that the highlight itself is slightly displaced (which is often a reasonable assumption), this is a pretty decent model. In fact, it you look at it closely, it's very similar to what was used for environment mapping. Because of this, you can simulate specular lighting by using an environment map. Due to its nature, it isn't necessary to use anything more than a spherical environment map. Once more, in the texture, you simply need to specify what color intensity you expect to be present for a given reflection angle, and the trick will be played. For this particular case, you should be looking at a sphere-like object, where a small portion at the center of the sphere is intensely lit. If you want to render such a texture in a fancy 3D rendering tool, you can do so by rendering a sphere and setting the specular component in that art tool to generate the highlight you would expect to see on your objects.

There was also a very popular and cool effect back in the old days that was commonly known as Phong mapping (sometimes incorrectly called Phong shading). In Gouraud shading, the color is interpolated from one vertex to another. In Phong mapping, the normal vector is interpolated from one vertex to another. This only works if your texture is itself curved, such as one generated for a sphere map. The problem with Gouraud shading is that it's unable to put the specular component in the center of a triangle because the colors are linearly interpolated. Phong mapping fixes this because the texture generation unit of the GPU interpolates the normals.

If you were able to use a diffuse map to change the color of an object, you can also use a map to modulate the intensity for the specular component. Such maps are called *gloss maps*. Since the diffuse maps determined the intensity of the color at $<x, y>$, the gloss maps determine the specular component at each point on the surface. For instance, you could build a crate with a highly specular liquid flowing on it merely by having the glossiness applied to the liquid via the gloss map. This is great when you want some parts of the objects to shine without having to cut a polygon into several smaller pieces to outline the shiny part. Take a look at Figure 18.4 for an example of a gun rendered with highlights.

Figure 18.4
A gun rendered with highlights

Bumpmapping

If you take a good look at a picture, you can tell that a house is a house, a dog is a dog, etc. More specifically, you can tell where the dog's shape begins and where the house begins. The information that tells you this is the color. If the dog was the same color as the house, you wouldn't be able to see the difference. Well, this isn't quite true. Because of lighting, you'll still be able to see the difference. When you look at a black and white photo, the only thing that tells you where the dog ends and the house begins is the darkness or the intensity of the image. Thanks to this chapter, you understand that if a section of the image is the dog, the darker areas are likely the ones that are shadowed, or at least the areas where the slope is likely to be steeper than the things facing the camera directly. So if you can generally deduce that a higher intensity implies a surface that's likely facing the camera, and one that has a lower intensity where light doesn't hit the surface perpendicularly, you get something really interesting. Take a look at Figures 18.5 and 18.6 for examples of bumpmapping. You can also see what Figure 18.6 looks like at the geometric level by looking at Figure 18.7.

Figure 18.5
A gun rendered using bumpmapping

Given a black and white photo, you can look at the difference between adjacent texels and take a decent guess at the inclination between these two texels. If the color

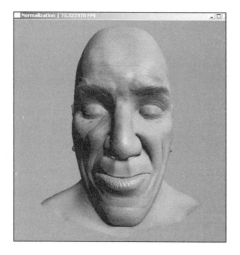

Figure 18.6
3D face rendered with bumpmapping

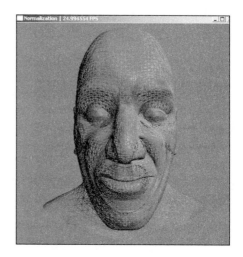

Figure 18.7
3D face rendered with lines only

remains the same, the normal on this surface is likely facing the light. If the color from left to right goes from dark to light, the normal of the surface is probably pointing towards the left. Similarly for a lighter/darker region, where the normal is likely to be pointing to the right.

So how can this help you at all? As you already know, a surface isn't perfectly flat. It's composed of carved pieces and extruding edges. If you can detect the places in the texture where parts extrude or carve, you can compute the light accordingly and light the texture depending on the angle of view (think Lambert shading on a per-pixel basis). In order to do the math on this, you need a normal vector for the surface. So how can you find a normal vector from a texture map?

Bumpmap Construction

Not all textures can be pushed into a generic bumpmap construction algorithm and yield decent results. The method that yields the best results is obviously one where you can fine-tune the normal vectors yourself. In other words, instead of computing the normal vector for each pixel, edit the normal vectors by hand and store the result in a texture. Instead of storing the texture as red, green, and blue components, you can store the texture as a normal map where each four-pair of values represents the four-vector of the normal. If you work with a 3D modeler and it can generate smooth objects, determining the normal for a texture generated with such a tool isn't too hard if it supports the feature. Unfortunately, the tools for this are not very common, and you're basically left to do the dirty work yourself.

The first thing you need to do is convert the image into an intensity map. The intensity map tells you how much light gets to a given position. A good way to guess the depth of a surface is to look at its intensity. The first step is to convert an RGB color image into a black and white intensity-based image. This is pretty easy, and it's done with the equation in the "Light a Ray Tracing Model" section earlier in this chapter. Once you have that, you need to compute a guess for the normal. Take the intensity map as a height map. In other words, consider the intensity map as a map where a white pixel is above a black pixel. That way, you can compute the slope in various directions. If you compute two slopes, and thus two vectors, you can compute a normal vector to both of them, and consequently the normal at that point. Mathematically, the following holds:

$$\mathbf{u}(x,y) = \langle 1, 0, h(x+1,y) - h(x-1,y) \rangle$$
$$\mathbf{v}(x,y) = \langle 1, 0, h(x,y+1) - h(x,y-1) \rangle$$
$$\mathbf{n}(x,y) = \langle -\mathbf{u}_z, -\mathbf{v}_z, 1 \rangle$$

You may have noticed that the two sample texels are not adjacent to one another. The reason is simply to preserve symmetry in the model. If you had to choose two adjacent texels, you would have to choose the texel either above or below the current one, and neither one yields a symmetric result. Of course, the preceding vector isn't necessarily normalized, so you should normalize it. You've already gone through the process before, so it shouldn't be news that this vector needs to be converted into a range of $[0, 1]$. You need to divide each component by 2 and add .5 to each, as was done for the cube map normal.

Tangent Space

So now you have a normal vector, which you can use to compute the amount of light on a surface's area. But you still have one problem: The vectors you come up with are all relative to a camera that looks down $<0, 0, 1>$. The texture you apply to an object could be on a backface, in which case any vector should actually point in the same direction as the camera. Yet the vectors you get from this calculation are all pointing towards the camera. You need to compare apples with apples. You need to convert one or the other so that they sit in the same space. You can either move the vectors into object space or move the object vectors into tangent space. These two techniques are equivalent; the only difference is the perspective. Tangent space can be defined as an orthonormal coordinate system where the normal of a given vertex $\mathbf{v}$ is $<0, 0, 1>$ and thus matches with what you have in the normal map. For example, if you had the vector running from the light to all three vertices of a triangle, you could convert this vector into tangent space and then interpolate this vector across the triangle as texture mapping does. The only real question is, how do you convert to such a coordinate system?

Arbitrarily, suppose that you want to convert from tangent space to object space. You want to transform the vector $<0, 0, 1>$ into object space. In this situation, you must be careful to maintain the texture mapping directions. In other words, you have to make sure that the square texturing directions $\mathbf{u}$ and $\mathbf{v}$ are maintained. $\mathbf{u}$ should correspond to the x axis in tangent space, and $\mathbf{t}$ should correspond to the y axis in tangent space. Tangent space is often defined by three components: the normal $\mathbf{n}$, the tangent $\mathbf{t}$, and the binormal $\mathbf{b}$. They often form an orthogonal basis, but there's no guarantee of this. It really all depends on the direction of your texturing coordinates. Suppose you have a triangle defined by three vertices {$\mathbf{a}$, $\mathbf{b}$, $\mathbf{c}$} and with corresponding texture coordinates $<\mathbf{u}_{\{a,b,c\}}, \mathbf{v}_{\{a,b,c\}}>$. The first and most obvious thing to do is to compute everything relative to the vertex for which you want to compute the tangent space. Suppose this vertex is $\mathbf{a}$. Thus, you have the following new definitions:

$$\mathbf{p} = \mathbf{b} - \mathbf{a}$$

$$\mathbf{q} = \mathbf{c} - \mathbf{a}$$

$$\langle u_1, v_1 \rangle = \langle u_b - u_a, v_b - v_a \rangle$$

$$\langle u_2, v_2 \rangle = \langle u_c - u_a, v_c - v_a \rangle$$

Because you want the texture mapping to be done along the same path when transformed, the following two equations must hold:

$$\mathbf{p} = u_1\mathbf{t} + v_1\mathbf{b}$$

$$\mathbf{q} = u_2\mathbf{t} + v_2\mathbf{b}$$

Thus, you can isolate for the two unknown directional vectors that make up the linear combination (the transformation) as follows for row-vectors $\mathbf{p}$, $\mathbf{q}$, $\mathbf{t}$, $\mathbf{b}$:

$$\begin{bmatrix} \mathbf{p} \\ \mathbf{q} \end{bmatrix} = \begin{bmatrix} u_1 & v_1 \\ u_2 & v_2 \end{bmatrix} \begin{bmatrix} \mathbf{t} \\ \mathbf{b} \end{bmatrix}$$

$$\begin{bmatrix} \mathbf{t} \\ \mathbf{b} \end{bmatrix} = \begin{bmatrix} u_1 & v_1 \\ u_2 & v_2 \end{bmatrix}^{-1} \begin{bmatrix} \mathbf{p} \\ \mathbf{q} \end{bmatrix}$$

This gives you a simple linear system where you can find and isolate for $\mathbf{t}$ and $\mathbf{b}$. Once you're equipped with this, you can easily compute the matrix $\mathbf{M}$, which converts from tangent space to object space:

$$\mathbf{M} = \begin{bmatrix} \mathbf{t} & \mathbf{b} & \mathbf{n} \end{bmatrix}$$

Here, $\mathbf{t}$, $\mathbf{b}$, and $\mathbf{n}$ are column vectors. Of course, the inverse matrix will perform the inverse transformation. It will convert from object space to tangent space. This goes by the very definition of an inverse given in Chapter 3, "Meet the Matrices." If the matrix is a rotation matrix, the inverse is pretty easy to compute because it equals the transpose. Thus, a more optimized inverse can be achieved here. Once you have this, you can use the hardware's capability to compute one dot product per vertex. This function is commonly referred to as the dot3 bumpmapping function, although it could be used for anything requiring one dot product per pixel.

Emission

Some objects may not only receive light, but also emit some light (without accounting for reflection). For instance, a neon sign can receive light, but it will also emit some light. This has the consequence of adding additional color to the overall model. Just as with the preceding methods, you can also generate an emission map that dictates how much color is emitted per texel. This isn't a very common map, but it's there if you need it.

PART FIVE

OPTIMIZATIONS

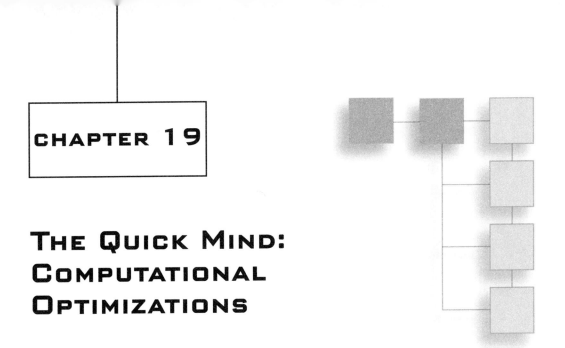

CHAPTER 19

THE QUICK MIND: COMPUTATIONAL OPTIMIZATIONS

What is the difference between a good programmer and a bad one? Chances are, you could come up with a list of 20 things that separate the good from the bad. In my opinion, however, the differentiator is not knowledge, which can be accumulated, but rather the thinking process. It doesn't matter if there are certain algorithms you don't know; you can easily grab that information off the Net. What does matter is the ability to solve a problem in an original fashion that is specifically tuned to the problem at hand.

Like most things, this is easier said than done. It's the equivalent of telling people not to bother remembering the qsort algorithm, and instead to understand the process behind it—or, more appropriately, the thinking process involved to solve the problem. When dealing with optimization, it is extremely important to understand the platform you are hacking on. Something like division, which can be reasonably fast on a PC, can be gruesomely slow on an ARMS processor that does not have hardware division instruction.

This chapter discusses not only PCs but also embedded devices—which typically are stripped-down versions of PCs. To understand the shortcomings of these devices, you will start by looking deep into the CPU/FPU to see how things are handled at the lowest level in a mathematical sense. (The FPU is the floating-point unit of the processor and is responsible for carrying out the complex math behind floats.) This is an important step in understanding why one function might be slower than another.

In this chapter, you will find many methods designed to replace the functions you have been using on the PC, and along the way, a few useful PC optimizations.

In short, the topics covered in this chapter are as follows:

- IEEE floating-point format and arithmetic
- Fixed-point format and arithmetic
- Condition arithmetic

Fixed Points

So you're working on one of these new state-of-the-art handheld devices and you just found out that they have absolutely no floating-point support. Luckily, your compiler does support floating point in software, but you really need all the speed you can squeeze out of that device. In the immortal words of Keanu Reeves, what do you do?

Floating points are too slow, and integers have no decimal precision; are you really stuck in the mud? Well, not quite. On embedded devices such as the latest phones and PDAs, FPUs are out of the question. Even if you did have an FPU in the latest processors, it run so slowly that you wouldn't even consider using it unless you needed the range it could provide or simply didn't care about speed—which in a game is rarely the case. Instead, developers started using fixed point. Unlike floating point, which describes a number in which the comma "floats" around, fixed-point numbers have a comma is fixed to a predetermined value.

What's even better? If you work in the embedded space, there are already a host of standards that allow for fixed point as input. Standards such as OpenGL-ES readily take fixed points as input, which makes understanding fixed points all the more important.

The idea behind fixed points is to use a rational number representation. Every rational number can be written in the form $\frac{a}{b}$ where a and b are two integers. The problem with using this general definition is that a division is tremendously slow, so you clearly want to stay away from that. But if, for example, you were to fix the value for b, and you were to use a value that is a pure power of 2, you could simply shift right in order to account for the division. A *shift* is an operation that takes the integer variable and pushes the bits left or right. If you convert from decimal to binary and vice versa by applying the shift, you will notice that shifting a binary number really multiplies or divides the number by two depending on which side the shift occurs. This is a pretty efficient operation.

To recap, for every number $\frac{a}{b}$ where b is actually implicit and a power of 2, you only carry the value a around. Again, assuming that b is a power of 2, if you take a close look at a, you will notice that the bits assigned to the decimal portion (mantissa) are completely different from the bits assigned to the integer. This is the beauty of this technique: It assigns the lower bits to the mantissa and the upper bits to the integer portion. For instance, if you were to choose a value of $b = 4$, every number a would be represented in the explicit form a/b. Thus you should be able to see that the 2 (because $2^2 = 4$) is the number of bits assigned to the mantissa and the remaining bits are assigned to the integer. If you take a number that is smaller than 4, you do not get an integer at all. On the other hand, any multiple of 4 will give you an integer value 8/4 = 2 and the partial values will give you a value with a certain degree of precision 9/4 = 2.25.

It should be pretty clear that this is fairly fast from the fact that a shift is pretty easy to implement conceptually. In fact, a shift is typically as fast as the addition. This is a nice way to set things up because if b is fixed, you do not have to carry any additional value around, thus every bit of precision is assigned to a for a number $\frac{a}{b}$.

There is another way to write a fixed point: You can cleanly separate the mantissa and the integer portion by multiplying it by a scalar. So a fixed-point $\frac{a}{b}$ represented as a with an implicit b can really be seen as $Integer \cdot b + Mantissa$. If you reverse the process by dividing the implicit fixed point by b, you'll notice that it is a logical deduction because if you divide the expression by b, you are left only with the integer portion (recall that this is an integer division).

In fact, b defines how much precision you will get out of a fixed point. Because you have only 32 bits, increasing the decimal precision also decreases the maximum number you can represent. If you decide to put 16 bits of precision for the decimal places, this only leaves you with 16 bits for the integer portion. This is something you have to think about when choosing the right integer:mantissa ratio for your needs. Do you need a large range or small and precise values?

This is all good, but how do you actually convert a floating-point value into a fixed-point value? It's pretty easy. If you take a fixed-point value k, you want to represent this value in fixed-point notation $\frac{a}{b}$ without losing significant precision. All you have to do to convert to a fixed-point is to multiply the floating point by b because the division by b is implicit. Thus, any floating-point k has its equivalent fixed-point value kb. What about converting back? This is easy: It's the inverse process. You simply need to divide by b, thus removing the implicit division. In fact, this was already done in the preceding example. If you reverse the process by multiplying by 4, you get back your original fixed point.

It is also interesting to look at fixed points in terms of memory bit-wise representation because there is a clear distinction between the integer portion of the number and the mantissa. If you look at Figure 19.1, which represents a 32-bit fixed-point value in memory, you'll notice that the integer portion of the bits and the mantissa (that is, the number following the point) share the 32-bit

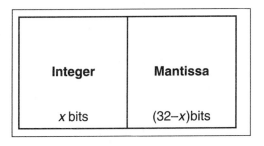

Figure 19.1
Single float memory representation

value. Thus you can easily compute the integer value with a mere shift (which is really equal to the division by b) by pushing the bits to the right such that the mantissa is reduced to 0 bits and the integer portion is represented with the entire 32 bits. It's that simple. Because the division by b is implicit, you can get the integer portion by shifting right.

Left alone, these numbers are a bit boring. For them to be useful, you need to give them a set of operations. So let's look at how you can compute various important operations on this set.

Fixed-Point Addition

With fixed-point addition, you get something similar to floating points by using integers only. For this to be worth your trouble, however, you need to make sure that the basic operations you wish to apply on these numbers are much faster than floating-point operations. To do this, you must take a look at the fixed-point operations. Besides, if you plan to use fixed points on embedded devices (and you should if you have no efficient FPU), you will need these as a clean separation of the integer portion and the decimal portion.

Let's consider two fixed-point numbers a and c. To make things easier on you, let's write them in the notation sb. Thus you have two numbers: $a = ib$ and $c = jb$. Any arithmetic operation on a fixed point should logically yield another fixed point, so the result of any fixed point should also be of the form sb. As it turns out, if you add the two fixed-point numbers in their floating-point representation, you get the following:

$$a + c = ib + jb = (i + j)b$$

The final answer is in fixed-point notation, so you are safe. This is most impressive because it means that adding two fixed-point numbers is no less complex than adding two integers. Fixed points are obviously pretty fast to add and subtract because subtraction is simply the addition of a negative number. You cannot do the math with the notation $\frac{a}{b}$ because you have to remember that the b is implicit in the value.

$$\frac{a}{b} + \frac{c}{b} = \frac{a+c}{b}$$

Fixed-Point Multiplication

Addition was a breeze to perform; multiplication, however, will give you a little more grief. When you multiply two fixed-point numbers, ab and cb, the result you would expect is acb. Unfortunately, if you multiply two fixed-point numbers together, you get an extra multiplication by b. This is not the end of the world; you can simply multiply your two numbers and thereafter shift right to divide by b. The only problem you may encounter is that multiplying a and b together may exceed the 32 bit limit. For this, you will have to juggle a little bit more. Literally. For now, this is the process that shows why you need to divide by b after a multiplication:

$$(b \cdot a)(b \cdot c) = b^2 a \cdot c$$

How do you take care of the overflow issues you may encounter? You can fine-tune this to fit your own bit-precision, but the idea is that you can split your variables a and c in two same-size separate parts. Suppose $a = [wx]$ and $c = [yz]$ such that for a 32-bit value, each sub-component represents the high/low 16 bits. Let k represent the value that is half the power carried by a and c. Thus, for 32-bit values, k would be 65536, which basically shifts a value in the upper 16 bits. The following reasoning ensues:

$$b^2 a \cdot c = (k \cdot w + x)(k \cdot y + z)$$

$$= k^2 \cdot w \cdot y + k(w \cdot z + x \cdot y) + x \cdot z$$

$$= k^2 \cdot w \cdot y + k(w \cdot z + x \cdot y) + x \cdot z + k^2 \left\lfloor \frac{w \cdot z + x \cdot y}{k} \right\rfloor - k^2 \left\lfloor \frac{w \cdot z + x \cdot y}{k} \right\rfloor$$

$$= k^2 \left(w \cdot y + \left\lfloor \frac{w \cdot z + x \cdot y}{k} \right\rfloor \right) + \left(\left((w \cdot z + x \cdot y) + -k^2 \left\lfloor \frac{w \cdot z + x \cdot y}{k} \right\rfloor \right) + x \cdot z \right)$$

This sounds like an incredibly winding and long process, but in terms of computing time, it's relatively simple. Notice how the two first-level parentheses are separated. In the first case, everything is multiplied by the square of k, while the other side does not have any implicit multiplication. The square of k is actually a shift of one complete element. Again, if you come back to the 32-bit example, k squared would in fact shift the entire value 32 bits up. Thus, the value contained in parentheses is actually the upper 32 bits of the multiplication, while the other parentheses carry the lower 32 bits.

The flooring function ensures that the number does not overflow. If you look at the elements in terms of how many bits of precision are carried around, you can see that everything matches as shown here for variables of n bits (recall that they represent the number of bits and not actual numbers, so the addition and multiplications are different in that respect):

$$= \left\{ \frac{n}{2} \right\}^2 \left(\left\{ \frac{n}{2} \right\} \cdot \left\{ \frac{n}{2} \right\} + \left\lfloor \frac{\left\{ \frac{n}{2} \right\} \cdot \left\{ \frac{n}{2} \right\} + \left\{ \frac{n}{2} \right\} \cdot \left\{ \frac{n}{2} \right\}}{\left\{ \frac{n}{2} \right\}} \right\rfloor \right) + \left(\left\{ \frac{n}{2} \right\} \left(\left\{ \frac{n}{2} \right\} \cdot \left\{ \frac{n}{2} \right\} + \left\{ \frac{n}{2} \right\} \cdot \left\{ \frac{n}{2} \right\} \right) - \left\{ \frac{n}{2} \right\} \left\lfloor \frac{\left\{ \frac{n}{2} \right\} \cdot \left\{ \frac{n}{2} \right\} + \left\{ \frac{n}{2} \right\} \cdot \left\{ \frac{n}{2} \right\}}{\left\{ \frac{n}{2} \right\}} \right\rfloor \right) + \left\lfloor \frac{n}{2} \right\rfloor$$

$$= \{n\} \left(\{n\} + \left\lfloor \frac{\{n\} + \{n\}}{\left\{ \frac{n}{2} \right\}} \right\rfloor \right) + \left(\left\{ \frac{n}{2} \right\} (\{n\} + \{n\}) - \left\{ \frac{n}{2} \right\} \left\lfloor \frac{\{n\} + \{n\}}{\left\{ \frac{n}{2} \right\}} \right\rfloor \right) + \{n\}$$

$$= \{n\} \left(\{n\} + \left\{ \frac{n}{2} \right\} \right) + \left(\left\{ \frac{n}{2} \right\} \left(\{n\} - \left\{ \frac{n}{2} \right\} \cdot \left\{ \frac{n}{2} \right\} \right) \right) + \{n\}$$

$$= \{n\} (\{n\}) + \left(\left\{ \frac{n}{2} \right\} (\{n\} - \{n\}) \right) + \{n\}$$

$$= \{n\} (\{n\}) + (\{n\} + \{n\})$$

$$= \{n\} (\{n\}) + (\{n\})$$

Of course, the additions could yield overflows, so you do have to carry one bit to the most significant n bits in each of these cases, but it's not that bad. That's because if you consider the fact that a process will typically cut the most significant bits when the multiplication overflows, you get the much more manageable formula, where the square brackets are used to represent the saturated multiplication:

$$b^2 a \cdot c = k^2 \left(w \cdot y + \left\lfloor \frac{w \cdot z + x \cdot y}{k} \right\rfloor \right) + \left(\left[k \left(w \cdot z + x \cdot y \right) \right] + x \cdot z \right)$$

At that point, you can divide each side by b to retrieve the final solution in fixed point. Of course, you can still get overflows with this technique, but the overflows will not be due to some bad calculations. Rather, they'll occur because the variables can only contain so much information, just like how multiplying two integers may overflow in 32 bits.

Although this is the general method for handling this type of situation, you can easily add a few shortcuts if you see that one of the computations (say, the upper 32 bits) is zero. The following code shows how you could go about implementing this:

```
FixedPoint FixMul(FixedPoint A, FixedPoint B)
{
        char            Negative;
        unsigned long AL, AH, BL, BH, RL, RH;
        // A = (AH << 16) + AL, B = (BH << 16) + BL, R = (RH << 16) + RL

        if (!(A | B))
                return 0;

        if (A < 0) {
                A               = -A;
                Negative        = 1;
        } else
                Negative        = 0;

        if (B < 0) {
                B               = -B;
                Negative        ^= 1;
        }

        AL = (unsigned long)(A & 0xFFFF);
        AH = (unsigned long)(A >> 16);
        BL = (unsigned long)(B & 0xFFFF);
        BH = (unsigned long)(B >> 16);
```

```
            // LSW
            RL = AL * BL;        // Calculate the lowest 32 bit value
            RH = AH * BH;        // Calculate the highest 32 bit value
                                 // Calculate the middle value
            AL = (AL * BH) + (BL * AH);        // It will never overflow because the
                                              // highs are signed thus 15 bits

            AH = AL << 16;
            AL = RL + AH;        // Add the low 16 bits to the high 16 bits

            If ((AL < AH) || (AL < RL))
                    RH++;        // Add the carry bit if it exists

            RH += (AL >> 16);
            RL  = (RL >> PRECISION) + (RH << (32 - PRECISION));

            return (FixedPoint)(Negative ? -((FixedPoint)RL) : RL);
}
```

This looks like an awful lot of work just to get a multiplication. As it turns out, though, it is significantly more efficient than a floating-point implementation. The section on floating points will help you appreciate why this is so, but for the time being, just know that on the PC, a Linux audio driver has tested floats versus fixed and found that on average, the fixed-point operations were two to three times faster. Mind you, this is on a system that is actually equipped with an FPU.

So why should you even bother to use floats? It's simple. Fixed points do not have a very great range, which means you cannot represent large numbers (or very small numbers) with them. As you will see later on, fixed-point numbers are more precise than floats, but they lack the range. Some things for the PC, such as TrueType fonts, are written using fixed points simply because they offer greater precision and speed. On an embedded device such a Game Boy or phone, however, things work up to six times slower depending on the device.

Fixed-Point Division

The multiplication of two fixed-point values is conceptually very simple. What makes it that more complicated is the fact that you have to consistently keep the precision at an all-time high. The division, as you may expect, is conceptually simple, but not so when it comes time to implement. The following similar logic ensues for two fixed-point values *ab* and *cb*:

$$\frac{ab}{cb} = \frac{a}{c}$$

In this scenario, you lack the multiplication by b. Thus, you have to multiply your final answer by b in order to retrieve the correct solution. This is another conceptually easy operation, but it's reasonably nasty to implement. In order to get full-blown accuracy, you cannot divide first. You must first multiply and then divide by c, which simply makes things worse than the multiplication alone.

If you divide a by c, what you get is the integer portion of the division. You lose all the details about the mantissa, which is not a good a thing. It's easy thereafter to multiply the integer portion by b. You could compute the remainder of the division to get the mantissa, but you still need to divide the remainder by c, which still does not solve the real problem. What you actually have to implement is a division algorithm.

You know that, by definition, the remainder is smaller than c. If you double the remainder and it ends up being greater than c, what does that tell you about it? Interestingly enough, it tells you that the remainder is at least half of c. Thus, you can add 0.5 to your value and the multiplication of the newfound value with c will be much closer to the real value of the division without being larger than it.

The question at this step is whether to add 0.5 to your value. If, for example, you take 63/128, doubling 63 shows that 63 is not at least half of 128; thus, you should not add 0.5 to your value. A floating-point calculation reveals that the number is indeed smaller than 0.5. If you had added 0.5 to the value, you would never have been able to generate a smaller value by adding any positive number. More precisely, by adding any other positive number, you would never be able to generate a function that converges toward the true answer.

You can apply this process recursively in order to get the most precise estimate of your number. If twice the remainder is larger than c, you can subtract c from it; if not, the number is already positioned to check for 0.25. The following example shows how this is performed:

$a = 63$

$c = 128$

Math Step	Number (Total of Adder)	Adder Step
$\dfrac{a}{c} = \dfrac{63}{128} = 0$	0.0	1
$2\dfrac{63}{128} = \dfrac{126}{128} = 0$	0.0	0.5
$2\dfrac{126}{128} = \dfrac{252}{128} = 1 + \dfrac{124}{128}$	0.25	0.25
$2\dfrac{124}{128} = \dfrac{248}{128} = 1 + \dfrac{120}{128}$	0.375	0.125
$2\dfrac{120}{128} = \dfrac{240}{128} = 1 + \dfrac{112}{128}$	0.4375	0.0625
$2\dfrac{112}{128} = \dfrac{224}{128} = 1 + \dfrac{96}{128}$	0.46875	0.03125
$2\dfrac{96}{128} = \dfrac{129}{128} = 1 + \dfrac{64}{128}$	0.484375	0.015625
$2\dfrac{64}{128} = 1$	0.4921875	0.0078125

In this case, you were able to repeat the process enough times to yield the exact solution—although that is not always possible. That's because fractions can yield infinite series.

You know that b specifies how many bits are available for the mantissa, and thus you should repeat this process for the only number of bits that b can represent.

In source code, the algorithm can be implemented as shown here:

```
typedef unsigned long FixedPoint;

FixedPoint FixDiv(FixedPoint A, FixedPoint C)
{
        unsigned long Rem;
        char Negative = 0;

        if (A < 0) {
                A = -A;
                Negative ^= 1;
```

```
        }
    if (C < 0) {
            C = -C;
            Negative ^= 1;
    }

    Rem = A % C;
    A   = A / C;

    for (char Bbit = PRECISION ; Bbit-- ;) {
            A   <<= 1;
            Rem <<= 1;
            if (Rem >= (unsigned long)C) {
                    Rem -= (unsigned long)C;
                    A++;
            }

    }

        return (FixedPoint)(Negative ? -((FixedPoint)A) : A);
}
```

As far as speed is concerned, is this function really better than what the processor can provide? One thing is certain: It isn't as nice as the multiplication or the addition. But if you grab any processor cycle count table, you will notice that division is always significantly slower than multiplication. Take today's Pentium 4, for example. A multiplication sits at seven CPU cycles, while a division goes up to a whopping 23—more than three times the number.

Would you expect the division function here to be three times slower than the multiplication? It depends where you run this code. On a PC, it is roughly equivalent to the division, barely beating it. On an embedded device where concepts such as branch prediction and out-of-order execution are not on the agenda, you really gain as much as you do with the multiplication, two to three times over floats—again, a pretty significant amount.

Integer Square Root

It is so easy to ask a computer to give you the square root of a number, but how does the computer go about computing it? On embedded devices, if you have no floating-point unit, it is very possible that a square-root function is completely out of the question. If that is the case, then you have to implement this function yourself. Fortunately, there is an easy and efficient way to implement it.

The idea is based on the one used for fixed-point division. You use a heuristic in order to determine whether you should toggle a bit, and this heuristic is meant for nothing else but to compute the square of your guess. You start by verifying the most significant bit of the square root (that is, bit 15 of a 32-bit square-root value). To do so, toggle the bit on initially; if the square of the value obtained by toggling the bit is smaller than the square of the square root you are looking for, then the bit should be toggled on. You can apply this process on all the lower-half bits in order to compute the square root. In other words, after you have verified that toggling bit 15 yields a number that is smaller than the square root of the number you are looking for, you can apply the same test for bit 14, keeping the previous bits toggled as per the test.

The following code illustrates the idea:

```
unsigned short sqrt(unsigned long X)
{
        unsigned long Guess = 0;
        unsigned long Bit = 1 << 15;

        do {
                Guess ^= Bit;
                // Verify if the bit should be toggled or not
                if (Guess * Guess > X)
                        Guess ^= Bit;
        } while (Bit >>= 1);

        return Guess;
}
```

This is grade-school stuff. For example, take 49 and compute its square root. You know that the 15th bit is not such a small number, so you can skip that one. Instead, start with 8, with the fourth bit being on. Table 19.1 illustrates the process.

Table 19.1 Sqrt(49) Computation

Bit On	Value with Bit Toggled	Test	Number So Far
4	8	$8 \cdot 8 <= 49$	no; 0
3	4	$4 \cdot 4 <= 49$	yes; 4
2	(4+2)=6	$6 \cdot 6 <= 49$	yes; 6
1	(6+1)=7	$7 \cdot 7 <= 49$	yes; 7

When you reach the last bit, you stop. Thus you find that sqrt(49) = 7.

This algorithm is good not only for integers, but also for fixed points. The only thing you have to be careful about is calculating the forward guess. (Source code for such a version will be given at the end of this section.) This is a very simple algorithm, but it is also very inefficient. The multiplication is the parasite, which would be nice to eradicate here. You can easily achieve this if you simply apply forward differentiation twice on it. What you get is the following, where x is your guess and b is the value added by the bit toggle:

$$\text{Guess}(x) = x^2$$
$$\text{Guess}(x+b) = x^2 + 2xb + b^2$$
$$= \text{Guess}(x) + (2xb + b^2)$$

and

$$\text{Guess'}(x) = 2xb + b^2$$
$$\text{Guess'}(x+b) = 2(x+b)b + b^2$$
$$= \text{Guess'}(x) + b^2$$

If you keep track of x^2 and $2x$, you can actually achieve this. Taking the square of b is easy because you can simply double the shift of the bit you wanted to test. And as for $2xb$, you can also compute it easily because b is actually just a shift of $2x$. If you keep track of the forward differentiation guess's two last terms, you can express the values of the forward differentiation as a combination of its last value and the square of the bits as shown here:

$$Bit_{n+1} = \frac{Bit_n}{4}$$
$$ForwardGuess_n = Bit_n \left(2Guess + Bit_n\right)$$
$$ForwardGuess_n = \frac{Bit_n}{2}\left(2Guess + \frac{Bit_n}{2}\right)$$
$$= \frac{1}{2}\left(2Guess \cdot Bit_n + \frac{Bit_n^2}{2}\right)$$
$$= \frac{1}{2}\left(2Guess \cdot Bit_n + \frac{Bit_n^2}{2} + \frac{Bit_n^2}{2} - \frac{Bit_n^2}{2}\right)$$
$$= \frac{1}{2}\left(2\left(Guess \cdot Bit_n + Bit_n^2\right) + 2\frac{Bit_n^2}{4}\right)$$
$$= \frac{1}{2}\left(ForwardGuess_n - 2Bit_{n+1}\right)$$

This yields the following source code:

```
unsigned short sqrt(unsigned long X)
{
        unsigned long Guess, SqrGuess, Bit, TwoSqrBit, ForwardGuess;

        Guess         = 0;
        SqrGuess      = 0;
        Bit           = 1 << 15;
        TwoSqrBit     = 1 << 31;        // 2*Bit^2
        ForwardGuess = 1 << 30;        // 2*Bit*Guess + Bit^2

        do {
                // Verify if the bit should be toggled or not
                if (SquGuess + ForwardGuess <= X) {
                        Guess          |= Bit;
                        SqrGuess       += ForwardGuess;
                        ForwardGuess += TwoSqrBit;
                }

                // Shift everything down to test the next bit
                Bit             >>= 1;
                TwoSqrBit     >>= 2;
                ForwardGuess          = (ForwardGuess - TwoSqrBit) >> 1;
        } while(Bit);

        return Guess;
}
```

You can optimize this source code even more if you evaluate ForwardGuess by keeping track of the actual bit number you are evaluating. If you are really that crazy about speed, you could easily unroll this loop to yield even greater results. The following source code shows how the non-unrolled version should be implemented:

```
unsigned short sqrt(unsigned long X)
{
        unsigned long Guess = 0, Bit = 0x8000, BitShift = 15;

        do {
                // 2*Bit*Guess + Bit^2
                unsigned long ForwardGuess = (Guess + Guess + Bit) << BitShift;
```

```
                    // Verify if the bit should be toggled or not
                    if (X   >= ForwardGuess) {
                            Guess           |= Bit;
                            X               -= ForwardGuess;
                    }

                    BitShift--;
            } while (Bit >>= 1);

            return Guess;
    }
```

But what about fixed points? If you want fixed points, you will have to do pretty much the same thing, but be a little more careful about the value of the guess. The following code shows such an implementation:

```
#define sqrt_Def_1(Bit)                             \
{                                                   \
    if (Sqr + (Val << Bit) <= (MMUInt32)a) {        \
        a   -= (Val << Bit) + Sqr;                  \
        Val |= 1 << (Bit - 1);                      \
    }                                               \
                                                    \
    Sqr >>= 2;                                      \
}


#define sqrt_Def_2(Bit)                             \
{                                                   \
    if (Sqr + (Val >> (8 - Bit)) <= (MMUInt32)a) {  \
        a   -= (Val >> (8 - Bit)) + Sqr;            \
        Val |= 1 << (Bit - 1);                      \
    }                                               \
                                                    \
    Sqr >>= 2;                                      \
}
FixedPoint fixSqrt(FixedPoint a)
{
    unsigned long Sqr = 0x40000000;
    unsigned long Val = 0;
    MMD_RUN(long Olda = a);

    // Verify that the result is a real number, not a complex
    MMD_ASSERT1(Olda >= 0, Olda, "I don't want to compute a negative square root!");
```

```
// Figure out the integer portion of our number
sqrt_Def_1(16);
sqrt_Def_1(15);
sqrt_Def_1(14);
sqrt_Def_1(13);
sqrt_Def_1(12);
sqrt_Def_1(11);
sqrt_Def_1(10);
sqrt_Def_1(9);
// Figure out the first byte of the decimal portion
sqrt_Def_1(8);
sqrt_Def_1(7);
sqrt_Def_1(6);
sqrt_Def_1(5);
sqrt_Def_1(4);
sqrt_Def_1(3);
sqrt_Def_1(2);
sqrt_Def_1(1);
// Discover the last byte of decimal precision
// 'Bit' starts at 8, thus move everything by 8
a    <<= 8;
Val <<= 8;
Sqr <<= 8;
sqrt_Def_2(8);
sqrt_Def_2(7);
sqrt_Def_2(6);
sqrt_Def_2(5);
sqrt_Def_2(4);
sqrt_Def_2(3);
sqrt_Def_2(2);
sqrt_Def_2(1);

    return Val;
}
```

IEEE Floating Points

A lot of programmers think that floating points can achieve pretty much anything they desire. If you have previously implemented a method to find the collision between game elements (such as a rocket or rail gun hitting a triangle), you know that this is completely false. To really understand why this is so and how bad the effect is, you have to look deep into the CPU and observe how things are done. You probably don't want to implement your own floating-point unit, but understanding the math behind it will help you understand where the slow functions are, and will also help you learn a few tricks.

The shocker about floating points is that they are not real numbers. Real numbers have the characteristic of potentially holding an infinite pattern of decimal digits. The square root of two is such an example. If you expand the value, you should never find a pattern repeating itself. In a game world, however, you deal with finite space; thus, you cannot represent real numbers directly unless you start to keep the numbers around in their original form (such as square root of 2, for example). Floats cannot accurately represent π, but how often (in game programming) do you need a 200-digit accurate value for π?

Floating points are actually rational numbers—that is, numbers that can be written as a fraction $\frac{a}{b}$. This can yield infinitely precise values such as $1/3$, but due to the finite aspect of the representation, there will always be a finite pattern in the decimal digits.

IEEE floating points can be any of 32, 64, or 80 bits on the PC. The interesting thing is that floats actually have quite a good range. Thus, necessarily, some bits in the number will be used to represent the number itself, and other bits will be used to represent the power by which it is multiplied. This means that a fixed point, for example, is actually more precise than a float if you want it to be. Another way to put it is that you can represent more numbers in the range $[0, 2^{32}]$ with a long (that is, fixed point) than with a single float that has only 19 bits for the actual number.

Many would not think that longs are "more precise" than single floats, but they truly are. This is all interesting, but it only pushes back the real question, which is, how are single floats represented according to the IEEE standard? It turns out that all floating-point formats can be expressed with the following formula, where the mantissa can be written as a rational number ranging from 0 on up and the exponent is an integer ranging from a negative to a positive:

$$\pm\left(1+2^{-mantissa}\right)2^{exponent}$$

Specifically, for 32-bit floats, the formula is as follows, where the mantissa ranges from $[0, 2^{23} - 1]$ and where the exponent has a range of $[0, 255]$:

$$\pm\left(1+\frac{mantissa}{2^{23}}\right)2^{127-exponent}$$

If you substitute the extrema in the equation, you get that a single float can produce numbers with a range of $[-3.4028 \cdot 10^{38}, 3.4028 \cdot 10^{38}]$ with the smallest positive number being $1.1754 \cdot 10^{-38}$. If you look at everything correctly, you will notice that 23 bits are assigned to the mantissa, eight bits to the exponent, and one bit used as the sign.

Sign	Exponent	Mantissa
1 bit	8 bits	23 bits

Figure 19.2
Single-float memory representation

The memory representation of a single float is shown in Figure 19.2. Table 19.2 contains a few examples of floating point representation in memory.

Table 19.2 Floating-Point Representation Examples

Float Value	Hex Value	Sign	Exponent	Mantissa
1.0	3F800000h	0b	01111111b (2^0)	00000000000000000000000b (0)
−4.0	C0800000h	1b	10000001b (2^2)	00000000000000000000000b (0)
$4.125*2^{42}$	55840000h	0b	10101011b (2^{44})	00001000000000000000000b (1.03125)

When designing the floating-point representation, the IEEE group could have used a bias for the sign of the floating-point value as well to span even more possible values, but they did not. This was a good decision, namely because floating-point values also take care of many other things with which integers have problems. Because many sets of bits are redundant, the IEEE group has also defined a set of values that the floating-point values can carry around, as shown in Table 19.3.

Table 19.3 Single Floating-Point Special Values

Name	Hex Range	Sign	Exponent	Mantissa
−QNaN	FFFFFFFFh– FFC00000h	1	11111111	1?????????????????????
−SNaN	FFBFFFFFh– FF800001h	1	11111111	0?????????????????????
−Inf	FF800000h	1	11111111	0000000000000000000000
−0	80000000h	1	00000000	0000000000000000000000
+0	00000000h	0	00000000	0000000000000000000000
Inf	7F800000h	0	11111111	0000000000000000000000
SNaN	7F800001h– 7FBFFFFFh	0	11111111	0?????????????????????
QNaN	7FC00000h–	0	11111111	1?????????????????????

Zero and infinity are pretty obvious values. As soon as you overflow the floating-point range, you get infinity. If you underflow, you get 0 (positive or negative, depending on where you come from). The more interesting ones are the NaNs. NaN stands for Not a Number. You could easily obtain one if, for example, you were to compute the square root of a negative number. The Q that precedes NaN stands for Quiet. Thus, when you do an operation, no exception is signaled. On the flipside, S stands for Signal, which does trigger an exception. Semantically, a QNaN stands for an indeterminate operation, while SNaN denotes an invalid operation.

There is one last nasty concept you need to be aware of: normal values against denormal values. What you have seen so far fits in the category of normal values. An exponent of 0 with a non-zero mantissa identifies a denormal value. Denormal values are a little different from their cousins, in that they try to extend the infinitesimal limit even further. A denormal value's equation is as follows:

$$\pm\left(\frac{mantissa}{2^{23}}\right)2^{-126}$$

In short, if you can remove the predominant one of a normal value, you can easily obtain the denormal value. All you can control in such a value is the mantissa. Thus, the values this equation can generate have a range of $[1.1754 \bullet 10^{-38}, 1.4012 \bullet 10^{-45}]$. If you are thinking about implementing your own version of floating point in software simply because you require large ranges and your device does not support it in software or hardware, then you could easily forget about denormalized values if they are not important to you.

Floats Addition

What is simple on paper is not always so trivial on a computer. Adding floating point values requires a bit of thinking. It probably isn't something you'd want to implement yourself unless your compiler was deprived of such a thing (which is typically not the case), but it is always nice to understand what goes on under the hood. This will help you understand why floats are so slow. In this section, your only concern will be the normalized values. You can abstract the fine details of the implementation by looking at them in terms of factors. Any floats can be represented as $a \bullet 2^b$.

For example, suppose that a is the mantissa factor with range $[1, 2]$ and b is the exponential factor. Thus, take two numbers $a2^b$ and $c2^d$. Without loss of generality, suppose that b is greater than d. The following logic can be deduced:

$$a \cdot 2^b + c \cdot 2^d = a \cdot 2^b + c \cdot 2^d \cdot (1)$$
$$= a \cdot 2^b + c \cdot 2^d \cdot \left(2^b \cdot 2^{-b}\right)$$
$$= a \cdot 2^b + \left(c \cdot 2^d \cdot 2^b\right) \cdot 2^{-b}$$
$$= \left(a + c \cdot 2^{d-b}\right)2^b$$

The idea behind the equations is rather simple. You should always discard the least significant bits. Thus, you take the greatest number between the two, and you try to change the second number such that its exponential factor can be factored out with the other number. Once they are factored out, the equation becomes easy to compute. It's a simple matter of shifting the value c to the right such that the power of d matches that of b. This is actually where you are losing precision, however, because you are killing all of the least significant bits here.

After the addition is done, you simply have to normalize the values such that the mantissa portion does not exceed a value of 2. If it does, the carry bit should be added to b automatically. This is the beauty of this representation. Let's see how this would work with an example:

$$a = 1.75$$
$$b = 10$$
$$c = 1.5$$
$$d = 5$$
$$
\begin{aligned}
a2^b + c2^d &= 1.75 \cdot 2^{10} + 1.5 \cdot 2^5 \\
&= 1.75 \cdot 2^{10} + 2^{10} \left(1.5 \cdot 2^{-5}\right) \\
&= 2^{10} \left(1.75 + 0.046875\right) \\
&= 1.796875 \cdot 2^{10}
\end{aligned}
$$

The same process can be applied to negative numbers as well (or subtraction, if you prefer). In this case, you simply have to make sure to check for borrowing bits. If the mantissa factor is less than 1, then you must make sure to reduce the power. This is the same type of thing you were doing in grade school but with a little more thinking involved. The process is a little bit messy because you have to take care of all these cases, which is also the reason why floating points were not too popular when there was no such thing as an FPU.

Floats Multiplication

If you understood the addition process, you will have no problem understanding the multiplication process because the same basic idea applies. The only difference is that you have to resort to a simple exponential identity. The following shows how you can achieve this:

$$a \cdot 2^b \cdot b \cdot 2^d = (a \cdot b) \cdot 2^{b+d}$$

It is in fact that simple. The only thing you have to be careful about is when you multiply a and b. For reasons you saw in the fixed-point section, you will have to shift right the result of $a \cdot b$ by the number of bits the mantissa carries (which is 23 for single floats). This may sound very strange at first, but it is the correct way to do things. Again, you have to remember to account for the overflow you may get from that multiplication. But once more, should there be any overflow, the bits will be shifted into the exponent's bits, which is exactly where the carry bits should be going. The following example illustrates how you would go about multiplying two floats together:

$$a = 1.75$$
$$b = 10$$
$$c = 1.5$$
$$d = 5$$
$$a2^b \cdot c2^d = 1.75 \cdot 2^{10} \cdot 1.5 \cdot 2^5$$
$$= 1.75 \cdot 1.5 \cdot 2^{15}$$
$$= 2.625 \cdot 2^{15}$$
$$= 1.3125 \cdot 2^{16}$$

Here, I did not shift the result of the multiplication by 23. I cheated by doing the multiplication in floats instead of with integers, which is how it should be done on the microprocessor. (After all, if you did have a floating point unit, why would you not use it?) The idea works in exactly the same fashion as fixed point for this specific section. The division can be performed with the same logic, but by subtracting the exponents and dividing the mantissa.

Double Floats

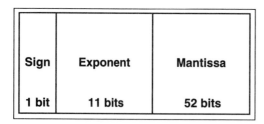

Figure 19.3
Double float memory representation

Double floats are very similar to single floats but they operate on 64 bits instead of 32 bits. The range is already pretty good for single floats, thus the IEEE organization opted to increase the accuracy more than the range. A double float has ratios of 1:11:52. That's one bit for the sign, 11 for the exponent, and 52 for the mantissa, as shown in Figure 19.3. Because of this ratio, the bias is half the maximum value. Thus, because 11 bits are reserved for the exponent, the bias for a 64-bit float is 1023.

The equation, which can represent any double float, is given by the following:

$$\pm\left(1+\frac{mantissa}{2^{52}}\right)2^{1023-exponent}$$

Given these details, you can easily check that the numbers have a range of $[-1.1897 \cdot 10^{4932}, 1.1897 \cdot 10^{4932}]$, with the smallest number being $3.3621 \cdot 10^{-4932}$ and $3.6451 \cdot 10^{-4951}$ for denormalized values. Denormalized values follow the exact same rules as mentioned previously with the noted exception of the added precision bits. Thus, all denormalized values have an exponent of 0 and their equations can be written as follows:

$$\pm\left(\frac{mantissa}{2^{52}}\right)2^{-1022}$$

The special cases follow the same rules they follow for single precision floats, but because it is always useful to have a table of values to look at, Table 19.4 shows all the exceptions in floating point representation.

Table 19.4 Double Floating-Point Special Values

Name	Hex Range	Sign	Exponent	Mantissa
−QNaN	FFFFFFFFFFFFFFFFh– FFF8000000000000h	1	11111111111	1?????????? ??????????? ??????????? ??????????? ???????
−SNaN	FFF7FFFFFFFFFFFFh– FFF0000000000001h	1	11111111111	0?????????? ??????????? ??????????? ??????????? ???????
−Inf	FFF0000000000000h	1	11111111111	00000000000 00000000000 00000000000 00000000000 0000000
−0	8000000000000000h	1	00000000000	00000000000 00000000000 00000000000 00000000000 0000000

(continued on next page)

Table 19.4 Double Floating-Point Special Values *(continued)*

Name	Hex Range	Sign	Exponent	Mantissa
+0	0000000000000000h	0	00000000000	00000000000 00000000000 00000000000 00000000000 0000000
Inf	7FF0000000000000h	0	11111111111	00000000000 00000000000 00000000000 00000000000 0000000
SNaN	7FF0000000000001h– 7FF7FFFFFFFFFFFFh	0	11111111111	0?????????? ?????????? ?????????? ?????????? ???????
QNaN	7FF8000000000000h– FFFFFFFFFFFFFFFFh	0	11111111111	1?????????? ?????????? ?????????? ?????????? ???????

Condition Arithmetic

Branches and conditions are two very separate entities. Branches modify the location of the instruction pointer, while conditions are functions that return a value.

Do you ever put a lot of effort into the way you present your conditions to the compiler? Would you rather say that the glass is half full or half empty? Trust me, simple questions like these can actually make a difference in your code. It is important that you take a careful look at your conditional expressions because the first expression that comes to mind is not always the best expression for the machine to understand what you want to achieve.

Before you start looking at methods for optimizing your conditions, let's first look at what a compiler generates when a condition is given. A simple condition is, well, simple. Instead, let's take an expression that is slightly more complicated—say, (A && B) where A and B are predicates. Believe it or not, this is actually converted into two branches, not one. The compiler typically converts the upper expression to the following:

```
if (A)
        if (B)
                DoIt();
```

This is exactly how it should be done according to the C standard. Because B is a function that returns a value, it should not be called unless A is true. This is obviously problematic for you because expressions can get pretty beefy.

This book is not an optimization book, so I won't really go into why this happens. However, you want to get rid of branches on your PC as best as possible because they can incur a penalty of up to 20% due to the branch prediction algorithm. In addition, if you are working with an expression carrying multiple conditions, then based on the preceding code, it is to your advantage to put the most likely case first. Sometimes, however, the cases are equally distributed, and you cannot really say if one atomic condition is more probable than the rest. For the rest of this section, assume that the conditions are more or less equiprobable.

For these reasons, the expressions in this section will be optimized in two steps. The first will consist of removing the multiple branches from the expression, and the second will look at optimizing the expression itself to minimize the number of checks you need to apply.

Removal Via Computation

Most programmers write code the way they think about it. This is not always the best way to do things, however, because the human way of thinking about a solution is not necessarily the best way to proceed for a machine. This section will contain many interesting formulas, but if you remember only one thing after reading it, it's to think about your problem from a machine's point of view.

Allow me to illustrate using examples. A very popular primitive is to calculate the minimum and the maximum of two values (say, integers). What is the first thing that comes to mind for the min? Whatever it is, it's probably one of these two solutions:

```
if (A < B)
        X = A;
else
        X = B;          // Solution 1
X = A < B ? A : B;  // Solution 2
```

Was I wrong? Both these functions are in fact the same, and end up having one conditional branch. This is what your typical compiler will output if you run an abs function from the math library. If you thought of the SIMD min functions, then you can give yourself one point for killing the branch, but that route is not very good in terms of speed if you are not planning to do parallel calculations.

So if it's not one of the preceding solutions, what could it be? How about the following:

$$\min\{a,b\} = \frac{a+b-|a-b|}{2}$$

This clearly does not have any branches, mathematically speaking, and if you think about it, it does work. If you do not see this, then perhaps re-working the equation as such will make more sense:

$$\min\{a,b\} = \frac{b+(a-|a-b|)}{2}$$

Without loss of generality, suppose that a is the largest number. By grouping the equation as done previously, and because a is the largest number, you get the following result:

$$\min\{a,b\} = \frac{b+(a-(a-b))}{2}$$
$$= \frac{b+b}{2}$$
$$= b$$

If, on the other hand, b is the largest number, simply change the parentheses and the order of the variables in the absolute value, and the result will be a. You may also change the sign before the absolute value in order to get the maximum instead of the minimum. Interesting way to look at it, is it not?

If I caught you by surprise, don't worry; I have another one for you. How would you calculate the absolute value of an integer? This one requires a little deeper knowledge of the PC. Stumped? Try the following:

$$x = ((x \gg 31) \wedge x) - (x \gg 31)$$

It's hard to believe that this function is faster than the condition, but trust me, it takes roughly 70 percent as long as the other function when tested. The key to understanding this one comes from the fact that a shift right for signed integers replaces the highest bits with 1. Thus, if the number is negative, you get the following:

$$x = (0xFFFFFFFF \wedge x) - 0xFFFFFFFF$$
$$= (-x) - 1$$

On the contrary, if x is positive, you get the following, which does absolutely nothing:

$$x = (0 \wedge x) - 0$$
$$= x$$

Combine the minimum function with this one, however, and you get roughly a 25 percent speed increase over the branch for a set of random numbers. Not too bad. It's not because you have found an equation for the general case that you do not need to think about your specific case. Many times, you can optimize your code by rethinking the problem with the specific things you know about the general solution.

Here is another challenge for you: Calculate the minimum of two unsigned integers. (Hint: you will require assembly instructions to achieve this.) Clearly, you could use the preceding code to achieve this, but let's try another approach. Assume that eax and ebx contain the two numbers, and you wish to find the minimum that is eventually stored in eax. The code follows:

```
sub     ebx, eax
sbb     ecx, ecx
and     ecx, ebx
add     eax, ecx
```

note

The fact that this is written in assembler code should not matter. The compiler does an excellent job optimizing C code in such small portions; for this reason, assembler code is generally comparable to C code for very small functions (unless you can use some special functions, such as in this case).

Some benchmarks on the preceding code show that it is in fact roughly 30 percent faster than the first version.

One thing you have to be careful about is that removing the branch does not imply removing the condition. Suppose, for example, that you have a function that returns an event—say, an event that tells you that a mouse button has been clicked. Further suppose that you need to flag a variable in your code to notify the main loop about this fact. When the main loop notices that the flag has been set, it can use this information to perform a certain action. Upon release, that same function is called but with some other event (for example, mouse unclicked). The traditional way to handle this is to write something along these lines:

```
If (Event == MOUSE_CLICKED)
        Flag = 1;
else
        Flag = 0;
```

A fancier method to achieve the exact same thing is to write the following:

```
Flag = (Event == MOUSE_CLICKED);
```

This does not convert into a branch because the compiler uses the internal condition flags for this. In this case, you save the branch. Another similar trick is to use a function that sets a given variable to 1 if a number is positive or −1 if it is negative. The solution? Very similar to what you have seen so far:

```
Sign = ((x > 0) << 1) - 1
```

The trick here is to recall that a conditional expression returns 0 or 1 depending on whether it is flagged as true or false. You are free to use this fact to your advantage in order to calculate the outcome of a variable based on an expression.

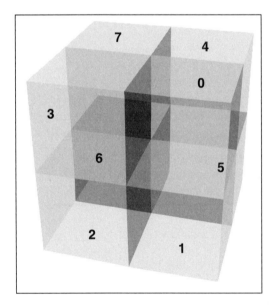

Figure 19.4
Octant index separation

You can also use lookup tables or, more interestingly, lookup values in order to obtain the final value you are looking for. One such example is a function to determine the octant (in an octree) in which a given vertex (x, y, z) sits. Assume that for some practical reason, you are forced to describe the octants in a clockwise fashion starting with octant 0 being the top-right octant. Furthermore, suppose that the frontmost half starts at 0, while the farthest half uses the same rule but starts at 4, as shown in Figure 19.4.

The trick at this point is to give a unique index to each octant. You can easily tell the difference between $z < 0$ and $z > 0$ by the computation $(z < 0)$, which yields 1 or 0. You can combine the same logic for x and y provided they do not lose the information you collected on z. If you assign them separate bits, then you should be good.

So suppose that the first bit is assigned for x, the second for y, and the third for z. You can shift the condition's result left to separate the bits. With three bits, you will generate eight possibilities and thus uniquely identify the eight octants. What you have computed so far is only an index, however. The index does not match the order you gave to your octants.

As a result, you have to map each of them to a different value between 0 and 7. Such a value can be represented on three bits; it just so happens that in a 32-bit number, you can store up to 10 3-bit values or up to eight 4-bit values.

The answer should be pretty obvious at this point: You can build a 32-bit value split into eight elements of four bits for which the index will offset the elements, and for which the offset i will map into the corresponding octant. Because every element is taken as a 4-bit element, the offset will have to be shifted left by 4 to correctly address the bits. All that remains at that point is to mask everything such that you only get the last three bits. The following code illustrates this:

```
unsigned long Index((X < 0) << 2);
Index |= (Y < 0) << 3;
Index |= (Z < 0) << 4;

Octant = (0x65742130 >> Index) & 7;
```

So how does this work? Well, the index value basically isolates the nibble, which is required. The possible values for the index are {0, 4, 8, 12, 16, 20, 24, 28}. Thus, the "magic value" is shifted by one of these values. The trick at that point is simply to match the case with an index and to match these two to an octant value. Each value is represented on 4 bits, which is why the index jumps in increments of 4bits. So for example, if you had the case <−2, 2, 2>, only the first test would pass. Consequently, your would get an index of 4, the second value in the set of possible values. This maps to octant 3 if you compute it using the preceding equation.

And Then There Were None

The title of this section stems from a famous book written by Agatha Christie—interesting, intriguing, not quite realistic, but still entertaining. It presents a story about guests who are invited to a house in order to be killed, one by one. Throughout the story, the refrain "And then there were x" is repeated; as expected, the book finishes with "And then there were none." Likewise, the goal of this section is to kill problematic operators one by one (perhaps not as radically as was done in Agatha's book, but I am sure that your imagination can yield many scenarios).

The Logical AND Operator

Let's start with the logical AND operator, denoted &&. The logical AND operator takes two variables. For example, suppose you have two predicates, A and B. Your condition (A && B) can also be converted into its bit-wise equivalent (A & B). This means that both predicates will be computed, but the bit-wise AND will guarantee the removal of one extra branch. So instead of converting to the sample code you saw earlier, you simply get one longer condition followed by the action.

The bit-wise AND operates on a bit-per-bit basis. For this to work, then, you must make sure that the intersection (AND) of all possible non-zero values will be non-zero, or else there isn't a one to one match. If you always use operators that convert your conditions to 0 or 1, then this is not a problem. But if you're like me and you prefer to use the shorter form to test non-zero elements, then a bitwise AND won't work correctly unless what is stated here is true:

```
if (a && b) DoIt();
```

Take, for example, a = 2 and b = 1. AND them together, and you will get 0, even though both of them are non-zero. Instead, what you need to do is to change the statement to something similar to the following, which converts the values to either 0 or 1:

```
if ((a != 0) & (b != 0))
```

The OR Operator

Now turn your attention to the OR primitive. The compiler typically converts the OR condition similarly to how it converted the AND condition. In essence, for two predicates, A and B, the expression (A || B) yields the following:

```
if (!A)
        goto Done;
If (!B)
        goto Done;

DoIt();
Done:
```

Again, you are presented with two branch structures and, as with the AND, you can express (A || B) to its equivalent bit-wise version (A | B). Be careful about one pitfall, however, which may surface as you do this. The AND bit-wise operator has a greater precedence than the XOR operator (^). Hence, make sure you have your parentheses set up correctly if you ever use an XOR inside your code. Besides this small hiccup, the OR operator does not present the same issue that the AND operator did, because the bits are additive.

Expressing Yourself Clearly

After you convert your expression into a single branch expression, you are ready to pipe it into the next step to reduce the number of verifications. There are two ways to achieve this:

- The first method is by creating a truth table and finding a minimal expression to represent the bits you want to be active in the expression.

- The second method makes use of algebraic notions by manipulating the expression with a set of identities until the expression can no longer be reduced.

Truth Tables to the Rescue

The idea here is ask yourself what the result of all possible inputs is. In order to do this, you have to clearly isolate your parameters, enumerate all possible values of these parameters in terms of bits, and to put them into a table. For example, suppose you have three input predicates A..C for which actions D..F happen as described by Table 19.5. A value of 1 implies that the result is taken, and a value of 0 implies that the result should not be taken.

Table 19.5 Bit Representation of a Function with Range [0..7]

A	B	C	D	E	F
0	0	0	-	0	1
0	0	1	0	0	0
0	1	0	-	0	1
0	1	1	0	0	0
1	0	0	-	1	0
1	0	1	0	0	0
1	1	0	-	1	1
1	1	1	0	0	1

This may sound very dull to some, but others who are very visual may prefer to have things set up this way. In this table, you find all possible predicates and all possible results of these predicates. (There may be only one if you are doing this process on only one branch.) For the predicates, you place a 0 when your condition fails, a 1 indicates that the condition must pass, and a dash represents no preference.

Now your task is to find a pattern within this table that minimally describes the result. Let's start with the result D. For every even value, D has no preference; for every odd value, it is set to 0. Henceforth, D should always be 0. This means that D is not a branch. In fact, this code should be promptly killed because it never needs to achieve that result.

For the next column, E, things are a little trickier. You may notice that A must be true to even consider having a bit. Furthermore, it seems like C must be false. Hence:

$$E = (A \& !C)$$

For the last column, F, in the worst case, you will have four comparisons, each with three checks on each predicate for a sum total of 12 branches. Let's try to do better than that. Notice that when A = C, you cover 75 percent of the cases and you get one wrong answer. The missing case you have not accounted for would work if you could invert B and C. This would not only take care of the wrong value, it would also include the missing value. You observe that this only happens when A is set. The reasoning is as follows: If A is set, swap B and C. The final test is that if A == C, the result is true. The final question is, how do you get the inversion going? The trick is to again consider the same types of questions you have previously seen in this chapter. Try to think it out by yourself for a little bit.

Give up? The equation that correctly solves the result for F is as follows:

$$F = \left(A == \left(\left((C + B + B) \gg A \right) | 1 \right) \right)$$

This example totals five operators instead of 16. It's a more cryptic solution, but a much leaner expression than the full expression, which would have been as follows:

$$F = (!A \& !B \& !C) | (!A \& B \& !C) | (A \& B \& !C) | (A \& B \& C)$$

At worst, you should always have fewer than half the total possibilities. If you suppose that it was possible to get more than half, take the complement (opposite) of that, and you will be left with fewer than half the cases.

This method is extremely useful to get you to think outside the box. It does not bind you by any strict algebraic rules. In general, this method can yield improvements much greater than a simple algebraic manipulation with a set of rules. The key to beat the next method is to think. Think about the relationship of every single operator, think about how they change the bits in a variable, and think about the logical operator ($>$, $<$, $==$, ...) but also the bit-wise operators ($<<$, $>>$, ^, |, &&, ...). In fact, algebraic expressions can help you to understand the behavior between these functions, so let's jump right into that topic.

Algebraic Identities

Why is it that so many high-school students claim that algebra is their worst nightmare? My belief is that it's because they never took analysis class, because that would have been their nightmare squared. Fortunately, this section sticks to algebra and skirts analysis altogether.

Algebra is built with definitions and axioms. The latter is a form of theorem that cannot be proven. Together, definitions and axioms are used to build theorems. This section is meant to deliver a set of theorems—more specifically, a set of equalities that you can use to simplify your conditional inequalities. Unfortunately, the list is not exhaustive, and some might sound very basic, but they are written here in case you forget. Capital letters are used to represent predicates (an atomic condition), while the remaining letters form the atomic elements of a predicate. I use the C/C++ notation for AND, OR, NOT, and so on.

I denote two types of mathematical equalities:

- The implication, which works on only one side. For example, suppose A ➔ B, A stands for "is a compiler," and B stands for "generates un-optimal code." You could say that if A is a compiler, then it generates un-optimal code. But you could not deduce that, given un-optimal code, the generator was a compiler. People write un-optimal code too.

- The operator • is an equality presented by a double-sided implication.

Table 19.6 expresses several algebraic identities.

Table 19.6 Algebraic Identities

Expressions

!!A	<–> A
(A & B) | (A & C)	<–> A & (B | C)
(A | B) & (A | C)	<–> A | (B & C)
(A & !B) | (!A & B)	<–> A ≠ B
A & !B	<–> A >= B
A | (A & B)	<–> A
A & (A | B)	<–> A
!A | !B	<–> !(A & B)
!A & !B	<–> !(A | B)
!(a > b)	<–> b >= a
!(a < b)	<–> b <= a
!(a == b)	<–> b ≠ a

You can also freely replace any predicate A with !A to yield new identities. Provided you do so everywhere in the expression, the relation will still be valid. In fact, this is a specific result of a more general rule: Any predicate A can also be substituted with a more complex expression. For instance, you could replace the predicate A with (B | (C & D)). Another important note is that sometimes, there are special relationships between predicates. For instance, if predicates A and B are (a > 3) and (a > 6) respectively, then you can see that B ➔ A, because (a > 6) ➔ (a > 3). The reverse, however, is not true. In other words, the first predicate gives information about the second one. Moreover, you can optimize your expressions even more if you take this fact into account. Table 19.7 shows a few identities with this in mind.

Table 19.7 More Algebraic Identities

Expressions

A ➔ B <–> !A | B
(A ➔ B) & (A ➔ C) <–> A ➔ (B & C)
(A ➔ C) & (B ➔ C) <–> (A | B) ➔ C
(A ➔ B) | (A ➔ C) <–> A ➔ (B | C)
((A ➔ C) | (B ➔ C)) ➔ ((A & B) ➔ C)

These lists are by no means exhaustive, but the good thing about them is that if you believe that you have found a relationship between a set of predicates, you can use a truth table to verify your claim. The unfortunate thing is that this method restricts you to thinking purely in algebraic terms and not outside of the box (the box being the algebraic rules). If you use some combination of both techniques shown so far coupled with a little thinking, you are bound to find a very good solution to your problem.

Float Comparisons

When writing code using a high-level language, most programmers do not put a lot of thought into the implications of the code they write. As the previous section has shown, however, some seemingly inoffensive operations can, in assembly, turn into something much more involved. A good assembler programmer can typically generate better high-level language code—not because they can convert slow portions of code into assembly, but because they generally have a better knowledge of the machine and a greater respect and appreciation for speed.

As it turns out, an integer comparison is faster than a floating-point comparison—not only in terms of pure cycle count but also in terms of process. A statement such as if (f > 1.0f) will typically be converted into something equivalent to the following:

```
float Memory(1.0f);
Compare(f, Memory);
EAX = _controlfp(0, 0)
If (EAX & 0x41)
...
```

For one, you cannot compare a float with an immediate value. Secondly, the architecture requires that you fetch the control word of the floating-point instruction, save that into the basic registers (PC internal variables), and follow up with a second test on the control word to determine the result of your floating-point comparison. That's a lot of operations to do.

If you treat the floating-point value as a raw address in memory, however, then you can optimize comparisons by simply using integer comparisons. The first and most obvious test you might wish to conduct is a pure equality test. Checking whether a floating point is equal to another floating point is the same thing as asking whether the bits of one float-ing point are exactly equal to the bits of the other floating point. As such, to test for strict equality, you can simply typecast to a long and do the comparison directly at that level, as the following code illustrates:

```
if (*(unsigned long *)&f == 0x3F800000)          // 1.0f =
0x3F800000
```

This also goes for strict inequality. You might think that you can achieve something sim-ilar with greater/lesser than operations, and the truth is, that is possible. Take 0, for exam-ple, which is a special case because it is the turning point of the sign. Thanks to that, you can check whether a floating-point value is greater than, equal to, or strictly smaller than by looking at the sign. But what happens to the strictly greater than and smaller than or equal cases? Well, you know that 0 in float is 0 in int, and that any negative number will have the most significant bit turned on. Hence, if you perform a signed comparison against 0, you essentially achieve the same thing as a floating-point comparison with 0. The following code shows this:

```
if (*(unsigned long *)&f & 0x80000000)       // Tests for f < 0.0f
if (!(*(unsigned long *)&f & 0x80000000))    // Tests for f >= 0.0f
if (*(long *)&f > 0)                            // Tests for f > 0.0f
if (*(long *)&f <= 0)                           // Tests for f <= 0.0f
```

What happens if the constant you want to compare against is non-zero? Let's first look at a positive constant floating-point value, and without loss of generality, let's choose 1.5f. You already know that 1.5f translates to 0x3FC00000. You know from the earlier section that any positive floating-point value is represented as $(1 + 2^{-mantissa}) * 2^{exponent - 127}$.

First, verify what happens when the mantissa is different. The mantissa of this number in bit representation is 0x400000. You can see that a smaller or greater mantissa gives a small-er or greater integer value, so for the mantissa, the comparison for raw memory is exact-ly the same for integers as it is for floats. If, on the other hand, the exponent is different, it can also be verified that the exact same logic ensues. The exponent is described as *expo-nent − 127*, and a smaller or greater exponent gives a smaller or greater integer value. If you combine both, it still works out correctly because the exponent lies before the man-tissa, hence giving it the prevalence when compared.

This is quite interesting because if you cast the float's memory block into a signed integer, you can then achieve comparisons against floating-point values by simply converting the constant to its integer equivalent and doing the comparisons in pure integers. The fol-lowing code demonstrates this:

```
if (*(long *)&f < 0x3FC00000)            // Tests for f < 1.5f
if (*(long *)&f >= 0x3FC00000)           // Tests for f >= 1.5f
```

```
if (*(long *)&f > 0x3fC00000)                  // Tests for f > 1.5f
if (*(long *)&f <= 0x3fC00000)                 // Tests for f <= 1.5f
```

So what about negative constants? Your main issue with negative constants is the sign. If you choose a negative number, then you have a number of the form 0x8. You treat the mantissa and the exponent as one because you have already seen that they are positioned correctly for your purposes and will start by examining the negative values. Both values are of the form 0x8.

What happens if the combined mantissa and exponent are greater? If you convert back from memory to float, you will notice that this actually means that the floating-point values are smaller. Similarly, for the smaller-than comparison, you have a greater number. If your variable is positive, you can also verify that this observation holds. Hence, for constants with negative values, you only need to invert the operand you wish to test and the equalities will hold for integers. Note that casting to sign is completely useless for you here. In fact, it's completely false when converted to a signed integer. The following code shows how the comparisons work for −1.5f:

```
if (*(unsigned long *)&f > 0xBfC00000)          // Tests for f < 1.5f
if (*(unsigned long *)&f <= 0xBfC00000)         // Tests for f >= 1.5f
if (*(unsigned long *)&f < 0xBfC00000)          // Tests for f > 1.5f
if (*(unsigned long *)&f >= 0xBfC00000)         // Tests for f <= 1.5f
```

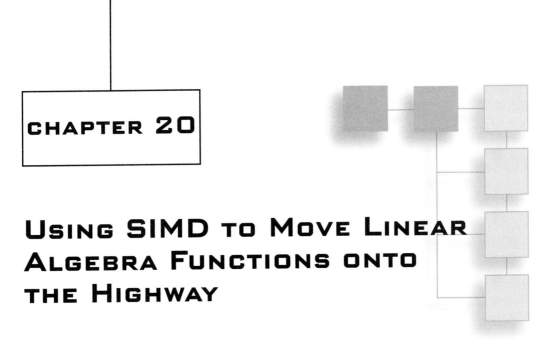

CHAPTER 20

USING SIMD TO MOVE LINEAR ALGEBRA FUNCTIONS ONTO THE HIGHWAY

Converting a math function over to efficient SIMD code can be difficult. It's not always easy to see the best way to compute a final value using parallel calculations, but this chapter will help you to "think SIMD." This chapter assumes that you have prior knowledge of SIMD instructions. SIMD was introduced briefly in the previous chapter, but if you don't know it very well, you should pick up a book covering the subject from top to bottom.

Throughout this chapter, I'll present various basic linear algebra functions in assembler using single-float calculations. If you only know intrinsic functions, you should be able to understand the meaning of the assembler functions because the two naming conventions are quite similar. Single floating points are used because you can do twice as many calculations as with double-float precision.

Compilers are getting better and better every day, but they still are horrible at scheduling instructions for complicated code. This is where the ASM tuning is required. In terms of code size, the functions may feel similar, but the actual order in which the equations are set makes a huge difference. Because these instructions are a critical part of any game's code loops, it is imperative to write the fastest possible functions. There are some libraries available to do this (such as the ones included in D3D), but a quick code inspection will reveal that the current version of that library isn't very well tuned to use SIMD (it does use SIMD, but it's far from being optimal). Eventually, I expect they'll get optimized to a point where it's no longer worth writing ASM code, but realistically speaking, a compiler will never be as fast as the latest stuff that comes out. Once the library is fine-tuned for today's architectures, it will be made obsolete by the next-gen CPU. Hence the importance of knowing assembly to reach for maximal throughput.

Besides a quick and dirty review of the principles from the previous chapters on vectors and matrices, the main topics for this chapter are

- Matrix storage format
- Matrix transposition
- Dot product
- Vector length and normalization
- Matrix-vector multiplication
- Matrix-matrix multiplication
- Matrix determinant
- Cross product
- Matrix division (inverse)

Matrix Storage Format

When you're writing SIMD code, it's important to choose the right structure. It makes a significant difference in your code. Unfortunately, the structure for your vectors depends on the number of calculations you need to apply. If you do few calculations, it may be more optimal to use vectors (X, Y, Z, W). If you must apply a lot of them, you might prefer the memory structure $X[]$, $Y[]$, $Z[]$, $W[]$. Again, this depends on the tasks you need to achieve and the input method your favorite 3D library takes. We will concentrate on the most pertinent storage methods, since each of the two mainstream 3D APIs (OpenGL, Direct3D) uses a different matrix storage format. In general, the OpenGL column-major matrices are faster than the row-major Direct3D matrices when SIMD is involved. Note that if you do a lot of computations for which an X-major matrix isn't as fast as the Y-major matrix format, you may want to transpose your matrix before doing any computation.

Matrix Transposition

A *transposition* is a geometrically simple operation for which, given the two matrices **A** and **B** and their respective elements a_{ij} and b_{ij}, **B** is the transpose of **A** and vice versa if and only if $a_{ij} = b_{ji}$. In other words, if you exchange every element about the diagonal of the matrix, you have calculated the transposition of your initial matrix. You can also see transposition as an exchange between rows and columns, where row i becomes column i and vice versa.

One possible solution to this operation is to swap the elements one by one. The problem is that you don't use the full capacity of the data bus. Instead, we'll attempt a SIMD approach to this problem. Shuffling instructions are tempting, but they're cycle eaters. You can do better than that.

The instructions that should attract you the most are the single precision unpacking functions. When you look at the details of these two instructions, you notice that, given two registers, the instructions convert two elements of the same column into adjacent rows. For the low version of the unpacking command, the two second elements are placed adjacent to each other in the third and fourth elements of the destination register, while the two first elements are placed adjacent to each other in the first and second elements of the destination register. This solves half of your problem because you can swap half the columns to rows. You can apply this to your two pairs of rows, once for the first two elements and once for the last two elements. All that's left is to move the high and low sections of the registers so that the elements of the same row end up as the elements of the same column, and you're done.

A diagram of the process is shown in Figure 20.1.

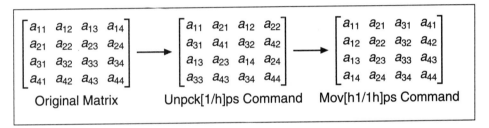

Figure 20.1
Step-by-step matrix transposition operation

The source code of the process follows:

```
lea         esi, [SrcMatrix]
movaps      xmm0, [esi + 0*4*4]
movaps      xmm2, xmm0
unpcklps    xmm0, [esi + 1*4*4]   // xmm0 = [a11, a21, a12, a22]

movaps      xmm1, [esi + 2*4*4]
movaps      xmm3, xmm1
unpcklps    xmm1, [esi + 3*4*4]   // xmm1 = [a31, a41, a32, a42]
movaps      xmm4, xmm0

Unpckhps    xmm2, [esi + 1*4*4]   // xmm2 = [a13, a23, a14, a24]
Lea         edi, [DstMatrix]
unpckhps    xmm3, [esi + 3*4*4]   // xmm3 = [a33, a43, a34, a44]
movaps      xmm5, xmm2

movlhps     xmm0, xmm1            // xmm0 = [a11, a21, a31, a41]
movaps      [edi + 0*4*4], xmm0
```

```
movhlps       xmm1, xmm4              // xmm1 = [a12, a22, a32, a42]
movaps        [edi + 1*4*4], xmm1
movlhps       xmm2, xmm3              // xmm2 = [a13, a23, a33, a43]
movaps        [edi + 2*4*4], xmm2
movhlps       xmm3, xmm5              // xmm3 = [a14, a24, a34, a44]
movaps        [edi + 3*4*4], xmm3
```

Dot Product

A while ago, when 3D was starting to be used more in software, a friend of mine was applying for jobs in the gaming industry. One interviewer asked, "What is the dot product?" My friend couldn't answer that question. This fundamental operation is crucial for any 3D game, and obviously, my friend was not called back.

Most game developers know the equation of a dot product, but do they actually know the geometrical representation of one? This is the key to solving certain geometrical problems. The dot product has the geometrical representation to be the length of a projected vector **a** upon a second vector **b** when the two vectors are centered at the origin. The operation is written as follows, where the last function is the geometrical representation initially given and theta is the angle between the two vectors:

$$\mathbf{a} \bullet \mathbf{b} = \sum_{i=0}^{n} \mathbf{a}_i \cdot \mathbf{b}_i = \|\mathbf{a}\|_2 \|\mathbf{b}\|_2 \cos(\phi)$$

The center equation is the equation of interest, mainly because it's easy to store and compute.

Array of Structure (AoS)

There are two ways to represent lists of vectors. Typically, creating a structure isn't the most optimal way. The OO gurus probably won't like this very much, but then again, most literally correct OO code seems to disregard speed in just about every possible way. Nonetheless, it may be more optimal to look at the problem as an array of structures with X, Y, Z, and W as members of the structure. You still have to come up with a way to calculate the dot product on the three components specified in the structure. The multiplication is easy to do in parallel (that is, <x . x, y . y, z . z, w . w>), but the one big issue here is the horizontal addition that needs to be performed to complete the dot product. If you need to calculate the dot product on four vectors or more, you may as well consider them as 4×4 matrices and calculate a matrix-vector multiplication. If they are not all multiplied by the same vector, you can take advantage of the horizontal add with four rows (shown later in the chapter). This will be faster.

If you only need to compute one dot product, you have little choice but to follow through with a horizontal addition of one element. You can split the vector into two vectors, where the two top elements are aligned with the two bottom elements, and add them in parallel. All that will remain at the end is to add the first and second elements. A shuffle can perform this task easily. (If this is unclear, the "Matrix-Vector Multiplication" section later in the chapter will explain the horizontal add with four vectors.)

The following code shows the idea illustrated in Figure 20.2.

Mulps	$[a_1\ a_2\ a_3\ a_4] \cdot [b_1\ b_2\ b_3\ b_4]$	$= [a_1b_1\ a_2b_2\ a_3b_3\ a_4b_4]$
Mov[h1l1h]ps	$[a_1b_1\ a_2b_2\ ...\ ...]+[a_3b_3\ a_4b_4\ ...\ ...]$	$= [a_1b_1+a_3b_3\ a_2b_2+a_4b_4\ ...\ ...]$
Pshufd	$[a_1b_1+a_3b_3\ ...\ ...\ ...]+[a_2b_2+a_4b_4\ ...\ ...\ ...]$ $= [a_1b_1+a_3b_3+a_2b_2+a_4b_4\ ...\ ...\ ...]$

Figure 20.2
Step-by-step AoS dot product calculation

```
movaps      xmm0, [SrcVectorA]
movaps      xmm1, [SrcVectorB]
mulps       xmm0, xmm1      // xmm0 = [a1, a2, a3, a4]
movhlps     xmm1, xmm0
addps       xmm0, xmm1      // xmm0 = [a1 + a3, a2 + a4, …]
pshufd      xmm1, xmm0, 01010101b
addss       xmm0, xmm1      // xmm0 = [a1 + a3 + a2 + a4, …]
movss       [Dest], xmm0
```

This will effectively enable you to compute dot products for a list of vectors if you have them set up such that each vector is contained by a structure. But there's another approach to data storage...

Structure of Array (SoA)

A structure of arrays is a much nicer way to represent vectors. Unfortunately, the 3D libraries aren't too friendly with this format. Nonetheless, we're not here to debate the best choice, because this is application-specific. We want to compute the dot product in SoA format. The SoA format does not require a structure because each component of the old structure is given a structure to itself. Thus you would end up with x, y and z containing the component values of the ith vector for that component. This is a very attractive way to set up the vectors. All you need to do is multiply each array by the ith element of the vector, and finish up by adding everything together, as these equations and code show:

$$\langle x_1, x_2, x_3, x_4 \rangle \bullet \langle a_1, a_2, a_3, a_4 \rangle = \langle a_1 x_1, a_2 x_2, a_3 x_3, a_4 x_4 \rangle$$
$$\langle y_1, y_2, y_3, y_4 \rangle \bullet \langle a_1, a_2, a_3, a_4 \rangle = \langle a_1 y_1, a_2 y_2, a_3 y_3, a_4 y_4 \rangle$$
$$\langle z_1, z_2, z_3, z_4 \rangle \bullet \langle a_1, a_2, a_3, a_4 \rangle = \langle a_1 z_1, a_2 z_2, a_3 z_3, a_4 z_4 \rangle$$

```
movaps      xmm7, [SrcVector]
pshufd      xmm4, xmm7, 11111111b
pshufd      xmm5, xmm7, 10101010b
pshufd      xmm6, xmm7, 01010101b
shufps      xmm7, xmm7, 00000000b
lea         eax, [X]
lea         ebx, [Y]
lea         ecx, [Z]
lea         edx, [W]
lea         edi, [DestValues]

Loop:
movaps      xmm0, [eax]
movaps      xmm1, [ebx]
movaps      xmm2, [ecx]
movaps      xmm3, [edx]
mulps       xmm0, xmm4
mulps       xmm1, xmm5
mulps       xmm2, xmm6
mulps       xmm3, xmm7
addps       xmm0, xmm1
addps       xmm2, xmm3
addps       xmm0, xmm2
movaps      [edi], xmm0
...
```

Vector Length and Normalization

Normalizing a vector is a common and slow task, and unfortunately it's required in many situations. The idea behind normalization is that, given a vector, you want to obtain a vector with the same direction but for which the norm (or if you prefer, the *length*) is 1. The typical norm used on vectors is the p-norm for $p = 2$. This is defined as the square root of the sum of squares. Simply put:

$$\|\mathbf{v}\|_2 = \sqrt{\mathbf{v} \bullet \mathbf{v}}$$
$$= \sqrt{\mathbf{v}_x^2 + \mathbf{v}_y^2 + \mathbf{v}_z^2}$$

If you want a vector with the same direction but a length of 1, you merely need to divide the vector by its length. Plain and simple.

Array of Structure (AoS)

There's not much you can do with this version. The best you can do is to calculate the dot product of the vector upon itself, followed by the inverse square root on it (using the SIMD operation). It's a little more interesting when you want to normalize more than one vector. Again, you can multiply every row by itself and apply the horizontal addition process to all four elements. You can see how this is done more efficiently with four rows by looking at the "Matrix-Vector Multiplication" section of this chapter. For now, let's look at the code that can do this on a single element:

```
movaps      xmm0, [SrcVectorA]
mulps       xmm0, xmm0      // xmm0 = [a1, a2, a3, a4]
movhlps     xmm1, xmm0
addps       xmm0, xmm1      // xmm0 = [a1 + a3, a2 + a4, …]
pshufd      xmm1, xmm0, 01010101b
addss       xmm0, xmm1      // xmm0 = [a1 + a3 + a2 + a4, …]
rsqrtss     xmm0, xmm0
shufps      xmm0, xmm0, 00000000b
mulps       xmm0, [SrcVectorA]
movaps      [Dest], xmm0
```

Structure of Array (SoA)

This version of the structure is a little friendlier to the way SIMD registers work. To compute this for four elements, all you need to do is a four-step algorithm: Compute the dot product of the vectors, sum all three arrays, calculate the reciprocal square root, and multiply each array by this vector. A little simpler than the previous method, is it not? Here's the source code:

```
movaps      xmm0, [X]
movaps      xmm1, [Y]
movaps      xmm2, [Z]
movaps      xmm4, xmm0          // xmm4 = X
mulps       xmm0, xmm0
movaps      xmm5, xmm1          // xmm5 = Y
mulps       xmm1, xmm1
movaps      xmm6, xmm2          // xmm6 = Z
mulps       xmm2, xmm2

addps       xmm0, xmm1
addps       xmm0, xmm2          // xmm0 = X + Y + Z
rsqrtps     xmm0, xmm0
mulps       xmm4, xmm0
```

```
mulps       xmm5, xmm0
mulps       xmm6, xmm0
movaps      [DestX], xmm4
movaps      [DestY], xmm5
movaps      [DestZ], xmm6
```

Matrix-Vector Multiplication

This is a fairly simple operation you can apply to a matrix. A vector can be defined as an *Nx1* matrix. Hence, a matrix-vector multiplication can be considered a special case of matrix multiplication. The product of two row-major matrices where the 2 indices are (row, column) is defined as follows:

$$x_{ij} = \sum_{j=1}^{4} a_{ij} \cdot b_{jk}$$

Column-Major

In the case where **b** is a vector, $k = 1$. Also recall that you're dealing with column-major matrices, so you have to invert the sub-indices. This gives the final equation, where the indices are in the traditional (column, row) format:

$$x_{1i} = \sum_{j=1}^{4} a_{ji} \cdot b_{1j}$$

Your data is stored in rows within the column matrix, so it would be much faster and more convenient to obtain a formula as a function of the rows instead of the single elements. You may notice that the row sub-index of *i* is equal for *x* and *a*. You can then convert these two elements to row-vectors and obtain the formula you were looking for, where **x** is a column-vector and b_j the j_{th} element of **b**:

$$\mathbf{x} = \sum_{j=1}^{4} \mathbf{r}_j \cdot b_j$$

The SIMD code for a column-major matrix follows. Note that this will work only on SSE2 (Pentium 4 and up). Feel free to change the pshufd to a series of shufps/movlps/movhps instructions in order to accomplish the same task on lower-end machines. The source code is a straightforward implementation of the process equations that follow:

$$\begin{bmatrix} a_{11} & a_{21} & a_{31} & a_{41} \\ a_{12} & a_{22} & a_{32} & a_{42} \\ a_{13} & a_{23} & a_{33} & a_{43} \\ a_{14} & a_{24} & a_{34} & a_{44} \end{bmatrix} \begin{bmatrix} b_1 & b_2 & b_3 & b_4 \end{bmatrix} = \begin{bmatrix} \mathbf{r}_1 \\ \mathbf{r}_2 \\ \mathbf{r}_3 \\ \mathbf{r}_4 \end{bmatrix} \begin{bmatrix} b_1 & b_2 & b_3 & b_4 \end{bmatrix}$$

$$= \begin{bmatrix} \mathbf{r}_1 \cdot b_1 & \mathbf{r}_2 \cdot b_2 & \mathbf{r}_3 \cdot b_3 & \mathbf{r}_4 \cdot b_4 \end{bmatrix}$$

```
movaps   xmm0, [SrcVector]
pshufd   xmm1, xmm0, 01010101b
lea      edi, [DstVector]
lea      esi, [Matrix]
pshufd xmm2, xmm0, 10101010b
pshufd xmm3, xmm0, 11111111b
pshufd xmm0, xmm0, 00000000b              // xmmi = {Vector[i]}


mulps   xmm0, [esi + 0*4*4]
mulps   xmm1, [esi + 1*4*4]
addps   xmm0, xmm1
mulps   xmm2, [esi + 2*4*4]
addps   xmm0, xmm2
mulps   xmm3, [esi + 3*4*4]
addps   xmm0, xmm3                        // xmm0 += xmmi * M[i]


movaps   [edi], xmm0
```

Row-Major

If you look at the equation for the transpose of the matrix A (row-major matrix with indices placed in order of (row, column)), it's clear that there are no easy algebraic conversions for row-based data:

$$x_{i1} = \sum_{j=1}^{4} a_{ij} \cdot b_{j1}$$

The simplification for this one changes the equation to

$$\mathbf{x} = \sum_{j=1}^{4} \mathbf{c}_j \cdot b_j$$

But your data isn't stored in columns. If you think about how the multiplications are done at a higher level, you'll realize that you multiply one row of the matrix by your column-vector, add all the values together, and that's your first value. You may apply this process to every row, yielding an Nx1 vector. This is nothing but the horizontal addition, as seen earlier, but applied four times. It turns out that this is the best way to proceed, so let's take a look at how a horizontal addition can be performed on four rows of elements.

The most obvious thing would be to shift everything around, but that's quite costly. Instead, you have to choose an approach that will divide the problem into smaller problems (the "Divide and Conquer" strategy). First, you need to add elements together. If you take two rows, let's say **U**, **V**, with *N* elements, you can split the problem in half by swapping the low half of **U** and the low half of **V**, followed by an addition of these two vectors. This yields one row for which half the elements of **U** and **V** are added together, and the vector is such that half of it is dedicated to **U** and the other half to **V**.

At this point, you can apply this recursively. Suppose two more vectors exist, **S**, **T**. Apply the same logic to them and you now have two vectors, the combined **UV** and the combined **ST**, each with half of its elements added together and half of the space dedicated to equal parts of its initial vectors. You can shuffle them around once more in the exact same way as before, but taking the divisions into account.

In other words, take **UV** and **ST**. Swap the internal variables such that **U** is divided in half. The first half is in the first vector, and the second half is in the second vector. Do the same for **V**, **S**, and **T**. This gives you two vectors, each with a quarter of the initial vectors. Add these two vectors together once more, and you've now successfully reduced the problem to a quarter of what it was before. Sure enough, your SIMD vectors are four elements in length, so you've added four rows horizontally. This process could be applied to matrices with more than four elements, but you need not in this case.

The source code follows, and Figure 20.3 illustrates the horizontal addition process.

$[a_1\ a_2\ a_3\ a_4],[b_1\ b_2\ b_3\ b_4],[c_1\ c_2\ c_3\ c_4],[d_1\ d_2\ d_3\ d_4]$

Mov[hl1]ps

$\begin{array}{l}[a_1\ a_2\ b_1\ b_2]\\ +\ [a_3\ a_4\ b_3\ b_4]\\ \hline [a_1+a_3\ a_2+a_4\ b_1+b_3\ b_2+b_4]\end{array}$, $\begin{array}{l}[c_1\ c_2\ d_1\ d_2]\\ +\ [c_3\ c_4\ d_3\ d_4]\\ \hline [c_1+c_3\ c_2+c_4\ d_1+d_3\ d_2+d_4]\end{array}$

Shufps

$\begin{array}{l}[a_1+a_3\ b_1+b_3\ c_1+c_3\ d_1+d_3]\\ +\ [a_2+a_4\ b_2+b_4\ c_2+c_4\ d_2+d_4]\\ \hline [a_1+a_2+a_3+a_4\ b_1+b_2+b_3+b_4\ c_1+c_2+c_3+c_4\ d_1+d_2+d_3+d_4]\end{array}$

Figure 20.3
Horizontal addition process (without the multiplication)

```
movaps  xmm0, [SrcVector]
pshufd  xmm1, xmm0, 11101110b      // xmm1 = [v2, v3, v2, v3]
lea           esi, [Matrix]
lea           edi, [DstVector]
pshufd  xmm0, xmm0, 01000100b      // xmm0 = [v0, v1, v0, v1]
```

```
movlps  xmm2, [esi + 0*4*4]
movhps  xmm2, [esi + 1*4*4]
mulps   xmm2, xmm0                      // xmm2 = [a11, a12, a21, a22]


movlps  xmm3, [esi + 0*4*4 + 2*4]
movhps  xmm3, [esi + 1*4*4 + 2*4]
mulps   xmm3, xmm1                      // xmm3 = [a13, a14, a23, a24]


movlps  xmm4, [esi + 2*4*4]
movhps  xmm4, [esi + 3*4*4]
mulps   xmm0, xmm4                      // xmm0 = [a31, a32, a41, a42]


movlps  xmm5, [esi + 2*4*4 + 2*4]
movhps  xmm5, [esi + 3*4*4 + 2*4]
mulps   xmm1, xmm5                      // xmm1 = [a33, a34, a43, a44]


addps   xmm2, xmm3                      // xmm2 = [a11+a13, a12+a14, a21+a23, a22+a24]
movaps  xmm3, xmm2
addps   xmm0, xmm1                      // xmm0 = [a31+a33, a32+a34, a41+a43, a42+a44]


shufps  xmm2, xmm0, 11011101b
shufps  xmm3, xmm0, 10001000b


addps   xmm3, xmm2                      // xmm0 = [a11+a12+a13+a14, a21+a22+a23+a24]
movaps  [edi], xmm3                     //         [a31+a32+a33+a34, a41+a42+a43+a44]
```

Now you probably have an idea why this version of the code doesn't work as well as the previous version. The difference is quite noticeable because this one takes about 2.75 times as long as the previous routine. The reason is simple: more instructions = slower code. If your vector's data structure is made up of three arrays and you require matrix-vector multiplication for many elements, you should consider this operation as a matrix-matrix multiplication, where one matrix is the same matrix used here, and the second is a matrix (a vector of a vector) made of four vectors: four elements of X, Y, Z, and W.

Matrix-Matrix Multiplication

Matrix multiplication is a computationally intensive operation. Thankfully, it isn't used too heavily on the CPU, but most 3D games still require a decent bit of matrix multiplication. You've already learned the rules for a matrix-matrix multiplication, but it helps to look at this operation at a higher level.

The most familiar matrix is the row-major matrix, so let's look at the multiplication of two row-major matrices, **A** and **B**, with result **C**. You have that **AB** = **C**. If you take the transposition on each side of the equation, you get that $\mathbf{B}^T\mathbf{A}^T = \mathbf{C}^T$. This is particularly interesting because there's a really simple relationship between the multiplication of row-major matrices and column-major matrices. As previously mentioned, the relationship between the two is just a transposition. This means that you merely need to swap $\mathbf{A}$ and $\mathbf{B}$ to multiply using the other mode. You can find the best way to multiply two matrices (either column-major or row-major), and this will automatically give you a way to calculate the other type.

Instinctively, the matrix-vector multiplication should be about four times faster than a matrix-matrix multiplication. The hint for this one is that a matrix-vector multiplication requires every field of a register, so you don't have any more space left for extra computations. The only way to fix this would be to change the algorithm altogether, but there doesn't seem to be an easier way to calculate a matrix-matrix multiplication than to apply the same idea you used in a matrix-vector multiplication.

So where is the advantage? For one thing, a matrix-vector multiplication stores the result as a row and not a column, which is the format you need for a column-major matrix. So a little bit of work will have to be done here. Another thing you can do is reduce resource usage and stalls by mixing the code a little bit, but this is pretty much the extent of the possible optimization.

By definition, you have that

$$x_{jk} = \sum_{j=1}^{4} a_{ij} \cdot b_{jk}$$

The most convenient method is always to consider rows of elements. So suppose the indices define a row-major matrix; i would represent the row and k the column. You want to consider an entire row, so let k range from 1 to 4. You come up with the following equation:

$$r_{x_i} = \sum_{j=1}^{4} a_{ij} \cdot r_{b_j}$$

This is the equation you can use to calculate every row (that is: $i = 1..4$). Because you've chosen the indices to represent a row-major matrix format, inverting the two matrices' order will actually compute the multiplication of a column-major matrix. Now all that's left is to optimize the assembly code such that the resources and stalls are minimized. The code to compute the multiplication of two row-major matrices follows:

```
// Row 1
lea     ebx, [MatrixA]                          // ebx = MatrixA
lea     esi, [MatrixB]                          // esi = MatrixB
movss   xmm0, [ebx + 0*4*4 + 0*4]
movaps  xmm4, [esi + 0*4*4]                     // xmm4 = Matrix2[0]
```

```
      shufps xmm0, xmm0, 00000000b              // xmm0 = [a11, a11, a11, a11]

      movss  xmm1, [ebx + 0*4*4 + 1*4]
      mulps  xmm0, xmm4
      movaps xmm5, [esi + 1*4*4]                // xmm5 = Matrix2[1]
      shufps xmm1, xmm1, 00000000b              // xmm1 = [a12, a12, a12, a12]

      movss  xmm2, [ebx + 0*4*4 + 2*4]
      mulps  xmm1, xmm5
      movaps xmm6, [esi + 2*4*4]                // xmm6 = Matrix2[2]
      shufps xmm2, xmm2, 00000000b              // xmm2 = [a13, a13, a13, a13]
      addps  xmm0, xmm1

      movss  xmm3, [ebx + 0*4*4 + 3*4]
      mulps  xmm2, xmm6
      movaps xmm7, [esi + 3*4*4]                // xmm7 = matrix2[3]
      shufps xmm3, xmm3, 00000000b              // xmm3 = [a14, a14, a14, a14]
      addps  xmm0, xmm2

      mulps  xmm3, xmm7
      lea    edi, [DstMatrix]                   // edi = DstMatrix
      addps  xmm3, xmm0                         // xmm3 += xmmi * xmm[i+4]

// Row 2
      movss  xmm0, [ebx + 1*4*4 + 0*4]
      shufps xmm0, xmm0, 00000000b              // xmm0 = [a21, a21, a21, a21]

      movss  xmm1, [ebx + 1*4*4 + 1*4]
      shufps xmm1, xmm1, 00000000b              // xmm1 = [a22, a22, a22, a22]

      movss  xmm2, [ebx + 1*4*4 + 2*4]
      shufps xmm2, xmm2, 00000000b              // xmm2 = [a23, a23, a23, a23]

      movaps [edi], xmm3
      movss  xmm3, [ebx + 1*4*4 + 3*4]
      shufps xmm3, xmm3, 00000000b              // xmm3 = [a24, a24, a24, a24]

      mulps  xmm0, xmm4
      mulps  xmm1, xmm5
      addps  xmm0, xmm1
      mulps  xmm2, xmm6
      addps  xmm0, xmm2
```

```
mulps   xmm3, xmm7
addps   xmm0, xmm3                              // xmm0 += xmmi * xmm[i+4]

movaps  [edi + 1*4*4], xmm0
// Row 3
movss   xmm0, [ebx + 2*4*4 + 0*4]
shufps  xmm0, xmm0, 00000000b                   // xmm0 = [a31, a31, a31, a31]

movss   xmm1, [ebx + 2*4*4 + 1*4]
shufps  xmm1, xmm1, 00000000b                   // xmm1 = [a32, a32, a32, a32]

movss   xmm2, [ebx + 2*4*4 + 2*4]
shufps  xmm2, xmm2, 00000000b                   // xmm2 = [a33, a33, a33, a33]

movss   xmm3, [ebx + 2*4*4 + 3*4]
shufps  xmm3, xmm3, 00000000b                   // xmm3 = [a34, a34, a34, a34]

mulps   xmm0, xmm4
mulps   xmm1, xmm5
addps   xmm0, xmm1
mulps   xmm2, xmm6
addps   xmm0, xmm2
mulps   xmm3, xmm7
addps   xmm0, xmm3                              // xmm0 += xmmi * xmm[i+4]

movaps  [edi + 2*4*4], xmm0
// Row 4
movss   xmm0, [ebx + 3*4*4 + 0*4]
shufps  xmm0, xmm0, 00000000b                   // xmm0 = [a41, a41, a41, a41]

movss   xmm1, [ebx + 3*4*4 + 1*4]
shufps  xmm1, xmm1, 00000000b                   // xmm1 = [a42, a42, a42, a42]

movss   xmm2, [ebx + 3*4*4 + 2*4]
shufps  xmm2, xmm2, 00000000b                   // xmm2 = [a43, a43, a43, a43]

mulps   xmm0, xmm4
movss   xmm3, [ebx + 3*4*4 + 3*4]
shufps  xmm3, xmm3, 00000000b                   // xmm3 = [a44, a44, a44, a44]

mulps   xmm1, xmm5
addps   xmm0, xmm1
```

```
mulps   xmm2, xmm6
addps   xmm0, xmm2
mulps   xmm3, xmm7
addps   xmm0, xmm3                    // xmm0 += xmmi * xmm[i+4]

movaps  [edi + 3*4*4], xmm0
```

Matrix Determinant

Calculating the determinant of a matrix is an often-useful function for computational geometry problems. Many problems can be converted into the calculation of a determinant, which makes this operation a must for many complex geometrical problems. The determinant of a 2×2 matrix is denoted |A| and is defined as $a_{11}a_{22} - a_{12}a_{21}$. Geometrically, you may see this as one diagonal less the mirrored diagonal. Define $\mathbf{M}_{ij}$ as the minor of the matrix $\mathbf{M}$. The minor matrix is the matrix obtained by removing row i and column j in a row-major matrix. You can define the determinant of square matrices greater than 2 by

$$|\mathbf{M}| = \sum_{j=1}^{n} (-1)^j a_{1j} |\mathbf{M}_{1j}|$$

The determinant has many properties, but the one we're interested in is the previous one, and the fact that $|\mathbf{M}| = |\mathbf{M}^T|$.

3×3 Matrix Determinant

For a 3×3 matrix, there's a really neat geometrical trick for computing the determinant. This trick is quite clear when the equation is expanded:

$$\begin{vmatrix} a_{11} & a_{12} & a_{13} \\ a_{21} & a_{22} & a_{23} \\ a_{31} & a_{32} & a_{33} \end{vmatrix} = a_{11} \begin{vmatrix} a_{22} & a_{23} \\ a_{32} & a_{44} \end{vmatrix} + a_{12} \begin{vmatrix} a_{23} & a_{21} \\ a_{33} & a_{31} \end{vmatrix} + a_{13} \begin{vmatrix} a_{21} & a_{22} \\ a_{31} & a_{32} \end{vmatrix}$$

Look back at your original matrix, and look at every single tri-term in the expanded equation. You'll notice that every tri-term is a diagonal. There's even more to it than this; every negative term is going from right to left, while the positive terms are going from left to right. This is pretty nice because it gives you an easy way to calculate this not only on paper, but also using SIMD. All you have to do is shift rows two and three such that they're aligned for one diagonal (let's say the right-left one) and then multiply them all together, as shown in Figure 20.4. Do the same for the left-right one, multiply them together, subtract the second from the first, and then apply a horizontal addition.

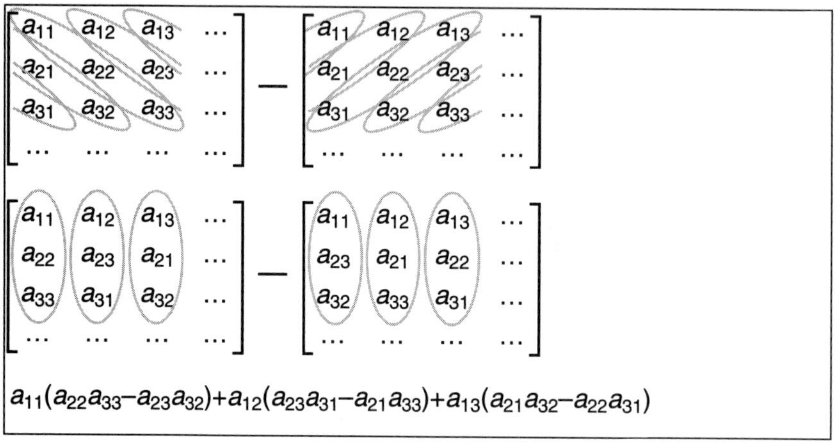

Figure 20.4
Computation of a 3×3 matrix determinant

3×3 matrices are much less costly than 4×4 matrices. Of course, this assumes that you store your 3×3 matrix in a 4×4 matrix (something you can do, typically). The source code for this follows:

```
lea          esi, [Matrix]
lea          edi, [D]
pshufd       xmm1, [esi + 4*4*1], 11001001b
pshufd       xmm2, [esi + 4*4*2], 11010010b
mulps        xmm1, xmm2                        // Multiply the 2 last rows

pshufd       xmm3, [esi + 4*4*1], 11010010b
pshufd       xmm4, [esi + 4*4*2], 11001001b
mulps        xmm3, xmm4                        // ^^ Again but reverse-crossing

subps        xmm1, xmm3
mulps        xmm1, [esi + 4*4*0]

movhlps      xmm0, xmm1
addss        xmm0, xmm1                        // xmm0 = [a1 + a3, a2 + a4, …]
pshufd       xmm1, xmm1, 01010101b
addss        xmm0, xmm1                        // xmm0 = [a1 + a3 + a2 + a4, …]
movss        [edi], xmm0
```

4×4 Matrix Determinant

If you can do with a 3×3 matrix determinant applied on a 4×4 matrix, do so. The computational requirements are that much better. If not, you still have to compute the determinant of a 4×4 matrix. If you expand the rather long equation, you quickly notice that there's no nice geometrical relation on the matrix, such as with the 3×3 matrix. In fact, the process is a bit painful and relies on the decomposition, as observed before.

Let's look at how you can compute this efficiently with SIMD by decomposing the determinant's definition. A 4×4 determinant is defined by

$$\mathbf{M}_1 = \begin{vmatrix} a_{22} & a_{23} & a_{24} \\ a_{32} & a_{33} & a_{34} \\ a_{42} & a_{43} & a_{44} \end{vmatrix}$$

$$= a_{22}\begin{vmatrix} a_{33} & a_{34} \\ a_{43} & a_{44} \end{vmatrix} + a_{23}\begin{vmatrix} a_{34} & a_{32} \\ a_{44} & a_{42} \end{vmatrix} + a_{24}\begin{vmatrix} a_{32} & a_{33} \\ a_{42} & a_{43} \end{vmatrix}$$

Thiking in terms of rows, we get

$$[\mathbf{M}_{11} \quad \mathbf{M}_{12} \quad \mathbf{M}_{13} \quad \mathbf{M}_{14}] = (\mathbf{r}_2 \ll 1)\begin{vmatrix} \mathbf{r}_2 \ll 2 & \mathbf{r}_3 \ll 3 \\ \mathbf{r}_4 \ll 2 & \mathbf{r}_4 \ll 3 \end{vmatrix} + (\mathbf{r}_2 \ll 2)\begin{vmatrix} \mathbf{r}_3 \ll 3 & \mathbf{r}_3 \ll 1 \\ \mathbf{r}_4 \ll 3 & \mathbf{r}_4 \ll 1 \end{vmatrix} + (\mathbf{r}_2 \ll 3)\begin{vmatrix} \mathbf{r}_3 \ll 1 & \mathbf{r}_3 \ll 2 \\ \mathbf{r}_4 \ll 1 & \mathbf{r}_4 \ll 2 \end{vmatrix}$$

This reduces the problem to computing the determinant of every 3×3 matrix. Notice one very interesting geometrical fact in the second-level determinant expression: If you look at the second index of the first element for each minor matrix, it always starts at one more than the second index of the coefficient the determinant is multiplied by. Furthermore, the numbers from left to right for that same second index are always increasing, and both rows have a cycle length of four.

This fact is very interesting because it implies that, for any of the first three minor matrices, the next minor matrix is in fact the same matrix in which all the elements of the 4×4 matrix have been shifted by one element to the left. In short, thanks to element cycling, you can think about how you will compute the determinant of a 3×3 matrix to compute the determinant of all first-level minor matrices. The only thing you have to be careful about is not to do any horizontal operations, because they break the symmetry you use to compute the four minor 3×3 determinants. This means that you cannot use the previous method to compute the determinants of 3×3 sub-matrices.

Let's turn our attention to computing the determinant of $\mathbf{M}_{11}$. By using SIMD's SSE 4-vector instructions, this will also compute $\mathbf{M}_{12}$, $\mathbf{M}_{13}$, and $\mathbf{M}_{14}$. By expanding the determinant some more, you get

$$\begin{vmatrix} a_{11} & a_{21} & a_{31} & a_{41} \\ a_{12} & a_{22} & a_{32} & a_{42} \\ a_{13} & a_{23} & a_{33} & a_{43} \\ a_{14} & a_{24} & a_{34} & a_{44} \end{vmatrix} = a_{11}\begin{vmatrix} a_{22} & a_{23} & a_{24} \\ a_{32} & a_{33} & a_{34} \\ a_{42} & a_{43} & a_{44} \end{vmatrix} + a_{12}\begin{vmatrix} a_{23} & a_{24} & a_{21} \\ a_{33} & a_{34} & a_{31} \\ a_{43} & a_{44} & a_{41} \end{vmatrix} + a_{13}\begin{vmatrix} a_{24} & a_{21} & a_{22} \\ a_{34} & a_{31} & a_{32} \\ a_{44} & a_{41} & a_{42} \end{vmatrix} + a_{14}\begin{vmatrix} a_{21} & a_{22} & a_{23} \\ a_{31} & a_{32} & a_{33} \\ a_{41} & a_{42} & a_{43} \end{vmatrix}$$

$$= a_{11}\mathbf{M}_{11} - a_{12}\mathbf{M}_{12} + a_{13}\mathbf{M}_{13} + a_{14}\mathbf{M}_{14}$$

$$= \mathbf{r}_1 \bullet [\mathbf{M}_{11} \quad \mathbf{M}_{12} \quad \mathbf{M}_{13} \quad \mathbf{M}_{14}]$$

You now have a way to compute a 4×4 matrix determinant, but you can minimally factor things out to obtain a nicer and more optimal form to express the formula. One of the first things you should notice is that there's a nice relationship between the first and last sub-determinants. Namely, the first sub-determinant is the same as the last determinant, but with a rotation of one element to the right. Another interesting observation is that the first row of the second sub-determinant is the same as the second row of that same sub-determinant, but rotated by two elements.

If you look back at your initial 4×4 matrix and look at the smallest center-determinant you can compute, the elements multiplied together are always two elements apart horizontally and one unit apart vertically. Going two units left or two units right is the exact same thing. Therefore, you can simply shift that row of two units when you want to multiply them together to compute the second sub-determinant.

This is pretty much the extent of factorizations you can apply here. The rest of the work will be to optimize resource usage and to keep the row shifts to a minimum. The following code shows this:

```
lea     esi, [Matrix]
pshufd  xmm6, [esi + 4*4*1], 10010011b        // xmm6 = [a24 a21 a22 a23]

movaps  xmm0, [esi + 4*4*3]                    // xmm0 = [a41 a42 a43 a44]
pshufd  xmm3, [esi + 4*4*2], 00111001b         // xmm3 = [a32 a33 a34 a31]

pshufd  xmm1, xmm0, 01001110b
mulps   xmm1, xmm3                             // xmm1 = [a32*a43 a33*a44 a34*a41
a31*a42]

pshufd  xmm2, xmm0, 10010011b
mulps   xmm2, xmm3                             // xmm2 = [a32*a44 a33*a41 a34*a42
a31*a43]
pshufd  xmm4, xmm6, 01001110b                  // xmm4 = [a22 a23 a24 a21]

mulps   xmm0, xmm3
pshufd  xmm0, xmm0, 00111001b                  // xmm0 = [a33*a42 a34*a43 a31*a44
a32*a41]
```

```
pshufd   xmm5, xmm6, 10010011b              // xmm5 = [a23 a24 a21 a22]

subps    xmm1, xmm0                         // xmm1 = [md13 ma13 mb13 mc13]
pshufd   xmm0, xmm1, 00111001b              // xmm0 = [md11 ma11 mb11 mc11]

pshufd   xmm3, xmm2, 01001110b
subps    xmm3, xmm2                         // xmm3 = [md12 ma12 mb12 mc12]

mulps    xmm0, xmm4
mulps    xmm1, xmm6
mulps    xmm3, xmm5

addps    xmm0, xmm1
addps    xmm0, xmm3                         // xmm0 = [M11 M12 M13 M14]
mulps    xmm0, [esi + 4*4*0]                // xmm0 = [a11*M11 a12*M12 a13*M13
a14*M14]

movhlps  xmm1, xmm0
addps    xmm0, xmm1                         // xmm0 = [A1 + A3, A2 + A4, …]
pshufd   xmm1, xmm0, 01010101b
subss    xmm0, xmm1                         // xmm0 = [A1 + A3 + A2 + A4, …]

movss    [Destination], xmm0
```

Cross Product

The cross product is another fundamental vector operation. Its geometrical representation, given two vectors, **A** and **B**, is that the resulting vector, $C = A[d]B$, is perpendicular to the plane generated by **AB**. The result is defined as

$$\left[a_y b_z - a_z b_y \quad a_z b_x - a_x b_z \quad a_x b_y - a_y b_x \right]$$

Or if you prefer, it can be represented in a matrix form as the determinant of the matrix for which the first row is the directional vector (**i, j, k**), and where the second and third vectors are **A** and **B**, respectively. Either way, this looks awfully close to a determinant, and the computation is in fact very much alike.

The computation of the cross product is as straightforward as you'd expect. All you need to do to compute it is rotate the vector **B** to the left, multiply it by **A**, subtract from that the multiplication of **B** and the rotation of **A** to the left, and you're done. Nothing to it, especially after having computed a determinant.

The AoS version of this calculation is too easy and will be left as an exercise. The source code for the SoA version follows:

```
pshufd   xmm0, [VectorA], 11001001b
pshufd   xmm1, [VectorB], 11010010b
mulps    xmm0, xmm1

pshufd   xmm2, [VectorB], 11001001b
pshufd   xmm3, [VectorA], 11010010b
mulps    xmm2, xmm3

subps    xmm0, xmm2
movaps   [DstVector], xmm0
```

Matrix Division (Inverse)

If you feel a sharp pain in the left side of your brain, it's probably because your artsy side feels a little neglected by this chapter. On the other hand, if you feel a sharp pain in the right side, it's probably because you've read the title of this next section and know what's involved.

Divisions have nearly always been slower to perform than multiplications, and matrices are no exception. The *easy* method that's taught in high school is to write the matrix followed by the identity matrix, and the task is to use Gauss-Jordan elimination to obtain the identity matrix on the left side. This method is efficient but lacks a few things. For starters, it doesn't readily tell you if it's possible to obtain an inverse. But the biggest issue with this method is that it's not very accurate. The values are reused many times, and many divisions are involved, making this method not only useless but also slow.

Another technique used to calculate this is to use the determinant. The inverse matrix can be defined as the transposed adjacent matrix divided by the absolute value of the determinant. What exactly is the adjacent matrix? It's a matrix for which every element a_{ij} equals the determinant of the minor matrix $\mathbf{M}_{ij}$:

$$\mathbf{M}^{-1} = \frac{\text{adj}(\mathbf{M})^{\mathrm{T}}}{|\mathbf{M}|}$$

$$= \frac{1}{|\mathbf{M}|}\begin{bmatrix} \mathbf{M}_{11} & \mathbf{M}_{21} & \mathbf{M}_{31} & \mathbf{M}_{41} \\ \mathbf{M}_{12} & \mathbf{M}_{22} & \mathbf{M}_{32} & \mathbf{M}_{42} \\ \mathbf{M}_{13} & \mathbf{M}_{23} & \mathbf{M}_{33} & \mathbf{M}_{43} \\ \mathbf{M}_{14} & \mathbf{M}_{24} & \mathbf{M}_{34} & \mathbf{M}_{44} \end{bmatrix}^{\mathrm{T}}$$

$$= \frac{1}{|\mathbf{M}|}\begin{bmatrix}
\begin{vmatrix} a_{22} & a_{23} & a_{24} \\ a_{32} & a_{33} & a_{34} \\ a_{42} & a_{43} & a_{44} \end{vmatrix} &
\begin{vmatrix} a_{21} & a_{23} & a_{24} \\ a_{31} & a_{33} & a_{34} \\ a_{41} & a_{43} & a_{44} \end{vmatrix} &
\begin{vmatrix} a_{21} & a_{22} & a_{24} \\ a_{31} & a_{32} & a_{34} \\ a_{41} & a_{42} & a_{44} \end{vmatrix} &
\begin{vmatrix} a_{21} & a_{22} & a_{23} \\ a_{31} & a_{32} & a_{33} \\ a_{41} & a_{42} & a_{43} \end{vmatrix} \\[3em]
\begin{vmatrix} a_{12} & a_{13} & a_{14} \\ a_{32} & a_{33} & a_{34} \\ a_{42} & a_{43} & a_{44} \end{vmatrix} &
\begin{vmatrix} a_{11} & a_{13} & a_{14} \\ a_{31} & a_{33} & a_{34} \\ a_{41} & a_{43} & a_{44} \end{vmatrix} &
\begin{vmatrix} a_{11} & a_{12} & a_{14} \\ a_{31} & a_{32} & a_{34} \\ a_{41} & a_{42} & a_{44} \end{vmatrix} &
\begin{vmatrix} a_{12} & a_{13} & a_{13} \\ a_{31} & a_{32} & a_{33} \\ a_{41} & a_{42} & a_{43} \end{vmatrix} \\[3em]
\begin{vmatrix} a_{12} & a_{13} & a_{14} \\ a_{22} & a_{23} & a_{24} \\ a_{42} & a_{43} & a_{44} \end{vmatrix} &
\begin{vmatrix} a_{11} & a_{13} & a_{14} \\ a_{21} & a_{23} & a_{24} \\ a_{41} & a_{43} & a_{44} \end{vmatrix} &
\begin{vmatrix} a_{11} & a_{12} & a_{14} \\ a_{21} & a_{22} & a_{24} \\ a_{41} & a_{42} & a_{44} \end{vmatrix} &
\begin{vmatrix} a_{12} & a_{13} & a_{13} \\ a_{21} & a_{22} & a_{33} \\ a_{41} & a_{42} & a_{43} \end{vmatrix} \\[3em]
\begin{vmatrix} a_{12} & a_{13} & a_{14} \\ a_{22} & a_{23} & a_{24} \\ a_{32} & a_{33} & a_{34} \end{vmatrix} &
\begin{vmatrix} a_{11} & a_{13} & a_{14} \\ a_{21} & a_{23} & a_{24} \\ a_{31} & a_{33} & a_{34} \end{vmatrix} &
\begin{vmatrix} a_{11} & a_{12} & a_{14} \\ a_{21} & a_{22} & a_{24} \\ a_{31} & a_{32} & a_{34} \end{vmatrix} &
\begin{vmatrix} a_{11} & a_{12} & a_{13} \\ a_{21} & a_{22} & a_{33} \\ a_{31} & a_{32} & a_{33} \end{vmatrix}
\end{bmatrix}$$

A few interesting things appear when you look at the redundancy in the adjacent matrix given with this notation. First off, you need to compute the determinant of $\mathbf{M}$, which means that at some point you must also compute the determinant of the minor matrices $\mathbf{M}_{11}$, $\mathbf{M}_{12}$, $\mathbf{M}_{13}$, and $\mathbf{M}_{14}$. It doesn't take a genius to notice that the first row of the inverse matrix contains exactly these four elements. So in other words, by computing the determinant of $\mathbf{M}$, you have also computed the first row of the adjacent matrix.

Notice that the last two rows of the determinants in the adjacent matrix's first and second row are identical. This means that you can precompute this value and use it when computing the determinant of the eight first minor matrices. The same goes for the determinant of the two last rows of the adjacent matrix. In this case, the two first rows of the determinant are identical. Recall that when computing a determinant, the actual order of the rows isn't important. Thanks to this, you can insert the last row of the determinants as the first row and apply the exact same process you used for the first and second row of the adjacent matrix.

Finally, you must finish off with a transposition and a multiplication of every element by the inverse of the determinant of **M**. From this point on, all that's left is to write the assembly code, which optimizes the resources as best as possible:

```
__declspec(align(16)) static const unsigned long Sign[4] =
       {0x00000000, 0x80000000, 0x00000000, 0x80000000};
// Row 1
lea          esi, [Matrix]
pshufd       xmm6, [esi + 4*4*1], 10010011b        // xmm6 = [a24 a21 a22 a23]

pshufd       xmm3, [esi + 4*4*2], 00111001b        // xmm3 = [a32 a33 a34 a31]
movaps       xmm0, [esi + 4*4*3]                    // xmm0 = [a41 a42 a43 a44]

pshufd       xmm1, xmm0, 01001110b
mulps        xmm1, xmm3                             // xmm1 = [a32*a43 a33*a44 a34*a41
a31*a42]

pshufd       xmm2, xmm0, 10010011b
mulps        xmm2, xmm3                             // xmm2 = [a32*a44 a33*a41 a34*a42
a31*a43]
pshufd       xmm7, xmm6, 01001110b                 // xmm7 = [a22 a23 a24 a21]

mulps        xmm0, xmm3
pshufd       xmm0, xmm0, 00111001b                 // xmm0 = [a33*a42 a34*a43 a31*a44
a32*a41]
pshufd       xmm5, xmm6, 10010011b                 // xmm5 = [a23 a24 a21 a22]

subps        xmm1, xmm0                             // xmm1 = [md13 ma13 mb13 mc13]
pshufd       xmm0, xmm1, 00111001b                 // xmm0 = [md11 ma11 mb11 mc11]

pshufd       xmm3, xmm2, 01001110b
subps        xmm3, xmm2                             // xmm3 = [md12 ma12 mb12 mc12]

mulps        xmm7, xmm0
mulps        xmm6, xmm1
mulps        xmm5, xmm3

addps        xmm7, xmm6
addps        xmm7, xmm5                             // xmm7 = [M11 M12 M13 M14]
movaps       xmm6, xmm7                             // xmm6 = [M11 M12 M13 M14]
pshufd       xmm2, [esi + 4*4*0], 10010011b        // xmm2 = [a14 a11 a12 a13]
// Determinant
```

```
mulps      xmm7, [esi + 4*4*0]                    // xmm0 = [a11*M11 a12*M12 a13*M13
a14*M14]

pshufd     xmm4, xmm2, 01001110b                  // xmm4 = [a12 a13 a14 a11]
movhlps    xmm5, xmm7
addps      xmm7, xmm5                              // xmm0 = [A1 + A3, A2 + A4, ...]
pshufd     xmm5, xmm7, 01010101b
subss      xmm7, xmm5                              // xmm0 = [A1 + A3 + A2 + A4, ...]
// Row 2
pshufd     xmm5, xmm2, 10010011b                  // xmm5 = [a13 a14 a11 a12]

mulps      xmm4, xmm0
mulps      xmm2, xmm1
mulps      xmm5, xmm3

addps      xmm4, xmm2
addps      xmm5, xmm4                              // xmm5 = [M21 M22 M23 M24]
// Row 3
pshufd     xmm4, [esi + 4*4*3], 00111001b          // xmm4 = [a42 a43 a44 a41]

movaps     xmm0, [esi + 4*4*1]                     // xmm0 = [a21 a22 a23 a24]
pshufd     xmm3, [esi + 4*4*0], 00111001b          // xmm3 = [a12 a13 a14 a11]

pshufd     xmm1, xmm0, 01001110b
mulps      xmm1, xmm3                              // xmm1 = [a12*a23 a13*a24 a14*a21
a11*a22]

pshufd     xmm2, xmm0, 10010011b
mulps      xmm2, xmm3                              // xmm2 = [a12*a24 a13*a21 a14*a22
a11*a23]

mulps      xmm0, xmm3
pshufd     xmm0, xmm0, 00111001b                   // xmm0 = [a13*a22 a14*a23 a11*a24
a12*a21]

subps      xmm1, xmm0                              // xmm1 = [md43 ma43 mb43 mc43]
pshufd     xmm0, xmm1, 00111001b                   // xmm0 = [md41 ma41 mb41 mc41]
mulps      xmm4, xmm0

pshufd     xmm3, xmm2, 01001110b
subps      xmm3, xmm2                              // xmm3 = [md42 ma42 mb42 mc42]
```

```
        pshufd      xmm2, [esi + 4*4*3], 10010011b      // xmm2 = [a44 a41 a42 a43]
        mulps       xmm2, xmm1
        addps       xmm4, xmm2


        pshufd      xmm2, [esi + 4*4*3], 01001110b      // xmm2 = [a43 a44 a41 a42]
        mulps       xmm2, xmm3
        addps       xmm4, xmm2                           // xmm4 = [M31 M32 M33 M34]
        // Row 4
        pshufd      xmm2, [esi + 4*4*2], 01001110b      // xmm2 = [a33 a34 a31 a32]
        mulps       xmm3, xmm2
        rcpss       xmm7, xmm7


        pshufd      xmm2, [esi + 4*4*2], 10010011b      // xmm2 = [a34 a31 a32 a33]
        mulps       xmm1, xmm2


        pshufd      xmm2, [esi + 4*4*2], 00111001b      // xmm2 = [a32 a33 a34 a31]
        mulps       xmm0, xmm2


        pshufd      xmm7, xmm7, 00000000b
        addps       xmm3, xmm1
        addps       xmm3, xmm0                           // xmm3 = [M41 M42 M43 M44]
        // Set the right signs
        // Multiply by the Determinant
        pxor        xmm7, [Sign]
        mulps       xmm6, xmm7
        mulps       xmm4, xmm7
        pshufd      xmm7, xmm7, 00010001b
        mulps       xmm5, xmm7
        mulps       xmm3, xmm7
        // Transpose
        movaps      xmm7, xmm6
        unpcklps    xmm6, xmm5                           // xmm6 = [a11, a21, a12, a22]


        movaps      xmm0, xmm4
        unpcklps    xmm4, xmm3                           // xmm4 = [a31, a41, a32, a42]
        movaps      xmm2, xmm6


        unpckhps    xmm7, xmm5                           // xmm2 = [a13, a23, a14, a24]
        lea         edi, [DstMatrix]
        unpckhps    xmm0, xmm3                           // xmm0 = [a33, a43, a34, a44]
        movaps      xmm1, xmm7
```

```
movlhps    xmm6, xmm4                // xmm6 = [a11, a21, a31, a41]
movaps     [edi + 0*4*4], xmm6
movhlps    xmm4, xmm2                // xmm4 = [a12, a22, a32, a42]
movaps     [edi + 1*4*4], xmm4
movlhps    xmm7, xmm0                // xmm2 = [a13, a23, a33, a43]
movaps     [edi + 2*4*4], xmm7
movhlps    xmm0, xmm1                // xmm0 = [a14, a24, a34, a44]
movaps     [edi + 3*4*4], xmm0
```

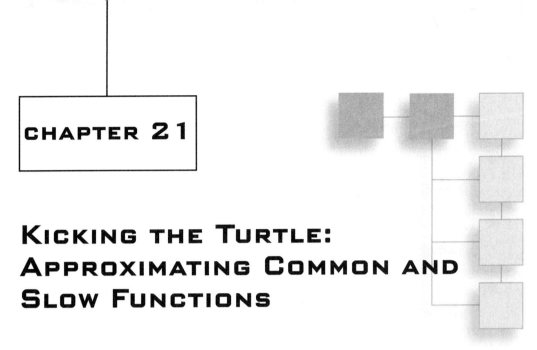

CHAPTER 21

KICKING THE TURTLE: APPROXIMATING COMMON AND SLOW FUNCTIONS

For a long time, one of the only ways to use functions such as sin/cos efficiently was to build a table. With a processor deprived of an FPU, and with few cycles to spare, a function such as sine was completely taboo in a real-time game. Tables worked pretty well and were used for quite a while, until the FPU became fast enough that reading an array became much less attractive than having a precise value. After all, the tables had a limited number of samples.

Unfortunately, these functions are part of the slowest group of instructions the PC has to offer today. In fact, they're so slow that a software-based approximation yielding the same amount of precision can actually outperform every complex function. This means that you can speed up a lot of interesting functions.

In Chapter 12, "Closing the Gap for Numerical Approximation," you learned about numerous approximation methods and how they can be used to approximate various functions. It's nice to have a good theoretical background, but it's not very useful if it doesn't have any application to creating games. This chapter goes one step further into approximation by completely reimplementing the costly FPU functions to make them faster. Clearly, you wouldn't want to do this unless there were practical uses for all of these functions, so this chapter will show the amazing things you can do with approximation, a few neat tricks, and a healthy, innovative mind.

More precisely, this chapter will cover the following:

- Approximating transcendental functions
- Physical simulation

Transcendental Function Evaluation

Transcendental. There's a word to put a spinning question mark over your head. The simplest definition of transcendental functions cannot be expressed in terms of algebra. Well-known examples of such functions are the set of trigonometry functions sine, cosine, tangent, e^x, and many more. This may come as a surprise, because cosine can be calculated on the computer. The truth is that such functions are approximated and not computed accurately.

If you cannot express such functions using algebra, the best you can do is *approximate* the functions using algebra. Because such functions aren't natural to our mathematics, they typically yield complex infinite algebraic approximation, and consequently yield extremely slow methods when compared with other algebraic functions. Anyone who has worked with trigonometric functions can attest to how slow these functions are, and looking at the Intel cycle count for such functions shows them to be the slowest of the pack. This is quite a shame, because these functions are extremely useful for anything natural under the spherical world coordinate (such as rotations).

The next section will present some series to accurately and efficiently compute such functions.

Cosine and Sine Approximation

If you want to approximate a cyclic curve, such as the sine or cosine functions, the first thing you should do is look for the easy symmetries and consider the simplest section only. Looking at a full period of the cosine wave, illustrated in Figure 21.1, you can remove the second half by symmetry:

$$\cos(Angle) = \cos(2\pi - Angle)$$

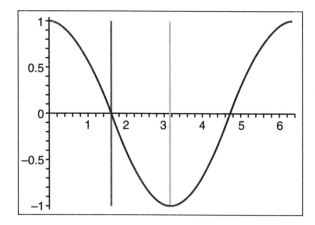

Figure 21.1
Cosine curve's symmetry

Furthermore, you can remove the second quarter by reflection and by inverting:

$$\cos(Angle) = -\cos(\pi - Angle)$$

Finally, you're left with approximating the cosine function from 0 to $\pi/2$, for which you can generate a much better approximation than a full-length cosine. In fact, any approximation that considers the entire period of the cosine will be prone to heavy precision penalties. The same idea can be applied to the sine function. Particularly interesting is the fact that the Taylor series becomes better than the Minimax series, in terms of computation speed versus precision, after about 16 bits of precision.

Tables 21.1 and 21.2 give the coefficient for the cosine and sine function when aiming for a given bit precision. Of course, for the Taylor series to be faster than the Minimax series, you will have to factor out the x^2. The code for the Minimax calculations of the cosine follows, as well as the tables for both cosine and sine. The code to set up the Taylor series will be slightly different, since it needs to precalculate x^2, but quite similar. A similar setup can be applied for sine.

Notice how the 90-degree case is handled. The sign is merely inverted, and the code still operates correctly. Note that this function only handles angles between 0 and 2π. It shouldn't be too hard to make sure that all arguments passed to this function fit that range, by continuously verifying for range overflows.

```
float cos(float X)
{
        float Result, Square;
        if (X > PI)
            X = 2.0f * PI - X;

        // 90° turnaround
        if (X <= PI / 2.0f) {
            Result  = XOCoEff;
            Square  = X;

        } else {
            Square  = X - PI;      // Invert the sign
            Result  = -XOCoEff;
            X       = -Square;
        }

        Result += Square * XiCoEff;
        Square *= X;              // The 2 last lines are repeated for every coeff.
        ...
```

```
        return Result;
}
```

Table 21.1 Cosine Best Computational Polynomial Coefficient Approximation for $x = [0..\pi/2]$

Precision	x^0	x^1	x^2	x^3	x^4	x^5	x^6
6 bits	0.1013851305E+1	-0.1336597009	-0.3314217715				
9 bits	0.998634052	0.296063466E-1	-0.6008541005	0.1125043249			
13 bits	0.9998923476	0.321957553E-2	-0.5152284612	0.2410259866E-1	0.2841899817E-1		
16 bits	0.1000007064E+1	-0.3342551E-3	-0.4974333054	-0.724957385E-2	0.5103547954E-1	-0.572168799E-2	
20 bits	1	$-2^{-1}x$	$24^{-1}x^2$	$-720^{-1}x^3$	$40320^{-1}x^4$	$-3628800^{-1}x^5$	
27 bits	1	$-2^{-1}x$	$24^{-1}x^2$	$-720^{-1}x^3$	$40320^{-1}x^4$	$-3628800^{-1}x^5$	$479001600^{-1}x^6$

Table 21.2 Sine Best Computational Polynomial Coefficient Approximation for $x = [0..\pi/2]$

Precision	x^0	x^1	x^2	x^3	x^4	x^5	x^6
6 bits	-0.13851306E-1	0.1174851861E+1	-0.3314217442				
9 bits	-0.13659477E-2	0.102525261E+1	-0.70689985E-1	-0.1125043144			
13 bits		x	$-6^{-1}x^2$	$120^{-1}x^3$	$-5040^{-1}x^4$		
18 bits		x	$-6^{-1}x^2$	$120^{-1}x^3$	$-5040^{-1}x^4$	$362880^{-1}x^5$	
24 bits		x	$-6^{-1}x^2$	$120^{-1}x^3$	$-5040^{-1}x^4$	$362880^{-1}x^5$	$39916800^{-1}x^6$

So the next question is, exactly how much faster is this code than the traditional C/C++ functions? All comparisons in this chapter are done with the Microsoft Visual C++ .NET compiler, which uses the FPU functions. The speed of the code is quite dependent on the compiler and the machine you're testing on. However, based on the tests I did, every single approximation presented above is faster than the library version (fcos). For the cosine, the last one takes about 70% of the original time. Once you reach 13 bits of precision, you've basically doubled the speed. For both cosine and sine, the first set of coefficient yields a three-times improvement. For the sine function, the slowest case is twice as fast as the original time. In either case, you achieve quite a good improvement in this area.

For any given row, Table 21.2 shows the fastest approximation, which is one notch more complex than the previous. Notice how the sine curve yields better approximations than the cosine values. For this reason, consider that the cosine curve is but a sine curve shifted by 90 degrees, and simply subtract $\pi/2$ from your input values. There are Minimax approximations, which are more complex than the 9 bits approximation. But clearly, the Taylor series is equally or less complex with more precision, as illustrated by the sine wave in Figure 21.2.

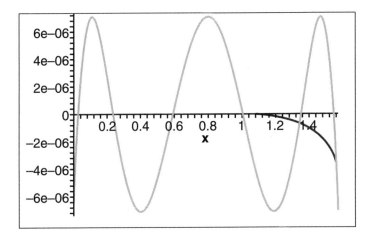

Figure 21.2
Approximation error of sin(x) with the Taylor series and the Minimax approximation for 18 bits

Now that you've seen how much of an improvement you can achieve with these functions, let's see what you can do with other quite popular transcendental functions.

Tangent Approximation

The sine and cosine functions are quite nice because they can be approximated with power series. These functions did not hold any singularity or extreme case, but that's all over now. The tangent function has an infinite number of singularities, but like the sine and cosine functions, we only consider one period. This function has singularities at $\mp\pi/2$. Consider the range $[0..\pi]$ for the tan function. You can easily change this to $[-\pi/2, \pi/2]$ or another similar range if you like. You know that the positive and negative side are mirrors of each other, so you can turn your attention to the range $[0..\pi/2]$. The big problem in approximating this function is the singularity, which exists at $\pi/2$. The function is asymptotic, and that's the real problem you have to fix. In general, any asymptotic curve will slowly converge, hence yielding very complex functions for a reasonable approximation. The key to speeding up the tangent function comes from a very simple identity, illustrated in Figure 21.3.

$$\tan(x) = \frac{1}{\tan\left(\dfrac{\pi}{2} - x\right)}$$

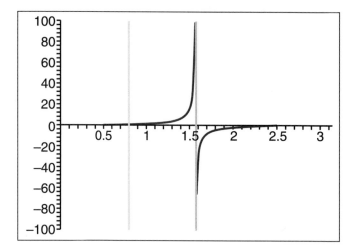

Figure 21.3
Tangent curve's symmetry

This means that you only need to approximate for the range $[0..\pi/4]$, because you can convert any other angle to that range with the identity. A division is really ugly, but in this case, it will save us. There are no more singularities and no more asymptotes, so you can now run some numerical analysis to compute the best coefficient for the tangent function. The code and Table 21.3 follow. Note that again, this code can only take angles from $0..\pi$. Hence, it's assumed that you can fit the angle into the range within your code, which is faster than taking the remainder of the modulus π (in floating point). Again, if you require a different range, such as $[-\pi/2..\pi/2]$, you should be able to achieve this with basic observations of the geometry of the tan function.

```
float tan(float X)
{
        float Result, Square;

        // 90° turnaround
        if (X <= PI/2) {
            Result    = X0CoEff;

            // 45° turnaround
            if (X > PI/4) {
                    Square = X = PI/2 - X;
                    Result += Square * XiCoEff;
                    Square *= X;     // The 2 last lines are repeated for every coeff.
                    ...
```

```
                            return 1/Result;


            } else {
                        Square = X;
                        Result += Square * XiCoEff;
                        Square *= X;     // The 2 last lines are repeated for every co.

                        ...
                        return Result;
            }
      } else {
            Result    = -XOCoEff;

            // 45° turnaround
            if (X < PI/2 + PI/4) {
                        Square     = PI - X - PI/2;
                        X       = -Square;
                        Square    = X;
                        Result += Square * XiCoEff;
                        Square *= X;     // The 2 last lines are repeated for every co.

                        ...
                        return 1/Result;

            } else {
                        Square     = X - PI;
                        X       = -Square;
                        Square    = X;
                        Result += Square * XiCoEff;
                        Square *= X;     // The 2 last lines are repeated for every co.

                        ...
                        return Result;
      }
}
```

Table 21.3 Tangent Best Computational Polynomial Coefficient Approximation for x = [0..π/4]

Precision	x^0	x^1	x^2	x^3	x^4	x^5	x^6	x^7	x^8
6 bits	0.1045977879E-1	0.7948298457	0.5752216385						
9 bits	-0.1507860077E-2	0.1051396471E+1	-0.263817587	0.6955414298					
11 bits	0.28624517E-3	0.9836760204	0.147441366	-0.1156751704	0.5044422587				
14 bits	-0.462938E-4	0.1002818329E+1	-0.5063428861E-1	0.5722670723	-0.4766239886	0.4917099099			
16 bits	0.8224682E-5	0.9990552968	0.1764544473E-1	0.2113610563	0.3905128158	-0.4724533695	0.4032294526		
19 bits	-0.1382595E-5	0.1000208836E+1	-0.5160125253E-2	0.3814473318	-0.2161735546	0.6420342794	-0.614525481	0.3658508231	
22 bits	0.240064E-6	0.9999536081	0.1472527626E-2	0.3154470199	0.1075857239	-0.2229558761	0.6687097787	-0.6272885679	0.3127296854

Before I get into the benchmarks, I should say a few words about the code. It seems to have been copied and pasted four times, and rightly so. If you take the common series calculation outside of the code, you must take care of the inverse for half the cases. You could add another if or gotos with two main polynomial expansions, but you'd take a large performance hit from the branch. Expanding the function, as was done here, results in a ~20% speed increase, which is quite considerable. Check out Chapter 19, "The Quick Mind: Computational Optimizations," with regards to branching for more details.

The Taylor series for this particular function performed really badly. The tables clearly show this, because every coefficient is from the Minimax and isn't in a nice rational format. For the speed analysis, it's not quite clear if you gained any speed or not. You require much more coefficient to achieve this, and one ugly division for half the cases. But in fact, looking at Intel's average clock cycles for the tan function clearly shows that this function suffers more than the previous two. When comparing the tan function with the series approximation, the results were roughly as good as what you achieved with *sin* and *cos*. For 14 bits of precision, the approximation is twice as fast as the C/C++ function. In the best case, you get a whopping four times speed increase, and the more precise case yields about 70% of the MS C/C++ implementation.

Again, a pretty good job was done of optimizing this function. This is nice, but let's raise a yellow flag here because there's a lot of computation going on. More precisely, the inverse function will hurt the precision beyond the theoretical amount. Hence, it's quite possible to run the approximation for 14 bits and end up with 9 bits of precision in practice. You have been warned. This is not a real issue with cos/sin.

ArcTangent Approximation

Here's another monster that's quite useful for geometry problems. Typically, the ArcTan is not something you want to use, because it's slower than all the other functions you have seen so far. Many times, you can get around calculating this function by looking at your problem in a different way. You can use slopes and four quadrants to remove the use of this function. So the moral is simple: If you can do without it, do without it, because approximating still won't be as fast as using, for example, slopes. Nonetheless, sometimes you just can't get away from using it, so let's analyze it.

The ArcTan function, illustrated in Figure 21.4, is yet another asymptotic curve. This makes approximating such curves a non-trivial task, and basically you have to look at the curve in a different way in order to obtain a good approximation. Right off the bat, notice the clear symmetry in X. Hence, you should only consider the positive section of the curve.

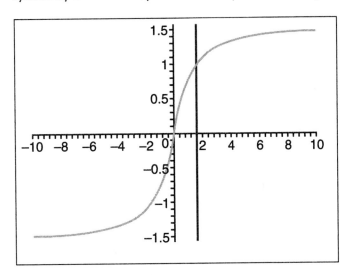

Figure 21.4
ArcTangent curve's symmetry

Once more, you can resort to a very nice identity:

$$\arctan(x) = \frac{\pi |x|}{2x} - \arctan\left(\frac{1}{x}\right)$$

Table 21.4 ArcTangent Best Computational Polynomial Coefficient Approximation for x = [0..1]

Precision	x^0	x^1	x^2	x^3	x^4	x^5	x^6	x^7	x^8
8 bits	-0.245220854E-2	0.106629478E+1	-0.275921995	-0.652734385E-1	0.1381076251				
9 bits	-0.110362645E-2	0.103662302E+1	-0.185954699	-0.338044841	0.2641311377	-0.4949954813E-1			
13 bits	-0.106190712e-3	1.003834532	-0.182871282e-1	-0.4511471648	0.1384985296	0.6584074532E-1	-0.3949398886E-1		
15 bits	0.20939139E-4	0.9982532521	0.236604866E-1	-0.3884985296		-0.556863294E-1	-0.2179607659	0.5122276497E-1	
17 bits	0.6385866E-5	0.9993825836	0.9668662E-2	-0.3309255465		0.3099892425	-0.2839751699	0.9057698416E-1	
21 bits	0.408069E-6	0.999974048	0.13775473E-3	-0.3231297466	-0.2703933342E-1	0.368096969			
22 bits	-0.189047E-6	0.10000032717E+1	-0.93189572E-3						0.9584986998E-2

Okay, so it isn't that nice, but it will suffice for our purposes. Moreover, if you only consider the positive values, you get the nicer form:

$$\arctan(x) = \frac{\pi}{2} - \arctan\left(\frac{1}{x}\right)$$

This is interesting, because now you can limit your approximation to the range [0..1] and effectively get rid of the asymptotic side of the equation. The code and Table 21.4 follow:

```
float atan(float X)
{
        float Result, Square;

        // 90° turnaround
        if (X <= 1) {
            Result = XOCoEff;
            Square = X;

        } else {
            Result = PI/2 - XOCoEff;
            X       = 1/X;
            Square = -X;
        }

        Result += Square * XiCoEff;
        Square *= X;      // The 2 last lines are
repeated for every coeff.
        ...
        return Result;
}
```

Again, the Taylor series is off the chart. Looking at the depth of the coefficient once again, this function is not an easy approximation. Speedwise, you might expect a good battle, but Intel claims that its ArcTan function ranges from 150–300 cycles. It has quite a wide range, but in some cases, it seems like it can beat cosine and sine. However, since you've already beaten the speed of the FPU's cosine and sine functions with approximations, it should come as no surprise that this function does very well also. When comparing with 15 bits of accuracy, the function is about 2.5 times faster than the built-in function. With the least amount of precision, it's a little less than four times faster, and with 22 bits of precision, it's still about 60% faster. Best of all, you're not losing precision like you were with the tan function, because the division is done before the approximation and not after.

ArcSin/ArcCos Approximation

This function terrorizes programmers even more than the ones seen previously. The ArcSin and the ArcCos are mere reflections of one another. These are very slow on PCs, mainly because there's no hardware ArcSin function. Typically, the solution is to calculate ArcTan and then use a trigonometry identity to convert from ArcTan to ArcSin and ArcCos. Just to bring even more to the discussion, one identity to convert from ArcSin using ArcTan is

$$\arcsin(x) = \arctan\left(\frac{x}{\sqrt{1-x^2}}\right)$$

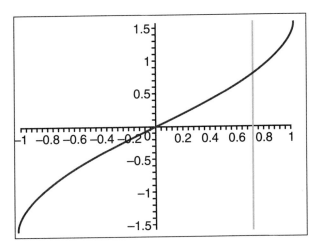

You may be able to get rid of the division with a few operations, but you sure won't be able to touch that square root, the square multiplication, and the ArcTan.

If Intel decided not to add an ArcSin function, there might be a good reason for this besides space and money. The ArcSin function illustrated in Figure 21.5 is one of the worst functions to approximate. It's very unnatural, or perhaps more properly put, unalgebraic. At first, though, this is some-what surprising because it only spans from −1 to 1, but its shape simply doesn't fit the power series pattern.

Figure 21.5
ArcSin curve's symmetry

The first thing you should notice is the symmetry, and hence you should consider only the top portion of the curve. If you tried to approximate the curve from 0 to 1, the precision would be extremely bad, to the point where 10 coefficient would yield about 8 bits of precision. Clearly, this is of no good use to us. Again, pull out nice identities known about ArcSin. Notably, the one of interest is

$$\arcsin(x) = \frac{\pi}{2} - \arcsin\left(\sqrt{1-x^2}\right)$$

This is still a rather ugly identity, but that's pretty much as good as it gets. At least you got rid of the division for the preceding identity. This gives us a span that's easier to approximate than the entire curve. One reason why this identity shouldn't bother you too much is that you only need to use it if x is greater than $2^{1/2}$, which is less than a third of the entire curve. As for ArcCos, it's easily expressed as

$$\arccos(x) = \frac{\pi}{2} - \arcsin(x)$$

A simpler way to put this is to simply adjust the first coefficient of the table and reverse all signs. This way, there's no added complexity to the equation. The code for the entire range $[-1..1]$ and its table (Table 21.5) follow:

```
float ArcSin(float X)
{
    float Result, Square;

    if (X >= 0) {
        if (X < 0.70710678118f) {
            Result = XOCoEff;
            Square = X;

        } else {
            Result = PI/2 - XOCoEff;
            X       = sqrtf(1 - X * X);
            Square = -X;
        }

    } else {
        if (X >= -0.70710678118f) {
            Result = -XOCoEff;
            Square = X;
            X       = -X;

        } else {
            Result = -PI/2 + XOCoEff;
            Square = X = sqrtf(1 - X * X);
```

Table 21.5 ArcSin Best Computational Polynomial Coefficient Approximation for x = [0..2^0.5]

Precision	x^0	x^1	x^2	x^3	x^4	x^5	x^6	x^7	x^8	x^9
7 bits	0.390516539E-2	0.9157107193	0.2601651471							
10 bits	-0.626570076E-3	0.1023174877E+1	-0.1289007245	0.357384868						
13 bits	0.142409784E-3	0.9912600081	0.847586401E-1	-0.1080609809	0.3200507049					
15 bits	-0.309810043E-4	0.1002762282E+1	-0.395589678E-1	0.3675987062	-0.4284585337	0.4144579268				
16 bits	0.7392498E-5	0.9990844198	0.184213283E-1	0.29971965E-1	0.464460866	-0.6844063045	0.5079377565			
18 bits	-0.1783422E-5	0.1000291568E+1	-0.77928038E-2	0.2451210611	-0.3792826008	0.1029652092E+1	-0.122055016E+1	0.6866194435		
21 bits	0.451287E-6	0.9999069216	0.319653809E-2	0.1247217679	0.271752664	-0.889521916	0.1923382206E+1	-0.2001980633E+1	0.9359964379	
23 bits	-0.11281E-6	0.1000029338E+1	-0.12575382E-2	0.1874599818	-0.1728256306	0.8862452458	-0.2254744452E+1	0.3740567555E+1	-0.3328418822E+1	0.1321618628E+1

```
      }
    }

    Result += Square * XiCoEff;
    Square *= X;      // The 2 last lines are
repeated for every coeff.

      ...

      return Result;
}
```

It should come as no surprise that you can do about as well as the ArcTan with this function. For 15 bits of precision, it's about 2.5 times faster than the built-in function. In the best case, it's four times faster than the system-provided function, and the worst case is about 54% faster than the original speed. Note that with these numbers, the square root function that was used is the one provided by the library. You could speed up the code even more if you approximated the square root.

Logarithm Approximation

Arguably, this isn't a very useful function for real-time games. But I know all too well that the second I say that, someone else will step up and give a counterexample. Mind you, physics and some complex simulations of air, water, or other similar phenomena may require such functions, so it's a good idea to see what you can do with them.

For starters, you know you can convert from any logarithm base to any other from this simple identity:

$$\log_b(x) = \frac{\log_a(x)}{\log_a(b)}$$

The last term is a constant, so you can easily precalculate it if you want to make a function with a fixed base. PCs are much better at doing calculations in base 2, so the most logical thing to do is create a function to calculate the base 2 logarithm, illustrated in Figure 21.6.

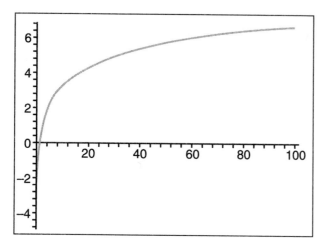

If you recall the way floating points are stored, you already know the integer base 2 logarithm of the x. Recall that floating points are written as $(1 + 2^{-mantissa}) * 2^{exponent-127}$. You can obtain the exponential part with just a bit mask and an offset. What will give you a harder time is the mantissa of the logarithm. From another log identity, you know that

Figure 21.6
Base 2 logarithm curve

$$log(xy) = log(x) + log(y)$$

Since you can calculate the logarithm of the exponential term, you just need to find the logarithm of the first term and then sum them up. Again, a quick look at the logarithm graph shows that you have another asymptote, which you will need to get rid of. Another thing you need to get rid of in order to produce a good approximation is the infinity to the right. But if you look at the expression for a floating-point value, this isn't a problem because you're guaranteed to have a number in the range [1..2]. The last thing you need to do is approximate the logarithm in that range. The code and Table 21.6 follow:

```
float log2(float X)
{
        float Result, Square;

        Result = (float)((*(unsigned long *)&X) >> 23) - 127 + x0CoEff;
        *(unsigned long *)&X = (*(unsigned long *)&X & 0x007FFFFF) | 0x3F800000;
        Square = X;

        Result += Square * XiCoEff;
        Square *= X;     // The 2 last lines are repeated for every coeff.
        ...

        return Result;
}
```

Table 21.6 Log$_2$ Best Computational Polynomial Coefficient Approximation for x = [1..2]

Precision	x^0	x^1	x^2	x^3	x^4	x^5	x^6	x^7	x^8
8 bits	-0.1674903474E+1	0.2024681754E+1	-0.344847634						
10 bits	-0.2153620718E+1	0.3047884161E+1	-0.1051875031E+1	0.1582487046					
13 bits	-0.2512854628E+1	0.4070090803E+1	-0.2120675146E+1	0.6451423713	-0.8161580995E-1				
16 bits	-0.2800364085E+1	0.5091710979E+1	-0.3550793149E+1	0.1631144891E+1	-0.416563 7343	0.4487361632E-1			
18 bits	-0.3040040971E+1	0.6112966147E+1	-0.5341994584E+1	0.3286533825E+1	-0.1266920898E+1	0.2751494963	-0.2569117106E-1		
21 bits	-0.3245537043E+1	0.713396534E+1	-0.7494120386E+1	0.5781427173E+1	-0.2985012428E+1	0.9780911032	-0.183938752	0.1515265932E-1	
22 bits	-0.189047E-6	0.1000032717E+1	-0.9318572E-3	-0.3231297466	-0.556863294E-1	0.368096969	-0.2839751699	0.9057698416E-1	-0.9584986 98E-2

First, a few notes about the source code. The first line of the function retrieves the integer part of the logarithm from the floating-point number (remember that you have to remove the 127 bias). The following line removes the exponent and masks in 127 (an exponent of 0) so that you can go on with your approximation, given a number in the range of [1..2]. Nothing too complex is going on.

As far as speed is concerned, the most precise case yields about 70% the speed of the original MS library function. The 16-bit case is a little less than twice as fast, and the fastest possible case is three times faster than the original version. Please note that these comparisons were done with the natural logarithm, and the *log2* function was multiplied by the constant using the aforementioned identity.

Powers Approximation

A power function isn't implicitly a transcendental function. For example, 2^8 can be calculated by multiplying 2 by itself eight times. Before we deal with the transcendental type, let's first optimize the algebraic types, which are much easier to deal with. Suppose you want to compute a power x^y, where x is a real number but y is a positive integer (natural number). The most obvious thing to try is to multiply x by y. But you can do much better than this, because it computes a lot of the same information repeatedly. It's a fundamental identity for exponentials that

$$x^{a+b} = x^a x^b$$

If you look at the binary representation of your natural number y, notice that it's in fact a bunch of additions. When the bit is turned on, you can add 2^i, and if not, you don't need to do anything. In essence, you have this:

$$x^{1+2+4+8+\ldots+2^i} = xx^2x^4x^8\cdots x^{2^i}$$

The right side is much more interesting because it means that, at most, you will need to compute $x^{2[\wedge i]}$. The rest is just a bunch of multiplications of these terms.

So the algorithm is simple. For a power x^y where y is a natural, loop until the exponent y is 0. But meanwhile, if the rightmost bit is turned on (in other words, if the number is odd), you may multiply your current power of x by the result. Regardless of the value, you have to multiply x by itself for every turn, hence calculating the increase in power. The source code follows:

```
float IntPow(float X, unsigned long n)
{
    float Result(1.0f);

    while (n) {
        if (n & 1)
            Result *= Square;

        X *= X;
        n >>= 1;
    }

    return Result;
}
```

This algorithm depends on the number of bits set in the integer, so if a lot of bits are set, you'll take a greater performance hit than if few of them are set. With the first 16-bits set, the algorithm is about three times faster than the pow function provided with the MS compiler. With 8-bits set, it's roughly five times faster. So either way, this function is much better than what the compiler provides. It has one big issue, though: It simply can't compute fractional exponents or negative ones. With many equations, you have a fixed power, so this isn't an issue. You can unroll the preceding algorithm to yield an efficient solution to this problem. Clearly, this cannot suit all of your needs, so you have to look for something else.

This function is extremely ugly because it's impossible for us to approximate this curve, given that you have two variables. You could do it, but the approximation would be so terrible that you wouldn't even want to use it. Instead, you can use an identity to convert to x^y. Moreover, the identity to choose is

$$x^y = 2^{y \log_2(x)}$$

Yes, this does imply another approximation, which isn't the greatest function you could hope for, but this function is that computationally expensive. You already know how to calculate a logarithm of 2, so the only thing you're currently lacking is a power function with base 2, illustrated in Figure 21.7. Of course, you can use any base you want, but 2 is chosen simply because the PC works more efficiently that way.

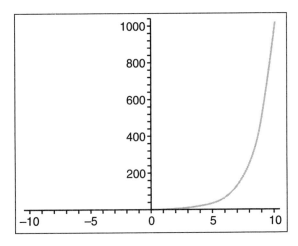

Figure 21.7
Power of 2 curve

By doing the analysis on the curve, again, you may find it to be an ugly curve because it has an asymptote and another infinite value for positive numbers. You must again reduce the approximated segment to have a good approximation. If you've followed the pattern so far, this is where an identity usually comes in and saves the day. Of course, this section is no different. You may summon the identity:

$$2^{a+b} = 2^a 2^b$$

As a matter of fact, it's the exact same identity as posted for $x = 2$. This identity can allow us to approximate the span from $[0..1]$. Particularly, the identity you will use is

$$2^{[n]+n-[n]} = 2^{[n]} 2^{n-[n]}$$

$(n - [n])$ is the fractional residue of n and $[n]$, the integer value of n. The function $2^{[n]}$ could be calculated with the preceding example, but you're working with PCs, so there's an easier way around this. To calculate this value, you can fetch the integer part of n and simply insert that value, plus the bias, into the exponent bits of the floating point. For the second term, you will once more require numerical approximation to a power series. This is easier said than done. Here are the code and table (Table 21.7):

```
float Exp2(float X)
{
    float Result, Square, IntPow;

    if (X < 0) {
        const unsigned long IntVal = *(unsigned long *)&X & 0x7FFFFFFF;
        const unsigned long Int    = (IntVal >> 23) - 127;

        if ((long)Int > 0) {
            *(unsigned long *)&IntPow    = ((((IntVal & 0x007FFFFF) |
```

```
                              0x00800000) >> (23 - Int)) + 127 + 1) << 23;
            *(unsigned long *)&X     = (((IntVal << Int) & 0x007FFFFF)
                         | 0x3F800000);
            X = 2.0f - X;

        } else {
            IntPow = 2.0f;
            X++;
        }

        Result = X0CoEff + Square * X1CoEff;
        Square *= X;     // The 2 last lines are repeated for every coeff.
        Result += Square * XiCoEff;
        ...
        return Result / IntPow;

    } else {
        const unsigned long IntVal = *(unsigned long *)&X;
        const unsigned long Int    = (IntVal >> 23) - 127;

        if ((long)Int > 0) {
            *(unsigned long *)&IntPow    = (((((IntVal & 0x007FFFFF) |
                         0x00800000) >> (23 - Int)) + 127) << 23;
            *(unsigned long *)&X     = (((IntVal << Int) & 0x007FFFFF)
                         | 0x3F800000);
            X--;

        } else
            IntPow = 1.0f;

        Square     = X;
        Result     = X0CoEff + Square * X1CoEff;
        Square *= X;     // The 2 last lines are repeated for every coeff.
        Result += Square * XiCoEff;
        ...
        return Result * IntPow;
    }
}
```

Table 21.7 2^x Best Computational Polynomial Coefficient Approximation for x = [0..1]

Precision	x^0	x^1	x^2	x^3	x^4	x^5
8 bits	0.1002475541E+1	0.6510478051	0.3440011131			
13 bits	0.9998929835	0.6964572484	0.224338518	0.792042337E-1		
18 bits	0.1000003704E+1	0.6929661329	0.2416384127	0.5169038746E-1	0.1369765902E-1	
23 bits	0.9999998931	0.6931547443	0.2401397705	0.5586608678E-1	0.8943010371E-2	0.189638812E-2

Now that the dust has settled, let's examine the code a little closer. There are two cases you need to handle: negative and positive exponents. The first one can be calculated without the negative and then you can calculate its inverse, which is by definition a negative exponent. The only catch with the negative values is that, when you round your integer, you'll have to make sure that it's floored, because it requires the approximated term to be between 0 and 1. For example, if you have −4.25, you want to do (−5 + 0.75) and not (−4 − 0.25).

Now, you may notice that the code doesn't have any floating-point calculations in assembly, such as *fscale* and *frndint*. The reason for this is simple. These ugly functions simply cannot be paired on the Pentium 3 without hogging the resources (the Pentium 4 does not have a second decoder). If you implement an integer version of these functions, which is what was done here, you'll benefit in terms of speed due to integer instructions. The difference is quite noticeable. It would be much easier if you used the floating-point functions, but alas, integers are faster.

The exponent of the number represents how many bits of the mantissa are describing the integer portion of the number. In essence, this is what the variable Int contains. Calculating IntPow, which is the term for the greatest power of 2, is just a matter of isolating the integer bits described by the mantissa (remember to add the implicit one 0x00800000) and shifting them in the exponent's position (with the bias). This is what the IntPow calculation does.

The next line computes the remainder for X. In this case, you can shift out the bits that describe the integer portion of the mantissa, keeping only the bits describing the non-integer bits. Then you have to get rid of the implicit 1. And then the algorithm is good to go, with the approximation and the final multiplication (or division, if you're dealing with the negative case).

This might look like a lot of computations for a simple assembly function that can do the same thing, but remember that these functions take 30 and 60 cycles each, according to Intel, and pairing up these already very fast instructions (if possible) means that you will outrun the slow FPU instructions. This is something you want to keep in mind when dealing with any choice of programming technology (SIMD, FPU, CPU).

This would be quite a pain if nothing good came out of it, but some good improvements were also made here. The function was compared against the compiler-provided power function, and with the duo log_2 and 2^x, which have been built so far. When the precision is set for both functions at about 16 bits, it runs about three times faster than the *pow* function. The best case is a little less than three times faster, while the best precision is more than twice as fast. The fact that Table 21.7 is so short implies that a power series approximates the curve fairly well, and it sure helps to speed things up. But again, the fact that you're using a set of integer functions to perform the task of fscale and frndint (which is what the compiler utilizes) definitely helps.

Shifting into Fourth Gear with SIMD

As if the speed you've gained so far wasn't enough, you can push the envelope even further with the help of SIMD instructions. One of the issues with SIMD instructions is that no transcendental functions are provided. If you require a calculation involving cosine/sine or any other transcendental function, you must calculate the value using floating-point values, followed by a conversion to a SIMD register.

Not anymore. The functions we came up with can apply very well if you require a lot of computation of transcendental functions, thereby increasing the speed limit even more. The unfortunate thing is that all of these operations require identities that change the function to be evaluated, depending on the input value. SIMD isn't very well suited to performing calculations on a single value, so in general, these cases will have to be taken care of before SIMD is used.

SIMD becomes useful when you compute the polynomial. For some functions, such as the cosine/sine, there are ways around all of these verifications before using SIMD, thereby removing all branches in the code.

Since you've already seen the cosine, let's look at the sine function with a twist of SSE instructions. Recall that the idea of the cosine code was to verify for symmetries where one was only a mirror and the other changed the sign. The method for changing the signs all over this code is to invert the sign of the first coefficient, and change the sign of the variable that multiplies X at every turn.

Now, you would obviously like to get rid of the jumps completely, and you can. The trick comes from the min/max instructions and another "bit" of playing around. The sine curve has two half reflections at $\pi/2$ and $3\pi/2$, and you can also consider the center of the curve (π) to be a reflection but with a sign inversion. For the sign, you can compute a bit mask with the *cmpss* SSE instruction, which you can then use at the end to invert the sign. The only step you're left with is to compute the reflection such that the number you chose is the one in the range $[0..\pi/2]$. This is easily achieved with the min/max instruction.

The code for the Taylor series version of the sinus function follows:

```
__declspec(align(16)) const static float Full[4] =
    {2 * PI, 2 * PI, 2 * PI, 2 * PI};
__declspec(align(16)) const static float Half[4] =
    {PI, PI, PI, PI};
__declspec(align(16)) const static unsigned long Mask[4] =
    {0x80000000, 0x80000000, 0x80000000, 0x80000000};
__declspec(align(16)) const static float CoEffi[4] = {...}
// ^^ Repeat this line for every Coefficient of the polynomial


void VectSin(float X[4])
{
    __asm {
        movaps    xmm0, [X]
        movaps    xmm1, [Full]
        subps     xmm1, xmm0            // xmm1 = 2PI - X
        movaps    xmm7, xmm1
        cmpps     xmm7, xmm0, 1
        andps     xmm7, [Mask]          // xmm7 = <sign mask>
        minps     xmm0, xmm1            // xmm0 = X[0..PI]

        movaps    xmm1, [Half]
        subps     xmm1, xmm0            // xmm1 = PI - X
        minps     xmm1, xmm0
        movaps    xmm2, xmm1            // xmm1 = X[0..PI/2]
        mulps     xmm2, xmm2            // xmm2 = X^2
        movaps    xmm0, xmm1            // xmm0 = X

        mulps     xmm1, xmm2            // xmm1 = X^3
        movaps    xmm3, [CoEffi]
        mulps     xmm3, xmm1
        addps     xmm0, xmm3            // xmm0 += X^3/6
        ...                             // Repeat the last block all coeff.

        xorps     xmm0, xmm7            // Change the sign accordingly
        movaps    [X], xmm0
    }
}
```

Speedwise, this code does very well. When compared to the compiler-provided sin function, it's a little less than 1.5 times faster for 20 bits of precision. It's about 75% the original speed for full precision, and roughly 60% for the worst precision. This is amazing, because with the SIMD version, you can approximate four numbers at a time and accomplish four times the work. Henceforth, in reality you're (6, 5.3, 6.6) times faster, in that order, than the compiler function. Comparatively, if you take Intel's average cycle count for this function, it ranges from 160–180.

With these improvements, the middle case enables us to achieve this in ~27–30 cycles on average, which is the reported speed of 2-integer multiplications. Because you're doing constant calculations, your code hasn't had a range. Hence, it takes about 28 cycles per sin. Converting the other functions to SIMD will most likely yield excellent results as well, but in general, the results shouldn't be as good. In this specific case, you were able to get rid of all branches completely, which isn't something you can achieve for most of the preceding functions.

Physical Model Approximation

When you're designing a game, typically you want to maximize resource usage. Resources include CPU power, GPU power, FPU power, sound IO, etc. If you have a lot of free resources, you can add some neat special effects, increase accuracy in various areas, or simply offload some weight from one resource to another to achieve higher frame rates. Of course, you have to consider that time is also a resource, and typically you don't have a lot of it to spare. But often, you can whip up some cool special effects in a day or two.

The idea behind physical model approximation is to model a physical process by a very rough, back-of-a-napkin equation. One of the demos that comes with this chapter includes a snowfall simulation coupled with a water effect, simulating an object falling into water. Of course, you can look in physics books and try to simulate the math behind the effect, but why do so when these effects are purely visual? The real test here is, "Does it look good?"

Snowfall Simulation

Many games have implemented a snowfall simulation, but pretty much all of them have used the most current technique, depending on the power of the PCs at the time they were released. The worst one I've seen used white square particles falling down in a straight line. Some more clever developers used a slightly different technique in 2D, which yields pretty decent results for a 2D game. The idea was to let the particle fall down linearly, but to shift the particle slightly by a small random number. This wasn't too bad, but it looked like the particle was shaking hysterically. A true physical model would take into account the air friction, the gravity, the surface of the snowflake, and many other details. This would make the simulation just too slow. If you've ever seen snow, you know how to describe the motion of a falling snowflake. It behaves more or less like a falling piece of paper, but with much less rotation.

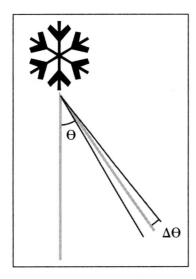

Figure 21.8
Falling angle of a snowflake given a randomized angle shift (phase shift)

The key to this one is that last word: *rotation*. If you want to simulate a snowflake, change its rotation instead of changing its position. As a snowflake falls, the air friction makes it sway left and right a little bit. This is the effect we want to simulate. Randomizing the particle's offset position wasn't a bad idea, but it wasn't smooth or gradual. If you randomize the angle of the particle, you get a really nice transition from left to right. This looks more natural.

Figure 21.8 shows the falling angle of the snowflake, as well as its random angle shift, which is computed every frame.

You don't want your snowflakes to start flying up into the sky, so you have to limit the values of the angle without a given range. If you wanted to be fancy, you could also use an angle delta, which is proportional to time. This would be more correct than a static angular delta. I chose to use the simpler method in the demo, though. What's implemented in the demo is the fact that the distance traveled by the particle is proportional to time, so that a user on a slower PC doesn't see really slow snow falling down. He only sees less drastic (X, Z) movements in the snowflakes, which should be acceptable.

Now we have to come up with an equation that will do all of this. It's pretty simple, actually, because this conversion is similar to converting spherical coordinates to Cartesian coordinates. The only difference is that you want the angles to have a range of $[-a, a]$. You can easily use the sine curve for which a value of 0 will not move the particle at all, and for which any of the boundary value will have a maximum movement for that range.

If this is a bit confusing, go back and look at the sine curve to see how it behaves for values with range $[-\pi/2, \pi/2]$, where the value Y is the shift that you apply in X or Z. What you have to wonder about is the value you should use for Y. You can increase Y by a fixed value, but it would look nicer if the particle didn't drop as fast if it moves a lot in X or Z, for example.

To achieve this, you can simply compute the cosine of each angle and multiply them together. Again, if you look at the cosine curve, its value is maximal at 0, and it drops when moving closer to your boundaries for your given range. In short, the equation is

$$\langle x, y, z \rangle = Speed \cdot Time \langle \sin(AngleX), \cos(AngleX)\cos(AngleZ), \sin(AngleZ) \rangle \rangle$$

There's no reason to chose this formula for *Y*, other than the fact that it decreases as the angles increase for any angle AngleZ or AngleX. An equally valid choice would be to compute the cosine of the addition for the absolute value of the angles. This would achieve roughly the same effect. As long as it's efficient and looks good, it should get the green light.

Bubble Simulation

Now that we have already talked about the snowflakes, this aspect should be pretty easy to simulate. When you go underwater, you may wish to simulate bubbles making their way up to the surface. In the snowflake's simulation, we required a function that was smoothly going from left to right because that's how light objects fall through gas. A bubble is a little different. Air has a much lower density than water, for example, and a bubble is never really spherical, even if we will use a sphere to approximate the bubble. Because of this, some pieces of the bubble tend to move up faster than some other areas of the bubble, and this causes a mass shift of air from one area to another. If you consider the bubble as a single point (its center), you will notice that the point actually moves from left to right rapidly (because of this mass shift, which you can observe). This is caused by the fluid's pressure. Given this, a formula to determine the position of a bubble becomes pretty easy. You can simply randomize the position of the bubble and you will effectively render a pretty decent simulation. In the demo, you may go under the water in order to see the bubbles. You do not always need to complicate the simulations more than that.

Simulating an Object Hitting a Fluid

One very neat (but rather costly) effect is to generate a ripple made by an object colliding with a fluid. The problem is that water is a rather complex physical object, and simulating it correctly takes a good deal of math. Clearly, you cannot afford this in a real-time game.

Let's assume that you're rendering a height map, and the ripples are computed by a function that simply adds a given height to your height map in order to generate the ripple. When an object penetrates a fluid, first it makes a hole by pushing some fluid to all sides. Once the fluid has sucked the object under it, because of the mass surrounding the hole, a high column of fluid is generated at the position where the object fell. Throughout this process, the fluid around the target area slowly starts to generate circular ripples extending as far as the viscosity of the fluid will allow.

You can see why this model isn't very common in games. It has a pretty high degree of complexity and takes some time on the CPU. All you want to do is *simulate* this effect. The first thing you should think about is the circular aspect of the pattern. It must have the same height for every angle given a fixed radius. Put in terms of equations, your input (X, Z) actually converts into the following value:

$$In = \sqrt{x^2 + z^2}$$

This is nice because you no longer need to think in 3D. You can think in 2D, because you've successfully collapsed your two input values into one. You can easily simulate small waves with a negative cosine curve. The cosine curve is chosen because it starts at a max, hence the hole. Furthermore, you choose the negative value of the cosine curve because you want a hole and not a lump. Otherwise, you would continuously generate a cosine curve as it tended towards infinity.

Unfortunately, there's a problem. When you jump into a pool, the waves are much smaller at the other end than at the point where you jump. You have to account for the fact that the farther away from 0 your input is, the smaller the waves are.

You have many choices for this, but for the demo I've chosen an exponential curve. Again, if you look at the graph of an exponential curve, you notice that the curve is pretty high for large values and tends towards zero for smaller values. This is exactly how you want your curve to behave. All you need to do here is choose a good starting point on the exponential curve, and scale your input such that the curve diminishes as fast as you want. The equation we have so far is similar to this:

$$e^{a - In \cdot Scale1} \cos(In \cdot Scale2)$$

At this point, you haven't done anything about the time that elapses while this curve is being rendered. For one thing, time should push the waves out from the focal point. You can achieve this effect simply by subtracting a scalar value of time from the cosine curve. Again, if you don't see this, look at the cosine curve and shift the entire curve towards the left. Just remember to scale down its height with the same function, and you should see it.

Finally, you have to account for the fact that the waves are concentrated around the target at first, but then disperse. This is a tricky effect, but it can be achieved in two steps. The first step is to create a wave where the affected span grows outwards. The second step is to make the entire wave decrease in height. This second step isn't too hard. The exponential curve tends towards zero when its value is negative and very small, so you can simply decrease a factor of time in the exponential for the second case.

But what about the first case? How can you simulate an expanding wave without adding much complexity? If you scale down the input value and let it expand gradually until it reaches its full span, you can achieve the desired effect easily. The best way to visualize this is to take the exponential curve in a given range and initially squeeze the curve such that it fits into a very small range. With time, let it expand to its normal range. This has the effect of expanding the affected region.

The equations for the first and second steps follow:

First Step:

$$a^{1-\frac{In \cdot Scale1}{Time \cdot Scale3}} \cos\left(In \cdot Scale2 - Time \cdot Scale4\right)$$

Second Step:

$$e^{a - In \cdot Scale1 - Time \cdot Scale3} \cos\left(In \cdot Scale2 - Time \cdot Scale4\right)$$

All in all, this is pretty complex. You have two inputs, {Time, In}, so you could approximate this function as a 3D surface. Instead, I chose to approximate the function in a piecemeal fashion. Take a look at the source code. By no means is it as optimal as it can get. As an exercise, study it and try to optimize the equations even more with the same desired effect. It *is* possible!

PART SIX

APPENDIXES

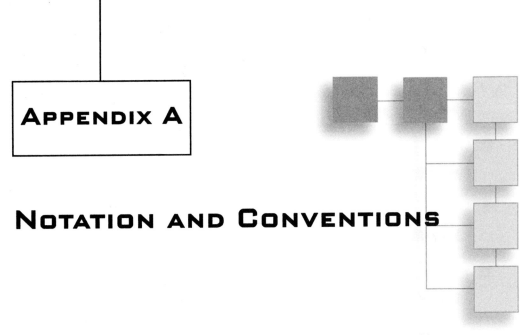

APPENDIX A

NOTATION AND CONVENTIONS

This book uses standard conventions and notations, as illustrated in Table A.1.

Table A.1 Conventions and Notations

Quantity/Operation/Symbol	Convention	Example
Scalars	Italic letters	a, b, x
Angles	Greek letters	ϕ, θ, π
Range including the limit	Square bracket with two scalars	$[a, b]$
Range excluding the limit	Parentheses with two scalars	(a, b)
Coordinate and expanded vectors	Bounded by < and > signs	$<x, y, z>$
Absolute value	Single bars	$\|a\|$
Vectors	Bold lowercase letters	$\mathbf{a}, \mathbf{b}, \mathbf{c}$
Matrices	Bold capital letters	$\mathbf{M}, \mathbf{U}, \mathbf{V}$
Quaternions	Bold Greek letters	$\boldsymbol{\phi}, \boldsymbol{\theta}, \boldsymbol{\pi}$
$\displaystyle\sum_{i=a}^{n} f(i)$	Sum of n elements described by $f(n, i)$, starting at $i = a$	$\displaystyle\sum_{i=1}^{n} i = 1 + 2 + \ldots + n$
$\displaystyle\prod_{i=a}^{n} f(i)$	Product of n elements described by $f(i)$ starting at $i = a$	$\displaystyle\prod_{i=1}^{n} i = 1 \cdot 2 \cdot \ldots \cdot n$
$\forall$	For every	$x, f(x) = 1$

(continued on next page)

Table A-1 Conventions and Notations *(continued)*

Quantity/Operation/Symbol	Convention	Example
$\exists$	There exists	x such that $f(x) > 1$
$\rightarrow$	Implies (a means b)	$\underline{a} = 2, a > 0$
$\leftrightarrow$	Two-way implication (a means b and b means a)	I win, you lose
$[k]$	Integer value of k	$[3.1415] = 3$
$\lfloor k \rfloor$	The floor of k defined as the greatest integer smaller or equal to k	$\lfloor 3.14 \rfloor = 3$
$\lceil k \rceil$	The ceil of k defined as the smallest integer greater or equal to k	$\lceil 3.14 \rceil = 4$

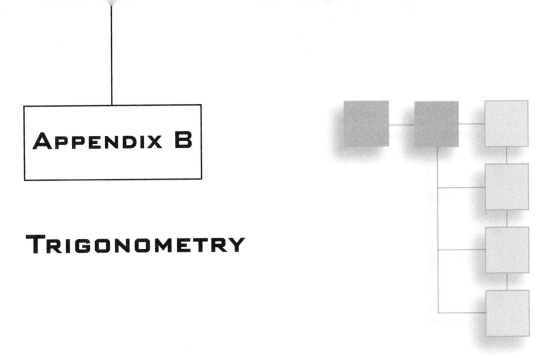

APPENDIX B

TRIGONOMETRY

For the uninitiated, trigonometry has a reputation for being a nasty field of math. The main reason people consider trigonometry to be difficult is because they've never looked at dynamic systems. Jokes aside, the real reason trigonometry is seen as a tough field is because it uses a gigantic set of identities that typically must be used in order to solve a problem easily. Trig uses so many identities simply because the functions are periodic and thus have a huge number of relationships between one another. Worse, the relationships can be recursively defined (that is, two relationships can be used to create one new relationship). Obviously, I will not be able to list every possible identity here, but you should be able to derive or minimally prove that a conjecture is true if you put one forward.

Trigonometric Definitions

Trigonometry is the branch of mathematics that deals with the relationship between the sides and angles of a triangle. This is thus the analysis of two well-known coordinate systems:

- The Cartesian coordinate system, which looks at the sides of the triangle
- The polar coordinate system, which looks at the angles and lengths

If you take a square triangle with sides x and y and hypotenuse r (that is, a triangle forming a 90-degree angle), as illustrated in Figure B.1, six trigonometry functions are defined as follows:

$$\sin(\theta) = \frac{y}{r} \quad \csc(\theta) = \frac{r}{y}$$

$$\cos(\theta) = \frac{x}{r} \quad \sec(\theta) = \frac{r}{x}$$

$$\tan(\theta) = \frac{y}{x} \quad \cot(\theta) = \frac{x}{y}$$

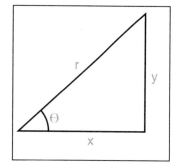

Figure B.1
A simple rectangular triangle

The angle is expressed in a unit called radians, which expresses the length of the arc of a unit circle. The radian is much easier to use than its brother, the degree, primarily because of this relationship. Whereas degrees range from 0 to 360, radians range from 0 to 2π. Thus, one could claim that the preceding trigonometric functions convert the length of a unit arc into a ratio of the sides of the triangle generated by that arc as shown in Figure B.1.

Due to the relationships between x, y, and r, you can also write another set of identities expressing trigonometric functions as a function of other trigonometric functions:

$$\tan(\theta) = \frac{\sin(\theta)}{\cos(\theta)} \quad \cot(\theta) = \frac{\cos(\theta)}{\sin(\theta)}$$

$$\sec(\theta) = \frac{1}{\cos(\theta)} \quad \csc(\theta) = \frac{1}{\sin(\theta)}$$

Symmetry

The rectangular triangle has a relationship that is expressed between its angle and its sides. <x, y>. In Figure B.1, this element sat in the first quadrant of the Cartesian coordinate space, but in reality, it does not have to be so. Indeed, it can be in the second, third, or fourth quadrant. This means that an expression such as <−x, y> is just as valid as its purely positive version. Because of this, you can clearly see that a set of symmetries exists because the same triangle can be obtained by simply changing a few things around. It becomes even more obvious if you render the set of functions on a graph as shown in Figures B.2–B.7.

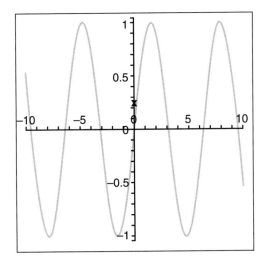

Figure B.2
The graph of sin(θ)

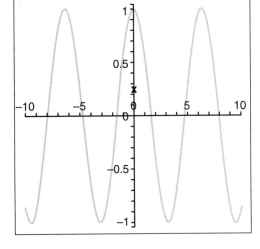

Figure B.3
The graph of cos(θ)

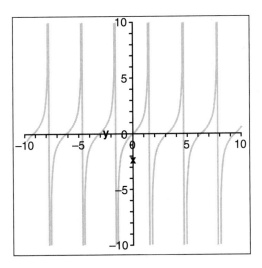

Figure B.4
The graph of tan(θ)

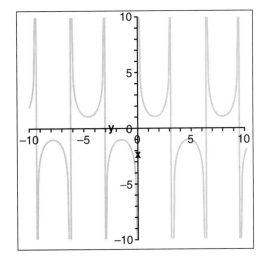

Figure B.5
The graph of csc(θ)

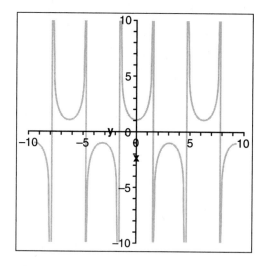

Figure B.6
The graph of sec(θ)

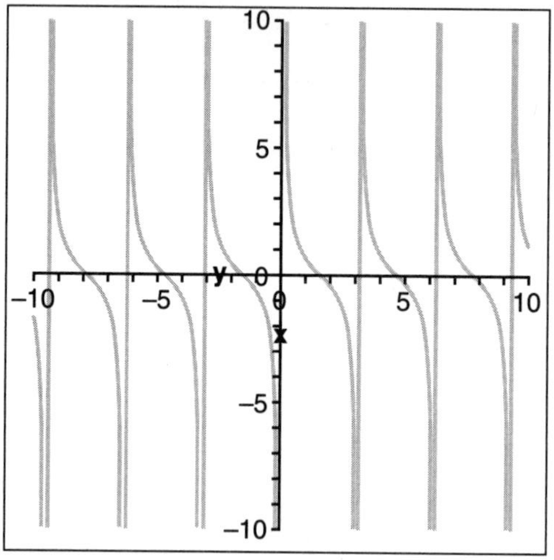

Figure B.7
The graph of cot(θ)

As can be clearly seen, relationships exist between various values of θ. You can start by looking at the relationship between negative angles and positive angles:

$$\sin(\theta) = -\sin(-\theta)$$
$$\cos(\theta) = \cos(-\theta)$$
$$\tan(\theta) = -\tan(-\theta)$$

There is also a relationship between the functions for a quarter period:

$$\sin(\theta) \;=\; -\cos\left(\theta + \frac{\pi}{2}\right) \;=\; \cos\left(\frac{\pi}{2} - \theta\right)$$
$$\cos(\theta) \;=\; \sin\left(\theta + \frac{\pi}{2}\right) \;=\; \sin\left(\frac{\pi}{2} - \theta\right)$$
$$\cot(\theta) \;=\; -\tan\left(\theta + \frac{\pi}{2}\right) \;=\; \tan\left(\frac{\pi}{2} - \theta\right)$$

You can also look at the relationship for a half period:

$$\begin{aligned} \sin(\theta) &= -\cos(\theta+\pi) = -\cos(\pi-\theta) \\ \cos(\theta) &= -\sin(\theta+\pi) = \sin(\pi-\theta) \\ \tan(\theta) &= \tan(\theta+\pi) = -\tan(\pi-\theta) \end{aligned}$$

As if this was not enough, there is another set of more obscure but equally important identities related to tan. The trick to this next identity comes from a careful observation of the tan as a function of x and y in the triangle. If you take a unit circle, all the trigonometry functions are on that, simply because given an angle ϕ, the position on the circle is $<\cos(\phi), \sin(\phi)>$. This is a mere application of the triangle's definition with the trigonometry functions. If you have already read Chapter 7, "Accelerated Vector Calculus for the Uninitiated," then you will understand that $\cot(\phi)$ is actually the slope of the circle for an angle of ϕ. cot is related to tan by a mere inverse, but where it becomes interesting is the observation that the slope is mirrored every 45 degrees along the circle. Because of this observation, you can deduce another identity relating tan for various angles:

$$\cot(\theta) = \tan\left(\frac{\pi}{2} - \theta\right)$$

$$\tan(\theta) = \cot\left(\frac{\pi}{2} - \theta\right)$$

Pythagorean Identities

If you take the definition of the trigonometric functions and multiply each side of the equations by the divider, you get simple relationships that rewrite x, y, and r as functions of a trigonometry function and one of $\{x, y, r\}$. You can thus rewrite Figure B.1 by using trigonometric functions. If you do so and write Pythagoras's identity $r^2 = x^2 + y^2$, you get a very useful relationship. You may thereafter divide this relationship by other trigonometry functions, and by keeping track of their relationships to x, y, and r, you can obtain another set of identities:

$$\sin^2(\theta) + \cos^2(\theta) = 1$$
$$\sec^2(\theta) - \tan^2(\theta) = 1$$
$$\csc^2(\theta) - \cot^2(\theta) = 1$$

You can also express the functions directly by computing the square root on each side of the equations:

$$\sin(\theta) = \sqrt{1 - \cos^2(\theta)}$$

$$\cos(\theta) = \sqrt{1 - \sin^2(\theta)}$$

$$\tan(\theta) = \sqrt{\sec^2(\theta) - 1}$$

Exponential Identities

The exponential identities are called such because they are all obtained by the DeMoivre formula, which is explained in Chapter 6, "Moving to Hyperspace Vectors: Quaternions." Due to exponential rules, you can write the exponential of an imaginary number Iθ as the function of a complex number where the real part is a cosine and the imaginary part a sine:

$$e^{\theta i} = \cos(\theta) + i\sin(\theta)$$

If you follow the rules of complex numbers and exponentials, you can write theta as a sum (or difference), and expanding the result yields the exponential trigonometric identities:

$$e^{(\theta + \phi)i} = \cos(\theta + \phi) + i\sin(\theta + \phi)$$

$$= e^{\theta i}e^{\phi i}$$

$$= \big(\cos(\theta) + i\sin(\theta)\big)\big(\cos(\phi) + i\sin(\phi)\big)$$

If you separate the real component from the imaginary component and write each equation separately, what you get are the trigonometric identities for the addition of two angles for the sine and cosine. The tangent can thus be deduced by using the prior identity that it is equal to the sine divided by the cosine:

$$\sin(\theta + \phi) = \sin(\theta)\cos(\phi) + \cos(\theta)\sin(\phi)$$

$$\cos(\theta + \phi) = \cos(\theta)\cos(\phi) - \sin(\theta)\sin(\phi)$$

$$\tan(\theta + \phi) = \frac{\tan(\theta) + \tan(\phi)}{1 + \tan(\theta)\tan(\phi)}$$

By combining these equations with those of the inversion of sign to the angle, you can obtain another slew of equations:

$$\sin(\theta - \phi) = \sin(\theta)\cos(\phi) - \cos(\theta)\sin(\phi)$$

$$\cos(\theta - \phi) = \cos(\theta)\cos(\phi) + \sin(\theta)\sin(\phi)$$

$$\tan(\theta - \phi) = \frac{\tan(\theta) - \tan(\phi)}{1 - \tan(\theta)\tan(\phi)}$$

If the angles are the same, you can obtain some more identities. Obviously, the subtraction of angles is not interesting because it yields zero, but the addition of two angles has some interesting properties:

$$\sin(2\theta) = 2\sin(\theta)\cos(\theta)$$

$$\cos(2\theta) = \cos^2(\theta) - \sin^2(\theta)$$

$$\tan(2\theta) = \frac{2\tan(\theta)}{1+\tan^2(\theta)}$$

For the cosine, you can find even more identities by mixing this one with the Pythagorean identity:

$$\cos(2\theta) = 1 - 2\sin^2(\theta)$$

$$\cos(2\theta) = 2\cos^2(\theta) - 1$$

If you consider the angle to be half of the angle you really want to compute, you can get the equation for the half angles:

$$\cos\left(2\frac{\theta}{2}\right) = 2\cos^2\left(\frac{\theta}{2}\right) - 1$$

Now simply isolate for the cosine of the half angle and you find a function as a function of the half angle. You can repeat the process for the sine and tangent function to yield the following set of identities:

$$\sin\left(\frac{\theta}{2}\right) = \sqrt{\frac{1-\cos(\theta)}{2}}$$

$$\cos\left(\frac{\theta}{2}\right) = \sqrt{\frac{\cos(\theta)+1}{2}}$$

$$\tan\left(\frac{\theta}{2}\right) = \frac{1+\cos(\theta)}{\cos(\theta)-1}$$

You can also compute the function of the product of two trigonometric functions if you add the two trigonometric identities of the addition/subtraction of angles for sine:

$$\sin(\theta+\phi)=\sin(\theta)\cos(\phi)+\cos(\theta)\sin(\phi)$$
$$+\sin(\theta-\phi)=\sin(\theta)\cos(\phi)-\cos(\theta)\sin(\phi)$$
$$\overline{\sin(\theta+\phi)+\sin(\theta-\phi)=\sin(\theta)\cos(\phi)+\cos(\theta)\sin(\phi)+\sin(\theta)\cos(\phi)-\cos(\theta)\sin(\phi)}$$

$$\sin(\theta+\phi)+\sin(\theta-\phi)=2\sin(\theta)\cos(\phi)$$

Isolate the product of the trigonometry function and you now have a function for the product of sine and cosine. A similar process can be applied to the cosine rule and the subtraction of the cosine rule to obtain identities for the product of sine and cosine functions:

$$\sin(\theta)\cos(\phi)=\frac{1}{2}\big(\sin(\theta-\phi)+\sin(\theta+\phi)\big)$$

$$\cos(\theta)\cos(\phi)=\frac{1}{2}\big(\cos(\theta-\phi)+\cos(\theta+\phi)\big)$$

$$\sin(\theta)\sin(\phi)=\frac{1}{2}\big(\cos(\theta-\phi)-\cos(\theta+\phi)\big)$$

Cosine and Sine Laws

So far, you have dealt only with rectangular triangles, but you can also look at non-rectangular triangles (scary thought, considering the number of identities you've already found). Let's start by the cosine rule. If you consider Figure B.8, you can start by establishing the Pythagorean relationship between the sides. Please note that ϕ_c is defined as the complement of ϕ and is thus defined by $[Pi]/2 - \phi$.

$$c^2 = h^2 + (a+d)^2$$
$$c^2 = \big(b*\sin(\pi-\Phi_c)\big)^2 + \big(a+b*\cos(\pi-\Phi_c)\big)^2$$
$$= b^2\sin^2(\pi-\Phi_c)+a^2+2ab\cos(\pi-\Phi_c)+b^2\cos^2(\pi-\Phi_c)$$
$$= b^2\big(\sin^2(\pi-\Phi_c)+\cos^2(\pi-\Phi_c)\big)+a^2-2ab\cos\Phi$$
$$= a^2+b^2-2ab\cos\Phi$$

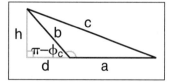

The sine law is much easier to obtain. It comes from a mere observation of the distances if you define ϕ_x as the angle opposite the segment x:

Figure B.8
Derivation of the cosine law

$$c * \sin \Phi_b = b * \sin (\pi - \Phi_c)$$
$$c * \sin \Phi_b = b * \sin \Phi_c$$
$$\frac{\sin \Phi_b}{b} = \frac{\sin \Phi_c}{c}$$

Inverse Functions

Given a ratio, you get an angle; this is the idea behind the inverse trigonometric functions. The domain of the functions (or input range, if you prefer) is $[-1, 1]$ for sine and cosine and $[-\infty, \infty]$ for tan. The range of the image (output range) is defined as $[-\pi/2, \pi/2]$, $[0, \pi]$, $[-\pi/2, \pi/2]$ for sine, cosine, and tan, respectively. The limits are necessary. Without them, there would be no inverse because the function is continuous; there would exist many possible values given an input. The inverse functions are such that the inverse function of the function itself is the input. In other words:

$$\arcsin(\sin(x)) = \sin(\arcsin(x)) = x$$

It's important to make the distinction between the inverse of a function and the inverse function. The inverse of a function is written as $f^1(x)$ and is such that the function multiplied by its inverse is 1. For instance, sin is the inverse of sec, but it is not the inverse function of sec. The notation to the power of -1 is often used to imply the inverse function and can be misleading with the inverse of a real number. Consequently, for trigonometry, the word "arc" is appended to the function to imply its inverse to minimize confusion. Obtaining the graph of these functions is very simple. You simply need to rotate the graph of the original functions 90 degrees. Just make sure that you cut the range correctly such that no two values for y can be obtained for a single x.

There are a few relationships if you want to compute the cosine, sine, or tangent of an inverse function. Due to the relationship of the triangle's $\{x, y, r\}$, you can determine some pretty interesting relationships between the inverse functions that can significantly cut down computation time. For instance, suppose you wanted to compute $\cos(\arcsin(w))$. It would be much easier if you were to decompose the functions into the triangle's components. You know that the input w is not an angle; it is a ratio. More precisely, it is the ratio y/r. You, in turn, are interested in computing x/r, but you already know that there is a tight relationship between x, y, and r via Pythagoras. If you suppose that $r = 1$, then $y = y/r$ and $x = x/r$. Now you only need to compute x to know the answer to x/r; this can be obtained by Pythagoras. If you apply this logic to all trig functions, you end up with the following identities:

$$\cos\left(\arcsin\left(w\right)\right)=\sqrt{1-w^2}\quad \tan\left(\arcsin\left(w\right)\right)=\frac{w}{\sqrt{1-w^2}}$$

$$\sin\left(\arccos\left(w\right)\right)=\sqrt{1-w^2}\quad \tan\left(\arccos\left(w\right)\right)=\frac{\sqrt{1-w^2}}{w}$$

$$\cos\left(\arctan\left(w\right)\right)=\frac{1}{\sqrt{w^2+1}}\quad \sin\left(\arctan\left(w\right)\right)=\frac{w}{\sqrt{w^2+1}}$$

Inverse trig functions are also equipped with interesting symmetries, as shown in Figures B.9–B.14. Sure enough, these are the same symmetries as expressed in the functions themselves because the graph of these functions is really the same graph but rotated and with a smaller range. For this reason, the identities will not be relisted here. You should be able to deduce them should you require them.

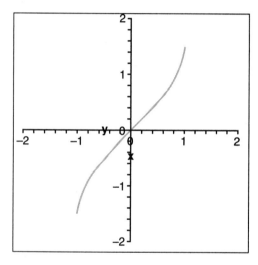

Figure B.9
The graph of arcsin(θ)

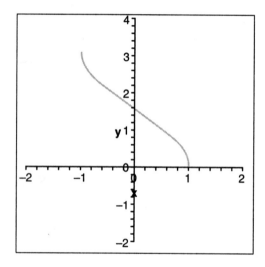

Figure B.10
The graph of arccos(θ)

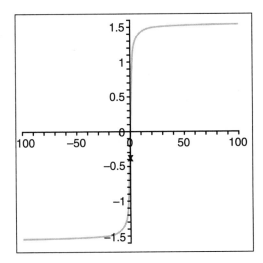

Figure B.11
The graph of arctan(θ)

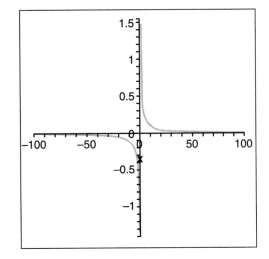

Figure B.12
The graph of arccsc(θ)

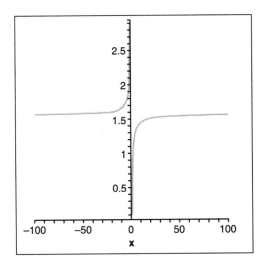

Figure B.13
The graph of arcsec(θ)

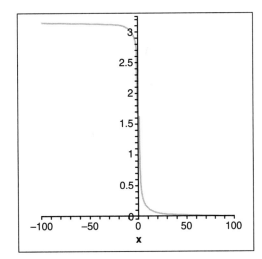

Figure B.14
The graph of arccot(θ)

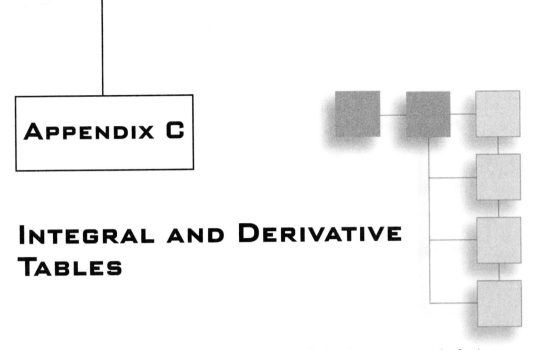

APPENDIX C

INTEGRAL AND DERIVATIVE TABLES

I t's pointless to derive the derivative or integral of a function every single time you want to use it. A more intelligent way to proceed is to use a table of derivatives (see Table C.1) and integrals (see Table C.2). Not every possible function will be listed in the table. Thus, the tables serve as tools to derive the equations, which need to be manipulated accordingly in order to obtain the answer you are looking for. Chapter 7, "Accelerated Vector Calculus for the Uninitiated," contains various techniques that can be used to find the solution to various integrals. The last thing you should take note of is that not all functions have an analytic solution (that is, a general solution as a function of parameters). Some solutions can only be integrated numerically (again, refer to Chapter 7 for further information). In the following equations, the only variable is x. f, u, and v, unless otherwise specified, are used to represent functions and implicitly mean $u(x)$ and $v(x)$. Every other character is thus a constant or a function. Throughout these tables, please recall that x can in fact be substituted with a function f, provided that the chain rule is followed. The chain rule is the 6th rule in the derivative table if x is substituted with $u(x)$.

Table C.1 Derivatives

Function	Derivative
k	0
kx	k
$u + v$	$u' + v'$

(continued on next page)

Table C.1 Derivatives *(continued)*

Function	Derivative
$u \cdot v$	$u \cdot v' + v \cdot u'$
$\dfrac{u}{v}$	$\dfrac{v \cdot u' - u \cdot v'}{v^2}$
$u(v)$	$u'(v) \cdot v'$
k^x	$k^x \cdot \ln(k)$
e^x	e^x
$k \cdot x^n$	$k \cdot n \cdot x^{n-1}$
$\log_k(x)$	$\dfrac{1}{x \cdot \log(k)}$
$\sin(x)$	$\cos(x)$
$\cos(x)$	$-\sin(x)$
$\tan(x)$	$\sec^2(x)$
$\cot(x)$	$-\csc(x)$
$\sec(x)$	$\tan(x) \cdot \sec(x)$
$\csc(x)$	$-\cot(x) \cdot \csc(x)$
$\arccos(x)$	$-\dfrac{1}{\sqrt{1-x^2}}$
$\arctan(x)$	$\dfrac{1}{1+x^2}$
$\text{arccot}(x)$	$-\dfrac{1}{1+x^2}$
$\text{arcsec}(x)$	$\dfrac{1}{x\sqrt{1-x^2}}$
$\text{arccsc}(x)$	$-\dfrac{1}{x\sqrt{1-x^2}}$

Without a doubt, integrals are harder to compute than derivatives. As always, the inverse is a pain in the butt. Luckily, if you know the derivative, you know a few integrals. It becomes pretty hard when you start to multiply terms, at which point it may not be obvious what the original integral is. The following table provides a few trivial and non-trivial integrals. In addition to the preceding definitions, a polynomial function p is defined as $p(x)$, and additional scalars are introduced $\{a, b, c, d\}$.

Table C.2 Integrals

Function	Integral
$x^k, k \neq$	$\dfrac{x^{k+1}}{k+1}$
$x^k \cdot \ln(x), k \neq -1$	$\dfrac{x^{k+1} \cdot \ln(x)}{k+1} - \dfrac{x^{k+1}}{(k+1)^2}$
$\dfrac{1}{x}$	$\log(\lvert x \rvert)$
k^x	$\dfrac{k^x}{\log(k)}$
e^x	e^{x}
$p \cdot e^{k \cdot x}$	$\dfrac{p \cdot e^{k \cdot x} - \int e^{k \cdot x} \cdot p'}{k}$
$\sin^k(x)$	$-\dfrac{\sin^{k-1}(x) \cdot \cos(x)}{k} + \dfrac{k-1}{k} \int \sin^{k-2}(x)$
$p \cdot \sin(kx)$	$-\dfrac{p \cdot \cos(k \cdot x) + \int \cos(k \cdot x) \cdot p'}{k}$
$\cos^k(x)$	$\dfrac{\cos^{n-1}(x) \cdot \sin(x)}{k} + \dfrac{k}{k-1} \int \cos^{k-2}(x)$
$p \cdot \cos(x)$	$\dfrac{p \cdot \sin(k \cdot x) - \int \sin(k \cdot x) \cdot p'}{k}$

(continued on next page)

Table C.2 Integrals *(continued)*

Function	Integral
$\tan(x)$	$-\log\left(\left|\cos(x)\right|\right)$
$\tan^k(x), k \neq 1$	$\dfrac{\tan^{k-1}(x)}{k-1} - \int \tan^{k-2}(x)$
$\cot(x)$	$\log\left(\left|\sin(x)\right|\right) a$
$\cot^k(x), n \neq 1$	$\dfrac{\cot^{k-1}(x)}{k-1} - \int \cot^{k-2}(x)$
$\sec(x)$	$\log\left(\left|\tan\left(\dfrac{2x+\pi}{4}\right)\right|\right)$
$\sec^k(x), n \neq 1$	$\dfrac{\tan(x)\cdot\sec^{k-2}(x)}{k-1} + \dfrac{k-2}{k-1}\int \sec^{k-2}(x)$
$\csc(x)$	$\log\left(\left|\tan\left(\dfrac{1}{2\cdot x}\right)\right|\right)$
$\csc^k(x), n \neq 1$	$\dfrac{\cot(x)\cdot\csc^{k-2}(x)}{k-1} + \dfrac{k-2}{k-1}\int \csc^{k-2}(x)$
$\dfrac{b\cdot x+c}{x^2+a^2}$	$\dfrac{b\ln\left(\left|x^2+a^2\right|\right)}{2} + \dfrac{c}{a}\arctan\left(\dfrac{x}{a}\right)$
$\dfrac{c\cdot x+d}{(x-a)(x-b)}$	$\dfrac{(a\cdot c+d)\ln\left(\left|x-a\right|\right) - (b\cdot c+d)\ln\left(\left|x-b\right|\right)}{a-b}$
$\dfrac{1}{\sqrt{k^2-x^2}}$	$\arcsin\left(\dfrac{x}{k}\right)$
$\dfrac{1}{\sqrt{x^2\pm a^2}}$	$\ln\left(\left|x+\sqrt{x^2\pm a^2}\right|\right)$
$\sqrt{a^2\pm x^2}$	$\dfrac{1}{2}\left(x\sqrt{a^2\pm x^2} + a^2\int\dfrac{1}{\sqrt{a^2\pm x^2}}\right)$

Table C-2 Integrals

Function	Integral
$\sqrt{x^2 - a^2}$	$\dfrac{1}{2}\left(x\sqrt{x^2 - a^2} - a^2 \displaystyle\int \dfrac{1}{\sqrt{x^2 - a^2}} \right)$
$\dfrac{1}{\sqrt{a \cdot x^2 + b \cdot x + c}}$	$\dfrac{\ln\left(\dfrac{b + 2a \cdot x}{2\sqrt{a}} + \sqrt{a \cdot x^2 + b \cdot x + c} \right)}{\sqrt{a}}$
$\dfrac{x}{\sqrt{a \cdot x^2 + b \cdot x + c}}$	$\dfrac{\sqrt{ax^2 + bx + c}}{a} - \dfrac{b}{2a} \displaystyle\int \dfrac{1}{\sqrt{ax^2 + bx + c}}$
$\dfrac{1}{x\sqrt{a \cdot x^2 + b \cdot x + c}}$	$\begin{cases} -\dfrac{1}{\sqrt{c}} \cdot \log\left(\left| \dfrac{2\sqrt{c} \cdot \sqrt{a \cdot x^2 + b \cdot x + c} + b \cdot x + 2c}{x} \right| \right) & c > 0 \\[2em] \dfrac{1}{\sqrt{c}} \cdot \arcsin\left(\dfrac{b \cdot x + 2c}{|x| \cdot \sqrt{b^2 - 4ac}} \right) & c < 0 \end{cases}$

Maple is always at your disposal if you ever need to find something involved. It is usually pretty good at finding complex and obscure integrals, but it is not, obviously, bulletproof. The remaining task if you use the tables is to think wisely about the relationships you have—trigonometric relationships, as well as the derivatives' relationships with the integral.

APPENDIX D

WHAT'S ON THE CD

Included on the CD is a link to a copy of SDL (Simple Direct Library). Maple is a mathematical analysis and computation tool that can do a lot of the offline computations for you. Whether you are looking for a derivative, an integral, an approximation, or a mere matrix multiplication, Maple can help. The version included with this book is a free evaluation version, which will be good for 30 days. Thereafter, you will have to buy the full version of the software to continue to use it. For more information, see Maple's Web site at http://maplesoft.com. If you're a student, special pricing plans are available.

Also included on the CD is a copy of SDL (Simple Direct Library). SDL is an abstraction layer that has been carefully crafted by a great designer/programmer who currently works for a game company called Blizzard Entertainment. SDL abstracts the entire event queue, video surface, sound mechanism, image loading, or networking library with minimal overhead. The beauty of SDL is the simplicity of the API and the fact that using code to write it guarantees that the code can be ported without changing a single line (or adding ugly #define tags) to the most popular OSes, such as Windows, Linux, and Mac. The latest version of the LGPLed library can be found at http://libsdl.org.

With each chapter also comes a specially tailored source code package that demonstrates some of the concepts explained in the chapter. Feel free to take a look at the source code to help yourself understand the chapter and expand your vision of things.

Two of the greatest math repositories can be found freely on the Web. The first is the commercial Web site http://mathworld.com, which hosts a very clean and rather complete repository of mathematical terms and definitions. The second is http://planetmath. com, which is another huge repository of mathematical definitions. The beauty of the latter one is that visitors can add definitions and concepts, thus making the site more complete than any others. Also available online for math questions is http://askdrmath.com, although this site is aimed more toward beginner-level questions.

With regards to game development, you can check out the following:

- http://flipcode.com
- http://gamedev.net
- http://gamasutra.com

All three sites are unique in their own way. Flipcode is geared toward game development news, while Gamedev is more of a blend between news and articles. At Gamedev, you may find some pretty interesting articles (especially if you are planning to do a car-racing game). Gamasutra is geared toward professionals, and features announcements for big game conferences in addition to covering the administrative and development aspects of gaming.

This book also has a corresponding Web site at http://mfgd.zapto.org, where all the fixes for the source code will be located. This site serves as an excellent spot for you to place demos you have created using the skills you have learned while reading this book, and to check out creations by fellow readers. In addition, you can check the forums on this site in the event you have any math-related questions.

INDEX

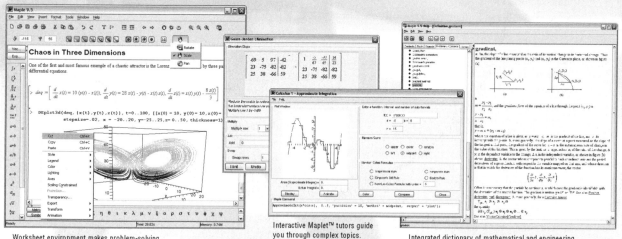

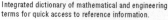

Gamedev.net

The most comprehensive game development resource

- The latest news in game development
- The most active forums and chatrooms anywhere, with insights and tips from experienced game developers
- Links to thousands of additional game development resources
- Thorough book and product reviews
- Over 1000 game development articles!
  Game design
  Graphics
  DirectX
  OpenGL
  AI
  Art
  Music
  Physics
  Source Code
  Sound
  Assembly
  And More!

Gamedev.net